Differentiating Normal and Abnormal Personality

Stephen Strack, PhD, is Director of Internship Training at the U.S. Department of Veterans Affairs Outpatient Clinic in Los Angeles and an adjunct faculty member at the University of Southern California, California School of Professional Psychology, and Fuller Graduate School of Psychology. He received his undergraduate training at the University of California at Berkeley, and graduate training in clinical psychology at the University of Miami in Florida. Dr. Strack has published numerous research articles and book chapters and is the author of the *Personality Adjective Check List*. He is a Fellow of the Society for Personality Assessment and serves on the editorial board of the *Journal of Personality Disorders*.

Maurice Lorr, PhD, is Professor Emeritus of Psychology at Catholic University of America, and Senior Fellow at the Life Cycle Institute in Washington, DC. He is widely known for his pioneering efforts in creating measures of psychopathology, interpersonal behavior, and mood, and for developing empirical models of psychotic syndromes and personality. Dr. Lorr's literary contributions include 3 books, 12 assessment devices, and over 200 published articles. He is a Fellow of the American Psychological Association and has served as President of the Society for Multivariate Experimental Psychology and District of Columbia Psychological Association. In 1982 he was recognized for his outstanding scientific contributions to psychology by the Maryland Psychological Association.

Differentiating
Normal and
Abnormal
Personality

Stephen Strack, PhD

Maurice Lorr, PhD

Editors

Springer Publishing Company

Springer Publishing Company, Inc.
536 Broadway
New York, NY 10012

94 95 96 97 98 / 5 4 3 2 1

Library of Congress Cataloging-in-Publication Data

Differentiating normal and abnormal personality / Stephen Strack, Maurice Lorr, editors.
    p. cm.
    Includes bibliographical references and index.
    ISBN 0-8261-8550-9
    1. Personality tests.   2. Personality disorders—Diagnosis.
3. Personality assessment.   I. Strack, Stephen.   II. Lorr, Maurice.
BF698.5054   1994
155.2'8—dc20   94-28761
                                             CIP

Printed in the United States of America

Contents

Contributors   vii

Foreword by Auke Tellegen   ix

Introduction   xiii

Part I Theoretical Perspectives

1 Normality–Abnormality and the Three-Factor Model of Personality   3
   Hans J. Eysenck

2 Psychopathology from the Perspective of the Five-Factor Model   26
   Robert R. McCrae

3 Differentiating Normal and Deviant Personality
   by the Seven-Factor Personality Model   40
   C. Robert Cloninger and Dragan M. Svrakic

4 Personality: A Cattellian Perspective   65
   Samuel E. Krug

5 Millon's Evolutionary Model of Normal and
   Abnormal Personality: Theory and Measures   79
   Theodore Millon and Roger D. Davis

6 The Interpersonal Circumplex and the Interpersonal Theory:
   Perspectives on Personality and its Pathology   114
   Aaron L. Pincus

7 Psychobiological Models and Issues   137
   Gordon Claridge

8 Normal versus Abnormal Personality from the Perspective
   of the DSM   158
   Thomas A. Widiger and Elizabeth M. Corbitt

Part II   Methodology

 9   Cluster Analysis: Aims, Methods, and Problems   179
     Maurice Lorr

10   Multidimensional Scaling Models of Personality Responding   196
     Mark L. Davison

11   Revealing Structure in the Data: Principles of Exploratory
     Factor Analysis   216
     Lewis R. Goldberg and John M. Digman

12   The Circumplex as a Tool for Studying Normal and
     Abnormal Personality: A Methodological Primer   243
     Michael B. Gurtman

13   Quantitative Genetic Methods for the Study of Abnormal
     and Normal Personality   264
     Steven O. Moldin

Part III   Measurement

14   The Personality Psychopathology Five (PSY-5): Issue from
     the Pages of a Diagnostic Manual Instead of a Dictionary   291
     Allan R. Harkness and John L. McNulty

15   Differentiating Normal and Abnormal Personality:
     An Interpersonal Approach Based on the Structural
     Analysis of Social Behavior   316
     William P. Henry

16   Evaluating Normal and Abnormal Personality Using the
     Same Set of Constructs   341
     Edward Helmes and Douglas N. Jackson

17   The MMPI and MMPI-2: Fifty Years of Differentiating
     Normal and Abnormal Personality   361
     Yossef S. Ben-Porath

18   The Personality Assessment Inventory and the Measurement
     of Normal and Abnormal Personality Constructs   402
     Leslie C. Morey and Joan H. Glutting

Summary and Perspective by Stephen Strack and Maurice Lorr   *421*

Author Index   *425*

Subject Index   *437*

Contributors

Yossef S. Ben-Porath, PhD
Assistant Professor of Psychology
Kent State University
Kent, OH

Gordon Claridge, PhD, DSc
University Lecturer in Abnormal
   Psychology
University of Oxford
and Tutorial Fellow in Psychology
Magdalen College
Oxford, England

C. Robert Cloninger, MD
Professor of Psychiatry
Washington University School
   of Medicine
St. Louis, MO

Elizabeth M. Corbitt, MA
Psychology Intern
Department of Psychiatry
Indiana University Medical Center
Indianapolis, IN

Roger D. Davis, BA
University Fellow and Doctoral
   Candidate
University of Miami
Coral Gables, FL

Mark L. Davison, PhD
Professor of Educational Psychology
and Professor of Psychology
University of Minnesota
Minneapolis, MN

John M. Digman, PhD
Research Psychologist
Oregon Research Institute
Eugene, OR

Hans J. Eysenck, PhD, DSc
Professor of Psychiatry, Emeritus
Institute of Psychiatry
University of London, England

Joan H. Glutting, BA
Doctoral Candidate in Clinical
   Psychology
Vanderbilt University
Nashville, TN

Lewis R. Goldberg, PhD
Professor of Psychology
University of Oregon
and Research Psychologist
Oregon Research Institute
Eugene, OR

Michael B. Gurtman, PhD
Professor of Psychology
University of Wisconsin-Parkside
Kenosha, WI

Allan R. Harkness, PhD
Assistant Professor of Psychology
University of Tulsa
Tulsa, OK

Edward Helmes, PhD
Clinical Psychologist
St. Joseph's Health Centre
and Adjunct Associate Professor
The University of Western Ontario
London, Ontario, Canada

William P. Henry, PhD
Assistant Professor of Psychology
The University of Utah
Salt Lake City, UT

Douglas N. Jackson, PhD
Senior Professor of Psychology
The University of Western Ontario
London, Ontario, Canada

Samuel E. Krug, PhD
President
Metritech, Inc.
Champaign, IL

Robert R. McCrae, PhD
Research Psychologist
Gerontology Research Center
National Institute on Aging, NIH
Baltimore, MD

John L. McNulty, MA
Doctoral Student in Clinical
  Psychology
University of Tulsa
Tulsa, OK

Theodore Millon, PhD
Professor of Psychology
University of Miami
Coral Gables, FL
and Professor in Psychiatry
Harvard Medical School
Cambridge, MA

Steven O. Moldin, PhD
Assistant Professor of Psychiatry and
  Director of the Center for
  Psychiatric Genetic Counseling
Washington University School
  of Medicine
St. Louis, MO

Leslie C. Morey, PhD
Professor of Psychology
Vanderbilt University
Nashville, TN

Aaron L. Pincus, PhD
Assistant Professor of Psychology
The Pennsylvania State University
University Park, PA

Dragan M. Svrakic, MD, PhD
Visiting Instructor in Psychiatry
Washington University School
  of Medicine
St. Louis, MO

Thomas A. Widiger, PhD
Professor of Psychology
University of Kentucky
Lexington, KY

Foreword

Most contemporary psychology textbooks and training programs treat personality psychology and psychopathology as separate areas, historically connected and adjacent, but essentially independent. This segregation is reflected in the division of subject matter among major psychology journals. Its beginnings can perhaps be traced to Gordon Allport's and Ross Stagner's pioneering textbooks, both written in 1937 and demarcating personality psychology as a distinct domain. Allport, and some of the "third force" humanistic psychologists later on, called specifically for personality psychology to emancipate itself from its psychopathological origins; it was to be a psychology of the healthy person, a discipline unburdened by clinical preconceptions.

Having achieved autonomy and a beginning maturity, personology in the United States slid into a kind of latency, or, rather, a period of invisibility during the 1970s and '80s. Productive theory development and research continued throughout this period. However, critics participating in the so-called person-versus-situation debate—peering through the thick lenses of narrow situationism—could not find the psychodynamic life or even the psychometric bones of which personologists had spoken. The crisis subsided when enough initial skeptics tried farther-sighted glasses and saw for themselves that lawful personality processes and structures exist after all.

Personality psychology is not only visible again, it is ready for expansion. Drs. Strack and Lorr have edited a volume that focuses on efforts to remove the customary boundary separating normal and abnormal personology and to reunite the two into one domain of empirical inquiry and integrative theory. Such a development would reaffirm personology's pre-Allportian past, even its ancient roots.

In the prescientific era, normal and abnormal behavioral phenomena were seen as manifestations of the same forces. Hippocrates and Galen explained human temperament and a variety of disorders within the same common organismic, even universal, framework of basic humors and elements. This tradition has proved durable and its organismic perspective is recognizable in some of today's temperament conceptions of human nature. In the beginning of this century, psychoanalysis established another influential tradition that incorporates the normal and abnormal in a single psychodynamic framework. And when psychological testing became prominent a few decades later, psychologists used the same instruments and constructs for assessing clinical and nonclinical populations. Contemporary representatives of these perspectives are well represented in the present volume.

Given their subject matter—namely, human nature and the nature of human inquiry itself—the variety of these viewpoints and approaches is not surprising. Some personality psychologists may worry that the diversity will be seen as anarchy and that this perception will fuel renewed skepticism, endangering the regained recognition of their discipline and precipitating another bout of invisibility. A personality psychology harboring a wide variety of perspectives is indeed not free of risks. However, the diversity of views characterizing the field is not inchoate; it offers possibilities for meaningful orderings that can guide informative empirical comparisons of differing but related models. Let me take examples from this volume.

Factor-analytic trait models come in three-, five-, and higher-dimensional versions forming an approximate hierarchy. In the family of circumplex models and measures we find alternative one- and three-ring versions to represent and record the fundamental social (or internalized social) relations postulated by interpersonal psychology. Still other sets of constructs are alternatively embodied in focused internally consistent measures, and in more sprawling complex measures primarily attuned to nontest external correlates.

Orderly arrangements of alternatives, by inviting systematic empirical comparisons, will help us evaluate from a predictive and explanatory viewpoint the integrative sufficiency of the more parsimonious models and the discriminative necessity (i.e., the incremental validity) of more complex ones. These evaluations will have to be tough-minded and must address questions of sufficiency and necessity in regard to both normal and abnormal phenomena. Possible qualitative and quantitative normal–abnormal distinctions must be examined, and those found genuine must be plausibly subsumed. This volume includes several reminders of the need for such examinations. To give one example, it not only introduces the purportedly all-purpose five-factor model, but invites its critical examination by also introducing a clinically focused "psychopathology five." The return to pre-Allportian desegregation of normal and abnormal personology must be shown to work in theory and practice. It must be a credible integration.

Crucial to the very feasibility of compelling empirical comparisons between alternative integrative models is that these models accord a central role to *constructs and measures of individual variation*. The diverse models Drs. Strack and Lorr have chosen to represent in this book meet this description. They have gathered original contributions by theorists and researchers who have pursued integrative normal–abnormal personology by assigning a central role to individual variations in personality functioning and their assessment. The editors have under-scored the importance of individual variability by incorporating relevant measure-ment- and assessment-oriented methodological chapters. May this set of contri-butions stimulate theoretical debates and empirical examinations needed to advance the normal–abnormal integrative cause.

AUKE TELLEGEN, PhD
Professor of Psychology
University of Minnesota

Introduction

Renewed interest in the interface between normality and pathology was ushered in by the inclusion of Axis II in the Third Edition of the *Diagnostic and Statistical Manual of Mental Disorders* (DSM, American Psychiatric Association, 1980). In trying to define what is pathological, we have come to understand that we must examine the nature of normal personality and the relationship between normality and pathology (Costa & McCrae, 1992a; Grove & Tellegen, 1991; Sabshin, 1989; Strack, 1987). Although diagnosis of personality disorders remains a categorical distinction in the revised Third Edition (American Psychiatric Association, 1987) and Fourth Edition (American Psychiatric Association, 1994) of the DSM, the belief that normal and abnormal traits are continuous and dimensional rather than categorical has become increasingly prevalent and accepted (Frances, Widiger, & Sabshin, 1991; Livesley, 1991). Furthermore, a number of fundamental questions still need to be answered: How many personality types, styles, and/or dimensions are needed to encompass the array of normal and abnormal individuals? What makes a personality normal or disordered? How are normal and abnormal personalities similar and different? Which traits are shared by normals and patients and which are unique to each population?

Publication of DSM-III in 1980 spawned a number of debates about diagnosis and classification of personality disorders (e.g., Millon & Klerman, 1986), as well as numerous empirical investigations into the similarities and differences between normal and disordered character (e.g., Shae & Hirschfeld, 1993). In addition, a handful of books and manuals have recently been published on such topics as the study of normality (Offer & Sabshin, 1991a), normal and abnormal personality development (Funder, Parke, Tomlinson-Keasey, & Widaman, 1993; Millon, 1990), how to extend existing models of normal personality to personality disorders (Costa & Widiger, 1993), and methods for measuring and understanding healthy and disordered personality styles (Benjamin, 1993; Clark, 1993). However, there are virtually no books that address the interface between normal and abnormal personality from a multitheoretical, multimethod perspective. Given the importance of answering the questions mentioned earlier, we believed there was need for a volume that would bring together major theorists, methodologists, and researchers in the area.

The chapters that comprise this volume are representative of the ideas, methods, and measures that inform us in our quest to differentiate and understand normal and abnormal personality. Contributions are divided into three main sections. The first concerns theory; namely, contemporary models of personality, temperament, and traits that address the differences between normality and pathology. The second section encompasses methodological strategies that have been, and continue to be, helpful in the search for knowledge of how traits, trait clusters, personality styles, types, and dimensions are organized. The third section presents empirical findings from a variety of productive research areas. We chose to focus on measurement instruments and systems rather than broadly based programs, because we felt that demonstrations of how current measures can be used to understand normality and pathology would be of greater use to clinicians and researchers.

In preparing their chapters, authors were asked to write for the growing number of mental health clinicians, researchers, and students who want to know about the interface between normal and abnormal personality, but may be unfamiliar with some concepts and methods. They were asked to cover all relevant material—even if technical—but to explain difficult or obscure terms and ideas. Authors were asked to stretch themselves to help bridge existing gaps and to suggest avenues for future research.

RECENT DEVELOPMENTS
IN PERSONALITY RESEARCH

Over the past 10 years, research in the area of normal personality has focused primarily on the lexical tradition that began with Allport and Odbert's (1936) search for terms to describe personality in natural language, and is now represented by the five-factor model (Digman, 1990; John, 1990). A majority now believe that factorial dimensions—as opposed to theoretically derived styles or types—most parsimoniously capture the variance in normal personality. There is less agreement about the number of factors that are needed to describe and predict normal behavior. The prominent view is that normal personality traits are hierarchically ordered, with as few as 2 or 3 super dimensions at the top of the hierarchy, and 16 or more first-order dimensions at the bottom (Costa & McCrae, 1992b; Goldberg, 1993; John, 1990; Mershon & Gorsuch, 1988; Royce & Powell, 1983).

The lead in the study of abnormal personality was taken in 1980 by the applied, descriptive system of DSM-III. Seeking to move beyond its psychoanalytic heritage, the DSM-III system of classifying personality disorders was designed to be atheortical. It was wrought from consensual agreement among DSM Task Force members who sought to distill empirical findings and clinical impressions into a medically oriented system that would capture most of the personality traits seen in clinical settings. The DSM system is frequently considered incomplete as a taxonomy. Many view categorical distinctions between normal and abnormal personality to be unsupported by empirical evidence. Most believe that all systems of personality must be based on theory or sound methodological roots. As a clinical entity, the DSM can boast neither of these. It has also been prone to shifting opinions: personality types are added and deleted at each revision and the rationale for the changes is not always compelling.

Regardless of its merits as a taxonomy, the development of DSM-III Axis II signaled the importance of personality per se in the diagnosis and treatment of psychiatric disorders. For the first time personality was clearly separated from other psychiatric conditions. The multiaxial system asked clinicians to evaluate the personalities of *all* their patients and to consider the relationship between enduring personality styles and more fleeting mental disorders. By altering the behavior of clinicians, ideas and opinions began to shift as well. For example, Millon (1969, 1981) found a growing audience for his arguments that psychiatric disorders emanate *from* personality, and that normal and abnormal personality exist within the same domain. In psychiatry, prominent members began questioning the relevancy of categorical diagnosis for personality disorders and started seeking alternative formulations (Frances, 1982). Changes such as these helped break down the artificial barriers that had existed between the separate traditions of normal and abnormal personality and have brought us to the present whirlwind of scientific activity centering on the questions raised earlier.

CONCEPTS OF NORMALITY AND PATHOLOGY

Although contributors to this volume differ widely in their approaches to personality, they are guided by similar sets of assumptions concerning the nature of normality and pathology. Offer and Sabshin (1991b) presented five models of normality–pathology that appear to encompass the viewpoints of practically all people in the field. The first of these conceptualizes *normality as health and pathology as illness.* Consistent with the traditional medical model, this perspective defines disorder by symptoms, syndromes, and physical and/or laboratory abnormalities. To be healthy is to be *reasonably free* of bothersome symptoms or disease—and this includes most people. Optimal or ideal functioning is not considered.

Normality as pathology, health as utopia is a viewpoint that conceptualizes the large majority of persons as being to some extent unhealthy. Health is defined as a perfect condition that few ever attain. According to this perspective, the average person falls considerably short of the ideal and is therefore viewed as suffering at least some pathology (e.g., possessing neurotic traits [Freud, 1937/1959]).

Defining *normality as average and pathology as deviant* takes into account cultural definitions of what is normal and healthy and what is not. In this perspective, behavior is defined according to what is acceptable and unacceptable within a given culture. The term "normal" is applied to typical or average behavior, while the term "abnormal" is applied to behavior outside this range.

The fourth model, *normality and pathology as transactional systems*, defines health and disorder according to an individual's ability to change and adapt within a social system that also changes. Patterns of adjustment are observed over long periods of time. Normal, healthy behavior is ascribed to those who adapt and respond effectively to ongoing internal (biological, psychological) and external (social) demands. Abnormal, unhealthy behavior occurs in persons who fail to adapt or respond adequately.

Normality and pathology as pragmatism asserts that consensual definition determines what is normal and what is abnormal. Relativistic in nature, this model suggests that any condition we recognize and treat as unhealthy or maladaptive is abnormal, whereas conditions that rarely, if ever, bring people in for help are normal. According to this perspective, normality and pathology are in the eye of the beholder and a given culture may have several definitions of what is healthy and unhealthy.

In addition to these broad, philosophical perspectives, most clinicians and researchers hold one of four views concerning the interface between normal and abnormal personalities. The first asserts that normal and disordered personalities are categorically distinct entities. Holders of this viewpoint assert that normal and abnormal personalities can be readily distinguished according to objective (ultimately biological or genetic) criteria. This perspective underlies the current system of DSM personality-disorder diagnosis. A second point of view holds that normal and abnormal personalities exist on the same plane and merge at some point on one or more sets of trait dimensions. Proponents of this viewpoint would agree that healthy and disordered personalities can sometimes be distinguished according to consensual definitions, but that these definitions are inherently arbitrary since personality traits are ultimately dimensional in nature.

Two additional perspectives combine elements of the categorical and dimensional approaches. The third viewpoint asserts that quantitative differences in normally distributed traits can produce qualitatively different normal and abnormal personality types. For example, certain combinations of extraversion, introversion, and emotional stability can lead to habitual patterns of behavior that are so pervasive and distinct that they can be defined as particular normal and abnormal personality styles (e.g., compulsive, histrionic). A fourth view holds that normal personality is based on dimensional traits, but abnormal personality results from biological processes and/or genetic elements that interact with these traits to produce categorically distinct disorders. For example, the presence of a genetic marker for schizophrenia in an otherwise normal introvert might result in disturbed thinking, a predisposition to psychotic breakdowns, and a schizotypal personality disorder.

Until the past several years traditional boundaries kept most researchers and clinicians within an academic or applied framework and within the scope of normality or pathology. Because of progress in defining the basic structures of personality and greater focus on personality by mental health practitioners, we are now seeing cross-fertilization and a willingness to expand existing models and methods across traditional lines. The current scene is marked by enthusiasm and hope for a better grasp of personality in all persons. We hope the chapters that follow will provide ample food for thought, will inform readers about the array of ideas, methods, and measures in the area of normal and abnormal personality, and inspire new opinions and avenues for research.

REFERENCES

Allport, G. W., & Odbert, H. S. (1936). Trait names: A psycho-lexical study. *Psychological Monographs, 47* (1, Whole No. 211).

American Psychiatric Association (1980). *Diagnostic and statistical manual of mental disorders.* (3rd ed.). Washington, DC: Author.

American Psychiatric Association (1987). *Diagnostic and statistical manual of mental disorders.* (3rd ed., rev.). Washington, DC: Author.

American Psychiatric Association (1994). *Diagnostic and statistical manual of mental disorders.* (4th ed.). Washington, DC: Author.

Benjamin, L. S. (1993). *Interpersonal diagnosis and treatment of personality disorders.* New York: Guilford.

Clark, L. A. (1993). *Schedule for Nonadaptive and Adaptive Personality (SNAP).* Minneapolis, MN: University of Minnesota Press.

Costa, P. T., & McCrae, R. R. (1992a). The five-factor model of personality and its relevance to personality disorders. *Journal of Personality Disorders, 6,* 343–359.

Costa, P. T., & McCrae, R. R. (1992b). *Revised NEO Personality Inventory (NEO-PI-R) and NEO Five Factor Inventory (NEO-FFI) professional manual.* Odessa, FL: Psychological Assessment Resources.

Costa, P. T., & Widiger, T. A. (Eds.). (1993). *Personality disorders and the five-factor model of personality.* Washington, DC: American Psychological Association.

Digman, J. M. (1990). Personality structure: Emergence of the five robust factors of personality. *Annual Review of Psychology, 41,* 417–440.

Frances, A. J. (1982). Categorical and dimensional systems of personality disorder. *Comprehensive Psychiatry, 23,* 516–527.

Frances, A. J., Widiger, T. A., & Sabshin, M. (1991). Psychiatric diagnosis and normality. In D. Offer & M. Sabshin (Eds.), *The diversity of normal behavior* (pp. 3–38). New York: Basic Books.

Freud, S. (1959). Analysis terminable and interminable. In J. Strachey (Ed.), *Collected papers of S. Freud (Vol. 5),* pp. 316–358. New York: Basic Books. Originally published in German in 1937.

Funder, D. C., Parke, R. D., Tomlinson-Keasey, C., & Widaman, K. (Eds.). (1993). *Studying lives through time: Personality and development.* Washington, DC: American Psychological Association.

Goldberg, L. R. (1993). The structure of phenotypic personality traits. *American Psychologist, 48,* 26–34.

Grove, W. M., & Tellegen, A. (1991). Problems in the classification of personality disorders. *Journal of Personality Disorders, 5,* 31–41.

John, O. P. (1990). The "Big Five" factor taxonomy: Dimensions of personality in the natural language and in questionnaires. In L. Pervin (Ed.), *Handbook of personality theory and research* (pp. 66–100). New York: Guilford Press.

Livesley, W. J. (1991). Classifying personality disorders: Ideal types, prototypes, or dimensions? *Journal of Personality Disorders, 5*, 52–59.

Mershon, B., & Gorsuch, R. L. (1988). Number of factors in the personality sphere: Does increase in factors increase predictability of real-life criteria? *Journal of Personality and Social Psychology, 55*, 675–680.

Millon, T. (1969). *Modern psychopathology*. Philadelphia: Saunders.

Millon, T. (1981). *Disorders of personality*. New York: John Wiley & Sons.

Millon, T. (1990). *Toward a new personology: An evolutionary model*. New York: John Wiley & Sons.

Millon, T., & Klerman, G. L. (Eds.). (1986). *Contemporary directions in psychopathology: Toward the DSM-IV*. New York: Guilford.

Offer, D., & Sabshin, M. (Eds.). (1991a). *The diversity of normal behavior*. New York: Basic Books.

Offer, D., & Sabshin, M. (1991b). Introduction. In D. Offer & M. Sabshin (Eds.), *The diversity of normal behavior* (pp. xi–xxi). New York: Basic Books.

Royce, J. R., & Powell, S. (1983). *Theory of personality and individual differences: Factors, systems, and processes*. Englewood Cliffs, NJ: Prentice-Hall.

Sabshin, M. (1989). Normality and the boundaries of psychopathology. *Journal of Personality Disorders, 3*, 259–273.

Shae, M. T., & Hirschfeld, R. M. A. (Eds.). (1993). The NIMH Williamsburg conference on personality disorders: What have we learned? [Special issue]. *Journal of Personality Disorders, 1*.

Strack, S. (1987). Development and validation of an adjective check list to assess the Millon personality types in a normal population. *Journal of Personality Assessment, 51*, 572–587.

I
Theoretical Perspectives

1

Normality–Abnormality and the Three-Factor Model of Personality

Hans J. Eysenck

INTRODUCTION

With a background in experimental and statistical psychology, I was suddenly plunged into the field of psychiatry and abnormal (clinical) psychology in the middle of the Second World War. I was appointed research psychologist at Mill Hill Emergency Hospital, which catered to members of the armed forces with neurotic or (rarely) psychotic disorders. It was staffed by members of Maudsley Hospital, which is the psychiatric teaching hospital of the University of London (Eysenck, 1990). After the war, I transferred to Maudsley Hospital, still a research psychologist, to become reader and then professor of psychology at the newly-founded Institute of Psychiatry, associated with Maudsley and Bethlem Hospitals, which provided patients for research and teaching in the new courses on clinical psychology. I had contracted to make clinical psychology into a profession in Great Britain (Eysenck, 1991b) where it had not existed before.

When I came to Mill Hill Emergency Hospital as a raw recruit, I knew very little about psychiatry, clinical and abnormal psychology, or personality; those had been my least favored topics in my very short professional career, so I set about trying to remedy these deficiencies, both by reading and by attending staff conferences. I became acquainted with the "medical model," which still governs psychiatry. This is a model that deals with disease entities like schizophrenia, hysteria, or personality disorder as if these were separate diseases that can be diagnosed reliably, leading to *specific* types of treatment that can actually be demonstrated to have a beneficial effect over and above their placebo effect. My attendance at case conferences taught me differently. Patients hardly ever fit into one or other of these taxonomic categories; there were endless arguments concerning the "correct" diagnosis, and treatment seemed to show little if any connection with diagnosis. Nor was there any evidence for the effectiveness of the therapy provided (Eysenck, 1952a). My work showed that the reliability of diagnoses was negligible (the superintendent forbade me to publish my results, on pain of instant dismissal [Eysenck, 1990]), and the major tools of diagnosis and research were unreliable projective techniques like the Rorschach (Eysenck, 1959b). It was not a reassuring picture.

CONSTRUCTING A MODEL

There were contrary voices. Several writers suggested a different taxonomic approach. Freud (1920) suggested a single continuum of regression, with psychotics classified as being most regressed, neurotics less so. Jung suggested a continuum from psychasthenia (extreme introversion) to hysteria (extreme extraversion). Kretschmer (1948) suggested a continuum from schizophrenia through schizotypy to dystonia, syntonia, cycloid personality and finally manic–depressive illness. His theory is shown in Figure 1.1. Many people tried to identify schizophrenia with introversion, cyclothymia with extraversion. MacKinnon (1944) wrote an excellent chapter summarizing the many attempts to relate psychiatric nosology and psychological taxonomy. All this set me to thinking.

Consider Figure 1.1. It seemed clear to me that this could only be part of a model. You cannot have "psychosis" at the two ends of a continuum without having to postulate a dimension of "psychoticism" at right angles. This would give you a dimension of severity of psychotic illness, or perhaps of psychotic disposition, or diathesis, with another dimension suggesting how there might be differing types of psychosis (Eysenck, 1970a,b). The same argument seemed to apply to Jung's (1921) scheme; there had to be a dimension or continuum of neuroticism to make possible the appearance of different neuroses at the two ends of his psychasthenia–hysteria continuum. All this suggested a three-dimensional system, both of personality description and of psychiatric nosology, incorporating psychoticism, neuroticism, and extraversion–introversion as the major orthogonal dimensions. (Eysenck, 1952b).

But there were obvious problems. Thus, Vernon (1938) had carried out a form of meta-analysis of published studies of introversion and neuroticism, showing that tests of either dimension correlated as highly with tests of the other dimension as they did with other tests of the same dimension; they completely failed to differentiate one from the other. Also there were theoretical problems; according to Freud, introversion was a lesser degree of neurosis, while for Jung they were quite independent. As I saw it, the questions to be tackled were determined by all these disagreements.

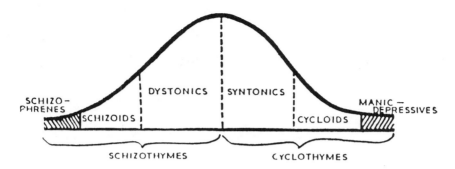

FIGURE 1.1. Diagrammatic representation of Kretschmer's theory.

From Eysenck, 1970a.

I listed them as follows: (1) Is mental disease *categorical* or continuous? (2) If continuous, is there one continuum, as Freud suggested, or two, as Kretschmer and Jung would suggest? (3) Is introversion a lesser degree of neuroticism, or is it orthogonal to it? (4) Is introversion related to psychasthenia, extraversion to hysteria? (5) Is schizothymia related to introversion, cyclothymia to extraversion? (6) And a final problem: Are these hypothetical entities subject to environmental determinants, genetic determinants, or to both, and to what degree? These problems, I thought, would keep me busy for a year or two. They did.

First I attacked the Jungian problem of the position of hysteria and psychasthenia (an old-fashioned name for which I substituted "dysthymia" as being more descriptive). I collected clinical ratings on 700 neurotic soldiers, using 39 categories, and subjected the resulting correlation to factor-analysis (Eysenck, 1947). Figure 1.2 shows the result; there seems to be good confirmation for my two-dimensional version of Jung's theory. Slater (1943) confirmed the main results on a sample of neurotic soldiers. Independently, he (Slater & Slater, 1944) and I developed a diathesis-stress theory of neurosis, in which a dispositional factor or trait, "neuroticism," form the diathesis which, under stress, develops into neurosis. Other British studies along similar lines have been discussed elsewhere (Eysenck, 1970a); they are seldom referred to in the American literature.

A similar picture is given by another analysis of data on 50 traits or notations on child guidance patients, the correlations between which have been published by Ackerson (1942). Both the factor interpreted as neuroticism, and the factor interpreted as introversion-extraversion appear quite clearly in the predicted form (Eysenck, 1970a). Figure 1.3 shows the outcome. Thus, the theory seems to apply equally well to children and adults.

My next endeavor was to find a way of testing the *continuum* theory of psychiatric abnormality as opposed to the medical model of distinct, categorical disease entities. To do this I introduced a method of analysis that I called

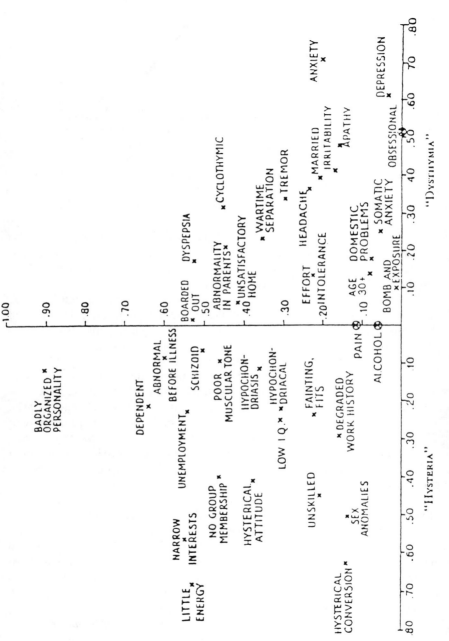

FIGURE 1.2. Factor analysis of clinical ratings.

From Eysenck, 1947.

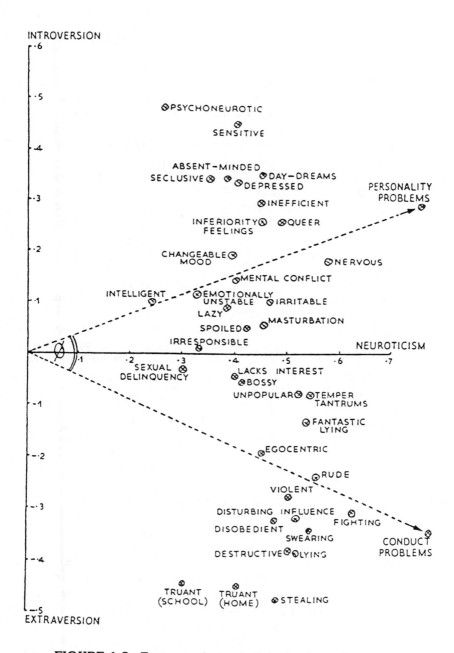

FIGURE 1.3. Factor analysis of clinical ratings of children.

From Eysenck, 1970a.

"criterion analysis." Let us consider neuroticism as a continuous variable (Eysenck, 1950).

Let us next assume the existence of a set of tests $T_1, T_2, T_3, \ldots T_n$, all of which have a linear regression on the hypothetical neuroticism factor. It will be immediately obvious that each of these tests will differentiate between groups of normals and neurotics. It will also be obvious that the degree of success with which the test differentiates between normals and neurotics is a function of its correlation with the hypothetical factor of neuroticism. We may calculate an index for the purpose of showing the degree of differentiation achieved by each test by correlating (biserial or tetrachoric) the test with the normal–neurotic dichotomy. Let us call these correlations "criterion correlations" and the set of correlations obtained in this way the "criterion column." If our hypothesis is correct, then the criterion correlation should be exactly proportional to the correlations of the tests with the hypothetical neuroticism continuum (factor loadings).

The only method of verifying this deduction consists in intercorrelating our n tests, factor analyzing the matrix of intercorrelations, and using the resulting factor coefficients as approximations to the correlations of our tests with the hypothetical neuroticism factor. If these saturations are proportional to the criterion column, then we may consider the various hypotheses outlined above verified, and we may safely and without semantic argument identify the factor thus isolated as one of emotional instability, or neuroticism. The crucial test of the original hypothesis then lies in the correlation between the factor saturations and the criterion correlations; we would not expect this correlation to be unity because some of the assumptions of linearity of regression and so forth are not likely to be fulfilled exactly by most existing test data; proper refinement of these tests, however, should lead us closer and closer to a perfect correlation.

The method demands that the factor analyses should be carried out *independently* on the normal and the neurotic groups and that the neuroticism factors extracted should have *similar loadings* for both groups (Eysenck, 1950). I shall illustrate the method as applied to psychoticism because, although few people would be likely to doubt that neurotic disability does form a continuum, many would doubt this as far as psychotic disorders are concerned.

The study is described elsewhere (Eysenck, 1952a). A normal group was constituted of 100 male subjects, and a psychotic group was composed of 50 schizophrenics and 50 manic–depressives. Twenty objective experimental tests were given, all of which differentiated between the groups. They were intercorrelated for normals and psychotics separately, and two factor analyses were undertaken; these give us factor loadings on psychoticism for normals and psychotics respectively. We also have a D (discrimination) column that tells us how well each test discriminates between normals and psychotics. The theory of continuity now states quite unambiguously that (1) the factor extracted from the normal group (F_n) should be proportional with the factor extracted from the psychotic group (F_p), and (2) both factors should be proportional with the discrimination (D) column (criterion column). These deductions would apply *if and only if* normality and psychosis form the extremes of a common continuum; if psychosis were a unique and separate disease, neither proportionately should apply.

The actual correlation of F_n with F_p was 0.871, and the two factors correlated with D 0.899 and 0.954. Note that the data were collected by an independent research worker who was "blind" to the hypothesis; and the psychometric analyses carried out by psychometrists also blind to the underlying hypothesis. The results leave little doubt about the truth of the continuity hypothesis. It seems curious to me that this study has never been properly criticized or replicated; the question it seeks to answer, one would imagine, is an important one (Claridge, 1985), and the method, if correct, would seem to provide an experimental answer.

We carried out several studies to answer the question of whether the neurotic and the psychotic dimensions were colinear, as Freud suggested, or orthogonal (Eysenck, 1970b); the answer has always been that they are orthogonal. A typical study shows the two factors that emerged from an analysis of clinical ratings; the interpretation of the two clusters of symptoms is clear (Trouton & Maxwell, 1956). Figure 1.4 shows the results; note that the item "depressed" has equal loadings on both factors, and of course it is widely accepted that these are neurotic (reactive) and psychotic (endogenous) forms of depression. These and many more studies summarized in the references given encouraged me to believe that the continuum hypothesis was true, and that neuroticism and psychoticism were orthogonal; the fact that psychiatrists still fail to admit to these facts seem to indicate a failure to take a scientific attitude to the nosological problem in such endeavors as *DSM-III* (Eysenck, Wakefield, & Friedman, 1983).

TOOLING UP FOR MEASUREMENT

This section is devoted to a brief discussion of the tests constructed to represent the major personality dimensions. Before doing so, I would like to discuss the principles underlying this construction, because they differ profoundly from those used by other psychologists. Most have followed one or the other of the two following methods.

The Heuristic Model

Tests like the Minnesota Multiphasic Personality Inventory (MMPI) and Gough's California Psychological Inventory (CPI) were designed to measure either psychiatric categories or commonly used traits; they were based on no theory and received no psychometric validation. The diagnostic categories on which the MMPI was based are arbitrary and are still rated as extremely unreliable, in spite of claims to the contrary (Kirk & Kutchins, 1992). When factor-analyzed, the MMPI breaks down into a quite different pattern to those hypothesized. The CPI,

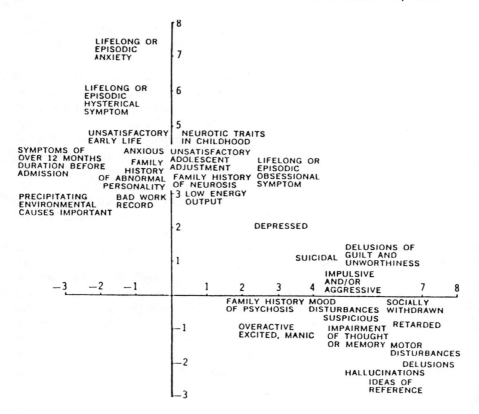

FIGURE 1.4. Factor analysis of 45 rated items on a random sample of 819 psychiatric patients.

From Trouton & Maxwell, 1950.

when factor-analyzed, shows two major factors identified as E (extraversion) and N (neuroticism). The same is true of many other similar tests (Eysenck & Eysenck, 1985).

An alternative approach is the psychometric one, adopted by Guilford, Cattell, Thurstone and many others, with the "Big Five" (John, 1990) the latest recruit. Lacking any theoretical background, they are simply pragmatic constructs depending on subjective views of their authors about what is important, or axiomatic and unproven notions, like the lexical hypothesis put forward by Cattell and the adherents of the Big Five, to wit, that our language system mysteriously identifies major personality factors and dimensions. Yet starting out with the same hypothesis, Cattell and the Big Five group arrived at quite different models. Furthermore, these models can be shown, when properly analyzed, to give rise to three superfactors very similar to P (psychoticism), E, and N (Eysenck & Eysenck, 1985). Similarly, in what amounts to a meta-analysis of existing psychometric studies Royce and Powell (1983) showed that quite generally there were three superfactors that closely resemble P, E, and N.

I have recently suggested that the lack of a paradigm in this field may be due to a lack of proper criteria for what may be regarded as a paradigm (Eysenck, 1991, 1992a), and that among the criteria most urgently required the most important is a fundamental theory underlying measurement. It is the virtue of the three-dimensional model that it is based on such a theory, tested and supported experimentally; we did not begin psychometric work on the construction of personality inventories until at least the outline of a proper theory had been established (Eysenck, 1983). It is this feature that distinguishes the three-factor theory from all the others; it uses factor analysis to test a theory, not to suggest one (Eysenck, 1991).

In the previous section, I have only dealt with psychiatric data and have interpreted some of the results, e.g., those shown in Figures 1.2 and 1.3, in terms of neuroticism and extraversion-introversion. But clearly these variables require separate measurement to be acceptable, and I have attempted through a whole series of inventories to nail down these factors as well as that of psychoticism, in measurable form. The first scale constructed on this theoretical basis was the Maudsley Medical Questionnaire (Eysenck, 1952c), a 40-item neuroticism questionnaire which, when applied to 1,000 normals and 1,000 diagnosed neurotics, misclassified 24% of normals, and 29% of neurotics—not a bad score when we remember that quite a few of the normals are liable to become diagnosed neurotic soon and that some at least of the neurotics have been diagnosed erroneously—the criterion of psychiatric diagnosis is notoriously unreliable.

This was followed by the Maudsley Personality Inventory (Eysenck, 1959b), which added extraversion to neuroticism; the Eysenck Personality Inventory (Eysenck & Eysenck, 1963), which added a dissimulation (Lie) scale; and the Eysenck Personality Questionnaire (EPQ) (Eysenck & Eysenck, 1975), which added a P scale. The most recent test is the revised EPQ-R (Eysenck & Eysenck, 1993), which incorporates psychometric improvements on the original EPQ. Each revision is based on large-scale psychometric studies of both adults and children, carried out by now in some 36 countries (Eysenck & Eysenck, 1983), refining and improving the scales. The tool most commonly used was factor-analysis, but other statistical techniques have also been employed.

Figure 1.5 shows the outcome of a study using multidimensional scaling (Hammond, 1987), using an Irish population. It will be seen that all the E items and all the L items are completely separated; two P items are found to have strayed marginally into the N space, but all the N items are in N space. Similar analyses have since been published for different nationalities, e.g., Russia (Hanin, Eysenck, Eysenck, & Barrett, 1991) and Canada (Eysenck, Barrett, & Barnes 1993).

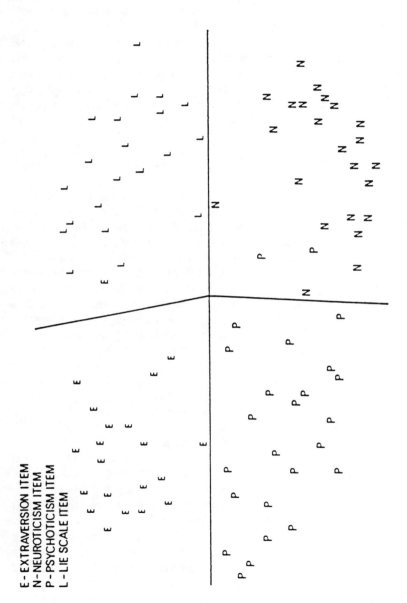

E - EXTRAVERSION ITEM
N - NEUROTICISM ITEM
P - PSYCHOTICISM ITEM
L - LIE SCALE ITEM

FIGURE 1.5. Analysis by multidimensional scaling of the EPQ.

From Hammond, 1987.

The Hierarchical Model

Underlying this model is the view that personality description requires a *hierarchical* model. Figure 1.6 shows the model applied to extraversion (Eysenck, 1947); it should be self-explanatory, starting with specific one-time behaviors, going up to reliable (repeated) behaviors, and arriving at the trait level when several different repeated behaviors are found to correlate together. Finally, the intercorrelations between traits define a type concept, although there is of course no implication of bimodality; as early as 1947 (Eysenck, 1947), I found normal distributions for E and N. Such a hierarchical model agrees well with the postulation of intercorrelated primary factors and with the view of higher-order factors based on the observed intercorrelations between primaries.

Such a model, of course, implies the danger that a given solution may mix up primaries and higher-order factors, as seems to have happened in the Big Five model, where primaries like conscientiousness and agreeableness are treated as if they were higher-order factors. Both correlate (negatively) quite highly with P, the disattenuated multiple R being 0.85; thus, they appear to be nothing but primary traits contributing one aspect of higher-order P (Eysenck, 1991).

One further point should be noted about the three-factor model as it appeared in my earlier books (Eysenck, 1947, 1952c): Reliance was not placed entirely on clinical judgments or self-report inventories; an attempt was made to use experimental tests to nail down differences more convincingly. Thus, we tested the hypothesis that neurotics would be more *suggestible* than normals by using the body-sway test (Eysenck, 1947) on groups of normals and neurotics showing varying degrees of neuroticism; the results are shown in Figure 1.7. Many other psychological and physiological tests were used and are described in those publications. They lend substance to the general picture.

At the same time, we used drugs to help define the major dimensions along physiological lines; Figure 1.8 shows the underlying theory that predicts how people would react to various types of drugs in changing their positions on the three personality dimensions (Eysenck, 1963, 1983). We also tried to put forward biological theories to account for the behaviors characteristic of P, E, and N (Eysenck, 1967; Eysenck & Eysenck, 1985). These studies and theories were based on the demonstration that both E and N were highly heritable (Eysenck, 1956; Eysenck & Prell, 1951), demonstrations that at the time proved highly controversial, but which are now more widely accepted (Eaves, Eysenck, & Martin, 1989). P, too, was found to be highly heritable.

THE NATURE OF PSYCHOTICISM

It remains to spell out the precise relationship between personality dimensions like P, E, and N and the nature of mental abnormality. The importance of E and N

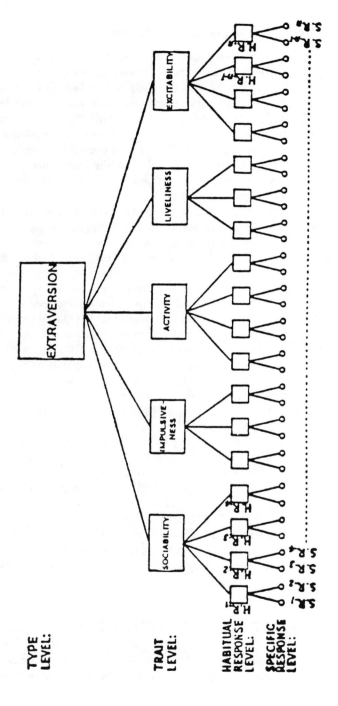

FIGURE 1.6. Hierarchical model of personality.

From Eysenck, 1947.

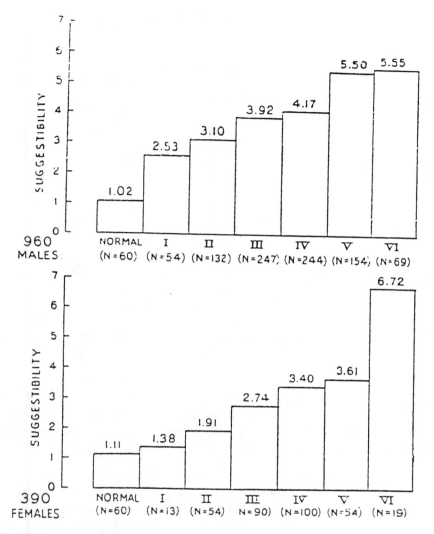

FIGURE 1.7. Behavioral measure of suggestibility as a test of neuroticism.
From Eysenck, 1947.

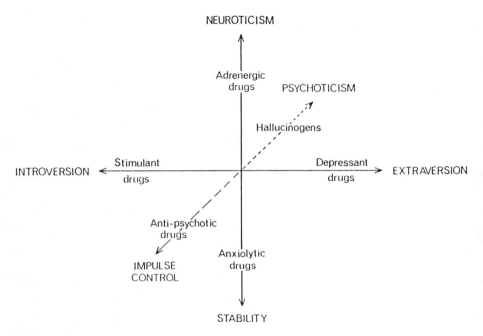

FIGURE 1.8. Psychotropic drugs and their effects on personality.
From Eysenck, 1983.

is by now fairly universally acknowledged; they constitute two of the Big Five, they emerge from factorial studies of Cattell's 16 PF and are universally found in most personality questionnaires (Eysenck & Eysenck, 1985). Psychoticism, however, has been less widely accepted and may repay a more detailed discussion (Eysenck, 1992b; Eysenck & Eysenck, 1976).

The theory underlying the concept is shown in Figure 1.9. We postulate a continuum of the psychotic diathesis ranging from P– qualities like altruistic behavior, good socialization, empathy, and conventional conformism to schizophrenia or affective disorder through schizoid types of behavior and hostile, impulsive, and aggressive conduct. P_A shows the probability of actually developing one of the functional psychoses, given a certain score of P. A similar diagram could be drawn for N, substituting traits like tense, anxious, depressed, shy, moody, emotional, and guilty feelings toward the right end of the continuum, ending in various diagnosed neurotic states.

This picture contradicts the usual Kraepelian dichotomy of schizophrenia and manic–depressive disorder, but the evidence indicates pretty clearly that such a distinction is not realistic. Contrasting clearly defined groups of schizophrenics and manic–depressives, Maxwell (1972) listed symptoms diagnosed with differ-

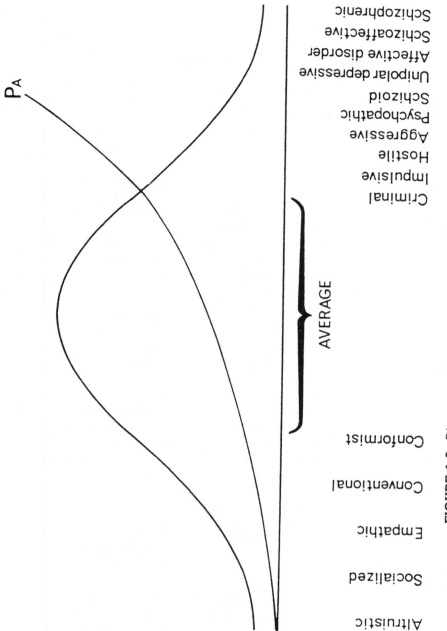

FIGURE 1.9. Diagrammatic representation of psychoticism dimension.

ential frequency in the two groups. The most diagnostic of these are reproduced in Figure 1.10; it will be seen that in the great majority of symptoms, there is very good agreement, and even the symptoms usually cited as most diagnostic show only small differences. The work by Kendall and Gourlay (1970), from which these data were taken, fails to show any U-shaped distribution of cases when optimal symptom combinations are scored; in one study the distribution was tri-modal, with the largest peak in the middle; in another, it was normal. There was little evidence for a Kraepelinian dichotomy.

A large number of other tests of the Kraepelin theory were surveyed (Eysenck, 1992), indicating in every instance that all functional psychoses shared a good deal of the variance, justifying the postulation of a dimensional concept like P. The remaining distribution between schizophrenia and affective disorder may be, as Kretschmer suggested, a function of some trait like E; Verma and Eysenck (1973) carried out a study suggesting some support for such a hypothesis. They also found that in a hospitalized group of functional psychotics, P correlated with severity of illness regardless of diagnosis. An alternative, preferred by many psychiatrists, would be that distinctions among functional psychotics are predicated on differences in severity of the disorder, with schizophrenia being the worst, schizo-affective disorders next, affective disorder (manic-depressive) following on, and unipolar depressive least severe. The evidence favors the second alternative, but it is impossible to come to any final conclusion; few experiments have addressed the issue.

The best evidence for the existence and relevance of such a type-continuum as psychoticism lies in what I have called the "proportionality criterion," which is a development of the criterion analysis. Let us take a test, T (verbal, experimental, or physiological), that discriminates clearly between psychotics and normals and which preferably has some degree of theoretical relevance to the distinction. Let us also administer the P scale to both groups. The proportionality criterion demands that in both groups (psychotic and normal), high scorers on the psychoticism scale (P +), as compared with low psychoticism scorers (P –) should score on T as psychotics compared with normals. I have surveyed the published literature, including purposely several different types of measures, such as biological variables (H2A B27; MAO; serotonin); laboratory behavior (eye-tracking, dichotic shadowing; sensitivity levels); learning-conditioning variables (latent inhibition, negative priming); psychological variables (creativity, word association, hallucinatory activity); and physiological variables (EMG, autonomic-perceptual inversion). For all these, positive results on the proportionality criterion were obtained, though in many cases only normal (P + vs. P –) subjects were submitted to testing. Obviously such results are not *final*, but they certainly give strong support to the theory.

There have been a number of criticisms of the P scale, some of which have led to improvements in the EPQ-R (Eysenck & Eysenck, 1993). Others have been answered in detail (Eysenck, 1992b). It may be useful to deal with one problem

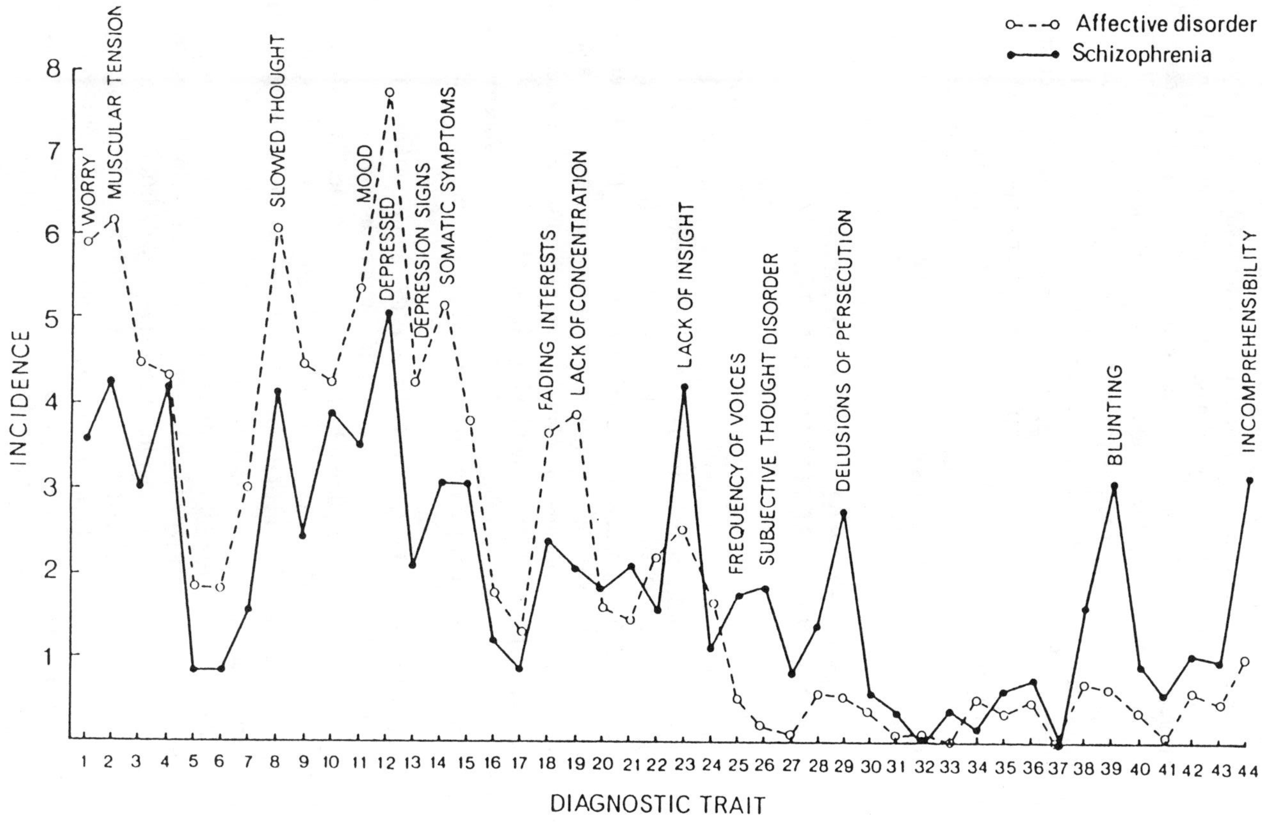

FIGURE 1.10. Diagnostic traits of schizophrenia and affective disorder.

From Eysenck, 1992.

which has puzzled many readers, namely the distinction between P and psychosis. The distinction is between a *predisposition* making a person more likely to succumb to stress and develop a psychotic illness and the actual psychosis itself (similarly for N and neurosis). The predisposition (diathesis) has a strong genetic basis (Eaves, Eysenck, & Martin, 1989), and I have suggested that there are additional genes that predispose persons to a particular *form* of breakdown (Eysenck, 1970a); again, a similar model is suggested for neurosis (Eysenck, 1987b). Thus, Torgersen (1979) has shown that not only does phobic reaction have a specific genetic background, but so does the specific form taken by the phobia, i.e., whether it is a phobia of height, of small animals, and so forth. Thus, the model is a complex one, involving genetic and environmental causes, but it is firmly centered on individual differences and combinations of the major dimensions of personality.

DIMENSIONAL ANALYSIS AND *DSM-III* PERSONALITY DISORDER

It may be useful to conclude with a specific application of the three-factor model to a particularly troublesome area of psychopathology, namely, that of the personality disorders. I have argued that criminal behavior is determined on the personality side by high P, high N, and high E, with the proviso that E is more important than N in childhood, E less than N in adult criminals (Eysenck, 1977; Eysenck & Gudjonsson, 1989); the evidence strongly supports such a view. I have also argued that psychopathic behavior, characteristic of personality disorders, is caused in a similar manner by high P, high N, and high E (Eysenck & Eysenck, 1978). Again, there is evidence to support this view. How, then, would we construct a model of the behavior that causes persons to be given the diagnosis of personality disorder?

I have suggested the following (Eysenck, 1987a). These three orthogonal dimensions give us a sphere as a model of personality, with orthogonal diameters corresponding to P, E, and N going through the center of the circle. They divide the sphere into octants, one of which contains people diagnosed with personality disorder. Only those at the outer rim of the octant are liable to come to the attention of psychiatrists or the law; those less extreme, and closer to the center, will be a great nuisance to their fellow citizens, lovers, and parents, but they are likely to escape significant encounters with the law. Some will be nearest to P, others to N, others yet to E; according to their position their behavior will differ. Some will be right in the center of the swarm of dots identifying the individuals in this octant, equidistant from P, E, and N, but high on all three dimensions. All possible combinations are possible, but of course more and more rare as we depart from the center point and drift toward the periphery (circumference). Neighboring octants such as P + N + E −, or P + N − E + will also contain somewhat less typical examples of the genus *personality disorder*, and quite generally, the further we depart from the P + N + E + octant, the less psychopathic will the behavior of the people be.

What about *DSM-III*? We may note the suggestion there made that personality disorders should be grouped into three clusters These clusters, as it happens, resemble quite closely the psychopathological personality dimensions of P, E, and N. The first cluster includes paranoid, schizoid, and schizotypal personality disorders; individuals with these disorders often appear to be odd or eccentric. This clearly is the essence of the psychoticism factor. The second cluster includes histrionic, narcissistic, antisocial, and borderline personality disorders, and it is stated that individuals with these disorders often appear dramatic, emotional, or erratic. These traits are characteristic of *extraversion*. The third class, then, includes avoidant, dependent, compulsive, and passive-aggressive personality disorders; and it is stated that individuals with these disorders often appear anxious or fearful. This description clearly resembles our *neuroticism* factor. (*DSM-III* also has a residual category, which is labeled "atypical, mixed or other personality disorder"; this is used for other specific personality disorders of all conditions that do not qualify as any of the specific personality disorders. Clearly this is a wastepaper category of no particular interest.) (Eysenck, 1987a).

We can see that on the descriptive side there is a good deal of agreement between *DSM-III* and the system of personality description elaborated by psychologists, the only point of argument really being whether a categorical or a dimensional system is better suited to the description of personality disorders. It would, I think, be difficult to argue in favor of a categorical system, which is really a relic of the medical diagnostic model erroneously applied to behavior that is by nature continuous in manifestations and impossible to categorize in this fashion. As the description in *DSM-III* makes clear, practically all the behavior used to describe the various types of personality disorders is conceived in terms of *more* or *less* rather than *either-or*; in other words, implicit in the description of *DSM-III* is the dimensional system rather than a categorical one, although this is not explicitly acknowledged by its authors.

Descriptively, there may seem to be little difference between the two approaches—diagnosing patients with personality disorders as belonging to one or more of the three clusters described in *DSM-III*, or stating their position in the three-dimensional space created by P, E, and N in a quantitative manner by reference to the three axes defining this space. There are, however, certain advantages to the system here suggested, which may be enumerated as follows.

1. A precise and quantitative statement is always to be preferred to a nonquantifiable one. The behavior that gives rise to assigning a person a position on the P, E, and N dimensions has been carefully selected on the basis of literally hundreds of descriptive studies using ratings, self-ratings, miniature situations, and experimental laboratory settings to study the interrelations between different

behavior and to quantitatively analyze these differences and demonstrate the existence of independent factors that serve to summarize a large body of knowledge. The precision gained by this empirical and statistical procedure would be thrown away if we regressed to a simple categorical nomenclature.

2. *DSM-III* is purely descriptive; it contains no mention of causal factors. It is thus purely heuristic and pragmatic, but science clearly seeks far more than simple descriptive convenience. Personality factors P, E, and N have been carefully investigated and related to biological causes that determine the behavior so described. In addition, there are many theories specifying the precise way in which these biological constraints determine behavior. Thus, antisocial behavior has been suggested to be linked with extraversion, and perhaps with psychoticism, through the failure of extraverts, and possibly high P scorers, to form the conditioned socialized responses that, through a process of Pavlovian conditioning, would produce a conscience in human beings as a consequence of thousands of experiences of praise and blame, reward and punishment (Eysenck, 1977). Such theories provide a mediating link between the genetic basis of the personality variables and the behavior actually observed. They are clearly testable and may be important in devising methods of treatment, which, in the case of personality disorders in particular, has hitherto proved rather unsuccessful. This lack of success may be due to the atheoretical approach of psychiatry illustrated in *DSM-III*.

How does all this relate to the question of whether the criteria for the personality disorder should be formulated in explicit and behavioral form or phrased in a conceptual and generalizable manner? Clearly the concepts involved, whether those incorporated in the three clusters postulated by *DSM-III* or the combination of three personality dimensions proposed by the writer, are all based on the explicit analysis of *behavior* whether observed, rated, or self-rated. This inevitably must be the basis of any descriptive system, and it is interesting (and perhaps important) to note that there is good agreement in these observations between the psychiatric authors responsible for *DSM-III* and the psychologists whose observations are incorporated in my proposed descriptive system. Such observations of behavior are absolutely fundamental for any descriptive system and must form the basis for any kind of theory. Furthermore, in coming to a diagnosis, whether categorical or phrased in dimensional terms, it is this behavior, made as explicit as possible, that must determine the final form this diagnosis takes. The more clear-cut the behavior in question and the more clearly defined, the more reliable will be the diagnosis.

We thus have two advantages implied in the use of a *dimensional* approach, as contrasted with a diagnostic one. The dimensional approach does justice to the *complexity* of the situation and to the infinite gradations involved; the diagnostic approach imposes a unique label on very heterogeneous material, confusing the different *types* of personality disorder, and disregarding problems of severity, thus ensuring low reliability of diagnosis. Communication is not helped by grouping together distinct variables in arbitrary combinations, nor is prediction or therapeutic choice helped by such a diagnostic procedure. P + N − E + patients require different treatment from P − N + E + patients; there is no proper provision for that in *DSM-III,* unless we accumulate diagnostic categories in abundant profusion (which is what *DSM-III* is drifting into); there were 106 separate diagnoses in *DSM-I,* 182 in *DSM-II,* 265 in *DSM-III,* and 292 in *DSM-III-R* (Kirk & Kutchins, 1992). This superabundance negates the alleged parsimony of adopting diagnostic labels; it would be much more parsimonious to have three dimensions and order patients in terms of their standing on these dimensions.

An obvious example of the application of dimensional analysis is the taxonomy of color. We have tens of thousands of discriminable colors, many of which have separate names (diagnostic principle); yet they can all find a meaningful and valid home in the combination of three dimensions! The advantage of this three-factor description (which of course is also aligned with the physiological color receptors) are so obvious that no one would even think of abandoning it. I am suggesting that a similar approach would be equally useful in the field of mental abnormality.

REFERENCES

Ackerson, L. (1942). *Children's behavior problems.* Chicago: University of Chicago Press.
Claridge, G. (1985). *Origins of mental illness.* Oxford: Basil Blackwell.
Eaves, L., Eysenck, H. J., & Martin, N. (1989). *Genes, culture and personality: An empirical approach.* New York: Academic Press.
Eysenck, H. J. (1947). *Dimensions of personality.* London: Routledge & Kegan Paul.
Eysenck, H. J. (1950). Criterion analysis: An application of the hypothetico-deductive method to factor analysis. *Psychological Review, 57,* 38–53.
Eysenck, H. J. (1952a). The effects of psychotherapy: An evaluation. *Journal of Consulting Psychology, 16,* 319–324.
Eysenck, H. J. (1952b). Schizothymia-cyclothymia as a dimension of personality. *Journal of Personality, 20,* 345–384.
Eysenck, H. J. (1952c). *The scientific study of personality.* London: Routledge & Kegan Paul.
Eysenck, H. J. (1956). The inheritance of extraverson-introversion. *Acta Psychologia, 12,* 95–110.
Eysenck, H. J. (1959a). *Maudsley personality inventory.* London: University of London Press.
Eysenck, H. J. (1959b). The Rorschach test. In K. Buros (Ed.), *The fifth mental measurement yearbook* (pp. 276–278). Nebraska: Gryphon.
Eysenck, H. J. (1960). Classification and the problem of diagnosis. In H. J. Eysenck (Ed.), *Handbook of abnormal psychology.* London: Pitman.
Eysenck, H. J. (1963). *Experiments with drugs.* London: Pergamon.
Eysenck, H. J. (1967). *The biological basis of personality.* Springfield, IL: Charles Thomas.
Eysenck, H. J. (1970a). A dimensional system of psychodiagnostics. In A. R. Mahrer (Ed.), *New approaches to personality classification* (pp. 169–207). New York: Columbia University Press.
Eysenck, H. J. (1970b). *The structure of personality.* London: Methuen.
Eysenck, H. J. (1970c). An experimental and genetic model of schizophrenia. In A. R. Kaplan (Ed.), *Genetic factors in schizophrenia.* Springfield, IL: Charles Thomas.

Eysenck, H. J. (1977). *Crime and personality.* London: Routledge & Kegan Paul.

Eysenck, H. J. (1983a). Is there a paradigm in personality research? *Journal of Research in Personality, 17,* 369-397.

Eysenck, H. J. (1983b). Psychopharmacology and personality. In W. Janke (Ed.), *Response variability to psychotropic drugs.* London: Pergamon Press.

Eysenck, H. J. (1987a). The definition of personality disorders and the criteria appropriate to their description. *Journal of Personality Disorders, 1,* 211–219.

Eysenck, H. J. (1987b). The role of heredity, environment, and "preparedness" in the genesis of neurosis. In H. J. Eysenck & I. Martin (Eds.), *Foundations of behavior therapy* (pp. 379–402). New York: Plenum.

Eysenck, H. J. (1990). *Rebel with a cause.* London: W. H. Allen.

Eysenck, H. J. (1991a). Dimensions of personality: 16, 5 or 3?—criteria for a taxonomic paradigm. *Personality and Individual Differences, 12,* 773–790.

Eysenck, H. J. (1991b). Maverick psychologist. In C. E. Walker (Ed.), *The history of clinical psychology in autobiography* (pp. 39–86). Pacific Grove, CA: Brooks/Cole.

Eysenck, H. J. (1992a). Four ways five factors are *not* basic. *Personality and Individual Differences, 13,* 667–673.

Eysenck, H. J. (1992b). The definition of measurement of psychoticism. *Personality and Individual Differences, 13,* 757–785.

Eysenck, H. J., & Eysenck, M. W. (1985). *Personality and individual differences: A natural science approach.* New York: Plenum.

Eysenck, H. J., & Eysenck, S. B. G. (1963). *Eysenck personality inventory.* London: University of London Press.

Eysenck, H. J., & Eysenck, S. B. G. (1975). *Eysenck personality questionnaire.* London: Hodder & Stoughton.

Eysenck, H. J., & Eysenck, S. B. G. (1976). *Psychoticism as a dimension of personality.* London: Hodder & Stoughton.

Eysenck, H. J., & Eysenck, S. B. G. (1978). Psychopathy, personality and genetics. In R. D. Hare & D. Schalling (Eds.), *Psychopathic behaviour* (pp. 197–223). London: Wiley.

Eysenck, H. J., & Eysenck, S. B. G. (1982). Recent advances: The cross-culture and study of personality. In C. D. Spielberger & J. N. Butcher (Eds.), *Advances in personality assessment, Vol. 2* (pp. 41–69). Hillsdale, N.J.: Lawrence Erlbaum.

Eysenck, H. J., & Eysenck, S. B. G. (1993). *The Eysenck personality questionnaire-revised.* London: Hodder & Stoughton.

Eysenck, H. J., & Gudjonsson, G. (1989). *The causes and cures of criminality.* New York: Plenum Press.

Eysenck, H. J., & Prell, D. B. (1951). The inheritance of neuroticism: An experimental study. *Journal of Mental Science, 97,* 441–465.

Eysenck, H. J., Wakefield, J. A., & Friedman, H. F. (1983). Diagnosis of clinical assessment: The *DSM-III. Annual Review of Psychology, 34,* 167–193.

Eysenck, S. B. G., Barrett, P. T., & Barnes, G. E. (1993). A cross-cultural study of personality: Canada and England. *Personality and Individual Differences, 14,* 1–10.

Freud, S. (1920). *General introduction to psychoanalysis.* New York: Liversedge.

Hammond, S. M. (1987). The item structure of the Eysenck Personality Questionnaire across method and culture. *Personality and Individual Differences, 8,* 541–549.

Hanin, Y., Eysenck, S. B. G., Eysenck, H. J., & Barrett, P. (1991). A cross-cultural study of personality: Russia and England. *Personality and Individual Differences, 12,* 265–271.

John, O. P. (1990). The "Big Five" factor taxonomy. In L. A. Pervin (Ed.), *Handbook of personality* (pp. 60–100). New York: Guilford.

Jung, C. G. (1921). *Psychological types*. London: Routledge & Kegan Paul.

Kendell, R. E., & Gourlay, J. (1970). The clinical distribution between the affective psychoses of schizophrenia. *British Journal of Psychiatry, 117*, 261–266.

Kirk, S. A., & Kutchins, H. (1992). *The selling of DSM: The rhetoric of science in psychiatry*. New York: Aldine de Grayer.

Kretschmer, E. (1948). *Korperban und charakter*. Berlin: Springer.

MacKinnon, D. W. (1944). The structure of personality. In J. McV. Hunt (Ed.), *Personality and the behavior disorders, Vol. 1*. New York: Ronald Press.

Maxwell, A. E. (1972). Difficulties in a dimensional description of symptomatology. *British Journal of Psychiatry, 121*, 19–26.

Royce, J. R., & Powell, S. (1983). *Theory of personality and individual differences*. Englewood Cliffs, N.J.: Prentice Hall.

Slater, E. (1943). The neurotic constitution. *Journal of Neurology and Psychiatry, 6*, 1–16.

Slater, E., & Slater, P. (1944). A heuristic theory of neurosis. *Journal of Neurology, Neurosurgery and Psychiatry, 7*, 49–55.

Torgersen, S. (1979). The nature and origin of common phobic fears. *British Journal of Psychiatry, 134*, 343–351.

Trouton, D. S., & Maxwell, A. E. (1956). The relation between neurosis and psychosis. *Journal of Mental Science, 102*, 1–21.

Verma, R. M., & Eysenck, H. J. (1973). Severity and type of psychotic illness as a function of personality. *British Journal of Psychiatry, 122*, 573–585.

Vernon, P. E. (1938). The assessment of psychological qualities by verbal methods. London: H.M.S.O.

2

Psychopathology from the Perspective of the Five-Factor Model

Robert R. McCrae

The five-factor model (FFM; Digman, 1990; McCrae, 1992) is a comprehensive classification of personality traits in terms of five broad dimensions: neuroticism (N), extraversion (E), openness to experience (O), agreeableness (A), and conscientiousness (C). It was first discovered in analyses of natural language trait terms (Tupes & Christal, 1961/1992), but it has been shown to account as well for the major dimensions underlying inventories based on a variety of formal personality theories. Jung's functions, Murray's needs, Guilford's temperaments, and Gough's folk concepts can all be understood in terms of these five factors (McCrae, 1989; McCrae, Costa, & Piedmont, 1993).

Strong links have also been shown between the FFM and measures of psychopathology (Costa & Widiger, 1994). In a series of studies in community samples (Costa & McCrae, 1990, 1992a; McCrae, 1991) using the NEO Personality Inventory (NEO-PI; Costa & McCrae, 1985) to operationalize the FFM, meaningful correlations have been shown with the scales of the Minnesota Multiphasic Personality Inventory (MMPI; Hathaway & McKinley, 1983), the Millon Clinical Multiaxial Inventory (MCMI; Millon, 1983), the Basic Personality Inventory (BPI; Jackson, 1989), and the Personality Assessment Inventory (PAI; Morey, 1991). Across all these instruments, only two scales—BPI Thinking Disorder and PAI Drug Problems—were unrelated to any of the five factors, and all five factors were related to at least one scale in each inventory of psychopathology. Studies conducted in clinical samples have shown similar results (e.g., Trull, 1992).

Were it not for the fact that there is a long tradition of segregating "normal" personality from "abnormal" personality, most of these associations would be considered unremarkable. In the NEO-PI, N is assessed by summing scales for

26

anxiety, angry hostility, depression, self-consciousness, impulsiveness, and vulnerability. Small wonder that it is related to measures of borderline personality disorder (Trull, 1992)! Individuals low in A are described as being suspicious, aggressive, and arrogant; the negative correlations of A with scales measuring paranoid, antisocial, and narcissistic personality disorders (Costa & McCrae, 1990) are confirmations of the continuity of normal and abnormal characteristics.

Further, personality traits are not mere correlates of personality disorders; they share with them the same five-factor structure. In 1989, Wiggins and Pincus showed that five and only five factors were needed to account for the communalities among personality disorder scales, and these five corresponded to the factors of the FFM. Clark (1990) and Livesley, Jackson, and Schroeder (1989) began at the level of individual personality disorder symptoms and found symptom dimensions that are readily interpretable in terms of the FFM (Clark & Livesley, 1994).

Many researchers have concluded from these data that the FFM can be a uniquely valuable tool for understanding DSM-III-R (American Psychiatric Association, 1987) personality disorders in psychiatric patients. On a theoretical level, analyses of the personality disorders in terms of the FFM can help to explain patterns of prevalence and comorbidity (Widiger & Trull, 1992) and to clarify divergences between alternate measures of the personality disorders (Costa & McCrae, 1990). On a practical level, assessment of individuals on measures of the FFM can facilitate personality disorder diagnoses (Widiger, Trull, Clarkin, Sanderson, & Costa, 1994). These possibilities have generated enormous interest in both researchers and clinicians (Costa & Widiger, 1994).

But there is also a more radical way to interpret the same data. We might conclude that normal personality and abnormal personality are not merely related phenomena but are in fact equivalent and that the personality disorders of the DSM-III-R are not qualitatively new forms of personality but are merely descriptions of individual differences in personality as they are seen in psychiatric patients.

Adopting this position does not require that we abandon the concept of psychopathology or deny that there are some kinds of psychopathology specifically related to personality. It does, however, change the nature of the problem posed by this book. Instead of differentiating normal personality from abnormal personality, it presumes that all individuals have personalities that can be adequately described in terms of standing on the five basic factors (and the more specific traits that define them), and then asks how, if at all, these personality traits are related to the various forms of psychopathology that some individuals manifest.

Thus, the FFM can be seen either as a way of understanding the DSM-III-R personality disorder categories or as the basis for an entirely different approach to personality and psychopathology. The more radical approach is justified by serious problems with the DSM-III-R system, which has been criticized as being arbitrary, overlapping, and without a clear empirical basis (e.g., Livesley, 1991; Widiger, 1993). In this chapter, I will note some of the problems of the DSM personality disorders and address ways of understanding personality-related psycho-pathology.

The editors of this volume asked me to approach the topic of abnormal personality from the theoretical perspective of the FFM. Insofar as the FFM is intended to be a *comprehensive* taxonomy of personality traits, collapsing normal and abnormal into a unified field of personality described by these five factors seems to be consistent with their charge. But the FFM is not itself a theory of psychopathology, and many different theories of psychopathology would be compatible with it. I will discuss some of my own ideas on the nature of psychopathology and its relation to personality, but other advocates of the FFM might have different and equally valid approaches to the topic.

THE DEFINITION OF PERSONALITY

Some readers may be puzzled by the assertion that there are no qualitative differences between normal personality and abnormal personality. Surely a hebephrenic schizophrenic or a severely demented individual has a qualitatively different psychological organization than the average person. If personality is defined broadly as, for example, "the entire mental organization of a human being at any stage of his development" (Warren & Carmichael, 1930, p. 333, cited in Allport, 1961) this objection is entirely appropriate. However, in the psychometric tradition of the FFM and of such measures of psychopathology as the MCMI, personality is more narrowly defined in terms of *traits*, that is, of relatively enduring and pervasive dispositions to act, think, and feel in consistent and characteristic ways.

The scope of personality traits, however, can also be broadly or narrowly construed. Traditionally, cognitive abilities (which clearly fit the above definition of traits) are excluded, and in joint analyses, general intelligence forms a sixth factor alongside the five personality factors (McCrae & Costa, 1985). A more difficult discrimination concerns specific psychiatric symptoms, which may also have trait-like qualities. Some individuals have chronic hallucinations that dramatically affect their thoughts, feelings, and behavior; other people have long-standing paraphilias that are consistent and characteristic. Yet most trait psychologists would probably not consider hallucination-proneness or transvestic fetishism to be personality traits.

One distinctive feature of personality traits seems to be that they are quasi-normally distributed. We can rate all people meaningfully on a scale of 1 to 10 on such traits as nervousness and orderliness, but hallucination-proneness and transvestic fetishism appear to be relevant constructs only for a small minority of individuals. In the language of Baumeister and Tice (1988), most people are *untraited* with respect to these characteristics. By contrast, everyone seems to be traited with respect to the dimensions of the FFM (McCrae, 1993).

AXIS I PSYCHOPATHOLOGY AND THE FFM

In the *DSM-III-R*, mental disorders are divided into *clinical syndromes* (Axis I) and maladaptive and inflexible traits that constitute *personality disorders* (Axis II). In general, this appears to be a useful distinction. Clinical syndromes are distinguishable from personality traits because they are acute rather than chronic (such as Major Depressive Episode), focalized rather than pervasive (such as Nicotine Dependence), or categorically distinct from normal behavior (such as Tourette's Disorder). A few of the disorders currently classified on Axis I do not fit these criteria—notably, Dysthymia and Social Phobia—and some writers have suggested that they might better be classified on Axis II (e.g., American Psychiatric Association, 1991; Widiger, 1992).

The fact that clinical syndromes are distinguishable from personality traits does not mean that they are necessarily unrelated. Widiger and Trull (1992) suggest four ways in which traits may be related to Axis I disorders: They may predispose individuals to a disorder, they may be consequences of the disorder, they may affect the manifestation and course of the disorder, or they may share a common etiology with the disorder. Empirical examples of the first three have been offered. Prospective studies have shown that high N predisposes individuals to experience depressive episodes as well as other psychiatric disorders (Hirshfeld et al., 1989; Zonderman, Herbst, Schmidt, Costa, & McCrae, 1993). Personality traits, notably C, are themselves altered in the course of dementing disorders (Siegler et al., 1991).

Perhaps of most clinical importance, personality traits affect response to therapy. Miller (1991) showed that high C scores predict better therapy outcomes, perhaps because conscientious patients work harder to solve their problems. In a randomized study of treatments for clinical depression, Shea (1988) found that drug treatment was more effective for introverts, whereas interpersonal therapies were more effective for extraverts. The comprehensive taxonomy offered by the FFM provides a framework for systematic exploration of such trait-by-treatment interactions.

AXIS II PSYCHOPATHOLOGY AND THE FFM

Although personality traits may be associated with Axis I disorders, they are, by definition, central features of Axis II personality disorders. *DSM-III-R* provides both a definition and a taxonomy of personality disorders that form the starting point of the remainder of this discussion. Personality disorders are defined as "inflexible and maladaptive" traits that "cause either significant functional impairment or subjective distress" (p. 335). The *DSM-III-R* taxonomy is a set of 11 disorders thought to meet this definition, together with "not otherwise specified" personality disorders.

The specified personality disorders are a non-systematic collection of syndromes derived from clinical lore and literature. On the one hand, the *DSM-III-R* is officially neutral on issues of etiology, so the diagnostic criteria tend to be simple descriptions of behaviors and reactions. On the other hand, it is an open secret that many of the personality disorders had their theoretical origins in psychoanalysis, where clinical formulations are often highly inferential. This discrepancy means that the *DSM-III-R* descriptions sometimes fail to capture the psychopathological essence of a disorder (cf. Kernberg, 1984).

For example, many clinicians have treated patients with severe psychological and interpersonal problems that might be attributed to a histrionic style. But the *DSM-III-R* histrionic personality disorder merely describes individuals who are excessively emotional and attention seeking. They are self-centered, vain, and dramatic, and their speech is impressionistic. Some of us would find the company of such individuals annoying, but it is by no means clear why these features themselves constitute a mental disorder. There is no clear implication of subjective distress, and although individuals meeting the *DSM-III-R* criteria for histrionic personality disorder might not be ideal candidates for occupations like forest ranger or accountant, that can hardly be considered a significant functional impairment. Of all the ways in which individuals can be distressed or impaired, why single out this one? The answer, of course, is that histrionic personality disorder is also called Hysterical Personality and evokes psychoanalytic associations stretching back to Breuer and Freud (1895).

Psychoanalysts often have brilliant clinical insights—as I will illustrate with Shapiro's (1965) treatment of the obsessive-compulsive style—but psychoanalytic theory often lacks empirical support, and the characteristics that define the histrionic personality disorder do not in fact covary as one would expect if they identified a naturally occurring category (Clark, 1990; Livesley, Jackson, & Schroeder, 1989). This creates problems for researchers who wish to develop internally consistent scales to measure the disorder, and item selection procedures typically result in scales that measure a narrower construct dominated by attention seeking (i.e., preference for social interaction) and emotionality (i.e., enthusiasm and excitement seeking). Thus, Millon's (1983) histrionic scale includes items like "I think I am a very sociable and outgoing person" and is so strongly correlated with measures of E (Costa & McCrae, 1990) that its discriminant validity is questionable. These versions of the histrionic personality disorder seem even further from psychopathology than the *DSM-III-R* description.[1]

Given their many conceptual and empirical problems, it would probably be a mistake to attempt to understand personality pathology by analyzing *DSM-III-R* syndromes. The *DSM* definition of personality disorders—inflexible and maladaptive traits causing distress or impairment—is less controversial, but it begs the question of what makes a trait maladaptive. I will consider three possibilities, two of which seem viable. To distinguish the conditions I will describe from the categorical personality disorders, I will use the term *personality-related disorders*. My basic premise is that when patients are characterized as having a personality disorder, they in fact have not a pathologic personality, but a personality-related pathology.

MODELS OF PERSONALITY-RELATED DISORDERS

All individuals have personalities that can be characterized in terms of standing on the five basic factors, and they are likely to encounter characteristic kinds of life problems, especially when there are conflicts between their dispositions and their life circumstances. To take a relatively benign example, individuals high in O may be frustrated by the monotony of their jobs; those who are low in O may be upset by technological innovation. Impaired occupational performance might result in either case. It is these problems, rather than the underlying traits, that bring people to psychotherapy. To define personality-related disorders, we need to understand the nature of these problems and their relation to personality traits.

Extremeness and inflexibility. The tradition of research associated with the interpersonal circumplex (Kiesler, 1983; Leary, 1957; Wiggins, 1979) has usually assumed that pathological interpersonal behavior is the result of extreme standing on interpersonal traits. Although Kiesler (1983) describes normal and abnormal interpersonal behavior as being qualitatively different, he appears to regard the abnormal versions as being merely exaggerations of the normal. Moderate levels of dominance are normal, but extremely high levels take on a pathological quality, much as extremely high levels of body weight become clinically significant obesity.

One basis of this argument is the assumed association of extremeness with inflexibility. If one exhibited dominant behavior in every social situation whether appropriate or not, one would score very high on measures of dominance and one would also be judged inflexible. Short of this absolute extreme, however, extremeness and inflexibility are essentially independent. A very dominant individual may be assertive in almost all aspects of life, but submissive in the few situations that realistically require it. Conversely, an individual could be average on the warm-cold dimension of the interpersonal circumplex but show inflexibility by being equally lukewarm to close friends and bitter foes.

Wakefield (1992) has discussed limitations of the statistical deviance view of mental disorders, arguing that it is neither a necessary nor a sufficient criterion. Extremeness is not, however, irrelevant. To the extent that problems are associated with a personality trait, those who rank higher on the trait will have a greater risk of encountering those problems. If open individuals require an occasional break from the monotony of routine at work, extremely open individuals may be unable to tolerate any routine.

The contribution of neuroticism. Subjective distress is one of the hallmarks of a personality disorder, and the tendency to be distressed is central to the definition of neuroticism (Watson & Clark, 1984). We might therefore argue that high standing on this dimension is prima facie evidence of a personality-related disorder. Trull (1992) noted that the borderline personality disorder in particular, with its symptoms of depression, hostility, and impulsiveness, is virtually isomorphic with N as measured by facets of the NEO-PI. Individuals with extremely high scores on scales measuring chronic anxiety, angry hostility, depression, self-consciousness, impulsiveness, and vulnerability would surely be at high risk for receiving a diagnosis of borderline personality disorder.

The combination of N with other personality factors could give rise to other kinds of disorder. Individuals with a diagnosis of histrionic personality disorder may in fact be extraverts who are also high in N. If so, we would expect that their distinctive features would have distressing implications not explicitly noted in *DSM-III-R*. They might be vain, but also be secretly terrified that they are losing their looks. They might seek out social contacts, but be painfully self-conscious when they receive the attention they seek.[2]

Distress is by far the most common reason individuals have for seeking psychotherapy, and patients with many different disorders share high levels of N (e.g., Fagan et al., 1991; Mutén, 1991). It is hard to understand why else an individual with schizoid characteristics—solitary, indifferent to social opinion, constricted in affect—would ever be found in treatment. Although antisocial patients are often thought to be callous and indifferent to psychological pain, those in voluntary treatment are in fact exceptionally high in N (as well as being low in A and C [Brooner et al., 1991]). Trull (1992) found that nine of the eleven personality disorders as assessed by the Personality Disorder Questionnaire-Revised (Hyler & Rieder, 1987) were significantly associated with N in a clinical sample.

The idea that personality disorders are merely the expression of different levels of E, O, A, and C in combination with high levels of N has considerable appeal; certainly most individuals diagnosed as having personality disorders could be described by that formula. The problem is that it is too broad. There are many individuals who have high N scores, yet do not seek and probably do not need psychotherapy. Jung (1933) noted this fact long ago:

> People whose own temperaments offer problems are often neurotic, but it would be a serious misunderstanding to confuse the existence of problems with neurosis. There is a marked distinction between the two in that the neurotic is ill because he is unconscious of his problems; while the man with a difficult temperament suffers from his conscious problems without being ill. (p. 101)

We may not wish to adopt Jung's view that psychopathology can be equated with unconscious problems, but there is a useful insight here: All people have problems—high N people more than most—but problems become disorders only when they exceed the individual's ability to deal with them. The borderline who is simply overwhelmed by affect, the abusive husband who cannot control his temper despite the likelihood of legal consequences, the narcissist who cannot understand why she has alienated all her friends, and the passive–aggressive individual whose career never advances have problems that require professional assistance. These people can be regarded as having personality-related disorders.

The contribution of disordered cognition. Most people solve their own problems, or require only temporary assistance in adjusting to new circumstances. People with personality-related disorders have chronic problems that they are unable to deal with effectively. The difference might be attributed to a disturbance in thinking.

This is perhaps clearest from a consideration of the *DSM-III-R* schizotypal personality disorder. Although some aspects of this disorder (e.g., extreme social anxiety) can be described in terms of the FFM, the most characteristic features are aberrant cognition: odd beliefs, unusual perceptions, ideas of reference. Very open individuals often entertain unconventional ideas of the sort measured by Epstein and Meier's (1989) Esoteric Thinking scale (McCrae & Costa, in press), but the resemblance of these ideas to schizotypal thinking is merely superficial. Schizotypal individuals are not open-minded, they are out of touch with conventional reality. This is not a feature captured by the FFM, and it is not surprising that there is no correlation between any of the five factors and Jackson's (1989) Thinking Disorder scale.

Cognitive distortions of one kind or another are also features of many of the other *DSM-III-R* disorders. Borderlines have identity disturbances, histrionics have impressionistic thinking, narcissists have an inflated sense of self-importance, paranoids have groundless suspicions, schizoids are vague and absent-minded. There is a sense in which all these disorders reflect misperceptions of reality, whether this is due to some defect in cognitive apparatus (as is probably the case with schizotypals), to the motivated repression hypothesized by psychoanalysts, or to a simple lack of insight into one's own personality traits and their interaction with the world.

Such cognitive distortions would help explain the persistence of maladaptive behaviors. Normal behavior is characterized by flexible adaptation. When we discover that our high opinions of ourselves are not shared by those around us, we may change our evaluations of ourselves (or of them), but we will not continue to be unpleasantly surprised by their lack of esteem for us. When our outbursts of temper fail to win others' submission, we learn to control our temper. But when we cannot understand the reasons for our problems we are likely to remain unable to resolve or accept them.

The definition's requirement that some form of cognitive distortion be present makes it readily understandable why personality-related disorders should be regarded as mental disorders: Those who suffer from them are, in greater or lesser degree, out of touch with reality—they are irrational. This requirement is also consistent with (though broader than) cognitive-behavioral views that identify dysfunctional cognitive schema as the source of personality disorders (Beck & Freeman, 1990).

In practice, deciding when a view of reality is a misperception can be difficult, although this difficulty is unavoidable in many psychiatric diagnoses. In
practice, also, psychological distress is probably sufficient to warrant treatment,
whether or not there is cognitive distortion. But a more theoretically satisfying (if
tentative) definition of a personality-related disorder is *a set of life problems that
(a) are characteristically related to the individual's personality traits, (b) cause
the individual significant distress, and (c) are maintained by misperceptions of
reality*. Extreme standing on a trait makes it more likely that one will encounter
the specific kinds of problems that are associated with the trait, and extreme standing on N makes it more likely that one will be significantly distressed by them,
but neither of these is required by the proposed definition.

This definition might be elaborated by allowing *functional impairment* as an
alternative to *distress* in (b), or by adopting some criterion of social harm as an
alternative to personal impairment (to accommodate such conditions as antisocial
personality disorder). But it seems likely that the basic definition would be suitable for the majority of individuals who appear for psychotherapy.

One notable feature of this definition is that it makes personality-related disorders, in principle, curable. *DSM-III-R* personality disorders by definition "continue throughout most of adult life" (p. 335), but that is not implied in the definition offered here. Although the underlying personality traits are very stable in
adulthood (McCrae & Costa, 1990), the particular problems they give rise to may
be acute. Psychotherapeutic interventions (e.g., Beck & Freeman, 1990) that give
people insight into their problems or teach them methods of dealing with distress
may justify discontinuation of the diagnosis.

AN EXAMPLE: THE OBSESSIVE-COMPULSIVE STYLE

Many of these ideas were anticipated by Shapiro in his 1965 classic, *Neurotic
Styles*. His description of *styles* as "forms of functioning—ways of thinking, experiencing, and behaving" is consistent with modern definitions of traits, and the
neurotic styles he so vividly described would probably be generally accepted today
as instances of personality disorders.

Consider the obsessive-compulsive style. Among the hallmarks of this style
are attention to detail; a strong sense of obligation, making "I should . . ." a
preoccupying thought; intense and continuous work; ceaseless efforts at self-
regulation; and a lack of spontaneity. These characteristics clearly call to mind
conscientiousness, a factor defined by such traits as order, dutifulness, achievement striving, self-discipline, and deliberation. It is thus not surprising that the
compulsive scale of the MCMI is strongly related to C (Costa & McCrae, 1990).
But traits related to C are normally considered desirable characteristics, contributing to a productive and fulfilling life (McCrae & Costa, 1991). If these are the
same traits, why are they pathological in the obsessive-compulsive's case?

Shapiro makes it clear that one difference is in the associated distress-proneness. Although they work ceaselessly, such people take little pleasure in their work. Instead, they do it because they feel that they must, and they suffer from an overwhelming sense of pressure, living a life "characterized by a more or less continuous experience of tense deliberateness, a sense of effort, of trying" (p. 31). At the same time, on vacations or weekends, "those occasions when the regular duties, responsibilities, and burdens of work, about which they have complained, are lifted, they show unmistakable signs of discomfort until they have located some new pressure or compelling duty" (p. 40). This damned-if-you-do, damned-if-you-don't phenomenon is characteristic of individuals high in N, who misattribute their intrinsic distress-proneness to some feature of their behavior. High N is also seen in the obsessive's worry about making the "right" decision, and in the common fear of losing control.

Shapiro also noted a loss of contact with reality in such individuals. They are preoccupied with detail to such an extent that they lose all perspective on their actions, devoting as much time and effort to trivial tasks as to major life concerns. Their thinking is dominated by "technical signs and indicators" (p. 52) rather than by a direct perception of their social reality, and this indirect view of the world can lead to either dogmatism or doubt when the signs and indicators misrepresent the reality of the situation. Technical, rule-guided thinking is consistent with the orderliness of high C individuals and contributes to disciplined thinking, notably in the sciences. Unless it is grounded in reality, however, it leads instead to maladaptive absurdities. For example, an obsessive–compulsive may believe that he "should" be more spontaneous and set about deliberately trying to act spontaneously, oblivious to the inherent contradiction in the attempt.

These elements of high C, high N, and cognitive distortion do not covary to form a discrete category. Livesley, Jackson, and Schroeder (1989), for example, found a Compulsive Behaviors factor defined by orderliness, precision, and organization, but they noted that "some dimensions usually associated with obsessive–compulsive personality disorder—namely, Perfectionism, Compulsive Activity, Frugality, Rigid cognitive Style, and Restricted Expression of Affect—were not salient on this component" (p. 299). But high C, high N, and cognitive distortion are also not mutually exclusive, and when they happen to coincide in the same individual, the obsessive–compulsive style may emerge.

PERSONALITY-RELATED DISORDERS AND THE DSM

Individuals have characteristic standings on all five factors; those who are high in N and who have impaired contact with reality are at risk for developing a personality-related disorder. The form of the disorder will be determined by the configuration of traits, and although it is perhaps easiest to identify styles associated chiefly with a single dimension (as the obsessive–compulsive style is with C), there are apt to be problems related to various combinations of traits. The comorbidity that is an embarrassment to the categorical system of the *DSM-III-R* is a perfectly understandable consequence of multidimensional personality structure.

Elsewhere (McCrae, 1994) I have described an alternative to the DSM system for the diagnosis of personality-related disorders. The alternative system requires the development of a compendium of problems in living that are associated with high or low standing on each of the five factors. For example, we might find that individuals very high in O are preoccupied with daydreaming to the point of impracticality, have diffuse and changing vocational interests, or find it difficult to conform to authoritarian structures like the military.

Diagnosis of individual patients begins with an assessment of standing on each of the five factors, either by clinical judgment (Miller, 1990) or by self-reports or observer ratings on standardized measures of the FFM. These assessments would identify potential problem areas in the compendium that should be systematically probed in the clinical interview. If problems are noted, and if they are a significant source of distress to the individual, they would justify the diagnosis of personality-related disorder (especially if they are also associated with some kind of cognitive distortion). Individuals could have from zero to five such diagnoses (e.g., Low Openness-Related Disorder; High Extraversion-Related Disorder).

This alternative has much to recommend it. It capitalizes on the solid empirical foundation of the FFM as a framework for diagnosis; it focuses attention on the patient's problems (which may be resolved) rather than the traits (which are less likely to be substantially changed by therapy); and through its systematic assessment of personality it identifies traits that may be relevant to prognosis and treatment (Miller, 1991), even if they are unrelated to a diagnosis.

Unfortunately, despite clear evidence on the limitations of the categorical system and lengthy debate on dimensional alternatives (Widiger, 1993), the American Psychiatric Association declined to make substantial changes in the diagnosis of personality disorders in the fourth edition of the DSM or to endorse any dimensional system. Perhaps by the time the fifth edition is prepared, there will be enough data to compel a change in thinking. In the meantime, however, the clinician who is obliged to render a DSM diagnosis yet who wishes to adopt some version of the alternative proposal can do so: The Task Force wisely left in place the diagnosis of Personality Disorder Not Otherwise Specified. All problems associated with the five basic dimensions of personality can be coded there.

ACKNOWLEDGMENTS

This chapter benefited from the comments of Paul T. Costa, Jr., Thomas A. Widiger, and the editors.

Official contribution of the National Institutes of Health; not subject to copyright in the United States.

NOTES

[1]Millon avoids this problem in part by restricting the recommended use of the MCMI to clinical populations, in which psychopathology can be assumed; the MCMI then need only identify the form of the pathology.

[2]This apparently incongruous combination of gregariousness and self-consciousness is not really implausible: Revised NEO-PI scales measuring these traits are only modestly negatively correlated, $r = -.23$ (Costa & McCrae, 1992b).

REFERENCES

Allport, G. W. (1961). *Pattern and growth in personality*. New York: Holt, Rinehart and Winston.

American Psychiatric Association. (1987). *Diagnostic and statistical manual of mental disorders* (3rd ed., rev.). Washington, DC: Author.

American Psychiatric Association. (1991). *DSM-IV options book: Work in progress* (9/1/91). Washington, DC: Author.

Baumeister, R. F., & Tice, D. M. (1988). Metatraits. *Journal of Personality, 56*, 571–598.

Beck, A. T., & Freeman, A. (1990). *Cognitive therapy of personality disorders*. New York: Guilford.

Breuer, J., & Freud, S. (1895). *Studies on hysteria. Collected works* (Vol. II). London: Hogarth.

Brooner, R. K., Costa, P. T., Jr., Fetch, L. J., Rousar, E. E., Bigelow, G. E., & Schmidt. (1991). The personality dimensions of male and female drug abusers with and without antisocial personality disorder. In L. S. Harris (Ed.), *Problems of drug dependence: Proceedings of the 53rd Annual Scientific Meeting, Committee on Problems of Drug Dependence*. Rockville, MD: National Institute on Drug Abuse.

Clark, L. A. (1990). Toward a consensual set of symptom clusters for assessment of personality disorder. In J. N. Butcher & C. D. Spielberger (Eds.), *Advances in personality assessment* (Vol. 8, pp. 243–266). Hillsdale, NJ: Lawrence Erlbaum Associates.

Clark, L. A., & Livesley, W. J. (1994). Two approaches to identifying dimensions of personality disorder: Convergence on the five-factor model. In P. T. Costa, Jr., & T. A. Widiger (Eds.), *Personality disorders and the five-factor model of personality* (pp. 261–277). Washington, DC: American Psychological Association.

Costa, P. T., Jr., & McCrae, R. R. (1985). *The NEO Personality Inventory manual*. Odessa, FL: Psychological Assessment Resources.

Costa, P. T., Jr., & McCrae, R. R. (1990). Personality disorders and the five-factor model of personality. *Journal of Personality Disorders, 4*, 362–371.

Costa, P. T., Jr., & McCrae, R. R. (1992a). Normal personality assessment in clinical practice: The NEO Personality Inventory. *Psychological Assessment, 4*, 5–13, 20–22.

Costa, P. T., Jr., & McCrae, R. R. (1992b). *Revised NEO Personality Inventory (NEO-PI-R) and NEO Five-Factor Inventory (NEO-FFI) professional manual*. Odessa, FL: Psychological Assessment Resources, Inc.

Costa, P. T., Jr., & Widiger, T. A. (Eds.). (1994). *Personality disorders and the five-factor model of personality*. Washington, DC: American Psychological Association.

Digman, J. M. (1990). Personality structure: Emergence of the five-factor model. *Annual Review of Psychology, 41*, 417–440.

Epstein, S., & Meier, P. (1989). Constructive thinking: A broad coping variable with specific components. *Journal of Personality and Social Psychology, 57,* 332–350.

Fagan, P. J., Wise, T. N., Schmidt, C. W., Ponticas, Y., Marshall, R. D., & Costa, P. T., Jr. (1991). A comparison of five-factor personality dimensions in males with sexual dysfunction and males with paraphilia. *Journal of Personality Assessment, 57,* 434–448.

Hathaway, S. R., & McKinley, J. C. (1983). *The Minnesota Multiphasic Personality Inventory manual.* New York: Psychological Corporation.

Hirschfeld, R. M. A., Klerman, G. L., Lavori, P., Keller, M. B., Griffith, P., & Coryell, W. (1989). Premorbid personality assessments of first onset of major depression. *Archives of General Psychiatry, 46,* 345–350.

Hyler, S. E., & Rieder, R. O. (1987). *Personality Diagnostic Questionnaire-Revised (PDQ-R).* New York: Author.

Jackson, D. N. (1989). *Basic Personality Inventory manual.* Port Huron, MI: Sigma Assessment Systems.

Jung, C. G. (1933). *Modern man in search of a soul* (W. S. Dell & C. F. Baynes, Trans.). New York: Harcourt Brace Jovanovich.

Kernberg, O. F. (1984). *Severe personality disorders.* New Haven, CT: Yale University Press.

Kiesler, D. J. (1983). The 1982 interpersonal circle: A taxonomy for complementarity in human transactions. *Psychological Review, 90,* 185–214.

Leary, T. (1957). *Interpersonal diagnosis of personality.* New York: Ronald Press.

Livesley, W. J. (1991). Classifying personality disorders: Ideal types, prototypes, or dimensions? *Journal of Personality Disorders, 5,* 52–59.

Livesley, W. J., Jackson, D. N., & Schroeder, M. L. (1989). A study of the factorial structure of personality pathology. *Journal of Personality Disorders, 3,* 292–306.

McCrae, R. R. (1989). Why I advocate the five-factor model: Joint analyses of the NEO-PI and other instruments. In D. M. Buss & N. Cantor (Eds.), *Personality psychology: Recent trends and emerging directions* (pp. 237–245). New York: Springer-Verlag.

McCrae, R. R. (1991). The five-factor model and its assessment in clinical settings. *Journal of Personality Assessment, 57,* 399–414.

McCrae, R. R. (Ed.) (1992). The Five-Factor Model: Issues and applications [Special issue]. *Journal of Personality, 60*(2).

McCrae, R. R. (1993). Moderated analyses of longitudinal personality stability. *Journal of Personality and Social Psychology, 65,* 577–585.

McCrae, R. R. (1994). A reformulation of Axis II: Personality and personality-related problems. In P. T. Costa, Jr., & T. A. Widiger (Eds.), *Personality disorders and the five-factor model of personality* (pp. 303–309). Washington, DC: American Psychological Association.

McCrae, R. R., & Costa, P. T., Jr. (1985). Updating Norman's "adequate taxonomy": Intelligence and personality dimensions in natural language and in questionnaires. *Journal of Personality and Social Psychology, 49,* 710–721.

McCrae, R. R., & Costa, P. T., Jr. (1990). *Personality in adulthood.* New York: Guilford.

McCrae, R. R., & Costa, P. T., Jr. (1991). Adding *Liebe und Arbeit*: The full five-factor model and well-being. *Personality and Social Psychology Bulletin, 17,* 227–232.

McCrae, R. R., & Costa, P. T., Jr. (in press). Conceptions and correlates of Openness to Experience. In R. Hogan, J. A. Johnson, & S. R. Briggs (Eds.), *Handbook of personality psychology.* New York: Academic Press.

McCrae, R. R., Costa, P. T., Jr., & Piedmont, R. L. (1993). Folk concepts, natural language, and psychological constructs: The California Psychological Inventory and the five-factor model. *Journal of Personality, 61,* 1–26.

Miller, M. J. (1990). The power of the "OCEAN": Another way to diagnose clients. *Counselor Education and Supervision, 29*, 283–290.

Miller, T. (1991). The psychotherapeutic utility of the five-factor model of personality: A clinician's experience. *Journal of Personality Assessment, 57*, 415–433.

Millon, T. (1983). *Millon Clinical Multiaxial Inventory manual* (3rd. ed.). Minneapolis: Interpretive Scoring Systems.

Morey, L. (1991). *Personality Assessment Inventory: Professional manual.* Odessa, FL: Psychological Assessment Resources.

Mutén, E. (1991). Self-reports, spouse ratings, and psychophysiological assessment in a behavioral medicine program: An application of the five-factor model. *Journal of Personality Assessment, 57*, 449–464.

Shapiro, D. (1965). *Neurotic styles.* New York: Basic Books.

Shea, M. T. (1988, August). *Interpersonal styles and short-term psychotherapy for depression.* Paper presented at the American Psychological Association Annual Convention, Atlanta, GA.

Siegler, I. C., Welsh, K. A., Dawson, D. V., Fillenbaum, G. G., Earl, N. L., Kaplan, E. B., & Clark, C. M. (1991). Ratings of personality change in patients being evaluated for memory disorders. *Alzheimer Disease and Associated Disorders, 5*, 240–250.

Trull, T. J. (1992). *DSM-III-R* personality disorders and the five-factor model of personality: An empirical comparison. *Journal of Abnormal Psychology, 101*, 553–560.

Tupes, E. C., & Christal, R. E. (1992). Recurrent personality factors based on trait ratings. *Journal of Personality, 60*, 225–251. (Original work published 1961.)

Wakefield, J. C. (1992). The concept of mental disorder: On the boundary between biological facts and social values. *American Psychologist, 47*, 373–388.

Warren, H. C., & Carmichael, L. (1930). *Elements of human psychology* (rev. ed.). Boston: Houghton Mifflin.

Watson, D., & Clark, L. A. (1984). Negative affectivity: The disposition to experience aversive emotional states. *Psychological Bulletin, 96*, 465–490.

Widiger, T. A. (1992). Generalized social phobia versus avoidant personality disorder: A commentary on three studies. *Journal of Abnormal Psychology, 101*, 340–343.

Widiger, T. A. (1993). The *DSM-III-R* categorical personality disorder diagnoses: A critique and an alternative. *Psychological Inquiry, 4*, 75–90.

Widiger, T. A., & Trull, T. J. (1992). Personality and psychopathology: An application of the five-factor model. *Journal of Personality, 60*, 363–393.

Widiger, T. A., Trull, T. J., Clarkin, J. F., Sanderson, C., & Costa, P. T., Jr. (1994). A description of the *DSM-III-R* and *DSM-IV* personality disorders with the five-factor model of personality. In P. T. Costa, Jr., & T. A. Widiger (Eds.), *Personality disorders and the five-factor model of personality* (pp. 41–56). Washington, DC: American Psychological Association.

Wiggins, J. S. (1979). A psychological taxonomy of trait-descriptive terms: The interpersonal domain. *Journal of Personality and Social Psychology, 37*, 395–412.

Wiggins, J. S., & Pincus, A. L. (1989). Conceptions of personality disorders and dimensions of personality. *Psychological Assessment: A Journal of Consulting and Clinical Psychology, 1*, 305–316.

Zonderman, A. B., Herbst, J. H, Schmidt, C., Jr., Costa, P. T., Jr., & McCrae, R. R. (1993). Depressive symptoms as a non-specific, graded risk for psychiatric diagnoses. *Journal of Abnormal Psychology, 102*, 544–552.

3

Differentiating Normal and Deviant Personality by the Seven-Factor Personality Model

C. Robert Cloninger and Dragan M. Svrakic

Thematically, this chapter consists of three main sections. The first section introduces a seven factor model of personality that describes four temperament and three character factors or higher order dimensions. The second section discusses the ability of the seven factor model to discriminate subjects with and without personality disorders (PDs) and to distinguish among individual PDs. The third section compares the ability of the seven factor model, measured by the Temperament and Character Inventory (TCI) (Cloninger, 1992), and the five factor model, measured by the NEO Personality Inventory (NEO-PI; Costa & McCrae, 1985), to diagnose the presence or absence of PDs and to differentially diagnose PD subtypes.

INTRODUCTION

PDs have become a serious scientific, psychiatric, and social problem. Between 11 and 23% of individuals in the general population have PD (Drake & Vaillant, 1988; Reich, Yates, & Nduaguba, 1989). These individuals have poor self-esteem and reduced ability to work and love (Drake & Vaillant, 1988). In addition, they are less educated, have marital difficulties, and tend to be unemployed (Reich et al., 1989). Many subclinical and clinical cases of alcoholism (Cloninger, 1987a) and criminal behavior in men (Guze, Goodwin, & Crane, 1969) and women (Cloninger & Guze, 1973) are associated with underlying PD.

Approximately 50% of psychiatric inpatients (Svrakic, Whitehead, Przybeck, & Cloninger, 1993) and outpatients (Trull, 1992) meet criteria for one or more PDs. In addition to generating chronic personal, social, or professional suffering (American Psychiatric Association, 1987, 1994), these disorders are predisposing, etiopathogenetic, and/or pathoplastic factors for many serious psychiatric conditions, such as psychoactive substance use (Cloninger, 1987a), affective (Akiskal, Hirschfeld, & Yerevanian, 1983), and anxiety disorders (Cloninger, 1986). Most critically, PDs or extreme personality traits interfere with treatment outcome in psychotherapy (Kernberg, 1976), pharmacotherapy (Joyce, Mulder, & Cloninger, 1993), or, even, electroconvulsive therapy (Zimmerman, Coryell, Pfohl, Corenthal, & Stangl, 1986) of Axis I syndromes.

A solid conceptual understanding and classification of PDs are critical to deal with these prevalent and chronic disorders efficiently. However, current diagnostic and classificatory systems for PDs have serious practical and theoretical limitations. The *DSM-III-R* and *DSM-IV* concept of PDs as sharply delineated categories is neither precise nor clinically practical. Furthermore, diagnostic indicators criteria for these disorders overlap and many individuals meet criteria for more than one diagnosis (Pfohl, Coryell, Zimmerman, & Stangl, 1986). This raises questions about the validity and utility of categorical personality diagnoses.

Consequently, many have argued for a dimensional approach emphasizing both the continuous nature of personality traits and the likelihood of more basic dimensions underlying PDs (Clark, 1990; Livesley, 1987; Tellegen, 1985). However, dimensional models of "normal" personality structure usually lack validation in clinical samples (Ben-Porath & Waller, 1992). Moreover, by assuming that PDs are extreme variants of adaptive traits, dimensional models do not answer the question "what is it about such traits that makes them disorders?" Extreme statistical deviation is not sufficient to be dysfunctional (e.g., some individuals are extremely extraverted or introverted without functional impairment).

Several dimensional models of PDs have been introduced (Millon, 1987; Schroeder, Wormworth, & Livesley, 1992; Tyrer & Alexander, 1988) and many studies have addressed the issue of the dimensional structure of PDs (Costa & McCrae, 1990; Trull, 1992; Tyrer & Alexander, 1988; Wiggins & Pincus, 1989). However, no consensus has been reached about the number or content of dimensions that purport to describe personality and its disorders most efficiently.

The Five Factor Model of normal personality, which describes higher order dimensions of Neuroticism, Extraversion, Openness, Agreeableness, and Conscientiousness (Costa & McCrae, 1985), has been advocated as a potential model for abnormal personality (Costa & McCrae, 1990; Trull, 1992; Wiggins & Pincus, 1989). However, clinical applications of this model are rare. The NEO-PI is usually applied to college students and/or adult community samples (Costa & McCrae, 1990; Wiggins & Pincus, 1989), questioning the generalizability of the results to clinical subjects with PDs. Only one study (Trull, 1992) applied the NEO-PI to a sample of psychiatric patients and found that Neuroticism, Extraversion, and Agreeableness were correlated with the number of PD symptoms. However, Axis I mood and anxiety states were not evaluated in this study, leaving open to question the soundness of the conclusions, especially the postulated specificity of neuroticism to PDs.

In summary, categorical systems for PDs have poor reliability (Mellsop, Varghese, Joshua, & Hicks, 1982), diagnostic validity and/or face validity (Blashfield & Breen, 1989). On the other hand, current dimensional models of these disorders have not been clinically validated as diagnostic tools for practical purposes.

I. A NOVEL APPROACH TO CONCEPTUALIZATION OF PERSONALITY DISORDERS

Several lines of evidence suggest that some core features, shared by all PDs, characterize discrete PDs classified in *DSM-III-R*. For example, *DSM-III-R* arranges 11 PDs into three clusters (A, B, and C) each characterized by similar symptomatology (odd/eccentric, dramatic/erratic, and fearful/anxious, respectively). Several studies have supported this clustering (except that the symptoms for compulsive PD tended to form a separate cluster) and suggested that the three clusters represent dimensions along which the *DSM-III-R* PDs vary (Hyler & Lyons, 1988; Kass, Skodol, Charles, Spitzer, & Williams, 1985). However, the ability of these dimensions to discriminate between subjects with and without PD and between PD subtypes has not been tested.

Cloninger, Svrakic, and Przybeck (1993) have recently outlined a general psychobiological model of personality that encompasses four temperament and three character higher order traits. The model introduces a novel approach to the conceptualization, definition, diagnosis, and differential diagnosis of PDs. It has been demonstrated (Svrakic, Przybeck, Whitehead, & Cloninger, 1993) that the characteristics of PDs can be decomposed to distinguish between the core features of all PDs, and features that permit discrimination among different PDs. From a clinical standpoint, identification of the core features is expected to provide an efficient guide to diagnosis and screening, whereas identification of the subtyping features is expected to improve differential diagnosis and treatment of patients with PDs.

A General Psychobiological Model of Personality

Initially, the model described behavioral and neurogenetic aspects of three higher order temperament traits called Novelty Seeking (NS), Harm Avoidance (HA), and Reward Dependence (RD) (Cloninger, 1987b). The structure of temperament was inferred largely from psychometric and genetic studies of personality in humans and neurobiological studies of the functional organization of brain networks underlying classical and operant learning responses to simple appetitive or aversive stimuli in humans and mammals. Behaviorally, the temperament dimensions were defined in terms of individual differences in associative learning in response to novelty, danger or punishment, and reward, respectively. In brief, NS is viewed as a heritable bias in the activation or initiation of behaviors such as frequent exploratory activity in response to novelty, impulsive decision making, extravagance in approach to cues of reward, quick loss of temper, and active avoidance of frustration. HA is viewed as a heritable bias in the inhibition or cessation of behaviors, such as pessimistic worry in anticipation of future problems, passive-avoidant behaviors (such as fear of uncertainty and shyness toward strangers), and rapid fatigability. RD is viewed as a heritable bias in the maintenance or continuation of ongoing behaviors, and is manifest as sentimentality, social attachment, and dependence on approval by others.

Differences between individuals on these temperament dimensions are observable in early childhood and are moderately predictive of adolescent and adult behavior (Sigvardsson, Bohman, & Cloninger, 1987).

The underlying dimensions of temperament and the psychometric properties of the Tridimensional Personality Questionnaire (TPQ), a self report inventory measuring these dimensions, have received empirical support with normative (Cloninger, Przybeck, & Svrakic, 1991) and clinical (Freedland et al., 1991) samples. The most noteworthy exception is that persistence (P), originally thought to be a component of RD, emerged as a distinct fourth dimension of temperament. Twin studies confirmed that each of these four temperament factors had heritability between 50–65% (Heath, Cloninger, & Martin, 1994).

However, combined analysis of the TPQ and the Eysenck Personality Questionnaire (EPQ) (A. Heath, personal communication, 1992) revealed evidence for two or three additional heritable dimensions of personality besides those measured by the TPQ (despite partial overlap of the TPQ and EPQ scales). Hence, three additional personality factors, called character dimensions: these include Self-directedness (SD), Cooperativeness (C), and Self-transcendence (ST) (Cloninger et al., in press). The character dimensions are described in terms of three aspects of self-concept, including identification and conceptualization of the self as an autonomous individual (SD), as an integral part of human society (C), and as an integral part of the universe (ST).

Temperament traits (NS, HA, RD, and P) are defined in terms of their genetic structure. Character dimensions (SD, C, and ST) are defined in terms of aspects of self-concept described in humanistic, transpersonal, and developmental psychology. Personality is defined as the interaction of temperament and character, with various aspects of self-concept modifying the significance and salience of percepts regulated by temperament (Cloninger et al., 1993). However, the most fundamental distinction between character and temperament appears to be that temperament (or the "emotional core" of personality) is defined in terms of perceptual memory and preconceptual biases in habit formation. Character (or the "conceptual core" of personality) is defined in terms of conceptual memory and insight learning or reorganization of self-concepts. More informatively, conceptual memory is regulated by the cortico-limbodiencephalic memory system underlying conscious processing of symbolic meaning and insight learning of concepts. Perceptual memory is regulated by the cortico-striatal memory system underlying the processing of visuospatial information, affective valence, and unconscious habit formation (Cloninger et al., 1993). The availability of measures for temperament and character should facilitate studies of inheritance, information processing, and development (cognitive, emotional, personal, social, moral, and spiritual).

The temperament dimensions are described in detail in prior publications (Cloninger, 1987b; Cloninger et al., 1991). In this chapter, we describe character dimensions in more detail.

The basic concept of Self-directedness (SD) refers to the ability of an individual to control, regulate, and adapt behavior to fit the situation in accordance with individually chosen goals and values. This character dimension can be formulated as a developmental process with several aspects. These include (1) responsibility versus blaming, (2) purposefulness versus lack of goal direction, (3) resourcefulness versus helplessness, (4) self-acceptance versus self-striving, and (5) congruent second-nature versus incongruent habits or personal distrust (Cloninger et al., 1993). These five aspects are lower order traits constituting the higher order character dimension of SD.

The second higher-order character factor of C was formulated to account for individual differences in identification with and acceptance of other people. C can be also formulated as a developmental process with several aspects. These include (1) social acceptance versus intolerance, (2) empathy versus social disinterest, (3) helpfulness versus unhelpfulness, (4) compassion versus revengefulness, and (5) principled versus self-advantage (Cloninger et al., 1993). Again, these five aspects are lower order traits constituting the higher order character dimension of C.

ST and traits associated with spirituality have usually been neglected in systematic research and personality inventories. The concept of ST used here refers to identification with everything conceived as essential and consequential parts of a unified whole. This involves a state of "unitive consciousness" in which everything is part of one totality. Similar to the other dimensions of character, ST can be formulated as a developmental process with several aspects. These aspects can be simplified to some basic experiences and ubiquitous behavior described in a broad spectrum of people and cultures: (1) self-forgetful versus self-conscious experience, (2) transpersonal identification (i.e., identification with nature versus self-differentiation), and (3) spiritual acceptance versus rational materialism (Cloninger et al., 1993).

Table 3.1 presents the TCI (Cloninger, 1992), a 226-item, self-report, true/false instrument developed to measure the 7 dimensions of personality and their corresponding lower order traits. As shown in Table 3.1, the TCI consists of 7 higher order scales, evaluating 4 temperament and 3 character dimensions, and 25 subscales, evaluating 12 temperament and 13 character lower order traits. The TCI has been tested in college students (Svrakic, Przybeck, Whitehead, &

TABLE 3.1 TCI Scales and Subscales

I Temperament:

NOVELTY SEEKING (NS) (40 items)
NS1: exploratory excitability vs. stoic rigidity (11 items)
NS2: impulsiveness vs. reflection (10 items)
NS3: extravagance vs. reserve (9 items)
NS4: disorderliness vs. orderliness (10 items)

HARM AVOIDANCE (HA) (35 items)
HA1: worry and pessimism vs. uninhibited optimism (11 items)
HA2: fear of uncertainty (7 items)
HA3: shyness vs. gregariousness (8 items)
HA4: fatigability vs. vigor (9 items)

REWARD DEPENDENCE (RD) (24 items)
RD1: sentimentality (10 items)
RD3: attachment vs. detachment (8 items)
RD4: dependence vs. independence (6 items)

PERSISTENCE (RD2) (8 items)

II Character:

SELF-DIRECTIVENESS (SD) (44 items)
SD1: responsibility vs. blaming (8 items)
SD2: purposefulness vs. lack of goal direction (8 items)
SD3: resourcefulness vs. helplessness (5 items)
SD4: self-acceptance vs. self-striving (11 items)
SD5: congruent second nature (12 items)

COOPERATIVENESS (C) (42 items)
C1: social acceptance vs. social intolerance (8 items)
C2: empathy vs. social disinterest (8 items)
C3: helpfulness (9 items)
C4: compassion vs. revenge (10 items)
C5: principled vs. self-serving (9 items)

SELF-TRANSCENDENCE (ST) (33 items)
ST1: self-forgetful vs. self-conscious (11 items)
ST2: transpersonal identification (9 items)
ST3: spiritual acceptance (13 items)

TOTAL: 226 ITEMS

Cloninger, 1993), general population (Cloninger et al., 1993), and clinical samples (Svrakic et al., 1993). We describe some of these studies below.

The general population sample (Cloninger et al., 1993) included 300 adults, 150 women and 150 men, who completed the TCI. The results for the temperament dimensions obtained in this sample were similar to those obtained in a national area probability sample of 1019 adults (Cloninger et al., 1991), suggesting that the sample was representative of the general adult population. The recruiters and administrators of the test were blind to the personality model measured by the TCI.

The mean age of the sample was 34.1 years (standard deviation = 12.9, range = 18–91). The sample consisted of 114 whites (62 men and 52 women) and 186 nonwhites (88 men and 98 women).

The internal consistency of the higher order scales was high, ranging from .76 to .87 for the temperament scales, and .84 to .89 for the character scales. Factor analysis of the character scales identified 3 factors. These accounted for 35%, 16%, and 8% of the variance, respectively (59% cumulatively). The standardized factor loadings following Promax rotation yielded a three factor solution which corresponded closely to the rationally defined dimensions of SD, C, and ST (with the exception that one of the SD subscales, i.e., self-acceptance, also loaded strongly with the C scales). This suggests that the ability to accept limitations about oneself is associated with the ability to tolerate and accept limitations in other people. Interfactor correlations were 0.52 for SD and C, −0.16 for C and ST, and 0.06 for SD and ST.

Factor analyses of the temperament *and* character scales identified 7 factors. In the Varimax solution the percents of variance explained by each factor were 14.2, 12.0, 10.1, 9.0, 7.6, 6.0, and 5.7, accounting for 65.0% of the total variance. The standardized factor loadings following Promax rotation are shown in Table 3.2. The derived seven factor solution corresponded closely to the rationally defined four dimensions of temperament (NS, HA, RD, and P) and three dimensions of character (SD, C, and ST). Interfactor correlations above .40 (Table 3.3) were observed for HA and SD (−.47), C and RD (.54), and C and SD (.57). These correlations suggest some reciprocal interaction.

II. DIFFERENTIATING NORMAL AND DEVIANT PERSONALITY BY THE SEVEN FACTOR PERSONALITY MODEL

The ability of the TCI to predict categorical symptoms and diagnoses of *DSM-III-R* PDs was tested in a clinical sample of psychiatric inpatients with and without PDs (Svrakic et al., 1993). In addition, the diagnostic power of the TCI was compared to that of a factor-analytically derived five-factor model, measured by the NEO-PI (section III).

TABLE 3.2 Factor Structure of the TCI Subscales (rotation by Promax)

	F1	F2	F3	F4	F5	F6	F7
NS1	.23	−.19	−.18	.13	**.37**	.33	.27
NS2	.15	−.32	−.32	−.01	**.56**	−.26	−.21
NS3	.04	.26	.25	.09	**.83**	.15	−.18
NS4	−.19	−.16	−.09	−.05	**.66**	−.05	.05
HA1	−.05	−.23	**.75**	−.01	.07	−.02	.07
HA2	.09	.00	**.81**	.02	−.16	.02	.04
HA3	.19	−.17	**.64**	−.26	.07	−.39	.08
HA4	−.24	−.05	**.48**	.15	.18	.06	−.37
RD1	**.63**	−.23	.15	.34	−.05	.11	.10
RD2	−.00	.16	.08	.09	−.13	−.10	**.85**
RD3	.07	−.00	−.07	.09	.02	**.82**	−.11
RD4	**.62**	−.16	.07	−.26	−.15	.40	−.24
C1	**.70**	.07	−.05	−.04	.07	−.06	.24
C2	**.60**	.15	−.14	.10	.07	.10	.00
C3	**.60**	.33	.04	−.18	.13	.11	−.01
C4	**.73**	.12	−.06	.27	−.12	−.18	−.04
C5	**.51**	.45	.19	.04	−.01	−.05	−.03
SD1	.07	**.64**	.21	−.18	.14	.07	.02
SD2	.00	**.53**	−.11	−.04	−.09	.37	.10
SD3	.07	**.56**	.21	−.08	−.05	−.00	.34
SD4	.13	**.64**	−.12	.10	−.08	−.22	−.27
SD5	−.01	**.68**	−.01	.04	−.06	−.05	.27
ST1	−.10	−.05	.13	**.73**	.24	−.02	.14
ST2	.01	−.18	−.18	**.79**	−.14	.09	.00
ST3	.22	.17	.00	**.70**	.02	.03	−.07

Highest loadings given in boldface.
Postulated factors underlined.

Legend:
NS1: exploratory excitability; NS2: impulsiveness; NS3: extravagance; NS4: disorderliness. HA1: worry/pessimism; HA2: fear of uncertainty; HA3: shyness with strangers; HA4: fatigability & asthenia. RD1: sentimentality vs. insensitiveness; RD2: persistence; RD3: attachment vs. detachment; RD4: dependence vs. independence. SD1: responsibility vs. blaming; SD2: purposefulness; SD3: resourcefulness; SD4: self-acceptance vs. self-striving; SD5: congruent second nature. C1: social acceptance vs. social intolerance; C2: empathy; C3: helpfulness; C4: compassion vs. revengefulness; C5: pure-hearted principles. ST1: self-forgetful vs. self-conscious experience; ST2: transpersonal identification vs. self-differentiation; ST3: spiritual acceptance vs. rational materialism.

The central hypotheses were: (1) Low scores on character dimensions of SD, C, and ST are universal (core) features of all PDs, which determine the presence or absence of these disorders; (2) temperament traits of NS, HA, RD, and P, distinguish among subtypes of PDs; (3) each PD category in the *DSM-III-R* (American Psychiatric Association, 1987) is associated with unique combinations of scores on the temperament and character dimensions; (4) the seven-factor model

TABLE 3.3 Correlations Among TCI Temperament and Character Scales

	NS	HA	P	RD	SD	C
NS						
HA	−.08					
P	−.14	−.27				
RD	.08	−.16	.03			
SD	−.26	**−.47**	.28	.21		
C	−.10	−.28	.18	**.54**	**.57**	
ST	.20	−.08	.11	.28	−.10	.15

Correlations above .40 indicated in bold

of personality supersedes the five-factor model as a descriptive and explanatory model of personality and its disorders.

Subjects were 136 psychiatric inpatients. There were 96 women (71%). The mean age was 42 years (standard deviation = 13, range = 18–74 years). 127 subjects (93%) were white.

Personality was assessed dimensionally by the TCI (Cloninger, 1992) and the NEO-PI (Costa & McCrae, 1985). Categorical diagnoses of PDs were based on the Structured Interview for *DSM-III-R* Personality Disorders–Revised (SIDP-R) (Pfohl, Blum, Zimmerman, & Stangl, 1989).

The *DSM-III-R* Axis I was assessed by self-reports and interviews. The self-reports were the Inventory of Depressive Symptomatology-Self Report (IDS-S) (Rush et al., 1986), and the Multiple Affective Adjective Checklist-Revised (MAACL-R; Zuckerman & Lubin, 1985). The interviews included the Washington University Psychiatric Patients Registry (Washington University School of Medicine, 1991) and the Inventory of Depressive Symptomatology-Clinician Rated (Rush et al., 1986). The former is a comprehensive clinical interview providing demographic information, attending physician's diagnosis, Axis I evaluation, evaluation of Antisocial personality (Axis II), medical history (Axis III), and global assessment of functioning (Axis V).

Results

Among the 136 patients, 134 had a primary Axis I diagnosis. 112 patients (82%) had a primary mood disorder, such as major depression, bipolar disorder, or dysthymia. The mean IDS-S score was 39.3 (standard deviation = 14.7). Compared to a mean score of 36.5 in a sample of psychiatric outpatients (Rush et al., 1986), the current sample appeared to be mildly depressed.

Among the 136 patients, 66 subjects (49%) had at least one *DSM-III-R* PD. Multiple diagnoses were frequent, ranging from one to seven per case. In general, the 66 subjects with PDs met criteria for 139 diagnoses, or more than 2 diagnoses per case. The mean number of PD symptoms for all 136 patients was 21.3 (standard deviation = 11.5). For the 70 non-PD subjects the mean was 14.0 (standard deviation = 6.9) and for the 66 cases with PDs the mean was 29.0 (standard deviation = 10.3).

The most frequent diagnoses were Histrionic (23 cases, 35%), Avoidant (20 cases, 30%), and Obsessive–Compulsive PD (20 cases, 30%). Other frequent diagnoses were Self-defeating (16), Borderline (11), Antisocial (10), and Narcissistic PD (8). The least frequent diagnoses were Paranoid (4) and Schizoid PD (1). Sadistic and Schizotypal PD were not observed in this sample. Among the 70 patients without PD, 17 were called "mixed" because they had all but one of the required criteria for at least two *DSM-III-R* PDs.

The mean scores, standard deviations, and alpha coefficients of the seven TCI dimensions are summarized in Table 3.4. Each dimension and its components showed extensive variability and high internal consistency in this patient sample, similar to those observed in community samples (Cloninger et al., 1993).

In order to examine the ability of TCI self-reports to predict independent interview diagnoses of PD, we first examined the correlations among the seven dimensional scores and PD symptom counts from the SIDP-R interview (Table 3.5). Low character dimensions, notably low SD and C, were associated with high symptom counts for all clusters of PD. In addition to being related to low character scores, Cluster A (aloof) symptoms were most highly associated with low RD ($r = -.37$), Cluster B (impulsive) symptoms with high NS ($r = .44$), and Cluster C (fearful) symptoms with high HA ($r = .43$), as predicted by Cloninger (1987).

Table 3.6 summarizes correlations among seven dimensional scores and symptom counts for 14 PDs. Again, SD and C were consistently negatively correlated with the number of symptoms for individual *DSM-III-R* PDs. In other words, the character dimensions appeared to be a common denominator extending across all categorical diagnoses of PDs. (The relationship between ST and PDs will be discussed later).

As shown in Table 3.6, individual PDs manifested specific combinations of high and low scores on the temperament dimensions of NS, HA, and RD. For example, Antisocial personality disorder was characterized by high NS and low RD, Histrionic personality disorder by high NS and high RD, and Dependent personality disorder primarily by high HA and high RD.

The correlational analyses suggested that temperament dimensions of NS, HA, and RD, and character dimensions of SD and C are most relevant to the *DSM-III-R* conceptualization of PDs (without controlling for age and depression). However, after controlling for age and depression, some of the TCI dimensions did not remain predictive of the PD symptoms. Stepwise multiple regression analyses (Table 3.7) showed that *the number of symptoms for PDs was predicted only by the TCI character scales of SD, C, and ST.*

TABLE 3.4 Mean Scores and Standard Deviations (as proportion of total items) and Cronbach's Alphas for TCI*

	# items	Mean	SD	Alpha
Novelty Seeking	**40**	**.45**	**.16**	**.81**
NS1	11	.38	.24	.71
NS2	10	.41	.25	.69
NS3	9	.55	.28	.77
NS4	10	.38	.21	.52
Harm Avoidance	**35**	**.64**	**.21**	**.89**
HA1	11	.60	.27	.81
HA2	7	.74	.24	.62
HA3	8	.65	.30	.80
HA4	9	.60	.29	.77
Reward Dependence	**24**	**.71**	**.17**	**.75**
RD1	10	.79	.19	.61
RD3	8	.61	.30	.79
RD4	6	.70	.22	.49
Persistence (RD2)	**8**	**.69**	**.21**	**.48**
Self-directiveness	**44**	**.60**	**.20**	**.90**
SD1	8	.59	.29	.74
SD2	8	.56	.29	.72
SD3	5	.50	.32	.64
SD4	11	.64	.24	.75
SD5	12	.63	.27	.82
Cooperativeness	**42**	**.82**	**.13**	**.83**
C1	8	.85	.17	.63
C2	7	.76	.21	.51
C3	8	.82	.16	.51
C4	10	.83	.21	.78
C5	9	.80	.15	.42
Self-transcendence	**33**	**.44**	**.18**	**.83**
ST1	11	.41	.24	.73
ST2	9	.37	.23	.68
ST3	13	.52	.22	.70

* For 136 psychiatric inpatients
NS1: exploratory excitability; **NS2**: impulsiveness; **NS3**: extravagance; **NS4**: disorderliness. **HA1**: anticipatory worry; **HA2**: fear of uncertainty; **HA3**: shyness with strangers; **HA4**: fatigability. **RD1**: sentimentality; **RD3**: attachment; **RD4**: dependence. **SD1**: responsibility; **SD2**: purposefulness; **SD3**: resourcefulness; **SD4**: self-acceptance; **SD5**: congruent second nature. **C1**: social acceptance; **C2**: empathy; **C3**: helpfulness; **C4**: compassion; **C5**: principled. **ST1**: self-forgetfulness; **ST2**: transpersonal identification; **ST3**: spiritual acceptance.

TABLE 3.5 Correlations Between TCI Scales and Total Number of Symptoms for PDs, DSM-III-R Cluster A, Cluster B, and Cluster C PDs

	Total # PD Symptoms	Cluster A Symptoms	Cluster B Symptoms	Cluster C Symptoms
Novelty Seeking	**.22[c]**	.02	**.44[a]**	−.06
Harm Avoidance	**.31[b]**	**.23[b]**	.08	**.43[a]**
Reward Dependence	−.14	**−.37[a]**	−.08	−.04
Persistence	.00	−.07	.04	−.01
Self-directedness	**−.56[a]**	**−.35[a]**	**−.43[a]**	**−.50[a]**
Cooperativeness	**−.44[a]**	**−.44[a]**	**−.40[a]**	**−.28[b]**
Self-transcendence	.02	−.08	.03	.04
Multiple R	.62	.50	.63	.56

Significant correlations shown in bold.
a = $p < .0001$; b = $p < .001$; c = $p < .01$.

Stepwise logistic regression was carried out to predict the presence or absence of any PD from the TCI scores. Only SD (partial R = −.54, $p < .001$) and C (partial R = −.30, $p < .05$) entered the model as substantial predictors of categorical PD diagnoses. Overall rank correlation between the logistic function and the presence or absence of PD was high (Somer's D = .59, model Chi-square = 38.7, $p < .0001$).

In the 34 patients with SD scores below 20, there was a high risk of PD regardless of their C score. Conversely, in subjects with a SD score higher than 30, the presence of PD was determined by their low C scores. In other words, high C reduces the risk of PD in those with moderate to high SD. This is clinically relevant for several PDs. For example, many narcissistic and/or antisocial personalities may have high scores on the SD dimension because they can be quite resourceful and purposeful (i.e., they are successful in pursuing their narcissistic or antisocial goals). However, low C (e.g., low empathy and helpfulness) makes these individuals maladaptive (i.e., they have PD).

SD scores predicted the number of PD diagnoses. Sixty-one percent of the subjects with high SD scores (30 to 44) were without PDs, 15% had one, and only 10% had two or more PD diagnoses. In contrast, only 6% of the subjects with low SD scores (below 20) were without PDs, 35% had one, and 56% two or more PD diagnoses. In general, patients with high SD scores had 0.6 diagnoses, those with medium scores had 0.9 diagnoses, and those with low scores had 2.3 diagnoses on average.

TABLE 3.6 Correlations between TCI Scales and Number of Symptoms for Individual PDs

PD Symptoms	TCI scales						
	NS	HA	RD	P	SD	C	ST
Antisocial (childhood)	.40[a]	−.09	−.17[c]	.02	−.20[c]	−.31[b]	.00
Antisocial (adult)	.40[a]	−.04	−.26[c]	−.02	−.23[c]	−.36[a]	−.07
Histrionic	.44[a]	−.04	.16	.06	−.29[b]	−.24[b]	.08
Borderline	.21[c]	.26[c]	−.08	.04	−.48[a]	−.29[c]	−.04
Narcissistic	.14	.13	.01	.01	−.26[c]	−.22[c]	.09
Passive-Aggressive	.24[c]	.12	−.11	−.19[c]	−.32[b]	−.29[b]	.03
Avoidant	−.30[b]	.51[a]	−.11	−.01	−.43[a]	−.15	−.05
Obsessive-Compulsive	−.12	.25[b]	−.15	.08	−.26[b]	−.20[c]	.00
Dependent	.00	.34[a]	.24[c]	.08	−.40[a]	−.13	.13
Schizoid	−.16	.14	−.33[a]	—	−.14	−.21[c]	−.23[c]
Schizotypal	−.05	.23[c]	−.28[b]	−.08	−.30[b]	−.29[b]	.09
Paranoid	.21[c]	.15	−.25[c]	−.08	−.32[a]	−. 47[a]	−.08
Sadistic	.18[c]	.05	−.13	−.05	−.23[c]	−.26[c]	.12
Self-Defeating	.09	.30[b]	−.00	—	−.41[a]	−.22[c]	.03

Significant correlations shown in bold.
a = $p < .0001$; b = $p < .001$; c = $p < .05$.

NS: Novelty Seeking; HA: Harm Avoidance; RD: Reward Dependence; P: Persistence; SD: Self-directedness; C: Cooperativeness; ST: Self-transcendence.

Thirty-three subjects had Cluster B (impulsive) PD, whereas 41 had Cluster C (anxious) PD. The TCI scores of patients in Cluster B or not, Cluster C or not, and in combinations of these two (B only, C only, both, and neither) were compared (Table 3.8). Multivariate analyses of variance revealed that the differences among the groups in each comparison were statistically significant ($p < .01$). Analyses of variance were used to indicate which scales differed among the groups. All clusters of PD were low in SD and C ($p < .01$). In addition, Cluster B patients were higher in NS, Cluster C patients were higher in HA, and the combination cases were higher in both, as expected.

TABLE 3.7 Stepwise Regression of SIDP-R PD Symptoms on TCI Scales Controlling for Age and Depression

Variables	PD Symptoms	
	Partial R^2	p
Age and Depression	.35	.0001
Novelty Seeking		
Harm avoidance		
Reward Dependence		
Persistence		
Self-directedness	.13	.0001
Cooperativeness	.03	.0076
Self-transcendence	.02	.0376
Cumulative R^2	.18	.0001
MODEL R^2	.53	. 0001

TABLE 3.8 Differences in TCI Scores for Cluster B vs. Non-B, Cluster C vs. Non-C, and for "All Groups"*

	Cluster B Impulsive PDs		Cluster C Fearful PDs		"All Groups"	
	F	p	F	p	F	p
Novelty Seeking	**16.14**	**.0001**	0.13	ns	**5.83**	**.0009**
Harm Avoidance	1.13	ns	13.48	**.0004**	5.16	**.0021**
Reward Dependence	0.75	ns	1.18	ns	1.41	ns
Persistence	0.01	ns	0.64	ns	0.27	ns
Self-Directedness	**13.39**	**.0004**	**14.98**	**.0002**	**10.40**	**.0001**
Cooperativeness	**13.79**	**.0003**	**8.0**	**.0054**	**6.69**	**.0003**
Self-transcendence	0.13	ns	0.22	ns	0.70	ns

Significant results shown in bold.

* "All groups" includes: Cluster B PDs; Cluster C PDs; Both Cluster B and C PDs; and Neither.

III. DIAGNOSTIC ASSESSMENT OF PERSONALITY DISORDERS FROM SEVEN FACTOR AND FIVE FACTOR PERSONALITY MODELS

This section presents data comparing the ability of the seven factor personality model, measured by the TCI, and the five factor personality model, measured by the NEO-PI, to diagnose the presence or absence of PD and to differentially diagnose PD subtypes in the same sample of 136 psychiatric patients.

The mean scores, standard deviations, and alpha coefficients for the NEO-PI scales and subscales are presented in Table 3.9. The internal consistency of the NEO-PI facet scales was high to very high, with alphas ranging from .79 to 93.

Several of the NEO-PI scales were moderately to highly intercorrelated. Neuroticism was related to Extraversion (−.40), Agreeableness (−.34), and Conscientiousness (−.27). Extraversion was related to Openness (.50) and Agreeable-

TABLE 3.9 Mean Scores, Standard Deviations, and Cronbach Alphas for NEO-PI Scales

	Men		Women		
	Mean	SD	Mean	SD	Alpha
Neuroticism	**105.0**	**26.0**	**113.4**	**25.0**	**.93**
N1: Anxiety	18.7	5.8	21.9	5.6	.82
N2: Hostility	24.6	5.3	14.2	5.8	.78
N3: Depression	19.8	6.3	21.8	6.9	.86
N4: Self-consciousness	17.8	5.3	19.4	5.2	.75
N5: Impulsiveness	18.7	4.7	18.0	4.9	.73
N6: Vulnerability	15.5	5.8	18.1	5.4	.81
Extraversion	**98.2**	**20.3**	**100.2**	**19.1**	**.87**
E1: Warmth	20.1	5.7	22.6	5.1	.81
E2: Gregariousness	14.0	5.1	15.3	4.6	.64
E3: Assertiveness	15.0	4.3	13.6	4.7	.65
E4: Activity	16.4	4.1	16.2	4.6	.62
E5: Excitement-Seeking	16.3	4.2	15.4	5.1	.62
E6: Positive Emotions	16.4	4.4	17.0	6.1	.80
Openness	**105.02**	**21.7**	**108.9**	**16.5**	**.87**
01: Fantasy	17.4	5.7	16.6	5.1	.75
02: Aesthetics	16.2	6.0	19.0	5.0	.79
03: Feelings	20.4	4.1	21.5	3.9	.57
04: Actions	14.0	4.1	14.4	4.2	.65
05: Ideas	16.9	5.2	17.8	5.4	.81
06: Values	20.1	4.0	19.6	3.7	.61
Agreeableness	**45.5**	**7.2**	**48.3**	**8.0**	**.79**
Conscientiousness	**42.4**	**9.8**	**46.8**	**8.1**	**.80**

The sample was composed of 136 psychiatric inpatients (40 men and 96 women).

ness (.22). Openness was related to Agreeableness (.30) and Agreeableness was related to Conscientiousness (.32).

Men were higher in Neuroticism, Agreeableness, and Conscientiousness than norms for adults in the community, whereas women were significantly higher in Neuroticism, Agreeableness, and Conscientiousness, and lower in Extraversion and Openness than published norms for adults in the general community. With the exception of Openness, the NEO-PI scales were related to depression. The correlation coefficients ranged from −.34 to .50. With the exception of Novelty Seeking, the TCI scales were related to depression, the correlation coefficients ranging from −.49 to .46.

One TCI scale, Novelty Seeking, was related to age (−.30). This is a postulated feature of this dimension (Cloninger, 1987b). In contrast, four NEO-PI scales (with the exception of Extraversion) were related to age, the coefficients ranging from −.28 to .25.

The TCI and NEO-PI scales were related in a meaningful and predictable way (Table 3.10). The highest positive correlations were between Harm Avoidance and Neuroticism (.71), and between Cooperativeness and Agreeableness (.64), whereas the highest negative correlations were observed between Self-directedness and Neuroticism (−.75) and between Harm Avoidance and Extraversion (−.65).

Table 3.10 also summarizes two sets of multiple regression analyses. The multiple Rs in the last column of the table reflect the variance in the TCI explained by the NEO-PI. The multiple Rs in the bottom row reflect the variance in the NEO-PI explained by the TCI. Overall, the five NEO-PI scales accounted for only 9%

TABLE 3.10 Correlations Among TCI and the NEO-PI Scales

	N	E	O	A	Con	**Multiple R**
NS	.06	.45[a]	.29[b]	−.20	−.41[a]	**.66[a]**
HA	.71[a]	−.65[a]	−.21	−.19	−.15	**.82[a]**
RD	−.08	.44[a]	.34[a]	.46[a]	.05	**.62[a]**
P	.02	.10	.02	.04	.31[b]	**.36[c]**
SD	−.75[a]	.35[a]	.16	.43[a]	.29[b]	**.79[a]**
C	−.38[a]	.32[a]	.25[c]	.64[a]	.33[a]	**.68[a]**
ST	−.02	.25[c]	.12	.07	.13	**.30**
Multiple R	**.84[a]**	**.79[a]**	**.46[a]**	**.69[a]**	**.57[a]**	

a = $p < .0001$; b = $p < .001$; c = $p < .01$. NS: Novelty Seeking; HA: Harm Avoidance; RD: Reward Dependence; P: Persistence; SD: Self-directedness; C: Cooperativeness; ST: Self-transcendence; N: Neuroticism; E: Extraversion; O: Openness; A: Agreeableness; Con: Conscientiousness.

of the variance in TCI Self-transcendence and 13% of the variance in TCI Persistence. However, the NEO-PI scales and the other five TCI scales shared about half their variance in common on average.

The seven TCI dimensions accounted for 21% of the variance in NEO-PI Openness, but other investigators have found Openness to be composed of clinically heterogeneous facets (Widiger & Trull, 1992). Accordingly, we regressed the 6 Openness facets on the 7 TCI dimensions, which accounted for about 30% of the variance in the NEO-PI Openness scale. Table 3.11 presents correlations between the NEO-PI dimensions and the number of symptoms for individual PDs. Most disorders were characterized by high Neuroticism (the exceptions were Antisocial, Schizoid, and Sadistic) and low Agreeableness (the exceptions were Dependent,

TABLE 3.11 Correlations of NEO-PI Dimensions with Number of Symptoms for Individual PDs

PD Symptoms	N	E	O	A	Con	Multiple R
Antisocial (child)	.16	.04	.05	**−.41**[a]	**−.36**[a]	.50[a]
Antisocial (adult)	.16	.02	.00	**−.41**[a]	**−.30**[b]	.46[a]
Histrionic	**.25**[c]	**.28**[b]	.14	**−.22**[c]	−.09	.52[a]
Borderline	**.53**[a]	−.07	.09	**−.37**[a]	**−.28**[b]	.60[a]
Narcissistic	**.30**[b]	.13	**.22**[c]	**−.23**[c]	**−.19**[c]	.46[a]
Passive-Aggressive	**.24**[c]	−.02	**.17**[c]	**−.22**[c]	**−.41**[a]	.46[a]
Avoidant	**.43**[a]	**−.40**[a]	.00	−.07	.00	.53[a]
Obsessive-Compulsive	**.18**[c]	**−.23**[c]	.00	−.08	.00	.27
Dependent	**.46**[a]	−.03	.14	.01	−.03	.53[a]
Schizoid	.08	**−.34**[a]	**−.22**[c]	−.16	−.02	.36[c]
Schizotypal	**.25**[b]	**−.25**[b]	.02	**−.20**[c]	−.14	.36[c]
Paranoid	**.29**[b]	**−.18**[c]	−.08	**−.48**[a]	**−.30**[b]	.52[a]
Sadistic	.15	.03	.07	**−.28**[b]	**−.21**[c]	.34[c]
Self-Defeating	**.37**[a]	−.13	.06	**−.20**[c]	−.14	.39[b]
Multiple R	.62[a]	.63[a]	.40	.61[a]	.54[a]	

N = 136. a = $p < .0001$; b = $p < .001$; c = $p < .05$. N: Neuroticism, E: Extraversion, O: Openness, A: Agreeableness, Con: Conscientiousness. The multiple Rs between the NEO-PI scales and each PD are presented in the last column. The multiple Rs between each NEO-PI scale and 11 PDs are presented in the bottom row. Significant correlations are shown in bold.

Avoidant, Schizoid, and Obsessive-Compulsive). Low Extraversion correlated with symptoms for "introverted and aloof" PDs (Paranoid, Schizoid, Schizotypal, and Obsessive-Compulsive), whereas high Extraversion characterized Histrionic PD. Low Conscientiousness characterized "impulsive" PDs such as Sadistic, Passive-Aggressive, Paranoid, Antisocial, Borderline and Narcissistic. Openness was largely unrelated to the number of symptoms for individual PDs.

Thus, without controlling for age and depression, the NEO-PI dimensions of Neuroticism, Extraversion, Agreeableness, and Conscientiousness appeared most relevant to the *DSM-III-R* conceptualization of PDs. However, stepwise regressions (Table 3.12) indicated that, after controlling for age and depression, the number of PD disorder symptoms was predicted only by high Neuroticism and low Agreeableness.

Stepwise multiple regressions of the total number of PD symptoms with 5 NEO-PI and 7 TCI scales considered together as predictors were performed to compare their relative predictive power (Table 3.13). After controlling for age and depression, the TCI character scales of SD, C, and ST were the only significant ($p < .05$) predictors of the number of PD symptoms. There was a trend for NEO-PI Openness as a fourth predictor, but it added only 1% additional variance and was not significant ($p = .08$).

In summary, controlling for age and depression, the TCI accounted for more of the personality-specific variance in number of PD symptoms than did the NEO-PI (18% versus 11%). Without age and depression as covariates, the TCI accounted for only slightly more variance than the NEO-PI (38% versus 36%), suggesting that Neuroticism is more confounded with nonspecific factors than is SD.

TABLE 3.12 Stepwise Regression of the Total Number of PD Symptoms on NEO-PI Scale Controlling for Age and Depression

	PD Symptoms	
Variables	Partial R^2	p
Age and Depression	.35	.0001
Neuroticism	.07	.0001
Extraversion		
Openness		
Agreeableness	.04	.003
Conscientiousness		
Cumulative R^2	.11	.0001
MODEL R^2	.46	. 0001

TABLE 3.13 Stepwise Regression of the Total Number of PD Symptoms on Both TCI and NEO-PI Scales Controlling for Age and Depression

	PD Symptoms	
Variables	Partial R^2	p
Age and Depression	.35	.0001
TCI Self-directedness	.13	.0001
TCI Cooperativeness	.03	.0076
TCI Self-transcendence	.02	.0376
NEO-PI Openness	.01	.0852
MODEL R^2	.54	. 0001

Note that no NEO-PI variables added significantly to the TCI variables

Logistic regressions of categorical PD diagnoses on both the TCI and the NEO-PI were performed to determine which scales predict the presence or absence of PD when the instruments are considered together. After controlling for age and depression, the only predictor that entered the model was the SD character scale (Chi square = 43.59, $p < .0001$). None of the other 11 TCI and NEO-PI scales was significant. Without age and depression as covariates, the two most significant predictors of the presence of categorical diagnoses were SD (parameter estimate .12, Wald Chi square 16.33, $p < .0001$) and C (parameter estimate .12, Wald Chi square 6.23, $p < .01$). The final predictor to enter the model was NEO-PI Openness (parameter estimate −.03, Wald Chi square 4.70, $p < .03$).

DISCUSSION

Normal personality traits described in the TCI and NEO-PI tended to generalize to PDs, suggesting that deviant traits may be conceptualized as extreme variants of normal behavior. Both the TCI and NEO-PI explained a substantial portion of the variance in PDs. The correlation matrix for the NEO-PI facet scales and symptoms of individual PDs (Table 3.12) is similar to that reported by Trull (1992), who found high correlations between the number of criterion *DSM-III-R* symptoms for PDs and the NEO-PI scales of Neuroticism, Extraversion, and Agreeableness. In the present study, only high Neuroticism and low Agreeableness were statistically significant when age and depression were controlled. This suggests that the NEO-PI may have difficulty discriminating clinical subjects with PDs (who are high in Neuroticism) from clinical subjects without PDs who have depression and anxiety and are high in Neuroticism as well.

The TCI appears more diagnostically specific for PDs than the NEO-PI. First, low scores on character dimensions appear to be a common denominator extending across the majority of discrete PDs. Second, subjects with PDs manifest specific combinations of high and/or low temperament dimensions. These combinations define the clinical subtype or diagnostic label for individual PDs. For example, Antisocial and Histrionic PD are expected to have low SD and/or C. In addition to this common feature, Antisocial personalities manifest high NS, low HA, and low RD, whereas Histrionic personalities manifests high NS, low HA, and high RD (the high RD makes Histrionic persons more suitable for psychotherapeutic corrections than Antisocial persons).

This subject sample has several limitations. The sample size was relatively small and some *DSM-III-R* PDs were under represented. However, it seems reasonable to suggest that low character dimensions may be universal (core) features of all PDs, which determine the presence or absence of these disorders. Temperament dimensions of NS, HA, and RD distinguish among subtypes of PDs. In other words, this study suggests that the characteristics of PDs can be decomposed to distinguish between the core features and the subtyping features of PDs. This has implications for the conceptualization, definition, diagnosis, differential diagnosis, and treatment of PDs; also, this provides an efficient guide to integration of categorical and dimensional models of PDs.

Conceptualization and Definition of Personality Disorder

The recent description of character by Cloninger et al. (1993) was, on the one hand, intended to account for some traits not covered in the TPQ (such as spirituality, hostility and revengefulness) and, on the other hand, to help clarify current concepts of what a personality disorder is in contrast to more optimal adaptation. As shown in this study, the character dimensions predict the presence or absence of PD. The temperament dimensions distinguish among subtypes of PDs and are critical for differential diagnosis of these disorders. Therefore, extreme temperament traits are expected to be associated with personal, social and/or occupational consequences that warrant the PD diagnosis only when accompanied by low character traits. This conception provides guidelines for the definition of PD (see Cloninger et al., 1993).

Diagnosis and Screening of Personality Disorders

The character traits of Self-directedness (SD) and Cooperativeness (C) can be measured and used for diagnosing and/or screening for the presence or absence of PD. Depending on these traits, the risk of PD in a clinical sample can vary from about 12% to 94% (Svrakic et al., 1993).

The Self-transcendence (ST) character trait, even though predictive of the number of PD symptoms, seems somewhat less relevant to the *DSM-III-R* conceptualization of PDs than SD and C. This probably reflects different age-specific developmental lines characteristic of ST and PDs. The latter usually develop in adolescence or early adulthood and the most severe symptoms tend to diminish after 35–40 years of age (American Psychiatric Association, 1987). In contrast, the significance of ST in early adulthood is arguable, but it becomes a major concern around 35 years of age (Koenig, Kvale, & Ferrel, 1988; Woodward, et al., 1992), that is, when people face death and misfortune (Cloninger et al., 1993). In other words, high ST may be correlated with indicators of maturity and integrity rather than with PD symptomatology. In this sample, psychiatric subjects with either Axis I or Axis II disorders manifested low SD (Cloninger et al., 1993) as compared to the general population subjects. In other words, low SD may be associated with psychopathology without specificity for PDs.

The Persistence dimension (P), which seems less relevant to the *DSM-III-R* conceptualization of PDs than the other three temperament dimensions, may prove critical for distinguishing neurotic (anxious) patients from those with other nonpsychotic psychiatric syndromes.

Differential Diagnosis of Personality Disorders

This study suggests that temperament dimensions discriminate among the *DSM-III-R* PDs. First, membership in Clusters A (aloof), B (impulsive), and C (fearful) is defined by low RD, high NS, and high HA, respectively. Next, discrete *DSM-III-R* PDs are characterized by specific combinations of high and/or low temperament dimensions; these combinations define the clinical subtype of PDs. Moreover, each individual PD category has a unique combination of scores in the seven factor model, indicating that the seven factor personality model could be used to replace or refine current PD criteria in order to reduce overlap among categories.

The TCI does not merely replicate the *DSM-III-R* clustering of PDs. Even though each of the temperament dimensions roughly corresponds to one of the *DSM-III-R* clusters of PDs (e.g., NS corresponds to the impulsive cluster, RD to the aloof cluster, and HA to the fearful cluster), it is the *combinations* of temperament dimensions (i.e., combinations of traits observable in each of the clusters) that define clinical subtypes of PDs. In other words, discrete PDs have features that characterize more than one cluster. These shared dimensions explain the overlap in categorical diagnoses of individual PDs.

Treatment of Personality Disorders

The distinction between character and temperament is expected to generate studies addressing the issue of specific and optimal treatment for PDs. For example, different therapeutic techniques may be relevant for the development of different aspects of character (Assagioli, 1965; Frankl, 1984; Goleman, 1988; Kirschenbaum & Henderson, 1989; Watson & Tharp, 1989; Wilbur, 1985). In contrast, temperament variables may be more responsive to psychopharmacological and behavioral interventions (Cloninger, 1986; Liebowitz, 1988; Sheard, Marini, Bridges, & Wagner, 1976). See also Cloninger et al., (1993) and Svrakic et al. (1993) for more details on this subject.

Integration of Categorical and Dimensional Models of Personality Disorders

The seven factor model of temperament and character provides guidelines for the integration of dimensional and categorical models of PDs. Low character traits are a common denominator (dimension) extending across all types of severe personality dysfunction currently classified as PDs. The *DSM-III-R* discrete PDs are categorical maladaptive syndromes, defined as unique combination of extreme temperament variants (low and high scores on temperament traits) related orthogonally to the basic dimension of low character traits.

This integrative model is consistent with the medical model approach to psychopathology and should provide a broader paradigm that can encourage both psychosocial and neurobiological progress. It retains the traditional notion of diagnosis and clinical decision making (each category of PD can be defined as a unique profile on the seven dimensions), yet, due to its dimensional character, the integrative model is expected to preserve more information about the patient and to suggest optimal treatment more precisely than current categorical systems.

ACKNOWLEDGMENTS

This research was supported in part by grant MH31302 from the National Institute of Mental Health, grants AA07982 and AA08028 from the National Institute of Alcoholism, and a pilot research grant from the MacArthur Foundation Mental Health Research Network I (Psychobiology of Depression).

REFERENCES

Akiskal, H. S., Hirschfeld, M. A., & Yerevanian, B. I. (1983). The relationship of personality to affective disorders: A critical review. *Archives of General Psychiatry, 40,* 801–810.

American Psychiatric Association (1987). *Diagnostic and statistical manual of mental disorders* (3rd ed.) (Rev.). Washington, D.C.: Author.

American Psychiatric Association (1994). *Diagnostic and statistical manual of mental disorders* (4th ed.). Washington, D.C.: Author.

Assagioli, R. (1965). *Psychosynthesis: A manual of principles and techniques*. New York: Viking.

Ben-Porath, Y. S., & Waller, N. G. (1992). "Normal" personality inventories in clinical assessment: General requirements and the potential for using the NEO Personality Inventory. *Psychological Assessment, 4,* 14–19.

Blashfield, R. K., & Breen, M. J. (1989). Face validity of the *DSM-III-R* personality disorders. *American Journal of Psychiatry, 146,* 1575–1579.

Clark, L. A. (1990). Toward a consensual set of symptom clusters for assessment of personality disorder. In J. N. Butcher & C. D. Speilberger (Eds.), *Advances in personality assessment* (pp. 243–266). Hillsdale, NJ: Lawrence Erlbaum Associates.

Cloninger, C. R. (1986). A unified biosocial theory of personality and its role in the development of anxiety states. *Psychiatric Developments, 3,* 167–226.

Cloninger, C. R. (1987a). Neurogenetic adaptive mechanisms in alcoholism. *Science, 236,* 410–416.

Cloninger, C. R. (1987b). A systematic method for clinical description and classification of personality variants. *Archives of General Psychiatry, 44,* 573–588.

Cloninger, C. R. (1992). *The temperament and character inventory.* (Available from C. R. Cloninger, M.D., Washington University School of Medicine, Department of Psychiatry, PO Box 8134, St. Louis, MO, 63110)

Cloninger, C. R., & Guze, S. B. (1973). Psychiatric illness and female criminality: The role of sociopathy and hysteria in the antisocial women. *American Journal of Psychiatry, 127,* 303–311.

Cloninger, C. R., Przybeck, T. R., & Svrakic, D. M. (1991). The Tridimensional Personality Questionnaire: U.S. normative data. *Psychological Reports, 69,* 1047–1057.

Cloninger, C. R., Svrakic, D. M., & Przybeck, T. R. (1993). A psychobiological model of temperament and character. *Archives of General Psychiatry, 50,* 975–990.

Costa, P. T. Jr., & McCrae, R. R. (1985). *The NEO personality inventory manual.* Odessa, FL: Psychological Assessment Resources.

Costa, P. T. Jr., & McCrae, R. R. (1990). Personality disorders and the Five Factor model of personality. *Journal of Personality Disorders, 4,* 362–371.

Drake, R. E., & Vaillant, G. E. (1985). A validity study of Axis II of DSM III. *American Journal of Psychiatry, 142,* 553–558.

Frankl, V. E. (1984). *Man's search for meaning: An introduction to logotherapy* (3rd ed.). New York: Touchstone.

Freedland, K. E., Carney, R. M., Krone, R. J., Smith, L. J., Rich, M. W., Eisenkramer, G., & Fisher, K. C. (1991). Psychological factors in silent myocardial ischemia. *Psychosomatic Medicine, 53,* 13–24.

Goleman, D. (1988). *The meditative mind: The varieties of meditative experience.* London: Crucible.

Guze, S. B., Goodwin, D. W., & Crane, J. B. (1969). Criminality and psychiatric disorders. *Archives of General Psychiatry, 20,* 583–591.

Heath, A. C., Cloninger, C. R., & Martin, N. G. (1994). Testing a model for the genetic structure of personality. *Journal of Personality and Social Psychology, 66,* 762–775.

Hyler, S., & Lyons, M. (1988). Factor analysis of the *DSM III* personality disorder clusters: A replication. *Comprehensive Psychiatry, 29,* 304–308.

Joyce, P., Mulder, R. T., & Cloninger, C. R. (1993). *Temperament predicts clomipramine and desipramine response in major depression.* Manuscript submitted for publication.

Jung, C. G. (1933). *Modern man in search of a soul.* London: Ark.

Kass, F., Skodol, A. E., Charles, E., Spitzer, R. L., & Williams, J. B. (1985). Scaled ratings of DSM III personality disorders. *American Journal of Psychiatry, 142,* 627–630.

Kernberg, O. F. (1976). *Object relations theory and clinical psychoanalysis*. New York: Jason Aronson.

Kirschenbaum, H., & Henderson, V. L. (1989). (Eds.). *The Carl Rogers reader*. Boston: Houghton Mifflin.

Koenig, H. G., Kvale, J. N., & Ferrel, C. (1988). Religion and well-being in later life. *Gerontologist, 28*, 18–28.

Liebowitz, M. R. (1988). Discussions arising from Cloninger, CR: A unified biosocial theory of personality and its role in the development of anxiety states. *Psychiatric Developments, 4*, 377–394.

Livesley, W. J. (1987). A systematic approach to the delineation of personality disorders. *American Journal of Psychiatry, 144*, 772–777.

Mellsop, G., Varghese, F., Joshua, S., & Hicks, A. (1982). The reliability of Axis II of DSM-III. *American Journal of Psychiatry, 139*, 1360–1361.

Millon, T. (1987). *Manual for the MCMI-II* (2nd ed.). Minneapolis: National Computer Systems.

Pfohl, B., Blum, N., Zimmerman, M., & Stangl, D. (1989). *Structured Interview for DSM-III-R Personality Disorders manual*. Iowa City, IA: Author.

Pfohl, B., Coryell, W., Zimmerman, M., & Stangl, D. A. (1986). *DSM III* personality disorders: Diagnostic overlap and internal consistency of individual *DSM III* criteria. *Comprehensive Psychiatry, 27*, 21–34.

Reich, J., Yates, W., & Nduaguba, M. (1989). Prevalence of *DSM III* personality disorders in the community. *Social Psychiatry and Psychiatric Epidemiology, 24*, 12–16.

Rush, J. A., Giles, D. E., Schlesser M. A., Fulton, C. L., Weissenburger, J., & Burns, C. (1986). The Inventory for Depressive Symptomatology (IDS): Preliminary findings. *Psychiatry Research, 18*, 65–87.

Schroeder, M. L., Wormworth, J. A., & Livesley, W. J. (1992). Dimensions of personality disorder and their relationships to the big five dimensions of personality. *Psychological Assessment, 4*, 47–53.

Sheard, M. H., Marini, S. L., Bridges, C. I., & Wagner, E. (1976). The effect of lithium on impulsive aggressive behavior in man. *American Journal of Psychiatry, 133*, 1409–1413.

Sigvardsson, S., Bohman, M., & Cloninger, C. R. (1987). Structure and stability of childhood personality: Prediction of later social adjustment. *Journal of Child Psychology and Psychiatry, 28*, 929–946.

Svrakic, D. M., Przybeck, T. R., Whitehead, C., & Cloninger, C. R. (1993). *Emotional traits and personality dimensions*. Manuscript submitted for publication.

Svrakic, D. M., Whitehead, C., Przybeck, T. R., & Cloninger, C. R. (in press). Differential diagnosis of personality disorders by the seven factor model of temperament and character. *Archives of General Psychiatry*.

Tellegen, A. (1985). Structures of mood and personality and their relevance to assessing anxiety, with an emphasis on self-report. In A.H. Tuma & J. Maser (Eds.), *Anxiety and the anxiety disorders* (pp. 681–706). Hillsdale NJ: Lawrence Erlbaum Associates.

Trull, T. (1992). *DSM-III-R* personality disorders and the five factor model of personality: An empirical comparison. *Journal of Abnormal Psychology, 101*, 553–560.

Tyrer, P., & Alexander, M. S. (1988). Personality Assessment Schedule. In P. Tyrer (Ed), *Personality disorders* (pp. 43–62). London: Wright.

Washington University School of Medicine (1991). *Washington university psychiatric patients registry*. (Available from the Department of Psychiatry, PO Box 8134, St. Louis, MO, 63110)

Watson, D. L., & Tharp, R. G. (1989). *Self-directed behavior: Self-modification for personal adjustment* (5th ed.). Pacific Grove, Calif: Brooks/Cole.

Widiger, T., & Trull, T. (1992). Personality and psychopathology: An application of the five factor model. *Journal of Personality, 60*, 363–393.

Wiggins, J. S., & Pincus, A. L. (1989). Conceptions of personality disorders and dimensions of personality. *Psychological Assessment: A Journal of Consulting and Clinical Psychology, 1*, 305–316.

Wilber, K. (1985). *No boundary: Eastern and Western approaches to personal growth.* Boston: Shambhala.

Woodward, K. L., Springen, K., Gordon, J., Glick, D., Talbot, M., Fisher, B. K., Miller, C., & Lewis, S. D. (1992, January 6). Talking to God. *Newsweek*, pp. 39–44.

Zimmerman, M., Coryell, W., Pfohl, B., Corenthal, C., & Stangl, D. (1986). ECT response in depressed patients with and without *DSM III* Personality Disorder. *American Journal of Psychiatry, 143*, 1030–1032.

Zuckerman, M., & Lubin, B. (1985). *Manual for the Multiple Affective Adjective Check List–Revised.* San Diego, CA: Educational and Industrial Testing Service.

4

Personality: A Cattellian Perspective

Samuel E. Krug

Throughout his prolific career, Raymond Cattell's contributions to personality research have been portrayed in a variety of different, often contradictory, ways. Perhaps this is no more than to be expected because the body of his work is already so vast, with more than 500 books, chapters, articles, and tests published at last count. Cattell remains personally and professionally active; research ideas continue to flow from his pen in a longhand few can understand (the handwriting, I mean, not the ideas).

Cattell takes a broad, integrative view of personality. He defines personality as that which tells what people will say, think, or do when placed in a given situation (Cattell, 1965, p. 25). In his view, ability and motivation, normal and abnormal characteristics, roles and states, thoughts and actions, verbal and nonverbal behavior, and a variety of other topics constitute legitimate targets for personality study. His work has implications for appreciating the importance of normal-range personality characteristics, understanding the distinction between normal and abnormal features, and recognizing the value of normal personality measurement in clinical decision making, a topic that Cattell first addressed more than a half century ago (Cattell, 1936).

This chapter begins with a brief history of Cattell's personality investigations. It then describes Cattell's structural model and relates that model to current thinking about the number and nature of phenotypic personality traits. Next, the chapter examines normal and abnormal personality characteristics from the vantage point of a set of well-defined, reliable variables that mark each domain. It then concludes with some summary reflections on the implications of Cattell's model for advancing personality research.

A BRIEF HISTORY OF CATTELL'S PERSONALITY RESEARCHES

Cattell completed his undergraduate studies at London University in chemistry and physics. As a graduate student, he turned to psychology and studied with Charles Spearman. It was Spearman who developed both classical test theory and factor analysis in order to organize and explain a vast array of sometimes contradictory findings related to human intellectual performance. Although Cattell's training in chemistry and physics undoubtedly helped, his exposure to Spearman's mathematically precise approach surely cemented a commitment to quantitative, empirical inquiry that correctly characterizes his entire body of work.

Cattell is usually identified as a factor analyst. However, he was not the only scientist to apply factor analysis to the study of personality, although he may well be most closely identified with this methodology. Guilford began to report his results in the early 1930s (Guilford & Guilford, 1933; 1936) and Thurstone published his 7-factor temperament schedule in 1949 (Thurstone, 1949). Factor analysis remained the method of choice for many later personality investigators.

Cattell began by exploring the entire universe of "trait elements" and attempted to identify the "larger unities" that explained the covariation among them (Cattell, 1943). He adopted the position that "all aspects of human personality which are or have been of importance, interest, or utility have already become recorded in the substance of language" (Cattell, 1943, p. 483). As an operational definition of the universe of trait elements, he took the anthology of 17,953 English-language terms that Allport and Odbert (1936) found in *Webster's New Unabridged International Dictionary*. Starting with the 4,504 terms in the group, Allport and Odbert called "personal traits," he and a colleague began to reduce this list to a more manageable number that could be analyzed empirically.

The first reduction proceeded logically. It resulted in a set of 171 variables that included not only such bipolar terms as "worrying–placid," "reliable–undependable," and "assertive–submissive," but also terms like "agoraphobic," "alcoholic," and "strong in personality." His final set of 171 variables included ability and interest variables as well, since Cattell saw both as subspecies within the general class of personality traits. This list of 171 variables was next reduced to 35 by applying informal cluster-analytic methods to a correlation matrix of peer ratings made by 100 adults. These 35 variables served as the basis for obtaining peer ratings on a sample of 208 adults. With the correlations among these peer ratings, Cattell began to apply factor analysis to the study of personality. Thus, the first personality factors he reported rested on rating data, not self-report data.

Cattell next generated a pool of questionnaire items hypothesized to represent the factors he had found in the rating studies. Cattell's insistence on linking personality factors across three observational media—self-report, observer ratings, and performance—undoubtedly contributed to the robustness of the dimensions with which he worked and their predictive utility in many kinds of situations.

Although some elements were unique to each method of observation, Cattell tried to focus on factors that showed the greatest replicability across all three media. The 16 that became the foundation for the test with which his name is most often associated, the 16 Personality Factor Questionnaire (16PF: Cattell, Eber, & Tatsuoka, 1970) are: A—Warmth; B—Intelligence; C—Emotional Stability; E—Dominance; F—Impulsivity; G—Conformity; H—Boldness; I—Sensitivity; L—Suspiciousness; M—Imagination; N—Shrewdness; O—Insecurity; Q1—Radicalism; Q2—Self-Sufficiency; Q3—Self-Discipline; Q4—Tension.

From these studies flowed an extensive series of theoretical papers, technological advances, and instruments for assessing personality. The 16PF was not the only one. Cattell and his colleagues published dozens more to fit other age ranges and serve other purposes. One of the more important from the perspective of this chapter is the Clinical Analysis Questionnaire (CAQ) (Krug, 1980). This test consists of 12 scales designed to measure factorially distinct aspects of depression and cognitive disturbance that complement the 16 normal dimensions.

ON THE DIMENSIONALITY AND STRUCTURE OF PERSONALITY (OR WHAT'S THE B. F. D.?[1])

During the late 1960s and the 1970s, much discussion focused on the number of "real" personality factors (Guilford, 1975). Interest in this topic greatly exceeded the level of agreement. Cattell (1975, 1986), Eysenck (1976, 1986), and Guilford (1975) were probably the most vocal, because their own structural models and tests were central to the debate. Each argued for a different, usually very different, number of factors that led to different conclusions about the nature of personality. Eysenck, for example, focussed at first on two factors, neuroticism and extraversion, then later added a third, psychoticism. Guilford, whose studies began in an attempt to separate hypothesized components of extroversion-introversion, argued for 13. Cattell, in turn, argued for no less than 23 factors and as many as 35 if the full domain of pathology was to be included (Cattell & Krug, 1986).

These debates were lively, spirited, and unrelenting. Although everyone conceded that differences in factor-analytic procedures, variable representation, and subject sampling could lead to differences in interpretation, no one gave in on the number or nature of personality structure. Now in a gentler, kinder research era we observe a very different phenomenon: people who normally make their living by studying differences are falling all over each other in attempts to embrace a common structural model: the Big Five. These five are identified as Extroversion (or Surgency), Agreeableness (or Friendliness), Conscientiousness (or Will), Emotional Stability (or Neuroticism), and Intellect (or Openness to Experience or Culture). The fact that so many "ors" are needed to describe these five suggests that consensus isn't quite as extensive as some would have us believe. On the other hand, Wiggins and Trapnell's (in press) thoughtful review of Big Five developments over the past half century points out that "different versions of the 'truth' may coexist without chaos."

In a recent overview of the current status of Big Five theory, Goldberg (1993) reported that "the intellectual 'father' of the Big Five factors, Raymond Cattell, has consistently denied his paternity and has yet to embrace the model" (p. 27). Because the courts are probably unclear on just what level of support to demand of an intellectual father, what reason could Cattell have for denying his paternity? Did he spend too many years at a Big Ten university to consider the Big Five a real possibility? Has Cattell really denied his paternity? Or is there another possibility?

Earlier I noted that from the beginning Cattell was concerned about the replication of structure across media of observation. Research with observer ratings and self-report led him to conclude that similarities across these two media were striking and compelling. When he analyzed the results from "objective test" or T-data, tasks that required the examinee to conduct no self-examination but only perform,[2] there were significant structural differences, at least at first glance. This led Cattell to focus more intently on the issue of different levels of personality structure.

In several key publications, Cattell showed that the factors in his questionnaires, which generally contained 12–16 scales, could be reliably resolved at a higher level of extraction in terms of a more limited set of second-order factors (Gorsuch & Cattell, 1967; Cattell & Nichols, 1972). Krug and Johns (1986) conducted the largest such study (N = 17,381). They concluded that the second-order structure of the 16PF could be explained in terms of the following factors: Extroversion, Anxiety, Tough Poise, Independence, Control, and Intelligence. The last factor is one that emerges regularly in 16PF second-order factor analyses, because Cattell initially chose to embed a set of cognitive ability items (mainly verbal analogies) in the test that retain their uniqueness even at the second-order level. Another factor, called Discreetness by Cattell (Cattell et al., 1970), was identified in the Krug and Johns factor analysis. However, it loads a single primary scale (N: Shrewdness). Considering the narrowness of its representation within the 16PF primaries and additional evidence from a joint factor analysis of normal and abnormal primaries to be described later in this chapter, Krug and Johns concluded that Discreetness was better conceptualized as Socialization and as a second-order factor belonging more to the abnormal than the normal domain. Among the clinical scales, the factor was found to have two important negative loadings on scales identified as Agitation and Psychopathic Deviation. These connections led Krug and Johns to speculate further whether 16PF primary factor N should continue to be interpreted as shrewd, polished, and astute, or whether these represented secondary characteristics of people who were highly controlled and sensitive to societal norms.

Krug and Johns (1986) found no support for another second-order factor Cattell called Prodigal Subjectivity (Cattell et al., 1970). Thus, excluding Intelligence, the second-order structure of the 16PF can essentially be explained by five factors. Karson and O'Dell (1974; 1976) appear to have come independently to the same general conclusion.

The titles of these second-order factors are those that Cattell originally used to describe them. At first glance, there appear to be some important differences between them and the Big Five structure described earlier. However, at least some of the differences are superficial. Extroversion, Anxiety, and Control link very directly to Big Five Factors I, IV, and III when the components of the patterns are compared closely (Goldberg, 1992).

What Cattell called Independence and Big Five theory calls Agreeableness have enough common elements to suggest that they represent two ends of a single continuum. That is, Agreeableness and Dependence share some important similarities. People categorized as dependent by the 16PF are described as trusting (Factor L–), cooperative (Factor E–), and group-oriented (Factor Q_2–), key adjectives that fit the pattern for Factor II (Goldberg, 1992). On the other hand, research has shown that lower scores on Independence are more often associated with clinical disorders (Krug, 1981). Thus, it seems inappropriate to conclude that Independence and Agreeableness represent two ends of the same continuum. In the 16PF tradition, the emphasis in this scale has been not so much on sociability as on internal versus external locus of control. Externally controlled people are likely to be perceived as more sociable and perhaps more agreeable in many contexts. However, the underlying dynamics are quite different.

The factor called Tough Poise by Cattell differentiates cool, emotionally detached, and analytic people from their more sensitive counterparts. The original label he proposed for it was Corticalertia (i.e., cortical alertness), later shortened to Cortertia, to suggest a link to cognitive processing speed. The most important 16PF primary factor involved in the pattern is Factor I, which Cattell often relates to the tender-minded vs. tough-minded dimension first described by William James. As with Independence and Agreeableness, there is a degree of resemblance to Factor V in the Big Five model: Intellect, Openness to Experience, or Culture. People who score high on Tough Poise are often described as perceptive and analytical, two main markers for the Factor V pattern (Goldberg, 1992). However, the critical difference between the two patterns lies in the fact that Cattell's variables, unlike most other personality researchers, include a direct measure of intellectual ability,[3] which is uncorrelated with Tough Poise. When Costa and McCrae (1992) describe high-O (Openness to Experience) individuals as people who are "imaginative and sensitive to art and beauty and have a rich and complex emotional life" (p. 6), they could quite easily be describing people who scored low on Tough Poise.

It should come as no surprise to anyone that we can find some level of description at which there is general agreement about the complexity of personality. In the cognitive area, for example, almost everyone agrees that g (general ability) exists and is important. Beyond that, there is considerable diversity of opinion. Cattell (1971), for example, initially argued for a refinement in Spearman's basic model by introducing the concepts of fluid (g_f) and crystallized (g_c) ability. Thurstone and others subsequently pursued a more complex primary ability model. More recently, some authors (e.g., Hunter, 1983; 1986) have argued that little is to be gained in predicting job performance from ability variables beyond g. But on that point, others disagree (Hartigan & Wigdor, 1989).

It seems likely that Cattell would concede that there are five important factors discernible within the domains of observer ratings and self-evaluations. This is the verdict of a programmatic series of researches begun about a half century ago that pursued the second-order structure of the 16PF across diverse samples, cultures, and populations. However, it seems unlikely that Cattell would agree that the present conceptualization of the Big Five model, even if we added a few more "ors" to the factor descriptions, represents the final word on personality structure. He probably would assert that the Big Five model places too much emphasis on a single level or layer of personality analysis, a level that in Cattell's thinking represents a second-order or secondary level of description. He also would probably disagree that the Big Five domains represent "the highest level that is still descriptive of behavior with only general evaluation located at a higher and more abstract level" (Goldberg, 1993, p. 27). For example,

> By the concept of factors as influence, the third order factor is one that influences growth of individual differences in second order factors. . . . However, these more remote influences need no longer be psychological. They might be economic, historical, biological, etc., embedded in the structure of society and race, and responsible only for the "arrangement" of lower order, truly psychological traits. (Cattell, 1975, p. 119)

Cattell's explorations of the objective test domain and his concern for linking findings across media probably would also give him concern about stopping with five. From his perspective, these five correspond well to factor patterns that have been discovered within the domain of objective test data (Cattell & Birkett, 1980): Extraversion with U.I. 32,[4] Anxiety with U.I. 24, Tough Poise with U.I. 22, Independence with U.I. 19, and Control with U.I. 17. However, there exist another half dozen replicated factor patterns in objective test data that remain to be mapped onto the rating and self-report domains. He appears willing to concede that some of these patterns may correspond more to abilities than personality dimensions (Cattell & Birkett, 1980). However, for Cattell it is probably too early in the history of personality research to conclude that *all* remaining T-data factors lie beyond the personality space defined by self-report and ratings.

Finally, Cattell probably would agree with Goldberg's (1993) suggestion that the development of reliable measures of job-related personality traits and measures for linking applicants' personality profiles with position requirements are important scientific activities. He would more likely disagree with the proposal that the five-factor model is the best level at which to work, as some have suggested (e.g., Barrick & Mount, 1991). In doing so, he would point to an extensive research literature stretching back a half century that links his primary level personality variables to important real-world outcomes (Krug & Johns, 1990). He also would argue that although the second-order variables capture much of the predictable variance in real-world prediction, they often miss some subtle but important differences that can be captured at the first-order level (Cattell et al., 1970). For example, two people may produce 16PF profiles that are very high on Extroversion but different on Factor A (Warmth), one of the key contributors to the second-order pattern. The low A extrovert will usually be perceived as more shallow and less sincere than the high A extrovert. As a result, people will respond differently to the two. Perhaps these kinds of differences in second-order expression help explain why even very ardent proponents of the Big Five model have simultaneously pursued the development of scores that break down Big Five dimensions into narrower subscales or facets (e.g., Costa & McCrae, 1985).

NORMAL AND ABNORMAL PERSONALITY (OR THE BIGGER TEN?)

The practical necessity to classify and diagnose as a preliminary step in treatment led to the development of many important personality assessment instruments, such as the Minnesota Multiphasic Personality Inventory (MMPI), which focuses almost exclusively on pathology. The assessment of normal-range personality characteristics for the most part proceeded independently. Two categories of instruments emerged: one oriented to pathology, one oriented to normality (or "normalcy" during the Harding administration).

The two types of tests differed most in the types of items they incorporated, and item selection criteria probably led to other differences in how each kind of scale performed (Krug, 1986). Scales oriented to normal-range characteristics usually produced the kinds of bell-shaped score distributions seen only in statistics books. However, it should come as no surprise to anyone that when scales are formed by aggregating responses to items such as "My thoughts are controlled by alien creatures," one would expect distinctly unusual score distributions except when parents of teenagers represent major sampling units within the study.

Test authors and personality theorists appeared to be unconcerned about linking the two domains. As often happens, the wisdom of practice forged the link. Clinicians found that tests like the MMPI were helpful in diagnosis but not sufficient when it came to developing treatment plans. On the other hand, tests like the 16PF and the California Psychological Inventory (Gough, 1975) were helpful in describing relatively permanent features of their clients' personalities but said little about current symptomology or psychiatric status. Although the two kinds of variables married in practice, they remained largely separate in theory, at least until the last 10 years or so (e.g., Millon, 1982).

Earlier I mentioned the CAQ, one instrument that attempted to combine both domains within a single profile. To the basic normal-range profile assessed by the 16PF, Cattell and his colleagues added 12 new scales to assess pathology. Seven represented factorially distinct aspects of depression: hypochondriasis, suicidal depression, agitation, anxious depression, low energy, guilt and resentment, boredom, and withdrawal (Cattell & Bjerstedt, 1967). Five others emerged from joint factor analyses of the MMPI and 16PF item pools: paranoia, psychopathic deviation, schizophrenia, psychasthenia, psychological inadequacy (Cattell & Bolton, 1969). The result was a 272-item test that encompassed 16 normal and 12 pathological personality features (Krug, 1980). In this way, the CAQ serves as a clinical extension of the 16PF by providing coverage of areas not well assessed by the 16 original scales, particularly depression and significant cognitive disturbance.

Krug and Laughlin (1977) conducted a large-scale structural analysis of the CAQ primary scales. The results of that study have some important implications for understanding the distinction between normal and abnormal characteristics. In this study, CAQ protocols from 1,915 normal and clinically diagnosed adults (roughly half of each type) were factor analyzed. Separate analyses by gender provided an opporunity to test the assumption that reliable structural differences might exist between men and women. Ten factors were extracted in each data set and rotated independently to oblique simple structure. The resulting factor patterns are shown in Table 4.1.

There are two columns for each second-order factor, one (M) corresponding to the pattern derived from the male data, the other (F) corresponding to the pattern derived from the female data. Values less than .30 in absolute value and decimal points have been omitted for clarity of presentation. As Table 4.1 shows, the agreement between results for men and women is very high. The median congruence coefficient across the 10 factors is .88.

The first five factors are those that were discussed extensively in the previous section of this chapter: Extroversion, Tough Poise, Independence, Control, and Anxiety. Four additional factors complete the picture. These were identified as Socialization, Depression, Psychoticism, and Neuroticism.

There are several important conclusions to be drawn from this study. First, as often happens, the clinicians were right: the overlap between the two sets of variables is small. Except for Anxiety, the other four major second-order, normal-range personality scales do not project far into the domain of psychopathology. Similarly, the loadings of the 12 pathological scales are largely restricted to the last four second-order dimensions. Anxiety (Emotional Instability) is the most notable exception to this rule. It has loadings both within the normal and abnormal domain. It is presented as the fifth factor here, rather than in its more typical forward position, to suggest that it represents a transitional dimension linking the normal and pathological domains.

Second, these results suggest that yet a second "Big Five" may exist, this time called Anxiety (or Emotional Instability), Depression, Socialization, Psychoticism, and Neuroticism, and that this set may help to organize the domain of psychopathology in the same way that the Big Five have helped to organize the domain of normal-range personality characteristics. From a structural perspective, a particularly intriguing feature of the two sets is that they share a common reference axis: Anxiety. Further developments within a joint structural model, using path analysis and structural equation modeling, for example, may lead to a better understanding of the etiology and progression of pathology. It may be possible, for example, to develop reliable normal-range indicators of subsequent psychiatric disturbance.

The factor-analytic evidence leads me to disagree with Costa and McCrae's (1992) assertion that "most dimensions of psychopathology have parallels in dimensions of individual differences in the normal range" (p. 9). However, although the two domains are largely factorially independent, there are correlations between the

TABLE 4.1 CAQ Second-Order Factor Pattern Matrix[a]

	Extroversion M	Extroversion F	Tough Poise M	Tough Poise F	Independence M	Independence F	Control M	Control F	Anxiety M	Anxiety F
A: Warmth	57	46								
B: Intelligence										
C: Emotional Stability									−57	−56
E: Dominance					34	56				
F: Impulsivity	63	63								
G: Conformity							42	41		
H: Boldness	65	61								
I: Sensitivity			−72	−37						
L: Suspiciousness									59	47
M: Imagination			−36	−45	32	38				
N: Shrewdness										
O: Insecurity									39	44
Q1: Radicalism						39				
Q2: Self-Sufficiency	−52	−57				52				
Q3: Self-Discipline				−30			58	83	−48	−53
Q4: Tension					36				63	74
D1: Hypochondriasis										
D2: Suicidal Depression										
D3: Agitation		44								
D4: Anxious Depression						−33				
D5: Low Energy Depression									31	
D6: Guilt and Resentment									33	35
D7: Boredom and Withdrawal	−34	−39								
Pa: Paranoia									30	
Pp: Psychopathic Deviation										
Sc: Schizophrenia										
As: Psychasthenia									42	34
Ps: Psychological Inadequacy										

(continued)

TABLE 4.1 (*Continued*)

		Socialization		Depression		Psychoticism		Neuroticism	
		M	F	M	F	M	F	M	F
A:	Warmth								
B:	Intelligence								
C:	Emotional Stability								
E:	Dominance							−54	−54
F:	Impulsivity								
G:	Conformity						−32		
H:	Boldness							-41	−37
I:	Sensitivity								31
L:	Suspiciousness						30		
M:	Imagination								31
N:	Shrewdness	36	34						
O:	Insecurity			34				42	45
Ql:	Radicalism								
Q2:	Self-Sufficiency								
Q3:	Self-Discipline								
Q4:	Tension							30	
Dl:	Hypochondriasis			76	80				
D2:	Suicidal Depression			79	75				
D3:	Agitation	−62	−60						
D4:	Anxious Depression			44	37				38
D5:	Low Energy Depression			78	77				
D6:	Guilt and Resentment			59	48				41
D7:	Boredom and Withdrawal			50	52				
Pa:	Paranoia					63	85		
Pp:	Psychopathic Deviation	−67	−41	−30					
Sc:	Schizophrenia			31	31	55	53		
As:	Psychasthenia					33	41		31
Ps:	Psychological Inadequacy			68	57		31		

[a]Adapted from a table presented in Krug and Laughlin (1977).

two: Extroversion with Depression (−.40), Anxiety with Depression (.50), Tough Poise with Psychoticism (−.30), and Independence with Socialization (−.40). The existence of these correlations suggests that additional interdomain structural analyses are likely to provide interesting and useful results. Moreover, the existence of such correlations causes me to agree with Costa and McCrae's suggestion that "one of the intriguing questions for future research concerns the nature of the relation between traits and psychiatric disorders" (1991, p. 9).

The second-order factors discovered here in the self-report realm that relate specifically to pathology appear, on the surface at least, to correspond to other of Cattell's objective test (T-data) factors: Socialization with U.I. 26, Depression with U.I. 27, Psychoticism with U.I. 25, and Neuroticism with U.I. 23 (Cattell,

1957). This linkage provides a broader theoretical base for interpreting these new second-order structures and suggests that alternative assessment procedures, relying on performance rather than on self-evaluations, may provide new insights into psychiatric disorders. There are some obvious practical implications that follow: for example, methodologies for confronting the problem of dissimulation and assessing factitious disorders.

SOME IMPLICATIONS OF CATTELL'S WORK

Normal-range personality variables have great predictive power. Approximately 4,000 research articles have established linkages between Cattell's primary personality characteristics and important real-world criteria. The ability of these scales to predict important aspects of job performance, for example, is already well documented (Krug & Johns, 1990). An extensive literature has accumulated regarding personality correlates of occupational preference and worker satisfaction, information that is helpful to those involved in guiding career choices and reenergizing cases of worker burnout.

Although the distinction between normal-range scales and pathological scales appears to be reasonably clear, normal-range scales offer the clinician significant information, as Costa and McCrae (1992) have correctly concluded. For example, researchers have found normal-range characteristics relevant in the treatment of substance abuse (Tuite & Luiten, 1986) and family violence (Engfer & Schneewind, 1982; Star, 1978). Correlates with physical, not just mental, health appear to be strong and useful as well. Sherman and Krug (1977) reviewed some of the early research in this area and research continues actively in this area (e.g., Duckitt & Broll, 1983; Lawrence, 1984).

Normal (and abnormal) dimensions must be studied and understood at various levels of personality organization. Although compatible with Cattell's view, this assertion is not uniquely Cattellian. Leary (1957), for example, encouraged both theorists and practitioners to examine personality on multiple levels. There now seems to be a personality model for which there is widespread agreement about dimensionality, if not the precise nature of those dimensions (Wiggins & Trapnell, in press). Our enthusiasm for consensus should not blur the reality that many differences still exist and, undoubtedly, many findings remain to be discovered.

Much study remains before we understand the full linkage between normal-range personality characteristics and psychiatric disorders. For a very long time, the study of normal-range personality and psychopathology has proceeded relatively independently. Now that we have at least some general agreement about one side of the equation, we should feel more comfortable exploring the other side of the equation more systematically. Who knows, maybe the Big Ten is more than an athletic conference?

NOTES

[1]Big Five Debate.

[2]T-data subsumes a broad array of observations and tasks: galvanic skin response changes in response to standard stimulus material, reaction time, perceptual tasks, response to humor, decision time, ability to follow directions, and many similar kinds of activities. Cattell describes the tests as objective because the score reflects a performance, not an evaluation of performance. That is, the examinee does not respond to a question such as "I generally follow directions carefully." Instead, the score is derived directly from an activity or simulation.

[3]Goldberg (1993) correctly notes that Cattell omitted variables related to Intellect in favor of an intelligence test but suggests that this test was omitted from Cattell's later studies. Factor B, a measure of verbal ability, has been part of the 16PF since the test was first published in 1949. Second-order studies have routinely included Factor B in the factor analysis. If a sufficient number of factors are extracted, the Factor B score will load on a single second-order factor that is essentially orthogonal to all other second-order factors.

[4]U.I. is an abbreviation for Universal Index, a system Cattell originally proposed for consistently indexing replicated factor patterns across media of observation.

REFERENCES

Allport, G. W., & Odbert, H. S. (1936). Trait-names, a psycho-lexical study. *Psychological Monographs, 47*.

Barrick, M. R., & Mount, M. K. (1991). The Big Five personality dimensions and job performance: A meta-analysis. *Personnel Psychology, 44*, 1–26.

Cattell, R. B. (1936). Temperament tests in clinical practice. *British Journal of Medical Psychology, 16*, 43–61.

Cattell, R. B. (1943). The description of personality: Basic traits resolved into clusters. *Journal of Abnormal and Social Psychology, 38*, 476–506.

Cattell, R. B. (1957). *Personality and motivation structure and measurement.* Yonkers-on-Hudson: World Book.

Cattell, R. B. (1965). *The scientific analysis of personality.* Baltimore: Penguin.

Cattell, R. B. (1971). *Abilities: Their structure, growth, and action.* Boston: Houghton Mifflin.

Cattell, R. B. (1975). Third-order personality structure in Q-data: Evidence from eleven experiments. *Journal of Multivariate Experimental Personality and Clinical Psychology, 1*, 118–149.

Cattell, R. B. (1986). The 16PF personality structure and Dr. Eysenck. *Journal of Social Behavior and Personality, 1*, 153–160.

Cattell, R. B., & Birkett, H. (1980). The known personality factors found aligned between first-order T-data and second-order Q-data factors, with new evidence on the inhibitory control, independence and regression traits. *Personality and Individual Differences, 1*, 229–238.

Cattell, R. B., & Bjerstedt, A. (1967). The structure of depression, by factoring Q-data, in relation to general personality source traits. *Scandinavian Journal of Psychology, 8,* 17–24.

Cattell, R. B., & Bolton, L. S. (1969). What pathological dimensions lie beyond the normal dimensions of the 16 PF? A comparison of MMPI and 16 PF factor domains. *Journal of Consulting and Clinical Psychology, 33,* 18–29.

Cattell, R. B., Eber, H. W., & Tatsuoka, M. M. (1970). *Handbook for the Sixteen Personality Factor Questionnaire (16PF).* Champaign, IL: IPAT.

Cattell, R. B., & Krug, S. E. (1986). The number of factors in the 16PF: A review of the evidence with special emphasis on methodological problems. *Educational and Psychological Measurement, 46,* 509–522.

Cattell, R. B.., & Nichols, K. E. (1972). An improved definition, from 10 researchers, of second-order personality factors in Q data (with cross-cultural checks). *Journal of Social Psychology, 86,* 187–203.

Costa, P. T., Jr., & McCrae, R. R. (1985). *The NEO Personality Inventory manual.* Odessa, FL: Psychological Assessment Resources.

Costa, P. T., Jr., & McCrae, R. R. (1992). Normal personality assessment in clinical practice: The NEO personality inventory. *Psychological Assessment, 4,* 5–13.

Duckitt, J. H., & Broll, T. (1983). Life stress, personality and illness behavior: A prospective study. *Psychological Reports, 53,* 51–57.

Engfer, A., & Schneewind, K. A. (1982). Causes and consequences of harsh parental punishment: An empirical investigation in a representative sample of 570 German families. *Child Abuse & Neglect, 6,* 129–139.

Eysenck, H. J. (1976). *The measurement of personality.* Lancaster, England: MTP Press.

Eysenck, H. J. (1986). Can personality study ever be scientific? *Journal of Social Behavior and Personality, 1,* 3–19.

Goldberg, L. R. (1992). The development of markers for the big-five factor structure. *Psychological Assessment, 4,* 26–42.

Goldberg, L. R. (1993). The structure of phenotypic personality traits. *American Psychologist, 48,* 26–34.

Gough, H. A. (1975). *California Psychological Inventory.* Palo Alto, CA: Consulting Psychologists Press.

Gorsuch, R. & Cattell, R. B. (1967). Second stratum personality factors defined in the questionnaire realm by the 16PF. *Multivariate Behavioral Research, 2,* 211–224.

Guilford, J. P. (1975). Factors and factors of personality. *Psychological Bulletin, 82,* 802–814.

Guilford, J. P., & Guilford, R. B. (1933). An analysis of the factors present in a typical test of introversion-extroversion. *Journal of Abnormal and Social Psychology, 28,* 377–399.

Guilford, J. P., & Guilford, R. B. (1936). Personality factors S, E, and M and their measurement. *Journal of Psychology, 2,* 109–127.

Hartigan, J. A., & Wigdor, A. K. (1989). *Fairness in employment testing: Validity generalization, minority issues, and the General Aptitude Test Battery.* Washington: National Academy Press.

Hunter, J. E. (1983). A causal analysis of cognitive ability, job knowledge, job performance, and supervisor ratings. In F. J. Landy, S. Zedeck, and J. Cleveland (Eds.) *Performance measurement and theory* (pp. 257–266). Hillsdale, NJ: Erlbaum.

Hunter, J. E. (1986). Cognitive ability, cognitive aptitudes, job knowledge, and job performance. *Journal of Vocational Behavior, 29,* 340–362.

Karson, S., & O'Dell, J. W. (1974). The personality makeup of the American air traffic controller. *Aerospace Medicine, 45,* 1001–1007.

Karson, S., & O'Dell, J.W. (1976). *A guide to the clinical use of the 16PF.* Champaign, IL: IPAT.

Krug, S. E. (1980). *Clinical Analysis Questionnaire manual.* Champaign, IL: Institute for Personality and Ability Testing.

Krug, S. E. (1981). *Interpreting 16PF profile patterns.* Champaign, IL: Institute for Personality and Ability Testing.

Krug, S. E. (1986). Self-report measures of personality. In B. Bolton (Ed.), *Handbook of measurement and evaluation in rehabilitation* (2nd ed.). Baltimore: Paul H. Brookes.

Krug, S. E., & Johns, E. F. (1986). A large scale cross-validation of second-order personality structure defined by the 16PF. *Psychological Reports, 59,* 683–693.

Krug, S. E., & Johns, E. F. (1990). The 16PF. In C. E. Watkins, Jr & V. L. Campbell (Eds.) *Testing in counseling practice.* Hillsdale, NJ: Erlbaum.

Krug, S. E., & Laughlin, J. E. (1977). Second-order factors among normal and pathological primary personality traits. *Journal of Consulting Psychology, 45,* 575–582.

Lawrence, R. A. (1984). Police stress and personality factors: A conceptual model. *Journal of Criminal Justice, 12,* 247–263.

Leary, T. (1957). Interpersonal diagnosis of personality. New York: Ronald.

Millon, T. (1982). *Millon Clinical Multiaxial Inventory.* Minneapolis: National Computer Systems.

Sherman, J. L., & Krug, S. E. (1977). Personality-somatic interactions: The research evidence. In S. E. Krug (Ed.), *Psychological assessment in medicine,* Champaign, IL: IPAT.

Star, B. (1978). Comparing battered and non-battered women. *Victimology: An International Journal, 3,* 32–44.

Thurstone, L. L. (1949). *Thurstone temperament schedule.* Chicago: SRA.

Tuite, D. R., & Luiten, J. W. (1986). 16PF research into addiction: Meta-analysis and extension. *The International Journal of the Addictions, 21,* 287–323.

Wiggins, J. S., & Trapnell, P. D. (In press). Personality structure: The return of the big five. In S. R. Briggs, R. Hogan, & W. H. Jones (Eds.), *Handbook of personality psychology.* Orlando, FL: Academic Press.

5

Millon's Evolutionary Model of Normal and Abnormal Personality: Theory and Measures

Theodore Millon and Roger D. Davis

Numerous attempts have been made to develop definitive criteria for distinguishing psychological normality from abnormality. Some of these criteria focus on features that characterize the so-called normal, or ideal, state of mental health, as illustrated in the writings of Offer and Sabshin (1974, 1991); others have sought to specify criteria for concepts such as abnormality or psychopathology. The most common criterion employed is a statistical one in which normality is determined by behavior that is found most frequently in a social group; and pathology or abnormality is determined by features that are uncommon in that population.

Central to our understanding of these terms is the recognition that normality and pathology are relative concepts; they represent arbitrary points on a continuum or gradient, because no sharp line divides normal from pathological behavior. Not only is personality so complex that certain areas of psychological functioning operate normally while others do not, but environmental circumstances change such that behaviors and strategies that prove adaptive at one time fail to do so at another. Moreover, features differentiating normal from abnormal functioning must be extracted from a complex of signs that not only wax and wane but often develop in an insidious and unpredictable manner.

Because the focus of this chapter is the construct termed personality, both normal and abnormal, we should ask at the outset, how do we conceive personality?

The word derives from the Greek term *persona* and originally represented the theatrical mask used by dramatic players. Its meaning has changed through history. As a mask assumed by an actor it suggested a pretense of appearance, that is, the possession of traits other than those that actually characterized the individual behind the mask. In time, the term *persona* lost its connotation of pretense and illusion and began to represent, not the mask, but the real person, his or her apparent, explicit, and manifest features. The third and final meaning that the term *personality* has acquired delves "beneath" the surface impression of the person and turns the spotlight on the inner, less revealed, and hidden psychological qualities of the individual. Thus, through history the term has shifted from meaning external illusion to surface reality to opaque or veiled inner traits. It is this third meaning that comes closest to contemporary use. Personality is seen today as a complex pattern of deeply embedded psychological characteristics that cannot be eradicated easily and express themselves automatically in most facets of functioning. Intrinsic and pervasive, they are composed of traits that emerge from a complicated matrix of biological dispositions and experiential learnings and now comprise the individual's distinctive pattern of perceiving, feeling, thinking, and coping.

Basic to the concept of personality is the notion that the traits of which it is composed are not a potpourri of unrelated perceptions, thoughts, and behavior but rather a tightly knit organization of attitudes, habits, and emotions. Although we may start in life with more or less random and diverse feelings and reactions, the repetitive sequences of reinforcing experiences to which we are exposed narrows our repertoire to particular behavioral strategies that become prepotent and characterize our personally distinctive way of coping with others and relating to ourselves.

This conception of personality breaks the long-entrenched habit of conceiving syndromes of personality disorder as one or another variant of a disease, that is, some "foreign" entity or lesion that intrudes insidiously within the person to undermine his or her so-called normal functions. The archaic notion that all mental disorders represent external intrusions or internal disease processes is an offshoot of prescientific ideas such as demons or spirits that ostensibly "possess" or cast spells on the person. The role of infectious agents and anatomical lesions in physical medicine has reawakened this archaic view. Of course, we no longer see demons, but many still see some alien or malevolent force as invading or unsettling the patient's otherwise healthy status. This view is an appealing simplification to the layman, who can attribute his or her irrationalities to some intrusive or upsetting agent. It also has its appeal to the less sophisticated clinician, for it enables him or her to believe that the insidious intruder can be identified, hunted down, and destroyed.

Such naive notions carry little weight among modern-day medical and behavioral scientists. Given our increasing awareness of the complex nature of both health and disease, we now recognize, for example, that most disorders, physical and psychological, result from a dynamic and changing interplay between individuals' capacities to cope and the environment within which they live. It is the patients' overall constitutional makeup that serves as a substrate that inclines them to resist or to succumb to potentially troublesome environmental forces. To illustrate: Infectious viruses and bacteria proliferate within the environment; it is the person's immunologic defenses that determine whether or not these microbes will take hold, spread, and, ultimately, be experienced as illness. Individuals with robust immune activity will counteract the usual range of infectious microbes with ease, whereas those with weakened immune capacities will be vulnerable, fail to handle these intrusions and quickly succumb. Psychic pathology should be conceived as reflecting the same interactive pattern. Here, however, it is not the immunologic defenses but the patient's personality pattern—that is, coping skills and adaptive flexibilities—that determines whether or not the person masters or succumbs to his or her psychosocial environment. Just as physical ill health is likely to be less a matter of some alien virus than it is a dysfunction in the body's capacity to deal with infectious agents, so too is psychological ill health likely to be less a product of some intrusive psychic strain than it is a dysfunction in the personality's capacity to cope with life's difficulties. Viewed this way, the structure and characteristics of personality, normal or abnormal, become the foundation for the individual's capacity to function in a mentally healthy or ill way.

Pathology of personality results from the same forces as involved in the development of normal personality. Important differences in the character, timing, and intensity of these influences lead some individuals to acquire pathological traits and others to develop adaptive traits. When an individual displays an ability to cope with the environment in a flexible manner, and when his or her typical perceptions and behavior foster increments in personal satisfaction, then the person may be said to possess a normal, healthy personality. Conversely, when average or everyday responsibilities are responded to inflexibly or defectively, or when the individual's perceptions and behavior result in increments in personal discomfort or curtail opportunities to learn and to grow, then we may speak of a pathological or maladaptive pattern. Despite the tenuous and fluctuating nature of the normality-pathology distinction, certain features may be abstracted from the flow of personality characteristics to serve as differentiating criteria; notable among them are an adaptive inflexibility, a tendency to foster vicious or self-defeating circles, and a tenuous emotional stability under conditions of stress (Millon, 1969, 1981, 1990).

In the following pages we present three major topics. First, we outline the orientation we have taken for conceptualizing personality, an orientation that argues in favor of grounding the concept in a firm theoretical foundation. Second, we propose that the most sturdy scaffolding for personality, normal and abnormal, is best constructed by employing the principles of evolutionary theory. Third, we describe a number of "operational definitions" of these constructs, that is, assessment tools that take the form of specific instruments and quantitative measures.

CONCEPTUALIZING PERSONALITY

The subject areas that subdivide the natural world differ in the degree to which their phenomena are inherently differentiated and organized. Some areas are "naturally" more articulated and quantifiable than others. To illustrate: The laws of physics relate to highly probabilistic processes in many of its most recondite spheres, but the features of our everyday physical world are highly ordered and predictable. Theories in this latter realm of physics (e.g., mechanics, electricity) serve largely to *uncover* the lawful relationships that do, in fact, exist in nature; it was the task of turn-of-the-century physicists to fashion a network of constructs that faithfully mirrored the universal nature of the phenomena they studied. By contrast, probabilistic realms of physical analysis (e.g., short-lived elementary particles) or systems of recent evolutionary development (e.g., human interactions) are inherently weakly organized, lacking either articulated or invariant connections among their constituent elements. In knowledge domains that relate to these less ordered spheres of nature (the "softer" sciences), classifiers and theorists find it necessary to impose a somewhat arbitrary measure of systematization; in so doing, they construct a degree of clarity and coherence that is not fully consonant with the "naturally" unsettled and indeterminate character of their subject. Rather than equivocate strategically, or succumb to the "futility of it all," noble or pretentious statistical or theoretical efforts are made to arrange and categorize these inexact and probabilistic elements so that they simulate a degree of precision and order transcending that which they intrinsically possess. To illustrate: In fields such as economics and psychopathology, categories and classifications are, in considerable measure, splendid fictions, compelling notions, or austere formulas devised to give coherence to their *inherently imprecise* subjects.

How can we best conceptualize and organize the clinical data that comprise normal and abnormal personality? Clearly, personality characteristics express themselves in a variety of ways approachable at different levels and from many frames of reference. Behaviorally, personality characteristics can be conceived as complicated response patterns to environmental stimuli. Phenomenologically, they can be understood as experiences of joy or anguish. Physiologically, they can be analyzed as sequences of complex neural and chemical activity. And intrapsychically, they can be inferred as unconscious processes that enable the person to enhance life or to defend against anxiety and conflict. Given these diverse possibilities, we can readily understand why both normal and pathologic states or processes may be classified in terms of any of several data levels we may wish to focus on, and any of a variety of attributes we may wish to identify and explain. Because the subject matter of personality is inherently diverse and complex, we must not narrow the data comprising a conceptual scheme to one level or one approach. Each source and each orientation has a legitimate and potentially fruitful contribution to make.

Manifest and Latent Taxa

Apart from the content of various personological constructs are the formal properties of a taxonomy itself. The elements that comprise such a classification system are called taxa (singular: taxon); they may be differentiated in a number of different ways. What may be labeled as *manifest* taxa involve classes that are based on observable or phenotypic commonalities (e.g., overt behavior). *Latent* taxa pertain to groupings formed on the basis of abstract mathematical derivations (factor or cluster analysis) or the propositional deductions of a theory, each of which ostensibly represents the presence of genotypic commonalities (e.g., etiologic origins or constitutional dispositions).

The polar distinction between manifest taxa, at the one end, and latent taxa, at the other, represents in part a broader epistemological dichotomy that exists between those who prefer to employ data derived from observational contexts versus those who prefer to draw their ideas from theoretical or mathematically-deduced sources. A parallel distinction was first drawn by Aristotle when he sought to contrast the understanding of disease with reference to knowledge of latent principles, which ostensibly deals with all instances of a disease, however diverse, versus direct observational knowledge, which deals presumably only with specific and individual instances. To Aristotle, knowledge based on direct experience alone represented a more primitive type of knowledge than that informed by mathematics or conceptual theory which could, through the application of principles, explain not only why a particular disease occurs, but illuminate commonalities among seemingly diverse ailments.

Manifest Personologic and Clinical Taxa

For the greater part of history, taxonomies of both normal and abnormal persons were formed on the basis of systematic observation, the witnessing of repetitive patterns of behavior and emotion among a small number of carefully studied individuals. Etiologic hypotheses were generated to give meaning to these patterns (e.g., Hippocrates anchored differences in observed temperament to his humoral theory and Kraepelin distinguished two major categories of severe pathology, dementia praecox and manic-depressive disease, in terms of their ostensive divergent prognostic course). The elements comprising these theoretical notions were *post hoc*, however, imposed on prior observational data rather than serving as a generative source for taxonomic categories. The most recent example of a clinical taxonomy, one tied explicitly to phenomenal observation and constructed by intention to be both atheoretical and nonquantitative, is, of course, the *Diagnostic and Statistical Manual of Mental Disorders-III* (DSM-III). Robert Spitzer, chairperson of the Task Force, stated in DSM-III that "clinicians can agree on the identification of mental disorders on the basis of their clinical manifestations without agreeing on how the disturbances came about" (p. 7).

DSM-III is implicitly a product of speculation regarding latent causes or structures. Nevertheless, a major goal of its Task Force committee was to eschew theoretic notions, adhering to as strict an observational philosophy as possible. In doing so, only those attributes that could be readily seen or consensually validated were to be permitted as diagnostic criteria. Numerous departures from this epistemology are notable, nevertheless, especially among the personality disorders, where trait ascriptions call for inferences beyond direct sensory inspection.

Not all who seek to render taxa on the basis of observational clinical data insist on keeping latent inferences to a minimum (Tversky, 1977). And by no means do those who draw their philosophical inspiration from a manifest mindset restrict themselves to the mere specification of surface similarities (Medin, Altom, Edelson, & Freko, 1982). It is not only those who employ mathematical procedures and who formulate theoretically generated nosologies who succumb to the explanatory power and heuristic value of pathogenic or statistical inferences. Feinstein (1977), a distinguished internist, provided an apt illustration of how one man's "factual" observations may be another's latent inference:

> In choosing an anchor or focus for taxonomy, we can engage in two distinctly different types of nosologic reasoning. The first is to form names, designations or denominations for the observed evidence, and to confine ourselves exclusively to what has actually been observed. The second is to draw inferences from the observed evidence, arriving at inferential titles representing entities that have not actually been observed. For example, if a patient says "I have substantial chest pain, provoked by exertion, and relieved by rest," I, as an internist, perform a denomination if I designate this observed entity as angina pectoris. If I call it coronary artery disease, however, I perform an inference, since I have not actually observed coronary artery disease. If a radiologist looking at a coronary arteriogram or a pathologist cutting open the coronary vasculature uses the diagnosis coronary artery disease, the decision is a denomination. If the radiologist or pathologist decides that the coronary disease was caused by cigarette smoking or by a high fat diet, the etiologic diagnosis is an inference unless simultaneous evidence exists that the patient did indeed smoke or use a high fat diet. (p. 192)

In large measure, observationally based taxa gain their import and prominence by virtue of consensus and authority. Cumulative experience and habit are crystallized and subsequently confirmed by official bodies such as the various DSM-III committees (Millon, 1986). Specified criteria are denoted and articulated, acquiring definitional, if not stipulative powers, at least in the eyes of those who come to accept the manifest attributes selected as infallible taxonomic indicators.

Latent Mathematical Taxa

Inasmuch as manifest taxa stem from the observations and inferences of, for example, clinical diagnosticians, they comprise, in circular fashion, the very qualities that clinicians are likely to see and deduce. Classes so constructed will not only direct future observers to focus on and to mirror these same taxa in their patients, but they may lead future nosologists away from potentially more useful constructs with which to fathom less obvious patterns of attribute covariation. Many taxonomists have turned either to numerical methods or to theoretical principles with the end of penetrating beneath the level of sensory appearances. The rapid proliferation of new and powerful techniques both for analyzing and synthesizing vast bodies of clinical data have greatly facilitated the mathematical approach. This expansion has been accelerated by the ready availability of inexpensive computer hardware and software programs. Unfortunately, such mushrooming has progressed more rapidly than its fruits can be digested.

The designation "factor analysis" is a generic term encompassing a variety of numerical procedures that serve to achieve different goals, the details of which are not relevant to this chapter. In essence, it seeks to reveal the underlying structure of its attributes by identifying factors which account for their covariation. Toward this end, linear combinations of the attributes are sequentially chosen to extract as much variance possible. Factors derived in this manner are often "rotated" after their initial mathematical solution to increase their psychological meaning.

In spite of the ostensibly productive lines of investigation that have resulted from the application of factor analytic techniques, serious questions continue to be raised about the methodology itself as well as the value of using factor analytic findings for the purpose of conceptualizing personality. Early in its application, Kendall (1975) reported that skepticism about factor analysis was widespread,

> largely because of the variety of different factor solutions that can be obtained from a single set of data and the lack of any satisfactory objective criterion for preferring one of these to the others. The number of factors obtained and their loadings are often affected considerably by relatively small changes in the size or composition of the subject sample, or in the range of test employed. (p. 108)

Several years later, Sprock and Blashfield (1984) noted that "deciding when to stop the process of selecting the number of factors, rotating the solutions, and interpreting the factors are all highly subjective and at the discretion of the user. Therefore, many distrust the results" (p. 108). In addition to these methodological caveats, a number of conceptual forewarnings must be kept in mind regarding the structural implications of factor analytic approaches. As is known among those involved in the development of psychometric instruments (Loevinger, 1957; Millon, 1983, 1987a), a reasonable degree of "fidelity" should exist between the pattern of relationships among the scales of a test and its structural model of normality or pathology.

Thus, despite its popularity with many distinguished psychometricians, the psychological composition of factorial structures are far from universally accepted. Not only do few personological or psychopathological entities give evidence of factorial "purity" or attribute independence, but factorial solutions tend to be antithetical to the predominant polythetic structure and overlapping relationships that exist among normal personalities and clinical conditions (e.g., Millon, 1969, 1981, 1990). Neither personologic nor syndromic taxa consist of entirely homogeneous and discrete attributes. Rather, taxa are comprised of diffuse and complex characteristics that share many attributes in common, factorially-derived or otherwise.

Nevertheless, a growing literature of impressive findings support one such model in the realm of normal personality, the five-factor model (FFM) (Costa & McCrae, 1990; Digman, 1990; Goldberg, 1990; McCrae & Costa, 1985). Costa and McCrae have provided strong evidence for the power of the FFM as a latent mathematical framework for unraveling diverse and complex structures of numerous personality instruments. In their recent writings (see McCrae, chapter 2 in this volume) they have made attempts to extend the FFM to the realm of personality disorders. This is not the chapter to comment on their efforts, but it should be noted in passing that other equally astute and productive investigators have registered disagreements concerning the sufficiency and scope of the FFM as a taxonomy of normal personality and its adequacy as a latent explicator of the personality disorders (e.g., Benjamin, 1993; Grove & Tellegen, 1991; Livesley, 1991; Tellegen, 1993).

Beyond these skeptics of the fruitfulness of the FFM are those who question the wisdom of employing latent mathematical methods at all. Kendall's comment of more than a decade ago (1975), on reviewing the preceding 20-year period, may be judged by some as no less apt today as then:

> Looking back on the various studies published in the last twenty years it is clear that many investigators, clinicians and statisticians, have had a naive, almost Baconian, attitude to the statistical techniques they were employing, putting in all data at their disposal on the assumption that the computer would sort out the relevant from the irrelevant and expose the underlying principles and regularities, and assuming all that was required of them was to collect the data assiduously beforehand.
>
> Moreover, any statistician worth his salt is likely to be able, by judicious choice of patients and items, and of factoring or clustering procedures, to produce more or less what he wants to. (p. 118)

We believe that the task of combining factor attributes into patterns and configurations that correspond to the personality, normal and abnormal, is one that transcends the powers of mathematical technique. To achieve this task one must still depend on clinical "artistry" or the deductive powers of a theory-based model, another approach to uncovering latent principles for constructing and classifying personality, and one to which we turn next.

Latent Theoretical Taxa

Whereas the biases of statisticians in shaping data are likely to be implicit or arcane, those of theorists are explicit and straightforward. Distinguished philoso phers such as Hempel (1965) and Quine (1977) consider that mature sciences must progress from an observationally based stage to one that is characterized by abstract concepts, or theoretical systemizations. It is their judgment that classification alone does not make a true scientific taxonomy, and that overt similarity among attributes does not necessarily comprise a scientific category (Smith & Medin, 1981). The card catalog of the library or an accountant's ledger sheet, for example are well-organized classifications, but hardly to be viewed as a taxonomy.

The characteristic which distinguishes what we term a latent theoretical as contrasted to a latent mathematical taxonomy is its success in grouping its elements according to logically consonant *explanatory* propositions. These propositions are formed when certain attributes which have been isolated or categorized have been shown or have been hypothesized to be dynamically or causally related to other attributes or categories. The latent taxa comprising a theoretical nosology are not, therefore, mere collections of overtly similar factors or categories, but are linked or unified into a pattern of known or presumed relationships among them. This theoretically grounded configuration of relationships is the foundation and essence of a heuristic taxonomy.

In short, what distinguishes a theoretically-grounded personality system from one that provides a mere descriptive summary of known observations and inferences is its power to *generate* observations and relationships other than those used to construct it. Such generative power Hempel (1965) termed the "systematic import" of a scientific classification. In contrasting what are familiarly known as "natural" (theoretically guided, deductively based) and "artificial" (conceptually barren, similarity-based) classifications, Hempel (1965) wrote:

> Distinctions between "natural" and "artificial" classifications may well be explicated as referring to the difference between classifications that are scientifically fruitful and those that are not; in a classification of the former kind, those characteristics of the elements which serve as criteria of membership in a given class are associated, universally or with high probability, with more or less extensive clusters of other characteristics.
>
> Classification of this sort should be viewed as somehow having objective existence in nature, as "carving nature at the joints" in contradistinction of "artificial" classifications, in which the defining characteristics have few explanatory or predictive connections with other traits.
>
> In the course of scientific development, classifications defined by reference to manifest, observable characteristics will tend to give way to systems based on theoretical concepts. (pp. 116, 148)

Ostensibly toward the end of pragmatic sobriety, those of an antitheory bias have sought to persuade the profession of the failings of premature formalization, warning us that we cannot arrive at the future we yearn for by lifting our science by its own bootstraps. To them, there is no way to traverse the road other sciences have traveled without paying the dues of an arduous program of empirical research.

Formalized axiomatics, they say, must await the accumulation of hard evidence that is simply not yet in. Shortcutting the route with ill-timed theoretical systematics, such as a latent taxonomy, will lead us down primrose paths, preoccupying our attentions as we wind fruitlessly through endless detours, each of which could be averted by holding fast to an empirical philosophy or a clinical methodology.

No one argues against the view that theories that float, so to speak, on their own, unconcerned with the empirical domain or clinical knowledge, should be seen as the fatuous achievements they are and recognized for the travesty they may make of the virtues of a truly coherent nosological system. Formal theory should not be pushed far beyond the data, and its derivations should be linked at all points to established clinical observations. Given the vast scope of personalities as well as the extent of knowledge still to be gathered, nosologic theories are best kept limited today both in their focus and specificity. As the senior author has written elsewhere (Millon, 1987), structurally weak theories make it impossible to derive systematic and logical nosologies; this results in conflicting derivations and circular reasoning. Most nosological theories of psychopathology have generated brilliant deductions and insights, but few of these ideas can be attributed to their structure, the precision of their concepts, or their formal procedures for hypothesis derivation.

In spite of the shortcomings of historic concepts of personality pathology, it is latent mathematical models and latent theories that will "facilitate a deeper seeing, a more penetrating vision that goes beyond superficial appearances to the order underlying them" (Bowers, 1977). We will turn next to a model that may provide us with this "deeper and more penetrating vision."

AN EVOLUTIONARY SCAFFOLD FOR PERSONALITY THEORY

What is proposed is akin to Freud's (1895) abandoned *Project for a Scientific Psychology* and Wilson's (1975) highly controversial *Sociobiology*. Both were worthy efforts to advance our understanding of human nature by exploring interconnections among disciplines that evolved ostensibly unrelated bodies of research and manifestly dissimilar languages.

Much of personology, no less psychology as a whole, remains adrift, divorced from broader spheres of scientific knowledge, isolated from firmly grounded, if not universal principles. Preoccupied with but a small part of the larger puzzle, or fearing accusations of reductionism, many fail to draw on the rich possibilities to be found in other realms of scholarly pursuit. With few exceptions, cohering concepts that would connect this subject to those of its sister sciences have not been developed. We must go beyond traditional conceptual boundaries in order to explore carefully reasoned, as well as intuitive, hypotheses that draw their principles, if not their substance, from the more established adjacent sciences such as physics and evolutionary biology. Not only may such steps bear new conceptual fruits, but they may provide a foundation that can undergird and guide our own discipline's explorations.

And what better sphere is there within the psychological sciences to undertake such syntheses than with the subject matter of personology? Persons are the only organically integrated system in the psychological domain, evolved through the millennia and inherently created from birth as natural entities, rather than culture-bound and experience-derived gestalts. The intrinsic cohesion of persons is not merely a rhetorical construction, but an authentic, substantive unity. Personologic features may often be dissonant and may be partitioned conceptually for pragmatic or scientific purposes, but they are also segments of an inseparable biopsychosocial entity, as well as a natural outgrowth of evolution's progression.

What makes evolutionary principles as relevant as we propose? Owing to mathematical and deductive insights from the field of physics, we have a deeper and clearer sense of the early evolution and structural relations among matter and energy. So, too, has knowledge progressed in the fields of physical chemistry, microbiology, evolutionary theory, population biology, ecology, and ethology. How odd it seems that we have only now again begun to investigate—as we did at the turn of the last century—the interface between the basic building blocks of physical nature and the nature of life as we experience and live it personally. How much more is known today, yet how hesitant people are to undertake a serious rapprochement. As Barash (1982) has commented:

> Like ships passing in the night, evolutionary biology and the social sciences have rarely even taken serious notice of each other, although admittedly, many introductory psychology texts give an obligatory toot of the Darwinian horn somewhere in the first chapter . . . before passing on to discuss human behavior as though it were determined only by environmental factors. (p. 7)

It is clear that each evolved species displays commonalities in its adaptive or survival style. Within each species, however, there are differences in style and differences in the success with which its various members adapt to the diverse and changing environments they face. In these simplest of terms, personality would be conceived as representing the more-or-less distinctive style of adaptive functioning that an organism of a particular species exhibits as it relates to its typical range of environments. "Disorders" of personality, so formulated, would represent particular styles of maladaptive functioning that can be traced to deficiencies, imbalances, or conflicts in a species' capacity to relate to the environments it faces.

Before elaborating where these "disorders" arise within the human species, a few more words must be said concerning analogies between evolution and ecology, on the one hand, and personality, on the other.

During its life history an organism develops an assemblage of traits that contribute to its individual survival and reproductive success, the two essential components of "fitness" formulated by Darwin. Such assemblages, termed "complex adaptations" and "strategies" in the literature of evolutionary ecology, are close biological equivalents to what psychologists have conceptualized as personality styles and structures. In biology, explanations of a life history strategy of adaptations refer primarily to biogenic variations among constituent traits, their overall covariance structure, and the nature and ratio of favorable to unfavorable ecologic resources that have been available for purposes of extending longevity and optimizing reproduction. Such explanations are not appreciably different from those used to account for the development of personality styles or functions.

Bypassing the usual complications of analogies, a relevant and intriguing parallel may be drawn between the phylogenic evolution of a species' genetic composition and the ontogenic development of an individual organism's adaptive strategies (i.e., its "personality style"). At any point in time a species will possess a limited set of genes that serve as trait potentials. Over succeeding generations the frequency distribution of these genes will likely change in their relative proportions depending on how well the traits they undergird contribute to the species' "fittedness" within its varying ecological habitats. In a similar fashion, individual organisms begin life with a limited subset of their species' genes and the trait potentials they subserve. Over time the *salience* of these trait potentials— not the proportion of the genes themselves—will become differentially prominent as the organism interacts with its environments. It "learns" from these experiences which of its traits "fit" best, that is, are most optimally suited to its ecosystem. In phylogenesis, then, actual gene *frequencies* change during the generation-to-generation adaptive progress, whereas in ontogenesis it is the *salience* or prominence of gene-based traits that changes as adaptive learning takes place. Parallel evolutionary processes occur, one within the life of a species, the other within the life of an organism. What is seen in the individual organism is a shaping of latent potentials into adaptive and manifest styles of perceiving, feeling, thinking and acting. These distinctive means of adaptation, engendered by the interaction of biologic endowment and social experience, comprise the elements of what is termed personality styles. It is a formative process in a single lifetime that parallels gene redistributions among species during their evolutionary history.

Humans are notable for unusual adaptive pliancy, acquiring a wide repertoire of "styles" or alternate modes of functioning for dealing both with predictable and novel environmental circumstances. Unfortunately, the malleability of early potentials for diverse learnings diminishes as maturation progresses. As a consequence, adaptive styles acquired in childhood that are usually suitable for comparable later environments become increasingly immutable, and resist modification and relearning. Problems arise in new settings when these deeply ingrained behavior patterns persist despite their lessened appropriateness. Simply stated, what was learned and was once adaptive may no longer "fit." Perhaps more important than environmental diversity, then, is the divergence between the circumstances of original learning and those of later life, a schism that has become more problematic as humans have progressed from stable and traditional to fluid and inconstant modern societies.

Lest the reader assume that those seeking to wed the sciences of evolution and ecology find themselves fully on solid ground, there are numerous conceptual and methodological impediments that face those who wish to bring these fields of biologic inquiry into fruitful synthesis—no less employing them to construe the styles and disorders of personality. Despite such concerns, recent developments bridging ecological and evolutionary theory are well underway, and hence do offer some justification for extending their principles to human styles of adaptation. To provide a conceptual background from these sciences and to furnish a rough model concerning the styles of personality, normal and abnormal, four spheres in which evolutionary and ecological principles can be applied are labeled Aims of Existence, Modes of Adaptation, Strategies of Replication, and Abstraction. The first area relates to the serendipitous transformation of random or less organized states into those possessing distinct structures of greater organization, the second refers to homeostatic processes employed to sustain survival in open ecosystems, the third pertains to reproductive styles that maximize the diversification and selection of ecologically effective attributes, and the fourth concerns the emergence of competencies that foster anticipatory planning and reasoned decision making. To illustrate normal and abnormal processes, we will restrict our discussion to the first three principles. The various components of the fourth sphere will be included in our description of the theory's coordinated assessment instruments.

Aims of Existence

The following pages summarize the rationale and characteristics of the first of the three segments of the polarity model to be described. In each section we will draw upon the model as a basis for establishing criteria for "normality" grounded in modern evolutionary and ecological theory.

Life Enhancement and Life Preservation: Pleasure–Pain Polarity

Two intertwined strategies are required, one to achieve existence, the other to preserve it. The aim of the first is the enhancement of life, that is, creating or strengthening ecologically survivable organisms; the aim of the second is the preservation of life, that is, avoiding events that might terminate it. Although we disagree with Freud's concept of a death instinct (Thanatos), we believe he was essentially correct in recognizing that a balanced yet fundamental biological bipolarity exists in nature, a bipolarity that has its parallel in the physical world. As he wrote in one of his last works, "The analogy of our two basic instincts extends from the sphere of living things to the pair of opposing forces—attraction and repulsion—which rule the inorganic world" (Freud 1940, p. 72). Among humans, the former may be seen in life-enhancing acts that are "attracted" to what we experientially record as "pleasurable" events (positive reinforcers), the latter in life-preserving behaviors oriented to repel events experientially characterized as "painful" (negative reinforcers).

Existence reflects a to-be or not-to-be issue. In the inorganic world, "to be" is essentially a matter of possessing qualities that distinguish a phenomenon from its surrounding field, that is, not being in a state of entropy. Among organic beings, "to be" is a matter of possessing the properties of life as well as being located in ecosystems that facilitate the enhancement and preservation of that life. In the phenomenological or experiential world of sentient organisms, events that extend life and preserve it correspond largely to metaphorical terms such as pleasure and pain, that is, recognizing and pursuing positive sensations and emotions on the one hand and recognizing and eschewing negative sensations and emotions on the other.

The pleasure–pain bipolarity not only places sensations, motivations, feelings, emotions, moods, and affect on two contrasting dimensions but recognizes that each possess separate and independent quantitative extremes. That is, events that are attractive, gratifying, rewarding, or positively reinforcing may be experienced as weak or strong, just as those that are aversive, distressful, sad, or negatively reinforcing can also be experienced as weak or strong.

Efforts to identify specific events or experiences that fit each pole of the pleasure–pain bipolarity are likely to distract from the essential distinction. Thus, the particular actions or objects that people find pleasurable (for example, sex, sports, art, or money) are legion, and for every patient who experiences a certain event as rewarding, one can find another who experiences that same event as distasteful or painful. In short, categorizations based on the specific properties of what may be subsumed under the broad constructs of pain or pleasure will prove not only futile and cumbersome but misguiding as well.

Although there are many philosophical and metapsychological issues associated with the "nature" of pain and pleasure as constructs, it is neither our intent nor our task to inquire into them here. That they recur as a polar dimension time and again in diverse psychological domains (for example, learned behaviors, unconscious processes, emotion and motivation as well as their biological substrates) has been elaborated elsewhere (Millon 1990). Let us examine their role as constructs for articulating criteria that may usefully define normality.

An interweaving and shifting balance between the two extremes that comprise the pain-pleasure bipolarity typifies normality. Both of the following criteria should be met in varying degrees as life circumstances require. In essence, a synchronous and coordinated personal style would have developed to answer the question of whether the person should focus on experiencing only the pleasures of life versus concentrating his or her efforts on avoiding its pains.

Life preservation: Avoiding danger and threat.   One might assume that a criterion based on the avoidance of psychic or physical pain would be sufficiently self-evident not to require specification. As is well known, debates have arisen in the literature as to whether mental health/normality reflects the absence of mental disorder, being merely the reverse side of the mental illness or abnormality coin. That there is a relationship between health and disease cannot be questioned; the two are intimately connected, conceptually and physically. However, to define health solely as the absence of disorder will not suffice. As a single criterion among several, however, features of behavior and experience that signify both the lack of, and an aversion to, pain in its many and diverse forms, provide a necessary foundation on which other, more positively constructed criteria may rest. Substantively, positive normality must comprise elements beyond mere nonnormality or abnormality. And despite the complexities and inconsistencies of personality, from a definitional point of view, normality does preclude non-normality.

Notable here are the contributions of Maslow (1968, 1970), particularly his hierarchical listing of "needs." Best known are the five fundamental needs that lead to self-actualization, the first two of which relate to our evolutionary criterion of life preservation. Included in the first group are the "physiologic" needs such as air, water, food, and sleep, qualities of the ecosystem essential for survival. Next, and equally necessary to avoid danger and threat, are what Maslow termed the *safety needs,* including the freedom from jeopardy, the security of physical protection and psychic stability, as well as the presence of social order and interpersonal predictability. That pathological consequences can ensue from the failure to attend to the realities that portend danger is obvious; the lack of air, water, and food are not issues of great concern in civilized societies today, although these are matters of considerable import to environmentalists of the future and to contemporary poverty-stricken nations.

It may be of interest to record some of the psychic pathologies of personality that can be traced to aberrations in meeting this first criterion of normality. For example, among those termed avoidant personalities (Millon 1969, 1981), we see an excessive preoccupation with threats to one's psychic security, an expectation of and hyperalertness to the signs of potential rejection that leads these persons to disengage from everyday relationships and pleasures. At the other extreme of the criterion we see a risk-taking attitude, a proclivity to chance hazards and to endanger one's life and liberty, a behavioral pattern characteristic of those we label antisocial personalities. Here, there is little of the caution and prudence expected in the normality criterion of avoiding danger and threat; rather, we observe its opposite, a rash willingness to put one's safety in jeopardy, to play with fire and throw caution to the wind.

Life enhancement: Seeking rewarding experiences.   At the other end of the "existence polarity" are attitudes and behaviors designed to foster and enrich life, to generate joy, pleasure, contentment, fulfillment, and thereby strengthen the capacity of the individual to remain vital and competent physically and psychically. This criterion asserts that existence/survival calls for more than life preservation alone; beyond pain avoidance is pleasure enhancement.

This criterion asks us to go at least one step further than Freud's parallel notion that life's motivation is chiefly that of "reducing tensions" (that is, avoiding/minimizing pain), maintaining thereby a steady state, if you will, a homeostatic balance and inner stability. In accord with our view of evolution's polarities, I would assert that normal humans are driven also by the desire to enrich their lives, to seek invigorating sensations and challenges, and to venture and explore, all to the end of magnifying if not escalating the probabilities of both individual viability and species replicability. Spencer (1870) put it well more than a century ago: "pleasures are the correlatives of actions conducive to [organismic] welfare . . . the incentives to life supporting acts" (pp. 279, 284). The view that there exists an organismic striving to expand one's inherent potentialities (as well as those of one's kin and species) has been implicit in the literature for ages. That "the pleasures" may be both sign and vehicle for this realization was recorded even in the ancient writings of the Talmud, where it states: "everyone will have to justify himself in the life hereafter for every failure to enjoy a legitimately offered pleasure in this world" (Jahoda, 1958, p. 45).

Turning to more recent psychological formulations, both Rogers (1963) and Maslow (1968) proposed concepts akin to the criterion of enhancing pleasure. In his notion of "openness to experience," Rogers asserted that the fully functioning person has no aspect of his or her nature closed off. Such individuals are not only receptive to the experiences that life offers but are able also to use them in expanding all of life's emotions, as well as being open to all forms of personal expression. Along a similar vein, Maslow spoke of the ability to maintain a freshness to experience, to keep up one's capacity to appreciate relationships and events. No matter how often events or persons are encountered, one is neither sated nor bored but is disposed to view them with an ongoing sense of "awe and wonder."

The pathological consequences of a failure to meet this criterion are seen most clearly in the personality disorders labeled schizoid and avoidant. In the former there is a marked hedonic deficiency, stemming either from an inherent deficit in affective substrates or the failure of stimulative experience to develop either or both attachment behaviors and affective capacity (Millon, 1981). Among those designated avoidant personalities, constitutional sensitivities or abusive life experiences have led to an intense attentional sensitivity to psychic pain and a consequent distrust in either the genuineness or durability of the "pleasures," such that these individuals can no longer permit themselves to experience them. Both of these personalities tend to be withdrawn and isolated, joyless and grim, neither seeking nor sharing in the rewards of life.

Modes of Adaptation

To maintain a unique structure, differentiated from the larger ecosystem of which the organism is a part, and to be sustained as a discrete entity among other phenomena that comprise the environmental field, requires good fortune and the presence of effective modes of functioning.

Ecologic Accommodation and Ecologic Modification: The Passive–Active Polarity

Like pleasure–pain, this evolutionary stage is also framed as a polarity. Passivity may best be characterized as the mode of ecologic accommodation, signifying inclinations to passively "fit in," to locate and remain securely anchored in a niche, subject to the vagaries and unpredictabilities of the environment, all acceded to with one crucial proviso, namely, that the elements comprising the surroundings will furnish both the nourishment and the protection needed to sustain existence. Though based on a somewhat simplistic bifurcation among adaptive strategies, this passive and accommodating mode is one of the two fundamental methods that living organisms have evolved as a means of survival, representing the core process employed in the evolution of what has come to be designated as the plant kingdom, a stationary, rooted, yet essentially pliant and dependent survival mode. By contrast, the second of the two major modes of adaptation is seen in the lifestyle of the animal kingdom. Here we observe a primary inclination toward ecologic modification, a tendency to change or rearrange the elements comprising the larger milieu, to intrude upon otherwise quiescent settings, a versatility in shifting from one niche to another as unpredictability arises, a mobile and interventional mode that actively stirs, maneuvers, yields, and, at the human level, substantially transforms the environment to meet its own survival aims. Both modes—passive and active—have proven impressively capable of both nourishing and preserving life. Whether the polarity sketched is phrased in terms of accommodating versus modifying, passive versus active, or plant versus animal, it represents, at the most basic level, the two fundamental modes that organisms have evolved to sustain their existence. This second aspect of evolution differs from the first stage, which is concerned with what may be called existential "becoming," in that it characterizes modes of "being," that is, how what has become endures.

Broadening the model to encompass human experience, the active–passive polarity means that the vast range of behaviors engaged in by humans may fundamentally be grouped in terms of whether initiative is taken in altering and shaping life's events or whether behaviors are reactive to and accommodate those events. Normal or optimal functioning, at least among humans, appears to call for a flexible balance that interweaves both polar extremes. In the first evolutionary stage, that relating to existence, behaviors encouraging both life enhancement (pleasure) and life preservation (pain avoidance) are likely to be more successful in achieving survival than actions limited to one or the other alone. Similarly, regarding adaptation, modes of functioning that exhibit both ecologic accommodation and ecologic modification are likely to be more successful than either by itself.

As with the pair of criteria representing the aims of existence, a balance should be achieved between the two criteria comprising modes of adaptation, those related to ecological accommodation and ecologic modification. Normality calls for a synchronous and coordinated personal style that weaves a balanced answer to the question of whether one should accept what the fates have brought forth or take the initiative in altering the circumstances of one's life.

Ecological accommodation: Abiding hospitable realities. On first reflection, it would seem to be less than optimal to submit meekly to what life presents, to "adjust" obligingly to one's destiny. As described earlier, however, the evolution of plants is essentially grounded (no pun intended) in environmental accommodation, in an adaptive acquiescence to the ecosystem. Crucial to this adaptive course, however, is the capacity of these surroundings to provide the nourishment and protection requisite to the thriving of a species. Nevertheless, to the extent that the events of life have been and continue to be caring and giving, is it not perhaps wisest, from an evolutionary perspective, to accept this good fortune and "let matters be?" Hence passivity, the yielding to environmental forces, may be in itself not only unproblematic but, where events and circumstances provide the "pleasures" of life and protect against their "pains," positively adaptive and constructive.

Maslow (1970) stated that "self-actualized" individuals accept their nature as it is, despite personal weaknesses and imperfections. Comfortable with themselves and the world around them, they do not seek to change "the water because it is wet, or the rocks because they are hard" (p. 153). They have learned to accept the natural order of things. Passively accepting nature, they need not hide behind false masks or transform others to fit "distorted needs." Accepting themselves without shame or apology, they are equally at peace with the shortcomings of those with whom they live and relate.

Where do we find clinical failures to meet the accommodating-abiding criterion? Some personality disorders exhibit an excess of passivity, failing thereby to give direction to their own lives. Several Axis II disorders demonstrate this passive style, although their passivity derives from and is expressed in appreciably different ways. For dependents, passivity stems from deficits in self-confidence and competence, leading to deficits in initiative and autonomous skills as well as a tendency to wait passively while others assume leadership and guide, if not control, them. Passivity among obsessive-compulsive personalities, however, stems from their fear of acting independently, owing to intrapsychic resolutions they have made to quell hidden thoughts and emotions generated by their intense self-other ambivalence. Dreading the possibility of making mistakes or engaging in disapproved behaviors, they become indecisive, immobilized, restrained, and passive. High on pain and low on both pleasure and self, self-defeating personalities operate on the assumption that they dare not expect nor deserve to have life go their way; giving up any efforts to achieve a life that accords with their "true" desires, they passively submit to others' wishes, acquiescently accepting their fate.

Finally, narcissists, especially high on "self" and low on "others," benignly assume that "good things" will come their way with little or no effort on their part; this passive exploitation of others is a consequence of the unexplored confidence that underlies their self-centered presumptions.

Ecologic modification: Mastering one's environment. The active end of the bipolarity signifies the taking of initiative in altering and shaping life's events. As stated previously, such persons are best characterized by their alertness, vigilance, liveliness, vigor, and forcefulness, their stimulus-seeking energy and drive.

White (1959) defined *effectance* as an intrinsic motivation that activates persons to impose their desires on environments. de Charms (1968) elaborated on this theme with reference to man as "Origin" and as "Pawn," constructs akin to the active polarity, on the one hand, and to the passive polarity, on the other. He described this distinction as follows:

> That man is the origin of his behavior means that he is constantly struggling against being confined and constrained by external forces, against being moved like a pawn into situations not of his own choosing. . . . An Origin is a person who perceives his behavior as determined by his own choosing; a Pawn is a person who perceives his behavior as determined by external forces beyond his control. . . . An Origin has strong feelings of personal causation, a feeling that the locus for causation of effects in his environment lies within himself. The feedback that reinforces this feeling comes from changes in his environment that are attributable to personal behavior. This is the crux of personal causation, and it is a powerful motivational force directing future behavior. (pp. 273–274)

In a similar vein, Fromm (1955) proposed a need on the part of man to rise above the roles of passive creatures in an accidental if not random world. To him, humans are driven to transcend the state of merely having been created; instead, humans seek to become the creators, the active shapers of their own destiny. Rising above the passive and accidental nature of existence, humans generate their own purposes and thereby provide themselves with a true basis of freedom.

Although it may sometimes be best to transform inhospitable realities, one can be too actively-oriented in doing so. One example of an inability to leave things as they are is seen in what the *DSM* terms the histrionic personality disorder. Their persistent and unrelenting manipulation of events is designed to maximize the receipt of attention and favors as well as to avoid social disinterest and disapproval. They show an insatiable if not indiscriminate search for stimulation and approval. Their clever and often artful social behaviors may give the appearance of an inner confidence and self-assurance, but beneath this guise lies a fear that a failure on their part to ensure the receipt of attention will, in short order, result in indifference or rejection, and hence their desperate need for reassurance and repeated signs of approval. Tribute and affection must constantly be replenished and are sought from every interpersonal source. As they are quickly bored and sated, they keep stirring up things, becoming enthusiastic about one activity and then another. There is a restless stimulus-seeking quality in which they cannot leave well enough alone.

Strategies of Replication

If an organism merely duplicates itself prior to death, then its replica is likely to repeat the same fate it suffered. However, if new potentials for extending existence can be fashioned by chance or routine events, then the possibility of achieving a different and conceivably superior outcome may be increased. And it is this co-occurrence of random and recombinant processes that leads to the prolongation of a species' existence. This third hallmark of evolution's procession also undergirds another of nature's fundamental polarities, that between self and other.

Reproductive Propagation and Reproductive Nurturance: The Self–Other Polarity

Recombinant replication, with its consequential benefits of selective diversification, requires the partnership of two "parents," each contributing its genetic resources in a distinctive and species-characteristic manner. Similarly, the attention and care given the offspring of a species' matings is also distinctive. Worthy of note is the difference between the mating parents in the degree to which they protect and nourish their joint offspring. Although the investment of energy devoted to upbringing is balanced and complementary, rarely is it identical or even comparable in either devotion or determination. This disparity in reproductive "investment" strategies, especially evident among animal species (insects, reptiles, birds, mammals), underlies the evolution of the male and female genders, the foundation for the third cardinal polarity we propose to account for evolution's procession.

Evolutionary biologists (Cole, 1954; Trivers, 1974; Wilson, 1975) have recorded marked differences among species in both the cycle and pattern of their reproductive behaviors. Of special interest is the extreme diversity among and within species in the number of offspring spawned and the consequent nurturing and protective investment the parents make in the survival of their progeny. Designated the r-strategy and the K-strategy in population biology, the former represents a pattern of propagating a vast number of offspring but exhibiting minimal attention to their survival; the latter is typified by the production of few progeny followed by considerable effort to assure their survival.

Not only do species differ in where they fall on the r- to K-strategy continuum, but *within* most animal species an important distinction may be drawn between male and female genders. It is this latter differentiation that undergirds what has been termed the self- versus other-oriented polarity. In effect, males tend to be self-oriented owing to the fact that competitive advantages that inhere within themselves maximize the replication of their genes. Conversely, females tend to be other-oriented owing to the fact that their competence in nurturing and protecting their limited progeny maximizes the replication of their genes. The consequences of the male's r-strategy are a broad range of what may be seen as self-oriented as opposed to other-oriented behaviors, such as acting in an egotistic, insensitive, inconsiderate, uncaring, and noncommunicative manner. In contrast, females are more disposed to be other-oriented, affiliative, intimate, empathic, protective, and solicitous (Gilligan, 1982; Wilson, 1978).

As before, we consider both of the following criteria necessary to the definition and determination of normality. We see no necessary antithesis between the two. Humans can be both self-actualizing and other-encouraging, although most persons are likely to lean toward one or the other side. A balance that coordinates the two provides a satisfactory answer to the question of whether one should be devoted to the support and welfare of others or fashion one's life in accord with one's own needs and desires.

Reproductive nurturance: Constructively loving others. As described earlier, recombinant replication achieved by sexual mating entails a balanced, though asymmetric, parental investment in both the genesis and nurturance of offspring.

Before we turn to some of the indices and views of the self–other polarity, readers should be mindful that these conceptually derived extremes do not evince themselves in sharp and distinct gender differences. Such proclivities are matters of degree, not absolutes, owing not only to the consequences of recombinant "shuffling" and gene "crossing over" but to the influential effects of cultural values and social learning. Consequently, most "normal" individuals exhibit intermediate characteristics on this as well as on the other two polarity sets.

More eloquent proposals related to this criterion have been formulated by the noted psychologists Maslow (1970), Allport (1937), and Fromm (1968). According to Maslow, once humans' basic safety and security needs are met, they next turn to satisfy the belonging and love needs. Here, we establish intimate and caring relationships with significant others in which it is just as important to give love as it is to receive it. Noting the difficulty in satisfying these needs in our unstable and changing modern world, Maslow saw the basis here for the immense popularity of communes and family therapy. These settings are ways to escape the isolation and loneliness that result from our failures to achieve love and belonging.

One of Allport's (1937) criteria of the "mature" personality, which he termed a warm relating of self to others, refers to the capability of displaying intimacy and love for a parent, child, spouse, or close friend. Here the person manifests an authentic oneness with the other and a deep concern for his or her welfare. Beyond one's intimate family and friends, there is an extension of warmth in the mature person to humankind at large, an understanding of the human condition, and a kinship with all peoples.

To Fromm (1968), humans are aware of the growing loss of their ties with nature as well as with each other and feel increasingly separate and alone. Fromm felt that humans must pursue new ties with others to replace those that have been lost or can no longer be depended on. To counter the loss of communion with nature, he believed that health requires that we fulfill our need by a brotherliness with mankind, a sense of involvement, concern, and relatedness with the world. And with those with whom ties have been maintained or reestablished, humans must fulfill their other-oriented needs by being vitally concerned with their well-being as well as fostering their growth and productivity.

The pathological consequences of a failure to embrace the polarity criterion of "others" are seen most clearly in the personality disorders termed antisocial and narcissistic. Both personalities exhibit an imbalance in their replication strategy; in this case, however, there is a primary reliance on self rather than others. They have learned that reproductive success as well as maximum pleasure and minimum pain is achieved by turning exclusively to themselves. The tendency to focus on self follows two major lines of development.

A pathological failure to love others is seen in the narcissistic personality, where development reflects the acquisition of a self-image of superior worth, learned largely in response to admiring and doting parents. Providing self-rewards is highly gratifying if one values oneself or possesses either a "real" or inflated sense of self-worth. Displaying manifest confidence, arrogance, and an exploitative ego-centricity in social contexts, this self-orientation has been termed the passive–independent style in the theory, as the individual "already" has all that is im-portant—him- or herself. They blithely assume that others will recognize their specialness. Hence, they maintain an air of arrogant self-assurance and, without much thought or even conscious intent, benignly exploit others to their own ad-vantage. Although the tributes of others are both welcome and encouraged, their air of snobbish and pretentious superiority requires little confirmation either through genuine accomplishment or social approval. Their sublime confidence that things will work out well provides them with little incentive to engage in the reciprocal give and take of social life. Those whom the theory characterizes as exhibiting the active-independent orientation resemble the outlook, temperament, and socially unacceptable behaviors of the *DSM* antisocial personality disorder. They act to counter the expectation of pain at the hand of others; this is done by actively engaging in duplicitous or illegal behaviors in which they seek to exploit others for self-gain. Skeptical regarding the motives of others, they desire au-tonomy and wish revenge for what are felt as past injustices. Many are irrespon-sible and impulsive, actions they see as justified because they judge others to be unreliable and disloyal. Insensitivity and ruthlessness with others are the primary means they have learned to head off abuse and victimization.

Reproductive propagation: Individuating and actualizing self. The converse of reproductive nurturance is not reproductive propagation but rather the lack of reproductive nurturance. Thus, to fail to love others constructively does not assure the actualization of one's potentials. Both may and should exist in normal, healthy individuals.

Jung's (1961) concept of individuation shares important features with that of actualization in that any deterrent to becoming the individual one may have become would be detrimental to life. Any imposed "collective standard is a serious check to individuality," injurious to the vitality of the person, a form of "artificial stunting."

Perhaps it was the first author's early mentor, Kurt Goldstein (1939, 1940), who coined the concept under review with the self-actualization designation. As he phrased it, "There is only one motive by which human activity is set going: the tendency to actualize oneself" (1939, p. 196).

The early views of Jung and Goldstein have been enriched by later theorists, among them Fromm (1968), Rogers (1963), and Maslow (1970). Following the views of his forerunners, Maslow stated that self-actualization is the "supreme development" and use of all our abilities, a state where we ultimately become what we have the potential to become. Noting that self-actualized individuals often require detachment and solitude, Maslow asserted that such persons are strongly self-centered and self-directed, make up their own minds, and reach their own decisions without the need to gain social approval.

In like manner, Rogers (1963) posited a single, overreaching motive for the normal, healthy person—maintaining, actualizing, and enhancing one's potential. The goal is not that of maintaining a homeostatic balance or a high degree of ease and comfort, but rather to move forward in becoming what is intrinsic to self and to enhance further that which one has already become. Believing that humans have an innate urge to create, Rogers stated that the most creative product of all is one's own self.

Where do we see failures in the achievement of self-actualization, a giving up of self to gain the approbation of others? The dependent personality disorder may be drawn on to illustrate forms of self-denial: Those with dependent personalities have learned that feeling good, secure, confident, and so on—that is, those feelings associated with pleasure or the avoidance of pain—are provided almost exclusively in their relationship with others. Behaviorally, these persons learn early that they themselves do not readily achieve rewarding experiences; the experiences are secured better by leaning on others. They learn not only to turn to others as their source of nurturance and security but to wait passively for others to take the initiative in providing safety and sustenance. Clinically, most are characterized as searching for relationships in which others will reliably furnish affection, protection, and leadership. Lacking both initiative and autonomy, they assume a dependent role in interpersonal relations, accepting what kindness and support they may find and willingly submitting to the wishes of others to maintain nurturance and security.

PERSONOLOGIC ASSESSMENT MEASURES

How do we measure the constructs we have proposed in prior pages? Are there "operational" gauges available that can appraise whether persons are suitably self-oriented, active in organizing their lives, over-reactive to the possibility of psychic pain, and so on? The answer to these questions is yes! Instruments exist to assess whether persons are clinically problematic in one or another combination of polarity extremes. Best known among these is the *Millon Clinical Multiaxial Inventory* (MCMI) (Millon, 1983, 1987a, 1994). Recent instruments geared to the theoretical model but focused essentially on nonclinical or "normal" populations have also been published. The *Personality Adjective Check List* (PACL) (Strack, 1987, 1991) was the first and most direct form of these tools. More recent is the *Millon Index of Personality Styles* (MIPS), developed by the authors and their associates (Millon, Millon, Davis, & Weiss, 1993). Both clinical and normal personality gauges will be briefly described below.

Clinical Instruments

The initial tools developed on the basis of the theoretical model were oriented primarily to assess personality *disorders*, although other clinical syndromes were appraised as well. Three instruments were constructed and published, the MCMI, the *Millon Behavioral Health Inventory* (MBHI) (Millon, Green, & Meagher, 1982b), and the *Millon Adolescent Personality Inventory* (MAPI) (Millon, Green, & Meagher, 1982a), recently replaced with the *Millon Adolescent Clinical Inventory* (MACI) (Millon, Millon, & Davis, 1993).

MCMI

A 175-item true-false self-report inventory, the MCMI and its subsequent revisions, MCMI-II (Millon, 1987a), and MCMI-III (Millon, 1994), include 14 personality disorder scales (all the personality disorders in both the main texts and appendices of the *DSM-III, III-R,* and *IV*), nine clinical syndrome scales, as well as three "modifying indices" to appraise problematic response tendencies.

Within the restrictions on validity set by the limits of the self-report mode, the narrow frontiers of psychometric technology, as well as the slender range of consensually shared diagnostic knowledge, all steps were taken to maximize the MCMI's concordance with its generative theory and the official classification system. Pragmatic and philosophical compromises were made where valued objectives could not be simultaneously achieved (e.g., instrument brevity versus item independence, representative national patient norms versus local base rate specificity, theoretical criterion considerations versus empirical data).

A major goal in constructing the MCMI was to keep the total number of items comprising the inventory small enough to encourage use in all types of diagnostic and treatment settings, yet large enough to permit the assessment of a wide range of clinically relevant behaviors. At 175 items, the final form is much shorter than comparable instruments. Potentially objectionable statements were screened out, and terminology was geared to an eighth-grade reading level. As a result, the great majority of patients can complete the MCMI in 20 to 30 minutes.

Unfortunately, as many have noted (Butcher, 1972), assessment techniques and personality theorizing have developed almost independently. As a result, few diagnostic measures have either been based on or have evolved from clinical theory. The MCMI is different. Each of its personality disorder and clinical syndrome scales was constructed as an operational measure of a syndrome derived from a theory of personality and psychopathology (Millon, 1969, 1981, 1990).

No less important than its link to theory is an instrument's coordination with the official diagnostic system and its syndromal categories. With the advent of the various recent *DSM*'s (American Psychiatric Association, 1980, 1987, 1994), diagnostic categories and labels have been precisely specified and defined operationally. Few diagnostic instruments currently available are as consonant with the nosological format and conceptual terminology of this official system as the MCMI.

Separate scales of the MCMI have been constructed in line with the DSM to distinguish the more enduring personality characteristics of patients (Axis II) from the acute clinical disorders they display (Axis I), a distinction judged to be of considerable use by both test developers and clinicians (Dahlstrom, 1972). This distinction should enable the clinician to separate those syndrome features of psychopathologic functioning that are persistent and pervasive from those that are transient or circumscribed. Moreover, profiles based on all 23 clinical scales illuminate the interplay between long-standing characterological patterns and the distinctive clinical symptomatology a patient manifests under psychic stress.

Similarly, it seemed useful to construct scales that distinguish syndromes in terms of their levels of psychopathologic severity. For example, the premorbid characterological pattern of a patient is assessed independently of its degree of pathology. To achieve this, separate scales are used to determine the style of traits comprising the basic personality structure (scales 1-8B) and the greater level of pathology of that structure (scales S, C, and P). In like manner, moderately severe clinical syndromes (scales A, H, N, D, B, and T), notably those of a "neurotic" form, are separated and independently assessed from those with parallel features but more of a "psychotic" nature (scales SS, CC, and PP).

Cross-validation data gathered with nondevelopment samples supported the measure's generalizability, dependability, and the accuracy of diagnostic scale cutting lines and profile interpretations. Large and diverse samples have been studied with the MCMI, but it is still necessary to achieve full domain coverage and engage in ongoing cross-validation studies. Moreover, local base rates and cutting lines must be developed for special settings. Nevertheless, validation data with a variety of populations (e.g., outpatients and inpatients, alcoholics and drug abusers) suggest that the MCMI can be used with reasonable confidence in most clinical settings.

As should be evident, the MCMI is not a general personality instrument to be used for "normal" populations or for purposes other than diagnostic screening or clinical assessment. Hence, it contrasts with other more broadly applied inventories whose presumed utility for diverse populations is often highly questionable.

Normative data and transformation scores for the MCMI are based on presumed clinical samples and are applicable therefore only to persons who evince psychological symptoms or are engaged in a program of professional psychotherapy or psychodiagnostic evaluation. As should also be noted, there are distinct boundaries to the accuracy of the self-report method of clinical data collection; by no means is it a perfect data source. The inherent psychometric limits of the tools, the tendency of similar patients to interpret questions differently, the effect of current affective states on trait measures, the effort of patients to effect certain false appearances and impressions, all narrow the upper boundaries of this method's potential accuracy. However, by constructing a self report instrument in line with accepted techniques of validation (Loevinger, 1957), an inventory should begin to approach these upper boundaries.

MBHI, MAPI, and MACI

In a manner similar to the various MCMI forms, these three instruments are best employed with individuals seeking professional assistance in medical, clinical, or counseling settings. In this regard they differ from the PACL and the MIPS, to be discussed shortly.

MBHI.   Using psychiatrically-oriented psychological tests in settings primarily of a medical nature requires that their concepts and indices be translated to fit new populations and purposes. Medical populations are not psychiatric populations, and viewing patients within traditional mental health constructs may prove neither valid nor useful. Of course, standard techniques can provide general information about overall emotional health or the presence of distinctive symptoms such as depression or anxiety. Problems arise, however, because of the unsuitability of norms, the questionable relevance of clinical signs, and the consequent inapplicability of interpretations. In brief, a "standard" interpretation of results obtained with a medical sample on a diagnostic test developed on and designed to assess a psychiatric population may not characterize sound test use. The MBHI (Millon, Green, & Meagher, 1982b) was developed specifically with physically ill patients and medical-behavioral decision-making issues in mind. Brevity, clarity, and ease of administration were added to the goal of elucidating salient and relevant dimensions of functioning.

Eight basic *coping styles* scales were derived from Millon's (1969, 1981) theory of personality. Six *psychogenic attitude* scales were developed additionally to reflect psychosocial stressors found in the research literature to be significant precipitators or exacerbators of physical illness. A final group of six scales were empirically derived either to appraise the extent to which emotional factors complicate particular psychosomatic ailments or to predict psychological complications associated with a number of diseases. All items were selected with data comparing groups of general medical populations or, in the case of specific disease scales, differentiating among sub-groups of patients with the same illness. This shift to a general medical reference population, rather than normal or psychiatric comparison groups, was expected to optimize the discrimination efficiency of the scales; the assumption that these steps should heighten diagnostic accuracy was supported in large part by cross-validation evidence.

MAPI and MACI. A variety of psychological tests have been developed through the years for use with adolescents. Often constructed in accordance with the sophistication then available, their shortcomings are now evident as psychometric advances have taken place. Although these older instruments provide useful information, they tend not to be tuned to current issues and behaviors, and lack a theoretically-grounded system of personality traits that can integrate the diverse features salient to the teen years. The MAPI (Millon, Green, & Meagher, 1982a) was normed on both clinical and nonclinical teenagers. The more recent MACI (Millon, Millon, & Davis, 1993) was based on clinical patients only and was developed to quantify relationships between traits and clinical states.

Both the MAPI and MACI were constructed specifically with an adolescent population in mind. The statements that comprise these inventories were written in a language that teenagers use and address matters they can understand and find relevant to their experiences. This contrasts with other commonly used personality inventories (e.g., the MMPI) which are designed for use with a broad and largely adult population. The most elegantly constructed psychometric tool is not likely to be widely accepted if its content, length and linguistic style make it unwieldy. A major goal for the MAPI and MACI was to construct an inventory with enough items to assess and illuminate accurately a variety of personality traits, psychological concerns and clinically relevant behaviors yet be of sufficient brevity to encourage its use in a variety of outpatient and residential settings. Both reading level and vocabulary were set to allow for ready comprehension by the vast majority of adolescents. The final 160-item inventory, geared to the sixth-grade reading level, can be completed by most teens in less than 20 minutes. The brevity and clarity of the instrument facilitates rapid administration with a minimum of client resistance.

Counselors, clinical psychologists, and psychiatrists were involved with the MAPI and MACI throughout all phases of their development. At an early stage clinicians were interviewed to ascertain issues relevant to both typical and troubled adolescents. The recent MACI includes 12 personality scales that parallel the DSM-IV disorders. There are eight "expressed concern" scales that address the phenomenological attitudes teenagers have regarding significant developmental problems. In addition, there are seven clinical syndrome scales that reflect major diagnostic categories associated with behaviors and thoughts that may pose serious difficulties for the adolescent (e.g., suicide ideation and substance abuse).

The capacity to differentiate each of the various clinical problem areas is a key to the effectiveness of the inventory. Hence, MACI item selections were made by comparing the targeted criterion group with a general, but troubled adolescent population. The utilization of reference groups such as these should substantially increase diagnostic discrimination efficiency.

Personality Instruments

As noted, the first group of instruments generated by the theoretical model focused on clinical diagnosis. As the theory was broadened to encompass personality traits and characteristics that fell within the so-called normal range (Millon, 1991), attention was directed to the development of suitably coordinated nonclinical assessment tools. Two such instruments have been constructed in line with this goal, the PACL (Strack, 1987) and the MIPS (Millon, Millon, Davis, & Weiss, 1993).

PACL

The first instrument specifically designed to assess the theoretically-derived personality types in a normal population was developed by a graduate research group led by the first author in the early 1980s. As the project progressed though its early revisions, the major responsibility for its further development was undertaken by one of its members, Stephen Strack. Using an adjective check list format, the initial forms (both clinician-rated and self-reported) were composed of 405 items that were intended to reflect the theory's eight basic personality types and its three more severe personality variants.

Item refinements and initial validation studies were based on data from over 2,000 "normal" adults from a variety of diverse national settings. A wide range of validity data have been gathered and reported (Strack, 1987, 1991, 1993), including correlations with various other gauges of personality and biographic data on current and past behavior. Each of the eight PACL personality scales appear consonant with theoretical expectations and measure normal versions of Millon's (1969, 1981) more severe, pathological styles. Thus, the PACL Inhibited scale (which reflects a milder variant of the theory's and *DSM*'s avoidant personality disorder) is positively correlated with measures of shyness, submissiveness, and social anxiety, while being negatively correlated with measure of sociability, dominance, and emotional well-being. Similarly, the PACL Forceful scale (a milder version of the theory's and *DSM*'s antisocial and sadistic disorders) is positively related to gauges of aggressiveness, arrogance, dominance, and negatively related to gauges of deference, submissiveness, and conscientiousness.

Owing to the common linkage in theory there is a possibility that the results of the PACL might be erroneously confused with parallel revisions of the MCMI. High scores on the PACL scales do not signify the presence of personality *disorders*, as they do on the MCMI; rather, they suggest the presence of distinctive personality traits. As Strack (1991) notes, all persons in the PACL development group were presumed to have normal personalities, hence the special utility of the instrument as a measure of normality rather than abnormality.

MIPS

This self-report inventory is composed of sentence-length items rather than adjectives. Both the MIPS and PACL are anchored to the theoretical model formulated by Millon from the mid-1960s to the mid-1980s. However, the PACL, like the MCMI, measures personality *types* as a composite or whole. In contrast, the MIPS focuses on constructs that *underlie* these personality types, the latent components that combine to give rise to them. To illustrate: The histrionic personality disorder of the MCMI, termed sociable personality style by the PACL, are the manifest abnormal and normal forms that take shape among those who are latently "active" on the active-passive polarity, and oriented to "other" on the self-other polarity. Focusing on these latent components, the first set of scales of the MIPS measure the three polarity pairs of the theory directly (e.g., pleasure–pain, active–passive, and self–other), rather than the manifest forms into which various combinations are exhibited.

Beyond breaking down the theory's manifest personality types into their constituent latent constructs, the theory as described in previous pages has been expanded substantially. Whereas the three polarities of the theory are still considered crucial elements of the model and serve as a particularly important gauge of personality *pathology*, they are now judged to be insufficient as a comprehensive scaffold for encompassing the highly diverse styles of normal personality.

This is not the chapter to elaborate both the full rationale and specifics of the expanded model; a recent essay on this theme may be found in the MIPS manual (Millon, Millon, Davis, & Weiss, 1993). However, we should briefly note that cognitive differences among individuals and the manner in which they are expressed has not been a sufficiently appreciated domain for generating personality traits. We have added a set of four polarities that reflect different "modes" of cognitive style to the MIPS. These follow the initial three polarities (eg., self-other), which have been termed "motivating aims." Similarly, we have added a third domain of polarities to those of "motivation" and "cognition," that termed "interpersonal behavior." We do not share the view of many who give the manifest forms of the interpersonal dimension primacy in their personality gauges, but we do judge them no less significant than either the motivational or cognitive, especially if they are organized in terms of the latent or fundamental polarities they express. Thus a third domain, comprising five interpersonal polarities, concludes the MIPS test form.

The following précis of the tripartite structure of the MIPS scales divides the test in the manner in which organisms function in their environment, one which we believe may be a useful theory-based schema for purposes of personological analysis. As noted previously, we have termed the first segment in this tripartite sequence as *motivating aims*, to signify that the behavior of organisms is prompted, energized, and directed by particular purposes and goals they wish to achieve. The second component of the sequence is labeled *cognitive modes* to indicate the manner in which human organisms seek out, regulate, internalize, and transform information about their environment and themselves, a step necessary if organisms are to achieve their aims effectively. The third segment in the sequence is referred to as *interpersonal behavior* to represent the different ways in which human organisms relate to and negotiate with other humans in their social environment in light of the aims that motivate them and the cognitions they have formed. To capture personality more-or-less fully we must find ways to characterize all three components of the sequence, namely, the deeper motives which orient individuals, the characteristic sources they utilize to construct and to transform their cognitions, and the particular behavior they have learned to relate to others interpersonally. By dimensionalizing and quantifying these three elements, we should be able to represent individual differences in accordance with the major features that characterize normal personality styles.

1. Closely akin to concepts such as need, drive, affect, and emotion, *motivating aims* pertain to the strivings and goals that spur and guide the organism, that is, the purposes and ends that stir them into one or another course of behavior. The aims of motivation reflect strivings for survival, which we see as composed of three elements, those referred to previously as "existence," "adaptation," and "replication" (Millon, 1990). In a manner akin to Freud (1915), these elements are organized as bipolarities, each of which comprise two contrasting scales. At one extreme of the first bipolarity is a motivation-based scale pertaining to the existential aim of strengthening one's life or reinforcing one's capacity to survive (phrased as *enhancing*); at the other extreme is an emotion-based scale that reflects the need to protect one's survival against life-threatening events (referred to as *preserving*). The second of the motivating aim bipolarities relates to adaptation, that is, methods by which one operates in one's environment to enhance and preserve life. One end of this bipolarity represents tendencies to actively and energetically alter the conditions of one's life, (termed *modifying*); the other end represents the inclination to passively accept in a neutral and nonresponsive manner one's life circumstances as they are given (referred to as *accommodating*). The third bipolarity comprising the motivating domain also differentiates two scales; one scale represents those who seek to realize and fulfill their own potentials before those of others (spoken of as *individuating*), as contrasted to those who are disposed to value the fortunes and potentials of relatives and companions to a greater degree than their own (called *nurturing*).

2. The second group of bipolarity scales relate to *cognitive modes*, incorporating both the sources employed to gather knowledge about life and the manner in which this information is transformed. In a manner akin to Jung (1923), four bipolarities, the constructs they reflect, and the eight scales developed to represent them, comprise this section of the MIPS. Here we are looking at contrasting "styles of cognizing," differences among people, first, in what they attend to in

order to experience and learn about life and, second, what they habitually do to make this knowledge meaningful and useful to themselves. The first two of these bipolarities refer to the *information sources* to which attention and perception are drawn to provide cognitions. One pair of scales contrasts individuals who are disposed to look outward for information, inspiration, and guidance (termed *extraversing*), versus those inclined to turn inward (referred to as *introversing*). The second pair of scales contrasts predilections for direct observational experiences of a tangible, material, and concrete nature (labeled *sensing*) with those geared more toward inferences regarding phenomena of an intangible, ambiguous, symbolic, and abstract character (named *intuiting*). The second set of cognitive mode bipolarities relate to *processes of transformation*, that is, ways in which information and experiences, once apprehended and incorporated, are subsequently evaluated and reconstructed mentally. The first pair of the transformation scales differentiates processes based essentially on intellect, logic, reason, and objectivity (entitled *thinking*) from those which depend on affective empathy, personal values, sentiment, and subjectivity (designated *feeling*). The second of the transformational scales are likewise divided into a bipolar pairing. At one end are reconstruction modes that transform new information so as to make it conserve and assimilate to preconceived formal, tradition-bound, well-standardized, and conventionally structured schemas (called *systematizing*); at the other bipolar scale are represented inclinations to avoid cognitive preconceptions, to distance from what is already known and to originate new ideas in an informal, open-minded, spontaneous, individualistic and often imaginative manner (termed *innovating*).

3. The third group of bipolar scales represent *interpersonal behavior*, reflecting how individuals prefer to relate to and conduct their transactions with others. These styles of social behavior derive in part from the interplay of the person's distinctive pattern of motivating aims and cognitive modes. Five bipolarities have been constructed to represent contrasting styles of relating behavior; in a broader context these behavioral styles may be considered to be located at the lower end of a continuum that shades progressively into the moderately severe personality disorders of *DSM-IV*. The first pair of scales in this, the third section of the MIPS, pertains to a bipolar dimension characterized by contrasting degrees of sociability. At one bipolar end are those persons whose high scale scores suggest that they relate to others in a socially distant, disengaged, affectless, and indifferent manner (termed *retiring*); on the other high scale end are those who seek to be engaged, are lively, talkative, and interpersonally gregarious (called *outgoing*). The second polarity pair relates to one's comfort and poise in social settings; it contrasts those who tend to be uncertain and fearful, are unsure of their personal worth, and are inclined to feel insecure and to withdraw socially (named *hesitating*), with those who are socially confident and self-possessed, as well as bold and decisive in their relationships (entitled *asserting*). The third pairing relates to contrasting degrees of conventionality and social deference; it differentiates those who are

disinclined more than most to adhere to public standards, cultural mores, and organizational regulations, act autonomously and insist on functioning socially on their own terms (labeled *dissenting*), as compared to those who are notably tradition-bound, socially compliant and responsible, respectful of authority, as well as appropriately diligent and dutiful (termed *conforming*). Facets of the interpersonal dimension of dominance-submission are tapped in the fourth polarity. High on one polar scale are those who are not only submissive, but also self-demeaning, diffident, overly modest, and self-depriving (designated *yielding*), as compared to those who, beyond being merely domineering, are also willful, ambitious, forceful, and power-seeking (termed *controlling*). The fifth and final set of polarities pertains to features of a dimension of social negativism versus social agreeableness. The former is seen among those who are dissatisfied with both themselves and others, who are generally displeased with the status quo, and tend to be resentful and oppositional (designated *complaining*); they contrast with those who are cooperative and compromising, not only considerate of others, but highly obliging and willing to adapt their behavior in accordance with the wishes of others (named *agreeing*).

CONCLUDING COMMENT

Our goal in this chapter was to connect the conceptual structure of both normal and abnormal personalities to their latent and common foundations in the natural world. What was proposed is akin to Freud's (1895) unfulfilled *Project for a Scientific Psychology*, an endeavor to advance our understanding of human behavior by exploring interconnections among diverse disciplines. It is also akin to Jung's (1961) effort to explicate the foundations of personality with reference to deeply rooted or latent polarities. In recent times, we have seen the emergence of sociobiology, a new "science" that explores the interface between human social functioning and evolutionary biology (Wilson, 1975, 1978). Our formulations, as briefly summarized here, have likewise proposed that substantial progress may be achieved by applying evolutionary notions to the study of both normal and abnormal personality traits.

REFERENCES

Allport, G. (1937). *Personality: A psychological interpretation*. New York: Holt.
American Psychiatric Association (1980). *Diagnostic and statistical manual of mental disorders* (3rd ed.). Washington, DC: Author.
American Psychiatric Association (1987). *Diagnostic and statistical manual of mental disorder* (3rd ed., Rev.). Washington, DC: Author.
American Psychiatric Association (1994). *Diagnostic and statistical manual of mental disorders* (4th ed.). Washington, DC: Author.

Barash, D. P. (1982). *Sociobiology and behavior* (2nd ed.). New York: Elsevier.

Benjamin, L. S. (1993). *Interpersonal diagnosis and treatment of personality disorders.* New York: Guilford.

Bowers, K. S. (1977). There's more to Iago than meets the eye: A clinical account of personality consistency. In D. Magnusson & N. S. Endler (Eds.), *Personality at the crossroads.* Hillsdale, NJ: Lawrence Erlbaum Associates.

Butcher, J. N. (Ed.) (1972). *Objective personality assessment.* New York: Academic Press.

Cole, L. C. (1954). The population consequences of life history phenomena. *Quarterly Review of Biology, 29,* 103–137.

Costa, P. T., & McCrae, R. R. (1990). Personality disorders and the five-factor model of personality. *Journal of Personality Disorders, 4,* 362–371.

Dahlstrom, W. G. (1972). Whither the MMPI? In J. N. Butcher (Ed.), *Objective personality assessment* (pp. 85–116). New York: Academic Press.

de Charms, R. (1968). *Personal causation: The internal affective determinants of behavior.* New York: Academic Press.

Digman, J. M. (1990). Personality structure: Emergence of the five-factor model. *Annual Review of Psychology, 41,* 417–440.

Feinstein, A. R. (1977). A critical overview of diagnosis in psychiatry. In V. M. Rakoff, H. C. Stancer, & H. B. Kedward (Eds.), *Psychiatric diagnosis* (pp. 189–206). New York: Bruner/Mazel.

Freud, S. (1895). Project for a scientific psychology. In *Standard edition* (English translation, Vol. 1). London: Hogarth.

Freud, S. (1915). The instincts and their vicissitudes. In *Collected papers* (English translation, Vol. 4). London: Hogarth.

Freud, S. (1940). *An outline of psychoanalysis.* New York: Liveright.

Fromm, E. (1955). *The sane society.* New York: Holt, Rinehart, & Winston.

Fromm, E. (1968). *The revolution of hope: Toward a humanized technology.* New York: Harper & Row.

Gilligan, C. (1982). *In a different voice.* Cambridge, MA: Harvard University Press.

Goldberg, L. R. (1990). An alternative "description of personality": The Big-Five factor structure. *Journal of Personality and Social Psychology, 59,* 1216–1229.

Goldstein, K. (1939). *The organism.* New York: American Book.

Goldstein, K. (1940). *Human nature in the light of psychopathology.* Cambridge, MA: Harvard University Press.

Grove, W. M., & Tellegen, A. (1991). Problems in the classification of personality disorders. *Journal of Personality Disorders, 5,* 31–41.

Hempel, C. G. (1965). *Aspects of scientific explanation.* New York: Free Press.

Jahoda, M. (1958). *Current concepts of positive mental health.* New York: Basic Books.

Jung, C. G. (1923). *Psychological types.* Zurich: Rasher.

Jung, C. G. (1961). *Memories, dreams, reflections.* New York: Vintage Books.

Kendall, R. E. (1975). *The role of diagnosis in psychiatry.* Oxford: Blackwell.

Livesley, W. J. (1991). Classifying personality disorders: Ideal types, prototypes, or dimensions? *Journal of Personality Disorders, 5,* 52–59.

Loevinger, J. (1957). Objective tests as instruments of psychological theory. *Psychological Reports, 3,* 635–694.

Maslow, A. H. (1968). *Toward a psychology of being* (2nd ed.). New York: Van Nostrand.

Maslow, A. H. (1970). *Motivation and personality* (2nd ed.). New York: Harper & Row.

McCrae, R. R., & Costa, P. T. (1985). Updating Norman's "adequate taxonomy": Intelligence and personality dimensions in natural language and in questionnaires. *Journal of Personality and Social Psychology, 49,* 710–721.

Medin, D. L., Altom, M. W., Edelson, S. M., & Freko, D. (1982). Correlated symptoms and simulated medical classification. *Journal of Experimental Psychology: Learning, Motivation, and Cognition, 8*, 37–50.

Millon, T. (1969). *Modern psychopathology: A biosocial approach to maladaptive learning and functioning.* Philadelphia: Saunders.

Millon, T. (1981). *Disorders of personality: DSM-III, Axis II.* New York: John Wiley.

Millon, T. (1983). *Millon clinical multiaxial inventory manual* (3rd ed.). Minneapolis, MN: National Computer Systems.

Millon, T. (1986). Personality prototypes and their diagnostic criteria. In T. Millon and G. L. Klerman (Eds.), *Contemporary directions in psychopathology: Toward the DSM-IV* (pp. 639–670). New York: Guilford Press.

Millon, T. (1987a). *Manual for the MCMI-II* (2nd ed.). Minneapolis, MN: National Computer Systems.

Millon, T. (1987b). On the nature of taxonomy in psychopathology. In C. Last and M. Hersen (Eds.), *Issues in diagnostic research* (pp. 3–85). New York: Plenum.

Millon, T. (1990). *Toward a new personology: An evolutionary model.* New York: Wiley.

Millon, T. (1991). Classification in psychopathology: Rationale, alternatives, and standards. *Journal of Abnormal Psychology, 100*, 245–261.

Millon, T. (1994). *Manual for the MCMI-III.* Minneapolis, MN: National Computer Systems.

Millon, T., Green, C. J., & Meagher, R. B., Jr. (1982a). *Millon Adolescent Personality Inventory manual.* Minneapolis, MN: National Computer Systems.

Millon, T., Green, C. J., & Meagher, R. B., Jr. (1982b). *Millon Behavioral Health Inventory manual* (3rd ed.). Minneapolis, MN: National Computer Systems.

Millon, T., Millon, C., & Davis, R. D. (1993). *Millon Adolescent Clinical Inventory manual.* Minneapolis, MN: National Computer Systems.

Millon, T., Millon, C., Davis, R. D., & Weiss, L. (1993). *Millon Index of Personality Styles manual.* San Antonio, TX: Psychological Corporation.

Offer, D., & Sabshin, M. (Eds.). (1974). *Normality.* New York: Basic Books.

Offer, D., & Sabshin, M. (Eds.) (1991). *The diversity of normal behavior.* New York: Basic Books.

Quine, W. V. O. (1977). Natural kinds. In S. P. Schwartz (Ed.), *Naming, necessity, and natural groups.* Ithaca: Cornell University Press.

Rogers, C. R. (1963). Toward a science of the person. *Journal of Humanistic Psychology, 3*, 79–92.

Smith, E. E., & Medin, D. L. (1981). *Categories and concepts.* Cambridge, MA: Harvard University Press.

Spencer, H. (1870). *The principles of psychology.* London: Williams and Norgate.

Sprock, J., & Blashfield, R. K. (1984). Classification and nosology. In M. Hersen, A. Kazdin, & A. Bellack (Eds.), *The clinical psychology handbook.* New York: Pergamon Press.

Strack, S. (1987). Development and validation of an adjective check list to assess the Millon personality types in a normal population. *Journal of Personality Assessment, 51*, 572–587.

Strack, S. (1991). *Manual for the Personality Adjective Check List (PACL)* (Rev.). South Pasadena, CA: 21st Century Assessment.

Strack, S. (1993). Measuring Millon's personality styles in normal adults. In R. J. Craig (Ed.), *The Millon Clinical Multiaxial Inventory: A clinical research information synthesis* (pp. 253–278). Hillsdale, NJ: Lawrence Erlbaum Associates.

Tellegen, A. (1993). Folk concepts and psychological concepts of personality and personality disorder. *Psychological Inquiry, 4*, 122–130.

Trivers, R. L. (1974). Parental investment and sexual selection. In B. Campbell (Ed.). *Sexual selection and the descent of man 1871–1971*. Chicago: Aldine.

Tversky, A. (1977). Features of similarity. *Psychological Review, 84*, 327–352.

White. R. W. (1959). Motivation reconsidered: The concept of competence. *Psychological Review, 66*, 297–323.

Wilson, E. O. (1975). *Sociobiology: The new synthesis*. Cambridge: Harvard University Press.

Wilson, E. O. (1978). *On human nature*. Cambridge: Harvard University Press.

6

The Interpersonal Circumplex and the Interpersonal Theory: Perspectives on Personality and its Pathology

Aaron L. Pincus

T he title of this chapter may appear to include a redundancy that I would like to immediately address. There is a common misconception that the structural model of interpersonal behavior known as the circumplex and the interpersonal theory of personality are one and the same. They are, in fact, distinct entities.[1] As such, the historical development of each can be traced separately; but if this is done, a complicating factor emerges. Although the psychologists developing the structural model have been guided *by the theory,* the model is not exactly an operationalization *of the theory.* However, since the articulation of the interpersonal circumplex, this structural model has had a significant impact on the evolution of its progenitor—the interpersonal theory itself. And, this is particularly clear when issues of personality pathology and normality are discussed. It is fitting that this state of affairs exists, as interpersonalists have consistently asserted that human behavior is best described within the context of transactional causality and reciprocal influence (Brokaw & McLemore, 1991). Persons A and B mutually and reciprocally influence each other, in that the behavior of each is both a response to and a stimulus for the other's behavior (Kiesler, 1983, 1988). It seems the same state of affairs applies to the ongoing dialogue between the interpersonal theory and the interpersonal circumplex.

In the last thirteen years, a number of reviews of the interpersonal circumplex have been published (e.g., Brokaw & McLemore, 1991; Kiesler, 1983, 1986a,

1991; Van Denburg, Schmidt, & Kiesler, 1992; Wiggins, 1980, 1982; Wiggins & Pincus, 1992). Generally, these reviews have emphasized the broad concepts of interpersonal personality theory, the implications for interpersonal diagnosis and intervention, and the empirical methods for assessing the interpersonal circumplex. To avoid significant redundancy with these reviews and to achieve the purpose of this edited volume, this chapter will begin with an introduction to the interpersonal circumplex model and will then proceed to discuss perspectives on maladaptive personality which can be clarified by the circular structure describing interpersonal behavior. Finally, recent advances in interpersonal assessment of maladaptive personality are discussed. Because of the bidirectionality of influence between the interpersonal theory and the interpersonal circumplex, I plan to review, describe, and propose perspectives on maladaptive personality guided by the theory and anchored to the model.

The interpersonal theory asserts that personality emerges and is best understood within the context of interpersonal relations with real, introjected, or fantasized amalgamations (personifications) of others (Carson, 1969; Sullivan, 1953a,b). The most emphatic statement of this perspective implies that personality exists only in an interpersonal context. Thus maladaptive or abnormal personality, from an interpersonal perspective, must involve maladaptive or abnormal social behavior. When maladaptive personality is discussed here, I am referring to some conceptualization of problematic interpersonal behavior, although only one real person need be present.

In focusing on conceptualizations of maladaptive personality anchored to the interpersonal circumplex, consideration of levels of behavioral analysis is necessary. When one reviews the development of the interpersonal circumplex and theory over the last 40 years, it is apparent that interpersonal conceptualizations of maladaptive personality have been described within the context of, and applied to, different levels of *interpersonal behavioral analysis*. These range from microanalytic behavioral sequences as when the behavior of person A is identified as a particular response and a particular stimulus in an ongoing transaction cycle with person B (e.g., Horowitz & Vitkus, 1986; Kiesler, 1988), to macroanalytic analyses of ongoing relationships emphasizing enduring patterns of behavior, such as the interpersonal description of a particular patient's relationship to his psychotherapy group across the course of treatment (Pincus & Wiggins, 1992) or the interpersonal description of a chronic schizophrenic's relationship with the voice he consistently hears (Benjamin, 1989).

The issue of levels has been given significant historical consideration in the interpersonal approach to personality. For instance, Leary (1957) proposed five levels to personality: Level I: public communication (or what the person does in social situations), Level II: conscious communication (or the individual's self-perceptions and perceptions of his interpersonal world), Level III: private perception (or the symbolic, fantastic, and preconscious aspects of interpersonal perception), Level IV: unexpressed (or unconscious aspects of personality), and Level V:

values (or the person's reported ego ideal). Brokaw and McLemore (1991) point out that most interpersonal theorists have focused on Leary's first two levels, and consideration of these two levels still appears to provide sufficient complexity for the discussion that follows. In fact, Leary's level of actual behavior (referred to as interpersonal mechanisms) and his level of perception of self and others (referred to as interpersonal traits) are inherently tied to microanalytic and macroanalytic interpersonal behavioral analyses, respectively.

This is not really a new proposition, as it can be discerned in the development of the first circumplex system (see below). However, the purpose here is to re-emphasize this distinction in order to capitalize on advances in trait theory and measurement (e.g., Funder, 1991; Funder & Colvin, 1991; McCrae & Costa, 1990; Wiggins & Pincus, 1992) and to clarify important concepts for differentiating normal and abnormal personality.

THE INTERPERSONAL CIRCUMPLEX

The first articulation of the interpersonal circumplex was developed from an ex-tensive investigation of group psychotherapy conducted by graduate students, clinicians, and faculty members primarily associated with the University of Cali-fornia and the Kaiser Foundation Health Plan in Oakland, California. The funda-mental goal of these studies was to understand the relations between group inter-action and personality structure (LaForge, Freedman, & Wiggins, 1985). The results of this work is documented in a series of articles which appeared in the early 1950's (Freedman, Leary, Ossorio, & Coffey, 1951; Laforge, Leary, Naboisek, Coffey, & Freedman, 1954; Laforge & Suczek, 1955; Leary & Coffey, 1955), and comprehensively summarized and expanded by Leary (1957). What is most important for the present purpose is to introduce the original circumplex model and some of its basic assumptions regarding maladaptive personality. In this regard, it is of significance that from the beginning, the structural model emerged from what Lewin (1931) referred to as a "Galileian mode of thought" (see also Wicklund & Gollwitzer, 1987). Such an approach is captured in the fol-lowing description by Rolfe LaForge, "We recognized the value of focusing on gross molar beginning-and-end situations mediating hypothetical inner forces. We understood that typological classification was of little utility, that psychological processes had to be related in terms of molar, integrated, goal-directed, dynamic laws" (LaForge, et al, 1985, p. 618). The goal was not simply a classification system, but a system of personality; and thus, the reciprocal influence between the interpersonal theory and the interpersonal circumplex had begun.

Although the theoretical influences on the first interpersonal system range from Henry Murray to Carl Jung, the central theoretical influence was the interpersonal theory of psychiatry developed by Harry Stack Sullivan (1953a, b). The initial set of interpersonal variables was derived from behavioral observations (Leary's

Level I) of patients engaged in group psychotherapy, whereby the investigators attempted to define "interpersonal mechanisms" of overt behavior. The definitions were developed in answer to the question, "What is the subject of the activity, e.g., the individual whose behavior is being rated, doing to the object or objects of the activity?" (Freedman et al., 1951, p. 149). The assumption was that behavior could be functionally understood when related to a dynamic theory of personality.

The comprehensive list of interpersonal mechanisms observed in patients was first presented on a circular continuum by Freedman et al. (1951). The most basic aspects of this circular structure representing interpersonal behavior have remained the same (see Figures 6.1 and 6.2), although a variety of interpersonal circumplex models have been elaborated over the years. However, Freedman points out that the circumplex was not a direct operationalization of theory:

> The circular continuum utilized to organize or systematize the interpersonal mechanisms did not emerge out of a priori or deductive reasoning. The first step after evolution of the concept of interpersonal mechanism was to list all the mechanisms that my colleagues and I could discern or distinguish at the beginning. The mechanisms were simply a list of verbs. Thousands of manipulations yielded a system and an orderly arrangement. Slowly the nodal points or axes of affiliation vs. aggression and dominance vs. submission emerged. (LaForge et al., 1985, p. 624)

Figure 6.1 presents an adaptation of the original circumplex of interpersonal mechanisms. Sixteen interpersonal variables are arranged in a circular continuum around the orthogonal dimensions of dominance-submission and hostility-affiliation. The circular arrangement of variables is meant to imply that, in some sense, variables close to one another are more "similar" than are variables that are more widely separated from one another. As can be noted from Figures 6.1 and 6.2, the original circumplexes were marked by "intensity" values increasing from the center of the circle. Wiggins (1982) points out that this feature necessitates that the model be considered a two-dimensional Euclidean space where variables that are located opposite to each other are considered bipolar contrasts (e.g., "to dominate" is the opposite of "to submit"). The basic dimensions making up the axes of the circumplex can be considered latent variables which give rise to the circular continuum. From this perspective, each of the interpersonal mechanisms (Figure 6.1) and interpersonal traits (Figure 6.2) may be thought of as representing a particular blend of dominance and affiliation. Gurtman (Chapter 12 of this volume) provides a psychometric and methodological discussion of these points and others made throughout this chapter.

The first circumplex was thus developed out of observations of specific behavior in group psychotherapy settings; that is, the interpersonal mechanisms were developed from a focus on microanalytic interpersonal behavioral analysis. "The interpersonal mechanisms are regarded as process variables of personality as dis-

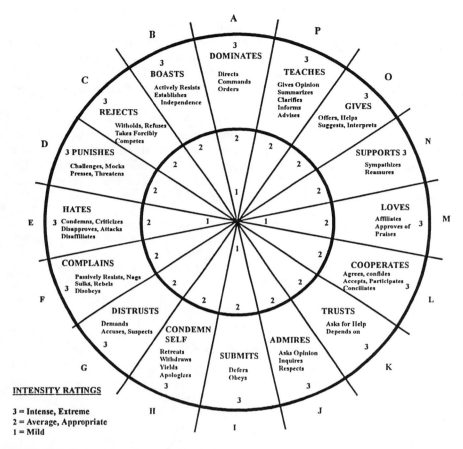

FIGURE 6.1. An adaptation of the original circumplex of interpersonal mechanisms (Freedman et al., 1951).

tinguished from structural variables of personality. They are regarded as descriptive of immediate interpersonal processes, the "personality in action," so to speak (Freedman et al., 1951, p. 156; see also Leary, 1957). When the circumplex representing interpersonal mechanisms is viewed as a two-dimensional Euclidean space, this level of analysis gives rise to a particular interpersonal perspective on maladaptive personality. The metric increasing from the center of the circle represents *behavioral intensity.*

The original presentation of the circumplex model additionally included discussion of Leary's Levels II and III, the conscious and symbolic levels of perception of self and others. Although Leary used the word "perception," it is clear that

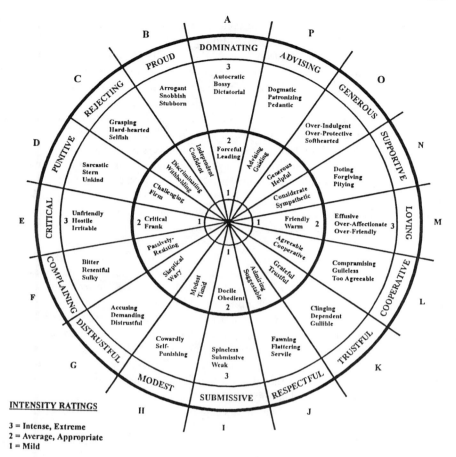

INTENSITY RATINGS

3 = Intense, Extreme
2 = Average, Appropriate
1 = Mild

FIGURE 6.2. An adaptation of the original circumplex of interpersonal traits (Freedman et al., 1951).

the second (and third) levels of personality refer to enduring qualities of interpersonal behavior. "The concept of *interpersonal trait* has been developed to systematize the structural variables or enduring tendencies of personality. The interpersonal mechanisms displayed by an individual in a social situation may be considered the outcome of an interplay between environmental forces impinging upon him and those enduring tendencies to action which he brings to the situation" (Freedman et al., 1951, p. 156; see also Leary, 1957).

The original circular ordering of interpersonal mechanisms was evaluated and translated with reference to adjectival trait descriptors (Freedman et al., 1951) which Leary (1957) defined as interpersonal motives attributed to self or others.

This suggests that Leary was using the concept of trait to mean a personality structure that has a causal link to behavior. Although this definition of trait is only one of many perspectives on trait ontology (e.g., Tellegen, 1991; Wiggins & Trapnell, in press), the important difference between Level II and Level I is the potential of the circumplex to be used to describe enduring patterns of interpersonal behavior, or macroanalytic interpersonal behavioral analysis (see Figure 6.2). The metric increasing from the center of a circumplex at this level of analysis represents a second perspective on maladaptive personality: *Behavioral Rigidity.*

In summary, the original structural model of interpersonal behavior was based on observations of behavior in group psychotherapy, which through extensive analyses yielded a circular continuum, or circumplex, based on two underlying orthogonal dimensions of Dominance–Submission and Hostility–Affiliativeness. Its configuration was not an a priori assumption nor should it be considered a strict operationalization of a particular theory. Initially, the structural model was applied to five levels of personality, two of which have continued to be particularly fruitful in the understanding of maladaptive personality. Specifically, microanalysis of interpersonal behaviors and macroanalysis of enduring patterns of behavior characterizing persons (e.g., personality traits) both can be represented by the interpersonal circumplex. The circumplex structures representing these two levels of analysis share the perspective that normal and abnormal personality lie on a continuum; thus, adaptive and maladaptive behaviors and behavior patterns can be described and measured along common dimensions. "Abnormality consists of the rigid reliance on a limited class of interpersonal behaviors regardless of situational influences or norms, that often are enacted at an inappropriate level of intensity. Normality, then, is simply the flexible and adaptive deployment, within moderate ranges of intensity, of behaviors encompassing the entire circle, as varied interpersonal situations dictate" (Carson, 1991, p. 190).

Kiesler (1991) points out that the levels of analysis discussed above are, in reality, only endpoints on a continuum. At one end is the "interaction unit" describing interpersonal behaviors of two actors in a reciprocally influential transaction cycle. At the other end is the enduring pattern of interpersonal behaviors enacted by a person which are presumed to demonstrate temporal stability and cross-situational consistency. Most theoretical and empirical study of maladaptive personality from an interpersonal perspective has been anchored at these two points. This is for the historical reasons discussed, and because "at the levels between micro and macro, A's interpersonal behavior can be characterized only with newly invented terms, because the language of psychology offers no appropriate words (Kiesler, 1991, p. 446).

INTERPERSONAL THEORY

To understand how interpersonal behaviors and interpersonal traits can be maladaptive, we must go beyond identifying the concepts of intensity and rigidity and our ability to describe and measure them with reference to the circumplex. Sullivan's (1953a,b) theory proposed that both our enacted behaviors and our perception of others' behaviors toward us is strongly affected by our concept of who we are, e.g., our "self." When we interact with others, we are attempting to define and present ourselves and negotiate the kinds of interactions and relationships we seek from others. Leary (1957) proposed the principle of reciprocal interpersonal relations as an explanation of how interpersonal behavior could fulfill such a self-definitional function: "Interpersonal reflexes tend (with probability significantly greater than chance) to initiate or invite reciprocal interpersonal responses from the other person that lead to a repetition of the original reflex" (p. 123). Kiesler (1988) points out that these relational "bids" are most often automatic and outside of awareness. (See also Sullivan's (1953b) discussion of the "self-system.")

Thus, the primary dynamic principle of interpersonal theory is that behavior serves the goal of self-definition and the mechanism through which this goal is attained is via the elicitation of a limited class of interpersonal reactions from others which are perceived as congruent with how one views oneself. Carson (1991) refers to this as an interbehavioral contingency process, that is, "There is a tendency for a given individual's interpersonal behavior to be constrained or controlled in more or less predictable ways by the behavior received from an interaction partner" (p. 191). To the extent that individuals can mutually satisfy their needs for interaction which is congruent with their self-definitions, the interpersonal situation will remain integrated; to the extent that this mutual satisfaction fails, the interpersonal situation will elicit anxiety and will disintegrate (Sullivan, 1953b).

With regard to the interpersonal circumplex, the ability to specify precisely which interpersonal behaviors are congruent with behaviorally implied self-definitions is based on the concept of complementarity. Carson (1969) first proposed that complementarity is based on reciprocity regarding the vertical circumplex axis (e.g., dominance pulls for submission; submission pulls for dominance) and correspondence regarding the horizontal axis (friendliness pulls for friendliness; hostility pulls for hostility).[2] Kiesler's (1983) seminal paper on complementarity expanded the concept significantly. Because any interpersonal behavior can be conceived of as a blend of dominance and affiliation, one can apply the principles of complementarity to identify complementary responses at any point on the circumplex. Although the empirical support for the principles of complementarity have been inconsistent (e.g., Bluhm, Widiger, & Miele, 1990; Orford, 1986), Kiesler (1991) points out that most tests have been significantly oversimplified and the theory itself requires clarification of a number of crucial issues.

The interpersonal theory of personality is based on dynamic principles that clearly imply a rich and meaningful intrapsychic life (Leary, 1957; Kiesler, 1982; Sullivan, 1953a,b). Thus, interpersonal complementarity (or any other conception of interbehavioral contingency) should not be conceived of as some sort of stimulus–response process based solely on overt behavioral actions and reactions. Most interpersonal theorists have emphasized some intrapsychic processes that color individuals' perceptions of their interpersonal world and thus their overt reactions to others, including personifications, selective inattention, and parataxic distortions (Sullivan, 1953a,b), emotions, action tendencies, and interpretations (Kiesler, 1987b), expectancies (Carson, 1982), fantasies and self-statements (Brokaw & McClemore, 1991) and cognitive interpersonal schemas (Foa & Foa, 1974; Safran, 1990, Wiggins, 1982).

Kiesler's (1986a, 1988, 1991) "Maladaptive Transaction Cycle" provides the most articulated discussion of the relations among overt and covert interpersonal behavior. Kiesler proposes that the basic components of an interpersonal transaction are (1) person A's covert experience of person B (including any of the intrapsychic experiences just described), (2) person A's overt behavior toward person B, (3) person B's covert experience in response to person A's action, and (4) person B's overt behavioral response to person A. These four components are part of an ongoing transactional chain of events. An interpersonal transaction becomes maladaptive when one interactant (person A) relies on a limited class of interpersonal behaviors, thus limiting the other interactant (person B) to a restricted class of complementary responses. The impact of person B's complementary responses is to confirm or validate person A's covert experiences of self, other, and the relationship and, thus escalate A's repetition of the rigid, and often extreme, interpersonal behaviors that began the cycle. Kiesler points out that the initial complementary responses feel mutually satisfying and the situation will remain integrated. However, as the transaction recycles, the narrow and extreme behaviors that person A can enact will have an aversive impact on person B. If person B cannot disintegrate the situation, complementary behavioral responses will be accompanied by subtle communication of the negative covert reactions to person A, thus leading to an escalation of person A's maladaptive interpersonal behaviors due to the experience of anxiety in response to the threat to person A's self-system these subtle negative messages evoke. Thus, the transaction cycles to "impasse—locked into a recurrent enactment of the cycle of maladaptive self-fulfilling prophecy and behavior" (Kiesler, 1986a, p. 59).

To understand maladaptive personality, we must combine concepts anchored to the interpersonal circumplex with a theory of interpersonal functioning. Kiesler (1991) describes the nature of this interface. The circumplex specifies the range of individual differences in normal and abnormal interpersonal behavior, and the model can be used to assess and describe the specific nature of an individual's interpersonal behavior. The maladaptive transaction cycle provides a dynamic theoretical depiction of the full range of overt and covert human experience involved in interpersonal interactions. It is only when we combine the interpersonal circumplex with interpersonal theory that we can locate "the person" in interpersonal interaction. There have been many revisions of the interpersonal circumplex since its original formulation. Most revisions have clarified the substantive ordering of segments and improved the psychometric and geometric properties of assessment instruments (e.g., Kiesler, 1983, 1985; Wiggins, Trapnell, &

Phillips, 1988). Figure 6.3 presents Kiesler's (1983) 1982 Interpersonal Circle, which can provide a structural reference for the discussions that follow.

BEHAVIORS, TRAITS, AND MALADAPTIVE PERSONALITY

Behaviors

Maladaptive behavioral intensity and rigidity, conceived of within a theoretical framework specifying the basis for interbehavioral contingencies, covert reactions, and overt responses, have different implications and applications at microanalytic and macroanalytic levels of analysis. At the microanalytic level, interpersonal approaches have provided a solid base for advancing the understanding of psychopathological states such as depression (e.g., Brokaw & McLemore, 1991; Horowitz & Vitkus, 1985; Kiesler, 1986a); as well as articulating psychotherapy process (e.g., Horowitz, Rosenberg, & Bartholomew, 1993; Horowitz, Rosenberg, & Kalehzan, 1992; Kiesler & Goldston, 1988; Talley, Strupp, & Morey, 1990), and generating unique psychotherapeutic interventions (Anchin & Kiesler, 1982; Kiesler, 1988).

Behavioral intensity can be of significance at the microanalytic level where a person's specific behavior can be characterized by a segment of the circumplex and rated as moderate and adaptive or extreme and maladaptive. A number of circumplex assessment instruments have been developed with the goal of articulating microanalytic levels of behavioral analysis in which intensity is a metric of the circle. Such inventories operationalize the circumplex through behavioral statements, typically verbs and phrase descriptors. These include the Interpersonal Behavior Inventory (IBI) (Lorr & McNair, 1963, 1965, 1966), the Check List of Interpersonal (or Psychotherapy) Transactions (CLOIT-CLOPT) (Kiesler, 1984, 1987a), and the 1982 Interpersonal Circle Acts Version (Kiesler, 1985). These instruments assess a two-dimensional Euclidean space where the intensity of a particular interpersonal behavior can be scaled as a distance from the origin of the circle.

If one chooses to employ a circumplex of interpersonal mechanisms such as Kiesler's (1985) Acts Version, it is possible to describe in some detail the nature of a specific interpersonal transaction. It has yet to be established what is the most useful duration to measure an interaction sequence. For example, one can adopt a sequential analytic strategy, attempting to code covert and overt action-reaction units stochastically (Kiesler, 1986a, 1991; Peterson, 1979, 1982). It is this point that creates a paradox for interpersonal assessment. Although a maladaptive transaction cycle may recycle only once, the interpersonal situation of interest will more often involve a significant number of cycles of covert and overt responses. At some point in the transaction, we begin to describe not a unit of specific interpersonal acts but a set of covert and overt interpersonal behavior patterns. Also, it is unlikely

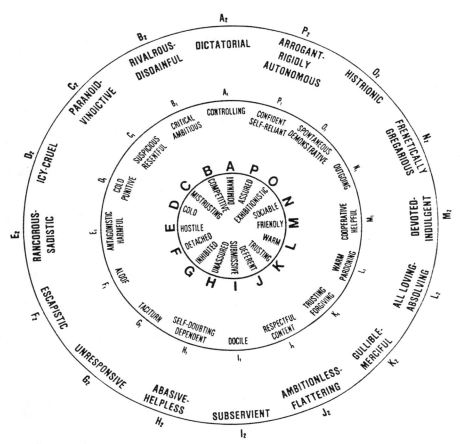

FIGURE 6.3. The 1982 Interpersonal Circle. From "The 1982 Interpersonal Circle: A taxonomy for complementarity in human transactions," by D. J. Kiesler, 1983, *Psychological Review, 90,* p. 189. Copyright © 1983 by the American Psychological Association. Reprinted by permission of the author.

that the majority of interpersonal transactions of importance in understanding maladaptive personality take place at "zero acquaintance" but are rather one point in an ongoing relationship. Therefore, I believe it is fundamental to understand maladaptive personality from the perspective of personality traits.

When we move from a stochastic form of analysis to an analysis of interpersonal behavioral patterns, maladaptiveness takes the form of rigidity (of both covert and overt interpersonal responses). It is possible to misinterpret much of the interpersonal literature as implying that, like intensity, rigidity is a property of *behavior*. Rigidity is, in fact, a property of the *person* who is interacting.

Traits and Maladaptive Personality

At the macroanalytic level, interpersonal approaches have been less articulated, although an immediate area of significant interest and convergence has emerged with the publication of the *Diagnostic and Statistical Manual of Mental Disorders* (*DSM*) *Axis II* personality disorder taxonomy (Wiggins & Pincus, 1989). The *DSM* defines personality disorders as "inflexible and maladaptive manifestations of personality traits (American Psychiatric Association, 1980, p. 305). Carson (1991) is cautious of the trait approach to measuring interpersonal behavior, suggesting that assessment of general propensities toward interpersonal behavior will often generate errors in predicting interpersonal responses of disordered individuals. It is my contention, however, that a consideration of modern trait theory (e.g., Buss, 1989; Funder, 1991; Tellegen, 1991; Wiggins & Trapnell, in press) and advances in the study of trait perception (e.g., Funder & Colvin, 1991) can provide important information to improve macroanalytic behavioral analysis, and increase our understanding of both interpersonal complementarity and maladaptive personality.

The logical necessity of developing a circumplex measure of enduring interpersonal patterns emerged quickly after articulation of the first circumplex of interpersonal mechanisms (Laforge et al., 1985). The first empirically based instrument assessing a circumplex of interpersonal traits was LaForge and Suczek's (1955) Interpersonal Check List (ICL). Although the ICL combined adjectival descriptors with verb phrases within its item pool, it was developed to describe the characteristics of persons rather than behaviors. The foremost effort to accurately describe and measure a circumplex of interpersonal traits is the ongoing development and revision of Wiggins' Interpersonal Adjective Scales (IAS) (Wiggins, 1979, 1991; Wiggins, Phillips, & Trapnell, 1989; Wiggins et al., 1988). Both the Wiggins' circumplex and Kiesler's 1982 Interpersonal Circle (see Figure 6.3) articulate a structure of enduring characteristics of persons (traits). These instruments operationalize a two-dimensional Euclidean space where the rigidity of an individual can be scaled as a vector length originating from the origin of the circle. The angular location of the vector indicates the segment of the circle which characterizes an individual's rigidly enacted interpersonal style (see Gurtman, this volume). Wiggins et al. (1989) demonstrated that when vector length is empirically derived, it is correlated with measures of psychological maladjustment.

If we return to the concept of personality disorders as inflexible and maladaptive expression of personality traits, we see that the current psychiatric nosology is quite consistent with the interpersonal perspective on personality pathology (Pincus & Wiggins, 1990; Wiggins & Pincus, 1989). From the interpersonal perspective, this inflexible and maladaptive expression of traits must consist of both rigid intrapsychic experiences (e.g., expectancies, action tendencies, or more generally, schemas) and the consequent overt behavioral enactments. When these characteristics of a person endure across time and interpersonal situation, they are observable in the consistent maladaptive transaction cycles of the individual, and can be described as interpersonal traits.

Although the presence of a trait can only be inferred on the basis of overt behavior, it refers to both overt behavior and the psychological structures and processes which give rise to it (Funder, 1991; Tellegen, 1991). Modern trait theory conceives of traits as descriptions of how a person behaves in certain situations; and of equal importance, traits describe something about the intraspsychic functioning of the individual's mind (Funder, 1991). Psychotherapeutic work with personality disordered individuals quickly demonstrates that their covert experiences of others are as rigid as their overt behavior. Thus, modern conceptions of traits encompass all parts of the maladaptive transaction cycles seen in personality disordered individuals.

Earlier, abnormality was described as rigid reliance on a limited class of interpersonal behaviors *regardless of situational influences or norms.* Trait psychology has endured and benefited from an ongoing debate over the primacy of influence on behavior ascribed to persons and situations (Buss, 1989; Kenrick & Funder, 1988). The legacy of this debate is the acknowledgment that both factors influence behavior and that psychologists must commit their efforts to understanding the complex interactions of the two. How is it that such situational and normative "data" fail to influence the personality disordered individual? Their rigid covert experiences act as distorting filters, deactivating normative situational influences and evoking actions that are, in fact, congruent with the personality disordered person's intrapsychic experience. For example, person A makes a helpful suggestion to person B, communicated in a friendly way. Person A's behavior may be characterized as falling in the friendly–dominant quadrant of the circumplex. Many personality disordered individuals rigidly experience such suggestions as punitive indications of mistrust and criticism, characterized as falling in the hostile-dominant quadrant of the circumplex.

Thus, the individual is truly "personality" disordered. The influence of the person on behavior is greater than "normal," while the situational influences are significantly weakened. However, this state of affairs quickly leads to disturbed interpersonal relations in which persons relating to a disordered individual quickly become reliant on a limited class of interpersonal responses. Thus, personality disordered individuals also have veridical interpersonal experiences as they continue to engage in maladaptive transaction cycles (Kiesler, 1991). The concept of "self-fulfilling prophecy" has never been more appropriate (Carson, 1982). McLemore and Brokaw (1987) provide an extended example in their discussion of rigid "thought-feeling-action patterns" in personality disordered individuals.

In the example just provided, the expected complementary response to person A's friendly–dominant behavior would be friendly–submissive acceptance of the suggestion as a helpful gesture (regardless of whether the suggestion is later acted on). However, the personality disordered individual actually experiences the suggestion as hostile–dominant and responds with complementary hostile–submissive behavior. Kiesler's (1991) suggestion that empirical tests of complementarity have been equivocal due to oversimplification appears correct. Many tests of complementarity have not incorporated covert responses into the experimental designs.

Recent research on trait perception is also congruent with the implications of the interpersonal approach to maladaptive personality and complementarity. Although the major goals of current work in trait perception include articulating the influences on, and improving the accuracy of, personality judgments by observers and peers (Funder, 1989); such work also identifies the influences on inaccuracy. Funder and Colvin (1991) suggest that lay judgments of personality are based on the coding of behaviors for social effect or psychological meaning (e.g., Cairns & Green, 1979). They also suggest that much of the consistency research in personality has focused on behavior, whereas people's perceptions of others focuses on an intuition of personality. Thus, individuals perceive others as decidedly more consistent than research has demonstrated. Similarly, I would suggest that individuals demonstrate complementarity more consistently than research has demonstrated because complementarity springs from the psychological meaning attributed to others' overt behavior, not from the behavior itself. In personality disordered individuals the processes generating such attributions are rigid and often wholly incongruent with normative interpretations of the interpersonal situation. It is significantly more difficult to assess covert responses of individuals. However, one instrument, the Impact Message Inventory (IMI; Kiesler, 1987b) attempts to assess the covert impacts of interactants. Currently, a circumplex version of this instrument is in development.

From an interpersonal perspective, personality is a complex set of interrelated intrapsychic and behavioral processes of persons which endure across time and situation. These enduring processes become maladaptive when they are rigid and inflexible, qualities which emerge only in the ongoing transactions of persons. This conception of maladaptive personality is congruent with advances in trait theory, where issues of behavioral consistency, intrapsychic processes, situational influence, and person perception continue to be addressed conceptually and empirically. The circumplex provides both a comprehensive structural model for the description and assessment of interpersonal personality traits and a framework for articulating dynamic psychological interpersonal processes involved in their maladaptive expression. Like its conception of personality, the nature of the relationship between interpersonal theory and the interpersonal circumplex is also transactional, a characteristic which will continue to promote theoretical and empirical advances. The final section of this chapter is devoted to a brief review of some recent trends in this ongoing theory–model transaction.

RECENT TRENDS IN INTERPERSONAL ASSESSMENT OF MALADAPTIVE PERSONALITY

Interpersonal Problems

Over the last 15 years, the work of Leonard Horowitz and his colleagues (e.g., Horowitz, 1979; Horowitz, Rosenberg, Baer, Ureno, & Villasenor, 1988) has added a significant dimension to the assessment and understanding of maladaptive interpersonal behavior. Horowitz (1979) noted that many individuals seeking psychotherapy present with difficulties encountered when interacting (or attempting to interact with others), e.g., interpersonal problems. To identify such problems, intake interviews of outpatients seeking psychotherapy were videotaped. Two observers recorded statements of problems reported in the interviews. After a series of item analyses, an Inventory of Interpersonal Problems was developed (IIP) (Horowitz et al., 1988). The item format of the IIP reflects the nature and content of such problems reported by patients seeking psychotherapy. Interpersonal problems are often reported in the form "It is hard for me to (do something desired)" or "I (do something undesired) too much" (Horowitz et al., 1993). A recent review of empirical research using the IIP can be found in Pincus and Wiggins (1992).

Two theoretical points are of significance for this chapter. First, the items of the IIP directly assess both self-reported and observer-reported judgments of interpersonal rigidity. In their discussion of personality disorders, Pincus and Wiggins (1990) proposed that two ways in which a traits could be expressed in a maladaptive and inflexible manner are: (a) in behavior one "does too much" and (b) in behavior one consistently finds "hard to do." Rigid *overt* interpersonal responses involve at minimum chronic behavioral excesses and chronic behavioral inhibitions, that is, interpersonal problems. Recent research relating attachment styles to interpersonal problems is beginning to address the potential developmental origins of enduring interpersonal rigidity (Bartholomew & Horowitz, 1991).

Second, when interpersonal rigidity conceived of as behavioral excess and inhibition is assessed directly, a circumplex structure of interpersonal problems robustly emerges. Thus, the IIP has been modified to assess a precise circumplex of interpersonal problems (IIP-C) (Alden, Wiggins, & Pincus, 1990). The IIP-C has shown perhaps the best circular structure of any instrument to date (Gurtman, 1993; see Gurtman this volume Chapter 12, for a figure of this circumplex), and the model has been related to conceptions of personality disorder (Pincus & Wiggins, 1990). The conceptual domain of interpersonal problems is a fertile area for further research in differentiating normal and abnormal personalities because of the fundamental conceptual link with interpersonal theory and the empirical development of a circumplex assessment instrument.

Configurational Analyses

Circumplex Profiles

Although the concepts behavioral intensity and interpersonal rigidity were derived from the interpersonal theory and operationalized (indirectly) via the development of the circumplex, the structural model itself provides a number of potentially useful indicators of personality abnormality. It can be noted that the assessment of the circumplex rests on a number of strong psychometric and geometric assumptions (Gurtman, this volume). The configuration of an individual's circumplex profile is constrained by certain semantic and substantive restraints which will, in normative samples, produce a characteristic profile, informally referred to as the "interpersonal spaceship" (Wiggins, 1991; Wiggins et al., 1989).

In Figure 6.4, an octant-based example of this configuration is shown at the top: The highest elevation occurs on the defining octant (DE), followed by adjacent octants (BC and FG), and diminishing to a highly truncated opposite octant (LM). "Normal" configurations will differ in location of the defining octant, but generally will not deviate in configurational pattern.

If an individual's profile configuration deviates significantly from the norm (as shown on the bottom of Figure 6.4), personality abnormality may be indicated. For instance, normal individuals recognize their flexible interpersonal repertoire, but when asked to indicate their *general tendencies,* rarely report that they are generally both dominant and submissive or both hostile and friendly. However, Kiesler (1986b) first theoretically proposed and later empirically demonstrated that personality disordered individuals may be identified by two or more peaks on segments of the interpersonal circumplex (Kiesler, Van Denburg, Sikes-Nova, Larus, & Goldston, 1990). Such deviant interpersonal profiles are consistent with conflicted or context-bound self-concepts often seen in personality disordered individuals (e.g., Dawson, 1988). Current research projects the author is associated with have also supported configurational complexity as a potential indicator of personality disorder.

The Five-Factor Model of Personality

In the last decade a consensus has emerged regarding the basic superordinate dimensions of personality referred to as the five-factor model of personality traits (for reviews see Digman, 1990; McCrae & John, 1992). The five broad factors include extraversion/dominance, agreeablness/nurturance, conscientiousness, neuroticism, and openness to experience. The first two dimensions of the model can be considered simple structure variants of the interpersonal personality dimensions (e.g., McCrae & Costa, 1989), or the interpersonal circumplex can be used to represent these two dimensions of the model (Pincus & Wiggins, 1992, Trapnell & Wiggins, 1990). The latter approach is termed the Dyadic-Interactional perspective (Wiggins & Pincus, 1992, 1994) and is presented in Figure 6.5.

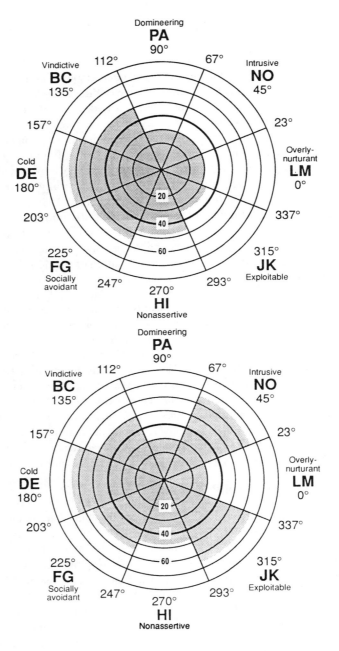

FIGURE 6.4. Normal and deviant circumplex profiles.

Five Factor Profile

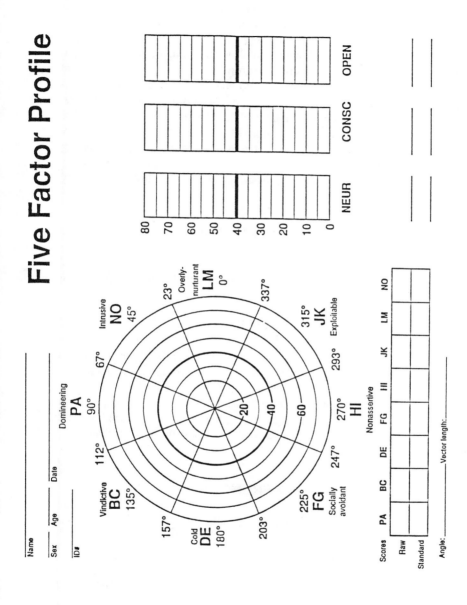

FIGURE 6.5. Dyadic-Interactional perspective on the five-factor model.

Of importance to the interpersonal approach to personality is the recognition that the circumplex is embedded within a broader model of personality structure, and interpersonal assessment can be interpreted within the five-factor model context. "Two individuals whose circumplex profiles are similar will probably present with distinctive patterns of behavioral rigidity depending on their relative standings on emotional lability and distress (neuroticism), impulse control, motivation, and responsibility (conscientiousness), and conformity, tolerance, and imagination (openness)" (Pincus & Wiggins, 1992, p. 94). For example, the rigid covert experiences of a disordered individual may be related to low openness, a significantly intrapsychic personality dimension (McCrae & Costa, 1985; Miller, 1991). The dyadic–interactional perspective on the five-factor model expands and applies interpersonal conceptions of behavioral rigidity to additional dimensions of personality without altering the theory's basic assumptions regarding normality and abnormality (Pincus, 1991).

ACKNOWLEDGMENTS

I thank Robert Carson, Lisa Feldman, Maurice Lorr, Stephen Strack, and Jerry Wiggins for comments on an earlier draft. I also thank Laura Boekman for her organizational help.

NOTES

[1] The present discussion is limited to the *interpersonal circumplex.* Other circumplex models have been articulated in diverse areas such as mood (Russell, 1980) and personality disorders (Millon, 1987).

[2] An alternative view on complementarity proposes that the opposite of dominance is the granting of autonomy; and, complementarity is affected by the symmetry or assymetry of status in a particular relationship (see Benjamin, 1974; Henry, this volume; Lorr, 1991).

REFERENCES

Alden, L. E., Wiggins, J. S., & Pincus, A. L. (1990). Construction of circumplex scales for the Inventory of Interpersonal Problems. *Journal of Personality Assessment, 55.* 521–536.

American Psychiatric Association. (1980). *Diagnostic and statistical manual of mental disorders* (3rd ed.). Washington DC: Author.

Anchin, J. C., & Kiesler, D. J. (Eds.). (1982). *Handbook of interpersonal psychotherapy.* New York: Pergamon

Bartholomew, K., & Horowitz, L. M. (1991). Attachment styles among young adults: A test of a four-category model. *Journal of Personality and Social Psychology, 61,* 226–244.

Benjamin, L. S. (1974). Structural analysis of social behavior. *Psychological Review, 81,* 392–425.

Benjamin, L. S. (1989). Is chronicity a function of the relationship between the person and the auditory hallucination? *Schizophrenia Bulletin, 15,* 291–310.

Bluhm, C., Widiger, T. A., & Miele, G. M. (1990). Interpersonal complementarity and individual differences. *Journal of Personality and Social Psychology, 58,* 464–471.

Brokaw, D. W., & McLemore, C. W. (1991). Interpersonal models of personality and psychopathology. In D. G. Gilbert and J. J. Connolly (Eds.), *Personality, social skills, and psychopathology: An individual differences approach* (pp. 49–83). New York: Plenum.

Buss, A. H. (1989). Personality as traits. *American Psychologist, 44,* 1378–1388.

Cairns, R. B., & Green, J. A. (1979). How to assess personality and social patterns: Observations or ratings? In R. B. Cairns (Ed.), *The analysis of social interactions: Methods, issues, and illustrations,* (pp. 209–226). Hillsdale, NJ: Erlbaum.

Carson, R. C. (1969). *Interaction concepts of personality.* Chicago: Aldine.

Carson, R. C. (1982). Self-fulfilling prophecy, maladaptive behavior, and psychotherapy. In J. C. Anchin and D. J.Kiesler (Eds.), *Handbook of Interpersonal Psychotherapy* (pp. 64–77). New York: Pergamon Press.

Carson, R. C. (1991). The social-interactional viewpoint. In M. Hersen, A. Kazdin, & A. Bellack (Eds.), *The Clinical Psychology Handbook* (pp. 185–199). New York: Pergamon.

Dawson, D. F. (1988). Treatment of the borderline patient: Relationship management. *Canadian Journal of Psychiatry, 33,* 370–374.

Digman, J. M. (1990). Personality Structure: Emergence of the five-factor model. *Annual Review of Psychology, 41,* 417–440.

Foa, U. G., & Foa, E. B. (1974). *Societal structures of the mind.* Springfield, Ill: Charles C. Thomas.

Freedman, M. B., Leary, T., Ossorio, A. G., & Coffey, H. S. (1951). The interpersonal dimension of personality. *Journal of Personality, 20,* 143–161.

Funder, D. C. (1989). Accuracy in personality judgement and the dancing bear. In D. M Buss & N. Cantor (Eds.), *Personalty psychology: Recent trends and emerging directions,* (pp. 246–260). New York: Springer-Verlag.

Funder, D. C. (1991). Global Traits: A neo-Allportian approach to personality. *Psychological Science, 2,* 31–39.

Funder, D. C., & Colvin, C. R. (1991). Explorations in behavioral consistency: Properties of persons, situations, and behaviors. *Journal of Personality and Social Psychology, 60,* 773–794.

Gurtman, M. B. (1993). Constructing personality tests to meet a structural criterion: Application of the interpersonal circumplex. *Journal of Personality, 61,* 237–263.

Horowitz, L. M. (1979). On the cognitive structure of interpersonal problems treated in psychotherapy. *Journal of Consulting and Clinical Psychology, 47,* 5–15.

Horowitz, L. M., Rosenberg, S. E., Baer, B. A., Ureno, G., & Villasenor, V. S. (1988). Inventory of Interpersonal Problems: Psychometric properties and clinical applications. *Journal of Consulting and Clinical Psychology, 56,* 885–892.

Horowitz, L. M., Rosenberg, S. E., & Bartholomew, K. (1993). Interpersonal problems in brief dynamic psychotherapy. *Journal of Consulting and Clinical Psychology, 61,* 549–560.

Horowitz, L. M., Rosenberg, S. E., & Kalehzan, B. M. (1992). The capacity to describe other people clearly: A predictor of interpersonal problems and outcome in brief dynamic psychotherapy. *Psychotherapy Research, 2,* 37–51.

Horowitz, L. M., & Vitkus, J. (1986). The interpersonal basis of psychiatric symptoms. *Clinical Psychology Review, 6,* 443–469.

Kenrick, D. T., & Funder, D. C. (1988). Profiting from controversy: Lessons from the person-situation debate. *American Psychologist, 43*, 23–34.

Kiesler, D. J. (1982). Interpersonal theory for personality and psychotherapy. In J. C. Anchin and D. J. Kiesler (Eds.), *Handbook of interpersonal psychotherapy* (pp. 3–24). Elmsford, NY: Pergamon Press.

Kiesler, D. J. (1983). The 1982 Interpersonal Circle: A taxonomy for complementarity in human transactions. *Psychological Review, 90*, 185–214.

Kiesler, D. J. (1984). *Check list of psychotherapy transactions* and *Check list of interpersonal transactions.* Richmond, VA: Virginia Commonwealth University.

Kiesler, D. J. (1985). *The 1982 interpersonal circle: Acts Version.* Unpublished manuscript, Virginia Commonwealth University, Richmond, VA.

Kiesler, D. J. (1986a). Interpersonal methods of diagnosis and treatment. In R. Michels and J. O. Cavenar (Eds.), *Psychiatry* (pp. 53–75). Philadelphia: Lippincott.

Kiesler, D. J. (1986b). The 1982 interpersonal circle: An analysis of DSM-III personality disorders. In T. Millon & G. Klerman (Eds.), *Contemporary directions in psychopathology: Toward DSM-IV* (pp. 571–597). New York: Guilford.

Kiesler, D. J. (1987a). *Check list of psychotherapy transactions-revised* and *Check list of interpersonal transactions-revised.* Richmond, VA: Virginia Commonwealth University.

Kiesler, D. J. (1987b). *Research manual for the impact message inventory.* Palo Alto, CA: Research Psychologists Press.

Kiesler, D. J. (1988). *Therapeutic Metacommunication.* Palo Alto, CA: Consulting Psychologists Press.

Kiesler, D. J. (1991). Interpersonal methods of assessment and diagnosis. In C. R. Snyder and D. R. Forsyth (Eds.), *Handbook of social and clinical psychology* (pp. 438–468). Elmsford, New York: Permagon.

Kiesler, D. J., & Goldston, C. S. (1988). Client-therapist complementarity: An analysis of the Gloria films. *Journal of Counseling Psychology, 35*, 127–133.

Kiesler, D. J., Van Denburg, T. F., Sikes-Nova, V. E., Larus, J. P., & Goldston, C. S. (1990). Interpersonal behavior profiles of eight cases of DSM-III personality disorder. *Journal of Clinical Psychology, 46*, 440–453.

Laforge, R., Freedman, M. B., & Wiggins, J. S. (1985). Interpersonal circumplex models: 1948–1983. *Journal of Personality Assessment, 49*, 613–631.

Laforge, R., Leary, T., Naboisek, H., Coffey, H. S., & Freedman, M. B. (1954). The interpersonal dimension of personality: II. An objective study of repression. *Journal of Personality, 23*, 129–153.

Laforge, R. & Suczek, R. F. (1955). The interpersonal dimension of personality: III. An interpersonal check list. *Journal of Personality, 24*, 94–112.

Leary, T. (1957). *Interpersonal diagnosis of personality.* New York: Ronald.

Leary, T., & Coffey, H.S. (1955). Interpersonal diagnosis: Some problems of methodology and validation. *Journal of Abnormal and Social Psychology, 50*, 110–124.

Lewin, K. (1931). The conflict between Aristotelian and Galileian modes of thought in contemporary psychology. *The Journal of General Psychology, 5*, 141-177.

Lorr, M. (1991). A redefinition of dominance. *Personality and Individual Differences, 12*, 877–879.

Lorr, M., & McNair, D. M. (1963). An interpersonal behavior circle. *Journal of Abnormal and Social Psychology, 67*, 68–75.

Lorr, M., & McNair, D. M. (1965). Expansion of the interpersonal behavior circle. *Journal of Personality and Social Psychology, 2*, 823–830.

Lorr, M., & McNair, D. M. (1966). Methods relating to evaluation and therapeutic outcome. In L. A. Gottschalk & A. H. Auerbach (Eds.), *Methods of research in psychotherapy.* New York: Appleton-Century-Crofts.

McCrae, R. R., & Costa, P. T., Jr. (1985). Openness to experience. In R. Hogan & W. H. Jones (Eds.), *Perspectives in personality, Volume 1* (pp. 145–172).

McCrae, R. R., & Costa, P. T., Jr. (1989). The structure of interpersonal traits: Wiggins' circumplex and the five-factor model. *Journal of Personality and Social Psychology, 56,* 586–595.

McCrae, R. R., & Costa, P. T., Jr. (1990). *Personality in adulthood.* New York: Guilford.

Miller, T. R. (1991). The psychotherapeutic utility of the five-factor model of personality: A clinician's experience. *Journal of Personality Assessment, 57,* 415–433.

Orford, J. (1986). The rules of interpersonal complemenarity: Does hostility beget hostility and dominance, submission? *Psychological Review, 93,* 365–377.

McLemore, C. W., & Brokaw, D. W. (1987). Personality disorders as dysfunctional interpersonal behavior. *Journal of Personality Disorders, 1,* 270–285.

Millon, T. (1987). *Manual for the MCMI-II (2nd Edition).* Minneapolis, MN: National Computer Systems.

Peterson, D. R. (1979). Assessing interpersonal relationships by means of interaction records. *Behavioral Assessment, 1,* 221–236.

Peterson, D. R. (1982). Functional analysis of interpersonal behavior. In J. C. Anchin & D. J. Kiesler (Eds.), *Handbook of interpersonal psychotherapy* (pp. 149–167). Elmsford, NY: Pergamon Press.

Pincus, A. L. (1991, August). Extending interpersonal problems to include the Big Five personality dimensions. Paper presented at the symposium on *Assessment of interpersonal problems: Implications for treatment and research,* L. E. Alden (Chair). American Psychological Association Annual Convention, San Francisco, CA.

Pincus, A. L., & Wiggins, J. S. (1990). Interpersonal problems and conceptions of personality disorders. *Journal of Personality Disorders, 4,* 342–352.

Pincus, A. L., & Wiggins, J. S. (1992). An expanded perspective on interpersonal assessment. *Journal of Counseling and Development, 71,* 91–94.

Russell, J. A. (1980). A circumplex model of affect. *Journal of Personality and Social Psychology, 39,* 1161–1178.

Safran, J. D. (1990). Towards a refinement of cognitive therapy in light of interpersonal theory: I. Theory. *Clinical Psychology Review, 10,* 87–105.

Sullivan, H. S. (1953a). *Conceptions of modern psychiatry.* New York: Norton.

Sullivan, H. S. (1953b). *The interpersonal theory of psychiatry.* New York: Norton.

Talley, P. F., Strupp, H. H., & Morey, L. C. (1990). Matchmaking in psychotherapy: patient-therapist dimensions and their impact on outcome. *Journal of Consulting and Clinical Psychology, 58,* 182–188.

Tellegen, A. (1991). Personality traits: Issues of definition, evidence, and assessment. In D. Cicchetti and W. Grove (Eds.), *Thinking clearly in psychology: Essays in honor of Paul Everett Meehl Volume 2—Personality and psychopathology* (pp. 10–35). Minneapolis: University of Minnesota Press.

Trapnell, P. D., & Wiggins, J. S. (1990). Extension of the Interpersonal Adjective Scales to include the Big Five dimensions of personality. *Journal of Personality and Social Psychology, 59,* 781–790.

Van Denburg, T. F., Schmidt, J. A., & Kiesler, D. J. (1992). Interpersonal assessment in counseling and psychotherapy. *Journal of Counseling and Development, 71,* 84–90.

Wicklund, R. A., & Gollwitzer, P. M. (1987). The fallacy of the private-public self-focus distinction. *Journal of Personality, 55,*491–523.

Wiggins, J. S. (1979). A psychological taxonomy of trait-descriptive terms: The interpersonal domain. *Journal of Personality and Social Psychology, 37,* 395–412.

Wiggins, J. S. (1980). Circumplex models of interpersonal behavior. In L. Wheeler (Ed.),

Review of personality and social psychology: Volume 1 (pp. 265–294). Beverly Hills, CA: Sage.

Wiggins, J. S. (1982). Circumplex models of interpersonal behavior in clinical psychology. In P. C. Kendall and J. N. Butcher (Eds.), *Handbook of research methods in clinical psychology.* (pp. 183–221). New York: Wiley.

Wiggins, J. S. (1991). *The Interpersonal Adjective Scales (IAS) Manual.* Odessa, FL: Psychological Assessment Resources, Inc.

Wiggins, J. S., Phillips, N., & Trapnell, P. D. (1989). Circular reasoning about interpersonal behavior: Evidence concerning some untested assumptions underlying diagnostic classification. *Journal of Personality and Social Psychology, 56,* 296–305.

Wiggins, J. S., & Pincus, A. L. (1989). Conceptions of personality disorders and dimensions of personality. *Psychological Assessment: A Journal of Consulting and Clinical Psychology, 1,* 305–316.

Wiggins, J. S., & Pincus, A. L. (1992). Personality: Structure and assessment. In M. R. Rosenszweig and L. W. Porter (Eds.), *Annual Review of Psychology, 43,* 473–504.

Wiggins, J. S., & Pincus, A. L. (1994). Personality structure and the structure of personality disorders. In P. T. Costa, Jr. & T. A. Widiger (Eds.), *Personality disorders and the five-factor model of personality* (pp. 73–93). Washington, DC: American Psychological Association.

Wiggins, J. S., & Trapnell, P. D. (in press). Personality Structure: The return of the Big Five. In S. R. Briggs, R. Hogan, and W. H. Jones (Eds.), *Handbook of personality psychology.* Orlando, FL: Academic Press.

Wiggins, J. S., Trapnell, P. D., & Phillips, N. (1988). Psychometric and geometric characteristics of the revised Interpersonal Adjective Scales (IAS-R). *Multivariate Behavioral Research, 23,* 17–30.

7

Psychobiological Models and Issues

Gordon Claridge

INTRODUCTORY REMARKS

Most commentators would surely agree that human personality variations, normal as well as abnormal, are "psychobiological," in the broad sense that for a complete understanding of an individual's uniqueness we require information about both psychological and biological functioning. It would be even more accurate to say that the span of necessary knowledge is "biosocial," and therefore wider still in scope. In practice, accounts of personality are not as integrative as this and, while theorists sometimes pay lip-service to the psychobiological (or biosocial) ideal, their actual formulations are more focused and self-contained within an experiential, cognitive, physiological, psychometric or other model. The result is a patchwork of differing perspectives that have so far failed to piece together entirely to form a recognizable whole. Among the more obvious reasons for this, one is the sheer complexity of the subject matter. In such circumstances, researchers are often understandably tempted, in the interests of coherence, to concentrate on some limited aspect of the phenomena to be explained; personality psychology, clinical psychology, and psychiatry are no exception in this regard. A further reason is that various viewpoints genuinely are difficult to assimilate to one another: research inevitably generates its own concepts, methods, and terminology, and translating between theories, even from reasonably adjacent domains (e.g., cognitive and behavioral) can be tricky. Finally, it also has to be said that there is sometimes a reluctance to attempt such assimilation anyway: theory builders have a habit of believing in the all-inclusive explanatory power of their own models!

Looking beyond these superficial causes, there is another, more substantive reason why the field under review has a rather untidy appearance. This stems from the way, historically, sociocultural influences have shaped research on and explanations of individual differences and psychological deviance. Constructions of the person and of personhood vary over time as well as geographically; scientific ideas that chime with expectations and attitudes—or serve professional or other needs—in one social climate might not do so in another. Consequently, quite different interpretations can be arrived at even among theoreticians starting from the same factual origin. Illustrating the point is a historical example I have quoted previously (Claridge, 1985) concerning the contrasting messages that European and North American psychologists drew from Pavlovian theory at the birth of and during the heyday of behaviorism. For J. B. Watson, Pavlov's account of the conditioned reflex offered a formula for elaborating a heavily environmental view of individual differences consonant with North American philosophy of personal equality and social opportunity. In contrast, it was left to writers in Europe—in Western Europe, mostly to Eysenck—to exploit on behalf of a more stratified social order Pavlov's concept of "nervous types" as a biological (and inferred genetic) explanation of human personality.

Of course, the precise issues contained in the above example are now out-of-date: extreme behaviorism is dead and so, hopefully, is crude hereditarianism. Yet, over time the *general* themes in the debate have scarcely changed. Appropriately spanning the psychobiological divide, a continuing source of tension has been between those who seek descriptions in the nervous system and those who prefer more macroscopic, whole person accounts, whether the latter are formulated in behavioral or, as is now more often the case, in cognitive terms. Furthermore, although not a necessary conjunction, these two positions have also been aligned with differing emphases on the relative influences of nature and nurture in human variation. Biological theorists are predictably drawn to the notion of genetic underpinning of the individual differences they study, but for the more psychologically minded, whose primary explanatory constructs lie further from the nervous system, the extrapolation has less appeal.

A relatively new factor in the situation is the recent rapid progress in the biological sciences, including, in the neurosciences, the invention of highly accurate scanning procedures for investigating brain structure and function and, in genetics, the discovery of precise methods for DNA analysis. Such advances are already yielding answers undreamed of a decade ago and promise to resolve once and for all some questions that have hitherto necessarily remained the subject of speculation and fuzzy debate. This could have two quite opposite consequences. Ideally it should help to promote a more sophisticated, empirically based, and integrated psychobiology. However, it could raise the expectations that most features of individual variation, especially in their pathological form, will soon yield to a biological probe of one kind or another, making discussion of their psychology redundant. The impression is that, in some quarters at least, the second of these two reactions is certainly now quite firmly in place and that the gaps in psychobiology waiting to be bridged are actually becoming wider rather than narrower. This is definitely true with respect to the psychotic states, which in psychiatry at least are now sometimes routinely spoken of as diseases whose organic etiology is now certain (Roberts, 1991; Crow, 1987). It is even the case for disorders that lie more obviously within the province of normal experience and behavior and which have always been regarded as equally the concern of the psychologist and of the biological scientist. Thus, it is currently possible to find putative explanations of the same condition that bear no resemblance to one another and where the authors have chosen (deliberately, we presume) to ignore an alternative opinion. An example is obsessive-compulsive disorder (OCD): here, cognitive/behavioral (Rachman & Hodgson, 1980; Salkovskis, 1985) and neurochemical (Montgomery, 1992) theories appear to coexist in a competitive isolation. Another is panic disorder, where those promoting a physiological etiology (Montgomery, 1993; Nutt & Lawson, 1992) may summarily dismiss or even fail to mention the demonstrable role of cognitive influences (Clark, 1986).

In such confrontations, the biological argument can always appear to have the edge. Apparent objectivity and precision of measurement give biological pronouncements a confident (and convincingly neutral) air, seeming to cushion them—apart from ethical concerns—against further discussion. However, this new materialism has not gone unchallenged or failed to stimulate debate; as witness the revived and burgeoning interest among neuroscientists in questions such as the nature of consciousness, the mind–brain relationship and so on (Blakemore & Greenfield, 1987; Churchland, 1986). Even closer to the present topic is the corresponding growth of movements concerned with the philosophical implications of psychiatry (Cawley, 1993) and with the need to pay more attention to the experience, as distinct from the observed data, of mental illness (*Schizophrenia Bulletin*, 1989). Both represent a worry that the scientific endeavor has already gone too far in dehumanizing the subject—and in any case is incapable of providing all of the answers. The contents of the present chapter are in a sense a particular case of these preoccupations.

REDUCTIONISM, ASYMMETRY, AND CONTINUITY

A major conceptual barrier to achieving a fully integrated psychobiological theory of personality is the widely held assumption that psychological events are potentially entirely explicable in biological terms, progressively reducible to neurophysiological, neurochemical, and genetic descriptors. Here, psychology can easily be construed—and is often regarded—as an unequal, second-rate partner in an exercise designed to get itself redefined as a branch of neuroscience. Willner (1985), in a succinct discussion of the nature of psychobiological explanation, criticizes this "reductionist fallacy" on several grounds. He points out, for example, that in a hierarchical organization of function—such as we have in this case—substituting a lower level of explanation of a phenomenon for an explanation at a higher level is generally not feasible, if only because the account gets too detailed and complex the further one moves down the hierarchy. For example, to describe even a simple perceptual experience would involve specifying an impossibly large number of neuronal connections: the opportunity and availability of data to describe it at a higher—in this case psychological—level is indispensable and in any case more meaningful. Willner's most telling criticism, however, makes use of the well-known phenomenon of emergent properties, whereby new qualities, not evident in simpler systems and not predictable from the latters' own features, become apparent as the level of organization increases in complexity. Here, the psychological data not only have *validity* in their own right but also their own *uniqueness*, simply by virtue of being psychological. Furthermore, as Willner stresses, they also have a certain precedence in psychobiological investigation: unless and until the variables of the psychological level are successfully specified they cannot sensibly be examined at a biological level.

As a contemporary example of what he judges to be a well thought out psychobiological model, Willner chooses Gray's (1982) theory of anxiety and its corollary concerning the mode of action of anti-anxiety drugs. Drawing a contrast with the crude "GABA hypothesis of anxiety"—which is merely correlative—Willner points out how Gray has systematically unpacked the hypothesis in order to try to specify mechanisms at each point in the hierarchy: "The relevant set of benzodiazepine receptors, the neural pathways involved, their role in normal brain function, and the relationship between functional changes and changes in experience."

Willner implicitly admits, however, that the model is weakest at the "upper" end, in not reflecting how complex the relationships are between functional brain processes and mental events; in other words, in not dealing properly with the emergent stage from the physiological to the psychological. Pursuing that comment further, it could indeed be argued that Gray's theory is itself, in its own way, overly reductionist. For it seems to fall short in the choice of interface between brain and psychological experience. Specifically, the "behavioral inhibition system" (and its corresponding neural circuitry), hypothesized by Gray as central in anxiety, is too low-level conceptually (and physiologically) to deal with the important introspective data of neurosis. This stems from the model's heritage, namely its origins in Eysenck's theory. The latter, and theories like it, have similarly always looked toward relatively primitive physiological systems to account for individual differences. This feature, which has a bearing on their contribution as psychobiological models of personality, will be taken up more fully in the next section. In the meantime, attention needs to be drawn to another important issue within the reductionist debate.

This concerns an apparent difference in the readiness with which biological reductionism is resorted to, and considered acceptable, according to whether the psychological phenomena to be explained fall within the domain of normal or of abnormal experience. Sass (1992), in a recent critique of biological psychiatry, refers to this as an "asymmetry" of explanation. He elaborates the idea as follows:

Normal (or healthy) forms of consciousness are assumed to be, to a great extent, under one's intentional control and, in addition, to operate according to rational principles and to be oriented toward the objective world. While these normal mental processes are certainly assumed to be *correlated* with physical events occurring in the brain, seldom are they viewed as being *mere* causal by-products of such events. . . . But *ab*normal modes of consciousness . . . have often been seen very differently: as involving a "fall into determinism", a lapse from dualism whereby the malfunctioning physical processes (in brain and nervous system) disrupt the mental or psychic stream, depriving it of its intrinsic rationality and meaningfulness.

Sass's remarks are directed mostly at explanations of psychosis. Yet, they easily generalize to other forms of psychological disorder, given psychiatry's growing preference, illustrated earlier with examples from the neuroses, for exclusively biological accounts of most forms of abnormal behavior. Several important questions are raised here about the continuity between normal and abnormal in psychological disorders and the relationship between personality, deviance, and illness.

In the case of personality and manifest illness, it could be argued that there *is* no such continuity, that the two form largely independent domains, and that the Sass criticism is misplaced. This is a view that seems to be encouraged by the Axis I/Axis II distinction in *DSM-IV* (American Psychiatric Association, 1994). It is also to be found in the early writings of Foulds (1965), who proposed that "personality" and "illness" refer to quite separate universes of discourse, revealed in two different kinds of feature—continuous syntonic traits in the case of personality and discrete dystonic signs and symptoms in the case of illness. Accordingly, he said, there is neither a necessary nor a sufficient connection between the type of illness an individual develops and his or her underlying personality structure. An asymmetric view of etiology would then appear perfectly valid, illness being perceivable as an intrusion into an otherwise healthy, functioning personality, with no reason to link them together either conceptually or causally.

However, two further points should be noted about Foulds. One is that he was eventually forced to admit that the distinction he was making was less clear-cut than he had originally thought (Foulds, 1971); a third kind of descriptor—*deviant traits*—is necessary to account for certain abnormalities (i.e., personality disorders) that lie outside the sphere of healthy adaptation but which do not constitute illness in the usual sense. The second point to note is that Foulds formulated his theory entirely in terms of interpersonal psychology. Both facts would actually set the theory in opposition to the naive organic psychiatry view at which the Sass criticism is aimed. Here it is not so much the perceived *continuity* or *discontinuity* in disorder that is crucial to the "Fouldsian" position; it is rather the extent to which disorder is seen as *psychological*, rather than biological or medical. If psychological, as Foulds argued, then asymmetry of explanation presents less of a problem, even in accounts of Axis I disorder. Furthermore, to the latter point, it is also of interest that Foulds went so far as to suggest a single continuum—of what he called 'personal illness'—connecting neurosis, personality disorder, and psychosis in one explanatory (psychological) model.

Organic medical models of disorder mostly ignore the problem referred to by Sass. Exclusively psychological explanations, of the general type proposed by Foulds, simply evade it by excluding the biological aspect altogether. Psycho*biological* theories, however, should be ideally placed to deal with the asymmetry question, for they assume *both* some continuity between normal and abnormal *and* a biological connection. Yet, for reasons already touched on, this interdisciplinary advantage may not be fully exploited—or indeed easily exploitable—and the "fall into determinism" is always a danger. Paradoxically, this may be equally the case—albeit in a different way—for the personality (and less serious psychiatric) disorders as it is for the major mental illnesses. In the latter there are certainly substantive issues about their "dimensionality" that still have to be resolved and it is temptingly easy, as Sass says, merely to attribute any abnormality to a lesion, without reference to the person. However, the discontinuities of function that such conditions entail should help to signal distinctions between person variables and illness variables; it should then be easier to recognize the two domains and to disentangle their respective contributions to the disordered state. In the personality disorders, as Foulds recognized, the boundary between normal and abnormal is altogether less clear. Consequently, explanatory constructs that serve to account for one can be readily taken up and extrapolated—in either direction— to the other. Any discrepancy that exists in the constructs that are used to describe normal personality and those used to describe its deviant forms should thus be minimized. But a problem can arise if the constructs themselves are biological, especially if they are interpreted in an overly reductionist way. Then the explanation of deviance may take on a medical flavor, the individual being seen merely as a "victim" of some aberration of nervous system functioning. Not being couched in the "existentialist" language in which Sass writes, such formulations will fail to address the point he is making—or actually slide into reductionist fallacy even about normal personality.

However these philosophical issues are eventually resolved, continuity remains a problem even at a working level for research and theory in the field. Models of illness that try to maintain firm boundaries between categories of disease have to cope with the failure to find definite "points of rarity" in the classification (Kendell & Brockington, 1980) and etiology (Taylor, 1992) even of the major psychoses. The existence of the borderline states is a constant source of embarrassment (Stone, 1980). Distinctions between neurotic and psychotic forms of the same illness may be difficult to maintain. Yet reinterpretation as mere variations in severity is not convincing and in use seems arbitrary and inconsistent; as, for example, in the coverage of depressive disorder in the recent revision of the international classification of mental disorders (ICD-10, 1992). It is not even always clear what writers mean when they talk of continuity. Do they imply continuity between illnesses, within illnesses, between illness and non-medical disorder, or simply between normal and abnormal? And how far do they incorporate *dis*continuity into their ideas? The personality disorders are uniquely problematical and articulate these ambiguities especially well. Explanations draw on ideas from both the neurosis and psychosis domains. Yet, they are set apart from both—and from the normal— by certain features, represented in Foulds's notion of deviant traits as descriptors of abnormality that are neither indicative of adaptive functioning nor a sign of ill-health. In these cases there seems to be more than the usual need to find models that can acknowledge both the dimensionality inherent in our constructions of normal personality and the discontinuity implicit in the concept of disorder.

Two broad questions emerge, then, from the discussion so far. First, how adequately do current psychobiological theories of personality and the personality disorders account for the latters' dysfunctional qualities? And, second, in discussing such disorders how can we best conceptualize the boundaries between them and the normal and between them and other clinical states, including the functional psychoses? Each of these issues will be considered in turn.

TEMPERAMENT, PERSONALITY, AND DEVIANCE

The notion that human individuality has its roots in biology is an ancient folklore belief, largely sustained in the prescientific era by the humoral theory of temperaments. In more modern times, its origins can be traced to Pavlov's attempts to explain differences in the behavior of his dogs in the conditioning stand according to variations in certain hypothetical properties of the nervous system. Furthermore, elaboration of this "theory of nervous types" in the former Soviet Union and its subsequent dissemination into the West (see Gray, 1971) has had a profound effect on human differential psychology. In adult personality theory, it has been responsible for creating an identifiable biological school, the members of which share a common interest in chasing personality to the nervous system. Their methods, terminology, and focus of interest vary, depending on the branch of the school to which they belong. East European psychologists, such as Strelau (1985) in Poland, have naturally stayed close to the original Pavlovian constructs, whereas those in West Europe and North America—for example, Zuckerman (1979)—have developed their own versions. In recent decades, there has been considerable interchange of ideas among workers in the field and, despite differences in approach and background tradition, some coherence of view has emerged, with the realization that although formulations may vary the phenomena to which they refer are substantially the same.

The collecting point for these ideas—and the person most responsible for their development—is of course Eysenck, whose own biological theory of personality, developed over nearly half a century, is the most extensively researched and publicized (Eysenck, 1952b, 1957, 1967). It is also the most comprehensive—in the sense of claiming to encompass a greater range of individual variation than any other theory—and has been offered by Eysenck as the definitive "paradigm for personality" (Eysenck & Eysenck, 1985). Others have challenged this claim; notably and most recently, adherents of the Big Five (Costa & McCrae, 1992). But the latter does not incorporate biological variables and, within its own terms of reference, when compared with similar efforts Eysenck's theory must surely be regarded as a major innovative contribution to individual differences research. Certainly the theory is invariably used as a referent by other workers in the field; while alternative formulations (e.g., Gray, 1982; Claridge, 1967) are usually accepted as derivative rather than fully original.

No attempt will be made in this paper to evaluate Eysenck's theory, or any part of it, comprehensively. The intention here is rather to note some relevant features of 'Eysenckian' theory, using the latter as a generic term for a class of personality models having certain features in common. One such feature has already been touched on, namely, the relatively reductionist nature of the theories. With Gray's model of anxiety as a notable (though only partial) exception, the theories are mostly correlative. That is to say, the bulk of the research they generate examines relationships—mostly in humans—between one or other descriptive personality characteristic and some laboratory phenomenon. The latter may be chosen from a vast array of possibilities—biochemical, physiological, psychophysical, or behavioral—the expressed aim being to discover the underlying biological determinants of the trait or traits in question.

Although this approach has generated a variety of conceptual nervous system models, the latter are of uniformly low level, in more senses than one. A typical integrative construct is "arousal," which has been used in several ways to account for a number of different personality traits (Strelau & Eysenck, 1987). The anatomical and physiological systems incorporated in the theories are correspondingly primitive. An example here is Eysenck's (1967) own identification of neuroticism and introversion with, respectively, limbic and reticular brain-stem sources of activation, a formulation that, although much refined in the hands of Gray (1982), remains the paradigm case for this style of theorizing about personality. As more than one member of the Eysenckian school has said to me privately, "it's what's happening down below in the brain that's important in personality; the top part's just a computer—a memory bank—being steered from underneath." Clearly such theories are not well set-up to deal with several of the issues raised earlier in this paper!

One of the problems with the Eysenckian theories is that they are overblown as theories of *personality*. Reinterpreted as accounts of *temperament*—which indeed they are described as by East European scientists—they begin to find their proper place. This becomes evident when comparisons are made with research on biological individual differences carried out within a *developmental* context. Developmentalists invariably use the term "temperament," there being no pretension that the subject matter is personality in the fullest sense. Interestingly, work on infant and childhood temperament has largely evolved independently of the

Western versions of Eysenckian theory, which has mostly ignored the developmental dimension. Indeed, only occasionally has there been detailed cross-reference between the two perspectives (e.g., Mangan, 1982). Yet, comparing them shows how closely they converge, in factual content, theoretical constructs, and explanatory range.

Contrasted with personality, temperament can be considered a simpler concept, both phylogenetically and ontogenetically. As used to describe infant behavior, temperamental traits refer to very basic (especially emotional) sources of variation that are highly heritable, observable in animals, and, as manifest signs of an individual's "tempo," appearing to be a quite direct reflection of nervous system differences (Buss & Plomin, 1984). In the Eysenckian school it is *personality* that is defined in that way, with similar reference to animal equivalents (Chamove, Eysenck, & Harlow, 1972) and strong genetic underpinning of the adult dimensions (Plomin, 1986). Not surprisingly, forms of the latter are recognizable in early life—for example, as sociability and emotionality—and justly regarded as precursors of later personality (Plomin & Dunn, 1986). Such equivalence, of course, helps to validate the adult theories, suggesting that they are tapping important sources of variation, even biological variation. But to assume that the theories thereby give comprehensive accounts of personality is surely too ambitious.

Despite their limitations, these temperament models of individual differences have generated some useful approaches to the description and explanation of the personality disorders. There is, for example, the suggestion that some forms of antisocial behavior are attempts to relieve the boredom of low arousal, driven by pathological stimulation-seeking (Quay, 1965), an idea Zuckerman (1978) later developed as the notion of *sensation* seeking. An alternative, but potentially relatable, interpretation introduced by Lykken (1957) has been to construe low arousal in this context as low *anxiety*, which is seen as acting to mediate antisocial behavior through its role in aversive conditioning and anticipatory and avoidance learning. Popularly used psychometric instruments to test these two formulations are, respectively, Zuckerman's (1978) Sensation Seeking Scales (SSS) and Lykken's Activity Preference Questionnaire (APQ), measuring situational anxiety reactivity (Lykken, Tellegen, & Katzenmeyer, 1973). Not surprisingly, there are some correlations between the two sets of scales, high sensation seekers generally tending to show low anxiety. But available evidence suggests that this is more true of normal subjects (Blankstein, 1975) than of the samples of behaviorally deviant individuals (prisoners) in whom it would have been of most interest (Hundleby & Ross, 1977). The picture is also complicated by somewhat uneven relationships between the various subscales of the SSS and the two—physical and social—components of anxiety tapped by the APQ; as well as between the latter and more general trait anxiety (Blankstein, 1976). An obvious overall conclusion would be that constructs like anxiety and sensation seeking are, by themselves, too global to be all-explanatory but that they can be usefully employed alongside other temperamental and life-history characteristics for profiling different forms of social deviance (see Af Klinteberg, Humble, & Schalling, 1992) for a contemporary example of such an approach).

A point at issue here is heterogeneity within the personality disorders, and Gray, writing in a more strictly Eysenckian tradition, has also commented on this. In modifying Eysenck's theory, Gray has mostly concentrated on dysfunctions associated with surplus anxiety (the High Neuroticism [N]/Low Extraversion [E] quadrant in Eysenckian terminology). But he has occasionally speculated on how the personality disorders might fit into his own version of Eysenck's theory (Gray, 1973). In the Gray scheme they could be associated with three quite different configurations of temperamental and biological traits. One is simply pathologically low anxiety. Such individuals would lie at the opposite end from dysthymic neurotics of Gray's major anxiety dimension (Low N/Low E); they would show correspondingly weak sensitivity to punishment, a quality accounting for some forms of incorrigible behavior due to failure to learn appropriate behavioral controls. A second possibility might be the extreme sensitivity to *reward* proposed by Gray as the biological basis of neurotic extraversion; this might have some affinity with sensation seeking and is the High N/High E combination that Eysenck himself originally considered most definitive of some personality disordered patients, including hysterical personalities and psychopaths. The third profile would involve the relatively newer dimension, "psychoticism" (P). Gray connects this to individual differences in the amygdaloid flight/fight system, thus allowing for an explanation of aggressive behavior in the personality disorders. Eysenck himself now also places considerable emphasis on P—and a proposed association to the biology of aggression—as the dimension in his theory that is most relevant here. This point will be returned to later, as part of the general discussion about the relationship of the personality disorders to psychosis.

Not all theorizing influenced by the Eysenckian approach to personality has remained at such a low level of explanation. A notable exception is to be found in the work of Hare and his colleagues on so-called primary psychopathy. Their accounts have followed an interesting progression over the years, from less to more sophisticated formulations of the disorder. The earliest explanations converged very much upon 'classic' temperament theory, drawing on ideas such as "arousal deficiency," "low anxiety," and "poor anticipation of punishment" as the biological sources of psychopathy (Hare, 1965). In the next phase Hare (1978) introduced a more cognitive element, albeit in a relatively primitive form indexed by psychophysiological response patterning. This made use of Lacey's (1967) "gating" hypothesis of directional heart rate change under stress and was thought to explain the psychopath's facility for tuning out unpleasant events, contributing to his deficiency in empathy, emotional response, and inability to learn from experience. However, even this attentional explanation of psychopathic behavior seemed too low-level to be satisfactory, and in recent years the Hare group has moved toward a more genuinely neurocognitive theory, based on the experimental study of hemisphere functioning in primary psychopaths. Two types of findings have emerged. One is suggestive of weakened, or even reversed, lateralization for language in such individuals (Hare & Jutai, 1988). The other indicates a semantic deficiency specifically concerned with the processing of affective aspects of language (Williamson, Harpur, & Hare, 1991), a result that the authors consider chimes well with an observation they quote about the primary psychopath, namely, that "he knows the words, but not the music." Such work represents an imaginative attempt to develop a more complete psychobiological account of personality disorder out of what on their purely Eysenckian form are still relatively reductionist—and therefore biologically primitive—temperament theories of individual differences. Other influences on Hare's research, discussed below, might be responsible for this more sophisticated approach.

PERSONALITY DISORDER AND PSYCHOSIS

Hare's investigations of primary psychopathy have been very much inspired by the writings of Cleckley, whose classic work, *The Mask of Sanity* (1976), articulates the second major theme to be taken up here. Historically, the notion that there is some connection between the personality disorders and the major psychoses has never been far from the agenda. As noted earlier, this has created—and still gives rise to—ambiguities of description, nosology, and causal theory. Cleckley's own writings are an excellent example of that indecision. In the fifth edition of *The Mask of Sanity* Cleckley notes that he originally believed that the people he was describing should be considered psychotic—as indeed the title of his book is intended to convey, namely, individuals concealing basic insanity behind an outward *persona* of intact function. Later, he changed that view. Yet, the book's title remained the same and empirical and theoretical developments since then have continued to keep the issue alive. Thus, several of Hare's laboratory findings on primary psychopaths find interesting parallels in schizophrenia research. These include observations about altered lateralization of brain function in schizophrenia (Gruzelier, 1991) and effects explicable according to the Lacey "gating" hypothesis of attention (Venables, 1973). It would seem that in some important biological and neurocognitive respects individuals meeting the criteria for primary psychopathy might indeed resemble psychotic patients.

Such speculation has formed only a small part of a wider debate about the nature of psychosis, especially about its clinical boundaries and whether these can be thought to enclose some forms of personality disorder (Siever, Kalus, & Keefe, 1993). On a theoretical front a crucial question has been that of dimensionality and whether models can be constructed that can account for facts both about serious forms of psychotic illness and about the lesser "borderline" conditions—as well as, in some versions of theory, about normal personality variations as well. In psychology, there have been two historically separate trains of thought on this issue. One, already mentioned, is Eysenck's introduction into his theory of a third dimension of psychoticism (P) (Eysenck & Eysenck, 1976); or, more correctly, his revival of what from the very beginning formed part of a three-dimensional scheme for personality description and psychiatric classification (Eysenck, 1952a). The other influence has stemmed from Meehl's development of the notion of 'schizotypy' as a way of conceptualizing and investigating dispositional, especially genetic, aspects of schizophrenia (Meehl, 1962, 1990).

Of the two approaches, Eysenck's is the more radical and comprehensive, as well as the one raising more openly the question of possible associations between psychosis, personality disorder, and normal individual differences. Meehl's theory focuses narrowly on schizophrenia, doing so on the genetics side through a single gene explanation of the condition. Logically speaking at least, this constrains the theory's references to dimensionality in two respects. First, it confines the area of interest within the personality disorders to those borderline conditions allegedly falling along the schizophrenia spectrum, i.e., schizotypal personality disorder (SPD) and, perhaps, among the milder personality disorders, the schizoid and paranoid forms. Second, it lays the groundwork for what elsewhere (Claridge, 1994) I have referred to as a "quasi-dimensional" (as contrasted with a "fully dimensional") view of the schizophrenia spectrum. This distinction refers to the two quite different interpretations that have been placed on continuity in psychological disorders, as follows.

The quasidimensional view confines continuity to the illness domain, construing it solely as a spectrum of severity of symptoms and making use of the notion of *forme fruste*, or reduced expression of some discrete disease process. A fully dimensional account, on the other hand, inextricably connects illness to personality. It includes the quasidimensional aspect, but it also proposes a further underlying continuum of normal personality and other individual differences traits that simultaneously define disposition to the disease to which they are relevant. An example of a fully dimensional model from the physical field that helps to draw apart the two usages is systemic disease associated with hypertension. There, blood pressure is a continuously variable trait-like feature that in health subserves a normal function but which also defines a factor of risk for vascular disease; the range of symptomatology that occurs in the disease itself constitutes the quasidimensional element.

Despite its putative links to schizotypy as "normal" variation Meehl's model of schizophrenia, with its emphasis on single gene explanation, is essentially quasidimensional. This means that for him, even personality aberrations falling short of psychotic illness still represent a clear discontinuity from healthy biological functioning and normal personality, being due to the same disease process as schizophrenia. In other words, SPD constitutes a *forme fruste* of schizophrenia and schizotypy (or schizoidia) a compensated expression of the schizophrenic genotype.

In contrast, Eysenck's opinion on continuity is a clearly stated dimensional one, apparently even dispensing with the notion of a symptom severity spectrum that defines the quasidimensional model. Eysenck also adopts an all-encompassing *Einheitpsychose* view of psychosis. Joined to his very broad, multigenetic formulation of normal personality, this gives his theory much more scope than Meehl's for considering the personality disorders as a whole as mild variants of the differing forms of psychotic behavior—capable of being represented, Eysenck would argue, as the different possible combinations of his three major dimensions of extraversion, neuroticism, and psychoticism. Unfortunately, the apparent advantage of such a sweeping synthesis of ideas is bought at the expense of some loss in conceptual clarity, in inattention to detail, and an ambiguity of terminology that considerably weakens the theory's explanatory power *vis-à-vis* the relationship between personality disorder and psychosis.

In assessing Eysenck's position on this issue, it is very important to distinguish the *principles* of his theory and how, *in practice*, the idea of psychoticism has been developed over the years since the theory was first proposed. On the former point, it seems a reasonable proposition that there might be a general dimension of psychoticism which, in combination with other characteristics, such as extraversion and neuroticism, accounts for a variety of personality disorders that fall short of, but have their reference point in, the major psychoses. A unifying and ecologically valid account of psychoticism within Eysenck's theory has proved elusive, however (Claridge, 1981, 1983). Of crucial significance here—and the basis of the drawn distinction between theory and practice in Eysenck's work— concerns the way in which the measurement of psychoticism by questionnaire has evolved. The latter is represented in the Eysenck P-scale, an instrument that has gone through several revisions (Eysenck & Eysenck, 1975, 1976; Eysenck, Eysenck, & Barrett, 1985). The most notable change has been the gradual shift in the item content of the scale, toward questions tapping broadly antisocial, nonconformist traits and away from those of a more manifestly psychotic nature. Indeed, as it now stands the P-scale could be said to have excellent validity as a measure of sociopathic characteristics, a point also emphasized by Zuckerman (1989), who sees Eysenckian P as overlapping somewhat with his own concept of sensation seeking.

One consequence of defining "psychoticism" as primarily antisocial behavior is that it forces Eysenck's theory into circularity: most of the personality disorders, virtually out of necessity, will form part of the psychosis spectrum. This would not matter if the Eysenckian concept was a strong one empirically and theoretically. But the evidence suggests otherwise; as shown in recent work examining the structure of psychosis-proneness or "psychoticism" from a different point of view. I am referring to research undertaken outside Eysenck's theory, within a more clinical context. This has been prompted by the appearance over the past decade of a glut of scales purporting to measure psychotic traits in general population subjects. Some of these scales were developed as a direct outgrowth of

Meehl's theory of schizotypy (e.g., Chapman & Chapman, 1980; Chapman, Chapman, & Miller, 1982); some as an attempt to find more clinically relevant alternatives to Eysenck's P-scale (Claridge & Broks, 1984); and some for special experimental or other purposes, such as high-risk research (Nielsen & Petersen, 1976; Venables, Wilkins, Mitchell, Raine, & Bailes, 1990). All the scales have in common the fact that, unlike the Eysenck questionnaire, their item content originated in clinical phenomena: they cover both the psychotic illnesses themselves—mostly schizophrenia, but also affective disorder—and the borderline states, especially SPD.

Several factor analyses of these instruments have now been reported, with results that are pertinent here (see Claridge, 1994, and Claridge & Beech, 1994 for more detailed accounts). Briefly, it turns out that schizotypy, psychoticism, or psychosis-proneness (however it is named) is multidimensional, breaking down into at least three, and possibly four, components. Not surprisingly, these correspond roughly to the symptom clusters observed in clinical psychosis itself. They include an affective factor that reflects anhedonia in the schizotypy domain and negative symptoms in schizophrenia; but especially prominent are strong cognitive components—of thought disorganization and aberrant perception and belief. Where, as in some studies, the Eysenck scale was included in an analysis it tended to behave unpredictably: P either floated across the other components just described or it defined another, weaker, factor—of antisocial, nonconformist behavior. In other words, contrary to Eysenck's view, the latter does *not* emerge as the central feature of psychoticism. It seems, instead, to constitute an ancillary set of traits, secondary to other, core characteristics of cognitive and affective dysfunction that are better tapped by more clinically focused scales. Of course, the fact that asociality appeared at all in these analyses is of interest and constitutes further evidence of an association between psychosis and certain aspects, or forms, of personality disorder. But its relatively minor status within the domain of psychosis-proneness traits suggests that the label "psychoticism" for the P-scale is confusing and misleading: among other considerations it perpetuates a societal myth about psychosis, reinforcing it through the proposed connection of P to the biology of aggressiveness.

The above conclusions find support in work on the experimental correlates of psychosis-proneness, using the various scales described. Again, a considerable amount of data has accumulated, using a range of laboratory procedures drawn from psychophysiology, cognitive psychology, and neuropsychology (see Claridge, 1994, for a summary, and Raine, Lencz, & Mednick, 1994, for detailed accounts of this literature). Compared with other measures of psychosis-proneness, especially those tapping its cognitive aspects, the Eysenck P-scale fares rather poorly; correlations with relevant objective indices are generally weaker and less consistent. Having said that, the picture in mainstream schizotypy research is still very confused. For example, it is still unclear which experimental paradigm (and corresponding theoretical model) will prove optimal for describing the underlying mechanisms of psychosis-proneness. And the latter's various components, identified in the factor analytic studies, have scarcely begun to be explored in the laboratory; it will probably turn out that the cognitive and affective—and perhaps even the asocial—components have identifiably different correlates, indicating that they are subserved by different underlying mechanisms. Furthermore, little effort has been expended so far on trying to answer detailed questions about the personality disorders. Rather, the focus has been on the implications for developing indicators of risk for major psychotic illness, especially schizophrenia. Where references have been made to personality disorder these have mostly been confined to its more serious forms, such as SPD, and even then generally from the viewpoint of medical genetics and pathophysiology rather than personality (Siever, Kalus, & Keefe, 1993).

A partial exception to the above, from within psychology, is the work of Raine. In a series of studies he has deliberately investigated the apparently overlapping domains of schizotypy, borderline disorder, psychopathy, and schizoid personality. In one questionnaire study Raine (1986) examined measures of these different features in a prison population, the assessments including Hare's Psychopathy Checklist, the Eysenck P-scale, and a specially constructed scale of schizoid traits. Correlations between the measures were rather low, suggesting separable sets of characteristics and especially some specificity, distinct from schizophrenia, for primary psychopathy. The latter finding is somewhat at variance with the speculations mentioned above, on the basis of laboratory studies, that there might be a connection between psychosis and primary psychopathy. In discussing this point Raine quotes Hare, who in turn quotes Cleckley, to the effect that deep-seated psychotic tendencies in psychopathic individuals might be difficult to probe with self-report inventories of subjective clinical procedures.

Results from the same study using more objective measures, and published separately by Raine (1987), were expected to throw more light on the issue, but they failed to do so. As Raine himself pointed out, this may have been because the laboratory index used was too low-level and non-specific to answer that particular question. Other findings from the same experiment (and elsewhere from Raine's research) are of interest, however. In his work Raine used a psychophysiological (electrodermal [EDA] orienting) procedure similar to that adopted in the ongoing Mauritius high-risk investigation of children thought vulnerable to later schizophrenia and/or antisocial personality disorder (Venables, Mednick, Schulsinger, Raman, Bell, Dalais, & Fletcher, 1978). Translating the paradigm to a study of normal adolescents, Raine and Venables (1984) demonstrated a relationship between EDA nonresponding and antisocial traits. But this was true only of a subset of schizoid individuals; in them, it was proposed, there is a deficit in sustained attention. The observation was consistent with the results of the prisoner study (Raine, 1987) where a subgroup of schizoid antisocials was also identified, characterized by reduced EDA orienting and high scores on a factor of schizotypy labeled "Anhedonia-Psychoticism." Also correlating with Anhedonia-Psychoticism, as well as with a second cognitive component of schizotypy, was an index of attention distraction, derived from the Wechsler Adult Intelligence Scale. Finally, and particularly striking about Raine's results, was that these various associations differed according to the quality of the subjects' early rearing environment: correlations between the objective measures and aspects of schizopathy—as Raine has sometimes called it—were much stronger in subjects rated as having come from intact, as distinct from broken, homes. Although collected on a rather narrow research front, such findings neatly demonstrate how environmental influences might modify endogenous predispositions in order to produce different outcomes; they also illustrate an important strategy for examining the interface between biological and social effects in antisocial behavior.

There seems little doubt that part of our understanding of the personality disorders will lie in examining their connections to the psychotic states, but two questions in particular still remain unanswered. One is how generalizable that association will prove to be. Is it confined to disorders solely relatable to the schizophrenia spectrum? Or does this only appear to be the case because the latter has been the most thoroughly researched? Is it possible that a set of continua defining a broader concept of psychoticism is viable, drawing within its compass all, or most, major forms of personality disorder? This could still be so given the multidimensional picture that is now beginning to emerge of what originated as the narrow concept of schizotypy. Eysenck's different use of the term "psychoticism" is a slight distraction here; but a deliberate attempt to align his dimensional framework with that used in mainstream psychosis-proneness research might itself be a profitable way of exploring the topic.

The second question remaining to be addressed concerns the nature of the *etiological* connection between personality disorder and psychosis, however limited or extensive that proves to be descriptively. Reference has already been made to the distinction between quasi- and fully dimensional interpretations of psychoticism, two differing perspectives on continuity that have important implications for how we view the personality disorders. A construction of the latter as *formes frustes* of the major psychoses—namely, as lesser and major varieties of illness caused by the same discrete brain pathophysiology—is clearly quite different from one seeking the origins of the personality disorders in the normal nervous system, that is, as biologically based temperamental differences, in the Pavlovian/Eysenckian tradition. The issue is of crucial significance theoretically. But it is also important for practical reasons; it has a bearing, for example, on discussions about where in classificatory schemes such as *DSM-IV* the personality disorders should be located—whether as minor organic illnesses or as extreme biological aberrations having their true reference point in normal personality functioning. The distinction is a subtle one, but it lies at the center of what eventually we might decide we mean by a psychobiological construction of personality disorder.

FINAL REMARKS

In their relatively recent book on personality disorders, Beck and his associates (1990) make absolutely no reference, even in passing, to the biological perspective; indeed they include none of the themes mentioned here, whether biological or not. The book is therefore a particularly telling example of the one-sided reporting referred to, with several other instances in psychiatry, at the beginning of this chapter. Of course, Beck is concerned in his writings with the cognitive, and particularly the cognitive-therapeutic, aspects of psychological disorder; in this case as an extension of his work in a similar vein on depression. The relative success of cognitive therapies in some forms of depressive illness (Williams, 1992) provides a good reason for extrapolating the same principles to the personality disorders and perhaps, in the interests of uncluttered presentation, concentrating exclusively on one approach. Another consideration is the neglect of psychological approaches to personality disorder within a modern cognitive framework. A further counterbalance to contemporary biological psychiatry is perhaps deserved, and the ideas discussed by Beck will certainly need to be incorporated into any future psychobiological theory of personality disorder. Within this last concern, there is, then, the hidden agenda of treatment policy, as implied in my remarks at the end of the previous section. If, for example, a strongly organic, heavily medically oriented explanation of personality disorders, such as SPD, were to prevail, then certain treatment preferences—presumably pharmacological—would flow from it. The more psychologically minded might feel that they should resist this, even at the expense of paying regard to only a limited set of data about the conditions they are trying to research and treat.

However, several criticisms can be made of such closed accounts—from whichever side of the psychobiological divide they emanate. One is general and intellectual and stems from the sheer unacceptability of explanations in psychiatry that do not at least try to *approach* the psychobiological. Where extensive psychobiological integration has been attempted—e.g., Willner (1985) for depression—the result is much more satisfying than the narrowly vested alternatives. It surely must always be right to seek as comprehensive an account as possible of any phenomenon. Of course, it could be that *truly* integrated psychobiological theories are impossible because of the linguistic and other constraints imposed on trying to bring together such differing levels or domains of explanation. Perhaps more important—and what we really mean when we refer to psychobiological modeling—is that investigators have within their repertoire of understanding the full spectrum of explanation and the facility (and willingness) to move between them as occasion demands. To take an example, a debate about vulnerability to psychological disorder might well draw heavily on biologically based theories of temperament but with a necessity to shift to the language of cognitive psychology to discuss the psychological mechanisms of symptom formation and maintenance.

The need for this interdisciplinary mentality is particularly evident in the case of the personality disorders, whose uniquely psychobiological nature must surely strike even the casual observer. On the one hand, they present a behavioral disturbance and emotional and cognitive dyscontrol of such severity as to seem endogenously rooted in the nervous system, tempting us to look only there for an explanation. On the other hand, their deviance contains a quality which, however fleetingly, we understand and feel to be within our psychological reach. Whichever stance we take is complicated by a further feature of the personality disorders, one that tends to set them apart from other psychological conditions. Mostly the psychiatric patient suffers and attracts our sympathy. But patients with personality disorders make others suffer; they evoke the anger and rejection, even of professionals (Lewis & Appleby, 1988). Given that the scientific endeavor always to a degree mirrors society's attitudes, this has special consequences for how as researchers we are inclined to construe the behavior. If taken to be merely aberrant examples of the human condition personality disordered individuals will be judged as such, responsible for their actions and lacking the protection of the label of illness; seen as victims of neurological impairment, their behavior will be morally neutralized but their personal integrity eroded. This is the classic "madness or badness" dilemma in psychiatry, exacerbated in this case by the fact that the alternatives are closer together than usual and less easy to distinguish objectively from each other. For this reason alone, the personality disorders deserve the special attention of psychobiology.

REFERENCES

Af Klinteberg, B., Humble, K., & Schalling, D. (1992). Personality and psychopathy of males with a history of early criminal behavior. *European Journal of Personality*, *6*, 245–266.

American Psychiatric Association. (1994). *Diagnostic and statistical manual of mental disorders* (4th ed.) Washington, DC: American Psychiatric Association.

Beck, A. T., Freeman, A., & Associates. (1990). *Cognitive therapy of personality disorders*. New York: The Guilford Press.

Blakemore, C., & Greenfield, S. (Eds.). (1987). *Mindwaves*. Oxford: Blackwell.

Blankstein, K. R. (1975). The sensation seeker and anxiety reactivity: Relationships between Sensation Seeking scales and the Activity Preference Questionnaire. *Journal of Clinical Psychology*, *31*, 677–681.

Blankstein, K. R. (1976). Relationships between Spielberger trait anxiety and Lykken social and physical trait anxiety. *Journal of Clinical Psychology*, *32*, 781–782.

Buss, A. H., & Plomin, R. (1984). *Temperament: Early developing personality traits.* Hillsdale, NJ: Lawrence Erlbaum Associates.

Cawley, R. H. (1993). Psychiatry is more than a science. *British Journal of Psychiatry*, *162*, 154–160.

Chamove, A. S., Eysenck, H. J., & Harlow, H. (1972). Factor analysis of rhesus social behaviour. *Quarterly Journal of Experimental Psychology*, *24*, 496–504.

Chapman, L. J., & Chapman, J. P. (1980). Scales for rating psychotic and psychotic-like experiences as continua. *Schizophrenia Bulletin, 6,* 476–489.

Chapman, L. J., Chapman, J. P., & Miller, E. N. (1982). Reliabilities and interrelations of eight measures of proneness to psychosis. *Journal of Consulting and Clinical Psychology, 50,* 187–195.

Churchland, P. S. (1986). *Neurophilosophy.* Cambridge, Mass.: The MIT Press.

Claridge, G. (1994). A single indicator or risk for schizophrenia: Probable fact or likely myth? *Schizophrenia Bulletin, 20,* 151–168.

Claridge, G. (1985). *Origins of mental illness.* Oxford: Blackwell.

Claridge, G. (1967). *Personality and arousal.* Oxford: Pergamon Press.

Claridge, G. (1981). Psychoticism. In R. Lynn (Ed.), *Dimensions of personality. Papers in Honour of H. J. Eysenck.* Oxford: Pergamon Press.

Claridge, G. (1983). The Eysenck Psychoticism Scale. In J. N. Butcher & C. D. Spielberger (Eds.),*Advances in Personality Assessment* (Vol. 2). Hillsdale, NJ: Lawrence Erlbaum Associates.

Claridge, G., & Beech, A. R. (1994). Fully and quasi-dimensional constructions of schizotypy. In A. Raine, T. Lencz, & S. Mednick (Eds.), *Schizotypal Personality.* Cambridge: Cambridge University Press.

Claridge, G., & Broks, P. (1984). Schizotypy and hemisphere function-I. Theoretical considerations and the measurement of schizotypy. *Personality and Individual Differences, 5,* 633–648.

Clark, D. M. (1986). A cognitive approach to panic. *Behavior Research and Therapy, 24,* 461–470.

Cleckley, H. (1976). *The Mask of Sanity.* (5th Ed.). St. Louis, MO: The C. V. Mosby Company.

Costa, P. T., Jr., & McCrae, R. R. (1992). Four ways five factors are basic. *Personality and Individual Differences, 13,* 653–665.

Crow, T. J. (Ed.). (1987). *Recurrent and chronic psychoses.* British Medical Bulletin, Vol. 43. Edinburgh: Churchill Livingstone.

Eysenck, H. J. (1957). *Dynamics of anxiety and hysteria.* London: Routledge and Kegan Paul.

Eysenck, H. J. (1952a). Schizothymia-cyclothymia as a dimension of personality. II. Experimental. *Journal of Personality, 20,* 345–384.

Eysenck, H. J. (1967). *The biological basis of personality.* Springfield, IL: Charles C. Thomas.

Eysenck, H. J. (1952b). *The scientific study of personality.* London: Routledge & Kegan Paul.

Eysenck, H. J., & Eysenck, M. W. (1985). *Personality and individual differences.* New York: Plenum Press.

Eysenck, H. J., & Eysenck, S. B. G. (1975). *Manual of the Eysenck Personality Questionnaire.* London: Hodder & Stoughton.

Eysenck, H. J., & Eysenck, S. B. G. (1976). *Psychoticism as a dimension of personality.* London: Hodder & Stoughton.

Eysenck, S. B. G., Eysenck, H. J., & Barrett, P. (1985). A revised version of the psychoticism scale. *Personality and Individual Differences, 6,* 21–29.

Foulds, G. A. (1965). *Personality and personal illness.* London: Tavistock.

Foulds, G. A. (1971). Personality deviance and personal symptomatology. *Psychological Medicine, 1,* 222–233.

Golden, R. R., & Meehl, P. E. (1979). Detection of the schizoid taxon with MMPI indicators. *Journal of Abnormal Psychology, 88,* 217–233.

Gray, J. A. (1973). Causal theories of personality and how to test them. In J. R. Royce (Ed.), *Multivariate analysis and psychological theory.* London: Academic Press.

Gray, J. A. (1964). *Pavlov's typology*. Oxford: Pergamon Press.

Gray, J. A. (1982). *The neuropsychology of anxiety*. Oxford: Oxford University Press.

Gruzelier, J. H. (1991). Hemisphere imbalance: syndromes of schizophrenia, premorbid personality, neurodevelopmental influences. In S. R. Steinhauer, J. H. Gruzelier, & J. Zubin (Eds.), *Handbook of schizophrenia, Vol. 5: Neuropsychology, psychophysiology and information Processing*. London: Elsevier.

Hare, R. D. (1978). Electrodermal and cardiovascular correlates of psychopathy. In R. D. Hare & D. Schalling (Eds.), *Psychopathic behavior*. Chichester: John Wiley.

Hare, R. D. (1965). Temporal gradient of fear arousal in psychopaths. *Journal of Abnormal Psychology, 70*, 442–445.

Hare, R. D., & Jutai, J. W. (1988). Psychopathy and cerebral asymmetry in semantic processing. *Personality and Individual Differences, 9*, 329–337.

Hundleby, J. D., & Rossm, B. E. (1977). Comparison of measures of psychopathy. *Journal of Consulting and Clinical Psychology, 45*, 702–703.

ICD-10 Classification of Mental and Behavioural Disorders (1992). Geneva: World Health Organization.

Kendell, R. E., & Brockington, I. F. (1980). The identification of disease entities and the relationship between schizophrenic and affective psychoses. *British Journal of Psychiatry, 137*, 324–331.

Lacey, J. I. (1967). Somatic response patterning and stress: Some revisions of activation theory. In N. H. Appley & R. Trumbell (Eds), *Psychological stress: Issues in research*. New York: Appleton-Century Crofts.

Lewis, G., & Appleby, L. (1988). Personality disorder: The patients psychiatrists dislike. *British Journal of Psychiatry, 153*, 44–49.

Lykken, D. T. (1957). A study of anxiety in the sociopathic personality. *Journal of Abnormal and Social Psychology, 55*, 6–10.

Lykken, D. T., Tellegen, A., & Katzenmeyer, C. (1973). *Manual of the Activity Preference Questionnaire*. Department of Psychiatry, University of Minnesota.

Mangan, G. (1982). *The biology of human conduct*. Oxford: Pergamon Press.

Meehl, P. E. (1962). Schizotaxia, schizotypy, and schizophrenia. *American Psychologist, 17*, 827–838.

Meehl, P. E. (1990). Toward an integrated theory of schizotaxia, schizotypy, and schizophrenia. *Journal of Personality Disorders, 4*, 1–99.

Montgomery, S. A. (Ed.). (1992). Obsessive compulsive disorder. *International Clinical Psychopharmacology*, Vol. 7, Supplement 1.

Montgomery, S. A. (1993). *Psychopharmacology of panic*. British Association for Psychopharmacology Monographs, No 12. Oxford University Press.

Nielsen, T. C., & Petersen, N. E. (1976). Electrodermal correlates of extraversion, trait anxiety, and schizophrenism. *Scandinavian Journal of Psychology, 17*, 73–80.

Nutt, D., & Lawson, C. (1992). Panic attacks. A neurochemical overview of models and mechanisms. *British Journal of Psychiatry, 160*, 165–178.

Plomin, R. (1986). *Development, genetics, and psychology*. Hillsdale, NJ: Lawrence Erlbaum Associates.

Plomin, R., & Dunn, J. (Eds.) (1986). *The study of temperament: Changes, continuities and challenges*. Hillsdale, NJ: Lawrence Erlbaum Associates.

Quay, H. C. (1965). Psychopathic personality as pathological stimulation-seeking. *American Journal of Psychiatry, 149*, 180–183.

Rachman, S., & Hodgson, R. (1980). *Obsessions and compulsions*. Englewood Cliffs, NJ: Prentice-Hall.

Raine, A. (1987). Effect of early environment on electrodermal and cognitive correlates of schizotypy and psychopathy in criminals. *International Journal of Psychophysiology, 4,* 277–287.

Raine, A. (1986). Psychopathy, schizoid personality and borderline/schizotypal personality disorder. *Personality and Individual Differences, 7,* 493–501.

Raine, A., & Venables, P. H. (1984). Electrodermal non-responding, antisocial behaviour, and schizoid tendencies in adolescents. *Psychophysiology, 21,* 424–432.

Raine, A., Lencz, T., & Mednick, S. (Eds.). (1994). *Schizotypal personality.* Cambridge: Cambridge University Press.

Roberts, G. W. (1991). Schizophrenia: A neuropathological perspective. *British Journal of Psychiatry, 158,* 8–17.

Salkovskis, P. M. (1985). Obsessional-compulsive problems: A cognitive-behavioural analysis. *Behaviour Research and Therapy, 23,* 571–583.

Sass, L. A. (1992). *Madness and modernism.* New York: Basic Books.

Schizophrenia Bulletin (1989). Issue theme: Subjective experiences of schizophrenia and related disorders. *15,* 177–337.

Siever, L. J., Kalus, O. F., & Keefe, R. S. E. (1993). The boundaries of schizophrenia. *Psychiatric Clinics of North America, 16,* 217–244.

Stone, M. H. (1980). *The borderline syndromes.* New York: McGraw-Hill.

Strelau, J. (Ed.). (1985). *Temperamental bases of behaviour: Warsaw studies of individual differences.* Lisse: Swets & Zeitlinger.

Strelau, J., & Eysenck, H. J. (Eds.) (1987). *Personality dimensions and arousal.* New York: Plenum Press.

Taylor, M. A. (1992). Are schizophrenia and affective disorder related? A selective literature review. *American Journal of Psychiatry, 149,* 22–32.

Venables, P. H. (1973). Input regulation and psychopathology. In M. Hammer, K. Salzinger, & S. Sutton (Eds.), *Psychopathology.* New York: Wiley.

Venables, P. H., Mednick, S. A., Schulsinger, F., Raman, A. C., Bell, B., Dalais, C., & Fletcher, R. P. (1978). Screening for risk of mental illness. In G. Serban (Ed.), *Cognitive defects in the development of mental illness.* New York: Brunner/Mazel.

Venables, P. H., Wilkins, S., Mitchell, D. A., Raine, A., & Bailes, K. (1990). A scale for the measurement of schizotypy. *Personality and Individual Differences, 11,* 481–495.

Williams, J. M. G. (1992). *The psychological treatment of depression.* (2nd ed.). London: Routledge.

Williamson, S. E., Harpur, T. J., & Hare, R. D. (1991). Abnormal processing of affective words by psychopaths. *Psychophysiology, 28,* 260–273.

Willner, P. (1985). *Depression.* New York: John Wiley.

Zuckerman, M. (1989). Personality in the third dimension: A psychobiological approach. *Personality and Individual Differences, 10,* 391–418.

Zuckerman, M. (1979). *Sensation seeking.* New York: Wiley.

Zuckerman, M. (1973). Sensation seeking and psychopathy. In R. D. Hare & D. Schalling (Eds.) *Psychopathic Behavior.* Chichester: John Wiley.

8

Normal Versus Abnormal Personality from the Perspective of the *DSM*

Thomas A. Widiger and
Elizabeth M. Corbitt

The purpose of this chapter is to discuss the distinction between normal and abnormal personality from the perspective of the American Psychiatric Association's (APA) *Diagnostic and Statistical Manual of Mental Disorders* (*DSM*). Our discussion will refer in particular to the third revised edition (*DSM-III-R*; APA, 1987) but we will also consider any changes or lack of changes to the fourth edition (*DSM-IV*; Task Force on *DSM-IV*, 1993). We will use the notation of *DSM-III-R(IV)* to refer to both editions. We will discuss in particular the *DSM-III-R(IV)* definition of a personality disorder and whether the threshold for diagnosis is consistent with this definition.

DSM-III-R(IV) PERSONALITY DISORDER DIAGNOSIS

It is stated in *DSM-III-R* that it is "when personality traits are inflexible and maladaptive and cause either significant functional impairment or subjective distress that they constitute Personality Disorders" (1987, p. 335). One can readily find a number of technical faults with this definition (Wakefield, 1992, 1993). However, it is likely that no infallible definition could ever be provided (Frances, Widiger, & Sabshin, 1991). Mental and personality disorders are hypothetical constructs that can not be reduced to a simple set of explicit observables (Widiger & Trull, 1991). The *DSM-III-R(IV)* definition of a personality disorder is at least a reasonable effort. The presence of a personality disorder is indicated when personality traits result in either significant social or occupational impairment or distress.

What is problematic for the *DSM-III-R(IV)* is the failure of the individual personality disorder diagnoses to be consistent with this definition. *DSM-III-R(IV)* diagnoses are not made at the point at which a personality trait becomes inflexible, maladaptive, or results in significant impairment or distress. The thresholds identify instead that point at which the number of features would be close enough to a prototypic case of a distinct type of personality disorder (PD) to warrant giving that particular diagnosis. Having fewer than four of the criteria for an avoidant PD did not appear to the *DSM-III-R* personality disorder Advisory Committee to be sufficiently close to a prototypic avoidant patient to warrant an avoidant PD diagnosis (Widiger, Frances, Spitzer, & Williams, 1988). Failing to meet this threshold does not necessarily imply an absence of maladaptive avoidant traits. A person who did not have four of the features but did have no close friends or confidants, was easily hurt by criticism or disapproval, and was unwilling to get involved with people unless certain of being liked would clearly have maladaptive avoidant traits that were resulting in social dysfunction and/or personal distress.

The presence of maladaptive avoidant, dependent, or borderline traits in persons who fail to meet the thresholds for these (and other) PD diagnoses is problematic empirically and clinically (McGlashan, 1987; Overholser, 1991). McGlashan, for example, was researching the comorbidity of borderline PD and depression, and he needed a comparison group of depressives without borderline personality disorder. He naturally used the *DSM-III* criteria for borderline PD and classified those who failed to meet these criteria as lacking the disorder. However, these persons had on average three *DSM-III* borderline features. "In short, the 'pure' . . . cohort was not pure" (McGlashan, 1987, p. 472). They did have borderline personality disorder pathology. As a result, they failed to be substantially different from the diagnosed borderlines. "Our comparison groups, although defined to be categorically exclusive, may not have been all that different" (p. 472).

Skodol (1989) made the same point with respect to clinical practice. Clinicians at the Columbia-Presbyterian Medical Center have observed avoidant, histrionic, compulsive, and other PD traits playing a significant role in treatment approach, course, and outcome in persons who failed to meet the *DSM-III-R* diagnostic criteria for the respective disorders. They therefore implemented a scaling system whereby these traits would be rated in those who failed to meet the *DSM-III-R* thresholds for diagnosis. "Using this system, we found that, in addition to the approximately 50% of clinic patients who meet criteria for a personality disorder, another 35% warrant information descriptive of their personality styles on Axis II" (Skodol, 1989, p. 386).

Should a clinician then diagnose the presence of avoidant personality disorder in persons who have just one of the avoidant criteria? The answer is perhaps no, given the purpose of the diagnostic criteria within the *DSM-III-R(IV)* categorical system. Diagnosing the presence of each of the individual PDs when only one feature is present could have the effect of providing six, seven, and even more PD diagnoses to most of one's patients. The average inpatient can meet the criteria for three or four PD diagnoses, using the *DSM-III-R* thresholds of four or more features (e.g., Skodol, Rosnick, Kellman, Oldham, & Hyler, 1988; Widiger, Trull, Hurt, Clarkin, & Frances, 1987; Zanarini, Frankenburg, Chauncey, & Gunderson, 1987). Imagine the number of diagnoses that would be given if the thresholds were reduced to just one maladaptive personality trait.

From the perspective of the *DSM-III-R(IV)* categorical model, it is desirable to give only one PD diagnosis per patient, or at most just two or three (Gunderson, 1992; Oldham et al., 1992). Beyond this number, the diagnoses become clinically confusing and theoretically meaningless (Widiger & Sanderson, in press). However, the *DSM-III-R* categorical system has not been successful in identifying which particular PD diagnosis should be given because many patients will meet the criteria for many PD diagnoses (Oldham et al., 1992). This was of substantial concern to the *DSM-IV* Personality Disorders Work Group (Gunderson, 1992). Options considered for *DSM-IV* were to raise the thresholds for diagnosis or to implement a hierarchical system whereby a few of the PDs (e.g., borderline) would trump the others (e.g., avoidant). The PD Work Group rejected these options (Widiger & Sanderson, in press), deciding instead to make it more difficult to meet the criteria for the individual symptoms and to make these symptoms more specific to a respective PD. For example, the *DSM-III-R* avoidant criterion of being reticent in social situations because of a fear of saying something inappropriate or foolish was revised to a restraint within intimate relationships due to the fear of being shamed or ridiculed, and being easily hurt by criticism or disapproval was revised to being preoccupied with being criticized or rejected in social situations. However, it is unlikely that *DSM-IV* will be any more successful than *DSM-III-R* in providing only one or two PD diagnoses per patient, and it will continue to fail to describe those persons with clinically significant maladaptive personality traits who fall below the arbitrary thresholds for diagnosis.

PERSONALITY DISORDER
NOT OTHERWISE SPECIFIED

There is a personality disorder diagnosis for when there are "features of more than one specific Personality Disorder that do not meet the full criteria for any one, yet cause significant impairment in social or occupational functioning, or subjective distress" (APA, 1987, p. 358). In *DSM-III*, this diagnosis was given the name of mixed personality disorder (the term mixed was deleted in *DSM-III-R* to minimize confusion with multiple personality disorder). The code number for this disorder is 301.90 (Personality Disorder, Not Otherwise Specified; PDNOS).

PDNOS can also be used for persons who have a personality disorder that is not officially recognized within the *DSM*. Options suggested in *DSM-III-R* included immature, impulsive, self-defeating, and sadistic (APA, 1987), but clinicians are free to use PDNOS for any personality disorder diagnosis they consider to be "appropriate" (APA, 1987, p. 358), including the pleonexic (Nikelly, 1992), racist (Hamlin, 1990), depressive (Phillips, Gunderson, Hirschfeld, & Smith, 1990), malovelent (Hurlbert & Apt, 1992), delusional-dominating (Pantony & Caplan, 1991), hyperthymic (Akiskal & Akiskal, 1992), and nonforgetannia (Farmer, Feldhous, Pelphrey, & Woods, 1992), as well as the sadistic and self-defeating (Cooper, 1993; Widiger et al., 1988).

It is stated in the introduction to the *DSM-III-R* that Axis II can also "be used to indicate specific personality traits . . . when no Personality Disorder exists" (APA, 1987, pp. 16–17). For example, one can indicate the presence of histrionic personality traits in persons who have just a few of the criteria for the histrionic PD. However, no code number would be provided "since a code number indicates a Personality Disorder" (APA, 1987, p. 17) and a person who fails to meet the *DSM-III-R* threshold for a diagnosis of histrionic PD would not have a histrionic PD. Nevertheless, the authors of *DSM-III-R* have actually suggested using PDNOS precisely for this purpose. For example, it was suggested in the *DSM-III-R Casebook* (Spitzer, Gibbon, Skodol, Williams, & First, 1989) that persons who are below the threshold for a specific PD be given the diagnosis of PDNOS.

> This woman's long-term functioning is characterized by excessive emotionality and attention-seeking; in her relationships with people she is vain, demanding, and dependent. These features suggest the additional diagnosis of Histrionic Personality Disorder. However, there is insufficient information about other symptoms of the disorder, such as inappropriate seductiveness and overconcern about physical attractiveness, to make this diagnosis. We therefore would add the diagnosis of Personality Disorder Not Otherwise Specified (with histrionic features). (Spitzer et al., 1989, p. 64)

The inclusion of PDNOS for persons who fail to meet the criteria for an officially recognized PD is an acknowledgment that persons who are below the diagnostic thresholds can have a personality disorder. The clinician is encouraged to give a diagnosis of a personality disorder (PDNOS) when the person fails to meet the criteria for any specific PD but (a) has features for more than one *DSM-III-R(IV)* PD, (b) has multiple features for just one of the *DSM-III-R(IV)* PDs, or (c) has maladaptive personality traits not included within the *DSM-III-R(IV)* nomenclature. PDNOS (mixed, atypical, or other) has in fact been the most prevalent personality disorder diagnosis in many studies (e.g., Fabrega, Ulrich, Pilkonis, & Mezzich, 1991; Kass, Skodol, Charles, Spitzer, & Williams, 1985; Koenigsberg, Kaplan, Gilmore, & Cooper, 1985; Loranger, 1990; Morey, 1988; Zimmerman & Coryell, 1989), occurring with more frequency than even the borderline personality disorder. The prevalence and popularity of PDNOS indicates clearly that the boundary between normal and abnormal personality bears little relationship to the presence versus absence of the 11 specific PDs (10 in *DSM-IV*; Task Force on *DSM-IV*, 1993).

NORMATIVE MALADAPTIVITY

Data on the prevalence of *DSM-III-R* personality disorder symptomatology within the normal population is very limited (Merikangas & Weissman, 1986; Weissman, 1993). The influential and often-cited National Institute of Mental Health (NIMH) Epidemiologic Catchment Area (ECA) study included only the antisocial personality disorder (APD). Lifetime prevalence rates for APD varied from 2.1% to 3.4% across ECA sites (Robins et al., 1984). Based largely on these data, it was stated in the *DSM-III-R* that "the estimate of the prevalence of Antisocial Personality Disorder among American males is about 3%, and for American females, less than 1%" (APA, 1987, p. 343). However, Robins, Tipp, and Przybeck (1991) indicated that the federal government "refused approval of questions about illegal occupations, such as fencing stolen goods, pimping, prostitution, and selling drugs, about infidelity and promiscuity, about financial irresponsibility, and about age at first sexual intercourse" (p. 262). In addition, two sites excluded questions concerning child abuse due to concerns regarding legal implications. The sites were therefore handicapped in assessing for APD symptomatology. The St. Louis site included the banned items by adding them to a 30-minute discretionary section not sponsored by the government. "When the banned questions were added, the St. Louis rate rose to 5.1%, an increase of 53%" (Robins et al., 1991, p. 262). Using the results obtained in the St. Louis site to correct for the truncated estimates obtained elsewhere, Robins et al. estimated the U.S. lifetime prevalence for APD to be 1% in females and 7.3% in males, a prevalence estimate substantially higher than provided in *DSM-III-R*.

Nestadt et al. (1990) provided data on the prevalence of histrionic personality disorder (HPD) symptomatology within the Baltimore ECA site, conducting two-stage interviews of 759 subjects (the assessments were again constrained by an inability to consider all of the HPD criteria). *DSM-III* HPD was diagnosed in only 2.1% of the subjects, but approximately 1.5% of the remaining subjects had six maladaptive histrionic traits, 2% had five, about 1% had four, approximately 4% had three, 4% had two, and 10% had one maladaptive histrionic trait. In other words, approximately 22.5% additional persons had at least one clinically significant maladaptive histrionic trait. Nestadt et al. (1991) conducted a similar analysis for five *DSM-III* compulsive PD (CPD) symptoms (perfectionism, stubbornness, indecision, excessive work devotion, and emotional constriction). Only 1.7% of the eastern Baltimore population was estimated to be diagnosed with *DSM-III* CPD based on their algorithm but 50% had at least one CPD trait. If one considers the most extreme level of rating (coded "severe") as suggesting a clinically significant level of maladaptivity, then 8% were assessed to be maladaptively perfectionistic, 12% were obsessively stubborn, 4% displayed severe emotional constriction, and 4% were excessively devoted to their work. Nestadt, Romanoski, Samuels, Folstein, & McHugh (1992) conducted the analysis for 21 APD features. Only 1.5% of the population met the algorithm for a *DSM-III* APD diagnosis but

14% had six or more features and 24% had at least one feature. The authors concluded that the *DSM-III* PD diagnoses underestimate substantially the rate of maladaptive personality traits within the general population.

Maier, Lichtermann, Klingler, Heun, and Hallmayer (1992) administered the Structured Clinical Interview for *DSM-III-R* Personality Disorders (SCID) to 109 community control probands, 57 of their mates, and 286 of their relatives. Ten percent met the *DSM-III-R* criteria for at least one PD. Zimmerman and Coryell (1989) administered the Structured Interview for *DSM-III* Personality Disorders (SIDP) to 797 relatives of normal controls and relatives of patients. Fourteen percent met the criteria for at least one *DSM-III* personality disorder. An additional 4% (29 persons) met their stringent criteria for a mixed personality disorder (only one symptom short of two or more personality disorders).

Neither Maier et al. (1992) nor Zimmerman and Coryell (1989) reported how many of the remaining "normal" persons had at least one feature of at least one personality disorder. Coryell and Zimmerman (1989) reported the mean number of PD symptoms assessed in each group of relatives (e.g., relatives of a schizophrenic proband, depressed proband, or normal proband). The average number of PD symptoms in the 185 relatives of the normal probands was 9.2 (SD=7.8), which is more than enough to meet the *DSM-III*(-R) criteria for a mixed personality disorder. Zimmerman and Coryell (1990b) subsequently reported the distribution of scores for each of the *DSM-III* PDs. For example, 60% of the ostensibly normal relatives had at least one antisocial feature; 61% had at least one histrionic feature; and 96% had at least one avoidant trait (this last figure, however, might include the *DSM-III* avoidant trait of desiring the affection or acceptance of others, which is not maladaptive). Zimmerman and Coryell did not report the number of subjects who failed to have at least one PD symptom across all of the PDs, but given the rate for each PD it was probably a very small minority (if any at all).

In addition, most of the SIDP assessments in the Zimmerman studies were done rather quickly by phone. Additional symptomatology would have been evident if the assessments had been more thorough. Zimmerman and Coryell (1990a) administered the Personality Diagnostic Questionnaire (PDQ; Hyler, Skodol, Kellman, Oldham, & Rosnick, 1990), a self-report measure of the *DSM-III* PD symptomatology, to 697 of the community subjects. More subjects were diagnosed with a PD using the SIDP than with the PDQ (13.5% vs 10.3%, p < .05) but the mean number of symptoms was statistically significantly higher for each one of the individual PDs when assessed by the PDQ. Johnson and Bornstein (1992) reported substantial rates for many of the PDs in an ostensibly normal sample of college students using conservative PDQ-R thresholds for diagnosis (e.g., 27% compulsive, 19% narcissistic, 30% borderline, and 13% avoidant). There are many studies to indicate that PD assessments are inflated with self-report measures (Loranger, 1992), but this is less problematic in "normal" subjects who lack substantial anxiety and mood disorder (Trull, 1993).

Zimmerman, Pfohl, Coryell, Stangl, and Corenthal (1988) have also indicated that SIDP interviews with a close friend or relative of the subject will identify additional PD symptomatology. This "informant" will be aware of additional insecurities, failings, and flaws that are not evident to or acknowledged by the subject. In an assessment of 66 depressed patients by Zimmerman et al., 36.4% were diagnosed with a PD based on a SIDP interview with the patient and 57.6% based on a SIDP interview with an informant. The final consensus assessment based on the data from both sources resulted in a prevalence rate of 65.2%, substantially higher than the prevalence of 36.4% based on the interview with just the patient.

Finally, it should also be noted that the Zimmerman studies were confined to the *DSM-III* taxonomy, which is hardly exhaustive or comprehensive in the sampling of maladaptive personality traits (e.g., Akiskal & Akiskal, 1992; Cooper, 1993; Hurlbert & Apt, 1992; Kiesler, 1986; Livesley, 1986; Nikelly, 1992; Pantony & Caplan, 1991; Phillips, Gunderson, Hirschfeld, & Smith, 1990; Widiger et al., 1988). In sum, it is evident that a thorough and comprehensive assessment of an ostensibly normal and healthy individual might identify at least one significant maladaptive personality trait. It would be of interest in future studies to determine systematically the extent to which normal persons actually lack any maladaptive personality traits.

The suggestion that all or most persons have maladaptive personality traits might appear on first blush to be ludicrous, but it may in fact be the case that each person has an Achilles heel, an area in which optimal functioning is hindered by the predominant personality traits. Any particular personality trait could be maladaptive within some particular situation or context. To the extent that a person's behavior is entirely flexible and adaptive to whatever situations arise, one might question the extent to which that person has a characteristic behavior pattern (Mischel, 1984).

Optimal personality functioning may represent an ideal that is achieved by no one, analogous to optimal physical functioning. "Health is a state of complete physical, mental, and social well-being, and not merely the absence of disease or infirmity" (World Health Organization, 1964, p. 1). There is no person who is entirely physically healthy throughout the lifetime or perhaps even at any one point in time. Everybody has and will continue to suffer from a variety of physical disorders and is probably currently hindered by at least one chronic physical impairment or disorder (e.g., myopia, allergies, herpes, or asthma).

Neuroticism is "the general tendency to experience negative affects such as fear, sadness, embarrassment, anger, guilt, and disgust" (Costa & McCrae, 1992, p. 14) and it is one of the more replicable and validated dimensions of normal personality (McCrae & Costa, 1990; Watson & Clark, 1984). "The most pervasive domain of personality . . . contrasts adjustment or emotional stability with maladjustment or neuroticism" (Costa & McCrae, 1992, p. 14). Persons who are beyond the *DSM-III-R(IV)* thresholds for a PD diagnosis will be characterized by a high degree of neuroticism, but persons at the normal or average level of neuroticism are not without neuroticism. Average neuroticism involves a degree of vulnerability, self-consciousness, and dysphoria (Costa & McCrae, 1992). Normal neuroticism is not normal in the sense of ideal health (or lacking any ill health), it is normal in the statistical (normative) sense of representing a common or average level of impairment and distress.

It is curious that we accept that we will suffer throughout our lives from many physical disorders and that our everyday functioning is hindered by chronic limitations and impairments, but we are very reluctant to acknowledge comparable dysfunctions and impairments in our psychosocial functioning. This "I'm O.K., you're O.K." mentality may reflect in part the stigmatization of mental illness. Seeing a doctor for a physical disorder is not usually an embarrassment or a threat to one's respect and esteem, but this is not the case with seeing a therapist for a mental disorder. Pehaps the concept of mental disorder implies to many the most severe variants (e.g., schizophrenia), as if seeing a doctor for a physical disorder implied that one had cancer or AIDS. The *DSM-III-R(IV)* contributes to this stigmatization by attempting to demarcate a boundary between mental disorders and normality at a point such that only a minority of the population would be diagnosable (Schacht, 1985).

CLINICALLY SIGNIFICANT MALADAPTIVITY

In the *DSM-III-R* definition of a personality disorder, it is stated that the impairment is "significant" (1987, p. 335), and in the definition of mental disorder it is stated that it involves a "clinically significant" (1987, p. xxii) syndrome or behavior pattern. Within the criteria sets for many of the disorders in *DSM-III-R* (and for more in *DSM-IV*) it is stated that the behavior pattern causes significant or marked impairment.

The purpose of these specifiers is to help establish the threshold when the symptomatic presentation is not clearly pathological (Task Force on *DSM-IV*, 1993). Presumably, the impairment should not be inconsequential, minor, or trivial. However, *DSM-III-R* and *DSM-IV* includes a mild level of impairment when the "symptoms result in no more than minor impairment in social or occupational functioning" (Task Force on *DSM-IV*, 1993, p. B:2). Apparently, only a minor impairment is actually sufficient for a mental disorder diagnosis. In fact, some diagnoses in *DSM-III-R(IV)* require no impairment and no distress. For example, a diagnosis of transvestic fetishism is made if a person has recurrent intense sexual urges and sexually arousing fantasies involving cross-dressing and has acted on these urges over a period of at least six months (1987, p. 289). A man who is experiencing no impairment in social or occupational functioning (e.g., has a fully satisfying marriage with a spouse who approves of and perhaps even enjoys the cross-dressing) and is fully comfortable with the cross-dressing (e.g., willfully cross-dresses in the privacy of his home) would meet the *DSM-III-R* (and *DSM-*

IV) criteria for a mental disorder as long as he engaged in the act for more than six months. One might presume that some degree of distress or impairment would be associated with cross-dressing for longer than six months, but aberrant sexual preferences can be ego-syntonic and within the control of the participant.

DSM-III-R and *DSM-IV* also fail to explain what is meant by "clinically significant." Spitzer and Williams (1982) defined the clinically significant threshold as that point at which the attention of a clinician was indicated: "there are many behavioral or psychological conditions that can be considered 'pathological' but the clinical manifestations of which are so mild that clinical attention is not indicated" (p. 19). Three examples were given: caffeine withdrawal, jet lag syndrome, and insomnia due to environmental noise. All three may represent pathological conditions but they "would not be justified as syndromes that were clinically significant to mental health professionals" (Spitzer & Williams, 1982, p. 20). Persons do not seek or need the intervention of a clinician for their treatment. However, it is of interest to note that jet lag syndrome was subsequently included in *DSM-III-R* (as a variant of sleep-wake schedule disorder; APA, 1987, p. 306) and a strong case was made for the inclusion of caffeine withdrawal in *DSM-IV* (Hughes, Oliveto, Helzer, Higgins, & Bickel, 1992).

Wakefield (1992) criticized the concept of clinical significance as providing a tautological definition (i.e., mental disorders are those conditions treated by a clinician). "A correct definition of disorder must classify every pathological condition as a disorder whether or not the condition is currently an object of professional attention. Otherwise, . . . it becomes impossible to argue that a condition for which people do not now seek clinical help is in fact a disorder" (Wakefield, 1992, p. 234). Spitzer and Williams (1982), however, were not defining clinical significance as those conditions that are receiving clinical attention but rather as a level of impairment that warrants clinical attention. A condition that warrants attention need not currently be an object of professional attention.

A level of impairment that does not warrant the attention of a clinician is perhaps too low to warrant a clinical diagnosis of a mental disorder. Some impairments are so trivial and inconsequential that it is perhaps meaningless to consider them to represent disorders. However, there are a variety of interpretations for the warranting of clinical attention. Each is viable, and each has different implications for a threshold. Four that we will discuss are (a) impairment for which treatment by a clinician would be beneficial, (b) impairment for which treatment by a clinician would be necessary, (c) impairment for which treatment is necessary, and (d) impairment for which treatment is desirable.

Treatment by a Clinician Would Be Beneficial

It is reasonable to suggest that a level of impairment that warrants clinical attention (and therefore a diagnosis) is one for which treatment of the condition would be beneficial. If treatment would help to ameliorate an impairment and thereby increase level of functioning, then treatment by a clinician would certainly be warranted.

A difficulty with this threshold for a *DSM-III-R(IV)* diagnosis is that it would apply to just about any maladaptive personality trait. It would be difficult to find a person who would not benefit from some form of psychotherapy. There may not be any person who is not hindered or impaired in some manner by his or her characteristic manner of behaving, thinking, and relating to others (Ellis, 1987; Freud, 1957). Everybody could be more flexible: either less passive or less asser- tive; more affectionate or less emotional; less dependent or less aloof; and so forth. Most anyone would meet this threshold.

Treatment by a Clinician Is Necessary

The threshold could be raised by requiring that treatment by a clinician is neces- sary for the amelioration of the impairment. Caffeine dependence does exist, but it was not included in *DSM-III-R* because one does not need the help or interven- tion of a clinician to overcome the dependence (Spitzer & Williams, 1982). It would be unusual for someone to seek the expertise of a clinical psychologist because they wanted to stop drinking coffee.

However, caffeine dependence is not inconsequential with respect to adaptive functioning and physical health (Hughes et al., 1992). If caffeine dependence is in fact a real disorder, perhaps it should be included within the manual. There are many physical disorders that also fail to need the intervention of a physician for their treatment (e.g., minor lacerations, colds, and influenza). The lack of a need for professional intervention does not make the condition normal (healthy). Fail- ing to include caffeine dependence in *DSM-IV* could suggest that it does not even exist. It would facilitate public recognition of the condition and public conscious- ness regarding mental and physical health if caffeine dependence was included.

In addition, the need for professional intervention does not really imply a more stringent threshold in the case of personality disorders. Persons will often need the expertise of clinicians for help in becoming less passive, submissive, antagonistic, or pessimistic, or more agreeable, conscientious, open, or affectionate. It is difficult to change one's personality, particularly when the impairment is mild (e.g., there are only minor costs or problems that are associated with the trait and therefore the reward or motivation for change is weak). People can make substantial changes to their personality without professional help, but this potential does not negate the fact that professional intervention can be very helpful and is often necessary.

Treatment Is Necessary

A more stringent threshold that could be commensurate with a *DSM-III-R(IV)* threshold for a personality disorder diagnosis is the level of impairment that re- sults in a need for professional intervention. It may be true that becoming more flexible, less passive, or less antagonistic would benefit most (or all) persons, but perhaps those persons with *DSM-III-R(IV)* personality disorders need professional intervention in order to obtain an adequate level of functioning, not just an improved level of functioning. Widiger and Trull (1991) suggested that "persons who are hindered in their ability to adapt flexibly to stress, to make optimal life decisions, to fulfill desired potentials, or to sustain meaningful or satisfying relationships . . . have a mental disorder" (p. 113). However, is it really necessary to always be making optimal life decisions or to fulfull all of one's potentials? Perhaps the persons with *DSM-III-R* mental disorders are not trying to grow, expand, or actualize; perhaps they are trying to survive.

The threshold of necessity, however, may only be useful for the clinical decision of hospitalization. Hospitalization is necessary if the person is suicidal and one makes the assumption that it is necessary to maintain physical survival. This assumption is defensible because the alternative is terminal and irreversible (although even the threshold of physical survival is debatable; Szasz, 1986; Widiger & Rinaldi, 1983). Beyond this point, it is never really certain that treatment is necessary. It is true that there is no necessity to fulfill all of one's potentials or to always be making optimal life decisions, but it is also unnecessary to obtain or maintain a relationship, to obtain or maintain employment, or to even enjoy life. There is no necessity to obtain and enjoy physical health. One can live with myopia, pain, or most any disability. It is not necessary to be free of pain, disability, and impairments, it is simply desirable.

It is common to have a patient ask if it is necessary to enter psychotherapy or to continue treatment beyond a certain point. There is never a certain or absolute answer to this question. There is always room for improvement and for additional progress (Freud, 1957). The question is not whether it is necessary to begin or to continue but whether it is sufficiently desirable or important enough to the person (and perhaps to others) to begin or to continue. Life can be sufficiently enjoyable or tolerable without a spouse, or with a disappointing, unfulfilling, or even abusive spouse; with a disappointing or unfulfilling job, or even without a job. To the extent that it is not necessary to fulfill one's potential in life or to make optimal life decisions, it is not necessary to obtain any particular level of functioning or to overcome any particular impairment.

Treatment Is Desirable

The threshold for impairment that is used by most persons who seek treatment is whether they desire to overcome whatever pathology or dysfunction is causing their distress and impairment. People will seek professional intervention when they are sufficiently distressed with their life that they desire a change and are unable to effect this change on their own. This threshold is consistent with the *DSM-III-R* and *DSM-IV* definition of a personality disorder as a maladaptive trait that causes "subjective distress" (1987, p. 335). However, the degree of impairment that is distressful or intolerable will vary across persons, and it will often bear little resemblance to the thresholds for the *DSM-III-R(IV)* PD diagnoses. Some persons who are distressed with their maladaptive submissiveness will be substantially below the threshold for a dependent personality disorder diagnosis, and some persons distressed with their social inhibition and introversion will be substantially below an avoidant personality disorder diagnosis. It would be appropriate to consider these persons as having clinically significant maladaptive personality traits (i.e., a personality disorder), but they could easily fail to meet the criteria for any *DSM-III-R* or *DSM-IV* PD diagnosis.

Desire for change and distress over the limitations or impairments of one's personality are not infallible indicators for the presence of a disorder. For example, a woman might seek professional assistance because her assertiveness results in vicious anger and abuse from her husband (Walker, 1987). She may already be excessively submissive and deferential, and yet wants the clinician to help her become an even more tolerant and forgiving spouse. In such a case, it would be desirable to help her become more assertive rather than more submissive.

An absence of distress or a desire for change will also fail to be infallible in suggesting the absence of any clinically significant impairment. Some persons may be significantly impaired by particular personality traits (e.g., mistrust, low empathy, antagonism, and anhedonia) but do not find them to be distressing. They may notice only the advantages that come from these traits (e.g., freedom from guilt and concern for others) and not the disadvantages (e.g., failure to sustain lasting relationships). These persons may be (appropriately and at times inappropriately) referred for treatment by someone else (e.g., by a spouse, employer, or the judicial system).

Because of the fallibility of distress and subjective desire, some have interpreted clinically significant impairment as that degree of impairment that a clinician would judge should be of concern to the person. Clinicians will often have more experience and knowledge regarding what is optimal, desirable, or adequate functioning. However, it is also clear that one would not want this judgment to be solely or essentially left to the clinician. Clinicians can be as mistaken and biased in their judgments as any other person.

AN ALTERNATIVE APPROACH

The *DSM-III-R(IV)* categorical system of diagnosis suggests that there is only a proportion of the population, perhaps even a small minority, that has a personality disorder. The rest of the population would be said to be free of clinically significant maladaptive traits. Perhaps a more realistic approach would be to provide a comprehensive description of the personality, and then assess precisely the manner and extent to which the respective personality traits are adaptive and/or maladaptive within the social and occupational context in which the person must function.

The same level of tough-minded antagonism that is maladaptive for a pastoral counselor could be adaptive for a police officer. *DSM-III-R* and *DSM-IV* fail to appreciate the adaptivity of the personality disorder traits. Authors have identified adaptive consequences for a variety of the *DSM-III-R* PDs, including the histrionic, compulsive, psychopathic, narcissistic, self-defeating, and even the borderline personality disorder (e.g., Leaf et al., 1990; Sutker, Bugg, & West, 1993; Walker, 1994). For example, the workaholism of the compulsive can be beneficial to career advancement at the same time that it is harmful to one's marital or familial relationships. This is particularly evident in the competitiveness and excessive achievement-striving of the Type A personality disorder (Garamoni & Schwartz, 1986). In other words, each personality style will have both adaptive and maladaptive consequences, and these can be understood only in the context of the person's aspirations, values, and social, occupational environment.

We would therefore suggest that a subject's personality be assessed comprehensively and independently of any presumed dysfunction. The Five-Factor model of personality, described in chapter 2 by McCrae, provides a particularly compelling alternative to the *DSM-IV* Axis II personality disorder diagnoses. The five factors of neuroticism, introversion vs extraversion, openness to experience, agreeableness vs antagonism, and conscientiousness have received substantial empirical support (Goldberg, 1993; McCrae & Costa, 1990; Wiggins & Pincus, 1992). The maladaptive traits that are contained within each of the *DSM-III-R(IV)* personality disorders are represented within this dimensional model, including (for example) the impulsivity, angry hostility, and depression of the borderline (neuroticism), the suspiciousness of the paranoid (antagonism), the anhedonia of the schizoid (introversion), the arrogance of the narcissist (antagonism), the submissiveness of the dependent (agreeableness), and the perfectionism, excessive discipline and organization, and workaholism of the compulsive (conscientiousness). A more complete and detailed explication of each *DSM-III-R* and *DSM-IV* personality disorder from the perspective of the Five-Factor model is presented in Widiger, Trull, Clarkin, Sanderson, & Costa (1994).

The Five-Factor model, however, goes beyond the *DSM-III-R(IV)* by being able to provide a quite specific description of each individual along the factors and facets of the five dimensions. Rather than try to summarize a personality by just one categorical label, such as schizoid, the Five-Factor model would provide a more precise description of the extent to which the person is low in warmth, positive emotions, and/or gregariousness. Rather than try to force a differential diagnosis between an avoidant and a schizoid personality disorder, the Five-Factor model would simply describe the extent to which the person who is elevated on facets of introversion (i.e., displays such schizoid traits as coldness, social withdrawal, and placidity) is also elevated on the facets of neuroticism (i.e., displays such avoidant traits as self-consciousness, anxiety, and vulnerability). It is apparent that persons do not come in neat, black–white categories; the most accurate and useful description of personality will be one that recognizes the various shades of grey (Widiger & Sanderson, in press). A Five-Factor description would also include not only traits that are likely to be maladaptive (e.g., excessive suspiciousness and arrogance) but also traits that are likely to be adaptive (e.g., openness to experience and assertiveness).

Once having described a personality from the perspective of the five factors, one would then assess the adaptivity and maladaptivity of the traits within the social, environmental context within which that person must function. One would inquire as to impairments in functioning that are likely to be associated with particular elevations (e.g., identify the specific nature of the vulnerability given an elevation on this facet of neuroticism, or assess for maladaptive gullibility, submissiveness, and acquiescence given a substantial elevation on agreeableness), and adaptive strengths that are likely to be assoociated with particular elevations (e.g., an openness to ideas that will be helpful in treatment, or evidence of warmth and agreeableness that can contribute to the resolution of marital conflicts).

To facilitate the assessment of maladaptivity, one might consider a systematic assessment of areas of dysfunction that commonly result from maladaptive personality traits. A potential instrument for such an assessment is the Psychiatric Epidemiology Research Interview (PERI) (Dohrenwend, Shrout, Egri, & Mendelsohn, 1980). The PERI was developed to assess important areas of dysfunction independent of any particular mental disorder. The instrument includes 38 scales, such as demoralization, suicidality, insomnia, drinking problems, job satisfaction, sexual problems, marital attainment, job performance, and housework. However, there are also many other available instruments, reviewed by Goldman, Skodol, and Lave (in press) in the process of considering a revision to Axis V of *DSM-III-R*.

In other words, we would recommend that clinicians (and researchers) (a) obtain a comprehensive and specific description of a patient's (or subject's) personality rather than forcing the patient into an overly simplistic, undifferentiated category, (b) obtain an independent assessment of the domain(s) of distress and social, occupational dysfunction that typically result from maladaptive personality traits (or those that are of most relevance to a particular social, clinical decision), and then (c) determine the contribution of the patient's (or subject's) personality traits to the specific areas of distress and/or impairment. Categorical distinctions may at times be necessary for pragmatic social and clinical decisions (e.g., decisions regarding hospitalization, disability, insurance coverage, or treatment). However, the type and degree of impairment that suggests the need for hospitalization, individual psychotherapy, behavioral therapy, disability, insurance coverage, or a particular form of group therapy will not be equivalent across these clinical decisions. Each clinical situation may need to emphasize a different domain of impairment (e.g., legal difficulties, physical well-being, financial condition, or parental skills) and/or a different threshold of impairment within a particular domain (e.g., the threshold of impairment that warrants disability may be higher than the threshold that warrants hospitalization, which may in turn be higher than a threshold that suggests a need for a particular form of therapy). No *DSM-III-R* or *DSM-IV* personality disorder diagnosis (e.g., presence vs. absence of borderline PD) provides enough information to make all of these different decisions. The *DSM-III-R(IV)* thresholds are fixed and may bear little relationship to the thresholds of impairment associated with the wide variety of clinical decisions that must be made. The most informative and useful decisions will be made by a comprehensive description of the patient's personality accompanied by an individualized assessment of the explicit type and specific degree of distress, social dysfunction, and occupational dysfunction that are resulting from these traits.

REFERENCES

Akiskal, H. S., & Akiskal, K. (1992). Cyclothymic, hyperthymic, and depressive temperaments as subaffective variants of mood disorders. In A. Tasman & M. B. Riba (Eds.), *Review of psychiatry* (Vol. 11, p. 43–62). Washington, DC: American Psychiatric Press.

American Psychiatric Association. (1987). *Diagnostic and statistical manual of mental disorders* (3rd ed., rev.). Washington, DC: Author.

Cooper, A. M. (1993). Psychotherapeutic approaches to masochism. *Journal of Psychotherapy Practice and Research, 2*, 1–13.

Coryell, W. H., & Zimmerman, M. (1989). Personality disorder in the families of depressed, schizophrenic, and never-ill probands. *American Journal of Psychiatry, 146*, 496–502.

Costa, P. T., & McCrae, R. R. (1992). *Revised NEO Personality Inventory (NEO PI-R) and NEO Five-Factor Inventory (NEO-FFI) professional manual*. Odessa, FL: Psychological Assessment Resources.

Dohrenwend, B., Shrout, P., Egri, G., & Mendelsohn, F. (1980). Nonspecific psychological distress and other dimensions of psychopathology. *Archives of General Psychiatry, 37*, 1229–1236.

Ellis, A. (1987). The impossibility of achieving consistently good mental health. *American Psychologist, 42*, 364–375.

Fabrega, H., Ulrich, R., Pilkonis, P., & Mezzich, J. (1991). On the homogeneity of personality disorder clusters. *Comprehensive Psychiatry, 32*, 373–386.

Farmer, N., Feldhaus, C., Pelphrey, A., & Woods, A. (1992). Christian defeat but a blugrass revival. *Journal of Seasonal Preoccupations, 54*, 19–78.

Frances, A. J., Widiger, T. A., & Sabshin, M. (1991). Psychiatriac diagnosis and normality. In D. Offer & M. Sabshin (Eds.), *The diversity of normal behavior* (pp. 3–38). NY: Basic Books.

Freud, S. (1957). Analysis terminable and interminable. In J. L. Strachey (Ed.), *Standard edition* (Vol. 23, pp. 209–254). London: Hogarth Press. (Originally published, 1937)

Garamoni, G. L., & Schwartz, R. M. (1986). Type A behavior pattern and compulsive personality: Toward a psychodynamic-behavioral integration. *Clinical Psychology Review, 6*, 311–336.

Goldberg, L. R. (1993). The structure of phenotypic personality traits. *American Psychologist, 48*, 26–34.

Goldman, H. H., Skodol, A. E., & Lave, T.R. (in press). Revising Axis V of DSM-IV: A review of measures of social functioning. In T. A. Widiger, A. J. Frances, H. Pincus, et al. (Eds.), *DSM-IV sourcebook*. Washington, DC: American Psychiatric Press.

Gunderson, J. G. (1992). Diagnostic controversies. In A. Tasman & M.B. Riba (Eds.),

Review of psychiatry (Vol. 11, pp. 9–24). Washington, DC: American Psychiatric Press.

Hamlin, W. T. (1990). *The chains of psychological slavery: The mental illness of racism.* Baltimore, MD: ICFP, Inc.

Hughes, J. R., Oliveto, A. H., Helzer, J. E., Higgins, S. T., & Bickel, W. K. (1992). Should caffeine abuse, dependence, or withdrawal be added to *DSM-IV* or ICD-10? *American Journal of Psychiatry, 149*, 33–40.

Hurlbert, D. F., & Apt, C. (1992). The malevolent personality disorder? *Psychological Reports, 70*, 979–991.

Hyler, S. E., Skodol, A. E., Kellman, H. D., Oldham, J. M., & Rosnick, L. (1990). Validity of the Personality Diagnostic Questionnaire - Revised: Comparison with two structured interviews. *American Journal of Psychiatry, 147*, 1043–1048.

Johnson, J. G., & Bornstein, R. F. (1992). Utility of the Personality Diagnostic Questionnaire - Revised in a nonclinical population. *Journal of Personality Disorders, 6*, 450–457.

Kass, F., Skodol, A. E., Charles, E., Spitzer, R. L., & Williams, J.B.W. (1985). Scaled ratings of DSM-III personality disorders. *American Journal of Psychiatry, 142*, 627–630.

Kiesler, D. J. (1986). The 1982 Interpersonal Circle: An analysis of DSM-III personality disorders. In T. Millon & G. L. Klerman (Eds.), *Contemporary directions in psychopathology. Toward the DSM-IV* (pp. 571–597). NY: Guilford.

Koenigsberg, H. W., Kaplan, R. D., Gilmore, M. M., & Cooper, A. M. (1985). The relationship between syndrome and personality disorder in DSM-III: Experience with 2,462 patients. *American Journal of Psychiatry, 142*, 207–212.

Leaf, R. C., DiGiuseppe, R., Ellis, A., Mass, R., Backx, W., Wolfe, J., & Alington, D. E. (1987). "Healthy" correlates of MCMI scales 4, 5, 6, and 7. *Journal of Personality Disorders, 4*, 312–328.

Livesley, W. J. (1986). Trait and behavioral prototypes of personality disorder. *American Journal of Psychiatry, 143*, 728–732.

Loranger, A. W. (1990). The impact of DSM-III on diagnostic practice in a university hospital. *Archives of General Psychiatry, 47*, 672–675.

Loranger, A. W. (1992). Are current self-report and interview measures adequate for epidemiological studies of personality disorders? *Journal of Personality Disorders, 6*, 313–325.

Maier, W., Lichtermann, D., Klingler, T., Heun, R., Hallmayer, J. (1992). Prevalences of personality disorders (DSM-III-R) in the community. *Journal of Personality Disorders, 6*, 187–196.

McCrae, R. R. (1994). Psychopathology from the perspective of the five-factor model. In S. Strack & M. Lorr (Eds.), *Differentiating normal and abnormal personality* (pp. 26–39). NY: Springer.

McCrae, R. R., & Costa, P. T. (1990). *Personality in adulthood.* NY: Guilford.

McGlashan, T. (1987). The borderline syndrome: II. Is it a variant or schizophrenia or affective disorder? *Archives of General Psychiatry, 40*, 1319–1323.

Merikangas, K. R., & Weissman, M. M. (1986). Epidemiology of DSM-III Axis II personality disorders. In A. J. Frances & R. E. Hales (Eds.), *Psychiatry update. American Psychiatric Association Annual review* (Vol. 5, pp. 258–278). Washington, DC: American Psychiatric Press.

Mischel, W. (1984). Convergences and challenges in the search for consistency. *American Psychologist, 39*, 351–364.

Morey, L. C. (1988). Personality disorders in DSM-III and DSM-III-R: Convergence, coverage, and internal consistency. *American Journal of Psychiatry, 145*, 573–577.

Nestadt, G., Romanoski, A. J., Brown, C. H., Chahal, R., Merchant, A., Folstein, M. F., Gruenberg, E. M., & McHugh, P. R. (1991). DSM-III compulsive personality disorder: An epidemiologic survey. *Psychological Medicine, 21,* 461–471.

Nestadt, G., Romanoski, A. J., Chahal, R., Merchant, A., Folstein, M. F., Gruenberg, E. M., & McHugh, P. R. (1990). An epidemiological study of histrionic personality disorder. *Psychological Medicine, 20,* 413–422.

Nestadt, G., Romanoski, A. J., Samuels, J. F., Folstein, M. F., & McHugh, P. R. (1992). The relationship between personality and DSM-III Axis I disorders in the population: Results from an epidemiological survey. *American Journal of Psychiatry, 149,* 1228–1233.

Nikelly, A. G. (1992). The pleonexic personality: A new provisional personality disorder. *Individual Psychology, 48,* 253–260.

Oldham, J. M., Skodol, A. E., Kellman, H. D., Hyler, S. E., Rosnick, L., & Davies, M. (1992). Diagnosis of DSM-III-R personality disorders by two structured interviews: Patterns of comorbidity. *American Journal of Psychiatry, 149,* 213–220.

Overholser, J. C. (1991). Categorical assessment of the dependent personality disorder in depressed inpatients. *Journal of Personality Disorders, 5,* 243–255.

Pantony, K., & Caplan, P. J. (1991). Delusional dominating personality disorder: A modest proposal for identifying some consequences of rigid masculine socialization. *Canadian Psychology, 32,* 120–133.

Phillips, K., Gunderson, J. G., Hirschfeld, R.M.A., & Smith, L. (1990). A review of the depressive personality. *American Journal of Psychiatry, 147,* 830–837.

Robins, L. N., Helzer, J. E., Weissman, M. M., Orvaschel, H., Gruenberg, E., Burke, J. D., & Regier, D. A. (1984). Lifetime prevalence of specific psychiatric disorders in three sites. *Archives of General Psychiatry, 41,* 949–958.

Robins, L. N., Tipp, J., & Przybeck, T. (1991). Antisocial personality. In L. N. Robins & D. A. Regier (Eds.), *Psychiatric disorders in America. The epidemiologic catchment area study* (pp. 258–290). NY: The Free Press.

Schacht, T. (1985). DSM-III and the politics of truth. *American Psychologist, 40,* 513–521.

Skodol, A. E. (1989). *Problems in differential diagnosis: From DSM-III to DSM-III-R in clinical practice.* Washington, DC: American Psychiatric Press.

Skodol, A. E., Rosnick, L., Kellman, H. D., Oldham, J. M., & Hyler, S. E. (1988). Validating structured DSM-III-R personality disorder assessments with longitudinal data. *American Journal of Psychiatry, 145,* 1297–1299.

Spitzer, R. L., Gibbon, M., Skodol, A. E., Williams, J.B.W., & First, M. B. (1989). *DSM-III-R Casebook.* Washington, DC: American Psychiatric Press.

Spitzer, R. L., & Williams, J.B. W. (1982). The definition and diagnosis of mental disorder. In W. Gove (Ed.), *Deviance and mental illness* (pp. 15–31). Beverly Hills, CA: Sage.

Sutker, P. B., Bugg, F., & West, J. A. (1993). Antisocial personality disorder. In P. B. Sutker & H. E. Adams (Eds.), *Comprehensive handbook of psychopathology* (2nd ed., pp. 337–370). NY: Plenum.

Szasz, T. (1986). The case against suicide prevention. *American Psychologist, 41,* 806–812.

Task Force on DSM-IV. (1993). *DSM-IV draft criteria.* Washington, DC: American Psychiatric Association.

Trull, T. J. (1993). Temporal stability and validity of two personality disorder inventories. *Psychological Assessment, 5,* 11–18..

Wakefield, J. C. (1992). Disorder as harmful dysfunction: A conceptual critique of DSM-III-R's definition of mental disorder. *Psychological Review, 99,* 232–247.

Wakefield, J. C. (1993). Limits of operationalization: A critique of Spitzer and Endicott's (1978) proposed operational criteria for mental disorder. *Journal of Abnormal Psychology, 102,* 160–172.

Walker, L. E. A. (1987). Inadequacies of the masochistic personality disorder diagnosis for women. *Journal of Personality Disorders, 1*, 183–189.

Walker, L. E. A. (1994). Are personality disorders gender biased? In S. A. Kirk & S. D. Einbinder (Eds.), *Controversial issues in mental health* (pp. 22–39). NY: Allyn & Bacon.

Watson, D., & Clark, L. A. (1984). Negative affectivity: The disposition to experience aversive emotional states. *Psychological Bulletin, 96*, 465–490.

Weissman, M. M. (1993). The epidemiology of personality disorders: A 1990 update. *Journal of Personality Disorders, 7*, 44–62.

Widiger, T. A., Frances, A. J., Spitzer, R. L., & Williams, J.B.W. (1988). The DSM-III-R personality disorders: An overview. *American Journal of Psychiatry, 145*, 786–795.

Widiger, T. A., & Rinaldi, M. (1983). An acceptance of suicide. *Psychotherapy: Theory, Research, and Practice, 20*, 263–273.

Widiger, T. A., & Sanderson, C. J. (in press). Towards a dimensional model of personality disorder in DSM-IV and DSM-V. In W. J. Livesley (Ed.), *DSM-IV personality disorders*. NY: Guilford.

Widiger, T. A., & Trull, T. J. (1991). Diagnosis and clinical assessment. *Annual Review of Psychology, 42*, 109–133.

Widiger, T. A., Trull, T. J., Clarkin, J. F., Sanderson, C., & Costa, P. T. (1994). A description of the DSM-III-R and DSM-IV personality disorders with the Five-Factor model of personality. In P. T. Costa & T. A. Widiger (Eds.), *Personality disorders and the Five-Factor model of personality* (pp. 41–56). Washington, DC: American Psychological Association.

Widiger, T. A., Trull, T. J., Hurt, S. W., Clarkin, J. F., & Frances, A. J. (1987). A multidimensional scaling of the DSM-III personality disorders. *Archives of General Psychiatry, 44*, 557–563.

Wiggins, J. S., & Pincus, A. L. (1992). Personality: Structure and assessment. *Annual Review of Psychology, 43*, 473–504.

World Health Organization. (1964). *Basic documents* (15th ed.). Geneva, Switzerland: Author.

Zanarini, M. C., Frankenburg, F. R., Chauncey, D. L., & Gunderson, J. G. (1987). The Diagnostic Interview for Personality Disorders: Interrater and test-retest reliability. *Comprehensive Psychiatry, 28*, 467–480.

Zimmerman, M., & Coryell, W. H. (1989). DSM-III personality disorder diagnoses in a nonpatient sample. *Archives of General Psychiatry, 46*, 682–689.

Zimmerman, M., & Coryell, W. H. (1990a). Diagnosing personality disorders in the community. A comparison of self-report and interview measures. *Archives of General Psychiatry, 47*, 527–531.

Zimmerman, M., & Coryell, W. H. (1990b). DSM-III personality disorder dimensions. *Journal of Nervous and Mental Disease, 178*, 686–692.

Zimmerman, M., Pfohl, B., Coryell, W. H., Stangl, D., & Corenthal, C. (1988). Diagnosing personality disorder in depressed patients. A comparison of patient and informant interviews. *Archives of General Psychiatry, 45*, 733–737.

II

Methodology

9

Cluster Analysis: Aims, Methods, and Problems

Maurice Lorr

luster Analysis represents a wide range of statistical techniques for classi fying entities (persons, plants, animals) into homogeneous subgroups on the basis of their similarities. The groupings are labelled classes, types or categories. The main aims of clustering are to identify natural groupings within a mixture, to generate a classificatory scheme, or to test for one or more hypothesized categories.

Clustering techniques have been developed and applied since the 1920s by anthropologists, archaeologists, biologists, ecologists, and psychologists as well as statisticians. Some of the first psychologists active in developing grouping procedures were Tryon (1939), McQuitty (1957), and Cattell (1944). A sharp rise in interest and a marked increase in publication occurred in the 1960s with the appearance and availability of high-speed computers. Another important stimulus was the appearance of Sokal and Sneath's *Principles of Numerical Taxonomy* (1963). A further impetus came from the formation of the Classification Society of North America in 1968.

The 1970s saw the appearance of a series of texts descriptive of available clustering techniques. Some of the better known are Everitt's *Cluster Analysis* (1974), Anderberg's *Cluster Analysis for Applications* (1975), and Hartigan's *Cluster Algorithms* (1975). More recent texts are Lorr's *Cluster Analysis for Social Scientists* (1983), Romesburg's (1984) *Cluster Analysis for Researchers*, and *Cluster Analysis* by Aldenderfer and Blashfield (1984). Scoltock (1982) reported in her survey of the literature that the bulk of the papers occur in biology, psychiatry, social science, geography/geology and pattern recognition. Most methodological articles are published in journals such as *Biometrics, Computer Journal, Multivariate Behavioral Research, Psychometrika*, and *Educational and Psychological Measurement*.

The aims of the present chapter are first to review the various steps involved in conducting a cluster analysis. Next, the major clustering methods will be sketched. Third, available approaches to assessing similarity will be described and discussed. Fourth, a brief summary of the empirical evaluations of the clustering methods will be given. With this review of clustering methodology, some readers could actually plan and conduct their own study.

THE PROCESS OF CLUSTERING

Clustering may be defined as the grouping of entities into subsets on the basis of their similarity across a set of attributes. Any well-designed study involves a sequence of steps such as the following:

1. Select a representative and adequately large sample of the entities to be studied. Clusters will be missed or poorly represented if sampled inadequately.
2. Select a representative sample of the attributes or characteristics in the domain of similarity chosen. The process should be similar to the selection and definition of traits in personality inventory construction. If attributes are complex and numerous, a dimensional analysis should be considered.
3. Describe or measure each entity in terms of the attributes sampled.
4. Choose a suitable metric and convert the variables into comparable units. In brief, consider standardizing the various measures to establish a common metric.
5. Select an appropriate index of similarity or difference such as distance, correlation coefficient or matching coefficient. Then assess the similarity between all pairs of entity profiles. Consider use of factor scores to increase measure reliability.
6. Choose a clustering method appropriate to the structure expected. Apply the procedure preferably to two samples and apply a criterion to determine the number of clusters present.
7. Apply a confirmatory clustering algorithm to the samples to check the generality of the finding. Because all methods find clusters, some confirmation is needed.

MEASURES OF SIMILARITY

To cluster entities, some measure of similarity or difference between entities is needed. Similarity, however, is not a general quality. It has meaning only with respect to some specified set of attributes. Entities alike with respect to one set of characteristics are not necessarily alike on another set. Cronbach and Gleser (1953) have introduced a widely accepted geometric model for the concept of similarity. Entities may be represented as points in K-dimensional attribute space. Then the measured dissimilarities correspond to the distance between the respective points. Given an N-by-K data matrix, each row of values in the matrix X defines the profile of an individual entity across the K attributes. The Euclidean distance between any two profiles is defined as:

$$D_{ih} = [\sum_{j}^{k} (x_{ji} - x_{jh})^2]^{\frac{1}{2}} \tag{1}$$

where D_{ih} represents the distance between entities i and h. To avoid the use of the square root, D_{ih}^2 is often used in computer programs.

As shown by Cronbach and Gleser, D^2 is composed of three components: elevation, scatter, and shape of the profiles. The *elevation* is the mean level of scores in the profile, the *scatter* represents the variation of entity scores, and *shape* refers to the configuration of scores. If the means are subtracted from the two sets of scores, information on elevation is lost. If the scores in the profiles are also standardized, information regarding score scatter is also lost.

Another common distance function is called the city-block or Manhattan metric. It is defined as the sum of the absolute values of the differences between entities on the profile elements as shown below:

$$d_{ih} = \sum_{j}^{k} |x_{ji} - x_{jh}| \tag{2}$$

The city-block metric has been used in many clustering algorithms.

The two distance measures, the Euclidean and the Manhattan, are special cases of a class of metric functions called the Minkowski metric, shown below (Sneath & Sokal, 1973).

$$d_{ih} = [\sum_{j}^{k} (x_{ji} - x_{jh})^p]^{1/p} \tag{3}$$

When p = 1 it is a city block metric, and when p = 2 the distance is Euclidean.

Correlations are equally useful and important for measuring score profile similarity. Q_{ih}, the correlation between entities i and h, is defined as follows:

$$Q_{ih} = \frac{\sum^{k}(x_{ji} - \bar{x}_i)(x_{jh} - \bar{x}_h)}{\sqrt{\sum^{k}(x_{ji} - \bar{x}_j)^2} \sqrt{\sum(x_{jh} - \bar{x}_h)^2}} \tag{4}$$

where $\bar{x}_i$ and $\bar{x}_h$ are the means and the denominators are measures of dispersion. Since the means are subtracted out and scatter is equalized by standardization,

Q_{ih} measures similarity in K-2 space. The correlations range between $+1$ and -1 with o denoting no relationship. Since scatter and elevation is removed, correlations reflect only the shape of the profiles.

If the raw scores in formula (1) are expressed algebraically in terms of deviation scores, the equation becomes:

$$D_{ih}^2 = K(\bar{x}_i - \bar{x}_h)^2 + (S_i - S_k)^2 - 2S_iS_h(1 - Q_{ih}) \tag{5}$$

The successive terms on the right represent (1) profile differences in elevation, (2) differences in scatter, and (3) differences in shape weighted by scatter. If the scores are standardized, the distance measure becomes:

$$D_{ih}^2 = 2(1 - Q_{ih}) \tag{6}$$

This formula can be used to convert distances into correlations.

Cattell (1949) developed another measure of correlation between two profiles, r_p, which ranges from $+1$ and -1. The transformation is based on Euclidean distance squared. Thus,

$$r_p = \frac{2K - \Sigma d^2}{2K + \Sigma d^2} \tag{7}$$

where 2K equals twice the median chi square for the number of variates and Σd^2 is simply D^2. Horn (1961) has developed a test of significance for use with r_p.

This index could be especially useful for testing whether a subject's profile, say on the MMPI, matches significantly with the profile of a reference group (neurotic, psychotic or sociopath).

COEFFICIENTS OF ASSOCIATION

There are numerous coefficients of association between entities when described by binary variables valued 0 and 1. These indices are also known as matching coefficients. Frequency of agreement and disagreement between two entities, i and h, is summarized in Table 9.1 below. Category *a* gives the number of agree-

TABLE 9.1 2 x 2 Contingency Table

		Entity i		
		0	1	Total
Entity h	1	b	a	a + b
	0	d	c	c + d
	Total	b + d	a + c	N

ments, while *b* gives the number of disagreements. Categories *b* and *c* indicate the number of disagreements. Some common matching coefficients given in Table 9.2 are the Jaccard, the Rand and the Kappa (Cohen, 1960). Kappa is a co-efficient of agreement for nominal scales when corrected for chance p_c. Holley's G index is much used in Q-factor analyses (Holley & Guilford, 1964).

CLUSTER METHODS

Clusters can be categorized by shape into two kinds. A *compact* cluster can be defined as a category of entities in which each member is more like every other member than like members in any other category. Such clusters are spherical or hyperspherical. An *extended* or *chained* cluster is defined as a category in which each member is more like *one* other member of the type when it is like an entity not on the type. Such clusters tend to be straggly, serpentine or amoebic (Lorr, 1983, p. 18). Cattell and Coulter (1966) termed such clusters *homostats* ("stat") and *segregates* ("aits").

Six major kinds of cluster analytic procedures have been developed. These are (1) hierarchical agglomerative, (2) hierarchical divisive, (3) iterative partitioning, (4) density search, (5) Q-type factor analysis, and (6) overlapping clustering.

HIERARCHICAL CLUSTERING

A hierarchy constitutes a family of nested multilevel classes. Hierarchical clustering techniques are both agglomerative and divisive. The agglomerative begins with each entity considered a separate cluster. At each level, the two closest clusters are merged or fused. The process of fusing continues until there is only one conjoint cluster. The agglomerative procedure builds a tree-like structure called a dendogram. The process is sequential, agglomerative, hierarchical, and non-overlapping. Clusters are *nested* insofar as each is a member of a more inclusive cluster.

TABLE 9.2 *Matching Coefficients*

1. Jaccard	$a / a + b + c$
2. Rand	$(a + d) / a + b + c + d$
3. Holley G	$(a + d) - (b + c) = p_a - p_n$
4. Kappa	$p_o - p_c / 1 - p_c$ p_o = observed; p_c = chance

Note. $p_a = a + d$ proportion of agreement.
$p_n = b + c$ proportion of non-agreement.

There are a half dozen agglomerative sorting techniques. These are single linkage, complete linkage, the centroid linkage method, the median linkage method, and the minimum variance method. All these methods of combining clusters have been shown by Lance and Williams (1967) to satisfy the same recurrence formula. In other words, the six procedures can be specified by the same formula. Let the distance between two clusters i and j be denoted d_{ij}. Suppose cluster i and j are merged to form a new cluster k. Then distance to the third cluster h is d_{hk}. The general formula is:

$$d_{hk} = Ad_{hj} + Bd_{hj} + Cd_{ij} + D \left| d_{hi} - d_{hj} \right|$$

where A, B, C, D are parameters whose values vary with the cluster method. Further illustrative material on the recurrence formula can be found in Everitt (1980), Lorr (1983) and Milligan (1979).

SINGLE-LINKAGE ANALYSIS

The method was independently proposed by Sneath (1957) and McQuitty (1957). A link is defined as the smallest distance between an entity and any other in the set. To begin a cluster, a search of the matrix is made for the closest pair ("nearest neighbor"). Then add the entity closest to either. The cluster is extended to all entities linked via at least one member. This extended cluster or chain is one in which each member is closest to at least one other member. Using single linkage, two clusters are merged in a hierarchy if at least one entity from each cluster is more similar to at least one member of the cluster than it is to any member of another cluster. In Monte Carlo studies of agglomerative hierarchical procedures, single-linkage has been found to be substantially inferior to other linkage methods.

COMPLETE LINKAGE CLUSTERING

The complete linkage method is also called the "furthest neighbor" method (Lance & Williams, 1967). The distance between clusters is defined as the distance between the most remote pair of entities. The distance between merging clusters is the diameter of the smallest sphere that can enclose them. In the resulting cluster, every member is more like *every* other member of the same cluster than it is like any other entity not in the cluster. Complete linkage tends to find compact hyperspherical clusters. This procedure was first proposed by Horn (1943) and by McQuitty (1967). Mezzich (1978) as well as Overall, Gibson and Novy (1993) found this procedure best in their studies.

AVERAGE LINKAGE CLUSTERING

An average linkage cluster is defined as a subset of entities in which each member is, on the average, more like every other entity than it is (on the average) like any entity in any other cluster. The method was first proposed by Sokal and Michener (1958). The procedure was developed to handle the limitations of single and complete linkage. Monte Carlo studies (Milligan, 1980) showed good recovery in known cluster structures. Overall, Gibson and Novy found that average linkage ranked below complete linkage and Ward's minimum variance. Among biologists, such as Sneath and Sokal, this method is preferred. It is labelled UPGMA (Unweighted Pair-Group Method Average).

Variations of average linkage are *centroid* and *median* linkage cluster analysis (Sokal & Sneath, 1973; Anderberg, 1973, p. 140). At each stage, the two clusters with the closest mean vector are merged for the updated distance. When two clusters differ substantially, the *median* can be used in merging clusters. On the whole, these methods are usually not as effective as average linkage cluster analysis.

MINIMUM-VARIANCE METHOD

In the beginning, each entity constitutes a cluster. At each stage in the procedure the aim is to form a group such that the sum of squared within-group deviations from the group mean of each profile variable is minimized for all profile variables at the same time. The objective function is known as the within-group sum of squares (ESS). The method joins clusters that result in the minimum increase in ESS. The number of clusters is systemically reduced from k to k-1, k-2 until all are combined in a conjoint cluster.

This popular procedure was designed by Ward (1963). The method tends to find clusters of relatively equal size. Moreover, the method is sensitive to profile elevation or mean score. Like all hierarchical procedures, a "stopping point" is needed to determine how many clusters are actually present. The biologist uses the entire hierarchy while the social scientist is mainly concerned with the number of groupings or clusters embedded in the data. Milligan and Cooper (1985) evaluated a large set of rules for determining the number of clusters present. About ten were found to be reasonably effective for deciding on the number of clusters present in the data. Mojena (1977) has proposed a useful rule.

THE DIVISIVE METHOD

A small number of hierarchical procedures are based on the division of the initial data set into subgroups. At each stage the group is bisected into subgroups. These methods can be classified as either monothetic or polythetic. Monothetic clusters are based on a single binary attribute. Such procedures are used for the construction of keys in botany and ecology. Polythetic clusters are based on several attributes shared by members of a cluster. Edwards and Cavalli-Sforza (1965) designed a method that uses the same partitioning procedure followed by Ward. They find the division that minimizes the within-cluster error sum of squares. Computer programs may be found in CLUSTAN (Wishart, 1978).

ITERATIVE PARTITIONING METHOD

Partitioning is the process of dividing a set of N entities into K mutually exclusive clusters. Most partitioning methods begin with a preliminary partition of a data set into a specific number of clusters. Next, the centroids of these clusters are computed. Usually the data points are then allocated to the nearest centroid. The new centroids can then be computed or updated. This process of iterative partitioning, however, reflects a major handicap. The most direct approach to finding an optimal partition is to form all possible partitions of (say) a data set of 25 into 5 nonoverlapping clusters and to select the best. Computationally, however, this approach is impractical. Even for a small data set the number of possible solutions is very great.

The partitioning methods differ in the following ways: (1) The method of selection of the initial "seed" points. Experience has shown that random sets work poorly. Milligan and Sokal (1980) found a K-means pass derived from average linkage provides a superior recovery of a known data set. Others suggest use of Ward's cluster solution represents a useful start. (2) The type of pass or assignment. The most common is the K-means pass in which each entity is allocated to the nearest centroid. (3) The type of statistical criterion employed by Friedman and Rubin (1967) use the ratio of two determinants $|T|/|W|$ or total dispersion over pooled within-group dispersions. Useful K-means programs are available in SPSS, BMDP, and SAS. The best known are: convergent K-means, Jancey K-means, Forgy K-means and MacQueen K-means.

DENSITY SEARCH METHOD

If entities are regarded as points in k-attribute space, it is plausible to regard clusters as regions of high density in multivariate space. A procedure called the Cartet Count had been suggested by Cattell and Coulter (1966). Convenient intervals are taken to define *Cartet's* two-dimensional squares. The computer program can then count the number of entities in each cube. Tryon and Bailey (1970) in their text construct what they called *Core* clusters that resemble Cattell's Cartets. The major difficulty is that there seldom is an a priori basis for such arbitrary sections.

In fact, natural clusters may have been sliced through. Carmichael and Sneath (1969), with similar aims, form clusters by single-linkage analysis to construct a "taxometric map." Wishart (1969) developed a single-linkage process called *mode analysis*. It searches for groupings of entities within a specified sphere with a given radius R. Use is made of single-linkage rules. A program is available in CLUSTAN (Wishart, 1978).

Another group of density search methods use the concept of a *mixture*. A mixture is a collection of samples from several populations of entities. Wolfe (1970) developed two procedures called NORMAP and NORMIX. These yield maximum likelihood estimates of the population parameters and give *probability* estimates of membership of each case to every cluster. These sophisticated procedures have failed to work out in practice. Large samples are needed, and the solutions reached are not likely to be optimal. As in the K-means procedure, some "seeds" from another cluster solution (such as Ward's) are needed as estimates for the final cluster solution.

OVERLAPPING CLUSTERS

Most methods of clustering are designed to yield mutually exclusive, non-overlapping clusters. A new clustering model (ADCLUS), recently developed, allows for the identification of overlapping clusters. The assumption made is that the similarity of two entities is an additive function of underlying weights associated with the characteristics shared by both entities (Shepard & Arabie, 1979). Another program, MAPCLUS, was later developed by Arabie and Caroll (1980) to replace ADCLUS.

It has long been known that diagnostic classes such as the Personality Disorders overlap. Psychiatric patients may belong to more than one diagnostic group despite the all-or-none disease model. For example, several overlapping categories such as Narcissistic, Histrionic, Antisocial and Borderline belong to one cluster. An example given by Arabie and Carroll shows that various drug brands may compete in more than one cluster of products. Bayer aspirin may compete with Bufferin to relieve pain and also compete with Anacin and Excederin to relieve arthritic pain. One possible approach to use of the method is to first cluster the sample by clustering procedures such as Ward's, construct a matrix of inter-entity similarities, and then submit these to the MAPCLUS algorithm.

THE METHOD OF Q-ANALYSIS

Stephenson (1936) was one of the first to conduct a factor analysis of correlations among entities (called Q-analysis) to discover types. The entity samples consisted of manic depressives, schizophrenics, and normals. The attributes were mood adjectives used to rate the subjects. The correlations among the subjects across the adjectives were subjected to a Q-analysis in contrast to an R-analysis of correlations among attributes. Biologists have long applied this process, which is called *ordination*, to obtain a low-dimensional mapping of the entities under study. The N x N matrix of intercorrelations among entities is subjected to a principal component analysis and three or four components are extracted. The points representing the entities are then plotted in two- or three-dimensional space. The space in which the *N* points are embedded can then be inspected to discover any groupings. Rohlf (1972), for example, analyzed nine different data sets such as butterflies, frogs, pigeons, rats and so on to discover groupings. Lorr (1983) computed the proximities among 33 warships listed in *Jane's Fighting Ships*. A multidimensional scaling analysis (INDSCAL) revealed a two-dimensional mapping of cruisers, battleships, destroyers and submarines. The 33 ships were clearly visible and most were separable into clusters. One problem here is that if an insufficient number of components is extracted, some clusters will not be visible.

Cattell has long asserted that Q-analysis is "not a method for finding types but for finding dimensions" (1978, p. 326). Horst likewise says, "It does not seem to be generally recognized that . . . it does not matter whether we factor one set of categories (attributes) or the other (entities)" (1965, p. 324). Burt developed a reciprocity principle in which he stated that "the factor loadings for persons obtained by correlating persons are identical with the factor measurements for persons obtained by covariating tests" (1940, p. 290). Since then, others have shown the equivalence of component analysis of the rows and columns of the data matrix, providing that a "basic structure" type of analysis (Horst, 1965) is followed. Thus, the dimensions from Q-analysis are systematically related to, and under proper conditions, the same as those resulting from an R-analysis.

Because Q-analysis is used for ordination and for deriving a classificatory scheme, a good understanding of the process is needed. Usually, it is best to standardize the attributes before computing indices of similarity. The process begins with an N x N matrix *Q* of correlations among entities which is analyzed by principal component analysis. The matrix of factor coefficients can then be rotated to simple structure.

When entity correlations are factored, the resulting factors are usually bipolar. Each factor identifies two subtypes—one positive and one negative. This means that there will be twice as many "types" as factors. The reason is that setting the entity means to zero and then factoring shifts the origins to the means of the variables. But setting the means of the variables to zero and then factoring them shifts the origin to the centroid of the entities. Overall and Klett (1972) suggested that a constant be added to all mean-corrected scores prior to factoring. Another solution is to analyze the sums of cross-products as suggested by Nunnally (1962) and others. More elaborate discussions of Q-analysis are available in Skinner (1979), Overall and Klett (1972), and Lorr (1983).

Illustrations of Q-analysis may be found in Overall and Klett (1972). Their analyses were concerned with the isolation of psychiatric "ideal types" such as paranoids, schizophrenics and depressives. Another example is found in McClung (1963). She administered a personality inventory comprised of 600 items to highly successful life-insurance salesmen, theoretical physicists, design engineers, ministers, and journalists. She used the Holley-Guilford *G* as an index of similarity. All five hypothesized factors emerged in the analysis. Skinner and Jackson (1978) sought to evaluate the Minnesota Multiphasic Personality Inventory (MMPI) code types from the Gilberstadt and Duker (1965) and Marks, Seeman and Haller (1974) systems. Using a Q-analysis procedure, they identified three "modal" profiles interpreted as representing neurotics, psychotics, and sociopaths.

EMPIRICAL STUDIES

Research concerning the accuracy and reliability of the various clustering methods has increased at a rapid rate. The basic problem is which clustering algorithm can recover the true cluster structure? Also, how many clusters are present? There are several empirical approaches to these problems.

Monte Carlo studies of artificial data sets with known cluster structure represent a major approach. Some analysts view clusters as mixtures of multivariate normal populations (Blashfield, 1976). Another approach is to assemble real data sets for which the actual structure is known. Cattell has called these *plasmodes*. One popular data set frequently included consists of Fisher's 150 specimens of *3* species of the plant Iris (Sneath & Sokal, 1973). Bartko, Strauss, and Carpenter (1971) generated data sets consisting of factitious psychiatric patients with distinctive symptom patterns. Cattell and Coulter (1966) have used classes of warships, dogs, and ethnic groups.

Several types of indices have been employed to assess the validity of a set of findings. The two most frequently applied measures are the Rand (1971) index and Cohen's statistic Kappa (1960). Rand's index varies from 0 to 1.0 where 1.0 represents perfect agreement; it represents the degree of recovery of a single partition. The formula is given in Table 9.2. Another index of the adequacy of cluster recovery is called Kappa. It is defined in Table 9.2. Here p_a is the observed proportion of classification agreement while p_c represents the proportion of agreement expected by chance.

Another important problem concerns the number of clusters present in a data set. Milligan and Cooper (1985) assessed the validity of 30 "stopping rules" for determining the number of clusters present in a data set when analyzed by hierarchical clustering. Monte Carlo evaluation of these procedures indicated excellent recovery of the true structure by at least five rules and reasonably good recovery by another five indices. One index, called the cubic clustering criterion, is included in the SAS package. Another rule was developed by Mojena (1977). The evidence indicated that the two-cluster case is the most difficult for the stopping rules to detect.

HIERARCHICAL CLUSTERING METHOD APPROACH

Validation results are best separated by clustering method. Kuiper and Fisher (1975) found Ward's method produced the best recovery for clusters of equal size. Complete linkage and group average linkage methods were superior for unequal-sized clusters. Blashfield (1975) found Ward's method was better than complete linkage and group average linkage. Mojena (1977) found that Ward's method gave better recovery than other methods. Mezzich (1978) found complete linkage superior.

In Milligan's (1980) extensive experiment, group average gave the best recovery, with Ward's method a close second. In general, Ward's method gave the best recovery with group average more erratic. Occasionally, complete linkage performed better than group average.

ITERATIVE PARTITIONING

Blashfield (1976) found best recovery of an iterative partition by CLUSTAN K-means and by two methods that used $|W|$ as criterion. Mezzich (1978) found the best partitioning technique was K-means with Euclidean distance. Milligan's (1980) study included four partitioning K-means. The best starting points came from group average linkage starting seeds. In summary, the convergent K-means method tended to give the best recovery of cluster structure for iterative partitioning.

ILLUSTRATIVE STUDIES

A few examples of the successful application of cluster analysis procedures will next be presented.

1. The study aim (Lorr and Suziedelis, 1982) was to identify the profile code types present in MMPI scale scores. One data set consisted of the 35 code types developed by Gilberstadt and Duker (1965) and by Marks, Seeman and Haller (1974). Another data set consisted of Lanyon's (1968) group profiles of 210 diagnostic classes. These profiles were divided into odd–even samples of 105. Ward's hierarchical procedure and an average linkage non-hierarchical cluster procedure were applied. Analysis of the 35 MMPI code types disclosed four code

type subsets: Neurotics (1-2-3), Depressed psychotics (2-7-8), Excited psychotics (8-9) and Sociopaths (4-9). Analysis of the Lanyon sample uncovered the same groupings and several normal clusters as well.

2. A typology of alcohol abusers was developed by Morey, Skinner, and Blashfield (1984). Using an extensive cluster analytic design, a sample of 725 persons seeking help for alcoholic-related problems were separated into Type A (Early-stage problem drinking), Type B (socially oriented moderate drinkers), and Type C (Schizoid, severely alcohol dependent persons who drank in binges). The Ward cluster procedure proved to be most effective of those used. The major assessment tools were the Michigan Alcoholism Screening Test and the Alcohol Use Inventory.

3. Kinder, Curtiss and Kalichman (1991) cluster analyzed the MMPI scores of male and female headache patients. Four distinct clusters were derived for both men and women on MMPI scores using Ward's procedure. The K-means iterative partitioning analysis was then performed to assign subjects to the clusters previously derived. Cattell's pattern similarity index was used as the measure of profile comparability.

4. Lorr and Strack (1993) sought to identify personality patterns in a college sample of 236 subjects administered the five-factor NEO-PI (Costa & McCrae, 1989). Application of Ward's hierarchical procedure to the score profiles disclosed six clusters that were replicated in a K-means partitioning process. The clusters were next compared by a one-way analysis of variance with respect to five higher-order factor scores of the Interpersonal Style Inventory (Lorr & Youniss, 1986). The F-tests confirmed the characteristics of the cluster profiles. The subgroups were interpreted as: (1) stable, extraverted and agreeable; (2) neurotic, disagreeable, but open to experience; (3) introverted, disorganized and disagreeable; (4) stable, introverted, conventional and conscientious; (5) highly disorganized and neurotic, and (6) flat profiles.

AN OVERVIEW

This chapter reflects the current debate on whether to retain the categorical conceptions of the personality disorders of *DSM-IIIR*. Many are now arguing for a conversion to a dimensional system of description and measurement of maladaptive interpersonal behavior (Widiger & Sanderson, 1993). Others, like Meehl (Golden and Meehl, 1979), believe that there are entities of a categorical kind (types or taxa). They have provided evidence for a schizoid taxon with MMPI indicators. Gangstead and Snyder (1985) have also examined the problem of discrete classes.

Thus, the researcher can experimentally check out any hypotheses concerning personality disorders or diagnostic groupings. The major cluster analytic procedures have been sketched out here. Latent or discrete classes can be examined by the taxometric methods outlined in Meehl and Golden (1982). The revised *DSM-IV*, which is about to be published, will not, to our knowledge, include any large-scale changes in viewpoint. It follows that cluster analytic procedures can be of potential use.

A related practical problem concerns the willingness of professionals to adopt or use profile patterns isolated. On the whole, psychiatry has been reluctant to adopt the groupings isolated by cluster analytic means. Another viewpoint strongly expressed by Paul Meehl is that "No accepted entity in psychopathology owed its initial discovery to formal cluster methods" (1979, p. 567). The facts are that Richard L. Jenkins (1973), a psychiatrist, first reported in 1946 and later confirmed at least four behavior disorders in children and adolescents through the application of clustering procedures. The categories discovered were labeled "undersocialized aggressive" disorder, "socialized conduct" disorder, "overanxious reaction," and "withdrawal reaction." These categories were first included in *DSM-II* (1968, pp. 50–51) and may also be found in *DSM-III* (1980). Recently (in a personal communication), Meehl acknowledged this contrary evidence, which I had presented to him.

REFERENCES

Aldenderfer, M. S. & Blashfield, R. K. (1984). *Cluster analysis*. Newbury Park, CA: Sage Publications.

Anderberg, M. R. (1973). *Cluster analysis for applications*. New York: Academic Press.

Arabie, P. & Carroll, J. D. (1980). MAPCLUS: A mathematical programming approach to fitting the ADCLUS model. *Psychometrika, 45,* 211–235.

Bartko, J. J., Strauss, J. S. & Carpenter, W. T. (1971). An evaluation of taxonomic techniques for psychiatric data. *Classification Society Bulletin, 2,* 2–28.

Blashfield, R. K. (1976). Mixture model tests of cluster analysis: Accuracy of four agglomerative hierarchical methods. *Psychological Bulletin, 83,* 377–388.

Blashfield, R. K. & Aldenderfer, M. S. (1988). The methods and problems of cluster analysis. In J. R. Nesselroade and R. B. Cattell (Eds.), *Handbook of multivariate experimental psychology* (2nd ed.). New York: Plenum Press.

Burt, C. (1940). *The factors of the mind*. London: London University Press.

Cattell, R. B. (1944). A note on correlation clusters and cluster search methods. *Psychometrika, 9,* 169–184.

Cattell, R. B. (1978). *The scientific use of factor analysis*. New York: Plenum Press.

Cattell, R. B. & Coulter, M. A. (1966). Principles of behavioral taxonomy and the mathematical basis of the taxonome computer program. *British Journal of Mathematical and Statistical Psychology, 19,* 237–269.

Cohen, J. (1960). A coefficient of agreement for nominal scales. *Educational and Psychological Measurement, 20,* 37–46.

Costa, P. T. & McCrae, R. R. (1989). *Revised NEO-personality inventory*. Florida: Psychological Assessment Resources.

Cronbach, L. & Gleser, G. (1953). Assessing similarity between profiles. *Psychological Bulletin, 50,* 456–473.

Edwards, A. W. F. & Cavalli-Sforza. (1965). A method for cluster analysis. *Biometrics, 21,* 362.

Everitt, B. S. (1980). *Cluster analysis.* New York: Halstead Press.

Friedman, H. P. & Rubin, J. (1967). On some invariant criteria for grouping data. *Journal of the American Statistical Association, 62,* 1159–1178.

Gangstead, S. & Snyder, M. (1985). "To carve nature at its joints:" On the existence of discrete classes in personality. *Psychological Review, 92,* 317–350.

Gilberstadt, H. & Duker, J. (1965). *Clinical and actuarial MMPI interpretation.* Philadelphia: Saunders.

Golden, R. R. & Meehl, P. E. (1979). Detection of the schizoid taxon with MMPI indicators. *Journal of Abnormal Psychology, 88,* 217–233.

Hartigan, J. A. (1975). *Clustering algorithms.* New York: Wiley.

Holley, J. W. & Guilford, J. P. (1964). A note on the G index of agreement. *Educational and Psychological Measurement, 24,* 749–753.

Horn, D. (1943). A study of personality syndromes. *Character and Personality, 12,* 257–274.

Horn, J. L. (1961). Significance tests for use with r_p and related profile statistics. *Educational and Psychological Measurement, 21,* 363–370.

Horst, P. (1965). *Factor Analysis of Data Matrices.* New York: Holt, Rinehart and Winston.

Jenkins, R. L. (1973). *Behavioral disorders of childhood and adolescence.* Springfield, IL: C. C. Thomas.

Kinder, B. N., Curtiss, G. & Kalichman, S. (1991). Cluster analyses of headache patients' MMPIs: A cross-validation study. *Psychological Assessment: A Journal of Consulting and Clinical Psychology, 3,* 226–231.

Kuiper, F. K. & Fisher, L. (1975). A Monte Carlo comparison of six clustering procedures. *Biometrics, 31,* 777–783.

Lance, G. & Williams, W. A. (1967). A general theory of classificatory sorting strategies. *Computer Journal, 9,* 373–380.

Lanyon, R. I. (1968). A handbook of MMPI group profiles. Minneapolis: University of Minnesota Press.

Lorr, M. (1983). *Cluster analysis for social scientists.* San Francisco: Jossey-Bass.

Lorr, M. & Strack, S. (1993). Some NEO-PI five-factor personality profiles. *Journal of Personality Assessment, 60,* 91–99.

Lorr, M. & Suziedelis, A. (1982). A cluster analytic approach to MMPI profile types. *Multivariate Behavioral Research, 17,* 285–299.

Lorr, M. & Youniss, R. L. (1986). *The Interpersonal Style Inventory.* Los Angeles: Western Psychological Services.

Marks, P. D., Seeman, W. & Haller, D. L. (1974). *The actuarial uses of the MMPI with adolescents and adults.* Baltimore, MD: Williams & Wilkens.

McClung, J. S. Guilford. (1963). Dimensional analyses of inventory responses in the establishment of group occupational types (Doctoral Dissertation, University of Southern California).

McIntyre, R. & Blashfield, R. K. (1980). A nearest-centroid technique for estimating cluster replication. *Multivariate Behavioral Research, 15,* 225–238.

McQuitty, L. L. (1957). Elementary linkage analysis for isolating orthogonal and oblique types and typal relevancies. *Educational and Psychological Measurement, 17,* 207–222.

Meehl, P. E. (1979). A funny thing happened to us on the way to the latent entities. *Journal of Personality Assessment, 43,* 564–576.

Meehl, P. E., & Golden, R. R. (1982). Taxometric methods. In P. Kendall & J. Butcher (Eds.) *Handbook of research methods in clinical psychology* (pp. 127–181). New York: John Wiley.

Mezzich, J. E. (1983). Comparing cluster analysis methods. In H. C. Hudson (Ed.), *Classifying Social Data: New Applications of Analytic Methods for Social Science Research*. San Francisco: Jossey-Bass.

Milligan, G. W. (1979). Ultrametric hierarchical clustering algorithms. *Psychometrika, 44*, 343–346.

Milligan, G. W. (1981). A Monte Carlo study of thirty internal criterion measures for cluster analyses. *Psychometrika, 46*, 186–199.

Milligan, G. W. (1981). A review of Monte Carlo tests of cluster analyses. *Multivariate Behavioral Research, 16*, 371–407.

Milligan, G. W. & Cooper, M. C. (1985). An examination of procedures for determining the number of clusters in a data set. *Psychometrika, 50*, 159–179.

Milligan, G. W. & Cooper, M. C. (1987). Methodology review: Clustering methods. *Applied Psychological Measurement, 11*, 329–354.

Milligan, G. W. & Sokal, L. M. (1980). A two-stage clustering algorithm with robust recovery characteristics. *Educational and Psychological Measurement, 40*, 755–759.

Mojena, R. (1977). Hierarchical grouping methods and stopping rules: An evaluation. *The Computer Journal, 20*, 359–363.

Morey, L. C., Blashfield, R. K. & Skinner, H. A. (1983). A comparison of cluster analysis techniques within a sequential validation framework. *Multivariate Behavioral Research, 18*, 309–329.

Morey, L. C., Skinner, H. A. & Blashfield, R. K. (1984). A typology of alcohol abusers: Correlates and implications. *Journal of Abnormal Psychology, 93*, 408–417.

Nunnally, J. C. (1962). The analysis of profile data. *Psychological Bulletin, 59*, 311–319.

Overall, J. E., Gibson, J. M. & Novy, D. M. (1993). Population recovery capabilities of 35 cluster analysis methods. *Journal of Clinical Psychology, 49*, 459–470.

Overall, J. E. & Klett, C. J. (1972). *Applied multivariate analysis*. New York: McGraw-Hill.

Rand, W. M. (1971). Objective criteria for evaluation of clustering methods. *Journal of the American Statistical Association, 66*, 846–850.

Rohlf, F. J. (1972). An empirical comparison of three ordination techniques in numerical taxonomy. *Systematic Zoology, 21*, 271–280.

Romesburg, H. C. (1984). *Cluster analysis for researchers*. Belmont, CA: Lifetime Learning Publications.

Scoltock, J. (1982). A Survey of the literature of cluster analysis. *Computer Journal, 25*, 130–134.

Shepard, R. N. & Arabie, P. (1979). Additive clustering: Representation of similarities as combinations of discrete overlapping properties. *Psychological Review, 86*, 87–123.

Skinner, H. A. (1978). Differentiating the contribution of elevation, scatter, and shape in profile similarity. *Educational and Psychological Measurement, 38*, 297–308.

Skinner, H. A. (1979). Dimensions and clusters: A hybrid approach to classification. *Applied Psychological Measurement, 3*, 327–341.

Skinner, H. A. & Jackson, D. N. (1978). A model of psychopathology based on an integration of MMPI Actuarial Systems. *Journal of Clinical and Consulting Psychology, 46*, 231–236.

Sneath, P.H.A. & Sokal, R. (1973). *Numerical taxonomy*. San Francisco: Freeman.

Sokal, R. R. & Michner, C. D. (1958). A statistical method for evaluating systematic relationships. *University of Kansas Scientific Bulletin, 38*, 1409–1438.

Sokal, R. R. & Sneath, P.H.A. (1963). *Principles of numerical taxonomy*. San Francisco: W. H. Freeman.

Stephenson, W. (1936). Introduction to inverted factor analysis with some application to studies in orexia. *Journal of Educational Psychology, 5*, 353–367.

Tryon, R. C. (1939). *Cluster analysis*. Ann Arbor: Edwards.

Tryon, R. C. & Bailey, D. E. (1970). *Cluster analysis*. New York: McGraw-Hill.

Ward, J. H. (1963). Hierarchical grouping to optimize an objective function. *Journal of the American Statistical Association, 58*, 236–244.

Widiger, T. A. & Sanderson. (1993). Toward a dimensional model of personality disorders in DSM-IV and DSM-V. In W. J. Livesly (Ed.), *DSM-IV Personality Disorders*. New York: Guilford.

Wishart, D. (1978). *CLUSTAN user's manual* (3rd ed.). Edinburgh: Program Library Unit.

Wolfe, J. H. (1970). Pattern clustering by multivariate mixture analysis. *Multivariate Behavioral Research, 5*, 329–350.

10

Multidimensional Scaling Models of Personality Responding

Mark L. Davison

R esearch psychologists have long used a variety of techniques to study structure, including factor analysis, cluster analysis, and multidimensional scal
ing (MDS). By representing structure in terms of discrete categories or
clusters, cluster analysis differs from factor analysis and MDS, both of which represent the structure spatially in terms of continuous latent variables called either
factors or dimensions.

Factor analysis and MDS differ in their assumptions about how the latent variables are related to observed data. These differing assumptions would be largely
academic except that they lead to major differences in the kinds of questions posed,
the character of the resulting structural representation, and the interpretation of
that representation.

Although there are exceptions (e.g., Bell & Jackson, 1992; Smith & Glass,
1977; Widiger, Trull, Hurt, Clarkin, & Frances, 1987), much of the MDS personality research can be divided into two major areas: research on interpersonal perception and research on personality inventories. The MDS interpersonal perception research begins from the premise that important personality variables manifest
themselves in interpersonal behavior. Interpersonal behavior is mediated by interpersonal perceptions, such as perceptions of self, others, roles, relationships, and
interpersonal episodes (Jones, 1983). MDS becomes a tool for mapping perceptions for purposes of studying the antecedents of those perceptions and the relationships between interpersonal perceptions and behavior.

Although the connection between MDS person perception research and interpersonal theories of personality is obvious, there is also a subtle connection between interpersonal theories of personality and MDS personality inventory re-

search. Circumplex models have played a prominent role in research on interpersonal dimensions of personality (Gurtman, 1992; Horowitz, 1979; Kiesler, 1983; Pincus & Wiggins, 1992; Wiggins, 1982). Because circumplex models have been prominent in theories of interpersonal personality dimensions and because MDS is particularly well suited to the study of circumplexes (Davison, 1985; Levin, 1991), MDS research on personality inventories is linked to interpersonal theories of personality and pathology.

The remainder of this chapter is divided into three major sections. The first section introduces basic statistical concepts in MDS. It is not intended as a thorough introduction to the method. Rather, it simply presents a brief overview of concepts used in succeeding sections. Readers interested in a more thorough treatment of MDS should consult Davison (1983) or Kruskal and Wish (1978). The second section covers MDS research designs for mapping social cognitions. Finally, the paper discusses MDS models for personality tests and inventories. These models are contrasted with the factor model. A new, profile interpretation of MDS dimensions is introduced.

BASIC STATISTICAL CONCEPTS

In classical MDS representations of structure, each object is represented as a point in a Euclidean space of continuous dimensions. While confirmatory techniques exist (e.g., Ramsey,1978; Heiser & Meulman, 1983), the most widely used MDS analyses are exploratory.

Sampling Subjects and Stimuli

As with any statistical technique, subjects must be drawn randomly or representatively if results are to be generalized to a wider population of people. Similarly, stimuli must be sampled randomly or representatively if results are to generalize beyond the sample of stimuli studied. An attribute of the stimuli cannot emerge as an MDS dimension if stimuli do not vary on that attribute. On the one hand, if the stimuli are descriptive personality statements and some refer to depression and others do not, then degree of relevance to depression can emerge as a dimension of statements in the MDS solution. On the other hand, if the statements are all equally relevant to depression, then depression relatedness is a constant across items and will not emerge as a dimension in the MDS solution. This seemingly obvious point will become important later in comparing components and MDS analyses of test intercorrelations.

Input Data

Input to a MDS analysis consists of proximity data. Proximity data are indices defined over pairs of stimulus objects which quantify the degree of similarity or association between each pair of objects. The best known proximity measure is the correlation coefficient defined over pairs of tests or test items. In the studies discussed below, researchers used two types of proximity data: direct proximity judgments and derived measures.

In collecting *direct proximity judgments*, the researcher asks subjects to directly judge the similarity or dissimilarity of two objects. For instance, the researcher may ask a subject to look at two interpersonal scenarios and then rate them in terms of similarity on a scale such as the following:

Highly Similar — — — — — — — — Highly Dissimilar

Although there are incomplete designs in which each subject judges only a subset of stimulus pairs, in a typical study, the subjects would judge the similarity of all possible pairs of stimuli. If each subject rated all possible pairs, the result would be one proximity data matrix for each subject, matrices like those at the top of Table 10.1.

If both individual differences parameters and stimulus scale values are to be estimated simultaneously, then each individual subject's judgements must be entered separately. If, however, only estimates of stimulus scale values are of interest, the researcher might average judgments over all subjects and enter just an average judgment matrix, such as the one at the bottom of Table 10.1.

Direct proximity judgments leave subjects free to select the attributes on which to base their judgments of similarity between stimuli. This contrasts with techniques, such as the Semantic Differential, in which unidimensional scales are specified by the researcher, and the result, while multidimensional, can only mirror the researcher's preconceptions embodied in those rating scales. Therefore, direct proximity judgments are particularly useful when the researcher wants to study the dimensions to which *subjects* attend and the salience of each such dimension.

In contrast to direct proximity judgments, derived proximity measures are ones computed from subject responses other than direct proximity judgments. For instance, the stimuli might be items from an adjective checklist. Subjects would select those adjectives which described them. Then the researcher would compute the correlation coefficient for each pair of adjectives. These correlation coefficients would be derived measures of proximity for stimulus adjective pairs. While the correlation coefficient is one possible derived measure, commonly available computer packages offer many others.

When the stimuli are test scores or test item scores, Davison and Skay (1991) argue that the squared Euclidean distance (SED) measure of proximity has a sound theoretical justification. Let m_{is} and $m_{i's}$ be the responses of subject s to stimulus measures i and i'. Then the SED proximity measure for stimulus measures i and i' will be

$$\delta^2_{ii'} = (1/S) \, \Sigma_s (m_{is} - m_{i's})^2 \tag{1}$$

where S is the number of subjects. If the measures i and i' are both in z-score form with mean 0.0 and variance 1.0, then the SED proximity measure is linearly re-

**TABLE 10.1 Hypothetical Ratings
of Dissimilarity for Two Subjects
and the Average Group**

Subject 1				
Stimulus	A	B	C	D
B	3			
C	4	3		
D	5	4	3	
E	6	5	4	3

Subject 2				
Stimulus	A	B	C	D
B	4			
C	3	3		
D	1	6	5	
E	5	2	4	4

Average Subject				
Stimulus	A	B	C	D
B	3.5			
C	3.5	3.0		
D	3.0	5.0	4.0	
E	5.5	3.5	4.0	3.5

lated to the correlation coefficient $d^2_{ii'} = 2 - 2r_{ii'}$, and hence, in a nonmetric MDS, which utilizes only the rank order information in the data, the two proximity measures ($d^2_{ii'}$ computed from z-scores and $r_{ii'}$) will yield identical MDS solutions. As is probably obvious to the reader, when a derived proximity measure is used, the nature of the solution can be materially influenced by the choice of proximity measure (Li, 1992).

MDS Models

Whatever the nature of the proximity data, there are various possible scaling models from which to choose. Such a model embodies a set of assumptions about the relationship between the proximity data and model parameters. Model parameters include the stimulus scale value parameters (locations of stimuli along "latent"

dimensions), and if the model is an individual differences model, person parameters. The various MDS analyses in the MDS family are based on different models;
that is, different assumptions about the relationship between observed proximity
data and parameters. The various MDS analyses are algorithms for estimating the
parameters in a model and quantifying the fit of the model to the data.

The best known and most frequently employed are the classical nonmetric
model and the weighted Euclidean model (WEM). In the nonmetric model, the
proximity data are assumed to have the following form:

$$\delta_{ii'} \approx f(d_{ii'}) \tag{2}$$

where f is a monotone function, $d_{ii'} = \sqrt{\Sigma_k(x_{ik} - x_{i'k})^2}$, and x_{ik} and $x_{i'k}$ are the scale
value parameters which locate stimuli i and i' respectively along dimension k. In
essence, this model posits that stimuli can be represented by points in a Euclidean
space of K dimensions. Except for measurement and sampling error, the rank order
of the distances between pairs of points, $d_{ii'}$, is the same as the rank order of the
data $\delta_{ii'}$. This model is said to be nonmetric because it utilizes only the rank order
of the input proximity data.

In an analysis based on the model of Equation 2, the goal is to estimate the
number of dimensions K needed to reproduce the data (unless K is known a priori),
the stimulus parameters x_{ik} and $x_{i'k}$, approximate the monotone function f (actually the inverse f^{-1}), and quantify the fit of the model to the data. In nonmetric
MDS, the most common measure of fit is Kruskal's (1964a, b) STRESS, a normalized, least squares measure of fit which equals 0.0 if the model can account
for the data perfectly and increases toward 1.00 as the model fit the data less well.

Unlike the nonmetric model of Equation 2, the weighted Euclidean model is
an individual differences model containing both stimulus scale value parameters
and person parameters. The basic input data consist of several proximity matrices, one for each person or subject group s with elements $\delta_{ii's}$. In its metric form,
the WEM is as follows:

$$\delta_{ii's} \approx \sqrt{\Sigma_k w_{ks}(x_{ik} - x_{i'k})^2}. \tag{3}$$

Except for measurement and sampling error, each data point equals a weighted
Euclidean distance between points. According to Equation 3, if the weight for
subject s, called the salience weight w_{ks}, equals zero along dimension k, then variation between stimuli along dimension k has no influence on the data of subject s.
As $w_{ks} > 0$ increases, then variation between stimuli along dimension k has an
increasing influence on the data of subject s. According to the model, it is as if
some subjects ignore the dimension, which would be reflected by a weight $w_{ks} = 0$,
while others heavily attend to it, as reflected in a large value of w_{ks}.

In analyses based on the WEM, the goal is to estimate the number of dimensions K (unless K is known a priori), the stimulus scale value parameters along
each dimension x_{ik}, the subject weights w_{ks}, and a measure of fit.

Various theories predict that the degree to which one attends to stimulus dimensions—particularly dimensions of interpersonal significance—is a function of personality variables, social roles, or demographic characteristics. The weights, w_{ks}, quantify the salience of stimulus dimensions. As we shall see below, one way to test such predictions is to study the relationship between dimension salience, as quantified by dimension weights w_{ks}, and personality measures, social roles, or demographic characteristics.

PERSON PERCEPTION

MDS has been used to study perceptions of various stimuli: personality prototypes (Broughton, 1990), avoidance strategies in intimate relationships (Belk & Snell, 1988), anger provoking experiences (Snell, McDonald & Koch, 1991), gender stereotypes (Six & Eckes, 1991), concepts of happiness (Thomas & Stock, 1988), and personal constructs in implicit personality theory (Rosenberg, Nelson & Vivekananthan, 1968; Voonk & Heiser, 1991). The literature on marital and family counseling contains several MDS studies; Ludlow and Howard (1990) and Diekhoff, Holder, and Burks (1988) used MDS to study perceptions of family members, and Amato (1990) examined perceptions of parent–child relationship concepts. Jones (1983) reviewed the literature to that date.

Research on interpersonal perceptions in small groups began with Jones' studies of social perceptions in an academic unit (Jones & Young, 1972) and an ROTC group (Davison & Jones, 1976). In these studies using direct proximity measures, group members rated all possible pairs of stimulus persons (group members) in terms of similarity, and a MDS representation of group structure was computed from these direct proximity measures using the WEM of Equation 3. In both studies, analyses of the salience weights, w_{ks} in Equation 3, revealed that perceptions varied as a function of perceived position in the group. For instance, Jones and Young found that faculty, who were higher than graduate students along MDS Dimension I (Status) seemed to attach more importance to Status as measured by their salience weights for Dimension I. In both studies, sociometric choice or sociometric preferences were related to perceived position in the group. Those perceived as more similar reported being more likely to interact. This association between sociometric behavior and interpersonal perceptions lends support to the hypothesis of a mediating relationship between interpersonal perceptions and interpersonal behavior.

Sprouse and Brush (1980) extended MDS research on small groups to the study of a therapy group. The authors used MDS to study how group members viewed one another, the consistency of those perceptions over time, the interpersonal dimensions underlying those perceptions, and the salience of the various dimensions to different members of the group.

At three points in time, each member rated the similarity of all possible pairs of group members. Using an analysis based on the WEM model of Equation 3, Sprouse and Bush (1980) found three dimensions underlying those perceived similarity ratings, high vs. low self-disclosure about alcohol problems, talkers vs. nontalkers, and race (black vs. white). From examining the average salience weights (w_{ks} in Equation 3) for blacks and whites, the authors concluded that blacks focused more (higher average weight w_{ks}) on the disclosure of alcohol problems dimension and the race dimension. Whites focused more heavily on the talker vs. nontalker dimension. The group leader focused heavily on the talker vs. nontalker dimension. The authors also examined changes in the salience weights over time. In importance, the disclosure dimension remained stable over time, the race dimension became less important, and the talker vs. nontalker dimension became more prominent in client's judgments about each other.

Like Jones and Young (1972) and Davison and Jones (1976), Sprouse and Bush (1980) found that the salience of interpersonal dimensions varied as a function of perceived position in the group. Their disclosure dimension raises the possibility of a relationship between personality variables, in this case self-disclosure, and interpersonal perceptions in small groups. Forgas' (1978) study confirms the relationship.

Like Jones and Young (1972) Forgas (1978) studied an academic unit, this time in England, by having group members rate each other in terms of similarity. According to Forgas, his first dimension was similar to Jones and Young's Status dimension, but it was more closely associated with task competence and several personality characteristics as rated by group members: dominance, self-confidence, and talkativeness. The second dimension, labeled Sociability, was correlated with group members' perceived friendliness, warmth, humor, and pleasantness. The last dimension, labeled Creativity, was correlated with extroversion and disclosing. Forgas also scaled social episodes and estimated salience weights for subjects on dimensions of social episodes. Analyses of the social episode salience weights revealed some interesting results. For instance, those perceived as sociable tended to discriminate little between tense vs. relaxed or pleasant vs. unpleasant social episodes as befits their social self-confidence.

To what extent are MDS dimensions of intact small group perceptions associated with personality variables? The Self-disclosure Dimension of Sprouse and Bush (1980) and the personality correlates of Forgas's (1978) dimensions suggest that such associations exist. Forgas's results further suggest that personality variables are associated both with individual differences in perceived position in the group and with individual differences in dimension saliences. If such associations exist, however, they will raise a host of issues. Presumably, the personality variables manifested in a small group will vary as a function of the group's activities. For instance, in therapy groups, self-disclosure seems more likely than some other personality characteristics. Are the MDS interpersonal dimensions more closely associated with self-reports or others' reports of personality? Do MDS dimensions correlate with personality characteristics which the individual displays only in the group studied or are they more generalized trait-like variables?

TESTS AND TEST ITEMS

Although factor analysis, including components analysis, remains the most common way to analyze the structure of tests or test items, MDS has been increasingly recommended. For instance, it has been used to study Locus of Control items (DuBois, 1985), Eysenck's Personality Questionnaire (Hammond, 1987), and the Interpersonal Checklist (Paddock & Nowicki, 1986). In two respects, the MDS research has rested on a shallower foundation than has the factor research. First, MDS research has not started from an explicit model of test/item responses m_{is}. Instead, it has started from a model of the derived proximity measure $d_{ii'}$. The second problem essentially stems from the first—the absence of an explicit model for test/item responses. Factor analysts can readily talk meaningfully about item parameters (the factor pattern matrix, the factor structure matrix, etc.), and person parameters (factor scores), because they begin from an explicit model of test/item responses which includes both person and test/item parameters. Many MDS studies refer only to test/item parameters, in part, because the study lacks an explicit model of test/item responses expressed in terms of both person and item parameters. Furthermore, it is more difficult to interpret MDS scale values. The scale values don't correspond to parameters in a model of test/item responses, and consequently one cannot readily relate dimensions back to the original test/item responses.

This section on tests/items will begin with a comparison of MDS and R-technique factor analyses of tests and items. Then I will describe two MDS approaches (Davison & Skay, 1991) that begin from two different explicit models for test and item responses. These MDS models will be contrasted with the factor model. For the first of the two MDS models, the vector model, a new profile interpretation of dimensions will be introduced.

MDS and Components Analyses of Correlation Matrices

In an earlier work (Davison, 1985), I compared MDS and components analyses based on the same input correlation matrix. That article began with an analytic comparison of *metric* MDS (Torgerson, 1958) and components analysis. Although the analytic results applied only to the relationship between *metric* MDS and components analyses, simulation and real data (Davison, 1985; Silverstein, 1987) confirmed that both metric and nonmetric MDS analyses of correlation matrices can be similarly related to components solutions. Silverstein (1987) found both components and common factor solutions to be related in similar fashions to nonmetric MDS solutions of the WAIS-R (Wechsler, 1981), WISC-R (Wechsler, 1974), and WPPSI (Wechsler, 1967). Thus, at least under some circumstances, the components/metric MDS relationship described below generalizes to nonmetric MDS and common factor analysis.

In components analysis, one takes the principle components of correlations, $r_{ii'}$, which are nothing more than average cross-products for measures m_{is} expressed in standard score form: $r_{ii'} = (1/S)\Sigma_s z_{is} z_{i's}$. Torgerson's metric scaling also involves taking principal components of an average cross-product matrix, with the only difference being that the scaling solution is based on z-scores expressed as deviations about person means. Let $z^*_{is} = z_{is} - z_{.s}$ where $z_{.s} = (1/I)\Sigma_i z_{is}$ is the mean score for person s and I is the number of measures. In other words, $z_{.s}$ is the level component of the standardized score profile for person s. The score z^*_{is} is an ipsatized standard score. In contrast to components analysis, which involves taking principal components of average cross-products between standardized scores $r_{ii'} = (1/S \Sigma_s z_{is} z_{i's}$, Torgerson's metric scaling involves taking principal components of average cross-products between standardized scores expressed in ipsative form: $\delta^*_{ii'} = (1/S \Sigma_s z^*_{is} z^*_{i's}$. In other words, the effect of switching from components analysis to classical metric MDS of a correlation matrix is tantamount to switching from components of correlations (computed from z-scores) to components of scalar products (computed from ipsatized z-scores). It is as if MDS implicitly removes the level component, the standardized person mean $z_{.s}$ from scores.

The link between MDS and the person mean $z_{.s}$ ties the MDS vs. factor analysis debate to some wider issues in personality research. First, what is the level component in personality responding? In several contexts, it has been identified as a General Distress/Complaint factor, intensity, or acquiescence (Alden, Wiggins & Pincus, 1990; Horowitz, Rosenberg, Baier, Urenono & Villasenor, 1988; Paddock & Nowicki, 1986; Ray, 1983). As Davison & Srichantra (1988) have pointed out, in order to fully evaluate MDS representations of structure, it is important to understand whether the variance implicitly removed by MDS—the level component $z_{.s}$—is valid, trait-related variance, merely response style variance, or some combination of the two. Where the level component carries substantial trait-related variance, MDS may be portraying only a selected portion of the valid psychological structure. Where the level component carries substantial acquiescence variance, factor analysis (including confirmatory techniques) confound valid trait-related variance with artifactual response style variance.

Second, the link between MDS and the level component $z_{.s}$ ties MDS to studies of the interpersonal problems circumplex, research in which partialing the level component before factoring has been used to reveal the circumplex structure of scales (e.g., Alden, Wiggins & Pincus, 1990; Horowitz et al., 1988; Strack, 1987). In most cases, doing so will yield a solution similar to that obtained from a MDS of the test intercorrelation matrix, and MDS offers a more convenient method of arriving at that solution. Furthermore, as we shall see below, the MDS dimensions have an intriguing personality prototype interpretation.

Factor and MDS Solutions

The relationship between MDS and component solutions is not entirely predictable (Davison, 1985). In one special case, where $z_{.s}$ equals zero for all people, ipsatizing scores has no effect and, consequently, MDS and components solutions should be identical. In what has proven to be a more interesting special case, where

z_s is orthogonal to the components of scalar products matrix $d^*_{ii'}$, the effect of ipsatization is to remove the first, unrotated component. That is, reproducing the correlation matrix requires one more component than MDS dimensions, and all of the unrotated components have a counterpart in the MDS solution *except* the general component.

This second, special case is illustrated in Table 10.2, which shows the first three unrotated principal components and the first two nonmetric scaling dimensions of the intercorrelations between six subtests in Holland's (1965) *Vocational Preference Inventory*.

The first principal component in Table 10.2 is the general component along which all loadings are high and positive. Neither scaling dimension fits this description (all high, positive scale values). Along the second component, however, each test's loading is of the same sign and approximately the same magnitude as its scale value along MDS Dimension 1. Similarly, for Component 3, each test's loading is of the same sign and approximately the same magnitude as its scale value along nonmetric MDS Dimension 2. Thus, in this example, the relationship between components and MDS solutions is as follows: it takes one more component than MDS dimensions to reproduce the intercorrelations of the subtests; all components except the first, general component, have a counterpart in the MDS solution. This same relationship between components/factor solutions and nonmetric MDS solutions was found in Davison's (1985) analysis of the GATB (U.S. Department of Labor, 1970), Silverstein's (1987) analysis of Wechsler Intelligence Tests, and the Levin/Nediger (Levin, 1991; Nediger & Chelladurai 1989) analyses of the *Life Styles Inventory*.

As noted above in discussing sampling of stimuli and as noted by Davison and Skay (1991), MDS dimensions represent sources of variation among stimuli. The general component in Table 10.2 represents that which the tests have in common, not something on which they differ. As the general component does *not* cor-

TABLE 10.2 Components Loadings and Nonmetric Scale Values for the Vocational Preference Inventory Scales

Scale	Component 1	Dimension 1	Component 2	Dimension 2	Component 3
Realistic	.595	.369	.324	.491	.598
Investigative	.555	.683	.685	.061	.158
Artistic	.568	.133	.335	−.696	−.607
Social	.736	−.236	−.080	−.294	−.371
Enterprising	.803	−.492	−.437	.020	−.055
Conventional	.711	−.456	−.496	.418	.307

Note: The scale values computed by KYST (Kruskal, Young and Seery, 1973) were all multiplied by −.475 to make the signs of scale values more nearly match those of loadings along Components 2 and 3 and to make the sum of squared scale values along Dimensions 1 and 2 equal the sum of squared loadings of Components 2 and 3.

respond to substantial variation among the tests, it has no counterpart in the MDS representation.

Furthermore, as can be seen in Figure 10.1, the circumplex structure of the stimuli is readily visible in the MDS scaling solution (or the plane defined by Components 2 and 3). To find the circumplex in the components solution, one must depart substantially from common practice—and justify the departures: specifically, one must throw out the component accounting for the largest proportion of variance and one must refrain from applying any rotation to simple structure. As when stimuli form a circumplex, structure has often emerged more clearly in a MDS than in an exploratory factor analysis with some rotation to simple structure (Rounds, Davison & Dawis, 1979; Levin, 1991).

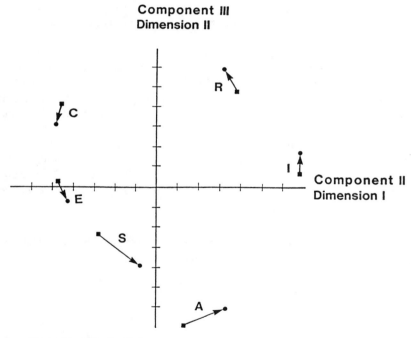

- ■ **Denotes Scale Values**
- ● **Denotes Component Loadings**

FIGURE 10.1. Scale values and component loadings for the *Vocational Preference Inventory* scales (*R* = Realistic, *I* = Investigative, *A* = Artistic, *S* = Social, *E* = Enterprising, *C* = Conventional).

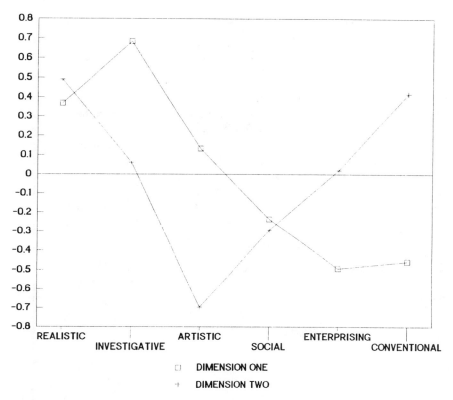

FIGURE 10.2. Scale values for Dimensions 1 and 2 in Table 2 plotted as profile prototypes.

An understanding of the complementarity between MDS and factor analysis requires more than just an understanding of how solutions, such as those in Table 10.2, compare. It also requires an understanding of the assumptions embodied in their respective models for personality test/item responses.

The Factor Model

If m_{is} is the response of subject s to measure i, the factor model posits that the observed responses m_{is} are related to latent factor scores f_{ks} by a function of the following form:

$$m_{is} = \Sigma_k a_{ik} f_{ks} + e_{is} \tag{4}$$

where a_{ik} is a weight for measure i on factor k, f_{ks} is the score of person s on factor k, and e_{is} is a deviation term combining unique and error variance. In the factor analytic tradition, the proximity measure (usually a correlation coefficient or co-variance) is derived from this model and standard assumptions:

$$\sigma_{ii'} = \Sigma_k a_{ik} a_{i'k}. \tag{5}$$

Here $\sigma_{ii'}$ is the covariance (or correlation if the measures are in standardized form) of measures i and i'. The various factor analytic algorithms solve for the weights a_{ik}.

One feature of the model in Equation 4 is noteworthy, because it contrasts with corresponding features of the MDS models below. The fundamental variables in the response model are factor scores, f_{ks}, latent individual differences variables. The test/item parameters, a_{ik}, are merely weighting parameters on those latent individual differences variables; if the factors are orthogonal, the test/item parameters reflect the amount of variance in measure i accounted for by factor s.

The MDS Vector Model

This MDS model, like the factor model, is linear, but it reverses the role of person and test/item parameters. The fundamental variables in the model are scores for test/items, the scale values x_{ik}. The person parameters, w_{ks}, are merely weighting parameters that are proportional to the amount of variance in the responses of person s, which can be accounted for by stimulus dimension k:

$$m_{is} = \Sigma_k w_{ks} x_{ik} + c_s + e_{is}. \tag{6}$$

From this model and some simplifying assumptions (Davison & Skay, 1991), one can show that the SED proximity measure (Equation 1) will be related to model parameters as follows: $\delta^2_{ii'} = \Sigma_k (x_{ik} - x_{i'k})^2 + 2\sigma^2$ where σ is the standard deviation of the error term in Equation 6. Hence, the MDS scale values represent estimates of the test/item parameters, x_{ik}.

How does one interpret those scale values? One can interpret them in terms of item content dimensions or features. Here, however, I will propose a profile, or personality prototype interpretation which borrows heavily from Tucker's (1972) "idealized individual" concept. As compared to the individual differences orientation of factor analysis, this profile interpretation has a more idiographic character.

In Equation 6, one can think of each MDS dimension as representing the score profile of a prototype individual. MMPI codes illustrate the conception of proto-type envisioned here in which the prototype is marked by its high and low scores. For instance, the MMPI 32 = 6 profile is a profile marked by high scores on the Depression and Hysteria Scales and a low score on the Paranoia Scale.

The MDS scale values along a dimension represent a profile of scores for a prototype with the level component removed (because scale values are standard-ized to have mean 0 along each dimension). That is, x_{ik} is the score of prototypical person k on measure i and the set of scale values x_{ik} ($i = 1, \ldots, I$) is the profile of prototypical person k on the I measures with the level component removed.

For instance, consider the MDS solution in Table 10.2 and Figure 10.1. This is a two-dimensional representation of the six Holland vocational interest scales in the *Vocational Preference Inventory* (Holland, 1965). These scale values are plotted in Figure 10.2 as two score profiles. In Figure 10.2, the profile corresponding to Dimension 1 represents a prototypical individual with high scores on Investigative (i.e., scientific) items and low scores on Enterprising (e.g., sales) and Conventional (e.g., bookkeeping, accounting) items. If one were to use MMPI-like codes, one might call this the I-EC prototype. The profile corresponding to Dimension 2 represents a prototypical individual with high scores on Conventional (e.g., accounting or bookkeeping) and Realistic (e.g., engineering or mechanics) items and low scores on Artistic items, a CR-A protype. When the dimensions are given a prototypical profile interpretation, the MDS vector model represents each person's responses, m_{is}, as a linear combination of the K prototypes x_{ik}.

Davison & Skay (1991) do not discuss how one can estimate the individual differences parameters, w_{ks}, in Equation 6. Given estimates of the scale values, x_{ik}, from an MDS analysis of the proximities $\delta_{ii'}$ and given the subject responses m_{is}, Davison (1983, pp. 159–163) shows how to estimate the subject salience weights w_{ks} and the subject's profile level parameter c_s by regressing the subject's responses m_{is} onto the dimension coordinates x_{ik}. If the dimensions are orthogonal, the subject weight estimates w_{ks} quantify the degree of correspondence between the score profile of subject s and the prototype profile corresponding to dimension k. Those subjects with the highest weights for dimension k, w_{ks}, are the ones whose score profile patterns most closely resemble the prototype pattern of dimension k. Subjects with negative weights display patterns which are the mirror image of prototype dimension k.

What is a "mirror image profile?" Consider the dimensions which would be expected in a study of the interpersonal personality circle. Dimension 1 might be a Dominant-Submissive Dimension, representing a Dominant Profile, with high scale values for dominant measures and low scale values for submissive measures. Dimension 2 might be a Friendly-Hostile Dimension, representing a Friendly Profile, with high scale values for friendly measures and low scale values for hostile measures. Scale values along Dimension 1 would reflect a Dominant Prototype individual with high scores on dominance measures and low scores on submissive measures. Large *positive* salience weights on the Dominant-Submissive Dimension would characterize people with a Dominant Profile. The mirror-image of the Dominant Profile is the Submissive Profile, characterized by high scores on submissive measures and low scores on dominance measures. Large *negative* salience weights would characterize subjects with a Submissive Profile. Likewise, the Hostile Profile is the mirror-image of the Friendly Profile. Subjects with a Hostile Profile would be characterized by large, *neqative* weights along Dimension

2, the Friendly-Hostile Dimension, while those with a Friendly Profile would be characterized by a large, *positive* weights along Dimension 2.

In interpreting MDS scale values, one need not rely on the profile interpretation outlined above. One can interpret dimensions in terms of content features or content orderings (e.g., item endorsement frequencies or depth of depression expressed in statements). For tests and items which rely heavily on idiographic interpretations, MDS may prove a particularly useful technique for representing structure in terms of prototypical profile patterns, each of which corresponds to an MDS dimension. Whereas the R-technique factor model represents observed individual differences variables, m_{is}, as linear combinations of "latent" individual differences variables f_{ks} called factors, the MDS vector model of Equation 6 can be interpreted as representing observed score profile patterns as a linear combination of "latent" or prototype profile patterns, x_{ik}.

The MDS Unfolding Model

The unfolding model below is a special case of the unfolding model proposed by Coombs (1964) for preference data. In personality research, the unfolding model is probably most useful in the study of developmental continua, such as those discussed by Loevinger (1966), Rest (1979), and Wohlwill (1973). Responses are assumed to be scored so that *low* scores indicate strong endorsement. Test/item responses are assumed to have the following form:

$$m_{is} = d_{is}^2 + c_s + e_{is} = \Sigma_k (x_{ik} - y_{sk})^2 + c_s + e_{is}. \tag{7}$$

Here y_{sk} refers to the location of person s along dimension k. The remaining terms, x_{ik}, m_{is}, c_s, and e_{is}, are defined as before. Each dimension k refers to a personality dimension, a developmental dimension, or a dimension of attitude/interest. Each stimulus statement i has a location along that dimension, x_{ik}, which refers to the level of content in that statement. According to this distance model, people will most strongly endorse those statements whose content closely resembles their own thinking or feeling Hence, according to the model, the smaller the distance between the point characterizing the subject's thinking, y_{sk}, and the point representing the thinking expressed in the statement, x_{sk}, the more strongly will the subject endorse the statement.

Davison and Skay (1991) have discussed how nonmetric MDS can be used to estimate the locations of stimulus items/tests that satisfy the model of Equation 7. Specifically, let m^*_{is} equal m_{is} expressed in deviation score form, $m^*_{is} = m_{is} - m_{i.}$, where $m_{i.} = (1/S) \Sigma_s m_{is}$ and S is the number of subjects. Davison and Skay suggest a MDS analysis based on the SED proximity measure computed over deviation scores m^*_{is} for all pairs of items:

$$\delta^2_{ii'} = (.25/S) \Sigma_s (m^*_{is} - m^*_{i's})^2. \tag{8}$$

Given certain simplifying assumptions, it can be shown that this proximity measure is directly related to the item scale values: $\delta_{ii'} = \Sigma_k(x_{ik} - x_{i'k})^2 + .5\sigma^2$. Because the proximity measures are monotonically related to distances in a Euclidean space, MDS can be used to solve for the model parameters x_{ik}, estimates of each statements' locations along the personality dimension k.

Clearly, this model assumes that statements, as well as people, are ordered along personality dimensions and that people most strongly endorse (or most frequently express) statements whose content resembles their own thinking. Most personality inventories make no such assumptions. However, some unidimensional, developmental personality models do (Loevinger, 1966; Rest, 1979). According to these models, statements can be ordered developmentally and people will most strongly endorse (or most frequently express) those statements which correspond to the subject's developmental level. Davison, Robbins, and Swanson (1977) studied the stage scores in Rest's *Defining Issues Test (DIT)* of moral judgment development. According to Rest (1979), each item is keyed to an ordered stage in Kohlberg's (1976) theory of moral development. Davison, Robbins, and Swanson (1977) found that the scales in Rest's test fell along a dimension in roughly stage order. The *D*-score reported for the *DIT* is proportional to a person's estimated location, y_{sk}, along the developmental continuum.

With the exception of Loevinger's *Sentence Completion Test* (1966) and Rest's (1979) *Defining Issues Test*, few personality instruments embody the assumption of statements ordered along one or more dimensions, the assumption of people ordered along those same dimensions, and the assumption that clients will most strongly endorse (or most frequently express) statements whose content most nearly expresses their own thinking/feeling. If the work of Loevinger and Rest are any indication, such assumptions—and hence the unfolding model of Equation 7 or some variation of it—will prove most useful in developmental models of personality in which the dimensions correspond to independent strands of personality development. In such models, statements vary in the developmental level of their expressed thinking/feeling indexed by scale values x_{ik}, people vary in their developmental levels indexed by person parameters y_{sk}, and people prefer statements which express thoughts and feelings characteristic of their developmental level.

DISCUSSION AND CONCLUSION

As MDS has been practiced to date, it has been tied to either interpersonal theories, the psychometric tradition of personality research, or both. The MDS interpersonal perception research has been premised on the assumption that important personality variables manifest themselves in interpersonal behavior and that interpersonal perceptions mediate interpersonal behavior. MDS has been used to map interpersonal perceptions. MDS maps of interpersonal perception have been viewed as a tool for studying the personality variables associated with individual differences in interpersonal perceptions, a tool for studying the personality variables which underlie interpersonal perceptions, and a tool for studying the relationships between interpersonal perception and interpersonal behavior.

In the psychometric tradition, MDS has served as an alternative to factor analysis in studying the structure of personality inventories and items. Although in theory the relationship between factor and MDS solutions based on the same correlation matrix is difficult to predict, often, in practice, each unrotated factor, except the general factor, has had a counterpart in the MDS solution. This has made MDS particularly useful for exploring certain types of structures, such as circumplex structures.

As a tool for personality research, MDS seems most promising in the following three areas. First, MDS can be used to map interpersonal perceptions for purposes of studying the relationships among personality variables, interpersonal perceptions, and interpersonal behavior. Second, the MDS vector model offers an idiographic alternative to nomothetic R-technique factor analysis, an alternative in which associations among tests or items are accounted for by a small number of dimensions interpreted as prototypical personality profiles, rather than in terms of factors interpreted as latent individual differences variables. Like Zevon and Tellegan (1982), I perceive the idiographic and nomothetic approaches as complementary viewpoints, but viewpoints often best served by different analyses of the same data. Finally (third), the MDS unfolding model offers a tool for studying developmental personality continua.

The various methods of studying structure—factor analysis, MDS, and cluster analysis—are usually viewed as complementary methods. Only with a more complete understanding of their complementarities will we be able to take full advantage of the techniques in building the body of knowledge we call personality psychology.

REFERENCES

Alden, L. E., Wiggins, J. S., & Pincus, A. L. (1990). Construction of circumplex scales for the Inventory of Interpersonal Problems. *Journal of Personality Assessment, 55*, 521–536.

Amato, P. R. (1990). Dimensions of the family environment as perceived by children: A multidimensional scaling analysis. *Journal of Marriage and the Family, 52*, 613–620.

Broughton, R. (1990). The prototype concept in personality assessment. *Canadian Psychology, 31*, 26–37.

Belk, S. S., & Snell, W. E., Jr. (1988). Avoidance strategy use in intimate relationships. *Journal of Social and Clinical Psychology, 7*, 80–96.

Bell, R. C., & Jackson, H. J. (1992). The structure of personality disorders in DSM-III. *Acta Psychiatrica Scandinavica, 85*, 279–287.

Coombs, C. H. (1964). *A theory of data.* New York: Wiley.

Davison, M. L. (1983). *Multidimensional scaling.* Wiley: New York.

Davison, M. L. (1985). Multidimensional scaling versus components analysis of test intercorrelations. *Psychological Bulletin, 97,* 94–105.

Davison, M. L., & Jones, L. E. (1976). A similarity-attraction model for predicting sociometric choice from perceived group structure. *Journal of Personality and Social Psychology, 33,* 601–612.

Davison, M. L., Robbins, S., & Swanson, D. (1978). Stage structure in objective moral judgments. *Developmental Psychology, 14,* 137–146.

Davison, M. L. & Skay, C. L. (1991). Multidimensional scaling and factor models of test and item responses. *Psychological Bulletin, 110,* 551–556.

Davison, M. L. & Srichantra, N. (1988). Acquiescence in components analysis and multidimensional scaling of self-rating items. *Applied Psychological Measurement, 12,* 339–351.

Diekhoff, G. M., Holder, B. A., & Burks, R. (1988). Social cognitive structures: Marriage counseling through multidimensional scaling. *Small Group Behavior, 19,* 185–206.

Dubois, N. (1985). The dimensionality of locus of control among French students. *Journal of Psychology, 119,* 549–555.

Forgas, J. P. (1978). Social episodes and social structure in an academic setting: The social environment of an intact group. *Journal of Personality and Social Psychology, 14,* 434–448.

Gurtman, M. B. (1992). Construct validity of interpersonal personality measures: The interpersonal circumplex as a nomological net. *Journal of Personality and Social Psychology, 63,* 105–118.

Hammond, S. M. (1987). The item structure of the Eysenck Personality questionnaire across method and culture. *Personality and Individual Differences, 8,* 541–549.

Heiser, W. J., & Meulman, J. (1983). Constrained multidimensional scaling, including confirmation. *Applied Psychological Measurement, 7,* 381–404.

Holland, J. L. (1965). *Manual for the vocational preference inventory* (6th ed.). Palo Alto, CA: Consulting Psychologists Press.

Horowitz, L. M. (1979). On the cognitive structure of interpersonal problems treated in psychotherapy. *Journal of Consulting and Clinical Psychology, 47,* 5–15.

Horowitz, L. M., Rosenberg, S. E., Baer, B. A., Ureno, G., & Villasenor, V. S. (1988). Inventory of interpersonal problems: Psychometric properties and clinical applications. *Journal of Consulting and Clinical Psychology, 56,* 885–892.

Jones, L. E. (1983). Multidimensional models of social perception, cognition, and behavior. *Applied Psychological Measurement, 7,* 451–472.

Jones, L. E. & Young, F. W. (1972). Structure of a social environment: Longitudinal individual differences scaling of an intact group. *Journal of Personality and Social Psychology, 24,* 108–121.

Kiesler, D. J. (1983). The 1982 interpersonal circle: A taxonomy for complementarity in human transactions. *Psychological Review, 90,* 185–214.

Kohlberg, L. (1976). Moral stages and moralization: The cognitive developmental approach. In T. Lickona (Ed.), *Moral development and behavior.* New York: Holt, Rinehart & Winston.

Kruskal, J. B. (1964a). Multidimensional scaling by optimizing goodness of fit to a nonmetric hypothesis. *Psychometrika, 29,* 1–27.

Kruskal, J. B. (1964b). Nonmetric multidimensional scaling: A numerical method. *Psychometrika, 29,* 115–129.

Kruskal, J. B., Young, F. W., & Seery, J. B. (1973). *How to use KYST, a very flexible program to do multidimensional scaling and unfolding.* Murray Hill, NJ: Unpublished manuscript, Bell Laboratories.

Kruskal, J. B., & Wish, M. (1978). *Multidimensional scaling.* Beverly Hills: Sage.

Levin, J. L. (1991). The circumplex pattern of the Life Styles Inventory: A reanalysis. *Educational and Psychological Measurement, 51*, 567–572.

Li, X. (1992). *An Investigation of Proximity Measures with Dichotomous Response Data in Nonmetric Multidimensional Scaling.* Unpublished doctoral dissertation, University of Minnesota, Minneapolis, MN.

Loevinger, J. (1966). The meaning and measurement of ego development. *American Psychologist, 21*, 195–206.

Ludlow, L. H., & Howard, E. (1990). The family map: A graphical representation of family systems theory. *Educational and Psychological Measurement, 50*, 245–255.

Nediger, W. G., & Chelladurai, P. (1989). Life Styles Inventory: Its applicability in the Canadian context. *Educational and Psychological Measurement, 49*, 900–909.

Paddock, J. R., & Nowicki, S., Jr. (1986). The circumplexity of Leary's interpersonal circle: A multidimensional scaling perspective. *Journal of Personality Assessment, 50*, 279–289.

Pincus, A. L., & Wiggins, J. S. (1990). Interpersonal problems and conceptions of personality disorders. *Journal of Personality Disorders, 4*, 342–352.

Ramsey, J. O. (1978). MULTISCALE: Four programs for multidimensional scaling by the method of maximum likelihood. Chicago: International Education Services.

Ray, J. J. (1983). Reviving the problem of acquiescent response bias. *Journal of Social Psychology, 121*, 81–96.

Rest, J. R. (1979). *Development in judging moral issues.* Minneapolis, MN: University of Minnesota Press.

Rosenberg, S., Nelson, C., & Vivekananthan, P. S. (1968). A multidimensional approach to the structure of personality impression. *Journal of Personality and Social Psychology, 9*, 283–294.

Rounds, J. B., Jr., Davison, M. L., & Dawis, R. V. (1979). The fit between Strong-Campbell Interest Inventory general occupational themes and Holland's hexagonal model. *Journal of Vocational Behavior, 15*, 303–315.

Silverstein, A. B. (1987). Multidimensional scaling vs. factor analysis of Wechsler's intelligence scales. *Journal of Clinical Psychology, 43*, 381–386.

Six, B., & Eckes, T. (1991). A closer look at complex structure of gender stereotypes. *Sex Roles, 24*, 57–71.

Smith, M. L. & Glass, G. V. (1977). Meta-analysis of psychotherapy outcomes. *American Psychologist, 32*, 752–760.

Snell, W. E., McDonald, K., & Koch, W. R. (1991). Anger provoking experiences: A multidimensional scaling analysis. *Personality and Individual Differences, 10*, 1095–1104.

Sprouse, C. L., & Brush, D. H. (1980). Assessing a quasi-therapy group by individual differences multidimensional scaling. *Small Group Behavior, 11*, 35–49.

Strack, S. (1987). Development and validation of an adjective checklist to assess the Millon personality types in a normal population. *Journal of Personality Assessment, 51*, 572–587. 17

Thomas, J. A., & Stock, W. A. (1988). The concept of happiness: A multidimensional scaling investigation. *International Journal of Aging and Human Development, 27*, 141–154.

Torgerson, W. S. (1958). Theory and methods of scaling. New York: Wiley.

Tucker, L. R. (1972). Relations between multidimensional scaling and three-mode factor analysis. Psychometrika, 37, 3–28.

U.S. Department of Labor. (1970). *Manual for the USTES.* Washington, D.C.: U.S. Government Printing Office.

Voonk, R., & Heiser, W. J. (1991). Implicit personality theory and social judgment: Effects of familiarity with a target person. *Multivariate Behavioral Research, 26*, 69–81.

Wechsler, D. (1967). *Manual for the Wechsler Preschool and Primary Scale of Intelligence.* New York: Psychological Corporation.

Wechsler, D. (1974). *Manual for the Wechsler Intelligence Scale for Children Revised.* New York: Psychological Corporation.

Wechsler, D. (1981). *WAIS-R Manual: Wechsler Adult Intelligence Scale Revised.* New York: Psychological Corporation.

Widiger, T. A., Trull, T. J., Hurt, S. W., Clarkin, J., & Frances, A. (1987). A multidimensional scaling of the DSM-III personality disorders. *Archives of General Psychiatry, 44,* 557–563.

Wiggins, J. S. (1982). Circumplex models of interpersonal behavior in clinical psychology. In P. S. Kendall & J. N. Butcher (Eds.), *Handbook of research methods in clinical psychology.* New York: Wiley, 183–211.

Wohlwill, J. F. (1973). *The study of behavioral development.* New York: Academic Press.

Zevon, M. A. & Tellegen, A. (1982). The structure of mood change: An idiographic/nomothetic analysis. *Journal of Personality and Social Psychology, 43,* 111–122.

Zygmond, M. J. & Denton, W. (1988). Gender bias in marital therapy: A multidimensional scaling analysis. *The American Journal of Family Therapy, 16,* 1988, 262–272.

11

Revealing Structure in the Data: Principles of Exploratory Factor Analysis

Lewis R. Goldberg and John M. Digman

One goal of science is to understand the relations among variables, and the object of factor analysis is to aid scientists in this quest. Factor analysis can be thought of as a variable-reduction procedure, in which many variables are replaced by a few factors which summarize the relations among the variables. Consequently, in its broadest sense factor analysis is a procedure for identifying summary constructs. If one already has a theory about the structure of a set of variables, one can investigate the extent to which that theory accounts for the relations among the variables in a sample of data; "confirmatory" factor procedures are used for this purpose.[1] "Exploratory" factor procedures, the subject of this chapter, are used to discover summary constructs when their nature is still unknown.

Over the years since its development, factor analysis has been used for a wide variety of purposes, and investigators have differed enormously in their views about the scientific status of factors. In the context of personality and psychopathology (the focus of the present chapter), the most "realist" position has been taken by Cattell (1957), who explicitly equates factors with motivational "causes" (neuropsychological structures that produce behavioral patterns). At the other end of this continuum are those investigators who use factor analysis merely as a substitute for cluster analysis, and thus who make no assumptions that factors have any meaning beyond a particular data set. Both authors of this chapter take an intermediate position, with JMD leaning more toward the realist viewpoint than LRG.

Factor analysis and its near relative, component analysis, are statistical techniques that were first introduced by Pearson (1901) and Spearman (1904) and later refined by Thurstone (1931, 1947) and Hotelling (1933). For many years after their introduction, however, their intense computational demands virtually prohibited their widespread use. Indeed, the prospect of spending weeks—perhaps months—on hand-calculations was certainly discouraging, if not completely disheartening, to most investigators. As time passed and the mathematical foundations of the techniques became more securely established, textbooks such as those by Harman (1976) and Mulaik (1972), linking the basic concepts of factor analysis to matrix algebra and the geometry of hyperspace, made these concepts accessible to the mathematically adept. The typical researcher, however, struggling with the mathematical complexity of the concepts and the intensive computational demands of the procedures, has had to await the arrival of the packaged statistical computer programs that have now become increasingly available. Today, with programs for factor analysis available even for notebook computers, anyone with a large, complex, or bemusing set of variables can consider using these techniques, in the hope that they will provide some sense and order to his or her data.

However, in consulting the manual for one's statistical package and finding the chapter on factor analysis, the user is likely to be confronted with several anxiety-arousing decision options, such as: (a) Should one conduct a factor analysis or a components analysis? (b) How does one decide on the number of factors to extract? (c) Should the factors be rotated, and if so should the rotation be an orthogonal or an oblique one? (d) Should one obtain factor scores, and if so, by which procedure? Such questions are puzzling to the first-time user, and even to the experienced researcher.

In this chapter, we will present some of the major features of exploratory factor analysis, as it used in the context of personality research. In so doing, we hope to answer some of the questions faced by the user when considering the various options commonly available in factor programs, such as those found in the SPSS, SAS, BMD, and SYSTAT statistical packages. As we describe these decisions, we shall comment on the choices faced by the researcher, pointing out, where applicable, our experiences and personal preferences. Obviously, this chapter is not intended as a comprehensive course in factor analysis, nor can it be regarded as a substitute for the major textbooks in the field, such as Gorsuch (1983) for the general reader and Mulaik (1972) for the specialist.[2]

There are many decisions that have to be made when carrying out a factor analysis. We will identify each of the relevant decision points, and some of the major options available at each decision point. Moreover, we will indicate which of the decisions we think are important (very few) and which are unimportant (all the rest). We assume the following fundamental principle: In general, the more highly structured are one's data, the less it matters what decisions one makes. The best way to assure oneself about a factor structure is to analyze the data several different ways: If one's conclusions are robust across alternative procedures, one may be on to something. However, if one's conclusions vary with the procedures that are used, we urge the investigator to collect another data set, or to think of some alternative procedures for studying that scientific problem.

DECISIONS TO BE MADE PRIOR TO COLLECTING THE DATA

Selection of Variables

This is by far the single most important decision to be made in any investigation, and it should be guided by theory and/or the findings from past research. In general, exploratory factor analysis will prove most useful when applied to variables from a single domain (e.g., intellect), rather than from several different domains (e.g., intellect, psychopathology, and religious preferences); confirmatory factor procedures may be more appropriate for across-domain investigations. In addition, the resulting factors are more likely to replicate in other subject samples when the variables are selected to be representative of the domain under study. And, finally, one needs to include at least a half dozen, and ideally more like a dozen, variables for each of the factors one is likely to obtain, which means that in the personality realm, where it seems that there are at least five broad factors, it will rarely be useful to apply factor analysis to sets of less than 50 variables. Later in this chapter, we will discuss other aspects of this problem as they relate to such issues as the hierarchical nature of personality-trait representations.

Selection of Subjects

Although this is a less important decision than that involving the selection of variables, it is far from trivial. Among the issues involved: (a) Should the investigator try to increase sample heterogeneity, and if so on what variables (e.g., race, social class)? (b) Alternatively, or in addition, should one select subjects who are relatively homogeneous on some variables (e.g., reading ability, general verbal facility, absence or presence of psychopathology), so as to discover relations that may be obscured in heterogeneous samples? These questions are not peculiar to factor analysis, of course; for example, the first question is directly related to the ever-present problem of generalizing from a sample to a population.

Among the most vexing problems involved in subject selection is the decision about the *number* of subjects to be included in the investigation. This problem is unusually thought-provoking because it always involves a trade-off between (a) the use of *many* subjects so as to increase statistical power and the generalizability of one's findings from the sample to the population and (b) the use of *few* subjects so as to decrease the cost of collecting the data. It is our belief that factor analysis is inherently a subject-intensive enterprise, and therefore robust findings are only likely when based on samples of at least a few hundred subjects; if research funds permit, we strongly recommend sample sizes in the 500 to 1,000 range.[3]

Selection of the Measurement Format

In personality research, subjects' responses can be obtained using a variety of item formats, including multi-step rating scales, dichotomous choices (e.g., True vs. False, Agree vs. Disagree, Like vs. Dislike), or check-lists (defined by instructions to check those items that apply). From the subject's point of view, the last of these is the most user-friendly, and the first is the most demanding. However, from a psychometric point of view, rating scales have some advantages over both of the less demanding formats. For example, dichotomous items are characterized by large differences in their response distributions, which affect the size of the correlations among them, and thus the nature of any factors derived from those correlations. Moreover, check-lists invite a huge range of individual differences in subjects' conscientiousness in considering each of the items, a serious problem that is reflected in an enormous range of individual differences in the number of items that are checked. In general, we recommend the use of rating scales (with no less than five response categories) over the use of dichotomous items. About one thing, however, we are adamant: Never use a check-list response format.

When subjects are requested to respond to hundreds of items on the same occasion, there are typically large individual differences in the means and the variances of the subjects' response distributions across the items. One way to eliminate such differences is to employ a Q-sort procedure, forcing every subject to use the same experimenter-imposed distribution. Q-sort methodology may sometimes be useful when the number of items is quite small (100 or less), and when both subjects and experimenters have relatively unlimited time. On the other hand, there are some disadvantages of Q-sort methodology: (a) Because the items must be compared with one another, the task tends to be difficult and time-consuming for the subjects, and as a consequence it is rarely feasible to Q-sort more than 100 items; (b) because the items are individually administered, far more experimenter time is needed than is required for group-administered procedures; (c) because the items are rank-ordered in respect to each other, no information is available about the absolute (as compared to the relative) values of the responses to the items.

To overcome these and other problems associated with Q-sort methodology, we recommend the administration of items in a single-stimulus format, ideally using five to nine category rating scales. When 100 or more items are administered on the same occasion, we also recommend that each subject's responses be separately standard (Z) scored across the total set of items, thereby attenuating the problems caused by individual differences in subjects' response distributions. We have found standard scoring to be useful for items rated on continuous scales, for dichotomous responses, and even for items administered in a check-list format; however, standard-scoring is rarely useful for bipolar rating scales. For a comparison between the findings from unipolar and bipolar scales, see Goldberg (1992).

DECISIONS TO BE MADE AFTER THE DATA HAVE BEEN OBTAINED

Cleansing the Data

(a) Examining the Distributions of Each of the Variables

We strongly recommend that investigators always examine each of the univariate frequency distributions to assure themselves that all variables are distributed in a reasonable manner, and that there are no outliers. If there are one or more extreme values, are they coding errors, or genuine freaks of nature? Clearly all of the errors should be corrected, and the few subjects that produce the freakish values should probably be omitted.

In addition, it is sometimes assumed that the correlation coefficient is free to vary between −1.00 and +1.00. However, this is true only when the shapes of the distributions of both variables are the same and they are both symmetric around their means. Two variables with distributions of different shapes can correlate neither +1.00 nor −1.00. Two variables with distributions of the same shape that are skewed in the same direction can correlate +1.00, but not −1.00; whereas two variables with distributions of the same shape but skewed in the opposite directions can correlate −1.00, but not +1.00. In general, differences in distributions serve to decrease the size of the correlations between variables, and this will affect any factors derived from such correlations.

(b) Handling Missing Data

Much has been written about this problem in the statistical and psychometric literature (e.g., Little & Rubin, 1987), so we will not cover the proposed solutions in this chapter. The presence of substantial amounts of missing data should alert the investigator to deficiencies in the procedures used to collect the data, including such problems as a lack of clarity in the instructions or in the response format. Stimuli that elicit extensive missing data may have been phrased ambiguously, and subjects who have omitted many responses may have found the task too difficult or demanding. In general, such problematic variables and subjects should not be included in the analyses.

(c) Checking to Make Sure that the Relations among All Pairs of Variables Are Monotonic

When possible, we recommend that each of the bivariate frequency distributions (scatter-plots) be examined to make sure that there are no U-shaped or inverted-

U-shaped distributions. Such non-monotonic relations are extremely rare in personality research. When one discovers such an occurrence, it is necessary to rescale the variable so that its relations with all other variables are monotonic.

Selecting an Index of Association

Basically, there are four major varieties of association indices (Zegers & ten Berge, 1985), each type being a mean value based upon one of the following: (a) Raw cross-products, which reflect differences between the two variables in their means, their standard deviations, and the correlation between them; (b) proportionality coefficients, or raw cross-products divided by the two standard deviations, which reflect differences between the variables in their means and their correlation but not their standard deviations, (c) covariances, or cross-products of deviation scores, which reflect differences between the variables in their standard deviations and correlation but not their means, and finally (d) correlations, or cross-products of standard scores, which are not affected by differences in either the means or the standard deviations. Neither raw cross-products nor proportionality coefficients have been much employed as indices of association among the variables included in exploratory factor analyses, although the latter (referred to as congruence coefficients) are widely used to assess the similarity between factors derived from different samples of subjects. Whereas covariances are often employed in confirmatory factor analyses, most applications of exploratory factor analysis have relied upon the correlation as an index of relation between variables. Thus, although this is a decision that should be guided by one's theoretical concerns, for the remainder of this chapter we will assume that the reader has selected the correlation as an index of association.[4]

In preparation for a factor analysis, then, one has a *data matrix*, which consists of N rows (one for each subject in the study) by K columns (one for each of the variables). From the data matrix, one begins by computing a *correlation matrix*, which consists of K rows and K columns. This matrix is square and symmetric, which means that it can be folded into two triangles along its main diagonal, with each of the values in one triangle equal to the corresponding value in the other triangle. Excluding the cells that lie along the main diagonal, there are $K \times (K - 1) / 2$ distinctive cells in the correlation matrix.

DECISIONS RELATED TO FACTOR ANALYSIS

Deciding Whether to Use the "Component" or the "Factor" Model

Much has been written about this decision, and some factor-analytic theorists consider it the most important decision of all. Others, however, have argued that the decision is unimportant because the results from both methods will usually be much the same (e.g., Fava & Velicer, 1992). We agree with the latter position. Readers who wish to make up their own minds should consult the special issue of the journal *Multivariate Behavioral Research* on this topic (January 1990, Volume 25, Number 1) in which Velicer and Jackson (1990) present a strong argument in favor of the use of component analysis in most applications, and a number of other factor theorists provide extensive commentaries on this target article.

We would argue that if this decision makes any substantial difference with personality data, the data are not well-structured enough for either variety of analysis. At a theoretical level, the models are different,[5] but in actual practice the difference lies in the values that are used in the main diagonal of the correlation matrix: In the component model, values of 1.00 (i.e., the standardized variances of the variables) are included in each cell of the main diagonal. In the factor model, the diagonal values are replaced by each variable's "communality" (the proportion of its variance that it shares with the factors); we will return to this topic latter in the chapter.

Of the two authors of this chapter, one (JMD) generally uses factor analysis, whereas the other (LRG) usually employs component analysis. However, we agree that in most cases any differences between the two procedures will be quite minor, and they will virtually disappear when the number of variables per factor is large and when many of the correlations are of substantial size. Indeed, we normally analyze our data by both procedures, so as to ascertain the robustness of the structure to procedural variations (e.g., Goldberg, 1990). For the remainder of this chapter, we will use the term "factor" to refer to *either* a factor *or* a component.

The General Component Model

Figure 11.1 presents a schematic flow-chart of the factor-analytic process, beginning with the correlation matrix. Such a matrix of K by K elements can be approximated by multiplying a smaller matrix of K rows by L columns, called a *factor matrix*, by its "transpose," which is the identical matrix with its rows and columns re-oriented and thus turned into a matrix of L rows by K columns. If the index of association one has selected is the correlation coefficient, then the entries in the factor matrix are also correlation coefficients, specifically the correlations between each particular variable and each of the factors.[6]

In the procedure referred to as "principal" factors, the loadings on the first factor are those that serve to best recreate the values in the correlation matrix, when that factor matrix is multiplied by its transpose. Thus, the first principal factor provides a measure of whatever is most in common to the variables that have been included in the analysis. In the case of measures of aptitude or knowledge, the first principal factor will normally be an index of general intelligence. In the case of personality variables, the first principal factor will typically be a blend of general evaluation (social desirability) and whatever particular content domain is most highly represented within the set of variables.

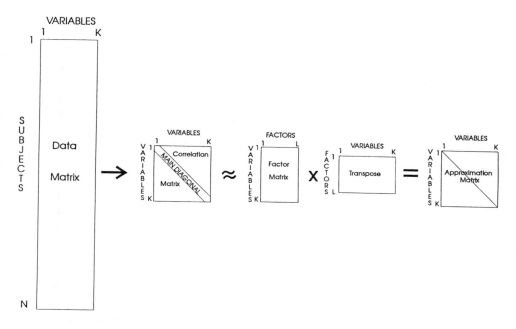

FIGURE 11.1. Schematic flow-chart of the factor-analytic process.

Moreover, each successive principal factor serves to best recreate the values in the correlation matrix *after taking into account the factors extracted before it.* Said another way, as each factor is extracted, the influence of that factor is partialed out of the correlations, leaving residual values that are independent of all factors that have been extracted. Thus, each factor is independent of all others; the intercorrelations among all pairs of factors are zero.

Extracting the Optimal Number of Factors

After the factors have been extracted, one can multiply the factor matrix by its transpose to form a new K by K matrix, which we will refer to as an "approximation" matrix of intercorrelations. As more factors are extracted, the differences between the values in the original and the approximation matrices become smaller and smaller. If each value in the approximation matrix is subtracted from its corresponding value in the original correlation matrix, the result is a K by K "residual" matrix, as shown in Figure 11.2. The more factors that are extracted, the better approximation of the original correlation matrix is provided by those factors, and thus the smaller are the values in the residual matrix. Consequently, if one's goal is to reproduce the original correlation matrix as precisely as possible, one will

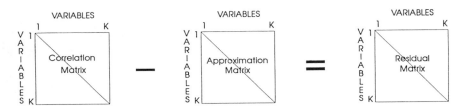

FIGURE 11.2. Relations among the correlation, the approximation and the residual matrices.

tend to extract many factors. On the other hand, the scientific principle of parsimony suggests that, other things being equal, fewer factors are better than many factors. One of the major decisions in factor analysis is the selection of the optimal number of factors, and this always involves a tradeoff between extracting as few factors as possible versus recreating the original correlation matrix as completely as possible.

Over the years, many rules have been proposed for deciding on the number of factors to extract (e.g., Zwick & Velicer, 1986). Unfortunately, none of these rules will invariably guide the researcher to the scientifically most satisfactory decision. Perhaps even more unfortunately, one of the least satisfactory rules (the "eigenvalues greater than one" criterion, which will be explained later) is so easy to implement that it has been incorporated as the standard "default" option in two of the four major statistical packages.

Figure 11.3 shows two indices that are typically derived from the factor matrix: "communalities" and "eigenvalues." A variable's communality is equal to the sum of the squared factor loadings *in its row* of the factor matrix. Thus, there are as many communality values as there are variables, and these values are normally presented as the final column of a factor matrix. The communality of a variable is the proportion of its variance that is associated with the total set of factors that have been extracted. That proportion can vary from zero to one: A variable with a communality of zero is completely independent of each of the factors. A variable with a communality of 1.00 can be perfectly predicted by the factors, when the factors are used as the predictors in a multiple regression equation and the variable itself is the criterion. In the "factor" model, these communalities are used to replace the original values of unity in the main diagonal of the correlation matrix.

The sums of the squared factor loadings *down the columns* of the principal factor matrix are equal to the first of the "eigenvalues" (or "latent roots") of the correlation matrix from which the factors were derived. These values are normally presented as the bottom row in a factor matrix. The eigenvalue associated with a factor is an index of its relative size: The eigenvalue associated with the first factor will always be at least as large, and normally much larger than, any of the others; and the eigenvalues of successive factors can never be larger, and will typically

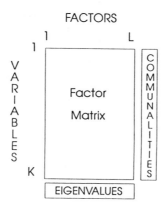

FIGURE 11.3. The unrotated factor matrix, with its communalities and eigenvalues.

be smaller, than those that precede them. A plot of the size of the eigenvalues as a function of their factor number will appear as a rapidly descending concave curve that eventually becomes nearly a horizontal line. An example of such an eigenvalue plot (sometimes referred to as a "scree" plot, after Cattell, 1966) is provided in Figure 11.4. Included in this figure are the eigenvalues from a principal components analysis of 100 personality trait adjectives, selected by Goldberg (1992) as markers of the Big-Five factor structure, in a sample of 636 self and peer ratings.

Some of the rules for deciding on the optimal number of factors are based on the characteristics of such eigenvalue plots (e.g., Cattell, 1966). For example, if there is a very sharp break in the curve, with earlier eigenvalues all quite large relative to later ones that are all of similar size, then there is presumptive evidence that only the factors above the break should be retained. However, as indicated in Figure 11.4, although this highly selected set of variables provides an extremely clear five-factor structure, subjective interpretations of this eigenvalue plot could lead to decisions to extract 2, 5, 7, 8, 10, or 16 factors, depending on the preconceptions of the investigator. Indeed, it is quite rare for a plot of the eigenvalues to reveal unambiguous evidence of factor specification, and therefore alternative rules must be invoked. For example, one might compare the eigenvalue plots from factoring two correlation matrices, one based on actual data and one based on random data for the same number of variables and the same number of subjects; the point at which the two eigenvalue plots intersect has been proposed as a likely stopping place (Horn, 1965). (Using the data displayed in Figure 11.4, such a rule would suggest the extraction of 7 factors.)

It is easier, however, merely to examine the numerical value of each eigenvalue and to retain those above some arbitrary cutting point. Kaiser (1958) proposed that principal components with eigenvalues of 1.00 or above should be

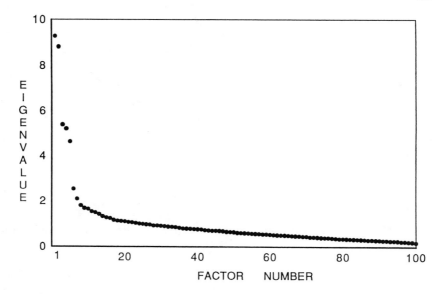

FIGURE 11.4. A plot of the sizes of the eigenvalues for 100 variables.

retained, and it is this quick-and-dirty heuristic that has been incorporated as the default option for factor extraction in two of the four major statistical packages. In fact, however, the number of components with eigenvalues greater than one is highly related to the number of variables included in the analysis. Specifically, the number of eigenvalues greater than one will typically be in the range between one-quarter and one-third of the number of variables included in the analysis. (The number of factors with eigenvalues of 1.00 or above is 24 in the data displayed in Figure 11.4.) If one assumes, as we do, that the number of broad factors in a domain should be independent of the number of variables included in the analysis, then the "eigenvalues greater than one" rule is not a reasonable procedure for deciding on the number of factors to extract.

In recommending procedures for deciding on the optimum number of factors, we are necessarily guided by our criteria for a useful structural model. Such a structure, in our view is one that (a) incorporates the distinction between higher-level and lower-level factors, and (b) is robust across variations in the selection of variables, subject samples, and measurement procedures. We will have more to say later in this chapter about the first criterion when we discuss the hierarchical nature of factor structures. For the present, we will point out that an optimal model differentiates between narrow oblique *clusters* of variables at the lower level of the trait hierarchy and the necessarily quite broad *factors* at the highest level of the structure.

In studies of personality traits, there appear to be only five broad higher-level factors (Digman, 1990; Goldberg, 1990; John, 1990; McCrae & John, 1992; Wiggins & Pincus, 1992), whereas at levels that are lower in the hierarchy the number of such factors varies enormously, reflecting the theoretical predilections of different investigators. In the explicitly hierarchical models of Cattell (1957) and of McCrae and Costa (1985, 1987), Cattell argues for 16 lower-level factors in analyses of the items in his Sixteen Personality Factors Questionnaire, whereas Costa and McCrae (1992) provide scales to measure 30 lower-level factors in the revised version of their NEO Personality Inventory. Both Cattell and Costa and McCrae claim substantial evidence of factor robustness across subject samples (although not of course across differing selections of variables), and their disagreements could simply reflect differences in the vertical locations of their factors (clusters) within the over-all hierarchical structure.

In any case, however, there seems to be widespread agreement that an optimal factor structure is one that is comparable over independent studies, and we advocate the incorporation of this principle into any procedure for deciding on the number of factors to extract (see Everett, 1983; Nunnally, 1978). What this means is that no single analysis is powerful enough to provide evidence of the viability of a factor structure; what is needed are two or more (preferably many more) analyses of at least somewhat different variables in different subject samples.[7]

Rotating the Factors

The factor matrix displayed in Figure 11.1 includes K rows (one row for each variable) and L columns (one column for each of the L factors that have been extracted). Multiplying the factor matrix by its transpose produces the K by K approximation matrix. However, there are an infinite number of K by L matrices which when multiplied by their transposes will produce that identical approximation matrix. Each of these "rotations" of the original factor matrix has the same set of communality values (the sums of the squared factor loadings within each row). Matrices included in this family of factor rotations differ from one another in the relative sizes of their factors, as indexed by the sums of squared factor loadings down the columns. Given any particular set of data, the unrotated principal factors have the steepest-possible descending pattern of factor sizes. At the other extreme, it is possible to obtain a factor matrix in which each factor is of approximately the same size.

However, neither of these two types of solutions has much scientific utility, except in a few quite limited contexts.[8] Instead, the criterion usually invoked for selecting the optimal rotation is that of "simple structure," which informally can be defined as a pattern of factor loadings that contains a few high values in each column, with the rest mostly around zero. Such a factor pattern is "simple" in the sense that most variables have high loadings on only one factor and each of the factors is defined by only a few variables, thus facilitating its interpretation. In practice, the various procedures for factor rotation search for a pattern of near zero and very high factor loadings, typically by maximizing the variance of the squared factor loadings and thereby maximizing the number of factor loadings that are approximately zero. Geometrically, one characteristic of such "simple-structured" factor patterns is that each of the factors is located near a dense cluster of variables. In such a factor pattern, there are relatively few variables that are located between the clusters, and which therefore would be interpreted as "blends" of two or more factors.

If one's aim was *solely* to maximize simple structure, one would locate the factors as close to the clusters as possible. In such a solution, however, the factors would no longer be unrelated to one another, but would be "oblique" (correlated with each other). If one desires "orthogonal" factors (each of which has a correlation of exactly zero with all of the other factors), the locations of the rotated factors are selected to be as close as possible to the positions that maximize simple structure, given the orthogonality restraint. As a consequence, oblique solutions are always at least as close if not closer to a simple-structure pattern than are their orthogonal counterparts. Thus, the decision to employ an oblique or an orthogonal rotational algorithm always involves a trade-off between the simplicity of a more simple structure (oblique) and the simplicity of uncorrelated factors (orthogonal). In our view, the relative advantages of each kind of rotation depend on the vertical location of one's factors in the hierarchical representation: If one seeks lower-level factors, we recommend the use of an oblique rotation. On the other hand, if one seeks broad higher-level factors so as to discover the over-all dimensionality of the domain, we recommend the use of an orthogonal rotation.

By far the most commonly used procedure for *orthogonal* factor rotation is the "varimax" algorithm of Kaiser (1958), which is available in all of the statistical packages. Because we have found the "equamax" algorithm (Saunders, 1961) to be a useful supplementary procedure, we recommend that, when possible, both methods be used, and the resulting solutions compared. The problem of providing an optimal algorithm for *oblique* rotations is far more complex than that for the orthogonal case, and there is less uniformity in the oblique rotational options provided by the major statistical packages. Indeed, the particular algorithm that we prefer, one called "promax" (Hendrickson & White, 1964), is not included in some of the most popular factor programs.

After an *orthogonal* rotation, the resulting factor matrix of K rows by L columns can be interpreted in the same way as the original unrotated matrix: Its entries are the correlations between each of the variables and each of the factors. The relative size of a particular unrotated or rotated factor can be indexed by the sum of its squared factor loadings down the column, but for the rotated factors these sums can no longer be referred to as "eigenvalues," which have distinct mathematical properties based on the original correlation matrix. When each of the sums of squared factor loadings down a column of a factor matrix is divided by the number of variables in the analysis, the resulting ratio indicates the proportion of the total variance from all variables that is provided by that factor.

In the case of an *oblique* rotation, there are three meaningful sets of factor loadings that can be interpreted: (a) the *factor pattern*, or the regression coefficients linking the factors to the variables; (b) the *factor structure*, or the correlations between the variables and each of the factors; and (c) the *reference vectors*, or the semi-partial (also called part) correlations between the variables and each of the factors, after the contributions of the other factors have been partialed out. In addition, it is necessary to obtain the correlations among the factors. With orthogonal factors, all three sets of factor-loading coefficients are the same, and the correlations among all pairs of factors are zero.

Figure 11.5 displays the locations of 20 hypothetical variables as determined by their correlations with two orthogonal factors. The first unrotated factor provides the vertical, and the second unrotated factor the horizontal, axes (the solid lines) in the figure; the positions of the factors after varimax rotation are shown by the dashed lines. Note that the first unrotated factor is located in the position that maximizes its variance across all 20 variables, and the second unrotated factor is orthogonal to the first. As is usually the case, however, these two unrotated factors do not pass through any of the dense clusters of variables, whereas the varimax factors are more likely to do so. Thus, the factors after rotation to a simple-structure position provide a more clear and easily interpretable factor representation.

Calculating Factor Scores

One important use of factor analysis is to discover the relations between factors in one domain and variables from other domains (which in turn might be other sets of rotated factors). One way to obtain such relations is to score each subject in the sample on each of the factors, and then to correlate these "factor scores" with the other variables included in the study. The major statistical computing packages provide such factor scores, if the investigator requests them. In component analyses, these factor scores are calculated directly, whereas in factor analysis they must be *estimated*, typically by multiple regression analysis.[9]

Moreover, when one requests factor scores from one of the major statistical packages, orthogonal components lead to orthogonal factor scores (unfortunately, this is not necessarily the case with orthogonal factors). However, even with orthogonal components, if one develops *scales* by selecting items with high factor loadings on each of those components, it is likely that these scales will be related to each other. In general, the reason for the sizeable correlations among scales derived from orthogonal factors is that (a) there are few factor-univocal items, most items having secondary factor loadings of substantial size, and (b) if one selects items solely on the basis of their highest factor loading, it is extremely unlikely that the secondary loadings will completely balance out. To decrease the intercorrelations among such scales, one needs to take secondary loadings into account, for which purpose one may want to use a procedure such as the AB5C model of Hofstee, de Raad, and Goldberg (1992), which will be described later.

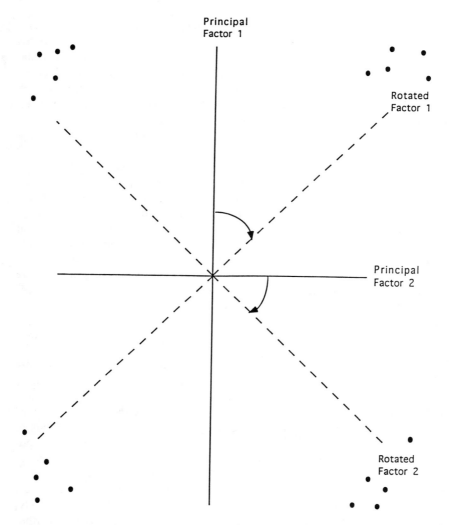

FIGURE 11.5. An illustration of two principal factors and their varimax-rotated counterparts.

VERTICAL AND HORIZONTAL ASPECTS OF FACTOR STRUCTURES[10]

Like most concepts, personality-trait constructs include both vertical and horizontal features. The vertical aspect refers to the hierarchical relations among traits (e.g., Reliability is a more abstract and general concept than Punctuality), whereas the horizontal aspect refers to the degree of similarity among traits at the same hierarchical level (e.g., Sociability involves aspects of both Warmth and Activity Level). Scientists who emphasize the vertical aspect of trait structure could employ multivariate techniques such as hierarchical cluster analysis, or they could employ oblique rotations in factor analysis, and then factor the correlations among the primary dimensions, thus constructing a hierarchical structure. Scientists who emphasize the horizontal aspect of trait structure could employ discrete cluster solutions or orthogonal factor rotations.

Historically, however, there has been no simple relation between the emphases of investigators and their methodological preferences. For example, both Eysenck (1970) and Cattell (1947) have developed explicitly hierarchical representations, Eysenck's leading to three highest-level factors, Cattell's to eight or nine. However, whereas Cattell has always advocated and used oblique factor procedures, Eysenck has typically preferred orthogonal methods. In the case of the more recent five-factor model, some of its proponents construe the model in an expressly hierarchical fashion (e.g., Costa, McCrae, & Dye, 1991; McCrae & Costa, 1992), whereas others emphasize its horizontal aspects (e.g., Peabody & Goldberg, 1989; Hofstee, de Raad, & Goldberg, 1992).

Vertical Approaches to Trait Structure

The defining feature of hierarchical models of personality traits is that they emphasize the vertical relations among variables (e.g., from the most specific to the most abstract), to the exclusion of the relations among variables at the same level. One of the most famous hierarchical models of individual differences is the classic Vernon-Burt hierarchical model of abilities (e.g., Vernon, 1950); specific test items are combined to form ability tests, which are the basis of specific factors, which in turn are the basis of the minor group factors, which in turn lead to the major group factors, which at their apex form the most general factor, "g" for general intelligence. Another classic example of a hierarchical structure is Eysenck's (1970) model of Extraversion; specific responses in particular situations (e.g., telling a joke, buying a new car) are considered as subordinate categories to habitual responses (e.g., entertaining strangers, making rapid decisions), which in turn make up such traits as Sociability and Impulsiveness, which finally form the superordinate attribute of Extraversion.

Horizontal Approaches to Trait Structure

The defining feature of horizontal models is that the relations among the variables are specified by the variables' locations in multidimensional factor space. When that space is limited to only two dimensions, and the locations of the variables are projected to some uniform distance from the origin, the resulting structures are referred to as "circumplex" representations. The most famous example of such models is the Interpersonal Circle (e.g., Wiggins, 1979, 1980; Kiesler, 1983), which is based on Factors I (Surgency) and II (Agreeableness) in the Big-Five model.

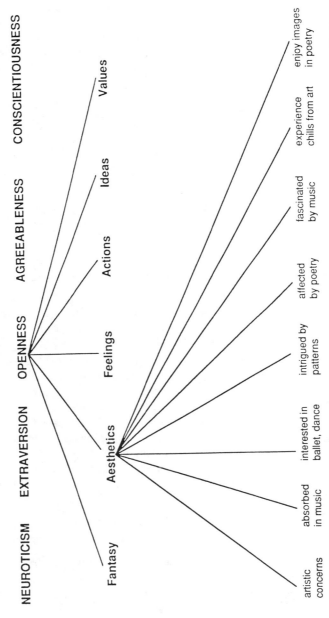

FIGURE 11.6. Portion of the hierarchical model of personality structure developed by Costa and McCrae (1992).

Other examples of circumplex models involve more than a single plane, including the three-dimensional structures that incorporate Big-Five Factors I, II, and III (Stern, 1970; Peabody & Goldberg, 1989), and Factors I, II, and IV (Saucier, 1992).

A more comprehensive circumplex representation has recently been proposed by Hofstee, de Raad, and Goldberg (1992). Dubbed the "AB5C" model, for Abridged Big Five-dimensional Circumplex, this representation includes the ten bivariate planes formed from all pairs of the Big-Five factors. In the AB5C model, each trait is assigned to the plane formed by the two factors with which it is most highly associated (e.g., its two highest factor loadings). In the AB5C model, each of the 10 circumplexes is divided into 12 segments, each of 30°, which form the facets of the AB5C model. Figure 11.6 presents one of the 10 circumplex representations from Hofstee, et al. (1992). The location of each trait variable is presented twice, once *within the circle* as defined by its angular position and its distance from the origin, and then again when projected onto the circumference of the circle. The triangles in Figure 11.7 indicate the locations of the factorially univocal terms, which by definition have very low secondary loadings, in planes other than the one containing their two highest loadings.

Comparing Vertical and Horizontal Perspectives

All structural representations based on factor-analytic methodology can be viewed from either vertical or horizontal perspectives. Factor analysis can be used to construct hierarchical models *explicitly* with oblique rotational procedures and *implicitly* even with orthogonal solutions, since any factor can be viewed as being located at a level above that of the variables being factored; that is, even orthogonal factors separate the common variance (the factors) from the total (common plus unique) variance of the measures. One could therefore emphasize the vertical aspect by grouping the variables by the factor with which they are most highly associated, thereby disregarding information about factorial blends. Alternatively, one could concentrate on the horizontal features of the representation, as in the AB5C model. What are the advantages associated with each perspective?

McCrae and Costa (1992) have argued that hierarchical structures are to be preferred to the extent to which the variances of the lower-level traits are trait-specific, as compared to the extent that they are related to the five broad factors. These investigators demonstrated that, after partialing out the five-factor common variance from both self and other ratings on the facet scales from the revised NEO Personality Inventory (Costa & McCrae, 1992), the residual variance in these scales was still substantial enough to elicit strong correlations among self ratings, spouse ratings, and peer ratings of the same lower-level trait. From this finding, they argued in favor of hierarchical representations, in which relatively small amounts of common variance produce the higher-level factors, with ample amounts of unique variance still available for predictive purposes.

Factor I and Factor II

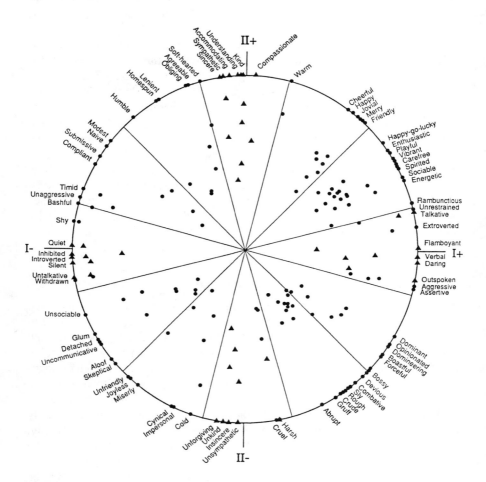

FIGURE 11.7. One of the 10 circumplex representations included in the AB5C model of Hofstee, de Raad, and Goldberg (1992).

This assumption has powerful implications for the role of trait measures when used in multiple regression analyses in applied contexts, such as personnel selection and classification. Because one loses some unique variance as one amalgamates measures, the optimal level of prediction is a function of statistical power, and thus of sample size. Other things being equal, the optimal number of predictors to be included in a regression analysis varies directly with the size of the subject sample; for large samples, one can include more variables than can be included in small samples, where one can more easily capitalize on the chance characteristics of the sample and thus lose predictive robustness when one applies the regression weights in new samples.

Although it is necessary to think hierarchically about the use of trait measures in applied contexts, it is equally necessary to think horizontally about basic taxonomic issues. Although McCrae and Costa (1992) have assumed that the amount of unique variance in the measures is the key to differentiating between the two types of representations, this assumption is incorrect. That is, the amount of unique as compared to common trait variance is not relevant to a comparison between the two models, because the models differ only in their representation of common variance. Specifically, the common variance is associated with a single factor in the NEO Personality Inventory, whereas it is represented as a blend of two factors in the AB5C model.

The need for horizontal representations of personality variables can be seen most clearly in analyses of the natural language of personality description (Goldberg, 1993a). Trait-descriptive terms are not clustered tightly in five-dimensional space, as would be true if the personality lexicon contained only semantically isolated sets of near-synonyms and near-antonyms; rather, most terms share some features of their meanings with one set of terms while they share other features with another set. Thus, even after rotation of the factors to a criterion of simple structure such as varimax, most terms have substantial secondary loadings, and thus must be viewed as blends of two or more factors.

Nor is it always easy to secure agreement on the optimal positions of the factor axes, even among personality theorists who share the same general orientation toward factor location. For example, Gray (1981) has long argued that Eysenck's two factors of Extraversion and Neuroticism are located 45° away from the theoretically most useful positions, which Gray labels Anxiety and Impulsivity. To best understand this theoretical disagreement, one should examine those personality descriptors located in the plane formed by Factors I and IV in the Big-Five model, the two factors that conform to Eysenck's dimensions of Extraversion and Neuroticism; one can then locate the variables that define Gray's two dimensions, which are blends of the factors proposed by Eysenck (or alternatively one can view the variables that are associated with Extraversion and Neuroticism as being blends of Anxiety and Impulsivity). Because hierarchical models deemphasize these horizontal aspects of trait relations, they provide no information about the nature of such factorial blends. For purposes of basic research on the structure of traits, therefore, models that emphasize horizontal relations (e.g., Hofstee et al., 1992) will typically be more informative.

SUMMARY AND CONCLUSIONS

Over more years than we'd like to admit, each of the two authors of this chapter has independently carried out hundreds of factor analyses. Although our intellectual roots differ substantially, the experience of writing this chapter surprised us: We found ourselves in agreement on most of the controversial issues in the field, and this chapter presents those agreements.

For example, with regard to two of the most vexing decisions—the use of factor analysis versus component analysis and the use of orthogonal versus oblique rotations—our experience suggests that in the realms of personality and psychopathology these choices are not very important, at least with well-structured data sets. In general, the more highly structured are one's data, the less it matters *which* factor-analytic decisions one makes. Indeed, the best way to assure oneself about a factor structure is to analyze the data different ways, and thereby test the robustness of one's solution across alternative procedures.

On the other hand, two decisions are of considerable importance: the initial selection of variables and the number of factors to extract. The selection of variables should be guided by theory and/or the findings from past research. Because we believe that an optimal factor structure is one that is comparable over independent studies, we advocate the incorporation of this principle into any procedure for deciding on the number of factors to extract. What this means is that no single analysis is powerful enough to provide evidence of the viability of a factor structure; what is needed are multiple analyses of at least somewhat different variables in different subject samples.

All structural representations based on factor-analytic methodology can be viewed from either vertical or horizontal perspectives. Factor analysis can be used to construct hierarchical models explicitly with oblique rotational procedures and implicitly even with orthogonal solutions, since any factor can be viewed as being located at a level above that of the variables being factored; that is, even orthogonal factors separate the common variance (the factors) from the total (common plus unique) variance of the measures. One could therefore emphasize the vertical aspect by grouping the variables by the factor with which they are most highly associated, thereby disregarding information about factorial blends. Alternatively, one could concentrate on the horizontal features of the representation, as in the AB5C model.

A hierarchical perspective has powerful implications for the role of trait measures when used in multiple regression analyses in applied contexts, such as personnel selection and classification. Because one loses some unique variance as one amalgamates measures, the optimal level of prediction is a function of statistical power, and thus of sample size. Other things being equal, the optimal number of predictors to be included in a regression analysis varies directly with the size of the subject sample; for large samples, one can include more variables than can be included in small samples, which more easily capitalize on chance characteristics and thus lose predictive robustness when one applies the regression weights in new samples.

However, a horizontal perspective is necessary for basic research on trait structure, because trait variables are not clustered tightly in five-dimensional space;

rather, most variables share some features with one set of variables while they share other features with another set. Thus, even after rotation of the factors to a criterion of simple structure such as varimax, most variables have substantial secondary loadings, and thus must be viewed as blends of two or more factors. Because hierarchical models de-emphasize these horizontal aspects of trait relations, they provide no information about the nature of such factorial blends. For purposes of basic research on the structure of traits, therefore, models that emphasize horizontal relations such as the AB5C model will typically be more informative.

In concluding this chapter, we acknowledge the fact that many investigators are now turning away from exploratory factor analysis altogether, in favor of confirmatory models and procedures; indeed, a spate of new textbooks deal exclusively with confirmatory models, whereas the most recent of the major textbooks that focus primarily on exploratory techniques was published a decade ago (Gorsuch, 1983). For readers who may be curious about our continued use of exploratory factor analysis in the face of the emerging concordance against it, we will try to provide some justification for our old-fashioned ways.

First of all, it is important to realize that most applications of confirmatory models involve, by our standards, extremely small sets of variables; a typical confirmatory analysis includes only a dozen or two variables, and applications of these models to variable sets of the sizes we work with (e.g., Goldberg, 1990, 1992) are still computationally prohibitive. In addition, repeated independent discoveries of the same structure derived from exploratory techniques seem to us to provide stronger evidence for that structure than would be provided by the same number of confirmatory analyses. Indeed, when a confirmatory analysis is used to reject a model (which will virtually always occur if the sample is large enough), the investigator's subsequent tinkering with the model can be viewed as a variant of exploratory analysis.

Although we have not been impressed with the substantive knowledge of personality structure that has yet accrued from findings based on confirmatory techniques, we applaud their development, and we encourage their use. We suspect that when theories of personality structure become specified more precisely, perhaps on the basis of findings from exploratory analyses, we will see the advantages of confirmatory factor models over exploratory ones. In the interim, we believe that there is a substantial role for both types of methodologies.

ACKNOWLEDGMENT

The writing of this chapter was supported by Grant MH-49227 from the National Institute of Mental Health. The authors are indebted to Shawn Boles, Frank B. Brokken, Norman Cliff, Lee J. Cronbach, Robert Cudeck, Robyn M. Dawes, Herbert W. Eber, Robert F. Fagot, Donald W. Fiske, Richard L. Gorsuch, Sarah E. Hampson, Paul A. Herzberg, Willem K. B. Hofstee, Henk A. L. Kiers, Daniel

J. Levitin, John C. Loehlin, Maurice Lorr, Clarence C. McCormick, Roderick P. McDonald, Roger E. Millsap, Stanley A. Mulaik, Warren T. Norman, William Revelle, William W. Rozeboom, Gerard Saucier, Lee B. Sechrest, Stephen Strack, Lawrence J. Stricker, Dennis Sweeney, Robert M. Thorndike, Wayne F. Velicer, Stephen G. West, Keith F. Widaman, and Jerry S. Wiggins for their thoughtful comments and suggestions.

NOTES

[1]Confirmatory factor procedures are part of most structural equation (or latent trait) programs, such as LISREL and EQS. For descriptions of confirmatory factor models, see Loehlin (1992) or Bollen (1989).

[2]Some other excellent sources include Chapters 13, 14, and 15 in Cliff (1987) for the beginner and Jackson (1991) for the mathematically adept.

[3]Our rationale for this recommendation is based on the sampling variability of the correlation coefficient. For example, with a population correlation of .50 and samples of size 50, one can expect the obtained correlations to vary between .26 and .74 from sample to sample. Such variability in the size of the correlations can affect the factors derived from them, thus causing the factors obtained in independent studies to appear to be different. Note that we do not consider the ratio of subjects to variables to be of any consequence in exploratory factor analysis, a point of view that has been reinforced by the analyses of Guadagnoli and Velicer (1988).

[4]As noted previously, the size of a correlation is attenuated to the extent that the shapes of the two distributions differ, and this problem is exacerbated when the values of one or both variables are dichotomous rather than continuous; for example, if two dichotomous variables both have frequency distributions of 10% and 90% in the same direction, the maximum possible negative correlation between them is −.11. In an attempt to solve this problem, some investigators have used statistical indices of association that are "corrected" for differences in distributions, such as phi/phimax, the tetrachoric correlation, the biserial correlation, and even r/r-max (Carroll, 1961). Neither of the two authors of this chapter has much experience with exploratory factor analyses based on these indices, and consequently we can provide little guidance about the conditions under which they should, or should not, be employed. In accord with our general recommendation for methodological pluralism, we suggest that whenever such estimates are used, the results should be compared with analyses based on the corresponding Pearson indices, such as the phi and point-biserial correlations.

[5]The precise difference between the models can only be specified by examining their mathematical formulations, which goes beyond the explicitly elementary treatment in this chapter. In general, however, *factors* are based solely on that portion of each variable that is related to the factors ("common variance"),

whereas *components* also incorporate that portion that is specific to the variable ("unique variance"). Another way of thinking of the difference between the two procedures is in terms of their function: Factors can be thought of as the *explanations* for the interrelations among the variables, whereas components are *summaries* of the information in the original data matrix. In the factor model each variable is a weighted sum of the factors, whereas in the component model each component is a weighted sum of the variables.

[6]The explanations in this section only apply to the original matrix of principal factors, which are "orthogonal," and not to the subsequent "rotated" matrices, which may be "oblique."

[7]To get started with the first such study, however, some common-sense rules can be invoked. Assuming that one is seeking broad factors at or near the top level of a hierarchical personality structure, one might invoke a rule that we will call the "magical law of five, plus or minus two." Structures of less than three factors are rarely interesting, and structures of more than seven factors are likely to include lower-level clusters of variables. Within any one data set, the investigator might examine the rotated factors from solutions that include three, four, five, six, and seven factors. The scientifically most reasonable solution from this set can then be used as one's *provisional* structure, pending replication in other samples.

[8]The first unrotated principal component has some properties that make it useful when all of the variables under analysis have been selected as measures of the exact same construct. For example, given that the first unrotated component provides an index of whatever is most in common to the variables, it can sometimes be used as a surrogate for the underlying "latent" construct, and its loadings then can be viewed as reflecting the correlations of each variable with that construct. In our experience, however, the most useful application of the first unrotated component is with tasks in which judges rate a common set of stimuli on some attribute. In such a situation, one can correlate the judges' ratings across the set of stimuli to index the extent to which pairs of raters agree with one another. The first unrotated principal component of this matrix of interjudge agreement correlations reflects the group consensus, and the factor loadings of each judge on this first component indicates that judge's correlation with the consensus. The factor scores for each stimulus on this component are the optimal scale values for that stimulus, when judges are weighted by their contribution to the group consensus. The Coefficient Alpha reliability of these factor scores is equal to $N / (N - 1) \times (E - 1) / E$, where E is the eigenvalue of the component and N is the number of judges (Serlin & Kaiser, 1976).

[9]In both models, however, the factor-score coefficients that are used to calculate these values may not be as robust across different subject samples as are other coefficients such as equal weights. One of the authors of this chapter (JMD) views factor-score coefficients as similar to regression weights in capitalizing on chance vagaries of the derivation sample (Dawes, 1979), and thus advocates the use of equal weights for those variables most highly related to each factor. The other

author (LRG), who sees most variables as blends of two or more factors rather than as univocally related to a single factor, prefers to use the exactly calculated factor scores provided by most factor programs. And, finally, a number of factor theorists eschew the use of factor scores altogether, preferring to use alternative "extension" methods of relating factors to other variables (McDonald, 1978).

[10]This section of the chapter has been adapted from Goldberg (1993b); readers interested in a more comprehensive discussion of these issues should consult that source.

REFERENCES

Bollen, K. A. (1989). *Structural equations with latent variables*. New York, NY: Wiley.

Carroll, J. B. (1961). The nature of the data, or how to choose a correlation coefficient. *Psychometrika, 26*, 347–372.

Cattell, R. B. (1947). Confirmation and clarification of primary personality factors. *Psychometrika, 12*, 197–220.

Cattell, R. B. (1957). *Personality and motivation structure and measurement*. Yonkers-on-Hudson, NY: World Book.

Cattell, R. B. (1966). The scree test for the number of factors. *Multivariate Behavioral Research, 1*, 245–276.

Cliff, N. (1987). *Analyzing multivariate data*. San Diego, CA: Harcourt Brace Jovanovich.

Costa, P. T., Jr., & McCrae, R. R. (1992). *Revised NEO Personality Inventory (NEO-PI-R) and NEO Five-Factor Inventory (NEO-FFI) professional manual*. Odessa, FL: Psychological Assessment Resources.

Costa, P. T., Jr., McCrae, R. R., & Dye, D. A. (1991). Facet scales for Agreeableness and Conscientiousness: A revision of the NEO Personality Inventory. *Personality and Individual Differences, 12*, 887–898.

Dawes, R. M. (1979). The robust beauty of improper linear models in decision making. *American Psychologist, 34*, 571–582.

Digman, J. M. (1990). Personality structure: Emergence of the five-factor model. In M. R. Rosenzweig & L. W. Porter (Eds.), *Annual Review of Psychology: Vol. 41* (Pp. 417–440). Palo Alto, CA: Annual Reviews.

Everett, J. E. (1983). Factor comparability as a means of determining the number of factors and their rotation. *Multivariate Behavioral Research, 18*, 197–218.

Eysenck, H. J. (1970). *The structure of human personality: Third edition*. London: Methuen.

Fava, J. L., & Velicer, W. F. (1992). An empirical comparison of factor, image, component, and scale scores. *Multivariate Behavioral Research, 27*, 301–322.

Goldberg, L. R. (1990). An alternative "Description of personality": The Big-Five factor structure. *Journal of Personality and Social Psychology, 59*, 1216–1229.

Goldberg, L. R. (1992). The development of markers for the Big-Five factor structure. *Psychological Assessment, 4*, 26–42.

Goldberg, L. R. (1993a). The structure of phenotypic personality traits. *American Psychologist, 48*, 26–34.

Goldberg, L. R. (1993b). The structure of personality traits: Vertical and horizontal aspects. In D. C. Funder, R. D. Parke, C. Tomlinson-Keasey, & K. Widaman (Eds.), *Studying lives through time: Personality and development* (Pp. 169-188). Washington, DC: American Psychological Association.

Gorsuch, R. L. (1983). *Factor analysis: Second Edition*. Hillsdale, NJ: Erlbaum.

Gray, J. A. (1981). A critique of Eysenck's theory of personality. In H. J. Eysenck (Ed.), *A model for personality* (pp. 246–276). Berlin, Germany: Springer-Verlag.

Guadagnoli, E., & Velicer, W. F. (1988). Relation of sample size to the stability of component patterns. *Psychological Bulletin, 103,* 265–275.

Harman, H. H. (1976). *Modern factor analysis: Third Edition.* Chicago, IL: University of Chicago.

Hendrickson, A. E., & White, P. O. (1964). Promax: A quick method of rotation to oblique simple structure. *British Journal of Statistical Psychology, 17,* 65–70.

Hofstee, W. K. B., de Raad, B., & Goldberg, L. R. (1992). Integration of the Big Five and circumplex taxonomies of traits. *Journal of Personality and Social Psychology, 63,* 146–163.

Horn, J. L. (1965). A rationale and test for the number of factors in factor analysis. *Psychometrika, 30,* 179–185.

Hotelling, H. (1933). Analysis of a complex of statistical variables into principal components. *Journal of Educational Psychology, 24,* 417–441, 498–520.

Jackson, J. E. (1991). *A user's guide to principal components.* New York, NY: Wiley.

John, O. P. (1990). The "Big-Five" factor taxonomy: Dimensions of personality in the natural language and in questionnaires. In L. A. Pervin (Ed.), *Handbook of personality theory and research* (pp. 66–100). New York, NY: Guilford.

Kaiser, H. F. (1958). The varimax criterion for analytic rotation in factor analysis. *Psychometrika, 23,* 187–200.

Kiesler, D. J. (1983). The 1982 interpersonal circle: A taxonomy for complementarity in human transactions. *Psychological Review, 90,* 185–214.

Little, R. J. A., & Rubin, D. B. (1987). *Statistical analysis with missing data.* New York, NY: Wiley.

Loehlin, J. C. (1992). *Latent variable models: An introduction to factor, path, and structural analysis: Second Edition.* Hillsdale, NJ: Erlbaum.

McCrae, R. R., & Costa, P. T., Jr. (1985). Updating Norman's "adequate taxonomy": Intelligence and personality dimensions in natural language and in questionnaires. *Journal of Personality and Social Psychology, 49,* 710–721.

McCrae, R. R., & Costa, P. T., Jr. (1987). Validation of the five-factor model of personality across instruments and observers. *Journal of Personality and Social Psychology, 52,* 81–90.

McCrae, R. R., & Costa, P. T., Jr. (1992). Discriminant validity of NEO-PIR facet scales. *Educational and Psychological Measurement, 52,* 229–237.

McCrae, R. R., & John, O. P. (1992). An introduction to the five-factor model and its applications. *Journal of Personality, 60,* 175–215.

McDonald, R. P. (1978). Some checking procedures for extension analysis. *Multivariate Behavioral Research, 13,* 319–325.

Mulaik, S. A. (1972). *The foundations of factor analysis.* New York, NY: McGraw-Hill.

Nunnally, J. (1978). *Psychometric theory: Second Edition.* New York, NY: McGraw-Hill.

Peabody, D., & Goldberg, L. R. (1989). Some determinants of factor structures from personality-trait descriptors. *Journal of Personality and Social Psychology, 57,* 552–567.

Pearson, K. (1901). On lines and planes of closest fit to systems of points in space. *Philosophical Magazine, Series B, 2,* 559–572.

Saucier, G. (1992). Benchmarks: Integrating affective and interpersonal circles with the Big-Five personality factors. *Journal of Personality and Social Psychology, 62,* 1025–1035.

Saunders, D. R. (1961). The rationale for an "oblimax" method of transformation in factor analysis. *Psychometrika, 26,* 317–324.

Serlin, R. C., & Kaiser, H. F. (1976). A computer program for item selection based on maximum internal consistency. *Educational and Psychological Measurement, 36,* 757–759.

Spearman, C. (1904). General intelligence, objectively determined and measured. *American Journal of Psychology, 15,* 201–293.

Stern, G. G. (1970). *People in context: Measuring person-environment congruence in education and industry.* New York, NY: Wiley.

Thurstone, L. L. (1931). Multiple factor analysis. *Psychological Review, 38,* 406–427.

Thurstone, L. L. (1947). *Multiple factor analysis.* Chicago, IL: University of Chicago.

Velicer, W. F., & Jackson, D. N. (1990). Component analysis versus common factor analysis: Some issues in selecting an appropriate procedure. *Multivariate Behavioral Research, 25,* 1–28.

Vernon, P. E. (1950). *The structure of human abilities.* London: Methuen.

Wiggins, J. S. (1979). A psychological taxonomy of trait-descriptive terms: The interpersonal domain. *Journal of Personality and Social Psychology, 37,* 395–412.

Wiggins, J. S. (1980). Circumplex models of interpersonal behavior. In L. Wheeler (Eds.), *Review of personality and social psychology* (Vol. 1, pp. 265–294). Beverly Hills, CA: Sage Publications.

Wiggins, J. S., & Pincus, A. L. (1992). Personality: Structure and assessment. In M. R. Rosenzweig & L. W. Porter (Eds.), *Annual Review of Psychology* (Vol. 43: pp. 473–504). Palo Alto, CA: Annual Reviews, Inc.

Zegers, F. E., & ten Berge, J. M. F. (1985). A family of association coefficients for metric scales. *Psychometrika, 50,* 17–24.

Zwick, W. R., & Velicer, W. F. (1986). Comparison of five rules for determining the number of components to retain. *Psychological Bulletin, 99,* 432–442.

12

The Circumplex as a Tool for Studying Normal and Abnormal Personality: A Methodological Primer

Michael B. Gurtman

O ver 40 years ago, the Kaiser Research group of Leary, LaForge, Freedman, and their collaborators developed a relatively simple, yet seemingly comprehensive, model of the interpersonal domain, the interpersonal circle (Freedman, Leary, Ossorio, & Coffey, 1951; Leary, 1957). The interpersonal circle, or, as it is more commonly referred to today, the *interpersonal circumplex* (Goldberg, 1993; Wiggins, 1979), depicts the array of possible interpersonal tendencies in terms of a circular continuum, with each point on the circle translatable into an interpersonal coordinate system of Dominance (power, control, agency) and Love (affection, affiliation, communion). In its total, the circumplex may be regarded as both a taxonomy of the interpersonal domain and a structural summary of how the domain is organized (e.g., Foa, 1961; Pincus, this volume; Wiggins, 1979). Figure 12.1 illustrates a circle of interpersonal problems proposed by Alden, Wiggins, and Pincus (1990). This circumplex will be used throughout the chapter as a demonstration tool.

The purpose of this chapter is to offer a primer for those interested in tapping the analytic potential of the circumplex for studying abnormal personality in its interpersonal forms. As part of that, I will present methods of analysis appropriate when individuals are assessed in reference to a circumplex model. Although it is possible to discuss principles of analysis independently of a particular application (as one would typically factor analysis, cluster analysis, and other topics

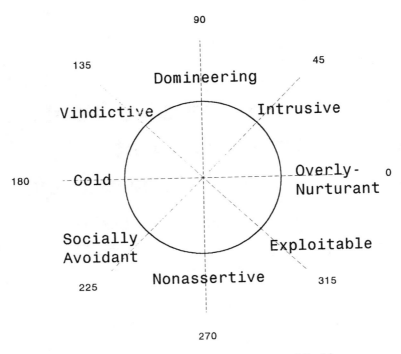

FIGURE 12.1. Circumplex of Interpersonal Problems.

Based on Alden et al. (1990)

covered in this section), they are greatly enriched by their close integration with what may be called collectively *interpersonal theory* (e.g., Carson, 1969; Kiesler, 1983; Leary, 1957; Sullivan, 1953). Indeed, it is to the credit of the Kaiser group, that, at the same time that the tenets of interpersonal theory were first being advanced, the methodological groundwork for applying those tenets to problems such as diagnosis and description was also being laid. This chapter, then, is a further development of the methodological side of this two-fold process. Pincus, in chapter 6 of this volume, provides a companion chapter on the *contents* side of the model in his presentation of the various theoretical formulations.

This chapter will be divided into three parts. The first part describes the structure of the circumplex and approaches to evaluating this structure. The second part presents a general method of profiling and graphically representing individuals within this space and the connection of these procedures to interpersonal aspects of adjustment. The final section relates the model to circular formulations of *DSM-III* personality disorders.

DEFINING AND EVALUATING CIRCUMPLEX STRUCTURE

Although the circumplex was originally conceived as a particular kind of correlation structure, a *circular matrix* (Guttman, 1954), the term today generally refers to the *geometric* representation of this matrix in a particular factor model. Consistent with the circle's geometry, a perfect circumplex of variables is defined by three properties (listed in order of increasing specificity): (a) differences among variables are reducible to differences in two-dimensions, or a plane (the circle as a *minimal representation*; (b) all variables have equal *projections* in this plane (the *constant radius* property); and (c) variables are uniformly distributed along the circle's circumference, generally translated into the property of *equal-spacing* when variables are discretely sampled as in Figure 12.1. Note that this third property effectively serves to differentiate between the circumplex and the simple structure (i.e., Big Five) version of the interpersonal space (e.g., Goldberg, 1993; Hofstee, de Raad, & Goldberg, 1992; McCrae & Costa, 1989).

By treating the circumplex as a factor model, it would follow that, for a perfect circle, the correlation, *r*, between any two points, *i* and *j*, on the circumference, can be exactly specified, and would equal:

$$r_{ij} = e + (1 - e) * \cos (\Theta_i - \Theta_j) \tag{1}$$

where *e*, or *elevation*, is the average intercorrelation among all points ($0 \le e < 1$), reflecting the size of the general factor; and Θ_i and Θ_j are the respective angular positions of points *i* and *j* on the circle. Adding property (c), or equal-spacing, Equation 1 essentially becomes a structural template for Guttman's (1954) circular matrix. Table 12.1 shows this matrix for two hypothetical circumplex structures, with and without a general factor (i.e., $e > 0$ and $e = 0$). As can be seen, both matrices have the defining circular-ordering of correlations of decreasing values followed by increases in a clear waveform pattern. Each new row looks like the previous row, with each column value, however, shifted one to the right and the last value returned back to the beginning. Note, too, that down any given diagonal, correlations are identical. In an equally-spaced circumplex, each row (or column) has the same average value, which returns the elevation term of Equation 1. Table 12.2 shows the obtained correlation matrix for the measure intended to operationalize the circumplex of Figure 12.1, the Inventory of Interpersonal Problems-Circumplex (IIP-C; Alden et al., 1990). The data are from a pool of 1,093 undergraduates who completed the IIP. The matrix seems to have this characteristic pattern.

It follows from the previous discussion that any putatively circular measure must conform, structurally, to the three defining features of a circumplex—two-dimensional representation, constant radius, and equal-spacing. Several methods

TABLE 12.1 Hypothetical Correlation Matrices for Two Perfect Circumplexes

No General Factor (e=0)

				Angular Position				
	0	45	90	135	180	225	270	315
0	1.000	0.707	0.000	−0.707	−1.000	−0.707	0.000	0.707
45	0.707	1.000	0.707	0.000	−0.707	−1.000	−0.707	0.000
90	0.000	0.707	1.000	0.707	0.000	−0.707	−1.000	−0.707
135	−0.707	0.000	0.707	1.000	0.707	0.000	−0.707	−1.000
180	−1.000	−0.707	0.000	0.707	1.000	0.707	0.000	−0.707
225	−0.707	−1.000	−0.707	0.000	0.707	1.000	0.707	0.000
270	0.000	−0.707	−1.000	−0.707	0.000	0.707	1.000	0.707
315	0.707	0.000	−0.707	−1.000	−0.707	0.000	0.707	1.000
e=	0.000	0.000	0.000	0.000	0.000	0.000	0.000	0.000

General Factor (e=.5)

				Angular Position				
	0	45	90	135	180	225	270	315
0	1.000	0.854	0.500	0.146	0.000	0.146	0.500	0.854
45	0.854	1.000	0.854	0.500	0.146	0.000	0.146	0.500
90	0.500	0.854	1.000	0.854	0.500	0.146	0.000	0.146
135	0.146	0.500	0.854	1.000	0.854	0.500	0.146	0.000
180	0.000	0.146	0.500	0.854	1.000	0.854	0.500	0.146
225	0.146	0.000	0.146	0.500	0.854	1.000	0.854	0.500
270	0.500	0.146	0.000	0.146	0.500	0.854	1.000	0.854
315	0.854	0.500	0.146	0.000	0.146	0.500	0.854	1.000
e=	0.500	0.500	0.500	0.500	0.500	0.500	0.500	0.500

have been used to evaluate instruments either implicitly or explicitly for these cardinal features. Recent articles by Browne (1992) and Tracey and Rounds (1993), and the references cited therein, offer rigorous and technically sophisticated statistical methods to evaluate the circumplex structure of tests (see also Romney & Bynner, 1989; and Wiggins, Steiger, & Gaelick, 1981). For the most part, however, researchers have relied on more familiar methods to evaluate test structure, notably principal components analysis (PCA; e.g., Alden et al., 1990; Wiggins, 1979; Wiggins, Phillips, & Trapnell, 1989) and multidimensional scaling (MDS; e.g., Gurtman, 1992b; Paddock & Nowicki, 1986). Although PCA and MDS are fundamentally exploratory rather than confirmatory techniques, they are arguably adequate as screening devices for most tests. Table 12.3 shows the results of a MDS analysis (Kruskal's nonmetric procedure) done on the correlation matrix given in Table 12.2. The results are in accord with the three goodness criteria proposed earlier. Stress values for 1, 2, and 3 dimensions were .332, .011, and .004. Stress indicates how well a given dimensional representation can account for the actual relations among objects; stress values close to 0 are desirable. These results then suggest that the matrix is reducible to two-dimensions. Projections for the variables (distances from the origin; vector length) were relatively uniform, as indicated by the small standard deviation (.09); thus, the projections are in accord with the constant radius property. Finally, when the vectors defined by the dimensional coordinates were rotated to maximum convergence with the target angles, the cosine-difference correlations averaged .996; thus, equal-spacing is also evident.

Although, as Davison (1985) has shown, results obtained with PCA and MDS (metric or nonmetric) are likely to be highly congruent (as could be demonstrated too for this example), in some circumstances one approach may be better suited than the other. For example, when a given matrix contains a general factor (equivalently, $e > 0$) as in Guttman's (1954) original example of the circumplex, MDS will generally produce the more parsimonious representation. In PCA, a general factor can confound the interpretation of results when rotated with other, substantive factors; indeed, two-factor solutions will often fail to reveal the underlying circumplexity of interpersonal variables when a general factor is present (see, e.g., Paulhus & Martin, 1987). Fortunately, the general factor can usually be effectively removed by ipsatizing profiles prior to PCA—that is, by expressing individuals' scores as deviations from the their own means. Compared to MDS, PCA has the advantage of allowing estimation of factor scores, which, as shown in Gurtman (1991) and Wiggins et al. (1989), can serve as the basis of a cross-validation of

TABLE 12.2 Correlation Matrix for Circumplex of Interpersonal Problems

Scale	Interpersonal Problem Category							
	PA	BC	DE	FG	HI	JK	LM	NO
Domineering	1.000	0.683	0.450	0.330	0.184	0.220	0.358	0.594
Vindictive	0.683	1.000	0.631	0.512	0.326	0.234	0.234	0.425
Cold	0.450	0.631	1.000	0.678	0.492	0.356	0.336	0.243
Socially Avoidant	0.330	0.512	0.678	1.000	0.714	0.504	0.401	0.206
Nonassertive	0.184	0.326	0.492	0.714	1.000	0.706	0.496	0.270
Exploitable	0.220	0.234	0.356	0.504	0.706	1.000	0.725	0.423
Overly-Nurturant	0.358	0.234	0.336	0.401	0.496	0.725	1.000	0.546
Intrusive	0.594	0.425	0.243	0.206	0.270	0.423	0.546	1.000
e (mean)=	0.477	0.506	0.523	0.543	0.523	0.521	0.512	0.463

n = 1,093

PA (90°) = Domineering, BC (135°) = Vindictive, DE (180°) = Cold, FG (225°) = Socially Avoidant, HI (270°) = Nonassertive, JK (315°) = Exploitable, LM (0°) = Overly-Nurturant, NO (45°) = Intrusive

TABLE 12.3 Multidimensional Scaling Analysis of Problem Matrix

| | Dimensional Coordinates | | | | | | | |
| | Original | | Rotated to Best-Fit | | | Angular Position | | |
Scale	1	2	1	2	Obtained	Target	Cosine–Difference	Vector Length
Domineering	1.07	0.30	1.10	−0.16	98.3	90.0	0.990	1.11
Vindictive	0.91	−0.41	0.67	−0.74	138.2	135.0	0.998	1.00
Cold	0.34	−0.82	−0.02	−0.89	181.4	180.0	1.000	0.89
Socially Avoidant	−0.34	−0.83	−0.65	−0.62	226.2	225.0	1.000	0.90
Nonassertive	−0.89	−0.40	−0.98	0.00	269.7	270.0	1.000	0.98
Exploitable	−0.96	0.30	−0.76	0.66	311.3	315.0	0.998	1.01
Overly-Nurturant	−0.54	0.81	−0.17	0.96	350.2	0.0	0.985	0.97
Intrusive	0.40	1.05	0.79	0.80	44.8	45.0	1.000	1.12
						Mean =	0.996	1.00
						SD =	0.006	0.09

A scale's vector length is its distance from the origin to its dimensional coordinates
Stress Values: 1-Dimension = .332
                           2-Dimensions = .011
                           3-Dimensions = .004

circumplex structure. Other technical differences are discussed by Davison both in this volume (Chapter 10) and in Davison (1985).

As indicated earlier, the circumplex and Big Five conceptualizations of the interpersonal domain vary in terms of whether traits are assumed to be evenly distributed around the circle or instead densely clustered at only certain points (presumably near the principal components)—in Goldberg's (1992) terms, whether the *interstitial space* between trait clusters in the personality *universe* is empty (simple structure) or populated (circumplex). At least two indices are available to differentiate between circumplex and simple structure. Mardia's (1972) important book on circular statistics advocates a uniformity measure, Kuiper's V_n, which was used by Fisher, Heise, Bohrnstedt, and Lucke (1985) in their analysis of a mood circumplex. Recently, Saucier (1992) developed a measure called the *squared loading index* (SQLI), that, in effect, serves to compare the theoretical loading pattern for simple structure space against that of a circumplex (see p. 1027). The measure ranges from 1 (perfect simple structure) to 2 (perfect circumplex), and appears promising.

Finding that a given test meets structural standards for goodness does not necessarily guarantee that it will have substantive merit as well. Here conceptual and quasiconceptual analyses of content are essential. For example, using purely conceptual criteria, Kiesler (1983) found important flaws in all four of the circumplex measures that he studied. His review highlights at least three critical substantive requirements for a measure: (a) categories at straight angles on the circle should be true semantic opposites (e.g., sociability vs. detachment); (b) a category's position on the circle should be correspond to its theoretical "weighting" of Dominance and Love; and (c) category referents occupying the same stratum ("level") on the circle should be comparable in their intensity or extremeness. To this may be added two further requirements: (d) Dominance and Love should fall at *exactly* 90° and 0°, respectively, on the circle; the proper alignment of axes is critical for testing complementarity, a central postulate of interpersonal theory (see Orford, 1986); and (e) all categories comprising the circle should be fundamentally "interpersonal" in nature, a requirement that, if logically followed, would force investigators to first confront their understanding of the interpersonal domain and frame that understanding in terms of a compelling theoretical model (e.g., Foa, 1961; Kiesler, 1983).

Turning to what I would call quasiconceptual methods, these involve formal analyses done on the products of informed judgments. As a ready example, Conte and Plutchik (1981) had Ph.D. psychologists provide similarity ratings on a large number of interpersonal trait adjectives; a complicated distance-scaling procedure yielded a circular arrangement of traits. This structure was then verified on a subset of traits through a factor analysis of a matrix of semantic differential ratings. In an often overlooked but excellent example of this method, McCormick and Kavanagh (1981) used various scaling procedures to examine the hypothesized circular structure of the Interpersonal Check List items (Leary, 1957); their results confirmed various inadequacies in the measure's coverage of the circle.

MEASURING INTERPERSONAL ADJUSTMENTS WITHIN THE CIRCUMPLEX SPACE

An important contribution of the Kaiser Foundation group was the development of methods for "charting" individuals within the space of the interpersonal circle. Leary's (1957) book, which brought to fruition the group's work toward "systematizing the complexity of personality" (p. 33) in interpersonal terms, describes two kinds of "quantifications" with relevance to measuring adjustment. The first, which has been the more influential and will be the starting point for this section, involves using the circle to summarize interpersonal tendencies, both graphically and numerically. The second, considerably less popular and successful as a methodological contribution, concerns the measurement of discrepancies (or "variability") both within and across different "levels" of personality. By "levels," Leary meant the different kinds of personality data necessary for a comprehensive assessment, these associated with particular areas of functioning, awareness, or perspective (e.g., public behavior, conscious description, private symbolization, etc.). The interested reader is referred to the third section of Leary's (1957) book for a discussion of this topic, a provocative, though never fully realized, integration of interpersonal measurement and theory.

As is evident throughout Leary (1957), the Kaiser group utilized two basic approaches to representing individuals within the circle. The first, which I will refer to as the *circular profile*, involves charting an individual's pattern of scores in the polar coordinate space defined by the particular circular measure. Figure 12.2 shows a case profile, using the preferred 8-octant breakdown of the circle. Other examples of either individual or averaged profiles can be found in Leary (1957), Gurtman (1992b), Pincus and Wiggins (1990), and Wiggins et al. (1989), among other places. Note that this profile, like most others presented in the litera-

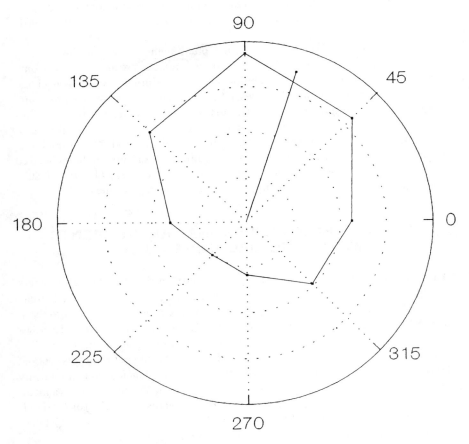

FIGURE 12.2. Circular profile for case study. Resultant vector is superimposed.

Measure is the Inventory of Interpersonal Problems-Circumplex (IIP-C).
Scales are as follows: Overly-Nurturant (0⁰), Intrusive (45⁰),
Domineering (90⁰), Vindictive (135⁰), Cold (180⁰),
Socially Avoidant (225⁰), Nonassertive (270⁰), Exploitable (315⁰).

ture, tends to have a particular pattern, which Wiggins and his associates (e.g., Wiggins et al., 1989) have dubbed the *interpersonal spaceship*. Technically, this profile is sinusoidal in form, which becomes apparent when the profile is plotted in the more typical rectangular coordinate system.

While the circular profile provides an informative view of an individual's interpersonal adjustments, the Kaiser group was also impressed by the need to develop what might be called a *structural summary* of profile data. Toward that end, LaForge, Leary, Naboisek, Coffey, and Freedman (1954) suggested measures of a profile's *general tendency* (vector angle) and *intensity* (vector length), which Leary (1957) later utilized in his system of interpersonal diagnosis and which have also figured prominently in the subsequent work by the Wiggins group (e.g., Wiggins et al., 1989; Wiggins & Broughton, 1991). Rather than present these directly, I will instead suggest a more comprehensive approach to profile analysis, one that fortunately incorporates the traditional methods and their implications.

As indicated earlier, the circular structure of measures tends to produce profile patterns having sinusoidal form. More specifically, it is possible to describe any interpersonal profile in terms of a *best-fit curve* to a cosine function, of the general form:

$$Z_{i'} = e + a * \cos(\Theta_i - \delta) \qquad (2)$$

where $Z_{i'}$ is the individual's predicted standard score on sector$_i$ of the circumplex; e is the mean level, or overall *elevation*, of the profile; a is the *amplitude* of the curve; Θ_i is the angle for sector$_i$; and δ is the *angular displacement* of the curve, the phase-shift that marks the curve's apex. As curve parameters, elevation, amplitude, and angular displacement can be estimated to produce a least-squares best-fit curve to the actual profile of scores. To this group may be added a fourth characteristic: the goodness-of-fit (R^2) between the curve and the profile itself. Figures 12.3 and 12.4 illustrate these concepts.

Elevation, amplitude, angular displacement, and goodness-of-fit provide what amounts to the *structural summary* of the key properties of an individual's circular profile.[1] Each too has a specific connection to interpersonal diagnosis and description. As seen in Figure 12.3, the curve's displacement is essentially a measure of the profile's central tendency; by definition, it indicates where the profile has its highest resultant value. Thus, the angle of the displacement conveys the predominant *quality*, or in Leary's (1957) terms, the *interpersonal typology* of the individual. A displacement of 45° would thus show a friendly-dominant adjustment; 110° a slightly hostile-form of dominance; 270°, submissiveness; and so on. It can be shown mathematically that the curve's displacement corresponds exactly to the measure of central tendency (vector angle) employed traditionally by interpersonal theorists (e.g., LaForge et al., 1954; Wiggins et al., 1989), and hence, it carries the same implications, interpretatively.[2]

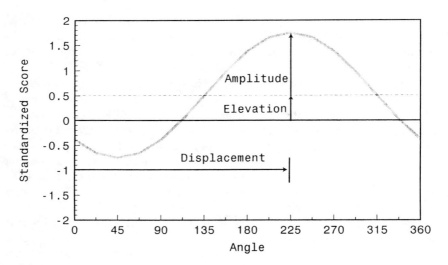

FIGURE 12.3. Cosine curve illustrating concepts of angular displacement, amplitude, and elevation.

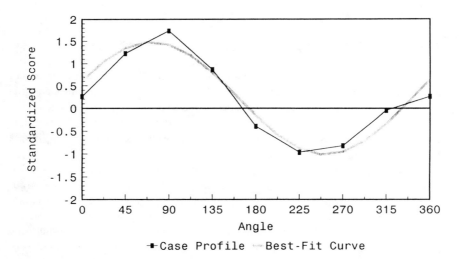

FIGURE 12.4. Best-fit cosine curve for earlier case study.

Measure is the Inventory of Interpersonal Problems-Circumplex (IIP-C). Scales are as follows: Overly-Nurturant (0^0), Intrusive (45^0), Domineering (90^0), Vindictive (135^0), Cold (180^0), Socially Avoidant (225^0), Nonassertive (270^0), Exploitable (315^0).

Returning to Figure 12.3, it can be seen that the amplitude of a profile curve indicates its interpersonal patterning—roughly speaking, the extent to which a person's interpersonal tendencies are constrained to a particular region of the circumplex. Amplitude will be high when the profile is "peaked" and will approach the floor of 0 when scores are comparable around the circle. Not surprisingly, perhaps, the curve's amplitude is mathematically identical to the traditional measure of profile *variability*, vector length. However, amplitude (and hence vector length) are not simple measures of variability (cf. Wiggins et al., 1989). More precisely, they are measures of *patterned* variability, as they describe variability constrained to a cosine curve function.[3]

As a measure of interpersonal variability, amplitude (vector length) can be easily linked to the notion of *interpersonal flexibility*, a key adjustment concept in interpersonal theory (Brokaw & McLemore, 1991; Leary, 1957; Paulhus & Martin, 1987; Pincus, Chapter 6 of this volume.) Theoretically, high amplitude (vector length) would suggest an extreme or intense interpersonal style, which may be associated with rigid rather than flexible adaptations to different interpersonal situations. Oddly enough, very few studies have empirically evaluated this important tenet of interpersonal theory. Wiggins et al. (1989) accrued evidence for this index's correlation with maladjustment, but Paulhus and Martin's (1988) study was less supportive.

The elevation, or mean level of the profile, has no counterpart in traditional interpersonal measurement, but has potential significance when the variables of the circumplex are related through a general factor, and hence, when a person's total score has meaning. For example, as a group, interpersonal problems tend to be positively related because of a shared "interpersonal distress" or complaint factor (e.g., Gurtman, 1992a, 1992b; Horowitz, Rosenberg, Baer, Ureño, & Villa-señor, 1988). Although this factor is related to the Big Five factor of Neuroticism (Pincus, Chapter 6 of this volume; Soldz, Budman, Demby, & Merry, 1993), Horowitz, Rosenberg, and Kalehzan (1992) have shown that it can be distinguished from general distress, and, moreover, has specific ramifications for psychotherapy process. Note that, unlike interpersonal problems, interpersonal traits (Wiggins, 1979) are theoretically devoid of a general factor (Wiggins et al., 1981); for this reason, when individuals are assessed in reference to a circumplex of interpersonal traits, any profile elevation would necessarily reflect a stylistic rather than substantive variable. In such a case, ipsatizing scores to remove the mean level would be appropriate.

Finally, the degree to which an individual's actual profile conforms to the best-fit cosine curve is an important, though previously unexamined, feature of the profile. Generally expressed as R^2, it indicates the extent to which an individual's profile can be *modeled* by its summary features; a poor-fit suggests that the complexity of an individual's profile cannot be adequately reproduced by knowing the central tendency (angular displacement), extremity (amplitude), and level (elevation). It is essentially, then, a measure of the discrepancy between the actual series of scores (Z_i) and the corresponding predicted scores $(Z_{i'})$. Conceptually, the degree-of-fit seems related to the *prototypicality* of an individual's interpersonal style, that is, its resemblance to an aggregate profile for individuals characterizing a particular, noncomplex interpersonal category (cf. Wiggins, 1982). For the purposes of interpersonal diagnosis, prototypic cases should be more easily classified than those with diverse or multiple-category features (e.g., Cantor, Smith, French, & Mezzich, 1980; Wiggins, 1982).

Before closing this section, it may be useful to make the connection between the structural measures developed here and the traditional profile measures of *elevation*, *scatter*, and *shape* (Cronbach & Gleser, 1953). In both approaches, elevation identifies the mean level of scores in the profile. Scatter, or the person's variability about his or her mean, is related to amplitude, though, as shown earlier, amplitude is scatter (variability) moderated by goodness-of-fit. Shape, which, according to Cronbach and Gleser (1953) is the profile's residual information after equating for elevation and scatter, is clearly then a function of a profile's displacement and its goodness-of-fit.

Computational Example

Table 12.4 provides a worksheet example for those who wish to apply either this or the traditional approach to profile analysis; the table was used to generate the curve presented in the earlier Figure 12.4. *Note that any method that returns the circular mean and variance (Mardia, 1972) can be used to derive the angular displacement and amplitude of the profile, as the respective terms are mathematically equivalent.* The most direct approach, then, is simple vector arithmetic, as developed by LaForge et al. (1954), and shown in the table. The individual's Dominance and Love coordinates would first be obtained through vector addition; because the space is theoretically circular, these Cartesian coordinates would then be converted into a polar coordinate system of vector angle (direction) and vector length (radius) using trigonometric principles. Note that ipsatizing scores for mean level or elevation is unnecessary when calculating angle and amplitude through the vector method, because level differences automatically cancel out in the summation process.

In many instances, an adequate alternative to this direct approach is to estimate an individual's Dominance and Love scores via principal components analysis (Wiggins et al., 1989). When measurements are taken from a well-constructed, two-factor circle, the first two components are likely to be rotated variants of Dominance and Love, and hence a person's factor scores will serve as orthogonal estimates of these interpersonal vectors. Two potential problems must be kept in mind, however: First, there is no assurance that the extracted components will correspond precisely to Dominance and Love, rather than some rotation of them (e.g., McCrae & Costa, 1989)[4]; a rotation to a target matrix would then be required,

TABLE 12.4 Deriving Structural Summary Components Using Vector Method (Refer to Case Data Depicted in Figure 4)

Calculation Steps and Formulas:

STEP 1.
Calculate resultant vector from circular profile of standard scores. Expressed in DOMinance and LOVe coordinates:

$$DOM = .25 * \Sigma (Z_i * \sin \Theta_i)$$

$$LOV = .25 * \Sigma (Z_i * \cos \Theta_i)$$

STEP 2.
Convert DOM and LOV to polar coordinates of vector angle and vector length, which are the least-squares estimates of angular displacement (δ) and amplitude (a), respectively:

$$\text{Vector angle } (\delta) = \text{atan} (DOM / LOV)$$

$$\text{Vector length } (a) = (DOM^2 + LOV^2)^{.5}$$

STEP 3. Calculate Elevation, e, as: $e = \Sigma (Z_i) / 8$

STEP 4. Construct best-fit curve, as: $Z_i' = e + a * \cos (\Theta_i - \delta)$

STEP 5. Calculate goodness-of-fit as: $R^2 = SS_{zi}' / SS_{zi}$

A computationally simpler formula is:

$R^2 = ka^2 / SS_{zi}$, where $k = 4$ for an 8-octant circle

Worksheet:

Θi	Zi	$\sin(\Theta i)$	$\cos(\Theta i)$	$Zi*\sin(\Theta i)$	$Zi*\cos(\Theta i)$	Zi'
0	0.26	0.00	1.00	0.00	0.26	0.62
45	1.23	0.71	0.71	0.87	0.87	1.35
90	1.74	1.00	0.00	1.74	0.00	1.42
135	0.87	0.71	−0.71	0.61	−0.61	0.80
180	−0.39	0.00	−1.00	0.00	0.39	−0.16
225	−0.96	−0.71	−0.71	0.68	0.68	−0.88
270	−0.82	−1.00	0.00	0.82	0.00	−0.95
315	−0.04	−0.71	0.71	0.03	−0.03	−0.33
Σ	1.86			4.75	1.56	
SS	6.65					6.24

Results:
DOM =	1.19
LOV =	0.39
Displacement =	71.85°
Amplitude =	1.25
Elevation =	0.23
R^2 =	0.94
Best-Fit Curve:	$Z_i' = .23 + 1.25 * \cos (\Theta_i - 71.85°)$

Note: Radians were used in all calculations, then converted to degrees for ease of interpretation. For purposes of display, terms are rounded to two decimal places.

eliminating the simplicity advantage of the PCA approach. Second, if the circular measure contains a general factor, individual scores should be ipsatized first to remove the person's mean level (in effect, removing the general factor), otherwise the first two components will almost certainly be confounded unsystematically with this factor. See Gurtman (1991) or Wiggins et al. (1989) for further details on using PCA to estimate Dominance and Love.

THE INTERPERSONAL CIRCUMPLEX AND PERSONALITY DISORDERS

Perhaps the most important proving ground for the circumplex model, and its attendant analytic tools, is the domain of personality disorders. As is probably familiar to most readers, the *DSM-III* defines personality disorders as maladaptive, rigidly-maintained, and relatively enduring patterns of thinking, feeling, and behaving (i.e., personality traits), which are associated with impaired functioning or distress. Since the inception of the *DSM-III*, there have been no shortage of attempts to accommodate the set of diagnosable personality disorders within a circular model (e.g., Blashfield, Sprock, Pinkston, & Hodgin, 1985; Kiesler, 1986; Morey, 1985; Pincus & Wiggins, 1990; Romney & Bynner, 1989; Soldz et al., 1993; Strack, Lorr, & Campbell, 1990; Wiggins, 1982; Wiggins & Pincus, 1989). In this section, I will briefly consider the circumplex approach to personality disorders. Following the aims of this chapter, the focus will be largely on methodological and analytic issues. As a quick orientation, Figure 12.5 shows a possible circumplex of personality disorders, informed by existing models (e.g., Wiggins, 1982) and empirical research (e.g., Soldz et al., 1993).

To a large extent, the potential strengths and weaknesses of the circumplex model, such as that of Figure 12.5, can be deduced from its structural and substantive characteristics. As revealed previously, the circumplex is a structurally-explicit taxonomy of the interpersonal domain: as a device for understanding PD's, it provides a picture of possible interpersonal dysfunctions and a model for how those dysfunctions are related to one another. Moreover, because of its close ties to interpersonal theory (e.g., complementarity), it is also a source of hypotheses, both clinically and scientifically, about the kinds of interpersonal transactions the individual is likely to experience, and the impacts he or she will typically produce (e.g., Kiesler, 1983).

The circumplex model, though, has some important limits, as well as logical requirements. First and foremost, the circumplex is a viable model only for personality disorders that are in large measure *interpersonal*. Although all personality disorders have interpersonal correlates and consequences (e.g., McLemore & Brokaw, 1987; Millon & Everly, 1985), the *interpersonalness* of a disorder, in this sense, refers to its factorial content as some combination of Dominance and Love (Gurtman, 1991), or more precisely, disturbances in these broad, interper-

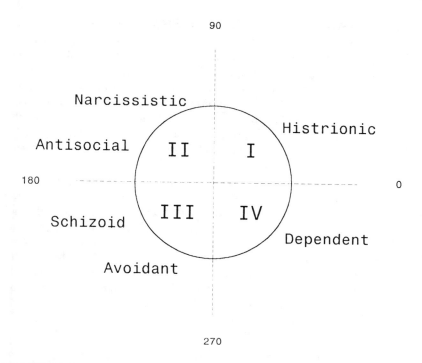

FIGURE 12.5. A possible interpersonal circumplex of personality disorders.

Roman numerals designate quadrants.

sonal tendencies. By this criterion, narcissism, a hostile-dominant form of adjustment (e.g., Horney, 1950; Leary, 1957; Wiggins, 1982), would qualify as interpersonal, but obsessive-compulsive disorders would probably be only marginally so (cf. Wiggins, 1982; Romney & Bynner, 1989). If one were to adopt a Big Five perspective, then such disorders would be defined by their *communality* with Factors I (Extraversion) and II (Agreeableness), which, as indicated earlier, are simply rotations of Dominance and Love (e.g., McCrae & Costa, 1989). Thus, some PD's do not have sizable projections in the interpersonal plane and would therefore not be represented in a circumplex plane. Still others, with significant interpersonal loading, may be poorly differentiated in circumplex space, because their defining features are found mainly in noninterpersonal attributes; an example would be the schizoid and avoidant PDs, both hostile-submissive adjustments, that are largely discriminated on the basis of their loadings on the Neuroticism factor of the Big Five (e.g., Wiggins & Pincus, 1994).

A second more subtle consideration is that disorders should be interpersonally homogeneous, that is, their interpersonal features should be largely contained within a relatively small and continuous segment of the circle. The PDs depicted in Figure 12.5 generally satisfy this requirement. PDs that are interpersonally diverse (complex), such as the so-called *ambivalent disorders* of the passive aggressive and compulsive styles (Millon & Everly, 1985), will show a diminished projection on the circle, even though their elemental features taken alone may be highly interpersonal. As an elaboration on this point, Kiesler's (1986) work in which he matched diagnostic criteria for 11 *DSM-III* PDs with their counterparts on his interpersonal circle deserves special attention. Among his findings were that PDs differed considerably in the breadth with which they sampled the circle, with at least 4 of 11 disorders spanning more than one octant (45°), and 2 disorders sampling noncontinuously.

Finally, the adequacy of the circumplex model rests, in part, on assumptions made about the nature of PDs themselves. Implicitly, the circumplex is a continuous, or dimensional, model of PDs, rather than a discrete, or categorical, model (e.g., Frances & Widiger, 1986). The continuous model, in its truest form, would represent PDs as essentially points (projections) in a circular space formed by the intersection of Dominance and Love. Note that *dimensionality* of this system is double; not only are individuals assessed along trait continua from normal to abnormal, but disorders themselves are dimensional in nature, conceived as particular "blends" of Dominance and Love. The boundaries then between disorders are eminently *fuzzy* (Wiggins, 1982).

From Model to Individual Assessment

The circumplex model carries with it important implications for how to assess individuals. On the one hand, it is possible to treat the circumplex space as a kind of *psychosocial alternative* (McLemore & Benjamin, 1979) to the Axis II taxonomy supplied by the *DSM-III*. McLemore and Benjamin's (1979) article is essentially the clarion call for this approach. Consistent with the broad principles of interpersonal diagnosis outlined by Leary (1957), the structural summary of an individual's interpersonal profile would serve as an interpretive medium. The previous section describes how angular displacement, amplitude, elevation, and goodness-of-fit could each contribute to the assessment of interpersonal tendencies. Note that, in a natively interpersonal system of diagnosis, these components can be related to principles of interpersonal influence, such as complementarity (e.g., Kiesler, 1983), which makes the system ultimately *prescriptive* when allied to the aims of psychotherapy (e.g., McLemore & Benjamin, 1979).

If the purpose of assessment is Axis II diagnosis (i.e., classification), then a somewhat different approach would be required. It is natural, perhaps even inevitable, that classification in this case be on the basis of comparisons to *interpersonal prototypes* (e.g., Blashfield et al., 1985; Wiggins, 1982). By prototype is meant here the composite circular profile produced by aggregating (i.e., averaging) the profiles of individuals who are exemplars of a particular PD. Importantly, if a PD has a significant projection on the circumplex, then its prototype will tend to conform closely to a cosine curve described earlier and can thus be summarized by its three properties of angular displacement, amplitude, and elevation (see Gurtman, 1992a). Figure 12.6 shows the prototype profiles that might be expected for the Narcissistic, Histrionic, and Avoidant PDs, assuming Figure 12.5 to be valid.

In a prototype scheme (e.g., Cantor et al., 1980), classification is essentially a probabilistic matter, in which the correspondence between the individual and the prototype serves to establish a degree of *category membership*. Euclidean distance is a common metric of profile similarity, yet its well-known disadvantage is that it indiscriminately lumps together all sources of profile difference (e.g., Cronbach & Gleser, 1953). A better method, especially if one is wedded to interpersonal measurement, is to compare each of the summary characteristics of the individual to those of the prototype. Here the person's correspondence in terms of interpersonal typology (angular displacement), extremity or patterning (amplitude), and distress (elevation) are meaningful dimensions of analysis. Of the three, however, the match between the angular positions of the individual and the prototype would usually be of greatest interest (e.g., Leary, 1957; Wiggins, 1982). Indeed, it can be shown that, when both profiles (individual and prototype) have reasonable goodness-of-fit, the cosine of their angular discrepancy (i.e., separation on the circle) is highly related to the Pearson correlation of their profiles. Thus, the dif-

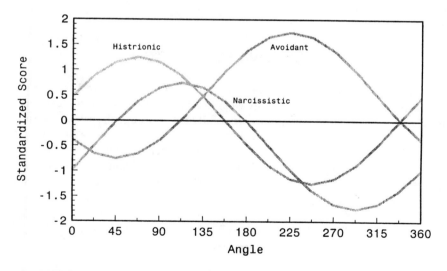

FIGURE 12.6. Prototypic interpersonal profiles for the Narcissistic, Histrionic, and Avoidant personality disorders. Note assumed differences in elevation (distress).

ference in the profiles' central tendencies becomes a simple measure of profile congruence.

BEYOND THE INTERPERSONAL CIRCUMPLEX

Although the focus of this paper has been the interpersonal domain, the methods developed here can be profitably extended to other domains having circumplex structure. Circular models, whether labeled so or not, have a long history in psychology, and continue to be popular. For example, in the personality area, Hofstee et al. (1992) and Saucier (1992) have recently shown that other crossings of Big Five factors (e.g., I and IV) yield statistically and substantively meaningful circumplexes. Russell (1980) is just one of many investigators who have now demonstrated that the "affective space" has circumplex properties. In applying the circumplex to vocational interests, Tracey's work (e.g., Tracey & Rounds, 1993) stands out. Of course, the structural components of displacement, amplitude, elevation, and fit are likely to have different interpretive significance in the noninterpersonal domains; nevertheless, when individuals are assessed in reference to a circular space, their profiles will have the same characteristic pattern described here, and thus can be analyzed in identical terms. I invite readers impressed by the geometric elegance of the circumplex to create those important links between theory and measurement.

ACKNOWLEDGMENTS

This chapter was written while I was a visiting scholar at Northwestern University. I sincerely thank the Psychology Department at Northwestern University for their generosity in hosting me; I also gratefully acknowledge the sabbatical support of the University of Wisconsin-Parkside. Terry Tracey, Steve Strack, and Maury Lorr provided valuable feedback on an earlier versions of this chapter. Those who contributed indirectly include Don Kiesler, Jim Schmidt, Chris Wagner, and Bill Revelle, in the last case through some free-ranging lunchtime conversations about personality theory and structure.

NOTES

[1]In previous papers (Gurtman 1992a, 1992b, 1993), I have explained the application of the best-fit curve method to issues such as construct validation and test construction. On a technical matter, goodness-of-fit is more of a metasummary, as it relates to the adequacy of the structural model.

[2]The caveat: *exactly* when scores are taken from a circumplex that theoretically is equally-spaced, which is virtually always the case.

[3]Consistent with this, it can be shown that:

$$a^2 = k^*R^2SS_{total}$$

where k is a constant, SS_{total} is the total variability of the individual's profile of scores expressed as sum-of-squares, and R^2 is the goodness-of-fit to the cosine curve. This equation also reveals the statistical identity of amplitude (vector length): it is essentially the nonstandardized regression weight, *beta*, for the best-fit cosine curve. (I thank William Revelle for helping me to see that connection.)

[4]Indeed, for a perfect circumplex, there is the problem that no one rotation of axes is statistically superior to any other. As a fortunate coincidence, factor analysis of the most widely-used circle measure, the Interpersonal Adjective Scales (IAS; Wiggins et al., 1989), tends to produce factors that are almost perfectly aligned to Dominance and Love, thus enabling the PCA estimation method.

REFERENCES

Alden, L. E., Wiggins, J. S., & Pincus, A. L. (1990). Construction of circumplex scales for the Inventory of Interpersonal Problems. *Journal of Personality Assessment, 55*, 521–536.

Blashfield, R., Sprock, J., Pinkston, K., & Hodgin, J. (1985). Exemplar prototypes of personality disorder diagnoses. *Comprehensive Psychiatry, 26*, 11–21.

Brokaw, D. W., & McLemore, C. W. (1991). Interpersonal models of personality and psychopathology. In D. G. Gilbert & J. J. Connolly (Eds.), *Personality, social skills, and psychopathology: An individual differences approach* (pp. 49–83). New York: Plenum.

Browne, M. W. (1992). Circumplex models for correlation matrices. *Psychometrika, 57*, 469–497.

Cantor, N., Smith, E. E., French, R. D., & Mezzich, J. (1980). Psychiatric diagnosis as prototype categorization. *Journal of Abnormal Psychology, 89*, 181–193.

Carson, R. C. (1969). *Interaction concepts of personality*. Chicago: Aldine.

Conte, H. R., & Plutchik, R. (1981). A circumplex model for interpersonal personality traits. *Journal of Personality and Social Psychology, 40*, 701–711.

Cronbach, L. J., & Gleser, G. C. (1953). Assessing similarity between profiles. *Psychological Bulletin, 50*, 456–473.

Davison, M. L. (1985). Multidimensional scaling versus components analysis of test intercorrelations. *Psychological Bulletin, 97*, 94–105.

Fisher, G. A., Heise, D. R., Bohrnstedt, G. W., & Lucke, J. F. (1985). Evidence for extending the circumplex model of personality trait language to self-reported moods. *Journal of Personality and Social Psychology, 49*, 233–242.

Foa, U. G. (1961). Convergences in the analysis of the structure of interpersonal behavior. *Psychological Review, 68*, 341–353.

Frances, A., & Widiger, T. A. (1986). Methodological issues in personality disorder diagnosis. In T. Millon & G. L. Klerman (Eds.), *Contemporary directions in psychopathology: Toward the DSM-IV* (pp. 381–400). New York: Guilford Press.

Freedman, M. B., Leary, T. F., Ossorio, A. G., & Coffey, H. S. (1951). The interpersonal dimension of personality. *Journal of Personality, 20*, 143–161.

Goldberg, L. R. (1992). The development of markers for the Big-Five factor structure. *Psychological Assessment, 4*, 26–42.

Goldberg, L. R. (1993). The structure of phenotypic personality traits. *American Psychologist, 48*, 26–34.

Gurtman, M. B. (1991). Evaluating the interpersonalness of personality scales. *Personality and Social Psychology Bulletin, 17*, 670–677.

Gurtman, M. B. (1992a). Construct validity of interpersonal personality measures: The interpersonal circumplex as a nomological net. *Journal of Personality and Social Psychology, 63*, 105–118.

Gurtman, M. B. (1992b). Trust, distrust, and interpersonal problems: A circumplex analysis. *Journal of Personality and Social Psychology, 62*, 989–1002.

Gurtman, M. B. (1993). Constructing personality tests to meet a structural criterion: Application of the interpersonal circumplex. *Journal of Personality, 61*, 237–263.

Guttman, L. (1954). A new approach to factor analysis: The radex. In P. F. Lazarsfeld (Ed.), *Mathematical thinking in the social sciences* (pp. 258–348). Glencoe, IL: Free Press.

Hofstee, W. K. B., de Raad, B., & Goldberg, L. R. (1992). Integration of the Big Five and circumplex approaches to trait structure. *Journal of Personality and Social Psychology, 63*, 146–163.

Horney, K. (1950). *Neurosis and human growth: The struggle toward self-realization*. New York: Norton.

Horowitz, L. M., Rosenberg, S. E., & Kalehzan, B. M. (1992). The capacity to describe other people clearly: A predictor of interpersonal problems in brief dynamic psychotherapy. *Psychotherapy Research, 2*, 37–51.

Horowitz, L. M., Rosenberg, S. E., Baer, B. A., Ureño, G., & Villaseñor, V. S. (1988). Inventory of Interpersonal Problems: Psychometric properties and clinical applications. *Journal of Consulting and Clinical Psychology, 56*, 885–892.

Kiesler, D. J. (1983). The 1982 interpersonal circle: A taxonomy for complementarity in human transactions. *Psychological Review, 90*, 185–214.

Kiesler, D. J. (1986). The 1982 interpersonal circle: An analysis of DSM-III personality disorders. In T. Millon & G. L. Klerman (Eds.), *Contemporary directions in psychopathology: Toward the DSM-IV* (pp. 571–597). New York: Guilford Press.

LaForge, R., Leary, T. F., Naboisek, H., Coffey, H. S., & Freedman, M. B. (1954). The interpersonal dimension of personality: II. An objective study of repression. *Journal of Personality, 23*, 129–153.

Leary, T. (1957). *Interpersonal diagnosis of personality*. New York: Ronald Press.

Mardia, K. V. (1972). *Statistics of directional data*. New York: Academic Press.

McCormick, C. C., & Kavanagh, J. A. (1981). Scaling interpersonal checklist items to a circular model. *Applied Psychological Measurement, 5*, 421–447.

McCrae, R. R., & Costa, P. T., Jr. (1989). The structure of interpersonal traits: Wiggins's circumplex and the five-factor model. *Journal of Personality and Social Psychology, 56*, 586–595.

McLemore, C. W., & Benjamin, L. S. (1979). Whatever happened to interpersonal diagnosis? A psychosocial alternative to DSM-III. *American Psychologist, 34*, 17–34.

McLemore, C. W., & Brokaw, D. W. (1987). Personality disorders as dysfunctional interpersonal behavior. *Journal of Personality Disorders, 1*, 270–285.

Millon, T., & Everly, G. S., Jr. (1985). *Personality and its disorders: A biosocial learning approach*. New York: Wiley.

Morey, L. C. (1985). An empirical comparison of interpersonal and DSM-III approaches to classification of personality disorders. *Psychiatry, 48,* 358–364.

Orford, J. (1986). The rules of interpersonal complementarity: Does hostility beget hostility and dominance, submission? *Psychological Review, 93,* 365–377.

Paddock, J. R., & Nowicki, S., Jr. (1986). The circumplexity of Leary's Interpersonal Circle: A multidimensional scaling perspective. *Journal of Personality Assessment, 50,* 279–289.

Paulhus, D. L., & Martin, C. L. (1987). The structure of personality capabilities. *Journal of Personality and Social Psychology, 52,* 354–365.

Paulhus, D. L., & Martin, C. L. (1988). Functional flexibility: A new conception of interpersonal flexibility. *Journal of Personality and Social Psychology, 55,* 88–101.

Pincus, A. L., & Wiggins, J. S. (1990). Interpersonal problems and conceptions of personality disorders. *Journal of Personality Disorders, 4,* 342–352.

Romney, D. M., & Bynner, J. M. (1989). Evaluation of circumplex model of DSM-III personality disorders. *Journal of Research in Personality, 23,* 525–538.

Russell, J. A. (1980). A circumplex model of affect. *Journal of Personality and Social Psychology, 39,* 1161–1178.

Saucier, G. (1992). Benchmarks: Integrating affective and interpersonal circles with the Big-Five personality factors. *Journal of Personality and Social Psychology, 62,* 1025–1035.

Soldz, S., Budman, S., Demby, A., & Merry, J. (1993). Representation of personality disorders in circumplex and five-factor space: Explorations with a clinical sample. *Psychological Assessment, 5,* 41–52.

Strack, S., Lorr, M., & Campbell, L. (1990). An evaluation of Millon's circular model of personality disorders. *Journal of Personality Disorders, 4,* 353–361.

Sullivan, H. S. (1953). *The interpersonal theory of psychiatry.* New York: Norton.

Tracey, T. J., & Rounds, J. (1993). Evaluating Holland's and Gati's vocational-interest models: A structural meta-analysis. *Psychological Bulletin, 113,* 229–246.

Wiggins, J. S. (1979). A psychological taxonomy of trait-descriptive terms: The interpersonal domain. *Journal of Personality and Social Psychology, 37,* 395–412.

Wiggins, J. S. (1982). Circumplex models of interpersonal behavior in clinical psychology. In P. C. Kendall & J. N. Butcher (Eds.), *Handbook of research methods in clinical psychology* (pp. 183–221). New York: Wiley.

Wiggins, J. S., & Broughton, R. (1991). A geometric taxonomy of personality scales. *European Journal of Personality, 5,* 343–365.

Wiggins, J. S., & Pincus, A. L. (1989). Conceptions of personality disorders and dimensions of personality. *Psychological Assessment: A Journal of Consulting and Clinical Psychology, 1,* 305–316.

Wiggins, J. S., & Pincus, A. L. (1994). Personality structure and the structure of personality disorders. In P. T. Costa Jr., & T. A. Widiger (Eds.), *Personality disorders and the five-factor model of personality* (pp. 73–93). Washington, DC: American Psychological Association.

Wiggins, J. S., Phillips, N., & Trapnell, P. (1989). Circular reasoning about interpersonal behavior: Evidence concerning some untested assumptions underlying diagnostic classification. *Journal of Personality and Social Psychology, 56,* 296–305.

Wiggins, J. S., Steiger, J. H., & Gaelick, L. (1981). Evaluating circumplexity in personality data. *Multivariate Behavioral Research, 16,* 263–289.

13

Quantitative Genetic Methods for the Study of Abnormal and Normal Personality

Steven O. Moldin

During the last two decades, behavior genetics research has made considerable progress toward identifying the origins of individual differences in personality. Family, twin, and adoption studies show that aspects of normal personality are moderately heritable, with genetic factors accounting for between 20 and 50% of phenotypic variance (Eaves, Eysenck, & Martin, 1989; Plomin, 1990; Plomin & Rende, 1991). A consistent finding is that about half of the variation measured in personality is due to environmental effects completely specific to the individual, i.e., social learning from parents and other contributions from shared family environment make a negligible contribution to the transmission of personality (Merikangas, 1982; Eaves et al., 1989).

Past research has focused primarily on the study of quantitative dimensions of personality in unselected populations, e.g., general population twin samples. Despite problems of classification and variations in the use of terminology, there is reasonably consistent evidence of a genetic component to several categories of abnormal personality—antisocial, anxious/avoidant, and schizoid/schizotypal personalities (McGuffin & Thapar, 1992).

The genetic investigation of normal and abnormal personality is made especially difficult because (1) most behavioral traits appear to be influenced by multiple genes, each of small effect; (2) nongenetic factors play a significant role in affecting behavior; (3) large sample sizes are likely required to differentiate among more realistic models of complex familial transmission and to estimate parameter values with precision; (4) both normal and abnormal personality are the end result of complex developmental processes, in which gene expression and social interaction change with time; and (5) accurate modeling of assortative mating is required, given that there are significant mate correlations for social attitudes and potentially for other elements of personality (Eaves et al., 1989).

Genetic analysis is a powerful methodology because it has the ability to evaluate the causative role of both nature and nurture in personality research. Human population and statistical genetics offer analytic techniques for rigorously testing hypotheses of familial transmission; however, explicit theories of personality are required to generate such hypotheses which can then in turn be subjected to the threat of refutation (Popper, 1976).

The work of Eysenck and Eysenck (1985) has provided such a paradigm in behavior genetics to guide many research endeavors. As discussed in Section B of this book, there are other comprehensive theories of personality that have yet to be as thoroughly applied in genetic investigations of personality; Cloninger's comprehensive theory appears to hold particular promise in terms of generating testable hypotheses of complex psychobiological dimensions (e.g. Cloninger et al., 1993). Regardless of which theory is tested, it is essential prior to the genetic analysis of abnormal and normal personality that three basic questions be addressed: (1) is personality defined as variation along continuous dimensions or is it defined as categorical variation for which there exists two or more discrete classes for each trait? (2) what is the precise relationship between normal and abnormal variants of personality (e.g., Moldin et al., 1994; Cloninger, Svrakic, & Przybeck, 1993)? and (3) how many dimensions of personality will be studied?

Most past behavior genetics studies have been concerned with normal personality or social attitudes and quantitative ratings were analyzed. Most studies in psychiatry that have investigated the biological basis of behavior assume that abnormal personality variants can be classified in prototypic classes that reflect underlying discrete pathophysiologic entities with natural diagnostic boundaries (Widiger and Frances, 1985), despite evidence of considerable diagnostic overlap and the failure to clearly demarcate boundaries between the presence/absence of a personality disorder (Widiger, Trull, Hurt, Clarkin, & Frances, 1987; Morey, 1988; Zimmerman & Coryell, 1989; Nurnberg et al., 1991; Oldham et al., 1992).

The objective of this chapter is to discuss the analytic procedures available for the genetic analysis of normal and abnormal personality. Answers to the above three questions are required beforehand and, as discussed below, will guide implementation of specific methods. A more technical discussion of some of the approaches mentioned here for investigating the inheritance of qualitative traits is provided elsewhere (Rice, Neuman, & Moldin, 1991).

DEFINITIONS OF ABNORMAL-NORMAL PERSONALITY

Continuous Phenotypic Variation

This model assumes that there exists an observable continuous range of values that can be measured by ratings, self-report items, and the like. The continuous model offers more power for genetic analysis given the greater information content of continuous vs. discrete variables and given that graded values on one or more dimensions are available on all members of a pedigree. It is important to note that while measurement is on a continuous level, there may be discontinuities observed at the *latent* level that reflect the existence of different classes of individuals. It is of interest to the behavior geneticist when different classes represent different *genotypes*, i.e., different genetic constitutions (see single locus model discussion below). In this model, dimensions of personality exist and both abnormal and normal variants fall along the same graded continuum—a personality disorder thus would represent an extreme at which one can draw an arbitrary threshold to distinguish it from "high normal" dimensional values. Transmission of a quantitative dimension of personality may be under any of the genetic models discussed below.

Discrete Phenotypic Variation

Discrete personality traits are those defined as present or absent; individuals are classified as "affected" or "unaffected" typically on the basis of clinical ratings or psychiatric diagnosis. The disadvantage of this model is that there is less information for genetic analysis in pedigree data, given that a particular personality variant is measured as a binary variable that is only observed to be present or absent. This conceptualization typifies the belief that abnormal personality is a distinct and discrete clinical entity with natural diagnostic boundaries. As is the case with continuous phenotypic variation, discrete phenotypic variation may be transmitted through a multifactorial factor or a single gene with background variation due to random nonfamilial factors or to genetic/environmental factors transmissible within families.

MODELS OF FAMILIAL TRANSMISSION

Several explicit models exist in quantitative genetics for rigorously testing hypotheses in the familial transmission of personality (Table 13.1). Hypothesis testing is conducted through the use of high-speed computers that implement sophisticated mathematical programs for the different methods of formal genetic analysis discussed in the next section of this chapter.

TABLE 13.1 Models of Familial Transmission

Model	Single Gene	Polygenes	Transmissible Environment
Multifactorial	No	Yes	Yes
Single Major Locus	Yes	No	No
Mixed	Yes	Yes	Yes
Oligogenic	No	Yes (limited number)	Yes

Multifactorial Model

The multifactorial model for transmission of quasicontinuous and continuous traits (Falconer, 1965; Reich, James, & Morris, 1972; Reich, Rice, & Cloninger, 1979; Rice & Reich, 1985) assumes that all relevant genetic and environmental contributions to variation can be combined into a latent standard normal variable termed liability. When phenotypic variation is discrete, and individuals are classified as affected or unaffected, there are one or more threshold values such that affected individuals are those with liability values that exceed the threshold. The model has been extended to include multiple thresholds (Reich et al., 1972), with individuals with scores between threshold values representing milder phenotypic classes of affection. For example, there may exist a dimension of social relatedness on which individuals above a threshold value are classified as schizoid and those above a second (higher) threshold as classified as schizotypal.

Familial inheritance is modeled through correlations in liability between family members, with the following assumptions: (a) many genes act additively and are each of small effect in relation to the total variation. Such genes are called *polygenes*; and (b) environmental contributions are due to many events whose effects are additive. A key assumption is that the joint distribution in latent liability of family members is multivariate normal (Figure 13.1). In the standard multifactorial model, liability is determined by both genetic and environmental factors.

Single Major Locus Model

The single major locus model assumes that all relevant genetic variation is due to the presence of alleles at a single locus, and that environmental variation is nonfamilial. The variance in a trait attributable to a single gene can be distinguished from the variance attributable to genes of small effect at multiple loci polygenes. *Mendelian* diseases or traits are those that result from a single mutant gene having a large effect on the phenotype and that are inherited in patterns similar or identical to those described by Mendel for certain discrete characteristics in garden peas. If the liability is the sum of effects due to the major gene and a normally distributed residual, than the distribution in the population will be as depicted in

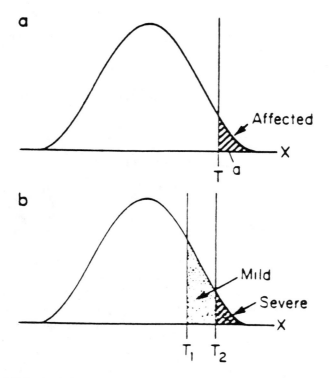

FIGURE 13.1. Liability distribution X with: (a) single threshold T and mean liability of affecteds denoted by a; and (b) two thresholds T_1 and T_2 used to model severity. In the case of a continuous trait phenotype, there is no threshold.

Figure 13.2. Assuming three possible genotypes (*AA, Aa, aa*) and letting q denote the frequency of the allele a in the population, under the assumptions of random mating the probabilities for the three genotypes AA, Aa, aa are $(1-q)^2$, $2q(1-q)$, and q^2 respectively. We further assume that the distributions within a genotype are normal with means z, $z + dt$, and $z + t$, respectively.

Although many human diseases are inherited as simple Mendelian traits, there is no robust evidence supporting the primary involvement of a major locus on behavior. However, researchers have not tested hypotheses that a personality trait is transmitted through a major locus of diminished effect in mixed models or transmitted under an oligogenic model (see below). Efforts continue to refine analytic strategies and molecular biological methods for detecting single genes of decreasing major effect that may be involved in the inheritance of complex behavioral traits (e.g., Moldin & Reich, 1993; Greenberg, 1993).

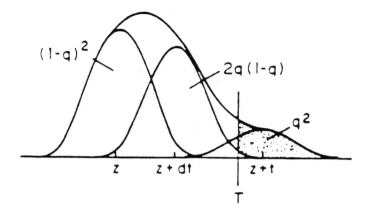

FIGURE 13.2. Commingled normal distributions of liability for three genotypes resulting from a single major locus. The overall composite distribution is nonnormal. In the case of a continuous trait phenotype, there is no threshold.

Mixed Model

The mixed model is a marriage of the single major locus and multifactorial models. An unobservable distribution of liability is determined by the effects of a major locus, a multifactorial transmissible background (polygenes and/or environmental factors), and residual nontransmissible environmental factors. A crucial distinction from the single major locus model is that the variation within a genotype for the major locus in the mixed model is in part familial.

This model and other related formulations have a number of conceptual and practical advantages over other approaches. It is the most comprehensive, given that traits may be transmitted through both a major locus and multifactorial (polygenes and/or common transmissible environment) causes. Rigorous tests of the mixed model have not been conducted in previous genetic investigations of personality or personality disorders.

Oligogenic Model

Oligogenic models are related to the multifactorial model in that a modest number of loci each of small effect, contribute to disease expression. Such models also allow for interactions (*epistasis*) among loci. Risch (1990) analyzed risk ratios for classes of relatives and found evidence for the potential interaction of a small number of such multiple disease susceptibility loci in the inheritance of schizophrenia. Similar results have been obtained in analyses of recurrence risk patterns from family studies of cleft lip with or without cleft palate (Mitchell & Risch,

1992). Oligogenic models have yet to be applied to study the transmission of personality traits or personality disorders.

PHENOTYPIC VS. LATENT MEASUREMENT

It is important to emphasize from the above discussion that phenotypic measurement is different from the latent distribution of the element of personality under investigation. Measuring a trait as discrete, with individuals classified as affected on unaffected, does not presume discontinuity at the latent level, i.e., single locus transmission. Likewise, quantitative assessment of a dimension of personality on a test like the Minnesota Multiphasic Personality Inventory (MMPI) does not presume continuity on an underlying latent scale (multifactorial inheritance). Both discrete and continuous phenotypic variation may reflect single major locus, multifactorial, or oligogenic inheritance or a mixture of these. Phenotypic assessment is driven by a substantive theory of personality and is independent of genetic inquiry; the behavior geneticist cannot employ sophisticated mathematical models to discern whether an element of personality is more correctly measured as a dichotomy or as a continuous dimension. Naturally, the measurements of the personality theorist should try to approximate nature as closely as possible, e.g., height should be measured on a continuous scale rather than dividing individuals into "tall" or "short" categories based on an arbitrary threshold.

RESEARCH DESIGNS

Several research designs can be applied to study normal and abnormal personality. The particular population studied and the sampling strategy in each design will depend on how personality is defined, i.e., as a quantitative dimension or as a categorical variable (affected vs. unaffected with a given personality disorder). If personality is defined as a continuous dimension, subjects from the general population typically will be sampled. In settings where ascertainment of pedigrees is through truncation on the distribution of the quantitative phenotype (e.g., an outpatient nonpsychotic sample) an appropriate method to correct for nonrandom sampling is required to yield unbiased estimates of transmission parameters (Hanis & Chakraborty, 1984; Rao & Wette, 1989). If personality is defined categorically according to a theory that places greater emphasis on personality disorder as a qualitatively different entity discontinuous with normal personality, sampling for genetic studies would be through a setting enriched for the personality disorder in question (e.g., an psychiatric outpatient clinic). An affected individual though which a pedigree is ascertained in this design is called a *proband*. An appropriate ascertainment correction would be required, given that pedigrees are nonrandomly sampled through an affected individual.

Family Studies

If genetic factors are involved in the transmission of personality, we will see familial resemblance on the trait in question. If abnormal personality is studied and individuals are classified as affected or unaffected with a given personality disorder, and if genetic factors are involved in the transmission of that disorder, we expect to see that disorder clustering in the families of affected members at a higher rate than in appropriate control populations. A family study can be conducted by ascertaining probands with personality disorder diagnoses from an outpatient or inpatient setting; the rate of illness is then assessed in their relatives. If personality is defined under a dimensional model, there are no probands to ascertain. Rather, pedigrees may be collected either by sampling from the general population or by sampling individuals in an outpatient or inpatient setting where you would expect truncation on the distribution of quantitative phenotypes. Familial resemblance is quantified by determination of parent–offspring, sib–sib, and other correlations. A variety of studies of quantitative dimensions of personality have found nonzero familial correlations (Ahern, Johnson, Wilson, McClearn, & Vandenberg, 1982; Loehlin, Willerman, & Horn, 1988; Eaves et al., 1989). Likewise, studies of *DSM-III-R* personality disorders have found evidence that personality disorders and personality disorder traits cluster in families (Loranger, Oldham, & Tulis, 1982; Siever et al., 1990; Silverman et al., 1993). However, a limitation of family study designs is that familial clustering of discrete traits or resemblance between relative classes on a dimension of personality does not in itself implicate a genetic mechanism: shared family environment may be responsible.

Twin Studies

The twin method has been an extremely popular research design to study the role of genetic factors in the familial transmission of dimensions of personality. Given that monozygotic (MZ) twins have identical genotypes, any dissimilarity between pair members must be due to unique environmental experiences. Dizygotic (DZ) twins have the same parents but share only 50% on average of their genes in common. If genetic differences are not important for familial resemblance on a dimension of personality, there should be no difference in MZ and DZ intraclass correlations. The difference between correlations is an estimate of the proportion of the total variance due to genetic factors within families. A comprehensive review of twin studies of personality (Eaves et al., 1989) concluded that there is a significant genetic component to the major dimensions of personality. Upwards of 50% of total phenotypic variation in personality may be assigned to nonshared environmental effects. Problems with previous studies include the use of different measures of personality across studies, small sample sizes, unspecified or too simple statistical models for familial transmission, and few attempts at replication across samples. Criticisms of the twin method include the fact that the degree of environmental resemblance for MZ twins is greater than that for DZ twins (Loehlin & Nichols, 1976). However, direct effects of the environment on twin behavior have not been demonstrated (Lytton, 1977; Kendler, Heath, Martin, & Eaves, 1986) and the alternate hypothesis has been proposed that environments individuals experience and create are actually functions of genetic differences.

Adoption Studies

Although twin data provides valuable information in building a model for human difference in personality, any model derived solely from twin studies needs to be tested against other kinds of data. Whereas twin studies endeavor to hold the effects of family environment constant, adoption studies permit the comparison of the effects of different types of rearing on groups that are assumed to be similar in their genetic predispositions. These studies attempt to separate the effects of genes and familial environment be capitalizing on the adoption process, in which children receive their rearing environment from a source different from which they receive their genes. Results of adoption studies investigating dimensions of personality in separated twins, adopted sibs, and foster parents and their adopted children are all consistent with the extensive data on twins reared together in supporting a genetic influence on dimensions of personality (Eaves et al., 1989). Furthermore, the findings of these studies support the involvement of a significant environmental component in the development of personality that is not shared among relatives but rather is unique. No adoption studies have been done ascertaining probands with personality disorders and examining rates of personality disorders in adoptees, adopting parents, or biological parents.

Association Studies

Transmission models incorporating a locus formally of major effect have not been tested in the study of personality disorders. One way to indirectly test such a hypothesis is to conduct an association study, in which the frequency of a particular form of a gene, an *allele*, in a group of individuals affected with a given personality disorder is compared to its frequency in a general population or other control group. Disorder-associations have been studied for many years; the best-known and best documented have been between the HLA system and several diseases that include insulin-dependent diabetes, multiple sclerosis, coeliac disease, and Graves disease (Mackintosh & Asquith, 1978; Farid et al., 1979; Haile, Hodge, & Iselius, 1983; Svejgaard & Ryder, 1989). Traditionally, associations between a genetic marker and a disorder have been detected by means of population-based association tests, which compare the frequency of the marker allele in affecteds versus those in controls. Recently, family-based association tests have become popular (Falk & Rubinstein, 1987; Hodge, 1993; Ott, Spielman, McGinnis, & Ewens, 1989). These tests use disorder and marker data within families and are appealing because the potential problems of population stratification in the selection of appropriate controls are circumvented.

Association studies must be conducted judiciously and the results interpreted cautiously because (1) there are no good candidate genes for use in the genetic investigation of personality disorders and (2) association studies likely cannot determine whether the association is due to true linkage of the disorder to a major locus necessary for illness expression or is due to the action of a susceptibility locus that is neither necessary nor sufficient for illness expression (Greenberg, 1993; Hodge, 1993).

ANALYTIC APPROACHES

A variety of analytic methods in quantitative genetics can be applied to the study of normal and abnormal personality (Table 13.2).

Estimation of Familial Correlations

Correlations among relatives are often used to measure the degree of familial aggregation of traits. Information regarding the genetic and environmental sources of familial resemblance is provided by such correlations. Familial correlations can be of several types: (1) correlations between classes of relatives on the same variable (e.g., parent–offspring correlations on a measure of introversion); (2) correlations between multiple members of the same class of relatives on the same variable (e.g., sib–sib correlations on introversion); (3) correlations between classes of relatives on different variables measured in each class (e.g. the correlation between parental introversion and child dominance); (4) correlations between members of the same class on different variables (e.g., the correlation between introversion in a child and extroversion in a sib; and (5) correlations between two different variables measured on the same person (e.g., the within person correlation between introversion and extroversion).

General methods for maximum-likelihood estimation of familial correlations derived under the assumption of a multivariate normal distribution have been presented (Donner & Koval, 1981; Rao, Vogler, McGue, & Russell, 1987; Shoukri & Ward, 1989). Recently, an analytic method has been described for estimating phenotypic familial correlations without requiring the assumption of a multivariate normal distribution (Zhao, Grove, & Quiaoit, 1992). It has been argued that, despite its boundary, the correlation is also useful for discrete phenotypes (Zhao & Prentice, 1990). Estimation of familial correlations is required for path analysis (see below).

TABLE 13.2 Research Designs and Methods in Quantitative Genetics

Approach	Goal
Family study	Establish familiarity
Twin study	Establish genetic effect
Adoption study	Disentangle genes from common environment
Association study	Detect a relationship between an allele and a disorder
Estimation of familial correlations	Establish familiality
Path analysis	Distinguish polygenes from transmissible environmental effects
Commingling analysis	Remove skewness or kurtosis from a distribution of continuous scores; detect two or more latent classes
Segregation analysis	Delineate a single locus effect
Linkage analysis	Assign chromosomal localization for a single major locus involved in transmission of a trait

Path Analysis

Path analysis was introduced as a mathematical technique to analyze correlations in order to evaluate the relative importance of varying causes influencing a variable of interest. The primary goal of path analysis in behavior genetic investigations of personality is to use twin and family or adoption data to resolve genetic from transmissible environmental effects common to parents and children (cultural inheritance) that contribute to familial aggregation of a dimension of personality or a personality disorder. When genetic transmission is present, additive polygenic effects cannot be distinguished from single locus effects.

Figure 13.3 shows a typical path model that might be applicable to the study of the transmission of personality. This figure shows a bivariate phenotype, i.e., a quantitative dimension of personality and a diagnosis of a given personality disorder may be measured on a person. The subscripts o, p_1, p_2 refer to an offspring, mother, and father, respectively. The model is parameterized to model inheritance of a quantitative dimension of personality x through a transmissible multifactorial component c. Liability to affection with a personality disorder is denoted by y. In this model, the quantitative trait x measures liability to affection directly and therefore defines the disorder (e.g, the relationship between blood glucose and diabetes; the potential relationship between a quantitative assessment of sociability and a DSM-III-R diagnosis of schizotypol personality disorder). The within-person correlation between liability to affection and the quantitative trait is given by the parameter r_w. Random environmental effects on y are denoted by w; random environmental effects on x are denoted by e (not shown in the diagram).

Path analytic techniques in behavior genetics can be implemented with the use of structural equation models that test cause and effect relationships involving both measured (observable) and latent (unobservable) variables. These relationships are analyzed by decomposing the variances and covariances of the measured variables into terms involving a set of unknown parameters which are used to model the effects of the latent variables. This general method of analysis is often referred to as covariance structure analysis (Jöreskog, 1973). Methods of analyzing covariance structures involve minimizing the difference between sample co-

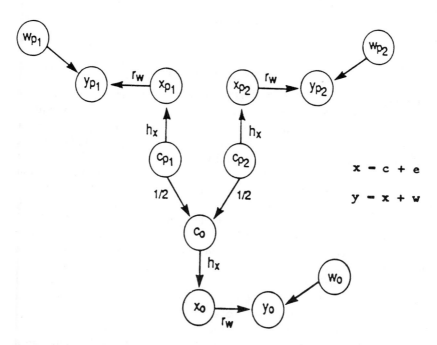

FIGURE 13.3. Representative path diagram depicting multifactorial transmission of a bivariate phenotype. A quantitative dimension of personality x is caused by a transmissible multifactorial component c and a random environment effect e. Liability y to a personality disorder diagnosis is correlated with x and is caused by x and a specific random environmental effect w.

variances and the covariance predicted by the model. LISREL is a computer program which was developed to estimate the unknown parameters in a set of structural equations developed by Jöreskog (1973). The program has become so widely used that the structural equation model introduced by Jöreskog has become known as the LISREL model and the general model is described in detail elsewhere (Jöreskog & Sörbom, 1989; Bollen, 1989; Rice et al., 1991). A comprehensive discussion of LISREL path analytic models and methods for analyzing twin and parental family data to distinguish genetic versus environmental transmission is presented by Neale and Cardon (1992). It is important to realize that typical path analytic approaches utilized in previous behavior genetic research of personality assume a multifactorial model of inheritance; genetic transmission is thus assumed to be through polygenes. Segregation analysis (see below) would be a useful analytic tool to refute the hypothesis of single locus transmission in pedigrees randomly selected from the general population *prior* to application of path analytic methods in twin and adoption samples, which generally are more difficult to locate and study.

Commingling Analysis

Commingling or admixture analysis (Day, 1969; Everitt & Hand, 1981; MacLean, Morton, Elston, & Yee, 1976) is a statistical technique used to fit mixtures of commingled normal distributions to a population distribution of quantitative trait values. Within a genetic context, discontinuity in the distribution of quantitative phenotype values may reflect discontinuity at the latent level and the existence of qualitatively different classes that correspond to different genotypes. Although such discontinuity is consistent with a single locus mode of transmission, segregation analysis (see below) is required to explicitly test the hypothesis of single locus transmission. This follows as discontinuity may be due to other factors, e.g., an artifact of the scale of measurement. Skewness and kurtosis can induce nonnormality in a distribution; the commonly used commingling analysis programs SKUMIX (MacLean et al., 1976) and ADMIX (Cloninger, von Knorring, & Oreland, 1985) both implement a power transform parameter to remove skewness from the data. The ADMIX program also implements an additional transform to remove kurtosis. Application of the ADMIX program to examine the distribution of scores on the Perceptual Aberration Scale (Chapman, Chapman, & Raulin, 1978), a psychometric measure of proneness to schizotypy, in a normal population sample led to the identification of three component distributions after skewness was removed through power transformation (Lenzenweger & Moldin, 1990).

Commingling analysis has two potential applications in the study of the familial transmission of quantitative dimensions of personality: (1) the estimation of power- and other transforms in a general population sample, in order to eliminate skewness and kurtosis from the data; and (2) the fitting of mixtures of normal distributions to the overall distribution of quantitative phenotype values. Both applications should precede estimation of transmission parameters for a quantitative personality trait in segregation analysis.

Segregation Analysis

Segregation analysis is a powerful method in human genetics for resolving a single major locus effect, but it cannot distinguish additive polygenic from environmental transmission. The unit of analysis is an entire pedigree and the object is to assess evidence for the segregation of a major gene in the presence of other sources of familial resemblance. Transmission of a major gene that is not fully penetrant can be modelled for qualitative phenotypes, i.e., it is not assumed that all individuals with the illness genotype(s) will in fact have the illness.

Segregation analysis has not been applied to the study of normal or abnormal personality. This likely has been so because (1) most personality researchers doubt on theoretical grounds that a major gene effects exists for dimensions of personality or personality disorders; and (2) there is no indirect evidence for a major gene effect from past behavior genetics research. However, no investigator has specifically conducted a segregation analysis to rigorously refuted the hypothesis of one or more incompletely penetrant major loci against a multifactorial background or of a limited number of oligogenes.

Linkage Analysis

Linkage analysis is a statistical technique by which family phenotypic and genetic marker data are examined to evaluate whether a quantitative or qualitative phenotype is co-segregating with a genetic marker at a known chromosomal location. Linkage analysis provides statistical evidence to identify on which chromosome lies a major gene involved in transmission of a phenotype. Linkage analysis has resulted in the chromosomal localization of a number of illnesses in human genetics that include neurofibromatosis, polycystic kidney disease, familial adenomatous polyposis, cystic fibrosis, Huntington's Disease, chronic granulomatous disease, Duchenne and Becker muscular dystrophy, and familial retinoblastoma.

No linkage studies of personality traits have been conducted. It is possible that digogenes or a small number of major genes in conjunction with additive genetic or environmental factors may be operative in the familial transmission of abnormal and normal personality. Two-locus models have been implemented in a linkage analysis program (Lathrop & Ott, 1990). Recently, a method for considering joint linkage of multiple loci for a complex disorder has been proposed (MacLean et al., 1993), but only for the case where all relevant information regarding the mode of transmission of the loci is known.

Nonparametric approaches to linkage analysis (Green & Woodrow, 1977;

Suarez & Van Eerdewegh, 1984; Suarez, Rice, & Reich, 1978) provide an attractive alternative to parametric lod score methods (Ott, 1991). This is true because specification of the mode of familial transmission is not required and other effects that can bias the results of parametric analyses (e.g., assortative mating, variable age-of-onset in the case of personality disorders) need not be modelled. If a categorical measurement model is employed and individuals are classified as affected or unaffected with a given personality disorder, sib-pairs in which both individuals are affected would be collected in a nonparametric analysis.

A difficulty in applying both affected sib-pair and parametric methods of linkage analysis is that there are no good candidate genes for the study of personality, i.e., one has no guidance in choosing among the ever-increasing number of available genetic markers, and conduction of a large number of independent linkage tests will lead to a commensurate increase in the probability of a false-positive finding (Kidd, 1993). Theories of personality that generate specific neurobiological hypotheses (e.g., Cloninger et al., 1993) are useful for delineating loci putative candidate.

Logistic Models for Genetic Analysis

An approach to mathematical computations in segregation and linkage analysis based on logistic regression models has been proposed (Bonney, 1984; Bonney, 1986). The major advantages of this approach compared to older models are that 1) integration of multivariate normal densities is not required and therefore numerical computations can be done much more quickly; and (2) an arbitrary number of covariates can be entertained. The utility of conveniently incorporating adjustments for a variety of factors relevant in the study of personality (sex, age, socio-economic status, environmental exposure) is very attractive. Logistic models offer a powerful methodology for understanding how genetic and environmental factors interact in the determination of complex personality traits in future research, and a one-to-one correspondence between the parameters of a regressive model and the mixed model has been established (Demenais, 1991).

CHALLENGES TO QUANTITATIVE GENETIC ANALYTIC APPROACHES

A striking result to emerge from previous studies of personality is that no one model has appeared to explain the variation and transmission of all the personality variables considered. It is very conceivable that transmission models that have been applied have not allowed consideration of the complexity of the underlying biological and psychosocial system, e.g., the fit of more sophisticated genetic models (mixed and oligogenic models) to family data has not been assessed. In addition, several factors may also be operative that complicate the genetic analysis of personality.

Assortative Mating

Several studies of spousal resemblance for personality show that mating is completely random for some traits like extraversion and neuroticism and only mildly assortative for psychoticism (Eaves et al., 1989). Transmission models that allow for phenotypic assortative mating, potential cultural inheritance, and additive genetic effects are necessary for future genetic investigations. The application of segregation analysis through logistic methods offers an opportunity to model assortative mating as a covariate.

Developmental Changes

Consideration of the developmental processes that lead to adult behavior is a requirement to fully describe the transmission of complex behavioral traits. A developmental perspective is necessary to understand why relevant genetic factors are turned off and on in the face of changing environments. Theory (e.g., Plomin & Daniels, 1987) and several longitudinal adoption studies suggest that the importance of nonshared environment increases with age. The results of a meta-analysis of twin studies (McCartney, Harris, & Bernieri, 1990) demonstrates such a developmental trend. New kinds of gene-environment interaction models that reflect the way in which gene expression and social interaction change with time are required. Such models may allow discrimination between two developmental explanations for increases or decreases in genetic effects on personality over time: (1) the same genetic effects are continually being reinforced by a series of successive environments; or (2) different genes are expressed during different "critical periods" in development. Neurodevelopmental models of fundamental brain structure and function have been proposed to explain the etiology of complex mental disorders (Bloom, 1993; Waddington, 1993), but have yet to be applied to the study of personality.

Gene-Environment Interactions

The weakest area in behavior genetics is undoubtedly in the modelling of gene-environment interaction. A major difficulty is knowing *what* aspect of the environment to measure. Investigators in genetic epidemiology (Rao et al., 1974; Rao & Wette, 1990) have developed environmental indices but it is crucial to consider potential genetic correlations between the phenotype and the index. Clearly, many so-called "environmental indices" behave just like any other inherited personality variable in twin studies (Eaves et al., 1989). Consequently, much more careful study of the environment is needed to assess those variables that might be actual factors involved in familial transmission, and not consequences of genetic differences. The delineation of environmental effects is made more difficult given that those most likely to be important are idiosyncratic and nonfamilial. Once accurate measurement of relevant environmental effects is achieved, it will become feasible to detect the genetic control of sensitivity to particular environmental oscillations (Eaves, 1984).

Multigenetic Control of Behavior

It likely will be necessary to include multiple genetic loci potentially in interaction when modelling complex biological systems important in the transmission of personality. The development of highly sophisticated quantitative methods in human genetics that incorporate such methods and that allow estimation of relevant transmission parameters has begun (MacLean et al., 1993). While computational difficulties in designing programs to estimate more and more parameters in complex pedigrees are daunting, Monte Carlo methods like Gibbs sampling (Geman & Geman, 1984; Gelfand & Smith, 1990) offer new and powerful approaches to estimating likelihood ratios for testing complicated transmission models. Gibbs sampling methods are being applied in genetic contexts to evaluate likelihood ratios in mixed model segregation analysis (Thompson & Guo, 1991), to estimate mixed model segregation parameters (Thomas & Cortessis, 1992), and to estimate linkage parameters (Thompson & Guo, 1991; Thomas & Cortessis, 1992; Thomas, 1992). Development and refinement of these new analytic methods will offer a powerful methodology to study the familial transmission of normal and abnormal personality under more realistic and sophisticated models incorporating genetic and environmental effects.

Uncertainties in Personality Theory

These questions cannot typically be answered by the behavior geneticist analyzing family data. The contributions of others in this book may be quite helpful in resolving basic definitional issues, e.g., the verisimilitude of continuous vs. a discrete models for personality, the relationship between normal and abnormal variants, the utility of studying normal or general population samples to learn about abnormal personality, etc. Theoretical models that have the greatest utility will prove to be those for which testable hypotheses of familial transmission can be specified for refutation; biologically meaningful theories of familial transmission will likely incorporate hypotheses to test oligogenic and mixed models.

CONCLUSION AND RECOMMENDATIONS

Continued careful application of increasingly sophisticated analytic methods from quantitative and human population genetics, together with clear theoretical models allowing explicit testable hypotheses, will enhance elucidation of genetic and environmental factors important in the transmission of normal and abnormal personality. While many behavior genetic studies have been conducted to date, questions still remain regarding the complex interplay of causative elements for several important dimensions of personality and for the personality disorders delineated in *DSM-III-R* and *DSM-IV*. The increasing sophistication and realism of mathematical models for complex inheritance, together with the ever-expanding number of more closely spaced DNA markers made available through molecular biology, will lead to more powerful analytic methods for studying the genetics of normal and abnormal personality. Now is the time to capitalize on the important work of previous investigators and apply current state-of-the-art genetic methodologies in personality research. Much of this work will of necessity be in the spirit of expanded hypothesis generation. Specific recommendations can be made for future research, and these apply to studies that collect quantitative or discrete data on either normal or abnormal personality:

1. Apply segregation analysis to personality data in multigenerational pedigrees. This may potentially lead to delineation of a single locus effect. Segregation analysis applications in personality research most likely will require implementation of oligogenic and mixed models, given that a single locus alone is unlikely to be involved in familial transmission. Quantitative dimensions of personality may best be investigated in general population samples and personality disorder pedigrees can be ascertained through psychiatric outpatient settings;

2. Identify candidate loci for use in association and linkage studies. To date, molecular neurobiologists have identified but a tiny fraction of the genes that are involved in determining the structure and function of the nervous system. Further identification will result in a very large number of putative candidate loci. Current psychobiological theories of personality (e.g., Cloninger et al., 1993) may serve to focus the search for such loci. The statistical complications of having to adjust and correct significance levels in association and linkage studies emphasizes the need in future genetic studies of personality to rely on replication as the best evidence for the verisimilitude of the findings of a single linkage or association study;

3. Conduct association studies as a screening method to provide indirect evidence for linkage, once candidate loci have been identified. An advantage

of association studies is that the mode of inheritance of a personality disorder under study does not have to be specified, and the study can be conducted by collecting a sample of affecteds and their parents as relevant controls (Falk & Rubinstein, 1987);

4. If segregation analyses or association studies yield promising results, conduct linkage analysis to establish chromosomal localization of a major locus. Given the likely genetic complexities of personality traits, it is crucial to conduct linkage analyses under models of oligogenic transmission and other multilocus systems. The importance of realizing that a single gene effect is likely to be diminished and to exist against a background of other genetic and environmental factors is crucial. Again, replication is essential. The collection of affected sib-pair data may prove to be an effective strategy, given that the mode of transmission of the major locus does not need to be modelled;

5. Reduce phenotypic measurement error and facilitate replication of findings by incorporating standardized assessments (e.g., objective personality inventories, highly structured diagnostic interviews). In the case of personality disorders, where there is no "gold standard" for diagnosis, studies need to be conducted to increase the reliability and accuracy of assessments. Rice and colleagues (1986; 1987; 1992) have developed a temporal stability model that they applied to the study of affective disorder diagnoses to allow consideration of clinical or other covariates (e.g., particular symptom ratings, treatment response, sex) that influence the likelihood that a positive case at time 1 will be positive at time 2. No longitudinal studies of personality disorders have been conducted that have a primary goal of identifying specific variables that predict temporal stability of diagnosis. Baron et al. (1990) demonstrated the utility of a caseness index derived from Rice et al.'s (1986, 1987, 1992) methods for grading the stability and severity of affective disorder diagnoses in linkage analysis;

6. Properly model the effects of age, sex, assortative mating, and other characteristics on transmission parameters. This is necessary for accurate estimation of segregation parameters and for establishment of the true mode of inheritance;

7. Apply logistic models for segregation and linkage analyses. These models allow flexible and direct incorporation of covariates into genetic analysis while offering a mathematical approach that does not require the underlying assumption of multivariate normal distributions;

8. Employ sophisticated path analytic and segregation analysis approaches that model developmental change and complex gene-environment interactions. Such strategies will facilitate identification of genes that exercise consistent and long-term effects on personality.

This is an exciting time for the application of biological paradigms to the study of normal and abnormal personality. Breathtaking advances in quantitative and molecular genetics in the last 10 years have led to a renewed excitement among behavior geneticists that identification of specific genetic effects on human behavior is possible. Carefully and thoughtfully conducted scientific research that relies on independent replication may likely lead to significant progress in delineating genetic factors that contribute to the familial transmission of personality.

ACKNOWLEDGMENTS

This work was supported in part by USPHS grant R29 MH48922, a Research Grant Award from the Scottish Rite Schizophrenia Research Program—Northern Masonic Jurisdiction, and by a Young Investigator Award from the National Alliance for Research on Schizophrenia and Depression.

REFERENCES

Ahern, F. M., Johnson, R. C., Wilson, J. R., McClearn, E. E., & Vandenberg, S. G. (1982). Family resemblances in personality. *Behavior Genetics, 12,* 261–280.

Baron, M., Hamburger, R., Sandkuyl, L. A., Risch, N. J.; Mandell, B., Endicott, J., Belmaker, R. H., & Ott, J. (1990). The impact of phenotypic variation on genetic analysis: application to X-linkage in manic-depressive illness. *Acta Psychiatrica Scandinavica, 82,* 196–203.

Bloom, F. E. (1993). Advancing a neurodevelopmental origin for schizophrenia. *Archives of General Psychiatry, 50,* 224–227.

Bollen, K. A. *Structural equations with latent variables* (1989). New York: John Wiley & Sons.

Bonney, G. E. (1984). On the statistical determination of major gene mechanisms in continuous human traits: Regressive models. *American Journal of Human Genetics, 18,* 731–749.

Bonney, G. E. (1986). Regressive models for familial disease and other binary traits. *Biometrics, 42,* 611–625.

Chapman, L. J., Chapman, J. P., & Raulin, M. L. (1978). Body-image aberration in schizophrenia. *Journal of Abnormal Psychology, 87,* 398–407.

Cloninger, C. R., Svrakic, D. M., & Przybeck, T. R. (1993). A psychobiological model of temperament and character. *Archives of General Psychiatry, 50,* 975–990.

Cloninger, C. R., von Knorring, L., & Oreland, L. (1985). Pentametric distribution of platelet monoamine oxidase activity. *Psychiatry Research, 15,* 133–143.

Day, N. E. (1969). Estimating the components of a mixture of normal distributions. *Biometrika, 56,* 463–474.

Demenais, F. M. (1991). Regressive logistic models for familial disease: a formulation assuming an underlying liability model. *American Journal of Human Genetics, 49,* 773–785.

Donner, A. & Koval, J. J. (1981). A multivariate analysis of family data. *American Journal of Epidemiology, 114,* 149–154.

Eaves, L. J. (1984). The resolution of genotype x environment interaction in segregation analysis of nuclear families. *Genetic Epidemiology, 1*, 215–228.

Eaves, L. J., Eysenck, H. J., & Martin, N. (1989). *Genes, culture, and personality*. New York: Academic Press.

Everitt, B. S. & Hand, D. J. (1981). *Finite mixture distributions*. New York: Chapman & Hall.

Eysenck, H. J. & Eysenck, M. W. *Personality and Individual Differences*. New York: Plenum Press, 1985.

Falconer, D. S. (1965). The inheritance of liability to certain diseases, estimated from the incidence among relatives. *Annals of Human Genetics, 29*, 51–76.

Falk, C. T. & Rubinstein, P. (1987). Haplotype relative risks: An easy reliable way to construct a proper control sample for risk calculations. *Annals of Human Genetics, 51*, 227–233.

Farid, N. R., Sampson, L., Noel, E. P., Bernard, J. M., Mandeville, R., Larsen, B., & Marshall, W. (1979). A study of human D locus related antigens in Graves' disease. *Journal of Clinical Investigation, 63*, 108–113.

Gelfand, A. E. & Smith, A. F. M. (1990). Sampling based approaches to calculating marginal densities. *Journal of the American Statistical Association, 85*, 398–409.

Geman, S. & Geman, D. (1984). Stochastic relaxation, Gibbs distribution and the Bayesian restoration of images. *IEEE Transactions on Pattern Analysis of Machine Intelligence, 6*, 721–741.

Green, J. R. & Woodrow, J. C. (1977). Sibling method for detecting HLA-linked genes in disease. *Tissue Antigens, 9*, 31–35.

Greenberg, D. A. (1993). Linkage analysis of "necessary" disease loci versus "susceptibility" loci. *American Journal of Human Genetics, 52*, 135–143.

Halle, R. W., Hodge, S. E., and Iselius, L. (1983). Genetic susceptibility to multiple sclerosis: A review. *International Journal of Epidemiology, 12*, 8–16.

Hanis, C. L. & Chakraborty, R. (1984). Nonrandom sampling in human genetics: Familial correlations. *IMA Journal of Mathematics Applied in Medicine and Biology, 1*, 193–213.

Hodge, S. E. (1993). Linkage analysis versus association analysis: Distinguishing between two models that explain disease-marker associations. *American Journal of Human Genetics, 53*, 367–384.

Jöreskog, K. G. (1973). A general method for estimating a linear structural equation system. In: Goldberger, A. S. & Duncan, O. D., eds. *Structural Equation Models in the Social Sciences*. New York: Academic Press, pp. 85–112.

Jöreskog, K. G. & Sörbom, D. (1989). *LISREL 7. A Guide to the Program and Applications (2nd ed.)*. Chicago: SPSS.

Kendler, K. S., Heath, A. C., Martin, N. G., & Eaves, L. J. (1986). Symptoms of anxiety and depression in a volunteer twin population: The etiologic role of genetic and environmental factors. *Archives of General Psychiatry, 43*, 213–221.

Kidd, K. K. (1993). Associations of disease with genetic markers: *Deja vu* all over again. *American Journal of Medical Genetics (Neuropsychiatric Genetics), 48*, 71–73.

Lathrop, G. M. & Ott, J. (1990). Analysis of complex diseases under oligogenic models and intrafamilial heterogeneity by the LINKAGE programs. *American Journal of Human Genetics, 47*, 188 (abstr.).

Lenzenweger, M. F., & Moldin, S. O. (1990). Discerning the latent structure of hypothetical psychosis proneness through admixture analysis. *Psychiatry Research, 33*, 243–257.

Loehlin, J. C., Willerman, L., & Horn, J. M. (1988). Human behavior genetics. *Annual Review of Psychology, 39*, 101–133.

Loehlin, J. C. & Nichols, R. C. (1976). *Heredity, Environment, and Personality: A Study of 850 Sets of Twins*. Austin: University of Texas Press.

Loranger, A. W., Oldham, J. M., & Tulis, E. H. (1982). Familial transmission of schizotypal and borderline personality disorders. *Archives of General Psychiatry, 39*, 795–799.

Lytton, H. (1977). Do parents create or respond to differences in twins? *Developmental Psychology, 13*, 456–459.

Mackintosh, P. & Asquith, P. (1978). HLA and coeliac disease. *British Medical Bulletin, 34*, 291–294.

MacLean, C. J., Morton, N. E., Elston, R. C., & Yee, S. (1976). Skewness in commingled distributions. *Biometrics, 32*, 695–699.

MacLean, C. J., Sham, P. C., & Kendler, K. S. (1993). Joint linkage of multiple loci for a complex disorder. *American Journal of Human Genetics, 53*, 353–368.

McCartney, K., Harris, M. J., & Bernieri, F. (1990). Growing up and growing apart: A developmental meta-analysis of twin studies. *Psychological Bulletin, 107*, 226–237.

McGuffin, P. & Thapar, A. (1992). The genetics of personality disorder. *British Journal of Psychiatry, 160*, 12–23.

Merikangas, K. R. (1982). Assortative mating for psychiatric disorders and psychological traits. *Archives of General Psychiatry, 39*, 1173–1180.

Mitchell, L. E. & Risch, N. (1992). Mode of inheritance of nonsyndromic cleft lip with or without cleft palate: A reanalysis. *American Journal of Human Genetics, 51*, 323–332.

Moldin, S. O., Rice, J. P., Erlenmeyer-Kimling, L., & Squires-Wheeler, E. (1994). Latent structure of DSM-III-R axis II psychopathology in a normal sample. *Journal of Abnormal Psychology, 103*, 259–266.

Moldin, S. O. & Reich, T. R. (1993). The genetic analysis of depression: Future directions. *Clinical Neuroscience, 1*, 139–145.

Morey, S. A. (1988). The categorical representation of personality disorder: A cluster analysis of DSM-III-R personality features. *Journal of Abnormal Psychology, 97*, 314–321.

Neale, M. C. & Cardon, L. R. (1992). *Methodology for Genetic Studies of Twins and Families*. Norwell: Kluwer Academic Publishers.

Nurnberg, H. G., Raskin, M., Levine, P., Pollack, S., Siegel, O., & Prince, R. (1991). The comorbidity of borderline personality disorder and other DSM-III-R axis II personality disorders. *American Journal of Psychiatry, 148*, 1371–1377.

Oldham, J. M., Skodol, A. E., Kellman, H. D., Hyler, S. E., Rosnick, L., & Davies, M. (1992). Diagnosis of DSM-III-R personality disorders by two structured interviews: Patterns of comorbidity. *American Journal of Psychiatry, 149*, 213–220.

Ott, J. (1989). Statistical properties of the haplotype relative risk. *Genetic Epidemiology, 6*, 127–130.

Ott, J. (1991). *Analysis of Human Genetic Linkage. (rev. ed.)*. Baltimore: Johns Hopkins University.

Plomin, R. & Daniels, D. (1987). Why are children in the same family so different from one another? *Behavioral Brain Science, 10*, 1–16.

Plomin, R. & Rende, R. (1991). Human behavioral genetics. *Annual Review of Psychology, 42*, 161–190.

Popper, K. R. (1976). A note on verisimilitude. *British Journal of the Philosophy of Science, 27*, 147–195.

Rao, D. C., Morton, N. E., & Yee, S. (1974). Analysis of family resemblance. II. A linear model for familial correlation. *American Journal of Human Genetics, 26*, 331–359.

Rao, D. C., Vogler, G. P., McGue, M., & Russell, J. M. (1987). Maximum-likelihood estimation of familial correlations from multivariate quantitative Data on Pedigrees: A general method of examples. *American Journal of Human Genetics, 41*, 1104–1116.

Rao, D. C. & Wette, R. (1989). Nonrandom sampling in genetic epidemiology: An implementation of the Hanis-Chakraborty method for multifactorial analysis. *Genetic Epidemiology, 6*, 461–470.

Rao, D. C. & Wette, R. (1990). Environmental index in genetic epidemiology: An investigation of its role, adequacy, and limitations. *American Journal of Human Genetics*, *46*, 168–178.

Reich, T., James, J. W. & Morris, C. A. (1972). The use of multiple thresholds in determining the mode of transmission of semi-continuous traits. *Annals of Human Genetics*, *36*, 163–184.

Reich, T., Rice, J. P. & Cloninger, C. R. (1979). The use of multiple thresholds and segregation analysis in analyzing the phenotypic heterogeneity of multifactorial traits. *Annals of Human Genetics*, *42*, 371–390.

Rice, J. P., McDonald-Scott, P., Endicott, J., Coryell, W., Grove, W. M., Keller, M. B. & Altis, D. (1986). The stability of diagnosis with an application in Bipolar II disorder. *Psychiatry Research*, *19*, 285–296.

Rice, J. P., Endicott, J., Knesevich, M. A., & Rochberg, N. (1987). The estimation of diagnostic sensitivity using stability data: An application to major depressive disorder. *Journal of Psychiatric Research*, *21*, 337–345.

Rice, J. P., Neumann, R., & Moldin, S. O. (1991). Methods for the inheritance of qualitative traits. In: Chakraborty, R. & Rao, C. R., eds. *Handbook of Statistics: VIII. Applications in Biological and Medical Sciences*. New York: Elsevier Press. pp. 1–27.

Rice, J. P., Rochberg, N., Endicott, J., Lavori, P. W., & Miller, C. (1992). Stability of psychiatric diagnoses: An application to the affective disorders. *Archives of General Psychiatry*, *49*, 824–830.

Rice, J. P. & Reich, T. (1985). Familial analysis of qualitative traits under multifactorial inheritance. *Genetic Epidemiology*, *2*, 301–315.

Risch, N. J. (1990). Linkage strategies for genetically complex traits: I. multilocus models. *American Journal of Human Genetics*, *46*, 222–228.

Shoukri, M. M. & Ward, R. H. (1989). Use of regression models to estimate genetic parameters and measures of familial resemblance in man. *Applied Statistics*, *38*, 467–479.

Siever, L. J., Silverman, J. M., Horvath, T. B., Klar, H., Coccaro, E., Keefe, R. S. E., Pinkham, L., Rinaldi, P., Mohs, R. C., & Davis, K. L. (1990). Increased morbid risk for schizophrenia-related disorders in relatives of schizotypal personality disordered patients. *Archives of General Psychiatry*, *47*, 634–641.

Silverman, J. M., Siever, L. J., Horvath, T. B., Coccaro, E. F., Klar, H., Davidson, M., Pinkham, L., Apter, S. H., Mohs, R. C., & Davis, K. L. (1993). Schizophrenia-related and affective personality disorder traits in relatives of probands with schizophrenia and personality disorders. *American Journal of Psychiatry*, *150*, 435–443.

Spielman, R. S., McGinnis, R. E., & Ewens, W. S. (1993). Transmission test for linkage disequilibrium: The insulin gene region and insulin-dependent diabetes mellitus (100m). *American Journal of Human Genetics*, *52*, 506–516.

Suarez, B. K., Rice, J. P., & Reich, T. (1978). The generalized sib pair IBD distribution: Its use in the detection of linkage. *Annals of Human Genetics*, *43*, 87–94.

Suarez, B. K. & Van Eerdewegh, P. A. (1984). A comparison of three affected-sib-pair scoring methods to detect HLA-linked disease susceptibility genes. *American Journal of Medical Genetics*, *18*, 135–146.

Svejgaard, A. & Ryder, L. R. (1989). HLA and insulin-dependent diabetes: An overview. *Genetic Epidemiology*, *6*, 1–14.

Thomas, D. C. (1992). Fitting genetic data using Gibbs sampling: An application to nevus counts in 38 Utah kindreds. *Cytogenetics and Cell Genetics*, *59*, 228–230.

Thomas, D. C. & Cortessis, V. A. (1992). Gibbs sampling approach to linkage analysis. *Human Heredity*, *42*, 63–76.

Thompson, E. A. & Guo, S. W. (1991). Evaluation of likelihood ratios for complex genetic models. *IMA Journal of Mathematics Applied in Medicine and Biology*, *8*, 149–169.

Waddington, J. L. (1993). Neurodynamics of abnormalities in cerebral metabolism and structure in schizophrenia. *Schizophrenia Bulletin, 19,* 55–69.

Widiger, T. A., Trull, T. J., Hurt, S. W., Clarkin, J., & Frances, A. (1987). A multidimensional scaling of the DSM-III personality disorders. *Archives of General Psychiatry, 44,* 557–563.

Widiger, T. A. & Frances, A. (1985). The DSM-III personality disorders: Perspectives from psychology. *Archives of General Psychiatry, 42,* 615–623.

Zhao, L. P., Grove, J., & Quiaoit, F. (1992). A method for assessing patterns of familial resemblance in complex human pedigrees, with an application to the Nevus-Count Data in Utah kindreds. *American Journal of Human Genetics, 51,* 178–190.

Zhao, L. P. & Prentice, R. L. (1990). Correlated binary regression using a quadratic exponential model. *Biometrika, 77,* 642–648.

Zimmerman, M. & Coryell, M. D. (1989). DSM-III personality disorder diagnoses in a nonpatient sample: Demographic correlates and co-morbidity. *Archives of General Psychiatry, 46,* 682–689.

III

Measurement

14

The Personality Psychopathology Five (PSY-5): Issue from the Pages of a Diagnostic Manual Instead of a Dictionary

Allan R. Harkness and
John L. McNulty

In this chapter, we will describe the questions that surround the application of a normal personality based five factor structural model to the descriptive problems of the personality disorder domain. We argue that a dedicated model, tailored specifically to the descriptive problems of the personality disorders, could potentially yield more informative clinical pictures. After introducing these issues, we then describe research in which we followed a strategy parallel to the researchers who developed the normal five factor models, with the exception that we began primarily with entries in a diagnostic manual rather than with entries in a common language dictionary. We then compare this psychopathology-based model to validated individual differences variables in the literature, and we highlight the similarities and differences between the psychopathology and normal structural models.

NORMAL FIVE-FACTOR MODELS AND ISSUES
SURROUNDING THEIR APPLICATION
TO PERSONALITY PSYCHOPATHOLOGY

Wiggins and Trapnell (in press) and Goldberg (1993) have detailed the rise to prominence of five factor models of personality (e.g., Costa & McCrae, 1985; Digman & Takemoto-Chock, 1981; Goldberg, 1990; Hogan, 1983; Norman, 1963; Tupes & Christal, 1961). These models, issuing from the lexical-semantic research tradition (John, Angleitner, & Ostendorf, 1988), attempt to depict the major vectors of variation, that is, the most powerful dimensions of stable individual differences in human personalities. Researchers in this tradition began with dictionaries and through selection and individual semantic similarity judgments, they culled personality terms. In later stages of research, they analyzed ratings and self-reports on the greatly reduced marker sets to yield five factor models. Goldberg (1993) describes the first four dimensions as: I. Surgency or Extraversion, II. Agreeableness, III. Conscientiousness, and IV. Emotional Stability versus Neuroticism. He notes that the fifth factor has been variously described as Culture, Intellect, and Openness to Experience, and he further describes the lack of agreement over this fifth factor as "somewhat of a scientific embarrassment."

Although five factor models have risen to prominence, several cautions appear to be in order. First, use of *the* as in *"The* Five Factor Model" leads to underestimation of the differences between several five factor models, and those differences have been noted and highlighted elsewhere (Briggs, 1989; John, Angleitner, & Ostendorf, 1988; Wiggins & Trapnell, in press, focus on differences in background theories; and a symposium at the Centennial meeting of the American Psychological Association was dedicated to differing interpretations placed upon the fifth factor). The next caution restraining enthusiasm for five factor models comes from examining the broader, hierarchical structure of personality variation.

In personality, many comprehensive structural models have been hierarchical (see, e.g., Cattell, 1946, especially pp.131–135; Eysenck, 1967; Goldberg, 1980; Guilford, 1975; Hampson, John, & Goldberg, 1986; Tellegen, 1982). That is, trait dimensions exist at various levels, such that at lower levels, there are many narrow trait dimensions, each engaging a narrow band of behavioral implications, and at higher levels, the trait dimensions are very broad, spanning a wide range of behavioral implications (Harkness, 1992). These trait dimensional hierarchies (unlike categorical hierarchies) are variance-covariance hierarchies: the covariance of the lower order dimensions becomes the variance of the higher order dimensions. For example, say that smiling covaries with talkativeness; and both covary with eye contact. The covariances of these lower order behavioral dispositions form the variance of the superordinate dimension of social engagement.

Two consequences of adopting the hierarchical viewpoint are the realizations that the once reasonable seeming question "how many dimensions are there to personality?" (a) probably does not fit the facts, and (b) probably arose as a theoretical habit dictated by computational limitations imposed by doing factor and component analyses in the era before cheap electronic computing. Slicing through the hierarchy at different levels provides different numbers of dimensions, and these different "coronal sections" can meet different descriptive needs (Hampson, John, & Goldberg, 1986). In component and factor analytic studies this approach does not demand a single solution with just one answer to the question: "how many factors do we extract?" Actual practice, such as the work of Zuckerman, Kuhlman, and Camac (1988) shows that there are frequently multiple highly coherent solutions. So rather than seeking a single point along the scree (Cattell, 1966), such as an elbow or other cutting point for eigen values, frequently there is a full range of mathematically acceptable and psychologically meaningful solutions.

Therefore, a second caution is that the five factor slice through the hierarchy may not be the best one for many of the descriptive problems faced by practicing clinicians. For example, lower levels of the hierarchy may offer descriptive resolution and predictive accuracy simply not available at the higher levels (see, e.g., Briggs, 1989; Mershon & Gorsuch, 1988; Harkness, 1992).

Some authors have suggested applying five factor models to the personality disorders (e.g., Costa & McCrae, 1990; McCrae & Costa, 1986), and a number of important additional questions have emerged. For example, questions have been raised about the relevance of "Openness to Experience" (Widiger, 1991) to personality disorders. Further, the need for some type of "cognitive disorganization factor" has been recognized (Costa & McCrae, 1990), in part because of the difficulty normal sample-based five factor models have had in separating Schizoid and Schizotypal disorders. That is, the power of five factor models based on normal samples to index major features of certain disorders has been questioned. For example, Romney and Bynner (1992) detailed a simplex that they identify as Impulsivity. This simplex provides an ordering going from compulsive at one end, to passive–aggressive, to avoidant, to borderline, and finally on to antisocial at the other end. The fact that this simplex that maximally spreads out an important subset of the personality disorders is not part of normal sample-based five factor models raises the possibility that there are better structural models for this descriptive problem.

ON THE NEED FOR A DEDICATED PSYCHOPATHOLOGY MODEL

Why might a new or modified model be needed when the population changes? Tellegen (1988, see p. 622) has distinguished between traits and *trait dimensions*, the latter being population concepts. That is, a trait dimension is composed of many people differing in trait levels. Thus a trait dimension is a population variance concept. It naturally follows that any trait dimensional system is *always situated in a given population*. Peabody and Goldberg (1989) demonstrated that structure can be made to dance to the tune of sample selection, expanding or contracting the size and coherence of the Agreeability factor, depending on the likability range of targets. Structural models are models of the major vectors of variation within a particular population. We contend that adding a strong complement of persons with diagnosable personality disorders could change the list of big variance dimensions.

The above reservations point to this fundamental question: Do normal sample-based five factor models optimally capture the essence of the clinical picture for personality disorder patients? Examine the following two sketches, excerpted from a casebook:

> A 21-year-old male was interviewed by a psychiatrist while he was being detained in jail awaiting trial for attempted robbery. The patient had a history of multiple arrests for drug charges, robbery, and assault and battery.
>
> Past history revealed that he had been expelled from junior high school for truancy, fighting, and generally poor performance in school. Following a car theft, when he was 14 years old, he was placed in a juvenile detention center. Subsequently, he spent brief periods in a variety of institutions, from which he usually ran away. At times his parents attempted to let him live at home, but he was disruptive and threatened them with physical harm. After one such incident during which he threatened them with a knife, he was admitted to a psychiatric hospital; but he signed himself out against medical advice, one day later. (Spitzer, Skodol, Gibbon, & Williams, 1981, p. 34)

Now while it is no doubt true that this patient is low in conscientiousness and agreeableness, these descriptions seem to be far too polite, too civil, and entirely too euphemistic. They seem to stop short of the essence of the clinical picture. Examine another patient excerpted from the same casebook, described as a 32-year-old female on welfare:

> Her feelings of detachment have gradually become stronger and more uncomfortable. For many hours each day she feels as if she were watching herself move through life, and the world around her seems unreal. She feels especially strange when she looks into a mirror. For many years she has felt able to read people's mind by a "kind of clairvoyance I don't understand." According to her, several people in her family apparently also have this ability. She is preoccupied by the thought that she has some special mission in life, but is not sure what it is; she is not particularly religious. She is very self-conscious in public, often feels that people are paying special attention to her, and sometimes thinks that strangers cross the street to avoid her. She is lonely and isolated and spends much of each day lost in fantasies or watching TV soap operas. (Spitzer, Skodol, Gibbon, & Williams, 1981, p. 95)

Although it makes sense to describe her as high in Neuroticism (in the psychometric, not psychoanalytic use of that term!) and low in surgency, there is clearly much more going on. To describe her problem as being too high in Openness, or having too much Culture or Intellect seems once again to miss the essence of the clinical picture.

The fact that normal sample-based five factor models may do an excellent job of summarizing the major vectors of variation in normal samples offers no guarantee that they will do the best possible job when they are transplanted into the personality disorders domain. Even if we know these dimensions work to *some* demonstrated degree with personality disorders, that does not guarantee that we have the best possible dimensions for this specific problem. After all, we could fit people's shoes by measuring their head size and then applying a regression equation, but it would be a shame not to simply measure their feet!

The fundamental point of this chapter is that the personality disorders might require a new or at least modified descriptive model; simply transplanting the structural models of normal personality to solve problems of descriptive psychopathology could be inefficient and underinformative. We decided to work directly on the following problem: *Which set of psychologically interpretable dimensions maximally spreads out markers of the personality disorders?*

To answer this question, we adopted a four point research strategy. Point One: We decided to stick consistently with internal semantic similarity data to generate candidate dimensions. These methods draw upon the fact that semantic similarity or "internal" data is known to produce structures resembling external data (e.g., ratings, self-reports) structures (a phenomenon known as Implicit Personality Theory, e.g., Block, Weiss, & Thorne, 1979; Lay & Jackson, 1969). This resemblance appears to hold, even in the domain of psychopathology (Stricker, Jacobs, & Kogan, 1974). Semantic similarity methods were heavily drawn upon by researchers who developed normal sample-based five factor models for much of the initial marker reduction (John, Angleitner, & Ostendorf, 1988). This semantic structure approach is particularly useful in psychopathological domains because it allows one to side-step, in initial research stages, methodological problems such as J-curve distributed variables (Maxwell, 1972) and the proper prevalence representation of low baserate, low catchment, or low ascertainment disorders. Point Two: Utilize methods that would allow (rather than dictate) the emergence of a hierarchical structure if it is present. Point Three: Compare emergent candidate dimensions to the existing literature. Are dimensions at the five factor level similar to normal sample-based five factor models? Or, are they different in important respects? Do emergent candidate dimensions link with other research traditions? And finally, Point Four: In later stages of research, develop measures of the candidate dimensions and compare their predictive and descriptive power to rival dimensional systems. This later stage checks the power of dimensions generated with internal data using external data.

We will now detail how the application of that strategy produced a five factor model called the Personality Psychopathology Five (PSY-5) that is specifically tailored for the personality disorders, is nested within a coherent hierarchy, and is linked to the existing literature.

METHOD

Subjects

Two hundred seven undergraduate students participated for extra credit in intro-
ductory psychology. Six students dropped out after the first session leaving complete sorting data from 201 subjects (97% completion rate). Nine of those 201
subjects chose not to complete the demographic information section; of the 192
providing such information, 97 were female, 95 male, with a mean age of 20.2,
(Sd = 2.94, ranging from 17 to 34).

Materials

Sixty phrase or sentence length descriptors of human behavior designed to widely
cover both normal and abnormal personality were each printed on a 4-by-6-inch
card. In developing a dimensional descriptive system, both normal and pathological personality markers are essential, otherwise, it could become impossible to index
a lack of pathology. That is, a system purely dedicated to differential diagnosis
runs the risk of becoming a false positive generator! The set of 60 descriptors was
composed of (a) 39 fundamental topic areas spanning the *DSM-III-R* (American
Psychiatric Association, 1987) Axis-II personality disorders (procedures detailing
the derivation of the 39 are given in Harkness, 1992), and (b) 26 markers spanning
primary dimensions of normal personality derived from Tellegen's exploratory
research program (Tellegen & Waller, in press; brief derivation of the 26 given in
Harkness, 1992, study #3, detailed description in Harkness, 1989/1990, pp. 88–108).
In five cases, descriptors from the two sets were judged to be substitutable and were
fused to become single descriptors (Harkness, 1989/1990, pp. 122–123), leaving
a total of 60 rather than 65 descriptors). The complete descriptor set, in order of
code numbers used in this study, is presented in Table 14.1.

In addition to the 60 piece descriptor card sets, each subject was also provided
with an "opposites booklet" that contained a random ordering of all 60 descriptors, with space after each to write out the code number of any descriptor that
seemed opposite or near opposite to the one under consideration. Four different
versions of the opposites booklets were prepared, each with a different random
order. Training materials were also provided: each subject was given a sample
problem based on physical descriptors, along with a sample "opposites booklet."

Procedure

Subjects were seen for two sessions. During the first session the subjects were
given a one-half hour consent, orientation and training period, followed by the
initial sorting task. Subjects were asked to examine all the descriptors and form
them into groups of their own choosing. They were asked to compose groups of
highly related descriptors ("fine grained sort" instructions, asking for 10 or more

groups). Each subject sorted the cards into groups on a large work table and left the cards out on the table.

The subjects then completed the "opposites" task. While the fine-grained sort results were still on the table, the subject went through the opposites booklet, listing any items thought to be opposite or nearly opposite to every descriptor. The results were recorded and the cards then counted sequentially into a fixed number of piles to break any structure in the deck and check the card count. The cards were then shuffled to prepare for the next subject.

When subjects returned for the second session, they were asked to sort the 60 descriptors again, but this time, they were told to make fewer groups of larger size. Called "coarse sort" instructions, the subjects were asked to make less than 10 groups, although they were always allowed to leave any number of descriptors as singlets.

Analyses

For each of the 201 subjects who examined the 60 topics, three 60 by 60 matrices were formed. In each of these matrices, X_{1-3}, the elements $X_{1-3}(j,k)$ and $X_{1-3}(k,j)$ represent the relationship between items j and k found in the subject's response to the three tasks (X_1 from the fine-grained sort, X_2 from the coarse sort, and X_3 from the opposites task). For each subject, the two positive sorts (fine-grained and coarse instructions) resulted in two conformable 60 by 60 cooccurrence matrices in which $X_{1-2}(j,k) = X_{1-2}(k,j) = + 1.0$ if the subject grouped items j and k together, and in which $X_{1-2}(j,k) = X_{1-2}(k,j) = 0$ if the subject did not group j and k together. These positive sorts quantify psychological similarity.

Psychological dissimilarity was quantified with data from the opposites task. All 60 items were listed in each of the opposites booklets, and subjects were asked to list any items opposite or near opposite to the item under consideration. Therefore, each pairing is potentially considered twice. That is, for items j and k, when the subject encounters j in the booklet, k is a potential opposite; when k is encountered, j is a potential opposite. Each dissimilarity matrix, X_3, was formed by first creating a 60 by 60 null matrix, and then adding a $- 1.0$ to element $X_3(j,k)$ and element $X_3(k,j)$ if the subject classed j as opposite to k, and then adding another $- 1.0$ if the subject classed k as opposite to j. This approach yields a symmetric matrix that represents consistent lack of oppositeness as 0, inconsistent oppositeness as $- 1.0$, and consistent oppositeness of an item pair as $- 2.0$.

The three matrices were added together to yield a full psychological similarity-distance matrix for each subject that quantifies short (very similar), medium (somewhat similar) and very long (opposite or near opposite) psychological distances. The 603 matrices from 201 subjects were then summed and rescaled to yield a consensus distance matrix with unities along the diagonal. The stability of the data due to high density of measurement is suggested by the correlation between the corresponding elements of two summary distance matrices formed from

TABLE 14.1 Set of 60 Markers Spanning DSM-III-R and Cleckley Personality Disorder Domain Plus Markers of Normal Personality Dimensions

1. Dislikes violence and does not seek revenge. M12
2. Does not remain upset or worried for long, is not generally prone to upset or worry. M18
3. Plans ahead, is thoughtful and careful. M9
4. Does not like to indulge in fantasy and is not easily caught up in sensory experiences. M17
5. Does not seek the company or help of others; has no close friends or confidants (or only one) other than close relatives (such as mother, father, sisters or brothers, and any children). M16, D5
6. Enjoys working hard; sticks to the job and sets her/himself high standards. M1
7. Is not overly concerned with moral standards, traditional values, or "proper" behavior. M15
8. Does not take advantage of others, does not enjoy others' misfortunes, disapproves of selfishness. M23
9. Is physically aggressive and cruel, enjoys frightening or hurting others; enjoys violence, seeks revenge. M10, D4
10. Tends not to feel victimized, exploited, or mistreated. M14
11. Is impulsive rather than planful, prefers spontaneous action. M19, D18
12. Believes in strict traditional moral standards for his or her own behavior and that of others. M4
13. Is very much afraid of being alone or being abandoned and feels lost when alone. D10
14. Is unreliable, neglects important obligations and responsibilities. D11
15. Has very odd or unusual beliefs and experiences that most people would consider unusual, strange, fantastic, or superstitious. D12
16. Is emotionally unstable, is prone to having big mood changes as well as unpredictable and sweeping changes in feelings toward others. D24
17. Engages repeatedly in illegal, antisocial actions. D1
18. Is uninterested in close personal or sexual relationships. D25
19. Offends, angers, or humiliates others but may feel bad in response to others' reactions. D35
20. Puts off decisions or seems unable to perform important tasks despite having the skills to do the work. D23
21. Overestimates own abilities, importance, and uniqueness. D17
22. Is resentful and obstructive, may sabotage work or be uncooperative when involved in tasks he or she does not want to do. D19
23. Feels envious, scornful of others; holds grudges. D36
24. Is odd in appearance and mannerisms, behaves in unusual or eccentric ways. D33
25. Has run away from home while living with parents or skipped school frequently. D32
26. Lacks remorse and shame. D28
27. Cannot make up his or her own mind; is too dependent on others for advice and help. D16
28. Generally shows little emotion or emotional responsiveness to others. D2
29. Lacks strong sense of self or values: lacks firm beliefs about self, life goals, and relationships. D39

(continued)

30. Speaks in an odd, vague, rambling, or imprecise way. D26
31. Is uneasy around people and is therefore shy and quiet or avoids social situations. D8
32. Controls or dominates others by frightening them or through cruelty. D14
33. Easily hurt or angered by others' criticism or disapproval. D7
34. Attempts to dominate and control family and friends in a possessive and mistrustful manner. D30
35. Enjoys taking risks; can be reckless or careless. M7
36. Rarely experiences pleasure, joy, or happiness. M22, D27
37. Shows heightened responsiveness to sights and sounds and fantasies; easily becomes absorbed in "inner" experiences, mental images, and imaginative events. M2
38. Is moody, is easily irritated and upset. M20
39. Is or would like to be powerful and influential, likes to be noticed. M6
40. Feels positive and optimistic about him or herself and life generally. M13
41. Does not seek or desire positions of authority, avoids leadership roles, avoids "visibility." M8
42. Enjoys close relationships with other people, is warm and sociable. M11
43. Lacks ambition, does not enjoy hard work, is not persistent. M5
44. Avoids risk taking; prefers safer activities without the excitement of adventure or danger. M24
45. Shows selfish unconcern for others in pursuit of own advantage. M26
46. Is nervous, tends to worry. M21
47. Questions authority, values rebelliousness. M25
48. Easily feels mistreated, exploited ("used"), or betrayed, is suspicious and distrusting of others' motives without good reason. M3, D3
49. Is promiscuous and seductive; invites and engages in casual (or "loose") sexual relationships. D22
50. Repeatedly threatens suicide without a motive to seriously harm him or herself, may show self-mutilating behavior. D34
51. Shows poor judgment and little forethought by acting recklessly and in ways that might harm self or others. D29
52. Can make a good first impression, but the apparent charm, intelligence, and personality shown to others are superficial rather than substantial. D37
53. Is quick to become angry; is aggressive and prone to be physically violent. D6
54. Rejects, resists, and resents advice or help from othes. D31
55. Is very self centered and selfish, not generous. D13
56. Repeatedly tells lies; is untruthful. D15
57. Needs constant attention, approval, and reassurance. D20
58. Is perfectionistic and overly concerned about doing things in an orderly and correct manner, to the point that little may actually be accomplished. D9
59. Appears to be "in touch with reality." D38
60. Plays the role of martyr, makes sacrifices against own best interests because of a strong need for approval and acceptance. D21

Note: Markers derived from Harkness (1992). Items marked with a "D" number came from DSM-III-R and Cleckley criteria; items marked with an "M" number came from Tellegen's MPQ; five fused items have both "D" and "M" designations.

two split halves of the sample: r = .982 (df = 1768; naturally all splitting is between, not within subjects).

Latent root methods followed by rotation toward simple structure allow for examination of such consensus structures (Clark, 1990; Watson, Clark, & Tellegen, 1984; Harkness, 1992). Full description of the mathematical basis of this approach wherein coocurrence matrices are in fact shown to be product matrices of each subject's rectangular group structure matrix multiplied by its own transpose, as suggested by Tellegen, can be found in Harkness (1989/1990, pp. 102–106, with explication of Harkness's extension of latent root methods to include opposites quantification on p. 133). A Multidimensional Scaling (MDS) of these data has been presented in Harkness (1989/1990, pp. 141–156) and is beyond the scope of the present chapter. However, it should be noted that the MDS results lack the clearer psychological interpretability of the rotated dimensions in the following report, and that the dimensions that follow can generally be visualized as regions or direction vectors in the two-space representations of the MDS.

Results and Preliminary Discussion

In line with the hierarchical approach discussed in the introduction, the results will not be presented as merely a single slice through a hierarchy, rather, the complete structure will be examined. Many principal components solutions, rotated toward simple structure using the varimax algorithm, taken at different levels of extraction, were used to examine the overall structure. It should be noted that the current method of separate principal components analyses, unlike a hierarchical agglomerative procedure, does not *impose* a hierarchical structure, and therefore, to the extent that a hierarchy does in fact emerge, it should be all the more persuasive.

Over what range should we extract components? Since coocurrence matrices rather than correlation matrices are being examined by latent root methods, most of the literature on extraction guidelines does not apply. The scree (Cattell, 1966) can still be viewed as indicating diminishing information returns with increasing extraction, and it therefore provides some guidance. However, with reduced mathematical guidance in extraction, the burden shifts decisively to psychological interpretability. Extracting more than 20 components begins to yield increasing numbers of components with single loading items. Extracting less than five results in very heterogeneous components and begins to miss quite a bit of the structure of the coocurrence relations. Figure 14.1 gives a distillation of the overall structure resulting from all of the rotated principal components solutions, going from 20 components extracted to 5 components extracted.

On Figure 14.1, the fate of each item (represented with an abbreviated label) can be traced from the lowest level of analysis, the 20-component solution, up to the highest level of analysis, the 5-component solution. For each rotated principal component solution, represented as a column in Figure 14.1, a letter is used to

```
                                            Level
                                     2111111111100000
                                     0987654321098765
                                     Low          High

48 SUSPICIOUS                        AAAAAAAAAAADDDDD
10 NOT FEEL EXPLOITED                AAAAAAARRRRRRRRT
33 EASILY HURT                       AAAAAAAADAADDDDD
23 ENVIOUS, SCORNFUL                 AAAAAAAAAAAIJIII
46 NERVOUS                           BBBBBBCCAAADDDDD
 2 NOT PRONE TO WORRY                BBBBBBRRRRRRRRRT
16 EMOTIONALLY UNSTABLE              CCCCCCCCAAADDDDD
38 MOODY, IRRITABLE                  CCCCCCCCAAADDDDD
57 NEEDS ATTENTION                   DDDDDDDDDDDDDDDD
27 TOO DEPENDENT                     DDDDDDDDDDDDDDDD
13 FEARS BEING ALONE                 DDDDDDDDDDDDDDDD
60 MARTYR, NEEDY                     DDDDDDDDDDDDDDDD
54 REJECTS HELP                      DDDADNNAFDDFFFFF
50 SUICIDE THREATS                   EEERRCNCAAADDDDD
29 LACK SENSE SELF                   EEEDDDDDDDDDDDDD
36 ANHEDONIA                         ESSSSSSSSSFFFFFF
18 UNINTERESTED SOC. RELS.           FFFFFFFFFFFFFFFF
 5 NO CLOSE FRIENDS                  FFFFFFFFFFFFFFFF
42 ENJOYS CLOSE RELS.                FFFFFFFFFFFFFFFF
31 SOC. ANXIETY, AVOID.              FFFFFFFFFFFFFFFF
28 UNRESPONSIVE TO Os                FFFFFFFFFFFFFFFF
41 AVOIDS LEADERSHIP                 GGGGGGGGGGFFFFFF
39 LIKES POWER                       GGGGGGGGGGJJJIII
52 SUPERFICIAL                       HHHHHGGGGJJJJIII
21 GRANDIOSE                         HHHHHGGGGJJJJIII
56 LIES                              HNNNNNNNNNNNIIIP
 9 AGGRESSIVE,CRUEL                  IIIIIIIIIIIIIIII
53 AGGRESSIVE, VIOLENT               IIIIIIIIIIIIIIII
32 CRUEL DOMINATION                  IIIIIIIIIIIIIIII
 1 DISLIKES VIOLENCE                 IIIIIIIIIIIIRRRT
34 DOMINATION & CONTROL              IIIIIIIIIIJIII
45 SELFISH                           JJJJJJJJJJJJJIII
55 SELF CENTERED                     JJJJJJJJJJJJJIII
 8 DOESN'T USE OTHERS                JJJJJJJJJRRRRRT
19 OFFENDS, CAN FEEL GUILT           KKKKJIIIIJIIJIII
26 LACKS REMORSE & SHAME             KKKKMMMNNNNNIIII
58 PERFECTIONISTIC                   LPHHHPPPPPPQPQPP
12 STRICT MORALS                     MMMMMMMNNNNNIQPT
 7 NOT TOO MORALISTIC                MMMMMMMNNNNNIQPP
49 PROMISCUOUS                       MMMMMMMNNNNNITPP
47 REBELLIOUS                        NNNNNNNNNNNNNIIPP
25 TRUANCY                           NNNNNNNNNNNNNIPPP
17 CRIMINALITY                       NNNNNNNNNNNNNIIIP
22 OBSTRUCTIVE                       NNNNNNNAIIIIIIIII
44 AVOIDS RISKS                      OOPPPPPPPPPPPPPP
35 RECKLESS, ENJOYS RISK             OOPPPPPPPPPPPPPP
11 IMPULSIVE                         PPPPPPPPPPPPPPPP
 3 PLANS AHEAD                       PPPPPPPPPPPPPPPT
51 POOR JUDGMENT,RECKLESS            PPPPPPPPPPPPPPPP
43 LACKS AMBITION                    QQQQQQQQQQQQQQPP
 6 ENJOYS WORKING HARD               QQQQQQQQQQQQQQRT
20 CAN'T DO JOB                      QQQQQQQQQQQQQQPP
14 UNRELIABLE                        QQQQQQQQQQQQQQPP
40 OPTIMISTIC,POSITIVE               RRRRRRRRRRRRRRRT
59 IN TOUCH REALITY                  RRRRRRRRRRRRTRRT
 4 NOT LIKE FANTASY                  SSSSSSSSSTTTTTTT
37 ABSORBED, INNER EXPER.            SSSSSSSSTTTTTTTT
24 ECCENTRIC BEHAVIOR                TTTTTTTTTTTTTTTT
15 UNUSUAL BELIEFS                   TTTTTTTTTTTTTTTT
30 ODD SPEECH                        TTTTTTTTTTTTTTTT
```

FIGURE 14.1. Rotated component analyses at different levels of extraction represented as columns.

indicate the items whose highest loading was associated with a unique principal component. Thus, every item marked with an "A" in the level 20 column had its highest loading on the same principal component; each item marked with a "B" had its highest loading on another component, and so on, down the column. The leftmost column of letters shows the results of extracting and rotating twenty components. All the items labeled "A" loaded most highly on one tight paranoid, suspicious component, all the "B" items loaded on a nervous, tense component, and so on. Although not indicated on this highly condensed Figure, the signs of the loadings were consistent with the item content: e.g., the loading of "not prone to worry" was opposite in sign to the loading of "nervous."

The second column from the left has one less letter: it is the 19-component solution. Moving all the way over to the right, the five component solution is shown. Naturally, we move from relative homogeneity to relative heterogeneity of item content as we move to higher levels of the hierarchy.

At the highest level (5), content becomes quite heterogeneous. The complete rotated five component solution is given in Table 14.2. In the following description of the structure, the elements comprising the dimensions at level 5 will be traced back to more homogeneous item groups in the lower levels. The general pattern that emerges is hierarchical. Tight, compact structures of narrow traits appearing on the left side of Figure 14.1 tend, in general, to combine to form related but broader traits toward the right side of the figure. One major exception will be discussed later.

Examining the first component on Table 14.2, we find a clear Aggressiveness dimension (these are the items marked "I" in the last column of Figure 14.1) that consists of such features as cruel domination, aggression, selfishness, superficiality, and enviousness. Elements of Sadistic Personality Disorder, Narcissistic Personality Disorder, and psychopathy appear on this dimension. If the elements of the "I" dimension at level 5 are traced back through the hierarchy and are examined at levels 15 to 20, one finds that more homogeneous item groups of aggressiveness, guilt potential, selfishness, and superficiality emerge.

The second component on Table 14.2 (represented by the "T"s in the rightmost column of Figure 14.1) is also quite heterogeneous. At its poles ("poles" refers to the greatest positive and negative loadings) it contrasts "appears to be in touch with reality" at one end with "has very odd or unusual beliefs and experiences" at the other. Using these poles, we have labelled this dimension (choosing to name the reflection) as "Psychoticism versus Good Models of Reality." In the remainder of the chapter, we will use the brief label "Psychoticism." Moving in from the poles, we find markers of Tellegen's Absorption. Within the shell of this reality-orientation dimension, however, there is great heterogeneity of item content.

It is within this second component that we find an apparent exception to the general hierarchical organization: the "positive valence" markers of diverse content areas combine to form one positive cluster of markers (in Figure 14.1, the "R" and "T" markers) from the middle level analyses on up through the higher level analyses. The "positive" ends of lower order dimensions are all drawn together

TABLE 14.2 Sorted Loadings on Five Varimax Rotated Components

ITEM	ABBREVIATION	AGGR 1	PSYCHOT 2	CONSTRAINT 3	NEUR/NE 4	EXTRO/PE 5
9	aggress, cruel	0.735				
32	cruel dominate	0.720				
53	aggress, violence	0.667				
34	control, dominance	0.639				
45	selfish	0.580				
55	self-centered	0.525				
23	envious, scorn	0.461				
22	obstructive	0.457		0.208		
39	likes power	0.413				−0.301
26	lacks remorse	0.357		0.289		
21	grandiose	0.287				
19	offends others	0.260				
59	in touch reality		0.689			
6	enjoys working		0.653	−0.233		
3	plans ahead		0.642	−0.451		
40	optimistic		0.630		−0.403	
2	not worry prone		0.568	0.243	−0.245	
8	not use others	−0.512	0.534			
1	not like violence	−0.494	0.500			
10	not feel exploited		0.455			
4	not like fantasy		0.398			0.251
12	strict morals		0.375	−0.374		
15	unusual beliefs		−0.292			
37	absorbed inner experience		−0.267			
24	eccentric behavior		−0.220			
35	reckless, enjoy risk			0.694		
11	impulsive			0.640		
51	poor judgment			0.626		
7	not too moral			0.501		
14	unreliable			0.500		
47	rebellious	0.293		0.497		
17	criminal	0.331		0.461		
25	truant hx			0.412		
44	avoids risks		0.313	−0.396	0.228	0.251
43	lacks ambition			0.349	0.207	0.282
49	promiscuous			0.339		−0.216
20	can't do job			0.316	0.279	0.203
56	lies	0.253		0.295		
58	perfectionistic			−0.248		
57	needs attention				0.705	−0.212
13	fears being alone				0.659	
27	too dependent				0.650	
33	easily hurt				0.614	
60	martyr, needy				0.540	
48	suspicious				0.481	

(*continued*)

TABLE 14.2 *(Continued)*

ITEM	ABBREVIATION	AGGR 1	PSYCHOT 2	CONSTRAINT 3	NEUR/NE 4	EXTRO/PE 5
46	nervous				0.473	
29	lack sense self			0.201	0.462	0.221
38	moody, irrit.	0.328			0.406	
16	unstable emot.	0.259			0.404	
50	suicide threats				0.318	
5	no close friends					0.783
18	uninterested soc. rels.					0.741
31	soc. anx., avoid					0.719
42	enjoy close	−0.204	0.477			−0.633
28	soc. unresponsive					0.596
41	avoid leader	−0.212			0.236	0.558
36	anhedonia				0.203	0.373
54	reject help	0.311				0.342
52	superficial					
30	odd speech					

Note: Loadings with absolute values equal to or less than .2 not shown.

into one higher level component. This shift of positive markers at the five-component level can be seen by looking down the rightmost column of Figure 14.1 and locating all the items marked "T," those with their highest loading on the second component. At this five-component level, looking down the column for the first "T" items, we find "does not feel exploited" and "not prone to worry" appearing on the second component, when they had started in the Negative Emotionality/Neuroticism cluster at the lower levels. Looking further down the column, within the "I" or Aggressiveness region, we see "dislikes violence" and "does not use others" appearing on the "T" component at the five-component level. Again, positive markers appear in a single grouping with smaller extraction numbers. Continuing further down, into the "P" or Constraint region, one will find that "strict morals" and "enjoys working hard" all appear on the second or "T" component at extraction level five.

This leads to the suggestion that the five component level is perhaps a bit underextracting, and that our second component represents an uneasy fusion of a relatively clear Psychoticism dimension and a collection of markers that represent the foreigners in the psychopathology marker set, the positive markers. It appears that the evaluation of markers, distinguishing the "good" markers versus "bad" markers (Osgood, Suci, & Tannenbaum, 1957) is a potent element in the responses of some judges. When we examined the first *unrotated* principal component of the distance matrix, we found all the markers of "goodness" at one pole and the markers of "badness" at the other pole. When many components are extracted and rotated, goodness and badness remain specific to coherent topic areas, such as "aggressive and violent" versus "dislikes violence." However, when few components are extracted, evaluative valence overpowers thematic coherence. This appears to be the primary exception to hierarchical organization along thematic lines. Tellegen and Waller (1987) have reported evaluative dimensions emerging at the seven factor level.

Because the PSY-5 is a model with a specific purpose, that of being a dimensional complement to PD diagnosis, and because there is a descriptive gap without a dimension tapping "cognitive aberration" (Costa & McCrae, 1990), and because the poles of our second component should most strongly guide its interpretation, and most of all because we can base our interpretation on the overall structure and not just on the five component level, we interpret the second component as Psychoticism rather than evaluation.

A third component emerging at level 5 (items marked "P" on Figure 14.1) resembles Tellegen's Constraint dimension (Tellegen & Waller, in press). Markers of Harmavoidance, Impulsivity, Control, Traditionalism, rebelliousness, and rule breaking criminality are all represented here, as is lack of productivity. Moving down the hierarchy, below level 6, criminality ("N" items) tends to be separated from impulse-control, poor judgment, and harmavoidance. At the lowest levels, below 18, harmavoidance ("O" items) and impulse control are separate.

The fourth component shown on Table 14.2 is a complex Negative Emotionality/Neuroticism dimension (items marked "D" at level 5 on Figure 14.1). This relatively heterogeneous component is comprised of elements of dependency, alienation, stress-reaction, emotional instability, and the making of suicidal threats and gestures. Below level 9, emotional instability ("C" items), nervousness ("B" items), and alienation ("A" items) are separate from dependency.

The fifth component on Table 14.2 ("F" items at level 5 on Figure 14.1) is well delineated by the positive and negative markers of Tellegen's Social Closeness. Markers of degree of interest in close social relations are mixed with markers of low reactiveness to others, markers of social anxiety and avoidance, of low hedonic capacity, and social potency. Thus, the features of Tellegen's superfactor Positive Emotionality are present, and Extroversion or Surgency elements are recognizable as well. Below level 11, this dimension is more purely comprised of markers of interest in and desire for social relations. Social anxiety and avoidance remain, as does reduced reactions to others, but below level 11, low hedonic capacity and social potency ("G" items) are separate from social closeness.

SUMMARY OF RESULTS
AND PRELIMINARY DISCUSSION

The interpretation of a single level (in this case the five component level) is enhanced by examining the full hierarchical structure. In general, at high levels of the hierarchy (such as the five component level where there are few dimensions), relatively heterogeneous item groups appear, and they resolve into highly interpretable and relatively homogeneous variable groups at lower levels, where there are many dimensions. Further, we contend that each of the dimensions emerging from our semantic analysis can be linked to psychological constructs already existing in the literature.

Looking at the five component level, our first impulse was to assimilate the results, to say, "That looks like the Big-Five" (e.g., Goldberg, 1990; Hogan, 1983; Norman, 1963; Digman & Takemoto-Chock, 1981; Costa & McCrae, 1985). However, true cognitive developments, in Piagetian form, require more than assimilation, and over time, as we took a closer, more careful look at the results, we began to shift to accommodation. We began to realize that our results pointed to a different model. Therefore, this model bears a different name: The Personality Psychopathology Five, or PSY-5. Since our dimensions emerged from internal, semantic data, it will be reassuring if they are clearly related to dimensions that are found in the literature and show coherence in external data. In the following section, we will detail trait constructs, that is, posited theoretical interpretations for each dimension of the PSY-5, along with their links to existing literature.

PSY-5 AS PSYCHOLOGICAL CONSTRUCTS

I. Aggressiveness

A glimpse at a newspaper, a few minutes of televised news, or perhaps the knowledge that our children pass through weapons detectors to get to class, readily convinces us of the pervasiveness and impact of human aggression. Our results suggest that measuring individual differences in aggressiveness would map important regions of the domain of personality disorders. Here is our construct: PSY-5 Aggressiveness entails general dispositions deriving from the systems controlling agonal behavior, particularly offensive aggression (Moyer, 1987). External data support the stability and power of individual differences in aggressiveness (Olweus, 1979). PSY-5 Aggressiveness also taps the status of systems promoting or inhibiting intraspecies aggression, that is, grandiosity versus egalitarianism. Elements of the desire for power and influence are also present.

PSY-5 Aggressiveness maps directly onto an important model of individual differences in interpersonal behavior, the Interpersonal Circle (IPC, e.g., Wiggins, 1982; Wiggins & Pincus, 1989). Specifically, the PSY-5 Aggression dimension should approximate a − 45° rotation from the dominance-submission axis, therefore extending from the upper left Domineering/Arrogant/Coldhearted quadrant down through the lower right quadrant of the IPC.

From Tellegen's exploratory study of personality (Tellegen & Waller, in press) two constructs are relevant. First, one of Tellegen's primary level factors is Aggression. As noted above, we link our construct with offensive aggression, whereas negative affect driven aggression may be more defensive, more responsive to frustration, pain, and delay. Aggression on Tellegen's MPQ may encompass both types, with an emphasis on the aggression responsive to negative affects. Second, one of Tellegen's higher order factors (in four factor solutions) has been called Agentic Positive Emotionality (Tellegen & Waller, in press). It may be that our PSY-5 Aggressiveness dimension, based upon judgments using extreme markers, may result in a fusion of Aggression and Agentic Positive Emotionality: that is, it may capture those who *enjoy* dominating, frightening, and controlling others.

II. Psychoticism

Although we borrowed the label from Eysenck (Eysenck & Eysenck, 1985), PSY-5 Psychoticism is entirely different from Eysenck's construct. Measures of our dimension should correlate poorly with Eysenck's "P" factor. Briefly, here is our construct. Across general psychology, older paradigms which viewed subjects as passive responders to stimulation have given way to perspectives which view subjects as builders of internal models of external reality. Examples include Tolman's latent learning experiments (see e.g., Tolman, 1960), Rescorla's (1988) revision of Pavlovian Conditioning, and the object relations developments in psychoanalysis (see, e.g., Greenberg & Mitchell, 1983), constituting an overall trend that has been called the cognitive revolution (see, e.g., Neisser, 1967). The trend has been to recognize the crucial role played by the internal representation of external reality. Psychoticism captures the gross verisimilitude of a person's inner models of the outer social and object world.

Psychoticism assesses the ability to model self, others, and the external object world in a manner that accurately reflects and predicts the events that surround us. From these internal models, we can run simulations of situations, allowing prediction and consideration of multiple outcomes. Depending on how well the models perform, they are counted upon, adjusted, or replaced. In Piaget's (1951) terms, the person low in Psychoticism seems able to stop assimilating data to a bad model and then start accommodating, revising the model to bring it into line with poorly fitting data. The balance between assimilation and accommodation to these inner working models is linked with the individual's general level of functioning. But the linkage is via *step-function*: all of us have illusions, misperceptions, and mistaken beliefs; only a few have delusions and hallucinations.

It becomes clear that our construct is related to features measured by the Chapmans (Chapman & Chapman, 1987) in their psychosis proneness research program, specifically, perceptual aberration (Chapman, Edell, & Chapman, 1980) and magical ideation (Eckblad & Chapman, 1983). In addition, our structural analysis also suggests a connection to Tellegen's (1982) primary factor of Absorption. In contrast to normal range Absorption, within Psychoticism, absorptive capacity entails "thinking away from reality," in a sense, a preference or tendency to emphasize primary over secondary process. PSY-5 Psychoticism, with Axis-II origins has many Axis-I implications.

III. Constraint

Constraint, as originally developed by Tellegen (1982) in his exploratory MPQ development project (Tellegen & Waller, in press) combines facets of Control versus Impulsiveness, as well as Harmavoidance and Traditionalism. In our analysis of marker structure, rule following versus rule breaking and criminality becomes a prominent feature of the mixture. This Constraint dimension is relevant to personality psychopathology in that it parallels Romney and Bynner's (1992) simplex that has Antisocial Personality at one end and Obsessive–Compulsive Personality Disorder at the other end.

Depue and Spoont (1986) and Spoont (1992) have postulated biological mechanisms that underlie individual reaction ranges in Constraint versus dyscontrol. To greatly condense, Spoont (1992) postulated general dampening effects of 5-HT (serotonin) systems on general signal processing in the nervous system. Thus low Constraint could tend to amplify effects from the other dimensions of the PSY-5. That is, aggression, odd form and content of thought, negative affects, and responsiveness to the hedonic engagements of positive emotionality could all be disinhibited by low Constraint. Although Siever and Davis (1991) couple impulsivity and aggression, we follow Spoont (1992) and Tellegen and Waller (in press) in treating Constraint as a separate dimension that can have modulating effects on all other systems.

IV. Negative Emotionality/Neuroticism

Negative Emotionality (Tellegen, 1982, 1985; Tellegen & Waller, in press; Watson & Clark, 1984; Watson, Clark, & Carey, 1988) / Neuroticism (Eysenck & Eysenck, 1985) is a broad affective disposition to experience negative emotions focusing on anxiety and nervousness, leading to internal suffering. Tellegen (1991) speculated on affective or temperamental dispositions as the limiting case on the trait notion, in that they can approach a context independent status: imagine the person who reacts to an unexpected raise and promotion with worries that he or she will now be exposed as incompetent and will be unable to handle the extra sum responsibly. Composed of markers of Tellegen's Stress-Reaction, and markers associated with certain Dependent, Borderline, and Paranoid personality features, plus markers of the research category Self-Defeating personality disorder, this affective component is recognizable in many current models of personality (e.g., Costa & McCrae, 1985; Siever & Davis, 1991; Trapnell & Wiggins, 1990).

V. Positive Emotionality/Extraversion

Positive Emotionality/Extraversion is a broad disposition to experience positive affects, to seek out and enjoy social experiences, and to have the energy to pursue goals and be engaged in life's tasks. The ready ability to experience positive emotions, feeling one's life is active and exciting, and generally feeling good about oneself and the future mark the high end of the affective component. A lack of pleasure or joy (especially in the face of potent species-relevant pleasure elicitors, e.g., a smiling, healthy baby) reflects the anhedonic pole. Tellegen's (Tellegen & Waller, in press) Well-being and the NEO-PI (Costa & McCrae, 1985) factor Positive Emotions, for example, reflect positive affective elements in common with this PSY-5 dimension.

Extraversion, or the interpersonal aspects of this dimension, include the enjoyment of affiliation and social interaction, the desire for close friends, and the seeking and valuing of close, intimate relationships. This is contrasted with a lack of aspirations for interpersonal relating, as well as lack of enjoyment of affiliation. Warmth and Gregariousness of the NEO-PI and the Social Closeness dimensions of Tellegen's MPQ have isomorphic features. Extraversion versus Introversion is a dimension on the IPC (the NO versus FG octants): it is a +45° rotation off of the Dominance-Submission axis. It then follows that PSY-5 Aggressiveness would be a 90° rotation from Positive Emotionality/ Extraversion. Working from very different methods, our work converges with that of Wiggins and Pincus (1989) in suggesting that the plane of the IPC is a crucial element of a five factor model purporting to assist in the description of personality disorders. Many of the markers of Cloninger's (1987) Reward Dependence dimension are consistent with Positive Emotionality/ Extraversion: desiring close, intimate relationships versus social detachment. However, Cloninger's Reward Dependence dimension also contains markers of dependence and neediness found on our Negative Emotionality/ Neuroticism dimension.

PSY-5 AND NORMAL-SAMPLE
FIVE-FACTOR MODELS COMPARED

One major point of our chapter is to compare and contrast the PSY-5 with normal sample-based five factor models. There are some shared dimensions and topic similarities in broad outline, but there are major differences as well. We will first discuss similarities and then progress to the differences.

PSY-5 and normal marker-based five factor models share two major dimensions, Negative Emotionality/ Neuroticism and Positive Emotionality/Extraversion. In both models, the two dimensions appear to be virtually substitutable. However, beyond these shared dimensions, there are important differences between the models, and we contend the differences make sense when one considers that a diagnostic manual rather than a dictionary was the primary source of markers.

In examining differences, we will begin by comparing PSY-5 Aggressiveness with Big-Five Agreeability. In this case, there are both differences of emphasis and differences of extremity in markers. PSY-5 Aggressiveness has more "tooth and claw" than the Agreeableness dimension of the Big-Five. PSY-5 markers include features such as aggressive, cruel, violent, and enjoys frightening others. These markers can be contrasted with Goldberg's (1992) markers of the negative end of Big-Five Agreeableness: cold, unkind, unsympathetic, distrustful, harsh, demanding, rude, selfish, uncooperative, and uncharitable. In the case of Aggressiveness and Agreeability, the differences between the two five factor models could be readily reconciled by adding the extreme PSY-5 markers to complement low Agreeability and by adding high Agreeability markers to fill out the low end of PSY-5 Aggressiveness. In the following cases however, such reconciliation is not possible.

PSY-5 Constraint is not comparable to normal sample-based Conscientiousness. This is not merely a difference in emphasis or extremity of markers, these are two different constructs. Constraint taps risk aversion, control versus impulsivity, traditional morality, rule following versus rule breaking, and criminality. Someone low in PSY-5 constraint would be impulsive, excitement seeking or at least not risk averse, rejecting of moral codes, and if very low on the dimension, a rule breaker and criminal. This can be contrasted with someone low in Conscientiousness. Here are Goldberg's (1992) markers of low Conscientiousness: disorganized, careless, unsystematic, inefficient, undependable, impractical, negligent, inconsistent, haphazard, and sloppy. It is interesting that this low end of Conscientiousness corresponds, perhaps, to a *DSM-II* (American Psychiatric Association, 1968) diagnostic concept, what used to be 301.82, Inadequate Personality. Although there may be more similarity at *high* levels of Constraint and Conscientiousness, the clear differences at low levels of Constraint and Conscientiousness suggest they are quite different dimensions.

We contend that it is descriptively inadequate to regard the case of the young man with the multiple robberies, the first case excerpted in the introduction, as merely low in Conscientiousness. Adding that he is also low in Agreeability, another status on a normal sample-based dimension, does not help much either. We contend that the young man can be far better described as being impulsive, as being a risk taker, as disregarding traditional morality, as being a rule breaker and criminal: in short someone very low in Constraint. The degree of Aggressiveness in a patient low in Constraint radically affects clinical management issues. This young man is also high on PSY-5 Aggressiveness. We contend that the low Constraint and high Aggressiveness picture provided by the PSY-5 gives a clearer description than to say that he is low in Agreeability and lacking in Conscientiousness. However, for the patient whose fundamental pattern is that of *DSM-II* Inadequate personality, the normal sample model may perform better than the PSY-5.

Psychoticism is a dramatically different construct compared to the so-called "fifth factor" in normal population five factor models. Examples of the different constructs of the fifth factor include Openness to Experience, Intellectance, and Culture, generally bearing on the cognitive style or capacity of the target. In the PSY-5, Psychoticism encompasses reduced reality contact, odd, unusual perception and mentation, and extensive absorption with fantasy. Referring to the second case presented in the introduction, that of the 32-year-old female, her derealization, depersonalization, her magical thinking, and her preference for fantasy rather than reality over extended periods of time all reflect features of elevated PSY-5 Psychoticism. These symptoms differentiate the diagnoses of Schizotypal and Schizoid Personality Disorders, a differentiation difficult to achieve with normal sample-based models as noted earlier. Further, the clinical implications extend to other personality disorders as well: for example, the Borderline patient high in PSY-5 Psychoticism presents different clinical management problems from the Borderline patient low in Psychoticism. We contend that Psychoticism is critical in any structural model that aims to map the full domain of personality psychopathology.

To summarize the comparison, the PSY-5 and normal sample-based five factor models share two virtually substitutable dimensions, Negative Emotionality/Neuroticism and Positive Emotionality/Extraversion. Aggression and Agreeability have a difference of emphasis and extremity that is potentially reconcilable. PSY-5 Constraint and Psychoticism are fundamentally different from their closest normal five counterparts. We contend that the PSY-5 is optimized for the dimensional description of the personality disorders, whereas normal sample-based five factor models do exactly what they were optimized to do: they reflect the big five vectors of personality individual differences in normal samples.

GENERAL SUMMARY

The five component picture is but one slice through a hierarchy in which evaluation clearly plays a strong role (Tellegen & Waller, 1987). However, at the level of broad, inclusive traits, the PSY-5 offers an optimized dimensional complement to categorical description of the personality disorders that arises predominantly from the pages of a diagnostic manual rather than from a dictionary. Currently, we are developing MMPI-2 based measurement scales for the PSY-5 (Harkness, McNulty, & Ben-Porath, 1993).

Although the PSY-5 was developed from semantic similarity judgments, its five dimensions are both psychologically interpretable and clearly recognizable in research programs that proceed from external data. Aggressiveness, Psychoticism, Constraint, Negative Emotionality/Neuroticism, Positive Emotionality/Extraversion are not found merely in the minds of marker sorters; they are clearly recognizable dimensions appearing in the many research programs cited above. In examining one of several dimensional options for DSM-IV, Widiger (1991, p. 395) noted, "The proposal for *DSM-IV* consists of seven dimensions: extraversion, neuroticism, constraint, agreeableness, openness, reward dependence, and cognitive disorganization (developed in consultation with Drs. Cloninger, Costa, Eysenck, McCrae, Siever, Tellegen, & Wiggins)." If Aggressiveness and Agreeability were reconciled as suggested above, the PSY-5 would cover five of the seven, and as noted above, extraversion covers much of the same terrain as reward dependence. This leaves out only openness. Widiger's distinguished panel and the quantitative study of semantic judgments produce a surprising degree of consensus.

ACKNOWLEDGMENTS

A portion of this research was supported by a Department of Veterans Affairs Health Systems Research and Development doctoral stipend for the first author. Portions of the project were part of the first author's doctoral dissertation in clinical psychology at the University of Minnesota. We wish to express our thanks to the editors and to Robert Hogan and Auke Tellegen for their thoughtful comments on earlier versions of this chapter.

REFERENCES

American Psychiatric Association. (1968). *Diagnostic and statistical manual of mental disorders* (2nd ed.). Washington, DC: Author.

American Psychiatric Association. (1987). *Diagnostic and statistical manual of mental disorders* (3rd ed., rev.). Washington, DC: Author.

Block, J., Weiss, D. S., & Thorne, A. (1979). How relevant is a semantic similarity interpretation of personality ratings? *Journal of Personality and Social Psychology, 37,* 1055–1074.

Briggs, S. R. (1989). The optimal level of measurement for personality constructs. In D. M. Buss & N. Cantor (Eds.) *Personality psychology: Recent trends and emerging directions.* New York: Springer.

Cattell, R. B. (1946). *Description and measurement of personality.* Yonkers, NY: World Book.

Cattell, R. B. (1966). The scree test for the number of factors. *Multivariate Behavioral Research, 1,* 245–276.

Chapman, L. J., & Chapman, J. P. (1987). The search for symptoms predictive of schizophrenia. *Schizophrenia Bulletin, 13,* 497–503.

Chapman, L. J., Edell, W. J., & Chapman, J. P. (1980). Physical anhedonia, perceptual aberration, and psychosis proneness. *Schizophrenia Bulletin, 6,* 639–653.

Clark, L. A. (1990). Toward a consensual set of symptom clusters for assessment of personality disorder. In J.N. Butcher & C.D. Spielberger (Eds.), *Advances in Personality Assessment* (Vol. 8). Hillsdale, NJ: Erlbaum.

Cloninger, C. R. (1987). A systematic method for clinical description and classification of personality disorders. *Archives of General Psychiatry, 44,* 573–588.

Costa, P. T., Jr., & McCrae, R. R. (1985). *The NEO Personality Inventory Manual.* Odessa, FL: Psychological Assessment Resources.

Costa, P. T., Jr., & McCrae, R. R. (1990). Personality disorders and the five-factor model of personality. *Journal of Personality Disorders, 4,* 362–371.

Depue, R. A., & Spoont, M. R. (1986). Conceptualizing a serotonin trait: A behavioral dimension of constraint. *Annals of the New York Academy of Sciences, 487,* 47–62.

Digman, J. M. & Takemoto-Chock, N. K. (1981). Factors in the natural language of personality: Re-analysis, comparison, and interpretation of six major studies. *Multivariate Behavioral Research, 16,* 149–170.

Eckblad, M. & Chapman, L. J. (1983). Magical ideation as an indicator of schizotypy. *Journal of Consulting and Clinical Psychology, 51*, 215–225.

Eysenck, H. J. (1967). *The biological basis of personality*. Springfield, IL: Thomas.

Eysenck, H. J. & Eysenck, M.M. (1985). *Personality and individual differences, a natural sciences approach*. New York: Plenum Press.

Goldberg, L. R. (1980, May). *Some ruminations about the structure of individual differences: Developing a common lexicon for the major characteristics of human personality*. Meeting of the Western Psychological Association, Honolulu.

Goldberg, L. R. (1990). An alternative "description of personality": The big-five factor structure. *Journal of Personality and Social Psychology, 59*, 1216–1229.

Goldberg, L. R. (1992). The development of markers for the big-five factor structure. *Psychological Assessment, 4*, 26–42.

Goldberg, L. R. (1993). The structure of phenotypic personality traits. *American Psychologist, 48*, 26–34.

Greenberg, J. R. & Mitchell, S. A. (1983). *Object relations in psychoanalytic theory*. Cambridge, MA: Harvard.

Guilford, J. P. (1975). Factors and factors of personality. *Psychological Bulletin, 82*, 802–814.

Hampson, S. E., John, O. P., & Goldberg, L. R. (1986). Category breadth and hierarchical structure in personality: Studies of asymmetries in judgments of trait implications. *Journal of Personality and Social Psychology, 51*, 37–54.

Harkness, A. R. (1990). Phenotypic dimensions of the personality disorders (Doctoral dissertation, University of Minnesota, 1989). *Dissertation Abstracts International, 50* (12B), 5880B.

Harkness, A. R. (1992). Fundamental topics in the personality disorders: Candidate trait dimensions from lower regions of the hierarchy. *Psychological Assessment, 4*, 251–259.

Harkness, A. R., McNulty, J. L., & Ben-Porath, Y. S. (1993, August). *The Personality Psychopathology Five (PSY-5) Constructs and Preliminary MMPI-2 Scales*. Paper presented at the 101st Annual Convention of the American Psychological Association, Toronto, Ontario, Canada.

Hogan, R. (1983). A socioanalytic theory of personality. In M. M. Page (Ed.), *1982 Nebraska Symposium on Motivation*. Lincoln: University of Nebraska Press.

John, O. P., Angleitner, A. & Ostendorf, F. (1988). The lexical approach to personality: A historical review of trait taxonomic research. *European Journal of Personality, 2*, 171–203.

Lay, C. H., & Jackson, D. N. (1969). Analysis of the generality of trait inferential relationships. *Journal of Personality and Social Psychology, 12*, 12–21.

Maxwell, A. E. (1972). Difficulties in a dimensional description of symptomatology. *British Journal of Psychiatry, 121*, 19–26.

McCrae, R. R., & Costa, P. T., Jr. (1986). Clinical assessment can benefit from recent advances in personality psychology. *American Psychologist, 41*, 1001–1003.

Mershon, B., & Gorsuch, R. L. (1988). Number of factors in the personality sphere: Does increase in factors increase predictability of real-life criteria? *Journal of Personality and Social Psychology, 55*, 675–680.

Moyer, K. E. (1987). *Violence and aggression: A physiological perspective*. New York: Paragon House.

Neisser, U. (1967). *Cognitive psychology*. New York: Appleton Century-Crofts.

Norman, W. T. (1963). Toward an adequate taxonomy of personality attributes: Replicated factor structure in peer nomination personality ratings. *Journal of Abnormal and Social Psychology, 66*, 574–583.

Olweus, D. (1979). Stability of aggressive reaction patterns in males: A review. *Psychological Bulletin, 86,* 852–875.

Osgood, C. E., Suci, G. J., & Tannenbaum, P. H. (1957). *The measurement of meaning.* Urbana: University of Illinois Press.

Peabody, D. & Goldberg, L. R. (1989). Some determinants of factor structures from personality-trait descriptors. *Journal of Personality and Social Psychology, 57,* 552–567.

Piaget, J. (1951). *The origins of intelligence in children.* New York: International Universities Press.

Rescorla, R. A. (1988). Pavlovian conditioning: It's not what you think it is. *American Psychologist, 43,* 151–160.

Romney, D. M., & Bynner, J. M. (1992). A simplex model of five DSM-III personality disorders. *Journal of Personality Disorders, 6,* 34–39.

Siever, L. J., & Davis, K. L. (1991). A psychobiological perspective on the personality disorders. *American Journal of Psychiatry, 148,* 1647–1658.

Spitzer, R. L., Skodol, A. E., Gibbon, M., & Williams, J.B.W. (1981). *DSM-III case book.* Washington, DC: American Psychiatric Association.

Spoont, M. R. (1992). Modulatory role of serotonin in neural information processing: Implications for human psychopathology. *Psychological Bulletin, 112,* 330–350.

Stricker, L. J., Jacobs, P. I., & Kogan, N. (1974). Trait interrelationships in implicit personality theories and questionnaire data. *Journal of Personality and Social Psychology, 30,* 198–207.

Tellegen, A. (1982). *Brief manual for the Differential Personality Questionnaire.* Unpublished manuscript, University of Minnesota, Minneapolis. [Since renamed Multidimensional Personality Questionnaire].

Tellegen, A. (1985). Structures of mood and personality and their relevance to assessing anxiety, with an emphasis on self-report. In A. H. Tuma & J. D. Maser (Eds.), *Anxiety and the anxiety disorders.* Hillsdale, New Jersey: Lawrence Erlbaum Associates.

Tellegen, A. (1988). The analysis of consistency in personality assessment. *Journal of Personality, 56,* 621–663.

Tellegen, A. (1991). Personality traits: Issues of definition, evidence, and assessment. In W. M. Grove & D. Cicchetti (Eds.), *Thinking clearly about psychology: Volume 2: personality and psychopathology.* Minneapolis, MN: University of Minnesota.

Tellegen, A., & Waller, N. G. (1987, August). *Re-examining basic dimensions of natural language trait descriptions.* Paper presented at the 95th Annual Convention of the American Psychological Association, New York.

Tellegen, A. & Waller, N. G. (in press). Exploring personality through test construction: Development of the Multidimensional Personality Questionnaire. In S. Briggs and J.M. Cheek (Eds.) *Personality measures: Development and evaluation (Vol. 1).* Greenwich, CN: JAI Press.

Tolman, E. C. (1960). *Purposive behavior in animals and men.* New York: Appleton-Century-Crofts.

Trapnell, P. D., & Wiggins, J. S. (1990). Extension of the interpersonal adjective scales to include the big five dimensions of personality. *Journal of Personality and Social Psychology, 59,* 781–790.

Tupes, E. C. & Christal, R. E. (1961). *Recurrent personality factors based on trait ratings.* USAF ASD Technical Report, No. 61–97.

Watson, D. & Clark, L. A. (1984). Negative affectivity: The disposition to experience aversive emotional states. *Psychological Bulletin, 96,* 465–490.

Watson, D., Clark, L. A., & Carey, G. (1988). Positive and negative affectivity and their relation to anxiety and depressive disorders. *Journal of Abnormal Psychology, 97,* 346–353.

Watson, D., Clark, L. A., & Tellegen, A. (1984). Cross-cultural convergence in the structure of mood: A Japanese replication and a comparison with U.S. findings. *Journal of Personality and Social Psychology, 47*, 127–144.

Widiger, T. A. (1991). Personality disorder dimensional models proposed for DSM-IV. *Journal of Personality Disorders, 5*, 386–398.

Wiggins, J. S. (1982). Circumplex models of interpersonal behavior in clinical psychology. In P. Kendall & J. N. Butcher (Eds.), *Handbook of research methods in clinical psychology*. New York: Wiley.

Wiggins, J. S. & Pincus, A. L. (1989). Conceptions of personality disorders and dimensions of personality. *Psychological Assessment, 1*, 305–316.

Wiggins, J. S. & Trapnell, P. D. (in press). Personality structure: The return of the big five. In S. R. Briggs, R. Hogan, & W. H. Jones (Eds.), *Handbook of Personality Psychology*. Orlando, FL: Academic Press.

Zuckerman, M., Kuhlman, D. M., & Camac, C. (1988). What lies beyond E and N ? Factor analyses of scales believed to measure basic dimensions of personality. *Journal of Personality and Social Psychology, 54*, 96–107.

15

Differentiating Normal and Abnormal Personality: An Interpersonal Approach Based on the Structural Analysis of Social Behavior

William P. Henry

Historically, "personality," however defined, has usually been seen as a quality that resides, as the name implies, in the person. For Hippocrates, personality was determined by the relative levels of four fluids, or humors, in the body. In this century, Freud's general drive model of personality was equally hydraulic, relying on the homeostatic balance of psychic energies within the individual. One of the most influential contemporary models of personality, Eysenck's three dimensional model (Eysenck & Eysenck, 1985), follows this tradition in the sense that each dimension (e.g., extraversion) is said to reflect heritable biological mechanisms that control the relative activation of certain autonomic nervous and endocrine system functions. Since the time of the Greeks, attempts to understand normal and abnormal behavior have often rested on somewhat mechanistic conceptions of personality as an *internal*, self-contained system that "emits" behavior.[1] In this context, the definition of normality becomes, at least theoretically, fairly straightforward—enough of this, not too much of that, etc. Pathology stems from a system that is somehow ill-constructed, "broken," or out of balance. For instance, an abnormal, depressive personality might result from too much black bile, or a neurotic personality might be rooted in an overactive nervous system that lowers the threshold for experiencing anxiety. In this chapter, I will take a somewhat different and, perhaps, paradoxical position. Specifically, I will propose a qualitative distinction between normal and abnormal personality while at the same time suggesting that nothing is actually "broken" in the abnormal personality. That is, normal and abnormal personality processes are essentially alike in most respects. Indeed, abnormal behavior may be seen as a normal response to an early *environment* that was out of balance.

AN INTERPERSONAL DEFINITION OF PERSONALITY

Regardless of one's theory, personality is by nature a hypothetical construct inferred from observable behavior. An interpersonal approach to personality emphasizes the transactional processes of behavior *between* people, rather than the purely internal determinants of behavior seen as the product of a closed system (Markus & Cross, 1990). Indeed, in many respects it is difficult to envision definitions of abnormality that do not ultimately make reference to interpersonal behavior. A person might be described as paranoid, anxious, angry, conforming, extraverted, rigid or conscientious, but these trait labels refer to the nature of the person's routine interactions with others, that is, their interpersonal behavior. Sullivan (1940, p.32) noted that "personality is made manifest in interpersonal situations, and not otherwise." From this standpoint, personality exists only in relationship to others. Writing on the nature of the self, Markus and Cross (1990) proposed that:

> What one "takes oneself to be" is an interpersonal achievement, deriving almost entirely from the individual's relations with others. . . . Even the appreciation of one's unique or unshared aspects of the self requires interaction with others. . . . it is difficult—perhaps impossible—to escape the influence of others, or to extract a 'pure' self from the interpersonal context. . . . Most current views of the self characterize it as a complex, dynamic entity that *reflects* ongoing behavior and that also *mediates* and *regulates* this behavior [italics added] . . . Whatever the name given to the structures of the self, there is consensus that they are social products. . . . Furthermore, a focus on the self in action overlaps almost entirely with characterizations of the functioning of personality. (pp. 576–578)

In general, interpersonal theories are based on the fundamental propositions that (1) early interpersonal interactions shape the personality;[2] (2) the self-structure, once established, is relatively stable because it tends to evoke interpersonal processes in the present which actively maintain the personality; and (3) personality both directs and is created by interpersonal behavior in a cyclical feedback loop (Carson, 1969; Kiesler, 1982). Models based on circumplex structure have become the standard for conceptualizing and measuring interpersonal behavior (Wiggins & Pincus, 1992). Many such models are available, but they share the common principle that all interpersonal behavior can be described as some combination of two basic underlying dimensions, namely, affiliation and control. In this chapter, Lorna Benjamin's (1974, 1993a) interpersonal circumplex system, called *Structural Analysis of Social Behavior* (SASB), is used as the conceptual and methodological base from which I discuss the broad issue of how to define normal and abnormal personality.

First I will provide a brief description of the SASB system. This will be followed by an overview of the basic developmental and behavioral principles necessary to derive an interpersonal definition of normality. Next, I discuss a number of fundamental, abstract questions: (1) *Why* might certain behavior be considered abnormal? (2) *Where* is psychopathology located (in perception, motivation, behavior, etc.)? (3) *How* should abnormality be measured (quantitatively, qualitatively, etc.)? Specific definitions of normal and abnormal personality are then presented, followed by a discussion of current research, and suggestions for future studies with SASB. It is hoped that the present analysis will ultimately point the way toward a more unified theory of personality.

STRUCTURAL ANALYSIS OF SOCIAL BEHAVIOR

SASB is a set of interrelated interpersonal and intrapsychic circumplexes developed by Lorna Benjamin (1974, 1993a), and was based on the work of such pioneers as Harry Stack Sullivan (1953), Henry Murray (1938), Timothy Leary (1957) and Earl Schaefer (1965). Murray developed a list of human needs that paralleled the early psychoanalytic concept of motivational drives. Leary and colleagues, influenced by Sullivan's thesis that interpersonal behavior rather than symptoms should be the basis for psychiatric diagnosis, took Murray's list of needs, reduced them to a smaller set of categories, and arranged them in circular form. This original interpersonal circumplex (IPC) was formed on the axes of affiliation (love-hate) and control (dominance-submission), which a large body of evidence has confirmed as the basic dimensions of interpersonal behavior (see Wiggins, 1982, for a review). Benjamin made two crucial refinements in the IPC. First, she recognized that the IPC was incomplete because its dominance-submission axis represented only one form of interpersonal control, namely, exchanges involving enmeshment. Schaefer developed a circumplex model of parenting behavior in which the opposite of dominance was not submission, but autonomy granting, or differentiation. To encompass both enmeshment and differentiation in human relations requires two separate control or interdependence axes containing four poles—dominance, submission, autonomy granting and autonomy taking (Benjamin, 1974).

SASB incorporates these four poles by introducing the concept of interpersonal focus, which yields two complementary circumplex surfaces capable of describing all interpersonal transactions. On all surfaces, the horizontal axis describes degree of affiliation and ranges from extremely attacking or rejecting on the left to extremely approaching or loving on the right. See Figure 15.1. Surface One, *Focus on Other*, describes transitive actions that are directed outward toward another individual. The vertical dimension ranges from extremes of control at the bottom to freeing or autonomy granting at the top. Surface Two, *Focus on Self*, describes intransitive behaviors focused on the self that are given in reaction to another person. The vertical dimension ranges from submission at the bottom to separation or autonomy taking at the top. The two surfaces are complementary in that the compliment of any Surface One action is found at the identical circumplex point on Surface Two. The bottom halves of each circumplex involve enmeshment (dominance and submission, respectively), while the top halves describe differentiation (autonomy granting and taking, respectively). SASB differs importantly from the traditional circumplex on which the opposite of control (dominance) is viewed as submission. In SASB, the opposite of control is autonomy granting, while the opposite of submission is autonomy taking, or separation.

Surface Three, the *Introject*, is an intrapsychic surface that reflects the Sullivanian notion of the self as the reflective appraisals of others (Sullivan, 1953). The introject surface describes actions directed by the self, toward the self, and represents the internalization of behavior directed toward the self by important others. Insofar as the way we treat ourselves mirrors the pattern of treatment historically received from others, the introject surface may also represent a generalized object model, or representation of general expectancies of other people. The vertical dimension, like Surface One, runs from control, at the bottom, to freeing, at the top.

The full SASB model contains 36 points around each of the three surfaces. These points may be collapsed into eight segments, called *clusters*, or four quadrants. In most applications the eight-cluster version of SASB has been used because it represents a good, workable compromise in complexity (and is the version typically referred to in this chapter). The complete cluster model is depicted in Figure 15.1. In referring to various points in SASB space, the convention is to use the surface number followed by the cluster number, such as 1–3 (Surface One, cluster three) to denote active love.

Three decisions are required to place a given interpersonal behavior in its SASB location. First, it must be decided whether the communication is focused on the self or on others. Next, a determination is made about how much affiliation or disaffiliation is present, and then the degree of interdependence is assessed. Finally, the affiliation and interdependence ratings are used as coordinates to place the communication into one of eight cluster segments on the appropriate surface.[3] SASB may be used to map the interpersonal process between interactants, the interpersonal content of spoken dialogue, or an individual's intrapsychic structure (Benjamin, 1993a). The system may be used by raters working from transcripts or tapes, and there is also a self-report version, the INTREX questionnaire (Benjamin, 1983, 1988).

DEVELOPMENTAL AND BEHAVIORAL PRINCIPLES

Principles of Interpersonal Behavior

As described by SASB, interpersonal behaviors have highly organized relationships to one another, and these relationships are guided by a set of predictive principles (Benjamin, 1984). The first principle is that actions tend to "pull for" reactions that are complementary. *Complementarity* is defined as corresponding behaviors on the affiliation dimension (e.g., friendliness pulls for friendliness and hostility begets hostility), and the interdependence dimension (e.g., control pulls for submission, and autonomy granting leads to autonomy taking or differentiation). Complementary behaviors are located at structurally homologous points on the SASB interpersonal surfaces. For example, hostile control (1–6: blame) tends to evoke hostile submission (2–6: sulk) and vice versa (sulking evokes criticism). This principle does not ensure that all interchanges will be complementary, but it does predict that for an interpersonal system to endure for any length of time a general pattern of complementarity must be achieved. The principle of complementarity has been empirically demonstrated with SASB, even within the rather structured bounds of the therapeutic relationship, in which theoretically, the therapist should deliberately avoid some complementary exchanges that are disaffiliative (Henry, 1986; Henry, Schacht & Strupp, 1986).

The *opposite* of any behavior is located at 180°, or directly across, on the same circumplex surface (such as 1–2: affirm vs. 1–6: blame or 1–4: protect vs. 1–8: ignore). Sometimes interpersonal behaviors simultaneously convey opposite messages, and these are called *complex communications*. For instance, a mother might say to her child in a sarcastic manner, "Go ahead and do it if you want!", with the intended message being, "You better not." This communication conveys a complex blend of affirmation (the surface content of friendly autonomy granting) and blame (the underlying command of hostile control). In SASB it would be coded 1–2/1–6.

The complement of the opposite is called the *antithesis*. Theoretically, maximum pull for change occurs when an individual responds antithetically to an undesired behavior. For example, if hostile power (1–6: blame) is responded to with its antithesis, friendly differentiation (2–2: disclose), rather than its complement (2–6: sulk), a *pull* is created for a new behavior in the first person, namely, affirmation (1–2).

The final principle is that of *introjection*. Introjection is sometimes referred to in this chapter as a developmental principle (see below), but it is also an ongoing process in daily adult encounters. The principle states that we absorb and encode the actions of others toward us, and treat ourselves as others have treated us and continue to treat us (Sullivan, 1953). The structure of our introjected experiences is presumably capable of development and change across the lifespan. In practice, however, this part of ourselves tends to be relatively stable because it is

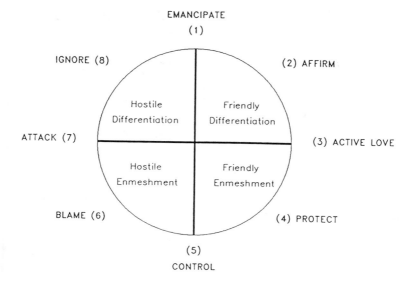

Surface One: Focus on Other

EMANCIPATE
(1)

IGNORE (8)

(2) AFFIRM

Hostile
Differentiation

Friendly
Differentiation

ATTACK (7)

(3) ACTIVE LOVE

Hostile
Enmeshment

Friendly
Enmeshment

BLAME (6)

(4) PROTECT

(5)
CONTROL

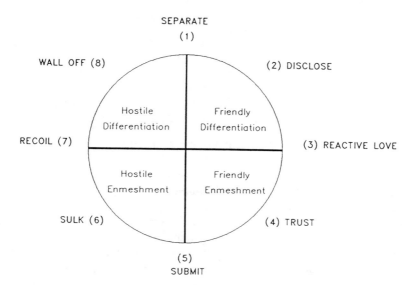

Surface Two: Focus on Self

SEPARATE
(1)

WALL OFF (8)

(2) DISCLOSE

Hostile
Differentiation

Friendly
Differentiation

RECOIL (7)

(3) REACTIVE LOVE

Hostile
Enmeshment

Friendly
Enmeshment

SULK (6)

(4) TRUST

(5)
SUBMIT

FIGURE 15.1. Benjamin's (1974, 1993a) Structural Analysis of Social Behavior cluster model. (A) Surface One: Focus on Other. (B) Surface Two: Focus on Self. (C) Surface Three: Actions Toward Self (Introject).

Surface Three: Actions Toward Self (Introject)

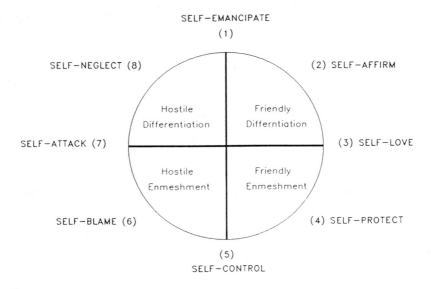

FIGURE 15.1. (Continued)

self-perpetuating through the mechanism of complementarity (see Henry, Schacht, & Strupp, 1990, for a more complete discussion of this point).

Developmental Principles

How early interactions with parental figures shape normal and abnormal personality is central to this chapter. There are three basic, interrelated mechanisms of socialization through which a child's interpersonal experiences determine the mental structures and representations that come to guide the behavior we label "personality": introjection, identification, and internalization. As just noted, *introjection* is the process by which early actions directed by important others toward the self become the ways in which the individual treats himself or herself. For example, a child who is constantly subjected to criticism (hostile control) is likely to become quite self-critical. *Identification* is the process of internalizing the behavior and characteristics of significant others through imitation. If a child is subjected to constant criticism, in addition to being self-critical the child is likely to imitate his or her accusers and become critical toward others. The principle of *internalization* states that people carry within themselves abstract representations of important others in the form of expectancies. These become a basic part of ongoing mental operations and are referred to by Benjamin (in press-b) as "important people or their internalized representations" (IPIR). These internalized representations shape our beliefs about the likely outcomes of interactions with others, and hence influence our perception of, and reaction to, ongoing interpersonal events. If an individual's internalized images of others are primarily critical, then the individual comes to expect criticism, perceive it (even when it may not be present), and react in a complementary manner to this perception with hostile submission (sulking and appeasing). Thus, an individual's Surface One actions are shaped by identification, Surface Two reactions are guided by internalization, and Surface Three actions toward self result from introjection. SASB's elegance stems in part from the fact that the system contains separate circumplex surfaces that correspond to these three basic mechanisms of socialization.

One final but critical theoretical element must be introduced in order to understand the distinction between normal and abnormal personality. In developing his theory of attachment, Bowlby (1977, 1988) drew on evolutionary biology to posit two basic and normative activities of the human infant—attachment seeking and exploration. He defined his theory as "a way of conceptualizing the propensity of human beings to make strong affectional bonds to particular others and of explaining the many forms of emotional distress and personality disturbance . . . to which unwilling separation and loss give rise," and described attachment behavior as "any form of behavior that results in a person attaining or retaining proximity to some other differentiated and preferred individual" (Bowlby, 1977, p. 201). Until the mid-1950s affectional bonds were thought to develop in order to satisfy primary needs or drives (food for the infant and sex for the adult). However, the work of Lorenz (1955) and Harlow (1958) demonstrated that animals seek attachments and form bonds in the absence of any reinforcing drive reduction. Bowlby drew on this work to support his hypothesis that seeking interpersonal attachment is a normative end in itself, and in fact, that attachment may form in spite of repeated punishments from the attachment figure. (These ideas will be important shortly in understanding how "abnormal" personality can arise from normal processes.) Bowlby additionally stated that once a child's primary attachment needs are satisfied, the primary attachment figure (usually the mother) serves as a base from which the child may venture forth to temporarily explore the environment before returning to renew the attachment bond. For a child to explore, however, the parent must allow the child some degree of autonomy or differentiation. Attachment seeking and exploration behaviors normally alternate in the healthy infant, and both have survival value.

Summary

Before moving on to discuss abnormal personality, let me first summarize the normative processes described by interpersonal theory. Personality consists of the mental operations associated with internal representations of self and others in interaction, and is made manifest in interpersonal behavior. All interpersonal behavior is comprised of some combination of values along two basic dimensions derived originally from primate research—affiliation and control (or interdependence). Any interpersonal behavior tends to "pull for" a complementary response, and stable behavior patterns between people are largely determined by the principle of complementarity. The developing child's personality is shaped by early interpersonal behaviors directed at the child by primary caregivers through the mechanisms of introjection, identification, and internalization. Humans have basic drives to seek attachment and explore the environment. The successful attainment of these goals is associated with the two basic interpersonal dimensions of affiliation and interdependence. As will be shown below, disruptions in attachment seeking and differentiation form the basis of personality disturbance.

INTERPERSONAL APPROACHES
TO ABNORMAL PERSONALITY

Description Versus Definition

There are three basic approaches to the study of abnormal personality utilizing the interpersonal circumplex. First, systems that detail categories of abnormal personality, pathological traits, or personality dimensions can be directly translated into, or mapped onto, the two fundamental interpersonal axes of affiliation and control. Various authors have reviewed the theoretical correspondence between circumplex models and the *Diagnostic and Statistical Manual of Mental Disorders (DSM)* (American Psychiatric Association, 1987) Axis II personality disorders (e.g., Widiger & Kelso, 1983; Kiesler, 1986). Most recently, Benjamin (1993a) has taken DSM descriptors for each of the eleven personality disorders and distilled them into interpersonal behaviors, wishes, and fears that correspond to SASB's circumplex surfaces.

A second approach has been to empirically establish the shared variance among the three major systems of organizing and describing normal and abnormal personality, namely, dimensional (e.g., McCrae & Costa, 1985), categorical (DSM) and circumplex models. Significant correlations have been obtained between interpersonal models and DSM personality disorder categories (Morey, 1985; DeJong, Van den Brink, Jansen, & Schippers, 1989). Horowitz (1979) constructed a list of common interpersonal problems and subsequent factor analyses have consistently revealed that these problems comprise two main factors corresponding to the circumplex axes of affiliation and control (Alden, Wiggins, & Pincus, 1990). Finally, it has recently been suggested that affiliation and control correspond to the first two of the "Big Five" personality factors, namely, extraversion and agreeableness (Wiggins & Pincus, 1992).

These two approaches have provided ample evidence for the assertion that interpersonal models can be used *descriptively*. There appears to be enough shared variance between categorical and dimensional models of personality and personality disorder, and the axes of affiliation and control, to suggest that the interpersonal circumplex might serve as a useful common language. A third, final approach is to directly *define* normal and abnormal personality in terms of interpersonal theory and circumplex structure, the ultimate aim of this chapter.

A comprehensive, theoretical definition of abnormal personality should address three interrelated questions: (1) *Why* or by what criteria are certain interpersonal behaviors considered abnormal? This entails a consideration of: (2) *What* is abnormal about a behavior and *where* in the behavioral sequence is pathology located (perception, motivation, behavior, environmental response, etc.)? Answers to these questions shape the possibilities for: (3) *How* is abnormal behavior to be measured or operationally defined? Should a classical or prototypic model be used? The emphasis throughout is on behavior because personality is envisioned not as a static structure or collection of traits but as a *process* that stems from interpersonal behavior and results in interpersonal behavior.

To begin with, it is unwise if not impossible to define normality or abnormality at the level of specific individual behavior. Under certain conditions, normal individuals may display behavior at all points on the interpersonal circumplex. For example, although complementarity is considered a normative behavioral principle, noncomplementary behavior, while nonnormative, is not *necessarily* abnormal. In fact, noncomplementary responses are often considered a virtue, such as meeting hostile control with friendly autonomy (i.e., turning the other cheek). Thus, we cannot say that any given interpersonal behavior is essentially normal or abnormal.

It is now generally accepted that models of personality should be hierarchical in nature (Eysenck, 1990). Eysenck (1990) asserted that personality systems should incorporate four levels: (1) singularly occurring acts or cognitions, (2) habitual acts or cognitions, (3) traits, composed of significantly intercorrelated habitual behaviors, and (4) higher order factors or dimensions composed of intercorrelated traits. For interpersonal behavior to be considered abnormal, it would seem reasonable to assume that such behavior must be at least at the habitual acts level (2), referred to by Benjamin (1993a) as an individual's *baseline*. Different types of habitual acts may also regularly follow one another in sequences, forming baseline behavioral patterns that might be considered traits. But we are still left with the problem of explaining *why* certain habitual acts are considered abnormal.

In defining Axis II personality disorders, *DSM* (American Psychiatric Association, 1987) opts for a pragmatic position, stating that behavior is pathological because of its *results*: "It is only when personality traits . . . cause either significant functional impairment or subjective distress that they constitute personality disorders" (p. 335). In short, personality is abnormal because it causes systematic distress to oneself or others. This generic definition is reasonable, and is in keeping with the descriptive aims of the *DSM* Task Force. However, concepts such as "functional impairment" are certainly culturally dependent value judgments. In this sense, such a description does not provide a satisfying universal definition of abnormality *per se*. Furthermore, there are many easily imagined circumstances in which "subjective distress," even if chronic, would not be considered dysfunctional. For example, an altruistic person might experience chronic distress in an environment populated by self-centered, antisocial individuals. Yet the altruistic person's distress would not be used, by itself, as evidence for a personality disorder.

In addition to broadly defining personality pathology, *DSM* provides a long list of descriptors that operationally answer the question "*what* is abnormal?" These descriptors cover a range of phenomena including *specific behaviors* (excessive spending, talking to oneself, suicide threats, stealing, volunteering to do demeaning things); *beliefs* (ideas of reference, unjustified belief that one's spouse is unfaithful); *thought processes* (inappropriately abstract, vague or digressive, magical thinking); *motivations* (little desire for sexual experiences, wants to be the center of attention at all times); *affect* (constricted or labile, inappropriately intense anger); *traits* (impulsivity, aggressiveness, social anxiety); and *behavioral results* (no close friends, devastated when relationships end, unstable and intense interpersonal relationships). At first glance, these descriptors do not seem to offer a unified framework for defining abnormal personality. They appear to be a grab bag of pathological features that are inconsistent in content (affects, cognitions, behavior, etc.), process (relating to inputs, mediation and outputs) and level of inference or abstraction. However, from an interpersonal perspective, all of the descriptors share a common feature, namely, they are associated with disrupted interpersonal relationships (either as cause or effect).

From an interpersonal standpoint, the theoretical foundation for considering personality abnormal must involve a disruption in the fundamental human drives for simultaneous attachment and differentiation. But the interpersonal behavior we view as personality is only the end product of a process involving learning, perception, motivation, goals, introjection, etc. Arriving at precise or universal definitions of what is abnormal in this process is difficult, and sometimes paradoxical, as I shall discuss below.

Normality and Abnormality as Defined by SASB

The definition of abnormal personality offered by Benjamin's (1974, 1993a) SASB model overlaps with, but is also distinct from, definitions offered by other interpersonal theorists. Leary (1957) distinguished normal and abnormal personality on the basis of behavioral intensity. Normal interpersonal behaviors are mild-to-moderate in intensity and occupy positions around the intersection of the affiliation and control axes (i.e., close to the center of the circle). Abnormal behavior (found near the outer edge of the circle) was defined as an extreme variant of normal behavior. For example, exploitive narcissism is viewed as the pathological extreme of confident, competitive behavior. Leary (1957), and later Carson (1969), emphasized that normal behavior is flexible while abnormal behavior is rigid. Individuals with disordered personality typically operate within a narrow slice of the circumplex, regardless of the situation, pulling for others to respond to them in the same stereotyped way. Thus, abnormal personality has frequently been defined in terms of a quantitative deviation from normal interpersonal processes that are marked by *moderation* and *flexibility*.

The definition of normality from the standpoint of SASB encompasses these traditional ideas of moderation and flexibility, but does so a way that leads to a *qualitative* definition of normality and pathology.[4] Benjamin (in press-b) stated that:

> Normality is not a mild version of pathology. It is qualitatively different. Along with showing a moderately separate and friendly position, a normal person also can become moderately enmeshed, share friendly interpersonal space. A normal person operates from a baseline of bondedness, moderate differentiation, and moderate enmeshment. A person with psychopathology does not. (p. 33)

In SASB language, an individual with a normal personality behaves primarily within a balanced range of clusters two, three, and four (see Figure 15.1), which have been referred to as the *attachment group* (AG) (Benjamin, in press-a). These clusters reflect affiliated, attached interpersonal processes accompanied by healthy flexibility in interdependence, ranging from moderately-friendly submission (enmeshment) to moderately-friendly differentiation or autonomy. Not by accident do these clusters correspond to Bowlby's (1977, 1988) postulates concerning the two major drives of attachment seeking and exploration. The circumplex space represented by clusters two through four also correspond to balanced, effective parenting. A good parent is able to provide a blend of emotional warmth and availability (cluster 3), acceptance and individuation (cluster 2), and structure, protection, and nurturant teaching (cluster 4). The 2–3–4 baseline[5] is considered to define "normal" because it corresponds to the satisfaction of the basic drives, or needs, as proposed by attachment theory. Benjamin (1993a) goes on to add that normality also involves the flexibility to respond, when necessary, with behavior that is outside the 2–3–4 baseline. For example, in responding to a threat to her child's safety, a mother might need to attack (cluster 7) or exercise pure control (cluster 5). In this sense, rigid adherence to the "normal" baseline regardless of the situation would be considered unhealthy.

In an ideal scenario, the developing child is acted upon by his or her parent figures with a blend of affirmation (1–2), active love (1–3), and protection (1–4). Through the mechanism of identification, the child comes to exhibit these behaviors toward others. The internalization of the parent's image (IPIR) directs the child's (and later the adult's) expectancies of treatment from others in general, acting as a perceptual filter that shapes baseline reactions to others. Introjection of the parents' 1–2, 1–3, and 1–4 behaviors results in an introject structure (3–2, 3–3, 3–4) that is a healthy blend of self-acceptance, self-love, and self-nurturance. However, if the child is treated with sufficient hostile control (1–6: blame) he or she may come to be routinely critical of others (identification), unduly sensitive to potential criticisms from others that may not actually be present (internalization), and highly self-condemning (introjection). The result might be an individual who is hostile, paranoid, insecure, and chronically depressed—a personality style most would consider abnormal. The consequence would be an impairment in the normal capacity for friendly attachment and mutual autonomy in a relationship.

Abnormal personality corresponds to interpersonal behaviors and introjects in clusters 6, 7, and 8, the *disrupted attachment group* (DAG) (Benjamin, in press-a). It is important to note that individuals with abnormal personalities may also display interpersonal behavior within the AG, perhaps with fair frequency. However, AG behavior is not likely to be characteristic of them. Abnormal persons typically interact with a high frequency of DAG behaviors, are likely to disregard or misinterpret the context of their interactions, and are likely to exhibit rapid, unpredictable shifts in their interpersonal posture (e.g., from friendliness to hostility and submission to separation). Disordered persons also tend to show normal behavior that is "contaminated," or complex—for example, behavior that is overtly friendly but have hostile intent (smiling sweetly to show disapproval), and those that are both granting of autonomy and controlling (directing someone to "be spontaneous"). Several authors (Duke & Nowicki, 1982; Kiesler, 1986; Watzlawick, Beavin, & Jackson, 1967) have noted that incongruent messages are a marker of disturbed functioning. In summary, normal interpersonal behavior is attached, moderate, flexible, stable, and congruent, while abnormal interpersonal patterns manifest disrupted attachment, extremes of interdependence (submission or separation), rigidity, instability, and complex messages.

To give an example of how this definition of abnormality provides a general theoretical framework, consider Teyber's (1989) typology of interpersonal coping styles related to dysfunction. Based on Horney's (1945) observations, Teyber noted that if a child's basic needs are unmet, anxiety arises with the need (such as feeling anxious when the need for affection arises). Individuals attempt to rise above the need and gain some active mastery over the helplessness and anxiety provoked by the need in one of three basic ways: (1) *moving toward others* by being overly attentive to others' needs, and overly submissive in an attempt to win approval and avoid rejection; (2) *moving against others* through aggression and resistance to others' efforts to establish control; and (3) *moving away* from others through avoidance, withdrawal and self-sufficiency to prevent rejection and block the arousal of needs for interpersonal nurturance.[6] Each of these styles can be seen to violate the basic SASB conditions of normality. Moving toward others involves excessive submission (2-4, 2-5, 2-6), violating the normal moderate balance of differentiation and enmeshment. Moving against others disrupts bonding through active attack (1-6, 1-7) and is also out of balance on both ends of the interdependence dimension; that is, the individual engages in reactive separation (2-8) to resist others as well as excessive control (1-5, 1-6). Finally, moving away from others entails insufficient affiliation and extreme differentiation (2-1, 2-8) at the expense of enmeshment.

THE ABNORMAL PARADOX

On the one hand, a case has been made that normal and abnormal personality are quite distinct (qualitatively different). On the other hand, normal and disordered personality processes may be identical in many ways. The definition of "abnormal" rests upon the observable interpersonal behaviors that differentiate normal from abnormal personalities. Tracing the underlying locus of pathology, however, is another matter, as there are a number of internal processes that might result in similar external behaviors. In most ways, normal and abnormal personality processes are the same, and in fact, abnormal behavior may be seen to arise from very normal mechanisms (hence the paradox).

Figure 15.2 illustrates a simplified model of interpersonal behavior based on the mechanisms of internalization, identification, and introjection of early experience. These mechanisms are thought to be universal and operate to create both normal and abnormal personality. It is also felt that all individuals manifest the basic motivation to seek interpersonal attachments, although overt behavior may seem to indicate otherwise.[7] Finally, all individuals ultimately share the same goals, or general wishes (the attachment group), and fears (the disrupted attachment group). That is, both normal and abnormal personalities alike wish for affirmation (1–2), love (1–3), and protection (1–4), and fear blame (1–6), attack (1–7), and abandonment (1–8). If normal and abnormal persons do not differ in formative mechanisms, motivations, or goals, where is the pathology located?

Abnormal personality is the result of normal processes operating within the context of an interpersonally damaging early environment. Experiences in an emotionally unhealthy environment create internalized object representations and introject structures that deviate from the normal baseline (clusters 2, 3, and 4). The internalized images create expectancies that in turn distort perceptions of new interpersonal events. Thus, a disordered person expects that specific wished-for behaviors from the AG (e.g., affirmation, love, protection) that were not provided by early caregivers will not be forthcoming in future interactions with others and that specific feared behavior from the DAG (e.g., blame, attack) that were frequently directed toward them in childhood will occur instead. Specific wishes and fears achieve a salience, or motivational prominence, in disordered persons that is not typically seen in normal individuals. Coupled with skewed perceptions, these central wishes and fears organize the disordered person's attempts to secure a balance of attachment and interdependence. Because the wishes and fears are so rigidly fixed in the minds of disordered persons, and the perceptions of others stereotyped by behaviorally-narrow IPIRs, the resulting attachment seeking behaviors are pathological.

The paradox—that abnormal personality arises from normal, adaptive processes—is based on the fundamental proposition that all mental operations are organized by attempts to achieve desired interpersonal conditions and avoid feared ones (Benjamin, in press-a). Benjamin (1993a, p.101) has stated that "Maladap-

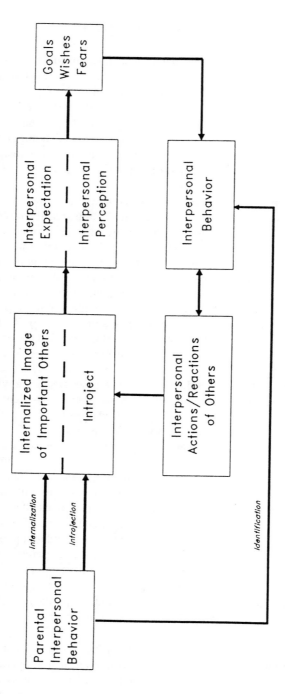

FIGURE 15.2. A simplified model of interpersonal behavior based on the mechanisms of internalization, identification, and introjection of early experience.

tive [personality] patterns are driven by wishes that internalized other persons will offer love, approval, forgiveness, apologies, admiration, reparation and so on." Take, for example, children who have been physically abused. As adolescents or adults, severely abused individuals often respond to anxiety or perceived abandonment from others with self-damaging acts, such as self-mutilation. Why? Because to treat oneself as the abuser did may reduce anxiety by providing feelings of attachment to the internalized image of the abuser. Another example might be the girl whose parents "tolerated" her as long as she was no bother, that is, quiet and out of the way. Active, attachment-seeking approaches by the girl were routinely met with rebuff by the parents while her nondemanding, passive behavior was at least tacitly rewarded. In this case, the early interpersonal environment taught the girl that maximum attachment, such as it is, is best achieved via passivity. As an adult, her apparent *lack* of attachment-seeking behavior may in fact represent an active attempt to maintain congruency with an internalized representation of parental attachment. In short, for normal and abnormal personalities alike, there is a logical relationship between internalization, perception, goals, and behavior. Abnormal personality emerges from attempts to adapt to an interpersonally unhealthy early environment.

A Clinical Example

SASB is an extremely useful heuristic tool that helps make clear the connections between early learning and maladaptive, abnormal interpersonal behavior. While specific early experiences may not be linked to specific *DSM* Axis II disorders, SASB's *dimensional representation* of early experiences has been demonstrated to be directly related to particular personality disorders (Benjamin, 1993a). As an example, Benjamin (1993a) explains a possible interpersonal etiology for the passive-aggressive or negativistic personality disorder (NEG):

1. The developmental cycle started . . . with nurturant parenting that built trust in the constancy and the competence of the caregivers. The consequence . . . is that the NEG expects nurturance . . .

2. The wonderful nurturance of early infancy was abruptly withdrawn and replaced with unfair demands for performance. The prototypic experience is that the NEG was a well-cared-for firstborn who abruptly lost nurturance when a younger sibling was born. . . . The [new] expectations were exacting, excessive, and oblivious to the legitimate needs of the NEG. . . . This made the NEG resentful of those (siblings) who were more fortunate. . . . The adult consequence is power sensitivity. The NEG sees authorities or caregivers as cruel, unfairly demanding, neglectful, and unfair.

3. There were very harsh punishments for the expression of anger. . . . The adult consequence is indirect expression of anger.

   There were also harsh punishments for any forms of autonomy that interfered with parental interests.

The consequence . . . is that, like anger, [autonomy] must be expressed indirectly. . . . The defiant-compliant pattern seems to the NEGs like the only way to cope. (pp. 270–271)

In SASB language, the parents in this case may have applied control that ignored the true needs of the child, a complex of 1–5/1–8. The complement of this behavior is 2–5/2–8, a complex of submission plus hostile separation or defiance. This is a classic passive-aggressive pattern. The NEG wishes for the return of nurturance (1–4), and fears control (1–5). The NEG struggles to achieve attachment by holding the caretaker at fault and hoping that his or her demonstrated misery will produce restitution (i.e., the return of mutual attachment behaviors). After all, the caretaker did originally provide nurturance. However, direct blame and attack of the negligent caregivers (1–6, 1–7) has been forbidden, permitting only indirect means. A normal degree of differentiation has also been forbidden, because to be autonomous means that attachment will be withdrawn. Therefore, the submission of the NEG (2–4, 2–5, 2–6) is in the service of attachment, but the NEG is then forced to achieve some measure of differentiation by indirect means.

Research Findings

There are two main types of SASB research methodologies. First, the actual interactions among people are rated for interpersonal process, or the content of the dialogue is scored for interpersonal process. Second, the INTREX questionnaire (Benjamin, 1983, 1988), a self-report instrument, is used to provide a detailed description of an individual's introject, his or her current significant relationships, and his or her early developmental interactions with parents (or between parents). These self reports can be made with instructions to describe how a relationship exists now, or how it exists in its "best" and "worst" states. Combining these possibilities yields a Person X State X Situation interaction.

There have been numerous empirical studies using SASB, and a complete review is beyond the scope of this chapter. Alpher (1988) summarizes the empirical development of SASB, cites relevant psychometric and validity data, and provides a representative bibliography of research to that time. For current purposes, I will cite a sampling of studies most directly relevant to the model of abnormal personality presented in this chapter. There are a number of possible approaches to empirically validating this model. At a minimum, it should be shown that individuals judged to have abnormal personalities by other accepted criteria (such as DSM) do indeed manifest interpersonal behaviors associated with SASB's DAG. Second, a correspondence should be demonstrated between abnormal behavior and early learning, as typified by parental behavior. Finally, it would lend credence to both interpersonal and traditional nosologies if specific interpersonal patterns could be associated with specific personality types or diagnostic categories. Fortunately, research to date has been promising on all of these fronts.

Humphrey (in press) provides excellent examples of the rating-based approach to SASB. She (1989) compared the interactions among the mother, the father, and teenage daughter in 74 families where the daughter was diagnosed as being anorexic, bulimic, bulimic–anorexic, or normal. The family's task (from which the interactions were extracted) was to discuss the daughters' separation from the family. Humphrey found that all clinical families manifested significantly more complex communications than the normal families. The families of anorexic patients and bulimic patients both violated the normative AG baseline, but in different ways. The anorexic parents communicated considerable nurturance, but in a manner that neglected the daughters' needs to express themselves (a complex blend of 1–3/1–8). Bulimic parents and their daughters tended to become hostilely enmeshed, exhibiting complementary cycles of blame and sulking (1–6 and 2–6). Humphrey (in press) has also showed that families of drug dependent daughters engaged in significantly more DAG behaviors, and significantly fewer AG behaviors, than normal control families.

Öhman and Armelius (1993) coded interviews with two schizophrenic patients for both interpersonal process and content. They reported that the patients' interpersonal process was marked by more hostile separation (cluster 8) when compared to a neurotic control subject, and they showed a complex interpersonal pattern of avoiding the interviewer through the continual disclosure of irrelevant details (2–2/2–8). Furthermore, they noted that the schizophrenic patients' dialogue had less interpersonal content, and they manifested a deviant use of interpersonal focus, when compared to the control subject. Specifically, they described only the actions, and never the reactions of others, while describing only their own reactions, not actions.

The relationship of early interpersonal experience to adult personality has also received empirical support. In an earlier study, Öhman and Armelius (1990) used data from the INTREX questionnaire to demonstrate that patients diagnosed with borderline personality disorders showed significantly higher levels of self-reported behavior in SASB clusters 6, 7 and 8 (the DAG) than 22 normal control subjects. They tied this to the borderline patients' developmental history, showing that the mothers of borderline patients had acted toward the patients at an early age with significantly lower levels of behavior in the AG (clusters 2, 3, and 4) as compared to controls.

I (1991) administered the INTREX battery and the Minnesota Multiphasic Personality Inventory (MMPI) (Hathaway & McKinley, 1951) to a sample of 83 inpatients and outpatients in psychotherapy. The MMPI personality disorder scales developed by Morey, Waugh, and Blashfield (1985) were scored and then factor analyzed. Three dimensions emerged and were labeled I, Dependent/Avoidant/Schizoid, II, Paranoid/Compulsive/Passive-Aggressive, and III, Borderline/Antisocial. Through a series of stepwise multiple regressions I attempted to predict the level of self-attack in the adult introject in its "best" and "worst" state from the degree of hostility in the patients' early interactions (ages 5–10) with their parents. I then predicted personality disorder factor scores from adult introject self-affiliation ratings. As expected, the early relationship with parents was significantly related to adult introject structure. The patients' actions toward their mother, and reactions to their mother, were the two significant predictors of self-attack in the introject "best" state. The patients' reactions to both their mother and father predicted the introject "worst" state. The patients' self-attack in both their "best" and "worst" states were significant predictors of their personality disorder Factor I scores. Factor III was related only to the introject at "worst." Although preliminary in nature, findings support the notion that early experience, adult introject, and personality dysfunction are meaningfully related. Interestingly, the patients' ratings of their relation-ship with their mother accounted for more variance in the adult introject than did the father ratings.

Another approach to research with SASB has been to demonstrate that patients with different DSM diagnoses exhibit predictable and distinct inter-personal and intrapsychic patterns on the INTREX questionnaire. Benjamin (1986) used discriminant function analysis to examine the utility of INTREX ratings made by patients in differentiating nine different DSM Axis I diagnostic groups. This study was particularly interesting in that circumplex methods have typically been applied to Axis II personality disorders, not Axis I symptom disorders. Benjamin obtained an overall classification accuracy rate of 48.8%, which compared more than favorably to the rates obtained with more traditional instruments such as the SCL-90R (26.1%) and the MMPI (40.9%). When INTREX ratings were made by nurse observers rather than the patients, the overall classification rate rose to 63.3%.

Finally, Alpher (1992a, 1992b, in press) has used the INTREX questionnaire as the chief assessment device in a programmatic study of patients with multiple personality disorder (MPD). He has used SASB to measure changes in the identity and self-organization of MPD patients (Alpher, 1992a), and to assess the different introjects of host and secondary personalities (Alpher, 1992b). Like Benjamin, he has used discriminant function analysis to distinguish a sample of problem drinkers from a MPD sample based on their self-rated introjects (Alpher, in press).

FUTURE DIRECTIONS

There is growing evidence to support the general validity of interpersonal theory (e.g., Wiggins & Pincus, 1992) as well as the ability of SASB to capture a full range of interpersonal and intrapsychic phenomena (see above). As a broadly-based descriptive system, the range of potential SASB research applications is limited only by the imagination of researchers. Nevertheless, there are certain logical directions for the application of SASB in personality research. As noted earlier, work has already begun in wedding the circumplex and factor analytic traditions in personality measurement. However, to date, this work has been accomplished within the confines of the traditional circumplex which ignores differentiation as well as intrapsychic processes. Factor analytic models of personality, such as the Big Five, are useful only insofar as they predict how different people behave. Differential behavior will still have to be described, and SASB provides an attractive unified metric for the descriptive measurement of behaviors associated with various dimensional models. In this vein, the interaction of biological or temperamental variables, and interpersonal or social learning history, is an important area for future study. What biological variables might enhance or retard the development of an AG or DAG baseline? Again, a common language is important to further such research, and SASB provides that language.

An obvious and important direction for research is the application of SASB to the study of personality disorders. It is debatable whether or not a "grand unified theory" of personality disorder is either possible or desirable. Nevertheless, current conceptions of personality can certainly be made more coherent and parsimonious, and etiological mechanisms shared among them can be made more explicit. In my opinion, SASB is better suited to the task of clarifying theory than the traditional circumplex. In the traditional approach, disorders or personality types are usually typified by a single point in circumplex space. The use of three surfaces, the focus on transactional behavior rather than behavioral type, and Benjamin's recent emphasis on the organizational properties of interpersonal wishes and fears (Benjamin, 1993a), all discourage thinking about personality as a point, and encourage thinking in terms of personality as process. Hopefully, SASB will encourage researchers to think more in terms of *sequential* patterns of behavior, the interpersonal triggers for the patterns, and the relationship between action, reaction, and introjection. The failure to find greater overlap between circumplex space and the *DSM* personality disorders (Morey, 1985) may be due in part to the fact that a categorical disorder is a complex of perceptions, behaviors, wishes, and fears, and cannot be reduced simply to a single point.

Benjamin (1993a) recently published a major work on the interpersonal diagnosis and treatment of personality disorders. She proposed a wealth of testable etiological hypotheses for each of the *DSM* Axis II personality disorders. From the standpoint of the theoretical model presented in this chapter, the most important research task is to show that while specific developmental experiences may vary, the interpersonal *dimensionality* of early experience corresponds to the dimensionality of the adult personality pattern or disorder. Current research with SASB has relied primarily on retrospective self reports. Ultimately, the strongest test of theory may come from longitudinal studies that utilize observer ratings as well as self reports.

A final task for researchers is to empirically develop and validate a reduced set of core interpersonal pathologies based on SASB. When individuals deviate from the AG baseline, surely they do so with some patterned regularities that could form the basis of a truly theoretical personality disorder nosology. For example, if Benjamin's (1993a) innovative list of wishes and fears for the eleven personality disorders is examined closely, two broad categories emerge. One group wishes to be granted autonomy (differentiation) and fears hostile control (enmeshment), while the other group wishes for nurturant control (enmeshment) and fears hostile abandonment (differentiation). Of course, such broad categorizations lose the specificity that SASB is capable of, and it is a task for future researchers to determine an optimum level of specificity to serve as a heuristic structure for different purposes.

SUMMARY: THE WHY, WHAT, AND WHERE OF ABNORMAL PERSONALITY

The model outlined in this chapter has many parents—Murray, Sullivan, Leary, Schaefer, Bowlby, and, most especially, Benjamin. It is by no means suggested that this model is the only valid approach to defining abnormal personality. The model does, however, enjoy the advantage of being based on primate and infant research, offers a theoretically-coherent account of the relationship between normal and abnormal personality, and is readily testable. Quite simply, personality is defined directly in terms of interpersonal behavior. Attachment seeking, and a balance of enmeshment and differentiation that enables both protection and exploration, are considered developmentally normal. In SASB terms, this is a balanced baseline of interpersonal and intrapsychic behavior corresponding to clusters 2, 3, and 4 (the AG). Thus, baseline patterns within the DAG (clusters 6, 7, and 8) are axiomatically abnormal because such behavior impedes satisfaction of the normal drives for interpersonal attachment and exploration.

The why and the what of abnormal personality are fairly straightforward. Locating the "where" of pathology is somewhat more ambiguous or perhaps arbitrary. It has been argued that there is actually nothing abnormal about "abnormal" personality processes. That is, the surface interpersonal behavior that is the defining feature of abnormal personality actually arises from the same processes (identification, internalization, introjection), motivations (wishes and fears), and goals (attachment) as normal personality. What actually makes abnormal personality abnormal is the internalized object images, based on early experience, which shape expectancies and hence perception. The locus of pathology is thus a somewhat arbitrary distinction. Pathology could be located externally in the environment or early learning history, or could be seen as internal in the form of object images. It is the programming that is faulty, and it makes little difference whether one blames the programmer or the resulting program.

Finally, it is interesting to consider whether this model is more nearly a classical model (monothetic) in which the defining features are all necessary and sufficient, or whether it is more of a prototypic model (polythetic) with multiple optional features, none of which is necessary or sufficient. At first glance, the definition of abnormal personality in terms of a deviation from the AG would seem to present a classical model. A baseline pattern that includes interpersonal behavior from the DAG is certainly *sufficient* for inclusion in the class abnormal. However, is it *necessary*? Technically, the answer is no, due to the fact that *rigid* adherence to the AG baseline, if situationally inappropriate, is also viewed as abnormal. Thus, neither of these models fit perfectly. In practice it may be more useful to adopt a polythetic approach. Abnormal personality is seen as manifested in interpersonal behavior that exhibits disrupted attachment, extremes of enmeshment or differentiation, response rigidity, instability, and complexity. SASB is capable of capturing all of these features of abnormal behavior, and it is hoped that the present model will stimulate the pursuit of a more theory-driven and unified approach to the study of normal and abnormal personality.

NOTES

[1]The word "personality" can be traced to the Latin *per* + *sonare*, which literally means "to sound through." It referred to the practice of placing small megaphones in the masks worn by actors so that their voices would project outward with greater amplification. Thus, the roots of the word are consistent with the idea that personality is something internal that is "emitted."

[2]I do not consider biological processes unimportant in shaping personality; however, a consideration of how biological variables interact with interpersonal experience is beyond the scope of this chapter.

[3]Occasionally, the ratings are extreme on both dimensions. For example, using normal scoring rules, an other-directed exchange rated at the extremes of control and attack would actually fall in a middle location (1–6: blame). However, in these extreme cases the middle point does not seem to truly capture the meaning. This problem is solved by the "axial intensity rule" (Benjamin, 1993a, pp. 62–63), according to which such communications are coded as complex (in this case 1–5/1–7), preserving the independent extremes of each dimension.

[4]Technically, SASB is a descriptive system that does not, in and of itself, define normality. The definition offered in this chapter stems from the thinking of Lorna Benjamin and myself as these ideas are operationalized with SASB.

[5]The basic position presented in this chapter is that normality is qualitatively distinct from abnormality rather than being a milder version of abnormality (or vice versa). It might be argued that this is a faulty conception because SASB's *baseline* seems to (and does) introduce a quantitative element. Certainly *baseline* is not defined precisely, and is a quantitative concept. However, if the concept of *baseline as habitual behavior* is accepted, then the distinction between normal and abnormal is qualitative in a manner distinct from the original IPC. In the original IPC, *abnormal* was defined according to vector length, not placement around the circumplex, while in SASB, abnormal behavior is located in distinct portions of the circumplex.

[6]Interestingly, these three interpersonal coping styles correspond closely to the typology of disturbed attachment styles proposed by Bartholomew and Horowitz (1991), namely, preoccupied, dismissing, and fearful.

[7]There may be biologically-based exceptions to this rule, particularly in the cases of schizoid and antisocial character. Nevertheless, the behavior of individuals with these personality styles still violates the SASB rule of normality, and even these possible exceptions fit the overall model.

REFERENCES

Alden, L. E., Wiggins, J. S., & Pincus, A. L. (1990). Construction of circumplex scales for the inventory of interpersonal problems. *Journal of Personality Assessment, 55,* 521–536.

Alpher, V. S. (1988). Structural Analysis of Social Behavior. In D. J. Keyser & R. C. Sweetland (Eds.), *Test critiques* (Vol. 7) (pp. 541–556). Kansas City, MO: Test Corporation of America.

Alpher, V. S. (1992a). Changes in identity and self-organization in psychotherapy of multiple personality disorder. *Psychotherapy, 29,* 570–579.

Alpher, V. S. (1992b). Introject and identity: Structural-interpersonal analysis and psychological assessment of multiple personality disorder. *Journal of Personality Assessment, 58,* 347–367.

Alpher, V. S. (in press). Introject and intrapsychic patterns in dissociative disorder patients reporting childhood psychosocial trauma. *Journal of Consulting and Clinical Psychology.*

American Psychiatric Association. (1987). *Diagnostic and statistical manual of mental disorders* (3rd ed., rev.). Washington, D.C.: Author.

Bartholomew, K., & Horowitz, L. M. (1991). Attachment styles among young adults: A test of a four-category model. *Journal of Personality and Social Psychology, 61,* 226–244.

Benjamin, L. S. (1974). Structural Analysis of Social Behavior. *Psychological Review, 81,* 392–425.

Benjamin, L. S. (1983). *The INTREX user's manual, Part I.* Madison, WI: INTREX Interpersonal Institute.

Benjamin, L. S. (1984). Principles of prediction using Structural Analysis of Social Behavior. In R. A. Zucker, J. Aronoff, & A. J. Rabin (Eds.), *Personality and the prediction of behavior* (pp. 121–174). New York: Academic Press.

Benjamin, L. S. (1986). Adding social and intrapsychic descriptors to Axis I of DSM-III. In T. Millon & G. R. Klerman (Eds.), *Contemporary directions in psychopathology* (pp. 599–638). New York: Guilford.

Benjamin, L. S. (1988). *Short form INTREX user's manual.* Madison, WI: INTREX Interpersonal Institute.

Benjamin, L. S. (1993a). *Interpersonal diagnosis and treatment of personality disorders.* New York: Guilford.

Benjamin, L. S. (in press-a). Good defenses make good neighbors. In H. Conte & R. Plutchik (Eds.), *Ego defenses: Theory and measurement.* New York: Wiley.

Benjamin, L. S. (in press-b). SASB: A bridge between personality theory and clinical psychology. *Psychological Inquiry.*

Bowlby, J. (1977). The making and breaking of affectional bonds: I. Aetiology and psychopathology in the light of attachment theory. *British Journal of Psychiatry, 130,* 201–210.

Bowlby, J. (1988). *A secure base: Parent child attachment and healthy human development.* New York: Basic Books.

Carson, R. C. (1969). *Interaction concepts of personality.* Chicago: Aldine.

DeJong, C. A. J., Van den Brink, W., Jansen, J. A. M., & Schippers, G. M. (1989). Interpersonal aspects of DSM-III axis II: Theoretical hypotheses and empirical findings. *Journal of Personality Disorders, 3,* 135–146.

Duke, M. P., & Nowicki, S. (1982). A social learning theory analysis of interactional theory concepts and a multidimensional model of human interaction constellations. In J. C. Anchin & D. J. Kiesler (Eds.), *Handbook of interpersonal psychotherapy* (pp. 78–94). New York: Pergamon Press.

Eysenck, H. J. (1990). Biological dimensions of personality. In L. A. Pervin (Ed.), *Handbook of personality: Theory and research* (pp. 244–276). New York: The Guilford Press.

Eysenck, H. J. & Eysenck, M. W. (1985). *Personality and individual differences.* New York: Plenum.

Harlow, H. F. (1958). The nature of love. *American Journal of Psychology, 13,* 673–85.

Hathaway, S. R., & McKinley, J. C. (1951). *The Minnesota Multiphasic Personality Inventory.* New York: Psychological Corporation.

Henry, W. P. (1986). *Interpersonal process in psychotherapy.* Unpublished doctoral dissertation. Vanderbilt University, Nashville, TN.

Henry, W. P., Schacht, T. E., & Strupp, H. H. (1986). Structural Analysis of Social Behavior: Application to a study of interpersonal process in differential psychotherapeutic outcome. *Journal of Consulting and Clinical Psychology, 54,* 27–31.

Henry, W. P., Schacht, T. E., & Strupp, H. H. (1990). Patient and therapist introject, interpersonal process, and differential psychotherapy outcome. *Journal of Consulting and Clinical Psychology, 58,* 768–774.

Henry, W. P. (1991, July). *Interpersonal antecedents of personality disorder dimensions.* Paper presented at the annual convention of the Society for Psychotherapy Research, Lyons, France.

Horney, K. (1945). *Our inner conflicts.* New York: Norton.

Horowitz, L. M. (1979). On the cognitive structure of interpersonal problems treated in psychotherapy. *Journal of Consulting and Clinical Psychology, 47,* 5–15.

Humphrey, L. L. (1989). Observed family interactions among subtypes of eating disorders using structural analysis of social behavior. *Journal of Consulting and Clinical Psychology, 57,* 206–214.

Humphrey, L. L. (in press). Individuation in families of adolescents: Multimethod measurement using structural analysis of social behavior. *Journal of Consulting and Clinical Psychology.*

Kiesler, D. J. (1982). Interpersonal theory for personality and psychotherapy. In J. C. Anchin & D. J. Kiesler (Eds.), *Handbook of interpersonal psychotherapy* (pp. 3–24). New York: Pergamon Press.

Kiesler, D. J. (1986). The 1982 interpersonal circle: An analysis of DSM-III personality disorders. In T. Millon & G. L. Klerman (Eds.), *Contemporary directions in psychopathology* (pp. 571–597). New York: Guilford.

Leary, T. (1957). *Interpersonal diagnosis of personality: A functional theory and methodology for personality evaluation.* New York: Ronald Press.

Lorenz, K. (1955). Morphology and behavior patterns in closely allied species. In B. Schaffner (Ed.), *Group processes.* New York: Macy Foundation.

Markus, H. & Cross, S. (1990). The interpersonal self. In L.A. Pervin (Ed.), *Handbook of personality: Theory and research*. New York: Guilford.

McCrae, R. R. & Costa, P. T. (1985). Updating Norman's adequate taxonomy: Intelligence and personality dimensions in natural language and in questionnaires. *Journal of Personality and Social Psychology, 49*, 710–721.

Morey, L. C. (1985). An empirical comparison of interpersonal and DSM-III approaches to classification of personality disorders. *Psychiatry, 48*, 358–364.

Morey, L. C., Waugh, M. H., & Blashfield, R. K. (1985). MMPI scales for DSM-III personality disorders: Their derivation and correlates. *Journal of Personality Assessment, 49*, 245–251.

Murray, H. A. (1938). *Explorations in personality*. New York: Oxford University Press.

Öhman, K. & Armelius, K. (1990). Schizophrenic and borderline patients: Introjection, relationship to mother and symptoms. *Acta Psychiatrica Scandinavica, 81*, 488–496.

Öhman, K. & Armelius, K. (1993). Interpersonal interactions and psychopathology—Five cases. *Psychotherapy Research, 3*, 208–223.

Schaefer, E. S. (1965). Configurational analysis of children's reports of parent behavior. *Journal of Consulting Psychology, 29*, 552–557.

Sullivan, H. S. (1940). *Conceptions of modern psychiatry*. New York: Norton.

Sullivan, H. S. (1953). *The interpersonal theory of psychiatry*. New York: Norton.

Teyber, E. (1989). *Interpersonal process in psychotherapy: A guide for clinical training*. Pacific Grove, CA: Brooks/Cole Publishing Co.

Watzlawick, P., Beavin, J., & Jackson, D. D. (1967). *Pragmatics of human communication*. New York: Norton.

Widiger, J. S. & Kelso, K. (1983). Psychodiagnosis of Axis II. *Clinical Psychology Review, 3*, 491–510.

Wiggins, J. S. (1982). Circumplex models of interpersonal behavior in clinical psychology. In P. C. Kendall & J. N. Butcher (Eds.), *Handbook of research methods in clinical psychology* (pp. 183–221). New York: Wiley.

Wiggins, J. S. & Pincus, A. L. (1992). Personality: Structure and assessment. In M. R. Rosenzweig & L. W. Porter (Eds.), *Annual Review of Psychology, 43*, 473–504.

16

Evaluating Normal and Abnormal Personality Using the Same Set of Constructs

Edward Helmes and Douglas N. Jackson

In this chapter we provide evidence bearing on the hypothesis that normal and abnormal personality can be conceptualized using the same set of personality constructs. We also examine the related question of whether or not abnormal personality can be considered as a more extreme form of behavioral disposition or constellation of dispositions that are also present in the general population, or if there are categorically distinct aspects of abnormal personality that do not share common ground with the range of normal personality. This forms a basic theoretical question concerning abnormal personality, as it is represented in the form of the personality disorders.

It is clear that the issue of dimensional versus categorical models can be addressed in different ways, as the chapters in the Methodology section illustrate. These different methods in turn will influence decisions as to how individuals will be regarded on the relevant dimensions or classified into the relevant categories. In addition, any discussion within the domain of psychological assessment of the distinction between normality and abnormality in personality is complicated by different usages of the term "personality." At times, this is taken to include a broad range of psychopathology, as implied by the Minnesota Multiphasic Personality Inventory (MMPI) (Hathaway & McKinley, 1967), and at others to imply a narrower range of interpersonal functioning. This latter definition, exemplified by *DSM* Axis II, would exclude aspects of mood, such as anxiety and depression, and pathological patterns of cognition, such as hypochondriasis and hallucinatory and delusional thought disorders. We feel that the term personality should be restricted to the latter, narrower usage, but wish to adopt momentarily the former usage in order to make a point concerning the measurement model for dimensional representations of the continuity between normal and abnormal or pathological states.

MODELS OF NORMALITY

The concept of normality in personality borrows heavily from the use of the term in medicine, in which the contrary state to the normal is one of injury or disease. Thus, many medical conceptions of disease are inherently categorical in that individuals either have been injured or infected by an organism or they have not. The conception of other medical disorders is clearly dimensional, in that the physiological property clearly extends on a continuum from normal values to ones that are clearly abnormal or pathological. Abnormal hormone levels and blood pressure are examples. Dimensional models generally incorporate the concept of a threshold or cutoff value, at which point a sufficient degree of the condition is present to consider the condition to be pathological.

Within the domains of personality and psychopathology, theoretical writings as to whether the disorders are categorical or dimensional have rarely been specific. Millon (1991a) discusses several of the issues that are relevant and notes the historical and current lack of consensus on this topic. Indeed, the general level of theoretical development of the concepts relating to disorders within the field of psychiatry leaves much to be desired (Brown, 1991). For some conditions, such as the affective disorders, there is a clear continuum between the normal fluctuations of mood and the pathological extremes of elation and despondency. The nature of other conditions is less clear at present, due to the ambiguous nature of current research. It is plausible, for example, that conditions such as schizophrenia and bipolar affective disorder are categorically distinct from a *normal* state (Meehl, 1973; Meehl & Golden, 1982). Taxometric evidence at the symptom level for a categorical model has been reported for Meehl's concept of schizotypy, which includes the more severe disorder of schizophrenia (Meehl, 1990).

Measurement of psychopathology should use a measurement model that corresponds with the theoretical model of that psychopathology (Livesley & Jackson, 1992). If the disorder is conceptualized as categorical, then the measurement model implies the attribution of a positive diagnosis when a critical number of diagnostic features is present. The presence of fewer features than the critical number implies the absence of the disorder. In contrast, the dimensional model implies that the accumulation of additional diagnostic features increases the severity of the disorder. The two inferences are not the same and should be distinguished in the same way that degree and kind are distinguished. Not to do so leads to the use of inappropriate statistical methods and incorrect inferences. The categorical model of pathology that underlies the MMPI clinical scales thus forms particular interpretive problems for users of that particular instrument (Helmes & Reddon, 1993), especially when they make inferences more appropriate to a dimensional model. In contrast, instruments developed from a clear conceptual framework to assess dimensional traits relevant to particular disorders can be interpreted in a more direct fashion.

The bulk of evidence in the realms of personality and mood supports the dimensional model (Clark, 1990; Eysenck, 1987). Individual traits are almost invariably continuously distributed, and quantitative evidence for discontinuities or overlapping independent distributions has been presented for only a few characteristics. The strongest evidence in the absence of discontinuities or clear points of rarity in a distribution (Kendell, 1975) is provided by maximum covariance analysis (Meehl, 1973; Meehl & Golden, 1982) and similar methods. Maximum covariance analysis uses a quantitative procedure to determine if there is evidence of two distinct but overlapping distributions of a symptom. This is somewhat analogous to finding the point of inflection between the modes of the bimodal distribution that should be apparent in such cases. To our knowledge, to date such evidence has been provided only for schizotypy and self-monitoring (Meehl, 1990; Gangstead & Snyder, 1985). Even with these two characteristics, the evidence suggests a continuous range of variation within the schizotypal or self-monitoring taxa. Within truly categorical disorders, the relevant traits may still be continuously distributed (Millon, 1991a).

The model used by the diagnostic committees in forming the Axis II diagnoses of personality disorder (American Psychiatric Association, 1987) is primarily categorical (Livesley & Jackson, 1991; Widiger & Kelso, 1983), with different diagnoses having varying emphasis upon theoretical or empirical constituents (Morey, 1991). The various criteria used within these and other diagnostic categories range from traits to individual behavioral acts. Such acts can be seen to parallel individual items in conventional personality inventories. At the same time as the *DSM* model relies upon a categorical approach to differentiating among diagnostic types, its view of disordered personality as a whole is less clear. In general, *DSM-III-R* does not take a stand for either categorical or dimensional models, acknowledging that "no definition adequately specifies precise boundaries for the concept 'mental disorder'" (American Psychiatric Association, 1987, p. xxii). The concept of mental disorder as applied to Axis I and II of the *DSM* does distinguish between clinical syndromes and personality functioning but does not makes a definite statement for a model for either concept. (See Widiger & Corbitt, chapter 8 of this volume, for a discussion of these issues in *DSM-IV*). British traditions may have been somewhat more strongly tied to dimensional approaches than have the American *DSM* models (Rutter, 1987).

MEASUREMENT ACROSS RELEVANT DIMENSIONS IN NORMAL AND ABNORMAL GROUPS

Despite the lack of commitment to either approach in the introduction to *DSM-III-R*, there is implicit agreement in other parts of *DSM* that disorders of personality are continuous with the range of normal personality. "It is only when *personality traits* are inflexible and maladaptive and cause either significant functional impairment of subjective distress that they constitute *Personality Disorders*" (American Psychiatric Association, 1987, p. 335). Of course, the critical questions here are *what* personality traits are inflexible and maladaptive, *how* inflexible must they be, and in *what situations* are they maladaptive. The range of normal personality encompasses a wide range of characteristics, most of which are clearly not pathological in the great majority of individuals (Offer & Sabshin, 1991). Persisting with a rigid adherence to old behavior patterns under changed circumstances can be maladaptive at times in even normal individuals. However, behavior characteristic of the extremes of normal personality characteristics may be persistently maladaptive in everyday life, as well as meeting the statistical definition of abnormality by being less common (Frances, Widiger, & Sabshin, 1991). Such extreme levels of a trait may be maladaptive both in an evolutionary sense, in that these individuals' social behavior is such as to minimize their likelihood of reproduction, and in common interpersonal relationships. Even if such individuals do not themselves experience distress, it is very likely that those around them are affected in a manner that does not promote harmonious social interactions.

To the extent that the same traits are found in groups defined in some way as abnormal and groups defined as normal, analyses of normal and abnormal populations using psychological assessment instruments should yield similar internal structures in order to maintain a common measurement model in both populations. This has been demonstrated with several populations with the Basic Personality Inventory (BPI) (Jackson, 1989): Hypochondriasis, Depression, Denial, Interpersonal Problems, Alienation, Persecutory Ideas, Anxiety, Thinking Disorder, Impulse Expression, Social Introversion, Self Depreciation, and Deviation. This instrument was developed to assess the constructs common the MMPI and the Differential Personality Inventory (DPI) (Jackson & Messick, 1986), and is intended to assess relatively distinct aspects of psychopathology. The BPI contains 240 items in a self-report format, using true and false as the response options. Reddon, Jackson, Reed, & Gill (1982) developed modal profiles (Skinner, 1977, 1978) from the 12 BPI scales and were able to demonstrate the congruence of these profiles across rural and urban samples of adolescents. Using a total of over 3,500 individuals, Chrisjohn, Jackson, and Lanigan (1984) used confirmatory factor analysis to show the presence of the same factor structure in 8 samples of normal and delinquent adolescents, normal adults, university students, and psychiatric patients. MacLean, Helmes, & Chrisjohn (1989) tested the structure of the 12 BPI scales under the strict assumptions of different models based upon item response theory. They used two samples, one of 813 psychiatric patients and another of 508 university undergraduates. The fit of two parameter models was acceptable for all 12 scales.

In many ways, the scoring key of an inventory provides a reasonable test of the congruence and stability of its structure for the purpose of determining the stability of a test's structure in different populations (Helmes, 1989). Holden, Reddon, Jackson, & Helmes (1983) rotated the responses of three samples (normal adults, psychiatric patients, and high school students) to a target matrix composed of the scoring key for the BPI scales. No item failed to load on its keyed scale in all three samples, and 205 of 220 items loaded appropriately in all samples. To date, in no other measure of psychopathology have the underlying constructs held up so well across different samples. This in turn illustrates the utility of construct based measures in which the theoretical and measurement models are congruent.

RESEARCH IN THE DIMENSIONAL ASSESSMENT OF PATHOLOGICAL PERSONALITY

For the past several years W. John Livesley and Douglas N. Jackson have undertaken a research program in the study of personality disorders using a systematically constructed measure of the dimensions underlying personality pathology. The availability of a psychometric procedure that shows acceptable levels of reliability has permitted a number of studies relevant to the nature of personality disorders and to how they might best be conceptualized and classified. One of the issues addressed relates to the issue of whether a categorical or dimensional model is most appropriate for describing personality disorders. Other questions relate to the structure of traits within normal and pathological populations as these apply to personality disorders, the question of whether patients diagnosed as having personality disorders can be classified in a manner consistent with extant diagnostic systems and how such classifications compare between clinical and normal samples.

Development of the Instrument

The development of the Dimensional Assessment of Personality Pathology (DAPP; Livesley & Jackson, in press) began by systematically perusing the literature on personality disorders and standard classification systems such as *DSM-III*. As a result of this review, 100 traits were identified as being linked to one or more personality disorder diagnosis, e.g., Guilt Proneness, Irritability, Failure to Adopt Social Norms, Restrictive Affective Expression, Sensation Seeking, and Suspiciousness. The identification of relevant traits was aided by earlier research (Livesley, 1986) that investigated descriptive features of each *DSM-III* diagnosis. Pooled judgements of panels of clinicians were used to obtain a consensus on the most prototypical features of each of the eleven major *DSM-III* diagnoses for personality disorder (Livesley, 1987). These judgements of diagnostic features were then ranked in terms of their prototypicality for each diagnosis. The next step was to evaluate highly prototypical features to determine whether or not they defined the same or distinct categories (for example, "Mistrustful" was combined with "Expects Trickery or Harm" into one category labelled "Suspiciousness"). These trait categories were in turn compared and contrasted across diagnoses with the goal of attempting to identify mutually exclusive trait categories that were judged to be relevant to at least one diagnostic category. The identification of trait categories was not limited to *DSM-III*, however. Some features had been identified in the literature and were judged to be highly prototypical of certain disorders, yet were not included in *DSM-III*. One example of such traits not included in *DSM-III* was the set of interpersonal features of anti-social personality (cf. Blackburn, 1988), such as Exploitation, Egocentrism, Externalization, and Contemptuousness. These were judged to be quite relevant to anti-social personality, even though they were not identified as salient features in *DSM-III-R*. Cleckley's (1976) widely accepted conception of antisocial personality incorporates other characteristics in addition to the emphasis on criminal activities in *DSM-III* (Frances, 1980).

The next step in the design of the questionnaire was to write items that were judged to capture the range of behavior relevant to each trait category. In this effort, the structured approach to personality scale development described by Jackson (1970, 1971) was employed. The aim of this scale development was to prepare sets of items that were maximally saturated with the trait categories for which they were prepared, minimally related to alternative trait categories, minimally related to Social Desirability, and showing sufficient differentiation between the normal and clinical populations and sufficient differentiation within each population that a reliable separation of respondents would result.

The task for respondents was to rate the appropriateness of each item on a five-point scale for describing themselves. The five response alternatives range from *Very unlike me* to *Very like me*. During the course of scale development the number of original scales was modified to accommodate trait categories that could be collapsed or could be subdivided. The final number of scales in the initial item pool was 100, although the initial number was somewhat smaller (79). Certain trait categories that were described as unitary in *DSM-III* actually were factorially complex and needed to be separated. For example, Schizotypal Personality Disorder is defined in terms of "deficits in interpersonal relatedness and peculiarities of ideation, appearance, and behavior" (American Psychiatric Association, 1987, p. 341). This definition carries the strong implication that there is a single dimension of "deficits and peculiarities" present in such individuals, but principal components factor analysis identified two distinct factors, *Cognitive Dysfunction* and *Social Apprehensiveness*. The first was marked by, among other scales, Schizotypal Cognition, and the second by Defective Social Skills. These factors can exist independently of one another.

Important issues in scale development that were addressed included the number of basic underlying dimensions that could be interpreted from the personality disorder domain and their nature and composition. A second important concern regarding the nature of personality pathology was also evaluated. We have already mentioned the controversy regarding whether personality disorders are best conceptualized in terms of a class or categorical model or of a dimensional model. We have noted that under a class model the distribution of variables describing members of the class should show discontinuities or points of rarity between normal populations and pathological populations. In addition, the intercorrelations between traits that describe personality disorders should be higher in the populations that show evidence of the personality disorder. If, for example, a class model is appropriate for describing a category such as Narcissistic Personality Disorder with salient features such as Grandiosity, Attention Seeking, and a strong Need for Adulation, then the correlation among these characteristics should be higher in a clinical sample than in a general population sample. This is so because a class model posits a different organization of traits in clinical groupings and seeks a constellation of features that are assumed to occur together and that define the particular diagnostic category. Thus, based on class model assumptions, one might expect more crystallized constellations of traits defining factors that are descriptive of personality pathology in a clinical group with clear pathology. Accordingly, there should be 18 dimensions that describe the domain of personality pathology that would encompass the constituent scales that were developed. The bases for the hypotheses were initial exploratory factor analyses (Livesley, Jackson, & Schroeder, 1992), conceptual analyses of the personality disorder literature, and clinical lore. Table 16.1 contains the hypothesized structure regarding the 18 dimensions of personality pathology together with the scales defining each dimension. A perusal of Table 16.1 indicates that, unlike *DSM-III-R* diagnostic criteria, the scales that define each factor show mutual independence, i.e., in no case was a given scale hypothesized to be linked to more than one dimension. The alternative, permitting a given dimension to be defined by scales or traits that also served to define other dimensions, is potentially a serious threat to the conceptual clarity and distinctiveness of the broad constructs of personality that serve to describe personality pathology.

In order to evaluate the degree to which this conceptualization of the personality disorder domain could be confirmed in an empirical structure, the DAPP was administered to both general population and clinical respondents. The general population sample consisted of a set of volunteers drawn from heterogeneous sources: community groups, hospital and university employees, university students, and other persons from the general population. A total of 149 women and 125 men volunteered. The clinical sample comprised 158 patients (95 women and 63 men) who had been assigned a primary diagnosis of personality disorder while patients of the psychiatry department of a general hospital. Excluded from the clinical group were individuals who also carried a diagnosis of organic brain pathology or of major (Axis I) psychiatric disorder.

The analysis consisted of a number of steps: (a) Obtaining means and standard deviations for each scale separately within each group. (b) Standardizing the

TABLE 16.1 Dimensions underlying the Dimensional Assessment of Personality Pathology

Dimension		Defining Scales
I.	Affective Lability	Affective Over-reactivity, Affective Lability, Labile Anger, Generalized Hypersensitivity, Irritability
II.	Anxiousness	Rumination, Guilt Proneness, Trait Anxiety, Indifference, Indecisiveness
III.	Cognitive Distortion	Schizotypal Cognition, Depersonalization or Derealization, Brief Stress Psychosis
IV.	Compulsivity	Orderliness, Precision, Conscientiousness
V.	Conduct Problems	Juvenile Antisocial Behavior, Addictive Behaviors, Interpersonal Violence, Failure to Adopt Social Norms
VI.	Diffidence	Suggestibility, Need for Advice and Reassurance, Submissiveness
VII.	Identity Problems	Chronic Feelings of Emptiness and Boredom, Anhedonia, Pessimism
VIII.	Insecure Attachment	Secure Base, Separation Protest, Proximity Seeking, Intolerance of Aloneness, Feared Loss
IX.	Interpersonal Disesteem	Remorselessness, Contemptuousness, Interpersonal Irresponsibility, Lack of Empathy, Exploitation, Egocentrism, Sadism
X.	Intimacy Problems	Inhibited Sexuality, Avoidant Attachment, Desire for Improved Attachment Relationships
XI.	Narcissism	Grandiosity, Need for Admiration, Attention Seeking, Need for Approval
XII.	Passive Opposition	Lack of Organization, Oppositionality, Passivity
XIII.	Rejection	Dominance, Interpersonal Hostility, Rigid Cognitive Style, Judgmental
XIV.	Restricted Expression	Self Reliance, Reluctance to Self-Disclose, Restricted Affective Expression, Avoidance Attachment, Restricted Expression of Positive Sentiments, Restricted Expression of Angry Affect
XV.	Self Harm	Self Damaging Acts, Ideas of Self Harm
XVI.	Social Avoidance	Social Apprehensiveness, Defective Social Skills, Desire for Improved Affiliative Relationships, Low Affiliation, Fear of Interpersonal Hurt
XVII.	Stimulus Seeking	Sensation Seeking, Recklessness, Impulsivity
XVIII.	Suspiciousness	Hypervigilence, Suspiciousness

clinical population data in terms of the normal sample. This standardization was important for subsequent numerical taxonomic work, but was not critical for the factor analysis. (c) Intercorrelating and factoring the 100 scales separately for the clinical and general population samples. (d) Undertaking a separate orthogonal procrustes rotation (Schönemann,1966). This rotation permitted an evaluation of the extent to which clinical and normal samples corresponded to our hypothesized structure. (e) Comparing the factors derived from the clinical and general samples. (f) Undertaking a modal profile analyses of the extent to which patients and general population individuals could be categorized into identifiable clusters using modal profile analyses (Jackson & Williams, 1975; Skinner, 1978). The results of the factor analyses and targeted rotation indicated a confirmation of the 18-dimensional structure hypothesized in Table 16.1. In addition, we identified a remarkably close degree of agreement between the factors derived in the clinical and general population samples, using the coefficient of congruence (Harman, 1976, pp. 343–346). Seventeen of the eighteen hypothesized factors were very similar in the two samples. Only two dimensions failed to show strong convergence in the two samples. Table 16.2 provides the results of the congruence analysis for the 18 dimensions of the DAPP.

An evaluation of the respective means and standard deviations from the clinical and general population groups and of the distributional plots supported the view that what are regarded as personality disorders can be conceptualized as behavioral tendencies that are more or less present in the general populations but that represent more extreme levels in clinical populations. There was no evidence of discontinuities between general population samples and clinical samples. Furthermore, the degree of congruence that emerged suggests that traits are organized in a similar manner in the general population and in clinical samples. What is remarkable about these findings is the high degree of convergence, although there were some exceptions. These exceptions can be attributed to the fact that some scales in the general population had a restricted range and, accordingly, low reliability. Thus, for example, pathological forms of suspiciousness in the general population were not present in a sufficient degree to provide a high loading for the Suspiciousness scale, although the loading was positive. Just as the correlation between two measures is limited by the respective reliabilities of these measures, so is the factor loading limited. In factor theory, a scale's communality cannot exceed its reliability. But it should be emphasized that these were exceptions. In general, the evidence strongly supports the hypothesis that scales defining dimensions of personality pathology are organized and structured in the same way in patient and general population samples. To us, this provides critical evidence supporting the hypothesis that personality pathology is best conceptualized within a dimensional framework, and, accordingly, personality pathology can be conceived of as representing more extreme forms of behavior and behavioral tendencies that are present to a lessor or greater extent in the general population.

TABLE 16.2 Convergence of Factor Structures of the Dimensional Assessment of Personality Pathology (DAPP) in Normal and Clinical Populations

Factor	DAPP Scale	Coefficient of Congruence
I.	Affective Lability	.971
II.	Anxiousness	.923
III.	Cognitive Distortion	.963
IV.	Compulsivity	.979
V.	Conduct Problems	.954
VI.	Diffidence	.905
VII.	Identity Problems	.963
VIII.	Insecure Attachment	.901
IX.	Interpersonal Disesteem	.986
X.	Intimacy Problems	.747
XI.	Narcissism	.970
XII.	Passive Opposition	.966
XIII.	Rejection	.956
XIV.	Restricted Expression	.980
XV.	Self Harm	.911
XVI.	Social Avoidance	.979
XVII.	Stimulus Seeking	.972
XVIII.	Suspiciousness	.832

MODAL PROFILE ANALYSIS OF DIMENSIONS OF PERSONALITY PATHOLOGY

In a further effort to evaluate the nature of and the degree of continuity between normal and clinical populations in personality pathology, an analysis that was designed to cluster individuals in categories defined by typal dimensions was used, modal profile analysis. This procedure addresses the question of the extent to which entities are distinguished by distinct profile patterns. It has been employed in the study of occupational classification in terms of vocational interest profile patterns (Jackson & Williams, 1975), as well as in a study evaluating the commonalities underlying MMPI profile types contained in popular classification schemes (Skinner & Jackson, 1978).

The technique involves a series of steps: (a) Starting with the principle component scores which represent linear combinations of the 100 DAPP scales organized into 18 dimensions, a matrix is formed with rows comprised of the component scores for each respondent and columns identified with each of the 18 dimensions described in Table 16.1. (b) This matrix is standardized in a manner similar to the manner in which tests are standardized in traditional factor analysis. (c) The matrix is subjected to a singular value decomposition which is equivalent to determining the eigenvalues and eigenvectors of the matrix. (d) The axes are transformed to meet a statistical criterion for *simple structure*, but in this case the simple structure is in terms of seeking to identify typal dimensions that have a few persons highly represented in terms of the dimension and others not. For this purpose, a univocal varimax criterion (Jackson & Skinner, 1975) was employed. (e) Finally, the resulting clusters need to be examined in terms of the classification efficiency, i.e., the number of persons classifiable into each category, and the degree to which results are generalizable across different populations—in this case, between clinical and general population samples.

The first feature of the results that is noteworthy is a substantial number of typal dimensions that could be identified in both the clinical and general population samples. In each sample, respondents could be classified into 17 modal types or modal profiles. Second, it was noteworthy that a large proportion of both the clinical and the general population samples were classifiable in terms of one of the clusters. For the clinical sample, a total of 134, or 84.8%, of the individuals were classifiable into one of the clusters, based on a correlation between their profile and the cluster profile of .5 or higher. In the general population sample, a total of 228, or 83.2%, of the individuals were classifiable, indicating that dimensions of personality pathology classify general population people almost as well as they do clinical patients. A third implication of our findings was the diversity and complexity of personality pathology as it is organized in terms of profile types.

Some idea of the results from such an analysis might be obtained from two of the seventeen profiles that emerged from the clinical sample. These are contained in Figure 16.1. Individuals can match either the positive pole of the modal profile or type or they can match its inverse or negative pole. Such individuals would have a negative correlation with the modal type and their profile would show the opposite pattern of peaks and valleys to the positive pole. The left side of Figure 16.1, in which 7 individuals in the clinical group could be classified positively, showed a pattern of Suspiciousness, Insecure Attachment (as represented by Proximity Seeking, Feared Loss, and Intolerance of Aloneness), and Compulsivity. They were also characterized as distinctly low in Anxiety. The right side of Figure 16.1, in which 4 individuals were classified positively and 7 negatively, represents a combination of Narcissism, Compulsivity, and Affective Lability. Such individuals seek out other people (the Social Avoidance dimension is low), a tendency that is consistent with the need for adulation, attention seeking, and need for approval that defines narcissism. Of equal interest was that substantially similar patterns emerged in the normal sample.

This research is continuing in comparing normal and pathological groups in terms of their profile patterns, but it is clear from this preliminary analysis that, although patients show some greater degree of elevation of scales, both groups are equally describable in terms of dimensions typically thought of as describing personality pathology.

APPLICATIONS WITH INVENTORIES FOR NORMAL PERSONALITY

Despite the plausibility of the argument for personality disorders as the extremes of normal personality, there are generally few other relevant empirical data. We have some additional relevant data in the form of preliminary results from an ongoing study of these issues in individuals with diagnosed personality disorders. Two of the instruments used are the Personality Research Form (PRF; Jackson, 1984) and the Jackson Personality Inventory (JPI) (Jackson, 1976, 1978). The PRF was developed to measure constructs from Murray's (1938) system of needs. The JPI was designed to evaluate a variety of traits and attributes with important implications for an individual's functioning, derived from modern research in personality and social psychology. Both are conventional self-report inventories using the true-false response format. Figure 16.2 reports mean scores for a group of psychiatric inpatients with personality disorders on the PRF, while Figure 16.3 reports the means on the JPI for a different group of inpatients. The majority of the sample were from a tertiary care psychiatric hospital and the remainder from the psychiatric unit of an urban general hospital. Half the group completed the JPI and the other half completed the PRF, along with other measures not reported here. The mean age was 33 (SD = 9.5), and 44% were males. Note that the means of all scales are within the range of 40 to 60 T scores. This would be regarded as the normal level by virtually any clinician experienced with these tests. The point of consistency in both figures is the relative high mean score on the Infrequency scales. In both samples there were some individuals whose scores on this scale would suggest doubtful validity of the test as a whole. The low mean scores are generally consistent with what might be expected in a hospitalized group in whom coping mechanisms had broken down and whose subjective distress might be higher than would be seen if the scales had been completed in the community. Thus, on the PRF the three scales with means just over $40T$ were Change, Endurance, and Sentience, along with low overall Desirability. On the JPI, the lowest means were on Energy Level and Self-Esteem.

Of course, to report means is to obscure individual variation. By the nature and definition of personality disorders, individuals with one personality disorder might be predicted to have low scores on one trait, while those with a different disorder might be predicted to have high scores on the same trait. At the same time, it is not clear to what extent individuals with personality disorders are extreme

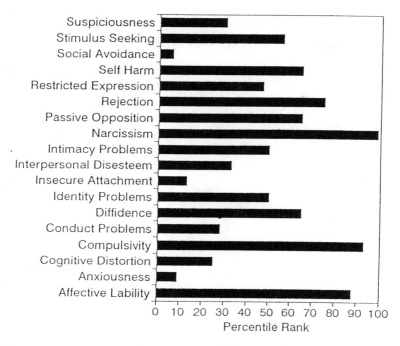

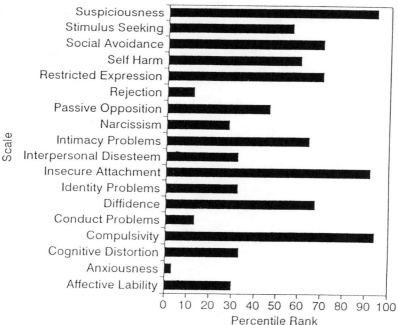

FIGURE 16.1. Modal profile for the positive pole of Type 5 (top figure) and the positive pole of Type 8 (bottom figure) using the Dimensional Assessment of Personality Pathology.

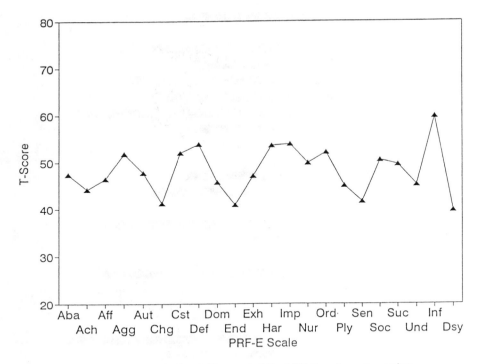

Note: Aba - Abasement; Ach - Achievement; Aff - Affiliation; Agg - Aggression;
Aut - Autonomy; Chg - Change; Cst - Cognitive Structure; Def - Defendence;
Dom - Dominance; End - Endurance; Exh - Exhibition; Har - Harm Avoidance;
Imp - Impulsivity; Nur - Nurturance; Ord - Order; Ply - Play; Sen - Sentience;
Soc - Social Recognition; Suc - Succorance; Und - Understanding; Inf - Infrequency;
Dsy - Social Desirability

FIGURE 16.2. *T*-scores for 25 cases of personality disorder on the Personality Research Form-E.

on normal personality traits, or even if all such individuals do have elevations on relevant traits. We present samples of profiles of two individuals from the study to demonstrate the point made earlier concerning aspects of Antisocial Personality Disorder that are not captured by the *DSM-III* definition.

Part A of Figure 16.4 provides the PRF-E profile of a 22-year-old man with the diagnosis of antisocial personality disorder. He had a history of street drug use, with an attempted suicide during one period of withdrawal. He also drank heavily and had several convictions for break-and-enter robberies and assaults. This profile is marked by both high and low points outside the average range. Endurance and Desirability provide the deepest low points, while Aggression and Defendence provide the peaks. Abasement, Achievement, and Understanding are

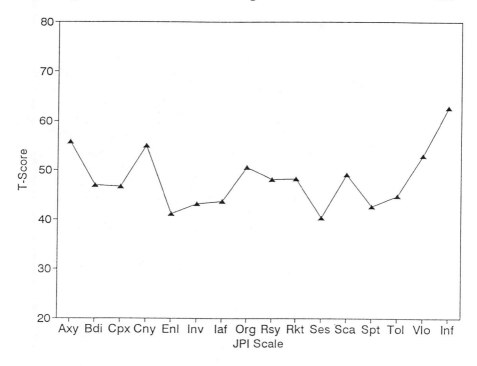

Note: Axy - Anxiety; Bdi - Breadth of Interest; Cpx - Complexity; Cny - Conformity;
Enl - Energy Level; Inv - Innovation; Iaf - Interpersonal Affect; Org - Organization;
Rsy - Responsibility; Rkt- Risk Taking; Ses - Self Esteem; Sca - Social Adroitness;
Spt - Social Participation; Vlo - Value Orthodoxy; Inf - Infrequency

FIGURE 16.3. *T*-scores for 26 cases of personality disorder on the Jackson Personality Inventory.

also low, while Impulsivity is elevated. This profile is marked by the expected anger and hostility, combined with a lack of perseverance and unpredictable, impulsive actions. This man's negative self-image is reflected in the low Desirability score.

Part B of Figure 16.4 illustrates the JPI profile of an unmarried 38-year-old man with a university education. He had a history of diagnosed antisocial personality disorder on previous hospital admissions, and his profile provides an interesting comparison with the first case. He too had a history of narcotic drug abuse and suicide attempts. His profile is marked by elevations on Anxiety and Risk Taking, together with low scores on Energy Level and Responsibility that might not be expected from the terms of the *DSM* framework. The profile is also marked by moderately low scores on Conformity, Interpersonal Affect, Self Esteem, and Social Participation.

CONCLUDING COMMENTS

The overall picture of these cases illustrates a greater degree of complexity then one might have anticipated on the basis of the apparently clear cut and relatively simple *DSM-III-R* criteria for the diagnosis of Antisocial Personality Disorder. Figure 16.4 also illustrates the different views of the same disorder that can be provided by different inventories. The choice of inventories is critical because of the importance of using traits that are relevant to the disorder (Clark, McEwen, Collard, & Hickok, 1993; Magaro & Smith, 1981). In dealing with abnormal personality, we are confronted with a level of differentiation and complexity that requires conceptual and measurement tools that are only beginning to be realized. But it is our firm conviction that if an understanding of personality pathology and a more refined, scientifically based diagnosis and classification of personality pathology is to be realized, then it is necessary to undertake the development of

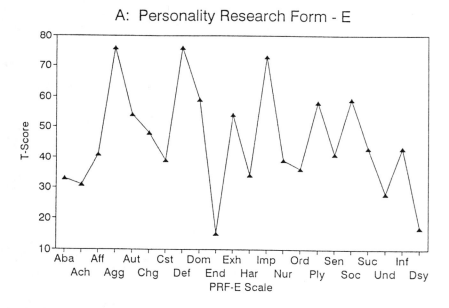

Note: Aba - Abasement; Ach - Achievement; Aff - Affiliation; Agg -Aggression; Aut - Autonomy; Chg - Change; Cst - Cognitive Structure; Def -Defendence; Dom - Dominance; End - Endurance; Exh -Exhibition; Har - Harm Avoidance; Imp - Impulsivity; Nur - Nurturance; Ord - Order; Ply - Play; Sen - Sentience; Soc - Social Recognition; Suc - Succorance; Und - Understanding; Inf - Infrequency; Dsy - Social Desirability

FIGURE 16.4. (A) Personality Research Form, and (B) Jackson Personality Inventory *T*-scores for two cases of Antisocial Personality Disorder.

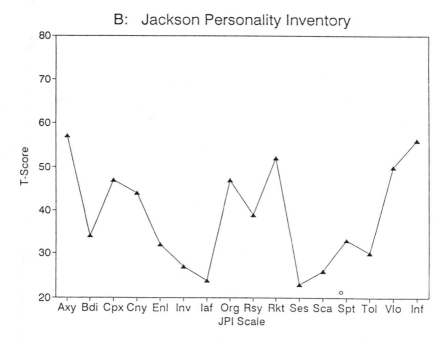

Note: Axy - Anxiety; Bdi - Breadth of Interest; Cpx - Complexity;
Cny - Conformity; Enl - Energy Level; Inv - Innovation; Iaf - Interpersonal
Affect; Org - Organization; Rsy - Responsibility; Rkt- Risk Taking;
Ses - Self Esteem; Sca - Social Adroitness; Spt - Social Participation;
Vlo - Value Orthodoxy; Inf - Infrequency

FIGURE 16.4. (Continued)

theories and of methods for the study of psychopathology that are equal to the challenge.

In doing so, it is also important in this venture to understand and delineate manifestations of personality pathology that fall in the normal range and those that might be identifiable as diagnostically significant or pathological. This might best be done through integrating abnormal personality into theories of personality development. Millon (1991b) provides a possible route. It is interesting to note that recently attempts have been made to evaluate the fit of *DSM* personality disorders into two modern theoretical frameworks: the interpersonal circle and the Big 5 traits. The fit was notably better for the Big 5 model (Soldz, Budman, Demby, & Merry, 1993). Other similar efforts are made in other chapters of this volume.

We feel this perspective on the use of construct based inventories shows benefits in the clear delineation of personality characteristics in individuals with obvious pathology in interpersonal functioning. Evidence is accumulating as to the relevant dimensions that characterize traditional diagnostic classifications. The issue of dimensional versus categorical models in personality is not settled, largely because relevant methods, such as maximum covariance analysis (Meehl, 1973), have not been rigorously applied. Nor has there been sufficient research directed towards the issues involved in the clinical decision process of diagnosing an individual as abnormal or pathological. Many interesting and important issues to be addressed in the future should increase our understanding of both abnormal and normal personality.

REFERENCES

American Psychiatric Association, (1987). *Diagnostic and statistical manual of mental disorders (3rd ed., rev.)*. Washington, DC: Author.

Blackburn, R. (1988). On moral judgements and personality disorders: The myth of psychopathic personality revisited. *British Journal of Psychiatry, 153*, 505–512.

Brown, T. (1991). Psychiatry's unholy marriage: Psychoanalysis and neuroscience. In: D. Offer & M. Sabshin (Eds.) *The diversity of normal behavior: Further contributions to normatology* (pp.305–355). New York: Basic Books.

Chrisjohn, R. D., Jackson, D. N., & Lanigan, C. B. (1984). *The stability of the factor structure of the Basic Personality Inventory*. Presented at the 45th annual meeting of the Canadian Psychological Association, Ottawa.

Clark, L. A. (1990). Toward a consensual set of symptom clusters for assessment of personality disorder. In J. N. Butcher & C. D. Spielberger (Eds.). *Advances in personality assessment* (8th ed.) (pp. 243–266). Hillsdale NJ: Lawrence Erlbaum Associates.

Clark, L. A., McEwen, J. L., Collard, L. M., & Hickok, L. G. (1993). Symptoms and traits of personality disorder: Two new methods for their assessment. *Psychological Assessment: A Journal of Consulting and Clinical Psychology, 5*, 81–91.

Cleckley, H. (1976). *The mask of sanity* 5th ed. St. Louis, MO: Mosby.

Eysenck, H. J. (1987). The definition of personality disorders and the criteria appropriate to their definition. *Journal of Personality Disorders, 1*, 211–219.

Frances, A. J. (1980). The DSM-III personality disorders section: A commentary. *American Journal of Psychiatry, 137*, 1050–1054.

Frances, A. J., Widiger, T. A., & Sabshin, M. (1991). Psychiatric diagnosis and normality. In: D. Offer & M. Sabshin (Eds.) *The diversity of normal behavior: Further contributions to normatology* (pp. 3–38). New York: Basic Books.

Gangstead, S., & Snyder, M. (1985). "To carve nature at its joints": On the existence of discrete classes in personality. *Psychological Review, 92*, 317–350.

Harman, H. F. (1976). *Modern factor analysis*. Chicago: University of Chicago Press.

Hathaway, S. R., & McKinley, J. C. (1967). *Minnesota Multiphasic Personality Inventory manual* (rev. ed). New York: Psychological Corp.

Helmes, E. (1989). Evaluating the internal structure of the Eysenck Personality Questionnaire: Objective criteria. *Multivariate Behavioral Research, 24*, 353–364.

Helmes, E., & Reddon, J. R. (1993). A perspective on developments in assessing psychopathology: A critical review of the MMPI and MMPI 2. *Psychological Bulletin, 113*, 453–471.

Holden, R. R., Reddon, J. R., Jackson, D. N., & Helmes, E. (1983). The construct heuristic applied to the measurement of psychopathology. *Multivariate Behavioral Research, 18*, 37–46.

Jackson, D. N. (1970). A sequential system for personality scale development. In C. D. Spielberger (Ed.) *Current topics in clinical and community psychology* (Vol. 2). (pp. 61–96).New York: Academic Press.

Jackson, D. N. (1971). The dynamics of structured personality tests: 1971. *Psychological Review, 78,* 229–248.

Jackson, D. N. (1976). *Jackson Personality Inventory manual.* Port Huron, MI: Research Psychologists Press.

Jackson, D. N. (1978). Interpreter's guide to the Jackson Personality Inventory. In P. McReynolds (Ed.) *Advances in psychological assessment* (Vol. 4). San Francisco: Jossey-Bass.

Jackson, D. N. (1984). *Personality Research Form manual* (3rd ed.) Port Huron, MI: Research Psychologists Press.

Jackson, D. N. (1989). *Basic Personality Inventory manual.* Port Huron, MI: Sigma Assessment Systems.

Jackson, D. N., & Messick, S. (1986). *The Differential Personality Inventory.* London, Ont.: Authors.

Jackson, D. N., & Skinner, H. A. (1975). Univocal varimax: An orthogonal factor rotation program for optimal simple structure. *Educational and Psychological Measurement, 35,* 663–665.

Jackson, D. N., & Williams, D. R. (1975). Occupational classification in terms of interest patterns. *Journal of Vocational Behavior, 6,* 269–280.

Kendell, R. E. (1975). *The role of diagnosis in psychiatry.* Oxford: Blackwell.

Livesley, W.J. (1986). Trait and behavioral prototypes of personality disorder. *American Journal of Psychiatry, 143,* 728–732.

Livesley, W. J. (1987). A systematic approach to the delineation of personality disorders. *American Journal of Psychiatry, 144,* 772–777.

Livesley, W. J., & Jackson, D. N. (1991). Construct validity and classification of personality disorders. In: J. M. Oldham (Ed.) *Personality disorders: New perspectives on diagnostic validity* (pp. 3–22). Washington,D.C.: American Psychiatric Press.

Livesley, W. J., & Jackson, D. N. (1992). Guidelines for developing, evaluating, and revising the classification of personality disorders. *Journal of Nervous and Mental Disease, 180,* 609–618.

Livesley, W. J., & Jackson, D. N. (in press). *Dimensional Assessment of Personality Pathology manual.* Port Huron, MI: Sigma Assessment Systems.

Livesley, W. J., Jackson, D. N., & Schroeder, M. L. (1992). Factorial structure of traits delineating personality disorders in clinical and general population samples. *Journal of Abnormal Psychology, 101,* 432–440.

MacLean, M., Helmes, E., & Chrisjohn, R. D. (1989). *A latent trait analysis of the Basic Personality Inventory in hospitalized and non hospitalized respondents.* Presented at the 50th annual meeting of the Canadian Psychological Association, Halifax.

Magaro, P. A., & Smith, P. (1981). The personality of clinical types: An empirically derived taxonomy. *Journal of Clinical Psychology, 37,* 796–809.

Meehl, P. E. (1973). MAXCOV HITMAX: A taxonomic search method for loose genetic syndromes. In: P. E. Meehl (Ed.) *Psychodiagnosis: Selected papers* (pp. 200–224). New York: W. W. Norton.

Meehl, P. E. (1990). Toward an integrated theory of schizotaxia, schizotypy, and schizophrenia. *Journal of Personality Disorders, 4,* 1–99.

Meehl, P. E., & Golden, R. R. (1982). Taxometric methods. In: J. M. Butcher & P. C. Kendall (Eds.) *The handbook of research methods in clinical psychology* (pp. 27–181). New York: John Wiley & Sons.

Millon, T. (1991a). Classification in psychopathology: Rationale, alternatives, and standards. *Journal of Abnormal Psychology, 100,* 245–261.

Millon, T. (1991b). Normality: What may we learn from evolutionary theory? In D. Offer & M. Sabshin (Eds.) *The diversity of normal behavior: Further contributions to normatology* (pp. 356–404). New York: Basic Books.

Morey, L C. (1991). Classification of mental disorder as a collection of hypothetical constructs. *Journal of Abnormal Psychology, 100,* 289–293.

Murray, H. A. (1938). *Explorations in personality.* New York: Oxford University Press.

Offer, D., & Sabshin, M. (1991). *The diversity of normal behavior: Further contributions to normatology.* Chicago: Basic Books.

Reddon, J. R., Jackson, D. N., Reed, P. L., & Gill, D. S. (1982). *Rural urban personality and adjustment.* Presented at the 43rd annual meeting of the Canadian Psychological Association, Montréal.

Rutter, M. (1987). Temperament, personality and personality disorder. *British Journal of Psychiatry, 150,* 443–458.

Schönnemann, P. H. (1966). A generalized solution of the orthogonal procrustes problem. *Psychometrika, 31,* 1–10.

Skinner, H. A. (1977). "The eyes that fix you": A model for classification research. *Canadian Psychological Review, 18,* 142–151.

Skinner, H. A. (1978). Differentiating the contribution of elevation, scatter and shape in profile similarity. *Educational and Psychological Measurement, 38,* 297–308.

Skinner, H.A., & Jackson, D. N. (1978). A model of psychopathology based on an integration of MMPI actuarial systems. *Journal of Consulting and Clinical Psychology, 46,* 231–238.

Soldz, S., Budman, S., Demby, A., & Merry, J. (1993). Representation of personality disorders in circumplex and five factor space: Explorations with a clinical sample. *Psychological Assessment: A Journal of Consulting and Clinical Psychology, 5,* 41–52.

Widiger, T. A., & Kelso, K. (1983). Psychodiagnosis of Axis II. *Clinical Psychology Review, 3,* 491–510.

17

The MMPI and MMPI-2: Fifty Years of Differentiating Normal and Abnormal Personality

Yossef S. Ben-Porath

The Minnesota Multiphasic Personality Inventory (MMPI) (Hathaway and Mckinley, 1943) has for several decades been the most widely studied and applied instrument in differentiating normal and abnormal personality. There are many reasons why the MMPI, and now its updated version the MMPI-2 (Butcher, Dahlstrom, Graham, Tellegen, & Kaemmer, 1989), have maintained this status. The longevity of the test is particularly striking given the skepticism and ambivalence that have characterized its perception among many personality researchers and repeated attempts to introduce psychometrically superior instruments designed to replace the MMPI. This chapter will discuss the theoretical background of the MMPI and MMPI-2, review the emergence of this instrument as a leading clinical tool in differentiating normal and abnormal personality, discuss the present status of the MMPI-2, and provide an outlook and recommendations for future directions in MMPI-2 research.

THE PSYCHOMETRIC PERSPECTIVE OF THE MMPI/MMPI-2

Developers of personality inventories have pursued their efforts from two broad, non–mutually-exclusive perspectives. One approach, which will be termed *the clinical perspective* in this chapter, is designed to produce clinically-useful instruments that help detect the presence of symptoms and syndromes of psychopathology. Test developers who follow this approach typically are clinical psychologists who conduct applied research. The MMPI is a leading example of instruments developed from the clinical perspective.

Test developers working from the *normal personality perspective*, however, seek to develop measures that may serve as tools in basic personality research and the assessment of normal personality characteristics. These tools are to be used to further our understanding of the development and function of personality traits. Tellegen's *Multidimensional Personality Questionnaire* is a prime example of a measure that evolved as part of a basic personality research program (Tellegen & Waller, in press).

As just noted, the two perspectives are not mutually exclusive. Tests developed from the clinical perspective have been found to be quite useful in the measurement and characterization of normal personality traits and characteristics. However, basic personality researchers have tended to refrain from using them in their investigations. Conversely, measures developed from the normal perspective provide descriptive information that may be quite useful to the clinician; however, practitioners do not routinely incorporate these tests in their assessment batteries.

An elaborate analysis of the reasons for the schism between normal and clinical perspectives on personality exceeds the scope of this chapter. However, one particular aspect of this divide, discrepancies between typological and dimensional approaches to personality, is central to the evolution of the MMPI. Historically, the Kraepelinian perspective on psychopathology has led to a typological view of abnormal personality. This approach continues to dominate current medical-model based diagnostic practices in which clinicians categorize individuals into distinct classes of disorder. The MMPI was developed initially to aid in the assignment of individuals to specific diagnostic categories. The empirical-keying method used to develop the eight original clinical scales of the MMPI assumed the existence of distinct classes of psychopathology.

Normal personality research has for the most part progressed from a dimensional perspective that grew out of differential psychology. The normal perspective views personality traits as dimensional constructs that are useful in the description of meaningful individual differences. This view allows for the characterization of quantitative differences between individuals, whereas the strict typological perspective allows only for the qualitative classification of individuals into distinct groups. Although current psychodiagnostic practice continues to be dominated by the Kraepelinian typological perspective, psychologists conducting clinical evaluations are well aware of the limitations of a strict categorical perspective. This awareness has played a vital role in the evolution of the MMPI from a strict typological instrument to a test that provides a wealth of information regarding the individual's standing along a variety of personality trait dimensions. The following sections explore the emergence and subsequent evolution of the MMPI.

THEORETICAL UNDERPINNINGS AND CONSTRUCTION OF THE MMPI

As chronicled by Dahlstrom (1992a) the MMPI was published during a period of increasing skepticism regarding the utility of self-report personality inventories (c.f., Landis & Katz, 1934; Landis Zubin, & Katz, 1935). The two major inventories of that time, the Bernreuter Psychoneurotic Inventory (Bernreuter, 1933) and the Humm-Wadsworth Temperament Scales (Humm & Wadsworth, 1935) were viewed as overly transparent, and, as a result, subject to manipulative distortion. They also were considered too narrow in scope to serve as omnibus measures of abnormal personality functioning. Thus, Hathaway and McKinley (1940) sought to "create a large reservoir of items from which various scales might be constructed in the hope of *evolving* a greater variety of valid personality descriptions than are available at the present time" (p. 249; italics added).

It is noteworthy that as early as 1940 Hathaway and McKinley viewed their initial efforts at scale development as a starting point in what they hoped would be the evolving nature of the test. In fact, a primary reason for the longevity of the MMPI has been the fruitfulness of its item pool and the continued research efforts that are among the important hallmarks of this test. Following are discussions of the theoretical underpinnings of the MMPI and a chronology of its evolution and emergence as the primary self-report measure of abnormal personality.

Theoretical Underpinnings

Although the method of scale development employed by Hathaway and McKinley was clearly empirical, it is a mistake to view the development of the MMPI as atheoretical. In constructing the MMPI, Hathaway and McKinley relied on a model of psychopathology and were influenced by behavioral and psychodynamic thinking and the psychometric knowledge of their time.

The MMPI was constructed in a medical setting, to be used as a screening instrument for the detection of psychopathology. In compiling the test items and constructing the scales Hathaway and McKinley were influenced strongly by psychiatric thinking and practices of the 1930s. In their words:

> The individual items were formulated partly on the basis of previous clinical experience. Mainly, however, the items were supplied from several psychiatric examination direction forms, from various textbooks of psychiatry, from certain of the directions for case taking in medicine and neurology, and from the earlier published scales of personal and social attitudes. (Hathaway & McKinley, 1940, p. 249)

Thus, in selecting items for the MMPI, Hathaway and McKinley followed the diagnostic classification system of the 1930s which was a derivative of the descriptive nosology developed by Kraepelin. In that respect, the MMPI was conceived originally in a manner that is quite consistent with current diagnostic practices of descriptive categorical classification.

Whereas Kraepelinian nosology supplied the model for the initial compilation of items and designation of scales, an interesting combination of behavioral, psychodynamic, and psychometric thinking can be found in early theoretical writings on the MMPI. All three elements can be found in Meehl's (1945) classic article, *The Dynamics of "Structured" Personality Tests*. Meehl (1945) wrote this article in response to a critique of self-report personality inventories that faulted them for relying on the assumption that test items must always have the same meaning to different individuals. While agreeing with the fallacy of this assumption, Meehl (1945) asserted that it was unnecessary for tests such as the MMPI. He stated:

> a "self-rating" constitutes an intrinsically interesting and significant bit of verbal behavior, the non-test correlates of which must be discovered by empirical means. Not only is this approach free from the restriction that the subject must be able to describe his own behavior accurately, but a careful study of structured personality tests built on this basis shows that such a restriction would falsify the actual relationships that hold between what a man says and what he *is*. (Meehl, 1945, p. 297)

Thus, according to Meehl (1945), the literal content of the stimulus (the item) is entirely unimportant, and even irrelevant and potentially misleading. Sophisticated psychometric use of test items dictates that the test interpreter ignore item content altogether lest he or she be misled. The empirical correlates of scales composed of responses to the item stimuli must be the sole source of test interpretation. Moreover, Meehl (1945) provided examples of MMPI items are scored in counter-intuitive or nonintuitive directions, thus laying the foundation for the psychodynamically-based assumptions of subtle measurement. In Meehl's words:

> The complex defense mechanisms of projection, rationalization, reaction formation, etc., appear dynamically to the interviewer as soon as he begins to take what the client *says* as itself motivated by other needs than those of giving an accurate verbal report. There is no good a-priori reason for denying the possibility of similar processes in the highly structured 'interview' which is the question-answer personality test. (Meehl, 1945, p. 298)

Although he provided a theoretical rationale for ignoring item content in test interpretation, Meehl (1945) was well aware that those who take the MMPI are attuned to the meaning of test items and may, for a variety of motivations, choose to distort their self-presentation through their responses. He recognized that item subtlety could only go so far in preventing such distortions and that other means must also be employed to counter this possibility. The MMPI validity scales *L* and *F* and the later addition of *K* (Meehl & Hathaway, 1946) provided additional psychometric means for detecting and correcting the effects of distortion.

In sum, the theoretical underpinnings of the MMPI included:

1. Initial selection of items and designation of scales based on the then-contemporary Kraepelinian descriptive nosology as a model of psycho-pathology.
2. Treatment of test items as stimuli for behavioral responses that may have certain empirical correlates including diagnostic group membership.
3. Rejection of content-based test interpretation as overly susceptible to the influences of overt (intentional) and covert (unconscious) distortion.

Scale Construction and Initial Use of the MMPI in Differentiating Normal and Abnormal Personality

Based on the theoretical foundations just outlined, the MMPI clinical scales were constructed by a method of empirical keying that involved the use of contrasted groups of differentially-diagnosed patients and non-patients. Statistical analyses were conducted to identify responses to test items that were correlated with diagnostic group membership. Essentially, items were selected based on their ability to differentiate grossly between normal and abnormal personality and discriminate more narrowly between various types of abnormal personality constellations corresponding to the Kraepelinian model of psychopathology. Hathaway and McKinley described the development of several of the original clinical scales of the MMPI in a series of articles (Hathaway & McKinley, 1940, 1942; McKinley & Hathaway, 1940, 1942, 1944).

The clinical scales were to be used by comparing the test-taker's responses to the items with those of a normative sample of individuals who were believed to be free of any major psychopathology and representative of the population of potential test takers. This sample was a subset of the normals used in constructing the scales. It was composed primarily of visitors to the University of Minnesota Hospital who volunteered to answer the test items. This group came to be known as the *Minnesota Normals*, most of whom were rural Minnesotans with an average of eight years of education and who were employed primarily as skilled and semi-skilled laborers and farmers.

Raw scores on a clinical scale were calculated by summing the number of items an individual answered in the same direction (True or False) as those who had a certain form of psychopathology (e.g., hypochondriasis). These were then converted to standardized T-scores with a mean of 50 and a standard deviation of 10.

The empirical method of scale construction employed by Hathaway and McKinley imposed an initially-limited ability to interpret standardized scale scores. Absent (as yet) any external correlates, T-scores could only be used to characterize the extent to which an individual responded to the test items in a manner similar to those who served as the criterion group for that scale. Thus, the higher the T-score on hypochondriasis, the more similar were the responses of the individual to those of known hypochondriacs and, by inference, the more likely was that individual to have hypochondriasis.

In spite of the care and ingenuity that characterized the work of Hathaway and McKinley, for various reasons the MMPI never worked as its authors had intended. Attempts to replicate the validity of the clinical scales as predictors of diagnostic group membership were only marginally successful for some scales, and primarily unsuccessful for others (Hathaway, 1960). However, rather than fade away as had many of its predecessors, the MMPI underwent a remarkable transformation. As quoted earlier in this chapter, Hathaway and McKinley (1940) viewed the initial development of the MMPI as a starting, not an end point. Led by Paul Meehl, Hathaway's students and followers reinvented the MMPI by directing its use away from the narrow task of differential diagnosis to a considerably broader application. Hathaway (1960) described this process as follows:

> The MMPI began with validity based upon the usefulness of the various diagnostic groups from which its scales were derived. Now the burden of its use rests upon construct validity. Only a small fraction of the published data relating clinical or experimental variables to its scales or profiles can be understood in terms of the original approach. If the validity views of 1941 were the only support for the inventory, it could not survive. What is happening is that the correlations observed with other variables in normal and abnormal subjects are filling out personality constructs that emerge, to be in turn tested for their ability to survive. It is significant that constructs, in the general sense of construct validity, can be the forerunners of diagnostic classes. (Hathaway, 1960, p. viii)

The MMPI's evolution into an omnibus measure of personality is described next.

EVOLUTION OF THE MMPI

Although no doubt disappointed by the test's failure to fulfill its original goal, early users of the MMPI observed consistency in the patterns of MMPI scale scores of individuals who shared certain personality characteristics. As a result, researchers began to shift their focus from the validity of individual scales, to the identification of replicable empirical correlates of patterns of scale scores. Authors began to use the term *profile* to refer to the complete set of scores on the eight clinical scales and *profile types* to identify certain patterns or combinations of scores. Gough (1946), Meehl (1946), and Schmidt (1945) published a series of articles on the utility of certain profile types in the task of differential diagnosis. Hathaway (1947) and then Welsh (1948) developed coding systems that provided convenient shorthand summaries of the pattern of scores on the profile. This led eventually to adoption of the term *code type* to designate certain classes of profiles. Most early code types were based on the highest one or two scales on the profile.

As investigators were studying the diagnostic accuracy of profile types they began to expand their studies to identify nondiagnostic correlates of MMPI profile types. Hathaway and Meehl (1951) developed an adjective checklist that was modified by Black (1953) in his study of the empirical correlates of MMPI code types. Examples of adjectives that appeared on Black's (1953) list include honest, orderly, conscientious, worrying, neurotic, cheerful, alert, seclusive, generous, foolish, incoherent, argumentative, peaceable, curious, and versatile.[1]

Within a decade of its initial publication, the nature of the MMPI had changed dramatically. The Kraepelinian nosological model was dropped in favor of a considerably broader and more ambitious goal of describing normal and abnormal personality characteristics, and code types, rather than individual scales, were viewed as the test's primary source of information. Reflecting this change, the original scale names that corresponded to the Kraepelinian nosological system were modified by using either abbreviations (e.g., *Hs* for Hypochondriasis) or digits (e.g., *Scale 1* for Hypochondriasis).

The empirical literature on the test was expanding at an exponential rate. By the time Welsh and Dahlstrom (1956) published their compendium of basic readings on the MMPI they were able to list 689 references. With such profound changes came a need to rethink the theoretical basis of the MMPI.

Revised Theoretical Foundations of the MMPI

As described earlier, the initial theoretical foundations of the MMPI were spelled out by Meehl (1945) and included elements of Kraepelinian nosology and behavioral, psychodynamic, and psychometric theory. With the move away from the initial intent of the MMPI, came a reframing of its theoretical base characterized by a sharpening of the focus on the empirical correlates of the test and a corresponding shift away from nosology and personality theory.

In 1954, Meehl published his seminal monograph on clinical versus statistical prediction. He presented a series of theoretical and empirical analyses leading to a call for clinical psychologists to use statistical or actuarial methods in predicting behavior. The thrust of his argument was that by using psychological test data and other sources of information to classify individuals into meaningful groups, we may then "enter a statistical or actuarial table which gives the statistical frequencies of behaviors or various sorts of persons belonging to the class" (Meehl, 1954, p. 3).

In effect, Meehl (1954) advocated that clinicians pursue a three-pronged task: First, they must identify meaningful classes within which individuals tend to cluster; second, they must develop reliable and valid ways of identifying to which class a given individual belongs; and finally clinicians were to identify statistical or actuarial correlates of belonging to different classes. This task would entail a fair amount of "bootstrapping" as we would learn to infer more about class membership than what we used initially to allow us to classify individuals into a given class. Eventually, by using actuarial tables clinicians would be able to predict a variety of behaviors and personality characteristics on the basis of knowing the individual's class membership. Moreover, the clinician would be able to attach a probability level to actuarial predictions.

Subsequently, in his presidential address to the Midwestern Psychological Association, Meehl (1956) described how such a method could be developed for the MMPI. In issuing his now famous call for an "MMPI Cookbook", Meehl (1956) described the cookbook method as one in which "any given configuration (holists please note—I said configuration, not sum!) of psychometric data is associated with each facet (or configuration) of personality description, and the closeness of this association is explicitly indicated by a number" (p. 121). Meehl (1956) did not provide a detailed prescription on how to develop a complete set of MMPI types but did note that the number of useful MMPI types is limited by the number of infallible criteria we wish to predict leading to a need to group different profiles into coarser types.

Meehl had now provided MMPI researchers with a theoretical rationale for developing actuarial methods of test interpretation and challenged them to do so. Instead of relying on now-antiquated Kraepelinian nosology, MMPI researchers were to identify a new, clinically-useful set of MMPI-based classes. After the development of an actuarial classification system, test interpretation would involve a simple clerical task of using the scores to reveal the individual's class and looking up the empirical correlates of class membership in actuarial tables. Investigators responded with a variety of efforts at developing such systems and demonstrating their validity and clinical utility.

The Codebook Approach to MMPI Interpretation

As reviewed in the preceding section, precursors to the codebook method of MMPI interpretation can be found in early research efforts such as those reported by Hathaway and Meehl (1951) Guthrie (1952), and Black (1953). In these early investigations profiles were classified based simply on the highest one or two scales in the Welsh code. Halbower (1955) took this approach a step further by beginning to introduce a more stringent set of criteria for code-type classification. Thus, for example, to be classified as a 13/31 code-type, a profile had to meet five criteria:

1. Scales 1 and 3 ≥ 70.
2. Scale 2 < Scales 1 and 3 by at least 10 T-score points.
3. Scales K or L > Scales ? (a T-score based on the number of item omissions) and F.
4. Scale F ≤ 65.
5. Scales 4, 5, 6, 7, 8, 9, 0 ≤ 70.

The advantage of following such a stringent set of criteria was the assurance of a relatively homogeneous set of individuals who would be classified as 13/31 code-types. Such homogeneity would minimize the error in prediction of the personality characteristics of the code type.

Halbower (1955) did not set out to develop an exhaustive set of code types. Drake & Oetting (1959), however, published a detailed codebook for counselors at college counseling centers which was based on the identification of empirical correlates of a large number of code types. These authors compiled the MMPI profiles of 2,634 college men and 1,564 college women who had been seen for counseling and whose records were culled for clinically-relevant personality descriptions that would serve as potential correlates for the various code types. In contrast to Halbower (1955), Drake and Oetting (1959) used a very relaxed method of code-type classification yielding a very large number of code types. This, coupled with the large number of potential descriptors, the large sample sizes involved, and the absence of correction for family-wise error in tests of statistical significance, resulted in a codebook containing many nondistinct code types with spurious lists of correlates.

A very different approach was taken by Marks and Seeman (1963) in their development of a codebook for MMPI interpretation. They investigated the empirical correlates of 16 code types that occurred frequently enough in their setting to allow for a minimum of 20 subjects in each code type. Rules for code type classification were quite stringent and detailed, even more so than those outlined by Halbower (1955). Therapists who were familiar with the subjects in this study but had not been exposed to their MMPI profiles provided Q sorts of 108 descriptive statements that served as the primary source of personality correlate data. Case history and additional psychometric data also were used in the identification of empirical correlates.

The stringency with which Marks and Seeman (1963) defined each of their code types ensured that there would be relatively little overlap in their correlates. However, there was a clear cost associated with this benefit. In contrast to Marks and Seeman's (1963) initial report that nearly 80% of the patients at their facility could be classified into one of the 16 code types, subsequent researchers found that as many as 80% of patients in other facilities *could not* be so classified (Briggs, Taylor, & Tellegen, 1966). Thus, stringent code-type definitions produced discrete, however nonexhaustive profile classes that had empirically replicable correlates.

Subsequent attempts to identify and study stringently-defined code types proved equally problematic. In response, researchers began to relax their code-type definitional criteria to allow for broader applicability of their systems. This, however reintroduced the problem of nondiscrete code types that had many overlapping correlates. Further discussion of this issue is offered by Tellegen and Ben-Porath (1993).

Another difficulty introduced by loosely-defined code types is that they are highly unstable. For example, the system developed by Gynther, Altman, and

Sletten (1973) was intended to be nearly exhaustive. A profile was classified based on the highest two scales on the profile regardless of how distant these two scales were from the remaining scales on the profile. Thus, in a hypothetical case in which an individual scores 70 on scales 1 and 2, and 69 on the remaining scales on the profile, should the MMPI be re-administered a change of one or two T-score points would be sufficient to move that individual into an entirely different code type.

Such instability is in fact found when this method of classification is employed. Graham, Smith, and Schwartz (1986) found that only 28% of psychiatric inpatients who were retested with the MMPI within an average of 80 days produced the same two-point code. Ben-Porath and Butcher (1989b) found approximately 40% agreement in the two-point codes of college students who completed the MMPI twice within one week.

A final question regarding the code-type approach to MMPI interpretation is the question of whether configural scale interpretation, implicit in profile coding, actually adds to the validity of MMPI interpretation. The most thoroughly documented answer (albeit limited in scope) to this question was provided by Goldberg (1965), who demonstrated that a linear combination of individual MMPI scale scores was more effective than the configural set of classification rules developed by Meehl and Dahlstrom (1960) to differentiate neurotics from psychotics with the MMPI.

In sum, the codebook method has received considerable research attention. Studies cited in this section have identified a broad range of normal and abnormal personality descriptors that are associated with adequately-defined code types. However, recent trends toward the relaxation of classification rules and the absence of empirical evidence that a code type is greater than the sum of its parts leave room for further research on code-type based profile interpretation. Suggestions for such research will be outlined in the final section of this chapter.

Other Developments in Empirical Assessment with the MMPI

The codebook approach just described, represented the primary approach to MMPI interpretation and continues to dominate MMPI-2 interpretation to date. However, soon after the initial publication of the inventory, researchers began harvesting additional scales from the MMPI item pool. These efforts can be viewed as a fulfillment of Hathaway's initial (Hathaway & McKinley, 1940) and continued (e.g., Hathaway, 1960, 1972) calls for improvements and refinements in the MMPI. In their initial collection of basic readings on the MMPI, Welsh and Dahlstrom (1956) reprinted articles describing eight new scales designed to supplement the original clinical scales. These included measurers of socioeconomic status (Gough, 1948), anti-semitism (Gough, 1951), dominance (Gough, McClosky, & Meehl, 1951), caudality (Williams, 1952), ego-strength (Barron, 1953), and control (Cuadra, 1953). An original chapter by Welsh (1956) describing his development of the factor-based scales *A* and *R* also was included, as was a reprinted article by Wiener (1948) describing his development of subtle and obvious keys for the MMPI.

These initial efforts at developing supplementary scales for the MMPI represented a variety of approaches to scale construction and conceptualization. Most followed in the footsteps of Hathaway and McKinley by using the contrasted-groups empirical-keying method to select items for their scales (e.g., Cuadra, 1953; Gough, 1948, 1951; Gough, McClosky, & Meehl, 1951; and Williams, 1952). In all these studies, the investigators identified two or more criterion groups and selected items based on their psychometric ability to differentiate between the groups.

This early work was followed by a near-avalanche of similar studies designed to construct empirically keyed scales for the MMPI. By 1975, Volume II of the *MMPI Handbook* (Dahlstrom, Welsh, & Dahlstrom, 1975) listed almost as many supplementary scales (455) as there were test items. With continued efforts, the number of supplementary scales eventually exceeded the number of test items. In contrast to the 10 clinical and three validity scales that were scored from only 383 of the 550 MMPI items, the supplementary scales made full use of the entire item pool. Most, however, remained highly obscure, and were used rarely in clinical practice.

The new empirically keyed scales, although introducing a near-endless number of personality traits and constructs for measurement with the MMPI, did not necessarily represent psychometric innovation or even advance. They were based on the same premises and theoretical formulations as were described earlier for the original clinical scales. There was, however, innovation to be found in some of the other scales and research efforts compiled by Welsh and Dahlstrom (1956). These were to lay the foundations for a new, innovative, and complementary approach to personality assessment with the MMPI—content-based interpretation.

Content-Based Personality Assessment with the MMPI

The content-based approach to MMPI interpretation has evolved considerably since the initial publication of the test. It began with attempts to control for the obvious nature of some of the MMPI items and continued with the identification of two major content dimensions of the MMPI, the development of content-based subscales to aid in the interpretation of the heterogeneous clinical scales and the compilation of lists of critical items, and it culminated in a set of content scales developed by Wiggins (1966). Following is a description of the origins of the content-based approach to MMPI interpretation and a discussion of the research foundations of various content-based strategies.

Origins of the Content-Based Approach

The content-based approach in some respects stands in contradiction to the original designation of the MMPI as a purely empirical instrument. It appears to have evolved more out of necessity than intent. Its origins may be found in early MMPI theoretical writings and scale-development efforts. As reviewed under the heading *Theoretical Underpinnings of the MMPI*, Meehl (1945) argued that the literal content of the item stimulus was irrelevant to test interpretation which should be based solely on the empirical correlates of the response. However, toward the end of his article Meehl (1945) noted:

> While it is true of many of the MMPI items, for example, that even a psychologist cannot predict on which scale they will appear or in what direction different sorts of abnormals will tend to answer them, still the relative acceptability of defensive answering would seem to be greater than is possible in responding to a set of inkblots. (p. 302)

In a later article Meehl and Hathaway (1946) commented further on this issue:

> One of the important failings of almost all structured personality tests is their susceptibility to "faking" or "lying" in one way or another, as well as their even greater susceptibility to unconscious self-deception and role-playing on the part of individuals who might consciously be quite honest and sincere in their responses. (p. 525)

The issue which was of considerable concern to the developers of the MMPI, was that it is possible for an individual completing a highly valid (criterion, construct, and otherwise) measure of personality, to produce an absolutely or relatively invalid test protocol. In other words, test validity is necessary, but not sufficient to guarantee the validity of individual test protocols, which may be tainted by any number of distorting strategies employed by the test-taker. Although in their initial empirical construction of the scales, Hathaway and McKinley ignored the content of the test items, they could not assume that individuals taking the test would do the same. In fact, they assumed, of course, that individual differences in the approach people take to responding to the test items, would be a function of both external circumstances (i.e., evaluation for need or eligibility for medical benefits) and internal states (e.g., the operation of unconscious defense mechanisms).

Meehl and Hathaway (1946) described the two initial validity scales *L* and *F* as relatively good indicators of conscious distortion. The *L* scale was made up of 15 items selected rationally (i.e., by examining their content) based on the honesty research of Hartshorne and May. It was keyed so that an elevated score would represent a conscious effort on the part of the individual to present her or himself in an overly positive manner. It was assumed that people who approach the entire test this way would be detected based on their score on *L*. Meehl and Hathaway (1946) reported the results of one of the very first simulation studies in which *L* proved successful at detecting individuals who were instructed to present an overly-favorable picture. The *F* scale, although not intended initially for this purpose, also proved capable of detecting intentional distortion. Meehl and Hathaway (1946) reported that it was successful at detecting subjects who were instructed to "fake bad".

Meehl and Hathaway (1946) were thus satisfied that scales L and F would be capable of alerting the test-interpreter that conscious distortion has occurred and recommended that profiles with elevated scores on these scales be designated invalid and not interpreted. They remained concerned that these scales would be far less successful at identifying people who were unconscious distorters. Consequently, Meehl set about developing a *subtle L* scale, one that would identify an unconscious, defensive approach to the MMPI. His work culminated in the K scale. Briefly, the K scale was developed by identifying a sample of 50 patients who had been hospitalized due primarily to behavioral acting out problems (e.g., alcoholism) and who had elevated scores on L and normal range scores on the clinical scales, and contrasting empirically their responses to the MMPI item pool with those of the normative reference group used in other MMPI scale construction efforts. Twenty-two of the K items were identified in this manner and were designated in early writings as scale L_6. Meehl was concerned that the L_6 scale somewhat underestimated the amount of true psychopathology reported by depressed or schizophrenic patients. To counteract this tendency, he added eight items that did not appear to be sensitive to test taking attitude but were answered differently (in the keyed direction) by depressed and schizophrenic patients when compared to the Minnesota Normals. K is thus made up of the 30 items identified empirically by the two approaches.

Meehl and Hathaway (1946) reported that K was not developed originally to be used as a third validity scale. Rather, it was intended to be used as a correction scale or suppressor variable to correct for the effects of unconscious distortion upon scores on the clinical scales. Through a series of empirical analyses Meehl devised a set of weights to be applied to the raw score on K to correct the raw scores on five of the clinical scales. It is noteworthy and often overlooked that the K-correction works in two ways. Elevated scores on K increase the level of elevation on the K-corrected T-score in comparison to the non-K-corrected T-score, on the assumption that the individual under-reported their abnormal personality characteristics. Conversely, a lower than average raw score on K leads to a decrease in the K-corrected T-score in comparison with the non-K-corrected T-score, on the assumption that the individual over-reported pathology.

In sum, it can be seen that awareness of the effect of individual differences in responsiveness to item content led to the development of the MMPI validity scales. These scales have proven to be one of the strongest and most enduring assets of the test. Their present status will be discussed further later in this chapter. These scales also represent the early view that item content was essentially a source of nuisance variance, the effect of which needed to be measured and, to the extent possible, corrected. Subsequent research efforts began gradually to reflect a view of item content as a source of valid variance in its own right.

Subtle and Obvious MMPI Scales

Concurrent with the development of the *K* scale, two early MMPI researchers (Wiener & Harmon, 1946) were developing an alternate approach for dealing with the problem of item content. Recognizing that some MMPI items were much more obviously related in content to the scale on which they were scored than were others, Wiener and Harmon (1946) sought to divide the clinical scales into obvious subscales, comprised of items whose scoring on a given scale was intuitively clear, and subtle subscales, made up of items whose connection to the scale was either unclear or counter-intuitive based on their scoring direction.

Wiener and Harmon (1946), who worked in a Veterans Administration counseling center, articulated two goals for their efforts: (1) "[To] detect symptoms of emotional disturbance in test-conscious veterans who did not want to indicate them" (p. 7); and (2) [To distinguish] invalidity on the separate scales of the Multiphasic Inventory" (p. 7). The first goal could be accomplished through the identification of elevated scores on one or more of the subtle scales in cases where the full scale score was not elevated. The second goal was to be accomplished by contrasting within each scale the individual's score on the subtle and obvious subscales. A considerably higher subtle than obvious subscale score would indicate under-reporting of pathology in the area measured by that scale, an opposite pattern would indicate over-reporting.

Each author examined independently all the items on each of the clinical scales and sorted them into those that were relatively obvious and those that were relatively subtle. Empirical evaluations suggested that useful subtle and obvious keys were developed for five of the clinical scales (Wiener & Harmon, 1946). It is important to note that an implicit and necessary assumption in using these scales for the purposes intended by Wiener and Harmon is that the subtle scales are valid and not susceptible to faking. That is, whereas the obvious scales are susceptible to faking and unconscious distortion, the subtle scales, by virtue of their non- or counter-intuitive content, are not.

Wiener (1948) conducted one of the first external validation studies of the subtle and obvious subscales. He compared the obvious and subtle T-scores of 100 veterans, half of whom had been successful and the other half unsuccessful in school and in on-the-job training. Previous analyses of this data set using the full scales indicated that "the MMPI showed consistent but generally insignificant differences favoring the emotional stability of the successful group" (Wiener, 1948, p. 168). In Wiener's new analyses, all five obvious scales were significantly higher for the unsuccessful group than the successful one, averaging a 6.5 T-score point difference. However, none of the subtle scales discriminated significantly between the two groups.

Wiener (1948) interpreted these findings as supporting the use of the subtle and obvious scales as the obvious scales were able to discriminate between the two groups much more successfully than the full scales. However, these findings *failed to provide any empirical support for the subtle scales*! They did, however, suggest that content-based assessment (as represented by the rationally-derived obvious scales) can yield clinically and statistically significant findings.

The history of the subtle and obvious scales of the MMPI is replete with debate and controversy. Wiener's (1948) findings are representative of much of the subsequent research with these scales. These investigations indicated that whereas the obvious scales can, in fact, be quite useful, there is very limited empirical support for the validity of the subtle scales as measures of psychopathology or as validity indicators. Their present status will be evaluated in the final section of this chapter.

The Welsh Factor Scales

Although they have never become widely used in clinical applications of the MMPI, the Welsh factor scales, *A* and *R*, represented important landmarks in the evolution of content-based MMPI interpretation. Welsh (1956) developed these scales to provide measures of two dimensions that appeared repeatedly in factor analyses of the MMPI scales. The method of construction for these two scales is less important for the present discussion than the manner by which Welsh (1956) went about analyzing them and recommending their use. Prominent among the analyses he reported was a detailed inspection of the content of items that appeared on each scale. His recommendations for their interpretation also were guided, to a significant degree, by their content. This approach, advocated by one of the leading figures in MMPI research, marked a significant departure from the early doctrine of test interpretation which was based exclusively on the empirical correlates of a response rather than its explicit meaning. Item content was no longer viewed solely as a potential cause of nuisance variance requiring sophisticated methods of correction. Rather, it was considered a potentially valid source of additional information. Although Welsh (1956) did not articulate this view explicitly, it is implied clearly in his methods of analysis.

The Harris-Lingoes Subscales

One of the most direct attempts to incorporate item content in MMPI interpretation was the development by Harris and Lingoes (1955) of a set of subscales for the clinical scales. These scales were designed to assist in the interpretation of the clinical scales whose item-content was highly heterogeneous. As noted previously, in assigning items to the clinical scales, Hathaway and McKinley were uninterested in content and unbothered by heterogeneity. However, as users and researchers of the MMPI began to inspect the content of these scales, they discovered that a given clinical scale may be comprised of a wide range of content areas.

Harris and Lingoes (1955) developed their subscales by examining the content of items on a given clinical scale and assigning them rationally to clusters of item-content. The scales were designed to aid the test-interpreter by allowing her or him to determine which of several sources of content may be contributing to an elevated score on the full clinical scale. In contrast to Wiener and Harmon's (1946) subtle and obvious subscales, the assumption underlying and guiding construction of the Harris-Lingoes subscales was that the obvious content of an item carried the brunt of its interpretive meaning. Thus, use of the Harris and Lingoes subscales was based on the assumption that people respond in meaningful ways to the content of MMPI items.

Critical Items

If the content of items to which an individual is responding is viewed as relevant to assessing their personality, a logical extension of this approach might be the examination of responses to individual items. After all, if one wishes to know what the test-taker said about himself or herself, there is no more direct way to find this out than to read their answers to specific test items. Grayson (1951) was the first to propose such an approach. He devised a list of 38 items that he believed to be highly indicative of severe psychopathology and should, if answered in the keyed direction, lead the test-interpreter to pause and take notice. They were designated *critical* or *stop* items. The Grayson list was generated on the basis of a rational inspection of item content and no empirical studies were ever published to support the selection and utility of these items. The same is true of a subsequent list of 68 items proposed by Caldwell (1969).

More recent attempts to develop critical item lists have employed empirical methods of item selection. Koss and Butcher (1973) based their selection of items on the responses of individuals known to be experiencing various types of crisis situations. Lachar and Wrobel (1979) selected their items by contrasting the responses of clinical and non-clinical samples. Both lists have received some additional empirical attention (e.g., Evans, 1984; Koss, Butcher, & Hoffman, 1976).

Critical item lists are, in some respects, the most radical of the content-based approaches to MMPI interpretation. The psychometric limitations of individual items are well-known, however developers of these lists have never proposed that they be used as psychometric indicators. Rather, they are viewed as a useful way for the test-interpreter to get a *flavor* for some of the specific issues that are of concern to the test-taker and as a means for identifying areas of functioning that might require additional evaluation.

Content Scales

Content scales are the most direct, *reliable* means for communication between the test-taker and test-interpreter. In contrast to critical items, when constructed properly, content scales provide psychometrically sound measures for discerning the major content themes of the individual's self-report. Wiggins (1966) set the standard for rigorous construction of content scales for the MMPI.

In providing a rationale for his project, Wiggins (1966) noted the dearth of attempts to develop content-based scales for the MMPI. He attributed this situation to the ambivalence, if not animosity, that existed among the originators of the MMPI toward any deviation from the strict empirical approach to scale construction and interpretation. Wiggins offered cogent arguments in favor of exploring the possibility of constructing content-based scales for the MMPI, citing research that had demonstrated equivalence, if not superiority, of content based measures over empirically-keyed ones, and the desirability of developing psychometrically sound, dimensional means of gauging the communication conveyed by the test-taker to its interpreter.

Wiggins (1966) began his study by examining the internal consistency of the 26 content-based item-groupings described originally (for descriptive, not prescriptive purposes) by Hathaway and McKinley (1940). He found some content areas to be quite promising for further scale-development efforts, whereas others, for a variety of reasons including a dearth of items, clearly were not. He then set about revising the content categories based on a rational-intuitive analysis followed by additional empirical analyses that yielded a set of 15 content dimensions that were promising enough to warrant further analyses. Empirical analyses involving the entire item pool of the MMPI yielded eventually a set of 13 internally consistent and relatively independent content scales.

The significance of Wiggins's (1966) efforts cannot be overstated. His methods served as the prototype for all subsequent efforts to develop content-based scales for the MMPI, and the psychometric success of his endeavor provided much-needed empirical support for the still-fledgling content-based approach to MMPI interpretation in particular and personality assessment in general. His method of scale construction was emulated in subsequent efforts to develop content-based measures for the MMPI (e.g., Morey, Waugh, & Blashfield [1985], in their development of *DSM-III*-based personality disorder scales for the MMPI). And, as will be described later, when the revisers of the MMPI sought to expand its item pool, they did so through the development of new content scales, following the tradition and methods originated by Wiggins (1966).

Evolution of the MMPI: Conclusions

As noted by Wiggins (1990), the evolution of the MMPI reflects, in many respects, some of the major developments, controversies, and advances in the area of personality assessment. Space limitations prohibit a detailed discussion of issues such as the impact (or lack thereof) of response styles on the MMPI, or further elaboration on the relative virtues and drawbacks of empirical-keying versus more contemporary methods of scale construction.

The developments chronicled in this section illustrate that by the 1980s, use of the MMPI followed only nominally the initial intent of its developers. Gone were both the nosological categories into which people were to be classified and the initial goal of developing an instrument to be used primarily for the differential diagnosis of psychopathology. Criticisms of the MMPI that cite its inadequacies in this area are irrelevant to its present applications.

After recognizing that the MMPI did not serve adequately its initial function, the test's developers and their students established two broad categories or methodologies for its application in clinical assessment and research: The empirical and content-based methods of interpretation. Of the two, the empirical method has dominated both in the extent of its research base and in its actual use in clinical evaluations. Within the empirical framework, the typologically-grounded codebook approach continues to prevail, however it is based on certain assumptions regarding configural scoring that merit further evaluation. A clear trend toward greater acceptance and incorporation of content-based approaches has characterized MMPI interpretation more recently.

The MMPI is without precedent in the amount, extent, and quality of the research efforts that have guided its application in differentiating normal and abnormal personality. Nevertheless, over the years, researchers and users of the MMPI became keenly aware of several shortcomings and deficiencies in the test that might be addressed through its update and revision. These considerations led eventually to the MMPI restandardization project and the publication of the MMPI-2.

THE MMPI-2

The publication, in 1989, of the revised version of the MMPI represented the culmination of nearly a decade of research. Although not without controversy and debate, four years after the MMPI-2's publication the revised version of the inventory is now replacing the original in the vast majority of clinical settings (Webb, Levitt & Rojdev, 1993). In the next sections, the rationale, goals, methods, and outcome of the revision will be described.

Rationale for the Revision

A need to update and revise the MMPI had been recognized and expressed for some time prior to the launching of the restandardization project (c.f. Butcher, 1972). However, for a variety of reasons, it was not until the early 1980s that the test-owner, the University of Minnesota Press, agreed to examine the feasibility of and eventually fund a major revision of what by then had become the most widely used self-report measure of personality (Lubin, Larsen, & Matarazzo, 1984). Following, is a list and discussion of the factors that led eventually to the revision.

Problematic Norms

Among the various arguments made in favor of revising the MMPI, none was more salient than the need to update the test's norms. As described earlier in this chapter, the MMPI normative sample was collected in the 1930s and consisted almost exclusively of caucasian working-class rural Minnesotans possessing an average of eight years of education who happened to be visiting the University Hospital at the time of the project and consented to serve as subjects. This sample, although appropriate for the test's initial application, became inadequate as the MMPI became more widely used in a variety of settings throughout the United States and the world over.

A second factor making the MMPI norms problematic was a significant shift from the way in which the test was administered originally when the norms were collected, to modern administration practices. Originally, the MMPI items were printed individually on index cards, and the test-taker was instructed to sort these cards (which were to be administered randomly) into three piles corresponding to the answers True, False, or Cannot Say. The Cannot Say option was presented as equally viable and was thus used frequently by the test-taker. In developing the original norms, a cannot say score reflecting 30 item omissions was set arbitrarily to a T-score 50. Dahlstrom, Welsh, & Dahlstrom (1972) report that this number corresponded closely to the actual mean number of item omissions in the Hathaway and Briggs (1957) normative data set. Although Hathaway & McKinley were aware that an excessive number of item omissions might deflate artificially an individual's scores on the remaining scales, they did not typically invalidate a protocol unless it had over 70 item omissions.

Presently, test-takers are asked to respond to all of the items, and if more than 10 are omitted, the protocol is interpreted cautiously. This change in administration procedure has compromised the appropriateness of the original norms. It is questionable whether the original norms of the MMPI should serve as a reference for standardizing raw scores that are obtained in a manner that deviates substantially from the way in which the normative raw scores were collected.

A third source of difficulty with the MMPI norms stemmed from overlapping use of the original normative data for scale development and standardization. Due to financial constraints that prevented Hathaway & McKinley from collecting a second normative sample, the clinical scales were developed and standardized using the same subjects. This could have introduced some contamination in the resultant standard scores.

These three factors in combination likely account for the recurrent research finding that nonclinical samples tended to produce elevated scores when referenced to the original norms (c.f. Pancoast & Archer, 1989; Pope, Butcher, & Seelen, 1993). Pancoast & Archer (1989) noted that this trend appeared as early as 1949 (Chyatte, 1949), and consistently through the 1980s. Thus, confronting the inadequacies of the original norms was a major task in the revision of the MMPI.

Problematic Items

Over the years, MMPI items had come under considerable criticism for a number of reasons. Foremost amongst these was the existence of items whose content was no longer clear, relevant, or appropriate based on modern linguistic patterns (e.g., "drop the handkerchief") and social norms. One set of MMPI items that had stirred controversy for many years posed questions regarding the test-taker's religious beliefs and practices. Other questions delved into such matters as excretory functions and sexual orientation. Butcher and Tellegen (1966) provided an empirically generated list of objectionable MMPI items. The test's revision was an opportunity to eliminate objectionable items and rewrite others that were worded archaically or contained gender-specific references.

A second issue pertaining to MMPI items was the existence of a relatively large set of items that was not scored on any of the clinical, validity, or widely used supplementary scales. These nonworking items were viewed as an unnecessary burden, and candidates for deletion and replacement.

A final item-level issue was the absence of item content dealing with issues that are relevant to contemporary clinical personality assessment (e.g., suicidal ideation, type A behavior, use of drugs such as marijuana, work-related difficulties, and treatment readiness). A tradeoff between nonworking and new items was viewed as the appropriate strategy for confronting both problems.

Goals for the Revision

Recognizing the needs and problems just noted, in 1982 the University of Minnesota Press, owner of the MMPI, appointed a committee of MMPI researchers that was charged with the task of carrying out a revision of the MMPI. The committee eventually included James N. Butcher, W. Grant Dahlstrom, John R. Graham, and Auke Tellegen. Beverly Kaemmer, test manager for the University of Minnesota Press, served as the coordinator for the committee that came to be known as the *MMPI Restandardization Committee.*

The restandardization committee was entrusted with two potentially discordant goals: Improve the test while maintaining as much continuity as possible with the original MMPI so as not to lose its vital research base. Improvement was to be attained by updating the normative base (hence the name *restandardization project*) and correcting the item-level deficiencies just noted. Continuity was to be accomplished by minimizing the amount of change to be introduced in the original validity and clinical scales so as to allow test-interpreters to continue to rely on decades of accumulated research and clinical experience with these scales.

Referring to the two main methodologies of MMPI interpretation reviewed earlier in this chapter, the MMPI restandardization committee decided to maintain continuity by retaining the test's ability to rely on the codebook database that had accumulated over the years and which served as the primary source of interpretive information, while developing an expanded item pool to be harvested for new content-based scales. The success of this two-pronged approach would depend in large part on the nature and extent of normative shifts between the original and new standardization samples.

Methods of the Revision

The first task of the restandardization committee was to develop an experimental MMPI booklet with which the new normative data would be collected and from which new items could be added to the test. The *MMPI-AX* was developed by retaining all 550 original MMPI items (although 82 were reworded slightly to correct for archaic or otherwise inappropriate language), dropping the 16 repeated items that had been added to the test for ease of scoring, and writing 154 new, experimental items as candidates for replacing non-working and objectionable items.[2] The new items were to cover content areas identified above as missing from the original MMPI.

Additional instruments developed for the restandardization project included a biographical data form that was used to collect extensive demographic data on normative and other subjects and a life events form designed to identify subjects who had been experiencing extreme stress in the six months prior to participating in the project. A subset of subjects who participated in the normative data collection along with their spouses or live-in partners also completed a modified version of the Katz and Lyerly (1963) Adjustment Scale and Spanier's (1976) Dyadic Adjustment Scale. These were to be used as sources of validity and correlate data for new scales that might be developed.

The MMPI-2 normative sample was collected throughout the United States, using a variety of procedures designed to produce an adequate sample of the population of individuals with whom the test is used. Over 2,900 individuals completed the test battery, of these, 2,600 (1,462 women and 1,138 men) produced valid and complete protocols and were included in the normative sample. Approximately 1,680 members of the normative sample who participated along with their spouses or live-in partners completed the two additional forms. Individual subjects were paid $15 for their participation; couples received $40.

The MMPI-2 manual (Butcher, Dahlstrom, Graham, Tellegen, & Kaemmer, 1989) provides comprehensive data regarding the geographic, ethnic, age, education, marital status, occupation, and income level distributions of members of the MMPI-2 normative sample. These data are compared to the 1980 U.S. census figures, and in most cases there is a close match. A noteworthy exception is the educational level of the normative sample which is considerably higher than that of the general population in 1980. The impact of this discrepancy is considered later in this chapter.

A number of additional clinical and non-clinical data sets were compiled and used in various scale development and validation studies. These included a sample of psychiatric inpatients (Graham & Butcher, 1988), individuals undergoing substance abuse treatment (McKenna & Butcher, 1987), patients at a pain-treatment clinic (Keller & Butcher, 1991), college students (Ben-Porath & Butcher, 1989a, 1989b; Butcher, Graham, Dahlstrom, & Bowman, 1990), military personnel (Butcher, Jeffrey, Cayton, Colligan, DeVore, & Mirmegawa, 1990), mothers at risk for child abuse (Egland, Erickson, Butcher, & Ben-Porath, 1991), and participants in the Boston Normative Aging Study (Butcher, Aldwin, Levenson, Ben-Porath, Spiro, & Bosse (1991). All tolled, over 10,000 subjects were tested in conjunction with the restandardization project.

Outcome of the Revision

The MMPI-2 consists of 567 items. Of the 383 items scored on the basic validity and clinical scales of the MMPI, 372 appear on the MMPI-2. Eleven items were deleted due to objectionable content. No basic scale lost more than four items; most scales did not lose any. A total of 64 of the MMPI-2's items were revised slightly. Ben-Porath & Butcher (1989b) found these changes to impact negligibly on the psychometric functioning of the scales on which they were scored. Thus, the basic validity and clinical scales of the MMPI-2 are nearly identical to those of the MMPI. This represents the main source of continuity between the two versions of the inventory. Following are specific aspects of continuity and change between the MMPI and MMPI-2:

Validity Scales

The original validity scales of the MMPI remain nearly identical in composition on the MMPI-2. The Cannot Say scale represents the total number of items unanswered or answered both True and False. In contrast to the original MMPI, there are no T-scores associated with the raw score on Cannot Say. This reflects the recent trend of relying upon the raw score to determine the effects of item omissions. The increasing availability of automated scoring systems for the MMPI-2 allows for more detailed examination of the effects of item omissions upon the test profile. For example, the *Minnesota Clinical Report* (Butcher, 1993) indicates the percentage of items answered on each of the scales, enabling the test-interpreter to consider scale-specific effects of item omission and, in some cases, providing indications of content areas that the test-taker is uncomfortable discussing.

The *L* scale of the MMPI-2 is made up of the same items as the original MMPI. The primary difference between the two versions of the test is at the T-score level.

As reported by Meehl & Hathaway (1946), T-scores for the original MMPI *L* scale were set arbitrarily since Hathaway & McKinley believed that the raw score distribution for this scale was overly skewed. The MMPI-2 T-scores for *L* are based on linear transformations of the raw score distribution in the new normative sample. As a result, T-scores on the MMPI-2 *L* scale are actually higher than their MMPI counterparts. The MMPI-2 *F* scale lost four objectionable items and is now composed of 60 items. T-scores on *F* are higher on the MMPI-2 than they were on the original MMPI for the same reason as they are on *L*. Here too, Hathaway & McKinley felt that the distribution of scores in the original normative sample was overly skewed, so they developed arbitrary T-scores instead of linear ones. The *K* scale is composed of the same 30 items on both versions of the inventory. On this scale, T-scores are lower on the MMPI-2 than they were originally on the MMPI.

In sum, the composition of scales *L*, *F*, and *K* is nearly identical on the two versions of the test. T-scores are somewhat different and may now be interpreted more directly as they represent the test-taker's standing in reference to the normative sample. This was not the case with arbitrarily-set T-scores for scales *L* and *F* on the original MMPI. Recently published research with the MMPI-2 indicates that these scales function in an identical manner to their original MMPI counterparts (e.g., Graham, Watts, & Timbrook, 1991; Wetter, Baer, Berry, Smith, & Larsen, 1992). Thus, there exists considerable continuity between the MMPI and MMPI-2 insofar as the original validity scales are concerned.

Along with continuity, the MMPI-2 offers new perspectives and possibilities for assessing protocol validity. Three new validity scales were developed for the MMPI-2. The *Fb* scale is very similar to the original *F* scale. It is made up of items that were endorsed infrequently by the MMPI-2 normative sample that appear in the second half of the booklet. The *Fb* scale allows the interpreter to detect any changes in the test-taker's response pattern that may have occurred after the first half of the booklet where nearly all of the *F* scale items are located.

Two new consistency scales were added to the MMPI-2. These scales, developed by Tellegen and Ben-Porath, were fashioned after the consistency scales developed by Tellegen (1982) for the MPQ. *Variable Response Inconsistency* (*VRIN*) is a measure of inconsistent, contradictory responding that is made up of pairs of items. These items were identified through a series of statistical and semantic analyses designed to identify item pairs that are identical or opposite in meaning. They are keyed so that for each item pair that an individual answers inconsistently, she or he will receive a point on *VRIN*. Raw scores are converted into linear T-scores that inform the test-interpreter regrading the extent of random responding in a given protocol.

VRIN is particularly useful in interpreting elevated scores on *F*. As reported by Meehl and Hathaway (1946), the *F* scale was intended originally for use as an index of careless responding. However, soon after its development, *F* was found to function well as an indicator of intentional exaggeration or malingering of psychological problems. Over the years, it became increasingly clear that there are essentially three non-mutually exclusive causes for elevated scores on *F*: (1) Random responding—whether intentional as in cases where the test-taker doesn't bother to read or respond to the test items, or unintentional, where the test-taker is not able to read, understand, and/or comprehend the test items due to reading limitations, concentration difficulties or similar problems; (2) Intentional exaggeration or malingering of psychological problems—a response pattern frequently labeled "Fake Bad"; and (3) The presence of severe psychopathology or psychological distress. The content of items on *F* is such that an individual who is experiencing severe (e.g., psychotic) symptoms of psychopathology or pronounced psychological distress, will, if he or she describes these symptoms accurately, produce an elevated score on *F*. Interpretation of *F* scale scores of inpatients is particularly problematic for this reason.

The *VRIN* scale can be used to evaluate the contribution of one of these three sources, random responding, to elevated scores on *F*. A more recently developed infrequent response indicator *F(p)* (Arbisi & Ben-Porath, 1993), helps to assess the extent to which true psychopathology may contribute to an elevated score on *F*. *F(p)* was developed by identifying 27 MMPI-2 items that are endorsed infrequently (i.e., less than 20% in the keyed direction) not only by the normative sample but also by various samples of inpatients. Thus, the *F(p)* scale is much less reflective of the effects of psychopathology and more exclusively affected by exaggeration, malingering, and or random responding. Use of *F*, *VRIN*, and *F(p)*, in combination, allows the test-interpreter to distinguish more effectively between the three sources of elevation on *F* just described.

A second new consistency scale developed for the MMPI-2 is *True Response Inconsistency (TRIN)*. This scale is made up of pairs of items that are opposite in meaning. Item pairs were identified through a series of statistical and semantic analyses. Because each item pair is opposite in meaning, answering both items True or False is inconsistent. Some pairs are inconsistent only when answered both True, others are inconsistent only when answered both False, and some are inconsistent with both combinations. The number of inconsistent True and inconsistent False responses is tallied separately, and T-scores were developed so that the test-interpreter can determine the predominant direction of inconsistency ("True" or "False"). *TRIN* can be used to detect two possible response sets—*yea saying* or *nay saying*. Knowledge of the presence of such response sets is particularly important given the asymmetrical keying that characterizes some of the MMPI-2 scales. For example, all of the items on *L* and all but one of the items on *K* are keyed false. Thus, a *nay saying* response set could produce artificially inflated scores on these scales. Examination of *TRIN* allows the test-interpreter to detect such response sets and consider their effects on the MMPI-2 scales in her or his interpretation. Even for scales with balanced keys, extreme *TRIN* scores, like high *VRIN* scores, indicate protocol invalidity.

In sum, the MMPI-2 offers a much more comprehensive set of scales to assist the test-interpreter in evaluating the validity of individual test protocols. Such scales are vital when using the MMPI-2 in clinical practice and can also be quite useful in identifying and deleting invalid records in research. The availability of an enhanced set of validity scales for the MMPI-2 represents an important advantage of the revised version of the inventory over the original.

The MMPI-2 Clinical Scales

The clinical scales of the MMPI-2 are nearly identical in composition to their MMPI counterparts. As mentioned, this represents a major source of continuity between the two versions of the inventory. A small number of wording changes has not affected the items' psychometric functioning (Ben-Porath & Butcher, 1989b), and the small number of items deleted from some of the scales has virtually no impact on the raw scores on these scales.

Whereas raw scores on the two versions of the inventory are, for all practical purposes, identical, T-scores are somewhat lower on the MMPI-2. This led the restandardization committee to lower the cutting point for clinically meaningful elevation from a T-score of 70 to 65. Given the high level of raw score comparability between the two versions of the inventory, it is clear that T-score differences are a function of changes in the response patterns of the original and new normative samples. As already discussed, one source of such differences is a change in the instructions given to test-takers regarding the cannot say option. Current instructions discourage the cannot say response which may account partially for the increase in the average raw scores of the new normative sample. This increase has led to a corresponding decrease in T-scores based on the new norms.

Another potential source of change at the T-score level is the development of *Uniform T-scores* for the MMPI-2 (Tellegen & Ben-Porath, 1992). Briefly, uniform T-scores were developed to correct a long-recognized problem with MMPI T-scores. Originally, T-scores were simple linear transformations based on the pattern of raw scores of the original normative sample. In adopting linear T-scores, Hathaway and McKinley retained the skewed distributions of the raw scores, allowing for T-scores to extend up to seven standard deviations above the mean. However, since the raw score distributions for the clinical scales are differentially skewed, the same T-score did not correspond to the same percentile across different scales. The lack of percentile equivalence across scales made direct comparisons of T-scores on different clinical scales potentially misleading.

The solution adopted by the restandardization committee was to compute the average distribution of non-K-corrected raw scores for men and women in the normative sample and correct each scale's distribution slightly to correspond to this composite. This is accomplished in the transformation of raw scores to T-scores. This approach yields percentile-equivalent T-scores while retaining the skewed nature of the clinical scales' distributions. An alternative approach would have been to develop normalized T-scores, however this solution would have altered substantially the nature of the MMPI profile by restricting T-scores elevation in nearly all cases to below 80. Details on the rationale, development, and functioning of the uniform T-scores are reported by Tellegen and Ben-Porath (1992).

By comparing profiles based on uniform versus traditional linear T-scores (both derived from the new normative sample), Graham, Timbrook, Ben-Porath, and Butcher (1991) demonstrated that the uniform T-scores do not alter substantially the nature and characteristics of the MMPI-2 profile. Ben-Porath and Butcher (1989a) also demonstrated considerable comparability at the level of the profile between the MMPI and MMPI-2. Nevertheless, some authors have suggested that when code-types are derived, the two versions of the inventory yield discrepant results. Initial data suggesting this possibility were provided in the MMPI-2 manual, in which it was reported that the same two-point code type is found in only two-thirds of cases where the same responses are plotted on MMPI and MMPI-2 norms. More recently, Dahlstrom (1992b) reported similar results.

The controversy regarding code-type congruence or comparability across the two sets of norms has resulted in concern regarding the applicability of nearly 50 years of research and clinical experience with the MMPI to MMPI-2 interpretation. *If*, in fact, in roughly one third of the cases the two sets of norms yield different code types, which set of empirical correlates should be used in interpreting the profile? Unfortunately, this debate has been based on misleading data analyses including those reported initially in the MMPI-2 manual.

As described earlier in this chapter, the codebook approach to MMPI interpretation has undergone tremendous change over the years. The method used to define code types in the analyses reported in the MMPI-2 manual and by Dahlstrom (1992b) yields highly unstable and thus unreliable code types. A change of one T-score point on two scales can lead to an entirely different code type designation. Because neither MMPI nor MMPI-2 scales are perfectly reliable, meaningful code-type classification schemes cannot be sensitive to such minuscule changes. Rather, a minimal degree of differentiation between the scales in the code type and the remaining scales on the profile must be present for the code type to be stable.

Analyses conducted by Graham, Timbrook, Ben-Porath, & Butcher (1991) suggest that scales in a code type need to be at least five points higher than the remaining scales in a profile for the code type to be sufficiently stable. Such well defined code types are also quite stable across the MMPI and MMPI-2. Graham et al. (1991) report congruence in 80 to 95% of clinical and nonclinical profiles when well defined code types are evaluated. In nearly all of the relatively small proportion of cases where the same code type does not emerge, at least one scale appears in both code types. Graham et al. (1991) attempted to compare the relative validity of this small number of discrepant code types, however, statistically significant differences were not found due to low power. Thus, at the very least, differing code types were equally valid. Tellegen & Ben-Porath (1993) discuss this issue in greater detail.

A final source of potential difficulty in interpreting scores on the clinical scales based on the new norms was the relatively high socio-economic status (SES) of the new normative sample when compared to the 1980 census figures. However, figures produced by Pope, Butcher, & Seelen (1993) illustrate that the correlation between the MMPI-2 clinical scales and SES indicators such as education does not yield clinically meaningful differences between the profiles of various SES groups. Additionally, the MMPI-2 normative sample is much closer in SES to the general population than was the original 1930s sample of rural working-class Minnesotans. As a consequence, the test-taker's level of education has a far lesser impact on interpreting MMPI-2 profiles than it did in MMPI interpretation.

In sum, in spite of some initial concerns, recent research has indicated that clinical scale profiles based on the two sets of norms are quite comparable. Thus, the product of nearly 50 years of research and clinical experience with codebook-based MMPI interpretation carries over directly to the MMPI-2. Because they are nearly identical in composition, the empirical correlates of individual clinical scales are unchanged for the two versions of the inventory. Content-based interpretation of the MMPI-2 clinical scales also remains viable since new norms were developed for the Harris and Lingoes subscales (Butcher, et al., 1989). Ben-Porath, Hostetler, Butcher, & Graham (1989) developed new subscales for the Social Introversion (Si) scale.

The MMPI-2 Supplementary Scales

One of the major challenges faced by the restandardization committee was to decide which of the hundreds of supplementary scales developed over the years for the MMPI should be protected and formally adapted for the MMPI-2. Protection meant that an attempt would be made to retain all or most of the items scored on a given supplementary scale. Adaption meant that new T-scores would be developed for a scale based on the MMPI-2 normative sample. Three primary criteria used in making these decisions were that a supplementary scale have a strong empirical foundation, proven clinical utility, and incremental validity (i.e., that the supplementary scale measure something that the clinical or other supplementary scales do not).

Based on these criteria, the restandardization committee decided to retain (in some cases with a slight loss of items) the Welsh (1956) A and R scales described earlier in this chapter, Barron's (1953) Ego Strength scale, MacAndrew's (1965) alcoholism scale, now called the MAC-R, in a slightly revised format with four new items replacing deleted objectionable items, the Megargee, Cook, & Mendelsohn (1967) Overcontrolled Hostility scale, the Gough, McClosky, & Meehl (1951) Dominance scale, the Gough, McClosky, & Meehl (1952) Social Responsibility scale, the Kleinmuntz (1961) College Maladjustment scale, and the Keane, Malloy, & Fairbank (1984) Post Traumatic Stress Disorder scale.

Three new supplementary scales introduced in the MMPI-2 manual were the Gender Role scales, GM and GF, described recently by Peterson and Dahlstrom (1992), and a new Post Traumatic Stress Disorder scale proposed by Schlenger and Kulka (1987). The clinical utility and incremental validity of these three new scales remain to be demonstrated.

Since the publication of the MMPI-2, three additional supplementary scales have been developed and are available for clinical use. These are the Marital Distress Scale developed by Hjemboe, Almagor, & Butcher (1992), and two new substance abuse scales—Addiction Potential (APS) and Addiction Acknowledgement (AAS) that were developed by Weed, Butcher, McKenna, & Ben-Porath (1992). These authors reported initial data indicating that APS and AAS are incrementally valid with respect to the MAC-R scale. Similar results were reported by Greene, Weed, Butcher, Arrendono, & Davis (1992).

The MMPI-2 Content Scales

As reviewed earlier in this chapter, over the years the content-based approach gained increasing acceptance as an aid and supplement to the codebook-based interpretation of scores on the MMPI clinical scales. The Wiggins (1966) content scales represented the most thorough and comprehensive application of this approach with the MMPI. The MMPI restandardization committee opted to introduce interpretive innovation through the adoption of a new set of content scales developed by Butcher, Graham, Williams, & Ben-Porath (1990).

The MMPI-2 Content Scales were developed through a series of rational-conceptual and empirical analyses fashioned after the ones used by Wiggins (1966) in developing the original content scales for the MMPI. Items were assigned first to potential scales based on consensus among judges who conducted a rational examination of their content. Then, a series of statistical analyses was carried out to eliminate items that did not contribute to the internal consistency of a scale and to identify potential items for inclusion that were missed in the first round of rational analyses. These candidate items were then inspected rationally and added if they were found by consensus to be related to the domain measured by a scale. Final statistical analyses were conducted to eliminate items that created excessive intercorrelation among the content scales.

This process yielded a set of 15 content scales. As might be expected, some of these scales are similar in composition to the ones developed by Wiggins (1966). Nearly all the scales have new items on them, some (e.g., Type A Behaviors and Negative Treatment Indicators) are composed predominantly of new items. As discussed earlier in this chapter, the interpretation of content scales can be based entirely on the actual content of the items endorsed. Empirical identification of correlates can substantiate and enhance content-based interpretation. Butcher et al. (1990) reported initial empirical correlates for the MMPI-2 Content Scales that lend considerable support for their use. More recently, Ben-Porath, Butcher, & Graham (1991) and Ben-Porath, McCully, & Almagor (1993) demonstrated that the MMPI-2 Content Scales possess considerable incremental validity in relation to the clinical scales. Such demonstration of incremental validity is crucial if the Content Scales are to be used as augments to the interpretation of the basic profile.

Recently, Ben-Porath and Sherwood (1993) have developed a set of subscales for the MMPI-2 Content scales—the Content Component Scales. These scales were derived through a series of principal component and item analyses that resulted in the development of 28 subscales that can augment interpretation of the MMPI-2 Content Scales in the same way as the Harris-Lingoes subscales aid in the interpretation of the clinical scales. Initial data reported by Ben-Porath and Sherwood (1993) indicate that the Component Scales have sufficient within-parent-scale discriminant validity to enable the test-interpreter to develop a more refined picture of the way in which the test-taker portrayed herself or himself.

PRESENT STATUS AND FUTURE DIRECTIONS

The length of this chapter and its accompanying list of references attest to the voluminous research base that guides users of the MMPI-2 in identifying and characterizing normal and abnormal personality characteristics. In the 50 years since its publication, the MMPI has undergone considerable change—first in the way in which it was used and more recently in the composition of its items and its normative data base. Throughout this time period, empirical research has guided clinicians as they have come increasingly to rely on the MMPI-2 in a variety of assessment tasks.

The MMPI-2 is used routinely in traditional clinical assessment, treatment planning, treatment outcome evaluation, medical settings, a wide variety of forensic applications, personnel screening for high-risk positions, and a broad array of additional tasks. Moreover, developers of new tests designed to augment or replace the MMPI-2, routinely compare the performance of their scales to those of the MMPI or MMPI-2 (c.f., Jackson & Hoffman, 1987; McCrae, 1991; Morey, 1991). As discussed by Ben-Porath and Waller (1992), tests that are intended to replace the MMPI-2 are faced with the daunting challenge of matching its empirical and experiential data base, whereas instruments designed to augment the MMPI-2 must be shown to possess incremental validity in the assessment of clinically relevant phenomena.

Present clinical assessment with the MMPI-2 continues to rely heavily on the empirical correlate method in general and the codebook approach in particular. Thus, the clinical scales continue to serve as the primary source of information for MMPI-2 interpretation. The content-based approach serves as a useful augment to the interpretation of the clinical scales and the content scales will likely assume an increasing role in this application. The availability of a cadre of validity scales for the MMPI-2 and increasingly-sophisticated methods for using these scales allow clinicians to maximize the amount of valid information that can be derived from an individual test protocol.

The introduction of new validity, supplementary, and content scales for the MMPI-2 will, it is hoped, spark a surge of research activity that will enhance further the utility of this instrument in the assessment of normal and abnormal personality. Following are some specific directions in which further MMPI-2 research is needed and likely to develop.

Updated Empirical Correlates

As emphasized throughout this chapter, interpretation of the MMPI-2 is based primarily on empirically identified correlates of scales scores and profile patterns. Although continuity between the original and revised versions of the test is well-established, identification of updated empirical correlates for the MMPI-2 is desirable for a number of reasons. First, many of the studies that generated the empirical correlates for the MMPI were conducted in the 1960s and 1970s. Thus, these correlates do not capture recent changes and advances in clinical practice, psychiatric nomenclature, personality theory and research, and other changes in potential dependent measures or criteria of interest in empirical-correlate research. Moreover, with the introduction of new items and scales on the MMPI-2, it is likely that the test's ability to predict empirical criteria has improved and expanded to cover areas not previously tapped by the MMPI. Finally, identification of comprehensive empirical correlates for the Harris and Lingoes subscales is long overdue.

Identification of empirical correlates requires collection of extremely large samples and use of sophisticated means to obtain reliable dependent measures or criteria. Large numbers of subjects are necessary to allow for the adequate sampling of various code types and to provide ample statistical power for analyses that require stringent control for family-wise error. For example, if a given set of criteria consists of 100 variables, an appropriate level for alpha might be .0005. Large sample sizes are required to maintain adequate power when alpha is set so low. Considerable attention must also be paid to maximizing the reliability of measures used as criteria for empirical-correlate identification. Unreliable measures yield reduced effect sizes and hence decrease power.

The sources for data used as criteria for empirical correlate studies need also to be considered. The potential for artifactual correlation when self-report data serve as criteria in such studies is well known. This does not, however, counterindicate any use of self-report data. The notion, for example, that structured interviews are somehow less contaminated by self-report bias is questionable given that they too rely ultimately on the report of the individual being assessed. Adding an intermediary to the process of recording these reports does not guarantee added objectivity. However, reliable assessment of clinical impressions of diagnostic issues, personality characteristics, treatment progress, etc. may add substantially to the more limited scope of data that can be collected only by self-report. Comprehensive and systematic reviews of clinical records may similarly broaden the range of criteria used in empirical-correlate studies.

Another potential enhancement of the empirical-correlate literature may come from the development of setting-specific correlates. Many of the original studies that identified empirical correlates of the MMPI were conducted in inpatient settings. Such settings have the advantage of offering greater familiarity with subjects and more controlled observation of their behavior. Nevertheless, it is likely that the base rates of some variables of interest will differ markedly from one setting to another, making the correlates of one inapplicable and incomplete when the test is used at a different setting. The extent of such differences is itself an empirical question that could be answered by collecting correlate data using similar measures at different settings.

In sum, although test-interpreters can continue to rely on the extensive and unparalleled data base that currently serves as the foundation for empirically-based MMPI-2 interpretation, there is room for considerable modernization, improvement, and enhancement of this data base.

Configural versus Linear Interpretation

Data collected to update the empirical data base of the MMPI-2 may also be useful in resolving a now decades-old question regarding the relative merits of configural versus linear interpretation of scores on the clinical scales. As described earlier in this chapter, the configural code-type approach has dominated much of the research and practice of clinical scale interpretation. This, in spite of the fact that there is no recent research to support the assumed superiority of configural interpretation.

The fundamental assumption of code-type-based interpretation is that the whole of the code type conveys more information than does the sum of its parts. Consider the 13/31 code type as an example. To support the configural approach, research must show one of two findings (1) that there exist certain correlates of the 13/31 code type that are not to be found among the list of correlates for scales 1 and 3 alone or in linear combination, *or* (2) the strength of the association between the 13/31 code type and certain correlates is significantly greater than the association between these criteria and each of the scales individually and in linear combination. In other words, research must show that the code type possesses incremental validity in comparison to an additive linear combination of the two scales.

Finding incremental validity for code types may be particularly challenging given the considerable loss of variance that occurs when they are used. Continuing with the 13/31 example, in a typical analysis of the correlates of this code type a set of profiles would be classified dichotomously as either meeting or not meet-ing the definitional criteria for the code type. Consequently, a 13/31 code type in which scales 1 and 3 are at T = 65 and the remaining scales fall below T = 55 would be treated the same as one in which scales 1 and 3 are at T = 90 and the remaining scales on the profile fall below T = 55. Although methods can be de-veloped to weight differentially these two profiles, they are not typically used. However, it is far simpler to use a continuous range of T-scores when working with individual scales.

In sum, although presently a majority of the empirical base of the MMPI-2 is based on the correlates of code types, there are no data to indicate the superiority of configural over linear interpretation of scale scores. Nearly 30 years ago, Goldberg (1965) demonstrated that as far as the differential diagnosis of neurot-icism and psychoticism was concerned, configural scoring of the MMPI offered no advantage. Briggs, Taylor, and Tellegen (1966) and more recently Tellegen and Ben-Porath (1993) have called for further analysis of this question. Collection of new empirical correlate data for the MMPI-2 would offer a unique opportunity to do so.

Item Subtlety and Subject Defensiveness

The grouping of item subtlety and subject defensiveness under one heading reflects the close association of these two topics in the history of the MMPI. As reviewed earlier in this chapter, the Wiener-Harmon subtle-obvious scales and the K-cor-rection were developed at the same time, in an effort to confront the same issue—a tendency on the part of some test-takers to approach the MMPI defensively. Wiener and Harmon (1946) believed that item subtlety, the nonintuitive or counter-intuitive presence of certain items on MMPI scales, offered a unique opportunity to circumvent the test-taker's defensive approach as the items would, in effect, fool the individual's defenses.

Although the concept of item subtlety continues to intrigue some authors (e.g., Greene, 1991) recent studies have failed to provide empirical support for using the Wiener-Harmon subtle-obvious keys as measures of psychopathology or validity indicators (Timbrook, Graham, Weiller, & Watts, 1993; Weed, Ben-Porath, & Butcher, 1990). It is likely that many of the items designated subtle by Wiener and Harmon are subtle to the point of invalidity. Had Hathaway & McKinley had the funds to cross-validate further the clinical scales, it is likely that many of these items would have been deleted. The question of whether some valid MMPI-2 items are more subtle than others remains open to empirical investigation. Advocates of subtle measurement might find their efforts more fruitful if they lay the Wiener Harmon scales to rest, and focus their research on the identification of such items.

At the time that Wiener & Harmon (1946) were developing subtle-obvious keys, Meehl & Hathaway (1946) developed a markedly different approach to dealing with subject-defensiveness. As described earlier in this chapter, the K-correction was developed to adjust an individual's score on MMPI clinical scales that were susceptible to the effects of defensiveness. There is, however, no recent research on the utility of the K-correction. Collection of new correlate data as suggested above, will allow researchers to re-examine the efficacy of K as a suppressor variable and the impact of the K-correction on the validity of MMPI-2 clinical scale correlates.

Interface with Five-Factor Models

As discussed earlier in this chapter, in spite of the MMPI-2's continued popularity among clinicians, the test frequently is ignored by normal personality researchers. The current popularity of factorially based theories of personality in general and five-factor models of personality in particular may account partially for this disparity. In chapter 14 in this volume, Harkness & McNulty discuss some of the reasons why clinicians have been reluctant to embrace five-factor models of normal personality. Harkness & McNulty describe their development of the Psychopathology Five (PSY-5), a five factor model that overlaps in some areas with the so-called Big-Five, while broadening considerably the clinically relevant scope of this model.

Recently, Harkness, McNulty, & Ben-Porath (1993) have developed MMPI-2 scales measuring the PSY-5 and their facets. The existence of such scales will, it is hoped, allow researchers interested in five-factor models of personality access to the MMPI-2, and more importantly to the vast amount of research data that have been collected over the years with the MMPI. The clinical utility of the PSY-5 scales remains to be examined. As is the case for all newly proposed MMPI-2 measures, the PSY-5 scales will have to demonstrate incremental validity in comparison to already existing scales on the MMPI-2. Similarly, other measures of five-factor models of normal personality will need to demonstrate incremental validity in comparison to the full set of MMPI-2 scales (including the PSY-5) to justify their use in clinical practice.

Computer Technology

Computers are playing an ever-increasing role in clinical personality assessment. In general, computers can be used to perform three tasks: Administration, scoring, and interpretation. Insofar as administration is concerned, computers are already used to administer the MMPI-2 on-line in a variety of settings, most notably the Veterans Administration system. On-line administration is faster and more reliable than booklet-based administration, and research indicates that well-written on-line administration programs produce results that are comparable to those of paper and pencil administration (Honaker, 1988).

Present on-line administration of the MMPI-2 does not take advantage of the flexibility offered by the computer. Adaptive testing, in which computer algorithms are developed to administer individually tailored versions of the test has only recently been considered. Item Response Theory (IRT)-based adaptive testing is problematic with the MMPI-2 in light of the multidimensional nature of the clinical scales. However, less sophisticated techniques such as the *Count-Down Method* (Butcher, Keller, & Bacon, 1985) have shown some promise (Ben-Porath, Slutske, and Butcher, 1989; Roper, Ben-Porath, and Butcher, 1991). The clinical applicability of these techniques remains to be demonstrated.

Automated, computerized scoring of MMPI-2 scales is now practiced routinely. The primary advantage of computerized scoring is speed and accuracy. The latter assumes that no errors are present in the software used to generate scale scores, an assumption that is more likely to be correct when officially licensed software is used for this purpose. Automated scoring is particularly useful given the proliferation of MMPI-2 scales and the complicated nature of scoring the new validity scales VRIN and TRIN.

Of the various applications of computer technology in personality assessment, computer-based test interpretation (CBTI) is clearly the most controversial. Essentially, an MMPI-2 CBTI system consists of software that generates interpretations on the basis of scale scores. In its most simple form, a CBTI system may simply generate a list of interpretive statements. More sophisticated systems produce elaborate narratives that take on the form of a clinician-generated report. The great advantage of CBTI systems is that they can incorporate vast amounts of information in the data base that is used to generate these reports. A clinician may have to spend hours compiling the information that the computer accesses in a matter of seconds.

CBTI systems are also far more reliable than is the individual clinician generating an MMPI-2 report. With the computer, the same scores will always yield the same interpretation. In fact, the optimal CBTI epitomizes the cookbook approach advocated by Meehl (1956) discussed earlier in this chapter. However, the perfect reliability of the CBTI system also represents a potential weakness of this technology. Although strides are continually being made, present systems are unable to incorporate much extra-test information in their interpretation. For example, although the Minnesota Clinical Report (Butcher, 1993), by far the most sophisticated of present MMPI-2 CBTI systems, now produces different reports for inpatient, outpatient, chemical dependency, correctional, college counseling, and other settings, it is still limited in the amount of extra-test information that can be incorporated.

Critics of CBTIs (Matarazzo, 1986) have complained of the lack of validity data regarding these products. Fowler and Butcher (1986) noted however, that CBTIs do not fall short of clinician-generated reports in this regard, and since Matarazzo's (1986) critique, a number of studies have now been published examining the relative efficacy of different MMPI CBTI programs (e.g., Eyde, Kowal, & Fishburne, 1991).

Although they have now been available for over 25 years, CBTI systems for MMPI and now MMPI-2 interpretation remain still in their infancy. Directions for further research and development of these systems include making them more user-interactive by allowing the user to pose specific questions to the system and research-interactive by developing more direct and efficient methods for updating these systems as new research becomes available. Further study of the clinical utility of these systems may also help shape their future.

CONCLUSIONS

This chapter has surveyed over 50 years of research and application of the MMPI. It is unlikely that Hathaway & McKinley could have envisioned the numerous and various developments and innovations that have occurred with the MMPI since its initial development. The longevity of the instrument is testimony to the ingenuity of its developers and the efforts of their followers. With the publication in 1989 of the MMPI-2, and more recently of the MMPI-A, the tradition of empirical research and thoughtful application of this venerable instrument will likely continue for many years to come.

ACKNOWLEDGMENTS

I thank Jim Butcher, Jack Graham, and Auke Tellegen for their helpful comments on a previous version of this chapter.

NOTES

[1]Examination of these examples should reassure adherents of five- and/or seven-factor models of personality that the MMPI research literature has long incorporated these dimensions of personality into the empirical correlate data base.

[2]A second booklet, the *MMPI-TX* was developed for a separate project designed to explore the feasibility of developing an adolescent version of the MMPI. This project culminated in the publication of the MMPI-A (Butcher, Williams, Graham, Archer, Tellegen, Ben-Porath, & Kaemmer, 1992).

REFERENCES

Arbisi, P. A., & Ben-Porath, Y. S. (March, 1993). Interpretation of inpatients' F scales: Moving from art to science. Paper presented at the *28th Annual Symposium on Recent Developments in the Use of the MMPI-2 and MMPI-A,* St. Petersburg Beach, FL.

Barron, F. (1953). An ego-strength scale which predicts response to psychotherapy. *Journal of Consulting Psychology, 17*, 327–333.

Ben-Porath, Y. S., & Butcher, J. N. (1989a). The psychometric stability of rewritten MMPI items. *Journal of Personality Assessment, 53*, 645–653.

Ben-Porath, Y. S., & Butcher, J. N. (1989b). The comparability of MMPI and MMPI-2 scales and profiles. *Psychological Assessment: A Journal of Consulting and Clinical Psychology, 1*, 345–347.

Ben-Porath, Y. S., Butcher, J. N., & Graham, J. R. (1991). Contribution of the MMPI-2 content scales to the differential diagnosis of psychopathology. *Psychological Assessment: A Journal of Consulting and Clinical Psychology, 3*, 634–640.

Ben-Porath, Y. S., Hostetler, K., Butcher, J. N., & Graham, J. R. (1989). New sub-scales for the MMPI-2 Social Introversion (Si) scale. *Psychological Assessment: A Journal of Consulting and Clinical Psychology, 1*, 169–174.

Ben-Porath, Y. S., McCully, E., & Almagor, M. (1993). Incremental validity of the MMPI-2 Content Scales in the assessment of personality and psychopathology by self-report. *Journal of Personality Assessment, 61*, 557–575.

Ben-Porath, Y. S., & Sherwood, N. E. (1993). *The MMPI-2 Content Component Scales: Development, psychometric characteristics. and clinical applications.* Minneapolis, MN: University of Minnesota Press.

Ben-Porath, Y. S., Slutske, W. S., & Butcher, J. N. (1989). A real-data simulation of computerized adaptive testing with the MMPI. *Psychological Assessment: A Journal of Consulting and Clinical Psychology, 1*, 18–22.

Ben-Porath, Y. S., & Waller, N. G. (1992). "Normal" personality inventories in clinical assessment: General requirements and the potential for using the NEO Personality Inventory. *Psychological Assessment, 4*, 14–19.

Bernreueter, R. J. (1933). Theory and construction of the personality inventory. *Journal of Social Psychology, 4*, 387–405.

Black, J. D. (1953). The interpretation of MMPI profiles of college women. *Dissertation Abstracts, 13*, 870–871.

Briggs, P. F., Taylor, M., & Tellegen, A. (1966) A study of the Marks and Seeman MMPI profile types as applied to a sample of 2,875 psychiatric patients. *Reports from the research laboratories of the Department of Psychiatry, University of Minnesota, Report Number PR-66-5.*

Butcher, J. N. (Ed.). (1972). *Objective personality assessment: Changing perspectives.* New York, NY: Academic Press.

Butcher, J. N. (1993). *User's guide for the Minnesota Clinical Report.* Minneapolis, MN: National Computer Systems.

Butcher, J. N., Aldwin, C. L., Levenson, M. R., Ben-Porath, Y. S., Spiro, A., & Bosse, R. (1991). Personality and aging: A study of the MMPI-2 aging elderly men. *Psychology of Aging, 6*, 361–370.

Butcher, J. N., Dahlstrom, W. G., Graham, J. R., Tellegen, A., & Kaemmer, B. (1989). *The Minnesota Multiphasic Personality Inventory-2 (MMPI-2): Manual for administration and scoring.* Minneapolis, MN: University of Minnesota Press.

Butcher, J. N., Graham, J. R., Dahlstrom, W. G., & Bowman, E. (1990). The MMPI-2 with college students. *Journal of Personality Assessment, 54*, 1–15.

Butcher, J. N., Graham, J. R., Williams, C. L., & Ben-Porath, Y. S. (1990). *Development and use of the MMPI-2 content scales.* Minneapolis, MN: University of Minnesota Press.

Butcher, J. N., Jeffrey, T., Cayton, T. G., Colligan, S., DeVore, J., & Minnegawa, R. (1990). A study of active duty military personnel with the MMPI-2. *Military Psychology, 2*, 47–61.

Butcher, J. N., & Tellegen, A. (1966). Objections to MMPI items. *Journal of Consulting Psychology, 46*, 527–534.

Butcher, J. N., Williams, C. L., Graham, J. R., Archer, R. P., Tellegen, A., Ben-Porath, Y. S., & Kaemmer, B. (1992). *Minnesota Multiphasic Personality Inventory (MMPI-A): Manual for administration, scoring and interpretation.* Minneapolis, MN: University of Minnesota Press.

Caldwell, A. B. (1969). *MMPI critical items.* Unpublished manuscript.

Chyatte, C. (1949). Personality traits of professional actors. *Occupations, 27*, 245–250.

Cuadra, C. A. (1953). *A psychometric investigation of control factors in psychological adjustment.* Unpublished doctoral dissertation, University of California.

Dahlstrom, W. G. (1992a). The growth in acceptance of the MMPI. *Professional Psychology: Research and Practice, 23*, 345–348.

Dahlstrom, W. G. (1992b). Comparability of two-point high-point code patterns from the original MMPI norms to MMPI-2 norms for the restandardization sample. *Journal of Personality Assessment, 59*, 153–164.

Dahlstrom, W. G., Welsh, G. S., & Dahlstrom, L. E. (1972). *An MMPI handbook, Volume I: Clinical Interpretation.* Minneapolis, MN: University of Minnesota Press.

Dahlstrom, W. G., Welsh, G. S., & Dahlstrom, L. E. (1975). *An MMPI handbook, Volume II: Research Applications.* Minneapolis, MN: University of Minnesota Press.

Drake, L. E., & Oetting, E. R. (1959). *An MMPI codebook for counselors.* Minneapolis, MN: University of Minnesota Press.

Egland, B., Erickson, M., Butcher, J. N., & Ben-Porath, Y. S. (1991). MMPI-2 profiles of women at risk for child abuse. *Journal of Personality Assessment, 57*, 254–263.

Evans, R. G. (1984). Normative data for two MMPI critical item 'sets. *Journal of Clinical Psychology, 40*, 512–515.

Eyde, L., Kowal, D., & Fishburne, F. (1991). A comparison of MMPI Interpretive systems. In T. B. Gutkin & S. L. Wise (Eds.), *The computer and the decision-making process*, (pp. 75–123). Hillsdale, NJ: Lawrence Erlbaum Associates.

Fowler, R. D., & Butcher, J. N. (1986). Critique of Matarazzo's views on computerized testing: All sigma and no meaning. *American Psychologist, 41*, 94–95

Goldberg, L. R., (1965). Diagnosticians vs. diagnostic signs: The diagnosis of psychosis versus neurosis for the MMPI. *Psychological Monographs, 79*, (9, Whole No. 602).

Gough, H. G. (1946). Diagnostic patterns on the MMPI. *Journal of Clinical Psychology, 2*, 23–37.

Gough, H. G. (1948). A new dimension of status: I. Development of a personality scale. *American Sociology Review, 13*, 401–409.

Gough, H. G. (1951). Studies of social intolerance: I. Psychological and sociological correlates of anti-semitism. *Journal of Social Psychology, 33*, 237–246.

Gough, H. G., McClosky, H., & Meehl, P. E. (1951). A personality scale for dominance. *Journal of Abnormal and Social Psychology, 46*, 360–366.

Gough, H. G., McClosky, H., & Meehl, P. E. (1952). A personality scale for social responsibility. *Journal of Abnormal and Social Psychology, 47*, 73–80.

Graham, J. R., & Butcher, J. N. (March, 1988). Differentiating schizophrenia and major affective disorders with the revised form of the MMPI. Paper presented at the *23rd Annual Symposium on Recent Developments in the Use of the MMPI*, St. Petersburg Beach, FL.

Graham, I. R., Smith, R. L., & Schwartz, G. F. (1986). Stability of MMPI configurations for psychiatric inpatients. *Journal of Consulting and Clinical Psychology, 54*, 375–380.

Graham, J. R., Timbrook, R. E., Ben-Porath, Y. S., & Butcher, J. N. (1991). Congruence between MMPI and MMPI-2: Separating fact from artifact. *Journal of Personality Assessment, 57*, 205–215.

Graham, J. R., Watts, D., & Timbrook, R. E. (1991). Detecting fake-good and fake-bad MMPI-2 profiles. *Journal of Personality Assessment, 57,* 264–277.

Greene, R. L., Weed, N. C., Butcher, J. N., Arrendono, R., & Davis, H. G. (1992). A cross-validation of the MMPI-2 substance abuse scales. *Journal of Personality Assessment, 58,* 405–410.

Guthrie, G. M. (1952). Common characteristics associated with frequent MMPI profile types. *Journal of Clinical Psychology, 8,* 141–145.

Gynther, M. D., Altman, H., & Sletten, I. W. (1973). Replicated correlates of MMPI two-point types: The Missouri actuarial system. *Journal of Clinical Psychology.* (suppl. 39).

Halbower, C. C. (1955). *A comparison of actuarial versus clinical prediction to classes discriminated by the MMPI.* Minneapolis, MN: Unpublished doctoral dissertation.

Harkness, A. R., McNulty, J. L., & Ben-Porath, Y. S. (March, 1993). The Mult does measure a five-factor model: Introducing the PSY-5. Paper presented at the 28th Ánnual Symposium on Recent Developments in the use of the MMPI-2 and MMPI-A, St. Petersburg Beach, FL.

Harris, R., & Lingoes, J. (1955). *Subscales for the Minnesota Multiphasic Personality Inventory.* Mimeographed materials, The Langley Porter Clinic.

Hathaway, S. R. (1947). A coding system for MMPI profiles. *Journal of Consulting Psychology, 11,* 334–337.

Hathaway, S. R. (1960). Forward. In W. G. Dahlstrom, & G. S. Welsh, *An MMPI handbook: A guide to use in clinical practice and research.* Minneapolis, MN: University of Minnesota Press.

Hathaway, S. R. (1972). Forward. In W. G. Dahlstrom, & G. S. Welsh, & L. E. Dahlstrom *An MMPI handbook, Volume 1: Clinical Interpretation.* Minneapolis, MN: University of Minnesota Press.

Hathaway, S. R., & Briggs, P. F. (1957). Some normative data on new MMPI scales. *Journal of Clinical Psvchology, 13,* 364–368.

Hathaway, S. R., & McKinley, J. C. (1940). A multiphasic personality schedule (Minnesota): I. Construction of the schedule. *Journal of Psychology, 10,* 249–254.

Hathaway, S. R., & McKinley, J. C. (1942). A multiphasic personality schedule (Minnesota): III. The measurement of symptomatic depression. *Journal of Psychology, 14,* 73–84.

Hathaway, S. R., & McKinley, J. C. (1943). *The Minnesota Multiphasic Personality Inventory.* Minneapolis, MN: University of Minnesota Press.

Hathaway, S. R., & Meehl, P. E., (1951). The Minnesota Multiphasic Personality Inventory. In *Military clinical psychology.* Department of the Army technical manual TM 8:242; Department of the Air Force Manual AFM 160–145. Washington, DC: U.S. Government Printing Office.

Honaker, L. M. (1988). The equivalency of computerized and conventional MMPI administration: A critical review. *Clinical Psychology Review, 8,* 561–577.

Humm, D. G., & Wadsworth, G. W. (1935). The Humm-Wadsworth temperament scale. *American Journal of Psychiatry, 92,* 163–200.

Hjemboe, S., Almagor, M., & Butcher, J. N. (1992). Empirical assessment of marital distress: The Marital Distress Scale (MDS) for the MMPI-2. In J. N. Butcher & C. D. Spielberger (Eds.), *Advances in Personality Assessment,* (Vol. 9). Hillsdale, NJ: Lawrence Erlbaum Associates.

Jackson, D. N., & Hoffman, H. (1987). Common dimensions of psychopathology from the MMPI and the Basic Personality Inventory. *Journal of Clinical Psychology, 43,* 661–669.

Katz, M. M., & Lyerly, S. B. (1963). Methods for measuring adjustment and social behavior in the community. *Psychological Reports, 13,* 503–535.

Keane, T. M., Malloy, P. F., & Fairbank, J. A. (1984). Empirical development of an MMPI subscale for the assessment of combat-related posttraumatic stress disorder. *Journal of Consulting and Clinical Psychology, 52,* 888–891.

Keller, L. S., & Butcher, J. N. (1991). *Use of the MMPI-2 with chronic pain patients.* Minneapolis, MN: University of Minnesota Press.

Kleinmuntz, B. (1961). The college maladjustment scale (MT): Norms and predictive validity. *Educational and Psychological Measurement, 21,* 1029–1033.

Koss, M. P., & Butcher, J. N. (1973). A comparison of psychiatric patients' self-report with other sources of clinical information. *Journal of Research in Personality, 7,* 225–236.

Koss, M. P., Butcher, J. N., & Hoffman, N. G. (1976). The MMPI critical items: How well do they work? *Journal of Consulting and Clinical Psychology, 44,* 921–928.

Lachar, D., & Wrobel, T. A. (1979). Validating clinicians' hunches: Construction of a new MMPI critical item set. *Journal of Consulting and Clinical Psychology, 47,* 277–284.

Landis, C. & Katz, S. E. (1934). The validity of certain questions which purport to measure neurotic tendencies. *Journal of Applied Psychology, 18,* 343–356.

Landis, C., Zubin, J., & Katz, S. E. (1935). Empirical validation of three personality adjustment inventories. *Journal of Educational Psychology, 26,* 321–330.

Lubin, B., Larsen, R. M., & Matarazzo, J. (1984). Patterns of psychological test usage in the United States 1935–1982. *American Psychologist, 39,* 451–454.

MacAndrew, C. (1965). The differentiation of male alcoholic outpatients from non-alcoholic psychiatric outpatients by means of the MMPI. *Quarterly Journal of Studies of Alcohol, 26,* 238246.

Marks, P. A. & Seeman, W. (1963). *The actuarial description of abnormal personality: An atlas for use with the MMPI.* Baltimore, MD: The Williams & Wilkins Company.

Matarazzo, J. D. (1986). Computerized psychological test interpretation: Unvalidated plus all mean and no sigma. *American Psychologist, 41,* 14–24.

McCrae, R. R., (1991). The five-factor model and its assessment in clinical settings. *Journal of Personality Assessment, 57,* 399–414.

McKenna, T., & Butcher, J. N. (March, 1987). Continuity of the MMPI with alcoholics. Paper presented at the *22nd Annual Symposium on Recent Developments in the use of the MMPI,* Seattle, WA.

McKinley, J. C., & Hathaway, S. R. (1940). A multiphasic personality schedule (Minnesota): II. A differential study of hypochondriasis. *Journal of Psychology, 10,* 255–268.

McKinley, J. C., & Hathaway, S. R. (1942). A multiphasic personality schedule (Minnesota): IV. Psychasthenia. *Journal of Applied Psychology, 26,* 614–624.

McKinley, J. C., & Hathaway, S. R. (1944). A multiphasic personality schedule (Minnesota): V. Hysteria, Hypomania, and Psychopathic Deviate. *Journal of Applied Psychology, 28,* 153–174.

Megargee, E. I., Cook, P. E., & Mendelsohn, G. A., (1967). Development and validation of an MMPI scale of assaultiveness in overcontrolled individuals. *Journal of Abnormal Psychology, 72,* 519–528.

Meehl, P. E. (1945). The dynamics of "structured" personality tests. *Journal of Clinical Psychology, 1,* 296–303.

Meehl, P. E. (1946). Profile analysis of the MMPI in differential diagnosis. *Journal of Applied Psychology, 30,* 517–524.

Meehl, P. E. (1954). *Clinical versus statistical prediction: A theoretical analysis and a review of the evidence.* Minneapolis, MN: University of Minnesota Press.

Meehl, P. E. (1956). Wanted—A good cookbook. *American Psychologist, 11*, 263–272.

Meehl, P. E., & Dahlstrom, W. G. (1960). Objective configural rules for discriminating psychotic from neurotic MMPI profiles. *Journal of Consulting Psychology, 24*, 375–387.

Meehl, P. E., & Hathaway, S. R. (1946). The K factor as a suppressor variable in the MMPI. *Journal of Applied Psychology, 30,* 525–564.

Morey, L. C. (1991). *Personality Assessment, Inventory.* Odessa, FL: Psychological Assessment Resources.

Morey, L. C., Waugh, M. H., & Blashfield, R. K. (1985). MMPI scales for DSM-III personality disorders: Their derivation and correlates. *Journal of Personality Assessment, 49*, 245–251.

Pancoast, D. L., & Archer, R. P. (1989). Original adult MMPI norms in normal samples: A review with implications for future developments. *Journal of Personality Assessment, 53*, 376–395.

Peterson, C. D., & Dahlstrom, W. G. (1992). The derivation of gender-role scales GM and GF for MMPI-2 and their relation to scale 5 (Mf). *Journal of Personality Assessment, 59*, 486–499.

Pope, K. S., Butcher, J. N., & Seelen, J. (1993). *MMPI, MMPI-2, & MMPI-A in court: A Practical guide for expert witnesses and attorneys.* Washington, DC: American Psychological Association.

Roper, B. L., Ben-Porath, Y. S., & Butcher, J. N. (1991). Comparability of computerized adaptive and conventional testing with the MMPI-2. *Journal of Personality Assessment, 57,* 278–290.

Schlenger, W. E., & Kulka, R. A. (August, 1987). Performance of the Keane-Fairbank and MMPI and other self-report measures in identifying post-traumatic stress disorder. Paper presented at the *95th Annual Meeting of the American Psychological Association*, New York, NY.

Schmidt, H. O. (1945). Test profiles as a diagnostic aid: the Minnesota Multiphasic Inventory. *Journal of Applied Psychology, 29*, 115–131.

Spanier, G. B. (1976). Measuring dyadic adjustment: New scales for assessing the quality of marriage and similar dyads. *Journal of Marriage and the Family, 38,* 15–28.

Tellegen, A., & Ben-Porath, Y. S. (1992). The new uniform T-scores for the MMPI-2: Rationale, derivation, and appraisal. *Psychological Assessment, 4*,145–155.

Tellegen, A. & Ben-Porath, Y.S. (1993). Code-type comparability of the MMPI and MMPI-2: Analysis of recent findings and criticisms. *Journal of Personality Assessment, 61*, 489–500.

Tellegen, A., & Waller, N. G. (in Press). Exploring personality through test construction: Development of the Multidimensional personality questionnaire. In S. R. Briggs & J. M. Cheek (Eds.), *Personality measures: Development and evaluation.* Greenwich, CN: JAI Press.

Webb, J. T., Levitt, E. E., & Rojdev, R. (March, 1993). After three years: A comparison of the clinical use of the MMPI and MMPI-2. Paper presented at the *53rd Annual Meeting of the Society for Personality Assessment*, San Francisco, CA.

Weed, N. C., Ben-Porath, Y. S., & Butcher, J. N. (1990). Failure of the MMPI Weiner and Harmon subtle scales as measures of personality and as validity indicators. *Psychological Assessment: A Journal of Consulting and Clinical Psvchology, 2*, 281–285.

Weed, N. C., Butcher, J. N., McKenna, T., & Ben-Porath, Y. S. (1992). New measures for assessing alcohol and drug abuse with the MMPI-2: The APS and AAS. *Journal of Personality Assessment, 58,* 389–404.

Welsh, G. S. (1948). An extension of Hathaway's MMPI profile coding system. *Journal of Consulting Psychology, 12*, 343–344.

Welsh, G. S. (1956). Factor dimensions A and R. In G. S. Welsh, & W. G. Dahlstrom, (Eds). *Basic readings on the MMPI in psychology and medicine* (pp. 264–281). Minneapolis, MN: University of Minnesota Press.

Welsh, G. S., & Dahlstrom, W. G. (Eds.). (1956). *Basic readings on the MMPI in psychology and medicine.* Minneapolis, MN: University of Minnesota Press.

Wetter, M. W., Baer, R. A., Berry, D. T. R., Smith, G. T., & Larsen, L. H. (1992). Sensitivity of MMPI-2 validity scales to random responding and malingering. *Psychological Assessment, 4,* 369374.

Wiener, D. N. (1948). Subtle and obvious keys for the MMPI. *Journal of Consulting Psychology, 12,* 164–170.

Wiener, D. N., & Harmon, L. R. (1946). *Subtle and obvious keys for the MMPI: Their development.* Minneapolis, V.A. Advisement Bulletin, No. 16.

Wiggins, J. S. (1966). Substantive dimensions of self-report in the MMPI item pool. *Psychological Monographs, 80,* (22, Whole No. 630)

Wiggins, J.S. (1990). Forward. In J. N. Butcher, J. R. Graham, C. L. Williams, & Y. S. Ben-Porath, *Development and use of the MMPI-2 content scales.* Minneapolis, MN: University of Minnesota Press.

Williams, H. L. (1952). The development of a cuadality scale for the MMPI. *Journal of Clinical Psychology, 8,* 293–297.

18

The Personality Assessment Inventory and the Measurement of Normal and Abnormal Personality Constructs

Leslie C. Morey and Joan H. Glutting

In attempting to measure important constructs related to normal and abnormal personality, the investigator is faced with a wide array of instruments of very different types. This chapter provides a brief overview of the guiding theory and procedures employed in developing one of these instruments, the *Personality Assessment Inventory* (PAI: Morey, 1991), to introduce the reader to a test that was introduced fairly recently by the standards of many instruments discussed in this volume. The remainder of the chapter is devoted to a discussion of the differences between instruments that purport to measure either normal or abnormal personality and to an examination of the PAI in the context of these differences.

AN OVERVIEW OF THE PAI

The PAI is a self-administered objective test of personality designed to provide information on critical client variables in professional settings. These include constructs relevant to variability in both normal and clinical populations, although from its inception it was constructed to be useful in clinical screening, diagnosis, and the planning, implementation, and evaluation of treatment. The development of the PAI was based on a construct validation framework that emphasized a rational as well as a quantitative method of scale development. This framework places a strong emphasis on a theoretically informed approach to the development and selection of items, as well as on the assessment of their stability and correlates. The theoretical articulation of the constructs to be measured is critical, because this articulation must serve as a guide to the content of information to be sampled and to the subsequent assessment of content validity. In this process, both the conceptual nature and empirical adequacy of the items play an important role in their inclusion in the final version of the inventory. The development of the test went through four iterations in a sequential construct validation strategy similar to that described by Loevinger (1957) and Jackson (1970), although a number of item parameters were considered in addition to those described by these authors. Of paramount importance in the development of the test was the assumption that no single quantitative item parameter should be used as the sole criterion for item selection. An overreliance on a single parameter in item selection typically leads to a scale with one desirable psychometric property and numerous undesirable ones.

As an example, each PAI scale was constructed to include items addressing the full range of severity of the construct, including its milder as well as its most severe forms. This approach rests on the assumption that there is meaningful dimensional information that distinguishes milder and more severe forms of any clinical construct. Such dimensional coverage would not be possible if a single item selection criterion was applied; *milder* items would be most effective in distinguishing clinical subjects from normals, while items reflecting more severe pathology would be more useful in discriminating among different clinical groups. Also, item-total correlations for such different items would be expected to vary as a composition of the sample, due to restriction of range considerations; milder items would display higher biserial correlations in a community sample, while more severe items would do so in an inpatient psychiatric sample. Thus, items selected according to a single criterion (such as discrimination between groups or item-total correlation) are doomed to provide limited coverage of the full range of severity of a clinical construct. The PAI sought to include items that struck a balance between different desirable item parameters, including content coverage as well as empirical characteristics, so that the scales could be useful across a number of different applications.

The clinical syndromes assessed by the PAI were selected on the basis of two criteria, namely, the stability of their importance within the nosology of mental disorder and their significance in contemporary clinical practice. These criteria were assessed through a review of the historical and contemporary literature as well as through a survey of practicing diagnosticians. In generating items for these syndromes, the literature on each clinical syndrome was examined to identify those components most central to the definition of the disorder, and items were written directed at providing an assessment of each component of the syndrome in question.

The test itself contains 344 items that are answered on a four-alternative scale, with the anchors Totally False, Slightly True, Mainly True, and Very True. Each response is weighted according to the intensity of the feature that the different alternatives represent; thus, a client who answers Very True to the question "Sometimes I think I'm worthless" adds three points to his or her raw score on the Depression scale, while a client who responds with Slightly True to the same item adds only one point. The 344 items comprise 22 nonoverlapping full scales: 4 validity, 11 clinical, 5 treatment consideration, and 2 interpersonal scales. Ten of the full scales contain conceptually derived subscales designed to facilitate interpretation and coverage of the full breadth of complex clinical constructs. Brief descriptions of the scales and subscales are provided later in this chapter.

Normative Data

The PAI was developed and standardized for use in the clinical assessment of individuals in the age range of 18 through adulthood. Reading level analyses of the PAI test items indicate that reading ability at the fourth-grade level is necessary to complete the inventory.

PAI scale and subscale raw scores are transformed to T scores in order to provide interpretation relative to a standardization sample of 1,000 community-dwelling adults. This sample was carefully selected to match 1995 U.S. census projections on the basis of gender, race, and age; the educational level of the standardization sample was selected to be representative given the required fourth-grade reading level. The only stipulation for inclusion in the standardization sample (other than stratification fit) was that subjects had to endorse more than 90% of PAI items; in other words, no more than 33 items could be left blank. No other restrictions based upon PAI data were applied in creating the census-matched standardization sample.

For each scale and subscale, the T scores were linearly transformed from the means and standard deviations derived from the census-matched standardization sample. Unlike many other similar instruments, the PAI does not calculate T scores differently for men and women; instead, the same (combined) norms are used for both genders. This is because separate norms distort natural epidemiological differences between genders. For example, women are less likely than men to receive a diagnosis of antisocial personality, and this is reflected in lower mean scores for women on the Antisocial Features (ANT) scale. A separate normative procedure for men and women would result in similar numbers of each gender scoring in the clinically significant range, a result that does not reflect the established gender ratio for this disorder. As it turns out, with the exception of ANT and Alcohol Problems (ALC), gender differences on the PAI scales were negligible in the community sample (Morey, 1991).

PAI T scores are calibrated to have a mean of 50 and a standard deviation of 10, using a standard linear transformation from the community sample norms. Thus, a T score value greater than 50 lies above the mean in comparison to the scores of subjects in the standardization sample. Roughly 84% of nonclinical subjects will have a *T* score below 60 (one standard deviation above the mean) on most scales, while 98% of nonclinical subjects will have scores below 70 (two standard deviations above the mean). Thus, a *T* score at or above 70 represents a pronounced deviation from the typical responses of adults living in the community.

The *T* score thus provides a useful means for determining if certain problems are clinically significant, because relatively few normal adults will obtain markedly elevated scores. However, other comparisons are often of equal importance in clinical decision-making. For example, nearly all patients report depression at their initial evaluation; the question confronting the clinician considering a diagnosis of major depression is one of *relative* severity of symptomatology. Knowing that an individual's score on the PAI Depression scale is elevated in comparison to the standardization sample is of value, but a comparison of the elevation relative to a clinical sample may be more critical in forming diagnostic hypotheses. To facilitate these comparisons, the PAI manual and profile form also provide information about normative expectancies referenced against a representative *clinical* sample of 1,246 adults (Morey, 1991, pp. 49–50). The clinical sample included 61% men and 39% women. Ages ranged from 18–70, and ethnic background was White, 79%; Black, 13%; and all others, 9%. Subjects for the sample came from over 80 sites and included inpatients, outpatients, prisoners, substance abusers, and general medical patients. Thus, interpretation of PAI profiles can be accomplished in comparison to both normal and clinical samples.

Reliability of the PAI

The reliability of the PAI has been examined in a number of different studies that have examined the internal consistency, test-retest reliability, and configural stability of the instrument. The internal consistency reliability of the PAI has been examined in a number of different populations (Morey, 1991). Median alpha coefficients for the full scales of .81, .82, and .86 for normative, college, and clinical samples, respectively, were obtained. Examination of internal consistency estimates for the PAI full scales for groups defined by various demographic characteristics indicated that there is very little variability in internal consistency as a function of race, gender, and age.

The temporal stability of PAI scales was determined by examining their test-retest reliability in samples of normal subjects over a four week retest period. Median reliability values for the eleven full clinical scales was .86, leading to standard error of measurement estimates for these scales on the order of three to four *T* score points.

The PAI Scales

The PAI scales may be divided into four broad areas—four *validity scales,* designed to measure the operation and influence of self-report response styles; eleven *clinical scales* that measure diagnostic constructs of contemporary relevance; five *treatment consideration* scales that provide information critical in treatment planning; and two *interpersonal scales* designed to identify the respondent's characteristic style of relating to others. The following paragraphs describe these scales and summarize some of the more noteworthy validity data available for them.

Validity Scales

The PAI validity scales were developed to provide an assessment of the potential influence of certain response tendencies on PAI test performance. Clinical measures are frequently given in contexts in which respondents might be motivated to distort their self-presentation or might be presenting with various conditions that could lead to distortions of which they themselves were unaware. As an example of the latter, many clients with severe depression tend to be very harsh in their self-appraisals and magnify their faults relentlessly. This tendency can potentially lead to more negative conclusions about the severity of the clinical picture that might be drawn from an independent observer. Although no self-report instrument can be impervious to this possibility, the PAI includes scales that can be useful in the detection of such response tendencies.

Two of these scales were developed to assess deviations from conscientious responding. The Inconsistency (ICN) scale consists of pairs of similar items that can be used to determine if the respondent is answering consistently throughout the inventory. The Infrequency (INF) scale consists of items that are neutral with respect to psychopathology and have extremely high or low endorsement rates in all populations. These items should only be endorsed if the respondent is answering questions idiosyncratically, carelessly, or randomly. Simulation studies have indicated that 99.4% of randomly generated PAI profiles were identified as such by either ICN or INF (Morey, 1991).

The remaining two validity scales attempt to capture test-taking styles that might distort the interpretation of self-reported information. The Positive Impression (PIM) scale was designed to identify individuals attempting to present a favorable impression or reluctant to admit to minor flaws. The Negative Impression (NIM) scale includes items tapping rare or unlikely clinical features that can be useful in identifying an exaggerated unfavorable impression or possible malingering. Various simulated studies have demonstrated that these scales can be useful in identifying individuals who are attempting to manage their impressions in either a positive or negative direction (Morey, 1991; Rogers, Ornduff, & Sewell, 1993).

Clinical Scales

The clinical scales of the PAI were assembled to provide information about critical diagnostic features of 11 important clinical constructs. A number of different validity indicators have been used to provide information on the convergent and discriminant validity of the PAI clinical scales; these indicators can be divided into measures of *neurotic features, psychotic features,* and *behavior disorder features.* There are four neurotic spectrum scales. The Somatic Complaints (SOM) scale has three subscales tapping facets of health functioning: Conversion (SOM-C), focusing on sensory or motor dysfunction of the type often reported in conversion disorders; Somatization (SOM-S), focusing on frequent complaints about common physical symptoms; and Health Concerns (SOM-H), measuring a preoccupation with health and physical functioning. The strongest correlates for SOM have been found to be the Wiggins (1966) Health Concerns (.80) and Organic Problems (.82) content scales from the MMPI (Hathaway & McKinley, 1967); the Wahler Physical Symptoms Inventory (Wahler, 1983), with a correlation of .72; and the MMPI Hypochondriasis (.60) scale. Each of these measures is a fairly straightforward assessment of complaints regarding physical functioning, so this pattern of correlations is consistent with expectations. The SOM scale also displays small to moderate relationships with measures of distress, such as anxiety and depression.

The Anxiety (ANX) scale focuses on the phenomenology and signs of anxiety as manifest across three response modalities, as measured by three subscales: Cognitive (ANX-C), assessing ruminative worry and concern; Affective (ANX-A), focusing on the perception of free-floating fear and anxiety; and Physiological (ANX-P), assessing overt physical signs of tension and stress. The ANX scale demonstrated substantial correlations with a number of measures of negative affect, including Neuroticism (.76) and Anxiety (.76) as measured by the NEO-PI (Costa & McCrae, 1985), Trait Anxiety (.73) as assessed by the State-Trait Anxiety Inventory (STAI) (Spielberger, 1983), and the Wiggins Depression content scale (.76). This finding is consistent with research results highlighting the prominent role of anxiety in many mental disorders; such a pattern should be anticipated, because ANX was intended to be a general measure of anxiety rather than a specific diagnostic indicator.

In contrast, the Anxiety-Related Disorders (ARD) scale was designed to provide content relevant to more specific diagnostic differentiations. Three subscales tap different disorders: Obsessive-Compulsive (ARD-O) focuses on rigidity, rumination, and affective constriction; Phobias (ARD-P) inquires about common phobic fears, including social situations; and Traumatic Stress (ARD-T) focuses on the experience of traumatic events that continue to be a source of marked distress for the respondent. Given the specificity of the disorders in question, the pattern of correlations tends to be more specific than that observed with ANX. The largest correlation for ARD was with the Mississippi Scale for Combat-Related Posttraumatic Stress Disorder (Mississippi PTSD; Keane, Caddell, & Taylor, 1988), and the second largest involved the Fear Survey Schedule (FSS) (Wolpe & Lang, 1964); each of these scales directly parallels a disorder for which ARD was designed to provide coverage.

The Depression (DEP) scale focuses on the phenomenology and symptoms of depression as manifest in three domains: Cognitive (DEP-C), focusing on thoughts of helplessness and personal failure; Affective (DEP-A), assessing anhedonia and sadness; and Physiological (DEP-P), vegetative signs of depression such as sleep and appetite disturbance and reduced drive. The DEP scale demonstrates its largest correlations with various well-validated indicators of depression, such as a .81 correlation with the Beck Depression Inventory (BDI) (Beck & Steer, 1987) and a .78 association with the Hamilton Rating Scale for Depression (HAM-D: Hamilton, 1960). This is consistent with expectations, because these measures are widely used in the assessment of depression and related symptomatology. Other noteworthy correlates of the Depression scale include the MMPI Depression scale (.66), the Wiggins Poor Morale scale (.74), and the NEO-PI Neuroticism (.69) and Depression (.70) scales.

The Mania (MAN) scale assesses three components of elevated mood and has three facets: Activity Level (MAN-A), measuring overinvolvement and accelerated thought processes; Grandiosity (MAN-G), focusing on inflated self-esteem and expansiveness; and Irritability (MAN-I), addressing frustrations in relationships with others resulting from overvalued or unrealistic ideas. MAN demonstrates strong correlations with Wiggins Hypomania (.63), Psychoticism (.58), and Hostility (.55) content scales, with clinical ratings on the Brief Psychiatric Rating Scale (Overall & Gorham, 1962) of Grandiosity (.48) and Conceptual Disorganization (.40), and with the MMPI Hypomania scale (.53).

The Paranoia (PAR) scale assesses three features typically associated with paranoid disorders of various types: Hypervigilance (PAR-H), involving a general suspicious and wariness in relationships; Persecution (PAR-P), involving specific beliefs that others are intentionally undermining one's interests; and Resentment (PAR-R), focusing on bitterness and an externalization of blame for misfortunes. The PAR scale demonstrated substantial correlations with the MMPI Paranoid personality disorder scale (Morey, Waugh, & Blashfield, 1985) (.70), the Wiggins Psychoticism scale (.60), and various measures of hostility such as the Wiggins Hostility content scale (.54) and the NEO-PI Hostility facet scale (.55). A moderate correlation with the MMPI Paranoia scale was also observed (.45).

The Schizophrenia (SCZ) scale includes three subscales tapping different components of schizophrenic spectrum disorders: Psychotic Experience (SCZ-P), assessing *positive* symptoms of schizophrenia ranging from magical thinking to the hallucinations and delusions characteristic of the active phase of a schizophrenic psychosis; Social Detachment (SCZ-S), involving *negative* symptoms of schizophrenia, such as social withdrawal and affective uninvolvement; and Thought Disorder (SCZ-T), focusing on confusion and concentration problems. The SCZ scale has been found to correlate with the Wiggins Psychoticism content scale (.76) and the MMPI Schizotypal (.67) and Paranoid (.66) personality disorder scales. The SCZ scale was also positively correlated with the MMPI Schizophrenia scale (.55) and negatively associated with indices of sociability and social effectiveness such as NEO-PI Agreeableness (−.49) and Gregariousness (−.57). This pattern indicates that scores on the SCZ scale reflect disruptions in both cognitive (e.g., delusions, hallucinations) and interpersonal (e.g., limited social competence) realms of functioning.

The Borderline Features (BOR) scale assesses four components of borderline personality functioning that have been replicated in a number of studies. The components include: Affective Instability (BOR-A), involving heightened emotional responsiveness and mood lability; Identity Problems (BOR-I), assessing feelings of emptiness and uncertainty about major life issues; Negative Relationships (BOR-N), involving a history of ambivalent and intense relationships; and Self-Harm (BOR-S), assessing self-damaging impulsivity. The strongest correlates of the BOR scale are the MMPI Borderline personality disorder scale (.77), the NEO-PI Neuroticism scale (.67), and several different measures of hostility, such as the NEO-PI Hostility facet (.70). The BOR scale also displayed substantial correlations with the Insecure Attachment scale (.63) from the Bell Object Relations Inventory (Bell, Billington, & Becker, 1985), with the NEO-PI Impulsiveness facet (.52), and with the Wiggins Family Problems (.63) and Psychoticism (.63) content scales. This pattern of anger, impulsiveness, and interpersonal clashes is consistent with the core features of the borderline syndrome.

The PAI Antisocial Features (ANT) scale includes both the behavioral component of antisocial personality, as measured by the Antisocial Behaviors (ANT-A) subscale, as well as two characterological components of the disorder: Egocentricity (ANT-E), involving a lack of empathy and remorse; and Stimulus Seeking (ANT-S), assessing recklessness and a low tolerance for boredom. The ANT scale demonstrated its largest correlations with the Hare (1985) Psychopathy Scale (.82) and the MMPI Antisocial personality disorder scale (.77). Other correlates included the Wiggins Hostility (.57) and Family Problems (.52) content scales, the NEO-PI excitement-seeking facet (.56), and the Interpersonal Adjectives Scale-Revised (IAS-R; Wiggins, Trapnell, & Phillips, 1988) cold interpersonal octant (.45). This pattern suggests that the personality, interpersonal, and behavioral elements of psychopathy are addressed by the scale. The correlation with the MMPI Psychopathic deviate scale is positive but not impressive (.34), suggesting that the two scales represent core features of the disorder somewhat differently.

The PAI Alcohol Problems (ALC) and Drug Problems DRG scales provide straightforward assessments of the type of problems typically associated with substance abuse and dependence. The scales demonstrate a similar pattern of correlates, namely, strong associations with corresponding measures of substance abuse and moderate links with indicators of antisocial personality. ALC yields a correlation of .89 with the Michigan Alcoholism Screening Test (MAST; Selzer, 1971), while DRG correlates .69 with the Drug Abuse Screening Test (DAST; Skinner, 1982).

Treatment Considerations Scales

The treatment consideration scales of the PAI were assembled to provide indicators of potential complications in treatment that would not necessarily be apparent from diagnostic information. There are five of these scales—two indicators of potential for harm to self or others, two measures of the subject's environmental circumstances, and one indicator of the subject's motivation for treatment.

The Aggression (AGG) scale is the only one of the five treatment scales to be organized around a subscale structure; it includes three such subscales: Aggressive Attitude (AGG-A), assessing hostility and poor control over anger; Verbal Aggression (AGG-V), involving verbal expressions of anger ranging from assertiveness to abusiveness; and Physical Aggression (AGG-P), which involves physical displays of anger. Substantial correlations have been identified between the AGG scale and NEO-PI Hostility scale (.83) and the Trait Anger (.75) scale from the State-Trait Anger Expression Inventory (STAXI; Spielberger, 1988). The AGG scale was also negatively correlated with the STAXI Anger Control scale (–.57).

The Suicidal Ideation (SUI) scale focuses on a range of attitudes and behavior related to suicide, ranging from hopelessness to thoughts and plans for suicide. SUI has demonstrated noteworthy correlations with the Beck Hopelessness Scale (Beck & Steer, 1988) (.64), the BDI (.61), the Suicidal Ideation (.56) and Total Score (.40) of the Suicide Probability Scale (SPS; Cull & Gill, 1982), and SUI was also found to be negatively correlated with perceived social support measures.

The Stress (STR) scale was designed to measure the impact of recent stressors in major life areas. It has been found to correlate substantially with the Schedule of Recent Events stress index developed by Holmes and Rahe (1967) as well as with various indicators of depression and poor morale. A second indicator of environmental characteristics, the Nonsupport (NON) scale, measures a lack of perceived social support, considering both the quality and quantity of support. As expected, the NON scale has been found to be highly and inversely correlated with measures of social support such as the Perceived Social Support scales (Procidano & Heller, 1983); –.67 with PSS-Family, and –.63 with PSS-Friends. NON was also moderately associated with numerous measures of distress and tension.

Finally, the Treatment Rejection (RXR) scale was designed to focus on attitudes theoretically predictive of interest and motivation in making changes of a psychological nature. RXR has been found to be negatively associated with Wiggins Poor Morale (–.78) and the NEO-PI Vulnerability (–.54) scales, consistent with the idea that distress can serve as a motivator for treatment. The Treatment Rejection scale has been shown to be positively associated with indices of social support (.26–.49), implying that people are less likely to be motivated for treatment if they have an intact and available support system as an alternative.

Interpersonal Scales

The interpersonal scales of the PAI were designed to provide an assessment of the interpersonal style of subjects along two dimensions: (a) a warmly affiliative vs. a cold rejecting axis—the WRM scale; and (b) a dominating, controlling vs. a meekly submissive style—the DOM scale. These axes provide a useful way of conceptualizing variation in normal personality as well as in many different mental disorders, and persons at the extremes of these dimensions may present with a variety of disorders. The PAI manual describes a number of studies indicating that diagnostic groups differ on these dimensions; for example, spouse-abusers are relatively high on the Dominance (DOM) scale, while schizophrenics are low on the Warmth (WRM) scale (Morey, 1991). Correlations with related measures also provides support for the construct validity of these scales. For example, the correlations with the IAS-R vector scores are consistent with expectations, with PAI DOM associated with the IAS-R dominance vector (.61) and PAI WRM associated with the IAS-R love vector (.65). The NEO-PI Extroversion scale roughly bisects the high DOM/high WRM quadrant, as it is moderately positively correlated with both scales; this finding is consistent with previous research (Trapnell & Wiggins, 1990). The WRM scale was also correlated with the NEO-PI Gregariousness scale (.46), while DOM was associated with the NEO-PI Assertiveness facet (.71).

In summary, the scales of the PAI have been found to associate with most major instruments for the assessment of diagnosis and treatment efficacy in theoretically concordant ways. Thus, the instrument appears quite promising with respect to its reliability and validity. However, the question remains: To what extent does the PAI provide comprehensive assessments of both normal and abnormal personality?

THE PAI AND THE DIFFERENTIATION OF NORMAL AND ABNORMAL PERSONALITY

The differentiation of normal and abnormal personality has been a particular challenge to the psychopathology researcher as well as to the mental health professional. In part, this difficulty stems from the heterogeneous behavior of individuals bearing diagnoses such as *personality disorder*, but it also reflects the vague and ill-defined nature of the boundaries between normal and abnormal personality, whether these boundaries are considered to be natural or artificial. As a further complication, the definition of *abnormal personality* (i.e., personality disorder) has undergone substantial changes in recent years, and the American Psychiatric Association's *Diagnostic and Statistical Manual of Mental Disorders*, despite admirable attempts to objectify many critical distinctions, is still unclear on distinctions between normal personality, abnormal personality, and clinical syndromes. Many of the other chapters in this volume detail the complexities of these definitional boundaries and the strengths and weaknesses of different approaches to resolving these issues.

Although the distinction between normal and abnormal aspects of personality has not been well articulated conceptually, in the psychometric field it is clear that there are differences between *instruments* as to whether they are designed to measure *normal* or *abnormal* constructs. For example, catalogs from test publishers often present such tests in separate sections, suggesting that the differences between the constructs is implicit in the minds of many. The remainder of this chapter proposes certain empirical criteria that we believe may help to identify whether a construct captures an element of *normal personality* or whether it represents something *abnormal*. Each of these criteria will be discussed with respect to the PAI, and the general conclusion will be drawn that the PAI measures elements of both normal and abnormal personality, although measurements of the latter type of constructs predominate. However, these criteria are easily applied to other instruments, and the further application of these criteria may also help to clarify some of the differences between psychopathology, abnormality personality, and normative personality traits.

Criterion 1. Normal and Abnormal Personality Constructs Differ in the Distribution of Their Related Features in the General Population

Differentiating normal and abnormal personality in this manner is similar to the approach taken by the late Graham Foulds (1971). Foulds separated what he called personality deviance from personal illness (i.e., psychopathology), and he proposed a model of the relationship between these conditions whereby they were viewed as overlapping but conceptually independent domains. In making this distinction, he focused upon quantitative aspects of these conditions, namely the distributions of symptoms (features of personal illness) and traits (features of personality deviance) in various populations.

In distinguishing between features associated with these conditions, Foulds hypothesized that abnormal symptoms should have distributions that have a marked positive skew (i.e., occur infrequently) in normal samples, while roughly normally distributed in clinical samples. In contrast, normative personality traits should be distributed in a roughly Gaussian (i.e., bell-shaped) manner in the general population; a sample of individuals with *deviant* personalities are distinguished by the personality trait being manifest to a degree rarely encountered in the general population. It should be noted that both types of constructs may be of clinical interest. Various regions of each type of construct may represent an area of concern; a person can be having difficulties because he or she manifests a particular normative trait to an extreme degree (e.g., introversion), or because he or she manifests an abnormal construct to even a slight degree (e.g., suicidal ideation). The primary difference is in the nature of the construct; the individual with a clinical trait (i.e., psychopathology) may be somehow qualitatively different from normals, while individuals with an *abnormal amount* of a normative personality trait are quantitatively distinct; that is, a difference of degree rather than kind.

The PAI was designed to be used with clinical populations, and as such many of the scales it includes would be considered to provide an assessment of psycho-pathological rather than normative personality constructs under this criterion. Support for this conclusion may be found in comparing the distributions of the PAI scales in community and clinical populations, as presented in Table 18.1. Most of the PAI scales and subscales demonstrate a pronounced positive skew in a community sample, with some (e.g., SUI, DRG) being quite skewed and as such meet this criterion as abnormal or pathological personality characteristics. Furthermore,

TABLE 18.1 Distributional Differences Between Clinical and Community Samples on PAI Full Scales

Scales by Group	Skewness		Mean Score	
	Community	Clinical	Community	Clinical
Validity				
ICN – Inconsistency	0.98	0.51	5.39	6.57
INF – Infrequency	1.59	1.03	2.66	3.18
NIM – Negative Impression	2.88	1.41	1.69	4.38
PIM – Positive Impression	−0.32	−0.01	15.07	12.24
Clinical				
SOM – Somatic Complaints	1.70	0.80	11.09	19.34
ANX – Anxiety	1.18	0.43	16.47	28.50
ARD – Anxiety-Related Disorders	0.86	0.40	19.91	28.27
DEP – Depression	1.24	0.42	14.28	27.38
MAN – Mania	0.52	0.43	23.01	25.34
PAR – Paranoia	0.64	0.54	18.45	24.86
SCZ – Schizophrenia	0.96	0.71	13.99	21.03
BOR – Borderline Features	0.79	0.21	18.03	31.39
ANT – Antisocial Features	1.18	0.72	13.16	18.88
ALC – Alcohol Problems	1.83	0.87	4.83	10.44
DRG – Drug Problems	1.95	1.01	4.09	8.62
Treatment Consideration				
AGG – Aggression	0.86	0.60	8.42	19.69
SUI – Suicidal Ideation	2.52	1.13	4.86	9.09
STR – Stress	1.18	0.12	5.80	11.91
NON – Nonsupport	1.09	0.48	4.90	8.44
RXR Treatment Rejection	−0.41	0.41	13.76	9.10
Interpersonal				
DOM – Dominance	−0.01	−0.27	20.60	19.41
WRM – Warmth	−0.21	−0.29	23.48	21.16

Notes. From Morey (1991, pp. 50 and 53). Community sample *n* = 1000; clinical sample *n* = 1246.

for most of the PAI scales, the distributions in clinical samples are more nearly Gaussian, as would be expected of a measure of a construct representing abnormality. For example, the distribution of the DEP scale is far more skewed in the community sample than in the clinical sample, suggesting that according to this criterion, depression qualifies as an *abnormal* facet of an individual's functioning.

However, some scales, in particular the interpersonal scales, demonstrate distributions that are quite similar in both community and clinical samples and are nearly normal. Furthermore, some of the clinical scales demonstrate rather small distributional differences across populations; for example, MAN and PAR have fairly similar skewness values in the two populations. These results suggest that there are important elements of *normal* personality measured by these two constructs, perhaps self-esteem and interpersonal wariness, respectively.

The PAI does include scales designed to provide an assessment of *personality disorder* concepts, conceptually represented in the *DSM* manual as being extreme manifestations of normal personality traits. The PAI scales for BOR and ANT are direct measures for antisocial personality disorder and borderline personality disorder. However, it is interesting to note that there are substantial skewness differences between populations for the BOR and ANT scales, suggesting that by this definition these are measures of abnormal aspects of functioning rather than of normative personality traits. This implies that the instantiation of these constructs on the PAI more resembles a psychopathological construct than an extreme manifestation of normal personality traits.

However, there are indications suggesting that other *DSM* personality disorder constructs may indeed reflect extremes of normal variation, if this criterion is applied to PAI data. For example, relationships between DOM and WRM dimensions of personality and personality disorders have been frequently identified (Dejong, van den Brink, Jansen, & Schippers, 1989; Morey, 1985; Wiggins, 1987), with the results obtained using the two PAI scales being quite similar to those found in previous research (Morey, 1991). For example, dependent and avoidant personality disorders were found to be negatively related to DOM and narcissistic personality disorder positively. Avoidant, schizotypal, and schizoid personalities are negatively associated with WRM. Histrionic personality is positively associated with both the WRM and DOM scales, with stronger associations for WRM. These consistent patterns of association support the conclusion that some of the personality disorder diagnoses included in the *DSM* may indeed be manifestations of extreme degrees of normative personality traits.

In summary, the criterion of distributional differences suggests that the preponderance of PAI scales would be considered to measure abnormal or psychopathological personality traits. However, this criterion also indicates that various aspects of personality constructs that are more normative in nature are assessed by certain PAI scales, particularly by the interpersonal scales.

Criterion 2. Normal and Abnormal Personality Constructs Differ Dramatically in Their Social Desirability

Assessment investigators have long recognized that self-report personality tests can be vulnerable to efforts at impression management. In particular, much concern has been expressed about the influence of efforts to respond in a socially desirable fashion on such tests. Various diverse and creative efforts have been directed at resolving this dilemma, including the empirical keying strategy behind the development of the original MMPI (Hathaway & McKinley, 1967) as well as the subsequent use of the *k*-correction and the forced choice matched item alternatives employed in the Edwards Personal Preference Schedule (Edwards, 1954). However, for self-report tests that focus on *abnormal* constructs, these strategies tend not to work very well. It is suggested that the reason for these problems is that abnormal constructs are inherently socially undesirable. As such, most measures of social desirability responding will correlate quite highly with measures of abnormal constructs. In contrast, the social desirability of normative personality features is more ambiguous, less evaluative, and more likely to be tied to a specific context. For example, the trait adjective *talkative* might be a socially desirable characteristic in a salesperson but not in a librarian. There is likely to be little consensus among people as to whether being talkative is a desirable or undesirable characteristic, whereas characteristics such as *depressed* or *delusional* will invariably be viewed consensually as undesirable.

This implies that the social desirability of a construct may be useful as an indicator of its status in capturing normal or abnormal variation between people. The desirability of the construct may be measured in many ways; for example, correlations with measures such as the Marlowe-Crowne (Crowne & Marlowe, 1960) social desirability scale can yield an estimate of the desirability loading of a measure of some construct. Another means to assess the desirability of a construct measured by a particular scale is to gauge the impact that efforts at impression management have upon scale scores. Each of these techniques was used in the development of the PAI, and the results of those studies suggested that these two desirability metrics are related although not identical. In these studies, two desirability metrics were examined: (1) intercorrelation with a short form of the Marlowe-Crowne (Reynolds, 1982); and (2) the *F* value from a one way analysis of variance comparing mean scale scores under positive impression, negative impression, and standard instructional sets (Morey, 1991). Some scales such as DOM and MAN-G demonstrated little correlation with the Marlowe-Crowne and were little effected by impression management, while others such as PAR-P and SCZ-T showed the opposite pattern, suggesting that features of persecutory beliefs and thought disorder have strong desirability connotations.

As was the case with the criterion of distributional differences, the use of social desirability to distinguish normal from abnormal constructs suggests that the preponderance of PAI scales appear to measure the latter. The majority of PAI scales demonstrate significant negative associations with social desirability measures and substantial effects of impression management instructional sets. Once again, however, this criterion also indicates that more normative aspects of personality are assessed as well, and again the interpersonal scales (particularly the DOM scale) appear as the strongest candidates as measures of normal personality traits by this criterion.

Criterion 3. Scores on Measures of Abnormal Personality Constructs Differ Dramatically Between Clinical and Community Samples, While Scores of Normal Constructs Do Not

This criterion is based upon the assumption that, in dealing with an abnormal personality construct, *more* is worse; that is, the more of the construct a person has, the greater the impairment the person manifests and the more likely the person is to come to the attention of mental health professionals. For example, when considering disordered thinking as a personal characteristic, greater amounts of thought disorder will be associated with greater impairment and need for intervention. Thus, a clinical population should invariably obtain higher scores on measures of such constructs than a community sample. In contrast, for a normative personality trait, the adaptive direction of scores is less clearcut. Given the assumption that such traits are normally distributed, then the traits are inherently bipolar, and extreme scores at *either* end of the trait may be maladaptive. Thus, even if clinical samples were restricted to persons with problems on a particular normative trait (e.g., extreme scores on introversion-extraversion), there would still be no reason to suspect mean differences between clinical and community subjects, as the extreme scores of the clinical subjects at either end of the continuum would be expected to balance out.

A comparison of mean PAI scale scores in community and clinical populations is presented in Table 18.1. Most of the PAI scales demonstrate much higher mean scores in a clinical sample, with the difference generally on the order of a standard deviation on many scales (standard deviations are presented in Morey, 1991). Particularly large differences are noted on the DEP and BOR scales, scales that have emerged on other criteria as noteworthy candidates for *abnormal* personality constructs. Once again, however, there are certain scales that demonstrate negligible mean differences between populations. For example, both of the interpersonal scales, as well as the MAN scale, seem to show little overall difference between community and clinical samples. These results once again point to the likelihood that these measures most heavily tap normative personality traits.

Criterion 4. Measures of Normative Personality Traits Should Demonstrate Factorial/Correlational Invariance Across Clinical and Community Samples, While Measures of Abnormal Traits May Not

The basic assumption behind this criterion is that the correlation pattern that gives abnormal constructs their syndromal coherence should only emerge in samples where there is adequate representation of individuals manifesting the syndrome (i.e., clinical samples). In community samples, which may include relatively few individuals who have a clinical syndrome, the association between features of the same syndrome may be no greater than that between any two features selected randomly. As an example, if depression were defined by five necessary and sufficient criteria and these five criteria were intercorrelated in a community sample that contained no depressed subjects, the average correlation between these features might well be zero. In a sample of nondepressed individuals, sleep problems and low self-esteem may only be associated at chance levels, because individuals who share the putative causal process that underlies the clinical association of these features have been removed from the sample. It is the covariation of these features in individuals considered to be depressed that lends a correlation pattern to these features. Thus, highly intercorrelated sets of features (i.e., syndromes) might emerge from a factor analysis of clinical subjects that would not be identified in a sample of subjects selected from the community.

In contrast, those traits that describe normal variation in personality would be expected to capture this variability among clinical as well as normal subjects. Even though the clinical subjects may be, as a group, more extreme on normal personality traits, similar correlational patterns among elements of the trait should be obtained. For example, the construct of introversion–extraversion should identify meaningful differences among clinical subjects as well as normal subjects, and the intercorrelation of the behavior that makes up this construct should be similar in the two populations. This should yield predictable empirical results with respect to the factor structure (for multifaceted scales/constructs) and the average item intercorrelation (i.e., coefficient alpha, for unidimensional constructs); for a normative trait, these results should be similar in clinical and nonclinical samples. In contrast, these values may well differ if an *abnormal* construct is being examined.

Interestingly, factor analyses of the PAI in clinical and community samples yields factor structures that are quite similar (Morey, 1991). In both samples, the first factor appears to involve negative affect and the second factor appears to involve impulsivity and poor judgment. The third factor, which emerges primarily in clinical samples rather than community samples, appears to involve egocentricity, callousness, and exploitativeness, once again suggesting that the construct of antisocial personality is better described as an abnormal construct rather than as an extreme of normal variation. The fourth and final factor was quite different in the two samples; in the clinical sample it appeared related to profile validity, while in the community sample it involved interpersonal sensitivity and detachment. This latter factor may again reflect a normal personality trait which, when extreme, may be maladaptive in either high (undue caution, paranoia) or low (dependency, gullibility) degree.

SUMMARY

In this chapter we presented four criteria for distinguishing between normal and pathological aspects of personality and demonstrated how the PAI illustrates empirical differences between the two types of constructs. The PAI was developed to provide assessments of constructs that for the most part would be considered in the *abnormal* spectrum. However, according to the criteria described above, the test includes many scales that are related to constructs which show considerable variation even within the general population. In part, this may be due to the assumption of inherent dimensionality of all clinical constructs that was the foundation of the development of the instrument. Despite the positive skew of most scales, they were constructed to have a relatively *soft floor* so that meaningful variation could be captured, even within the normal range. Nonetheless, with the exception of the interpersonal scales, the PAI was designed for the ascertainment of abnormality, not to capture the possible variants of normality. As noted, the four criteria discussed above suggest strongly that the PAI is heavily slanted in that direction. To provide a thorough evaluation of both domains of interest, the PAI is probably best used in conjunction with an instrument designed specifically for the assessment of normative personality traits. However, the criteria we proposed for distinguishing abnormal from normative personality features have many implications for clarifying the differences between normal personality, personality disorder, and psychopathology.

REFERENCES

Beck, A. T., & Steer, R. A. (1987). *Beck Depression Inventory manual.* San Antonio: The Psychological Corporation.

Beck, A. T., & Steer, R. A. (1988). *Beck Hopelessness Scale manual.* San Antonio: The Psychological Corporation.

Bell, M. J., Billington, R., & Becker, B. (1985). A scale for the assessment of object relations: Reliability, validity, and factorial invariance. *Journal of Clinical Psychology, 42,* 733–741.

Costa, P. T., & McCrae, R. R. (1985). *The NEO Personality Inventory manual.* Odessa, FL: Psychological Assessment Resources.

Crowne, D. P., & Marlowe, D. (1960). A new scale of social desirability independent of psychopathology. *Journal of Consulting Psychology, 24,* 349–354.

Cull, J. G., & Gill, W. S. (1982). *Suicide Probability Scale manual.* Los Angeles, CA: Western Psychological Services.

DeJong, C. A. J., van den Brink, W., Jansen, J. A. M., & Schippers, G. M. (1989). Interpersonal aspects of DSM-III axis II: Theoretical hypotheses and empirical findings. *Journal of Personality Disorders, 3,* 135–146.

Edwards, A. L. (1954). *Manual for the Edwards Personal Preference Schedule.* New York: Psychological Corporation.

Foulds, G. A. (1971) Personality deviance and personal symptomatology. *Psychological Medicine. 1,* 222–233.

Hamilton, M. (1960). A rating scale for depression. *Journal of Neurology, Neurosurgery and Psychiatry, 23,* 56–62.

Hare, R. D. (1985). Comparison of procedures for the assessment of psychopathy. *Journal of Consulting and Clinical Psychology, 53,* 7–16.

Hathaway, S. R., & McKinley, J. C. (1967). *MMPI manual (revised edition).* New York: Psychological Corporation.

Holmes, T. H., & Rahe, R. H. (1967). The social readjustment rating scale. *Journal of Psychosomatic Research, 11,* 213–218.

Jackson, D. N. (1970). A sequential system for personality scale development. In C. D. Spielberger (Ed.), *Current topics in clinical and community psychology, volume 2,* pp. 62–97. New York: Academic Press.

Keane, T. M., Caddell, J. M., & Taylor, K. L. (1988). Mississippi scale for combat-related posttraumatic stress disorder: Three studies in reliability and validity. *Journal of Consulting and Clinical Psychology, 56,* 85–90.

Loevinger, J. (1957). Objective tests as instruments of psychological theory. *Psychological Reports, 3,* 635–694.

Morey, L. C. (1985). An empirical comparison of interpersonal and DSM-III approaches to classification of personality disorders. *Psychiatry, 48,* 358–364.

Morey, L. C. (1991). *The Personality Assessment Inventory Professional Manual.* Odessa, FL: Psychological Assessment Resources, Inc.

Morey, L. C., Waugh, M. H., & Blashfield, R. K. (1985). MMPI scales for DSM-III personality disorders: Their derivation and correlates. *Journal of Personality Assessment, 49,* 245–251.

Overall, J. E., & Gorham, D. R. (1962). The brief psychiatric rating scale. *Psychological Reports, 10,* 799–812.

Procidano, M. E., & Heller, K. (1983). Measures of perceived social support from friends and from family: Three validation studies. *American Journal of Community Psychology, 11,* 1–24.

Reynolds, W. M. (1982). Development of reliable and valid short forms of the Marlowe-Crowne Social Desirability Scale. *Journal of Clinical Psychology, 38,* 119–125.

Rogers, R., Ornduff, S. R., & Sewell, K. W. (1993). Feigning specific disorders: A study of the Personality Assessment Inventory (PAI). *Journal of Personality Assessment, 60,* 554–560.

Selzer, M. L. (1971). The Michigan Alcoholism Screening Test: The quest for a new diagnostic instrument. *American Journal of Psychiatry, 127,* 1653–1658.

Skinner, H. A. (1982). The drug abuse screening test. *Addictive Behaviors, 7,* 363–371.

Spielberger, C. D. (1983). *Manual for the State-Trait Anxiety Inventory.* Palo Alto, CA: Consulting Psychologists Press.

Spielberger, C. D. (1988). *State-Trait Anger Expression Inventory.* Odessa, FL: Psychological Assessment Resources.

Trapnell, P. D., & Wiggins, J. S. (1990). Extension of the Interpersonal Adjective Scale to include the big five dimensions of personality. *Journal of Personality and Social Psychology, 59,* 781–790.

Wahler, H. J. (1983). *Wahler Physical Symptoms Inventory, 1983 edition.* Los Angeles: Western Psychological Services.

Wiggins, J. S. (1966). Substantive dimensions of self-report in the MMPI item pool. *Psychological Monographs, 80, 22* (whole No. 630).

Wiggins, J. S. (1987, August). How interpersonal are the MMPI personality disorder scales? Paper presented at the meeting of the American Psychological Association, New York.

Wiggins, J. S., Trapnell, P., & Phillips, N. (1988). Psychometric and geometric characteristics of the revised Interpersonal Adjectives Scale (IAS-R). *Multivariate Behavioral Research, 23,* 517–530.

Wolpe, J., & Lang, P. (1964). A fear survey schedule for use in behavior therapy. *Behavior Research and Therapy, 2,* 27–30.

Summary and Perspective

The modern tradition of examining healthy and disordered personality separately may be viewed by future psychologists as a scientific detour necessitated by the psychoanalytic conceptions that dominated the field in the first half of the twentieth century. The bifurcation may perhaps be lamented for its division of resources along with ideas, but it did help counterbalance the often one-sided elaborations that paid lip service to health but focused almost exclusively on pathology, and established a legitimate domain for the study of normal functioning.

This volume is a strong argument for reuniting personologists in the service of developing a better grasp of personality in all individuals. As a whole, the chapters demonstrate that a wealth of theories, methods, and measures is available to clinicians and researchers to address the interface between normality and pathology. Comprehensive models of personality are represented in this volume by the dimensional views of Cattell, Cloninger, and Eysenck, the five-factor model of Costa and McCrae, Millon's evolutionary theory, and the interpersonal approaches of Benjamin, Kiesler, and Wiggins. Somewhat more specific conceptualizations are noted in the DSM, MMPI, and psychobiological models presented by Claridge. In the realm of methodology, three statistical techniques are presented for finding formal structure in multivariate data sets—namely, cluster analysis, multidimensional scaling, and factor analysis. Gurtman proposes some rigorous procedures for fitting data into a circumplex, which is the foundation for the interpersonal circle. Moldin presents ways of assessing the contribution of genetics to personality characteristics. With regard to measurement, both old and new assessment devices are offered as helpful in differentiating normal and abnormal traits. Ben-Porath presents novel and traditional ways of using the MMPI data set for measuring personality, while Harkness and McNulty argue for a new psychopathology based five-factor approach. Henry presents Benjamin's three-circle SASB extension of the two-dimensional interpersonal circumplex, Helmes and Jackson offer the new DAPP, and Morey and Glutting describe the PAI.

Surveying these contributions, as well as others that we could not include on such topics as schizotypy (e.g., Chapman & Chapman, 1987), schizophrenia (Meehl, 1990), the *Schedule for Nonadaptive and Adaptive Personality* (Clark, 1990, 1993), and Tellegen's (1993; Tellegen & Waller, in press) *Multidimensional*

Personality Questionnaire, we are assured that scientists have at their disposal many useful tools for differentiating normal and abnormal personality. So where do we go from here?

It is clear from the many definitions for normality and abnormality presented in the Introduction that it is unrealistic to expect the emergence of a single, wholistic conception of personality that will satisfy everyone. This is because how we define normality and abnormality determines the nature of our theories. Thus, a belief in normality as health and personality disorder as a manifestation of genetic abnormality or disease leads to theories that explain abnormality from a biological point of view. By contrast, viewing normality as that which is not problematic, and disordered personality as a manifestation of problems in living, leads to explanations that focus on interpersonal functioning within a particular context or culture.

As long as we generate multiple views of normality and abnormality, we shall have multiple theories. Because of this, we believe that a near-future goal should not be to assert the superiority of one viewpoint over another, but rather to make explicit in our theories and empirical investigations what our assumptions are. This cuts two ways. We should be clear about how we define normality and pathology—for example, average versus deviant or health versus disease—and how we conceptualize normal and abnormal personality—for example, in terms of dimensions, categories, styles, types, or some combination of these. If we can do this we should be able to make more meaningful comparisons among models and research investigations that *share* assumptions, and avoid misleading contrasts.

The theories that we now have are quite impressive in their scope and potential explanatory power. Nevertheless, improvements can be made in most of them by more precisely specifying the elements of human functioning they are attempting to address, the hierarchical levels and/or domains their explanatory principles are aimed toward, and how their concepts and variables are linked across levels and domains. Further, it is still relatively easy to find somewhat lopsided treatments of either normal or abnormal character, and somewhat vague distinctions between healthy and disordered traits, styles, or types. In the new age of research that addresses both normal and abnormal personality, we need greater clarity and specification of similarities and differences between the two, as well as better operating principles for distinguishing one from the other.

Following the division of research lines, most available personality instruments were created to measure either normal or abnormal traits, but not both. Greater availability of assessment devices that tap healthy *and* disordered character elements in children, adolescents, and adults will make progress in the field easier to come by. In this regard, we are pleased that there are a handful of promising instruments now on the market (see, for example, the chapters by Cloninger and Svrakic; Eysenck; Helmes and Jackson; Henry; Krug; McCrae; and Pincus).

Considerable progress has been made in the search for a taxonomy of personality traits in the realm of normal character (Digman, 1990; John, 1990), and it is important to expand this effort to the domain of personality disorders. Doing so should greatly assist our efforts to understand how normal and abnormal personalities differ and how they are the same. Of course, developing a taxonomy that encompasses normal and abnormal traits will not be easy. The population of abnormal persons is much smaller than that of normal persons, and changing definitions continue to shift the boundaries of psychopathology (note the DSM). Furthermore, the stability that characterizes most normal persons is frequently absent in psychiatric patients. Research on state versus trait issues will hopefully assist us in the task of sorting out the effects of transient psychiatric conditions on presumably more pervasive personality traits.

Concerning empirical studies, longitudinal investigations are needed for testing hypotheses about the course of personality disorders. Findings in the realm of normal personality have demonstrated remarkable stability of traits after age 30 (e.g., McCrae & Costa, 1990). Are personality disorders likely to show similar stability? In some cases we would expect the answer to be "yes," but in others "no," because of the potentially unsettling influence of the DSM Axis I psychiatric conditions that some disordered personalities are susceptible to, such as substance abuse and depression. In any event, longitudinal scrutiny is needed to provide critical evidence.

Studies that compare and contrast different samples, models, methods, and measures will also be helpful in the next generation of research. Most reports to date have focused on single groups of normal or abnormal individuals and have utilized single theories, methodologies (like factor analysis), and measures (like the MMPI). The value of more frequent use of well-matched and well-defined samples of healthy and disordered persons cannot be underestimated. Studies of this type will provide pertinent data for mapping the fundamental similarities and differences between these populations. Examination of multiple models, statistical techniques, and instruments should give us a clearer perspective on the strengths and limitations of competing systems.

On a practical front, clinicians and researchers should continue to push for a more empirically sound diagnostic system that acknowledges dimensional traits and normal personality. The current DSM multiaxial system is much improved over that employed before 1980. However, it is limited as a descriptive, categorical system that endorses only pathological character. Everyone has a unique personality, and it is important for clinicians making Axis I psychiatric diagnoses and treatment plans to understand the strengths and limitations of the person with the illness. Incorporating dimensional traits into the diagnostic system will help make it more empirically sound and, hopefully, encourage clinicians to consider the healthy aspects of their patients' personalities.

Ten years from now we hope to edit a book on the same topic that demonstrates substantial improvements in our understanding. Our vision includes more complete theoretical explications, improved methodologies and measures, and sound empirical evidence from a wide variety of research areas. We trust that the manifest contributions found in the current volume will serve as inspiration to both new and experienced scholars to tackle the problems and issues that challenge us in this important field of inquiry.

REFERENCES

Chapman, L. J., & Chapman, J. P. (1987). The search for symptoms predictive of schizophrenia. *Schizophrenia Bulletin, 13*, 497–503.

Clark, L. A. (1990). Toward a consensual set of symptom clusters for assessment of personality disorder. In J. N. Butcher & C. D. Spielberger (Eds.), *Advances in personality assessment* (Vol. 8) (pp. 243–266). Hillsdale, NJ: Lawrence Erlbaum Associates.

Clark, L. A. (1993). *Schedule for Nonadaptive and Adaptive Personality (SNAP)*. Minneapolis, MN: University of Minnesota Press.

Digman, J. M. (1990). Personality structure: Emergence of the five robust factors of personality. *Annual Review of Psychology, 41*, 417–440.

John, O. P. (1990). The "Big Five" factor taxonomy: Dimensions of personality in the natural language and in questionnaires. In L. Pervin (Ed.), *Handbook of personality theory and research* (pp. 66–100). New York: Guilford Press.

McCrae, R. R., & Costa, P. T., Jr. (1990). *Personality in adulthood*. New York: Guilford.

Meehl, P. (1990). Toward an integrated theory of schizotaxia, schizotypy, and schizophrenia. *Journal of Personality Disorders, 4*, 1–99.

Tellegen, A. (1993). Folk concepts and psychological concepts of personality and personality disorder. *Psychological Inquiry, 4*, 122–130.

Tellegen, A., & Waller, N. G. (in press). Exploring personality through test construction: Development of the multidimensional personality questionnaire. In S. Briggs & J. M. Cheek (Eds.), *Personality measures: Development and evaluation*. Greenwich, CT: JAI Press.

Author Index

Ahern, F. M., 271, 283
Akiskal, H. S., 41, 61, 161, 164, 172
Akiskal, K., 161, 164, 172
Alden, L. E., 128, 132, 204, 212, 243–
    246, 261, 324, 338
Aldwin, C. L., 382, 396
Alexander, M. S., 41, 63
Allport, G., 66, 76, 99, 110
Almagor, M., 388–389, 396, 398
Alpher, V. S., 332, 334, 338
Altman, H., 369, 398
Altom, M. W., 84, 112
Amato, P. R., 201, 212
Anchin, J. C., 123, 132
Anderberg, M. R., 185, 192
Angleitner, A., 292, 295, 313
Appleby, L., 154, 156
Apt, C., 161, 164, 173
Arabie, P., 187, 192, 194
Arbisi, P. A., 384, 395
Archer, R. P., 379, 395, 397, 400
Armelius, K., 333, 340
Arrendono, R., 388, 398
Asquith, P., 273, 285
Assagioli, R., 61

Bacon, 394
Baer, B. A., 128, 133, 253, 262, 383, 401
Baier, B. A., 204, 213
Bailes, K., 150, 157
Bailey, D. E., 186, 195
Barash, D. P., 89, 111
Barnes, G. E., 11, 24

Baron, M., 282–283
Barrett, P., 11, 24, 149, 155
Barrick, M. R., 71, 76
Barron, F., 370, 387, 396
Bartholomew, K., 123, 128, 132–133,
    338
Bartko, J. J., 189, 192
Beavin, J., 328, 340
Beck, A. T., 153–154, 408, 418
Becker, B., 409, 418
Beech, A. R., 150, 154
Belk, S. S., 201, 212
Bell, B., 151, 157
Bell, M. J., 409, 418
Bell, R. C., 196, 212
Ben-Porath, Y. S., 41, 62, 311, 313,
    369–370, 382, 384–389, 392–398,
    400
Benjamin, L., 86, 111, 115, 132–133,
    258, 262, 318–320, 322, 324–329,
    331–332, 334–335, 337–338
Bernieri, F., 279, 285
Bernreuter, R. J., 363, 396
Berry, D. T. R., 383, 401
Bickel, W. K., 166, 173
Billington, R., 409, 418
Birkett, H., 70, 76
Bjerstedt, A., 72, 77
Bolton, L. S., 72, 77
Black, J. D., 367–368, 396
Blackburn, R., 346, 358
Blakemore, C., 139, 154
Blankstein, K. R., 145, 154

Blashfield, R., 42, 62, 85, 112, 179,
    189–191, 193–194, 256, 258, 261,
    333, 340, 377, 400
Block, J., 295, 312
Bloom, F. E., 279, 283
Bluhm, C., 121, 133
Blum, N., 48, 63
Bohman, M., 43, 63
Bohrnstedt, G. W., 248, 261
Bollen, K. A., 238, 240, 276, 283
Bonney, G. E., 278, 283
Bornstein, R. F., 163, 173
Bosse, R., 382, 396
Bowers, K. S., 88, 111
Bowlby, J., 323, 327, 336, 339
Bowman, E., 382, 396
Breen, M. J., 42, 62
Bridges, C. I., 61, 63
Briggs, P. F., 369, 379, 392, 396, 398
Briggs, S. R., 292–293, 312
Brockington, I. F., 142, 156
Brokaw, D. W., 114, 116, 122–123, 126,
    133, 135, 150, 154
Broll, T., 75, 77
Broughton, R., 201, 212, 251, 263
Brown, T., 342, 358
Browne, M. W., 246, 261
Brush, D. H., 201–202, 214
Budman, S., 253, 263, 357, 360
Bugg, F., 170, 174
Burks, R., 201, 213
Buss, A., 125–126, 133, 145, 154
Butcher, J. N., 102, 111, 283, 361, 370,
    376, 378–382, 385–389, 392, 394–
    400
Bynner, J. M., 246, 256–257, 263, 293,
    308, 314

Caddell, J. M., 407, 419
Cairns, R. B., 127, 133
Caldwell, A. B., 376, 397
Camac, C., 293, 315
Campbell, L., 256, 263
Cantor, N., 254, 259, 261
Caplan, P. J., 161, 164, 174
Cardon, L. R., 276, 285
Carey, G., 308, 314

Carmichael, 187
Carpenter, W. T., 189, 192
Carroll, J. B., 238, 240
Carroll, J. D., 187, 192
Carson, R. C., 115, 120–122, 125–126,
    133, 244, 261, 317, 326, 339
Cattell, R. B., 65–72, 74, 76–77, 179,
    182–183, 186, 189, 192, 216, 225,
    227, 231, 240, 293, 300, 312
Cavalli-Sforza, 186, 192
Cawley, R. H., 139, 154
Cayton, T. G., 382, 396
Chakraborty, R., 270, 284
Chapman, J. P., 150, 155, 276, 283, 307,
    312
Chapman, L. J., 150, 155, 276, 283, 307,
    312–313
Charles, E., 42, 62, 161, 173
Chasmove, A. S., 145, 154
Chauncey, D. L., 160, 175
Chelladurai, P., 205, 214
Chrisjohn, R. D., 344, 358–359
Christal, R. E., 292, 314
Churchland, P. S., 139, 155
Chyatte, C., 379, 397
Claridge, G., 9, 23, 138, 144, 149–150,
    154
Clark, D. M., 139, 155
Clark, L. A., 41, 62, 164, 175, 300, 308,
    312, 314–315, 343, 356, 358
Clarkin, J., 160, 170, 175, 196, 215, 265,
    286
Cleckley, H., 346, 358
Cliff, N., 238, 240
Cloninger, C. R., 40–42, 46, 48–49, 55,
    59–63, 267, 276, 283, 286, 309,
    311–312
Coffey, H. S., 116, 133–134, 243, 251,
    262
Cohen, J., 183, 189
Cole, L. C., 98, 111
Collard, L., 356, 358
Colligan, S., 382, 396
Colvin, C. R., 116, 125, 127, 133
Conte, H. R., 249, 261
Cook, P. E., 387, 399
Coombs, C. H., 210, 212

Cooper, A. M., 161, 164, 172–173
Cooper, M., 185, 189, 194
Corbitt, 343
Corenthal, C., 41, 63, 164, 175
Cortessis, V. A., 280, 286
Coryell, M. D., 265, 287
Coryell, W., 41, 63, 163, 164, 172, 175
Costa, P. T., Jr., 40–41, 48, 62, 69, 71, 73–75, 77, 86, 111, 116, 129, 132, 135, 144, 155, 164–165, 170, 172–173, 175, 191–192, 227, 231–233, 235, 240–241, 245, 254, 257, 262, 292–293, 305–306, 309, 311–313, 324, 340, 407, 418–419
Coulter, M. A., 183, 186, 189
Crane J. B., 41, 62
Cronbach, L., 181, 192, 254, 259, 261
Cross, S., 317, 340
Crow, T. J., 139, 155
Cuadra, C. A., 370–371, 397
Cull, J. G., 410, 419
Curtiss, G., 191, 193

Dahlstrom, L. E., 370–371, 397
Dahlstrom, W. G., 361, 363, 367, 370–371, 379, 381–382, 386, 388, 396–397, 400–401
Dalais, C., 151, 157
Daniels, D., 279, 285
Davis, H. G., 388, 398
Davis, K. L., 308, 314
Davis, R. D., 102, 106–107, 112
Davison, M. L., 197–198, 201–204, 206, 208–214, 247–248, 261
Dawes, R. M., 238, 240
Dawis, R. V., 206, 214
Dawson, D. F., 129, 133
Day, N. E., 276, 283
de Charms, R., 97, 111
de Raad, B., 229, 231, 233–234, 241, 245, 262
De Vore, J., 382, 396
DeJong, C. A. J., 324, 339, 414, 419
Demby, A., 253, 263, 357, 360
Demenais, F. M., 278, 283
Depue, R. A., 308, 312

Diekhoff, G. M., 201, 213
Digman, J. M., 86, 111, 129, 133, 227, 240, 292, 306, 312
Dohrenwend, B., 171, 172
Donner, A., 274, 283
Drake, L. E., 369, 397
Drake, R. E., 40, 62
DuBois, N., 203, 213
Duckitt, J. H., 75, 77
Duke, M. P., 328, 339
Duker, J., 189–190, 193
Dye, D. A., 231, 240

Eaves, L., 13, 20, 23, 264–265, 271–272, 279–280, 283
Eber, H. W., 67, 77
Eckblad, M., 307, 313
Eckes, T., 201, 214
Edell, W. J., 307, 312
Edelson, S. M., 84, 112
Edwards, A. W. F., 186, 192
Egland, B., 283, 397
Egri, G., 171–172
Ellis, A., 167, 172
Elston, R. C., 276, 285
Engfer, A., 75, 77
Erickson, M., 382, 397
Evans, R. G., 376, 397
Everett, J. E., 227, 240
Everitt, B. S., 184, 193, 276, 284
Everly, G. S., Jr., 256, 258, 262
Eyde, L., 394, 397
Eysenck, H. J., 3–5, 8–11, 13–16, 18–22, 67, 77, 143–145, 148–149, 154, 231, 240, 264–265, 284, 292, 307–308, 311, 313, 316, 325, 339, 343, 358
Eysenck, M. M., 265, 284, 307–308, 313, 316, 339
Eysenck, S. B. G., 144, 148–149
Eysenck, S. B. J., 10–11, 13, 18, 20

Fabrega, H., 161, 172
Fairbank, J. A., 388, 399
Falconer, D. S., 267, 284
Falk, C. T., 273, 282, 284
Farid, N. R., 273, 284
Farmer, N., 161, 172

Fava, J. L., 222, 240
Feinstein, A. R., 84, 111
Feldhous, C., 161, 172
Ferrel, C., 60, 63
First, M. B., 161, 174
Fishburne, F., 394, 397
Fisher, G. A., 248, 261
Fisher, L., 190, 193
Fletcher, R. P., 151, 157
Foa, E. B., 122, 133
Foa, U. G., 122, 133, 243, 249, 261
Folstein, M. F., 162, 173–174
Forgas, J. P., 202, 213
Foulds, G. A., 141, 155, 412, 419
Fowler, R. D., 394, 397
Frances, A., 158–160, 172, 175, 196, 215,
      258, 261, 265, 286, 344, 346, 358
Frankenburg, F. R., 160, 175
Frankl, V. E., 61–62
Freedland, K. E., 43, 63
Freedman, M. B., 116–119, 133–134,
      243, 251, 262
Freko, D., 84, 112
French, R. D., 254, 261
Freud, S., 88, 91, 108, 110–111, 167–
      168, 172
Friedman, H. F., 9, 24
Friedman, H. P., 186, 193
Fromm, E., 97, 99, 101, 111
Funder, D. C., 116, 125–127, 133–134

Gaelick, L., 246, 263
Gangstead, S., 191, 193, 343, 358
Garamoni, G. L., 170, 172
Gelfand, A. E., 280, 284
Geman, D., 280, 284
Geman, S., 280, 284
Gibbon, M., 161, 174, 294, 314
Gibson, J. M., 184
Gilberstadt, H., 189, 190, 193
Gill, D. S., 344, 360
Gill, W. S., 410, 419
Gilligan, C., 99, 111
Gilmore, M. M., 161, 173
Glass, G. V., 196, 214
Gleser, G., 181, 192, 254, 259, 261
Goldberg, L. R., 68–70, 76–77, 86, 111,

170, 172, 220, 222, 225, 227, 229,
      231, 233–235, 237, 240–241, 243,
      245, 248, 262, 292–293, 306, 310,
      313–314, 370, 392, 397
Golden, R., 191–193, 342–343, 359
Goldman, H. H., 171–172
Goldstein, K., 101, 111
Goldston, C. S., 123, 129, 134
Goleman, D., 61–62
Goodwin, D. W., 41, 62
Gollwitzer, P. M., 116, 135
Gorham, 408
Gorsuch, H. A., 68, 77
Gorsuch, R. L., 217, 237, 240, 293, 313
Gough, H. A., 71, 77
Gough, H. G., 366, 370–371, 387, 397
Gourlay, J., 18, 25
Graham, J. R., 361, 370, 381–383, 386–
      389, 392, 395–398
Gray, J. A., 140, 143–144, 146, 235,
      241
Grayson, 376
Green, C. J., 102, 104–105, 112
Green, J. A., 127, 133
Green, J. R., 278, 284
Greenberg, J. A., 268, 273, 284
Greenberg, J. R., 307
Green, J. R., 278, 284
Greenberg, J. A., 268, 273, 284
Greenberg, J. R., 307
Greene, R. L., 388, 392, 398
Greenfield, S., 139, 154
Grove, J., 274, 287
Grove, W. M., 86, 111
Gruzelier, J. H., 147, 156
Guadagnoli, E., 238, 241
Gudjonsson, G., 20, 24
Guilford, J. P., 66–67, 77, 183, 193, 292,
      313
Guilford, R. B., 66, 77
Gunderson, J. G., 160–161, 164, 172,
      174–175
Guo, S. W., 280, 286
Gurtman, M. B., 128–129, 133, 197, 213,
      246–247, 250, 253, 256, 259–260,
      262
Guthrie, G. M., 368, 398

Guttman, L., 245, 247
Guze, S. B., 41, 62
Gynther, M. D., 369, 398

Halbower, C. C., 368–369, 398
Halle, R. W., 273, 284
Haller, D. L., 189–190, 193
Hallmayer, J., 163, 173
Hamilton, M., 408, 419
Hamlin, W. T., 161, 173
Hammond, S. M., 11–12, 24, 203, 213
Hampson, S. E., 292–293, 313
Hand, D. J., 276, 284
Hanin, Y., 11, 24
Hanis, C. L., 270, 284
Hare, R. D., 146–147, 156–157
Harkness, A. R., 292–293, 296, 300, 311, 313, 393, 398
Harlow, H., 145, 154
Harlow, H. F., 323, 339
Harman, H. F., 349, 358
Harman, H. H., 217, 241
Harmon, L. R., 374, 376, 392, 401
Harpur, T. J., 147, 157
Harris, M. J., 279, 285
Harris, R., 375, 398
Hartigan, J. A., 70, 77
Hathaway, S. R., 333, 339, 341, 358, 361, 363, 365–368, 370–373, 377, 379, 383, 392, 398–400
Heath, A. C., 43, 62, 272, 284
Heise, D. R., 248, 261
Heiser, W. J., 197, 201, 213–214
Heller, K., 410, 419
Helmes, E., 342, 344–345, 358–359
Helzer, J. E., 166, 173–174
Hempel, C. G., 87, 111
Henderson, V. L., 61, 63
Hendrickson, A. E., 228, 241
Henry, 132
Henry, W. P., 320, 322, 339
Heun, R., 163, 173
Hickok, L. G., 356, 358
Hicks, A., 42, 63
Higgins, S. T., 166, 173
Hirschfeld, R. M. A., 161, 164, 174
Hirschfield, M. A., 41, 61

Hjemboe, S., 388, 398
Hodge, S. E., 273, 284
Hodgin, J., 256, 261
Hodgson, R., 139, 156
Hoffman, H., 389, 398
Hoffman, N. G., 376, 399
Hofstee, W. K. B., 229, 231, 233–235, 241, 245, 260, 262
Hogan, R., 292, 306, 313
Holden, R. R., 345, 358
Holder, B. A., 201, 213
Holland, J. L., 205, 209, 213
Holley, J. W., 183, 193
Holmes, T. H., 410, 419
Honaker, L. M., 393, 398
Horn, D., 184, 193
Horn, J. L., 182, 193, 225, 241
Horn, J. M., 271, 284
Horney, K., 257, 262, 328, 339
Horowitz, L. M., 115, 123, 128, 132–133, 197, 204, 213, 253, 262, 324, 338–339
Horst, P., 188, 193
Hostetler, K., 387, 396
Hotelling, H., 217, 241
Howard, E., 201, 214
Hughes, J. R., 166, 167, 173
Humble, K., 146, 154
Humm, D. G., 363, 398
Humphrey, L. L., 333, 339
Hundleby, J. D., 145, 156
Hunter, J. E., 70, 77
Hurlbert, D. F., 161, 164, 173
Hurt, S. W., 160, 175, 196, 215, 265, 284
Hyler, S. E., 42, 62, 160, 163, 173–174

Iselius, L., 273, 284

Jackson, D. D., 328, 340
Jackson, D. N., 189, 194, 295, 313, 342–347, 349–352, 358–360, 389, 398, 403, 419
Jackson, H. J., 196, 212
Jackson, J. E., 222, 238, 241–242
Jacobs, P. I., 295, 314
Jahoda, M., 94, 111
James, J. W., 267, 285

Jansen, J. A. M., 324, 339, 414, 419
Jeffrey, T., 382, 396
Jenkins, Richard L., 192–193
John, O. P., 10, 24, 129, 227, 241,
  292–293, 295, 313
Johns, E. F., 68, 71, 75, 78
Johnson, J. G., 163, 173
Johnson, R. C., 271, 283
Jones, L. E., 196, 201–202, 213
Joreskog, K. G., 276, 284
Joshua, S., 42, 63
Joyce, P., 41, 62
Jung, C. G., 101, 108, 110
Jutai, J. W., 147, 156

Kaemmer, B., 361, 381, 395, 397
Kaiser, H. F., 225, 228, 238, 241–
  242
Kalehzan, B. M., 123, 133
Kalichman, S., 191, 193
Kalus, O. F., 147, 151, 157
Kaplan, R. D., 161, 173
Karson, S., 69, 77–78
Kass, F., 42, 62, 161, 173
Katz, M. M., 381, 399
Katz, S. E., 363, 399
Katzenmeyer, C., 145, 156
Kavanagh, J. A., 249, 262
Keane, T. M., 388, 399, 407, 419
Keefe, R. S. E., 147, 151, 157
Keller, L. S., 382, 394, 399
Kellman, H. D., 160, 163, 173–174
Kelso, K., 324, 340, 343, 360
Kendall, R. E., 18, 25, 85, 111, 142, 156,
  343, 359
Kendler, K. S., 272, 284
Kenrick, D. T., 126, 134
Kernberg, O. F., 41, 62
Kidd, K. K., 278, 284
Kiesler, D. J., 114–115, 120–127, 129,
  134–135, 164, 173, 197, 213, 231,
  241, 244, 248–249, 256, 258, 262,
  317, 328, 339
Kinder, B. N., 191, 193
Kirk, S. A., 9, 25
Kirschenbaum, H., 61, 63
Kleinmuntz, B., 388, 399

Klett, C. J., 188–189, 194
Klingler, T., 163, 173
Klinteberg, B., 146, 154
Koch, W. R., 201, 214
Koenig, H. G., 60, 63
Koenigsberg, H. W., 161, 173
Kogan, N., 295, 314
Koss, M. P., 376, 399
Koval, J. J., 274, 283
Kowal, D., 394, 397
Krug, S. E., 67, 69, 71–72, 74–75, 77–78
Kruskal, J. B., 197, 200, 205, 213
Kuhlman, D. M., 293, 315
Kuiper, F. K., 190, 193
Kulka, R. A., 388, 400
Kutchins, H., 9, 25
Kvale, J. N., 60, 63

Lacey, J. I., 146, 156
Lachar, D., 376, 399
LaForge, R., 116–117, 125, 134, 243,
  251, 254, 262
Lance, G., 184, 193
Landis, C., 363, 399
Lang, P., 407, 420
Lanigan, C. B., 344, 358
Lanyon, R. I., 190, 193
Larsen, L. H., 383, 401
Larsen, R. M., 378, 399
Larus, J. P., 129, 134
Lathrop, G. M., 278, 284
Laughlin, J. E., 72, 74, 78
Lave, T. R., 171–172
Lawrence, R. A., 75, 78
Lawson, C., 139, 156
Lay, C. H., 295, 313
Leaf, R. C., 170, 173
Leary, T., 75, 78, 115–116, 118–119,
  121, 133–134, 318, 326, 336, 339
Leary, T. F., 243–244, 249–251, 253,
  257–259, 262
Lencz, T., 150, 157
Levenson, M. R., 382, 396
Levitt, E. E., 378, 400
Levin, J. L., 197, 205–206, 214
Lewin, K., 116, 134
Lewis, G., 154, 156

Li, X., 199, 214
Lichtermann, D., 163, 173
Liebowitz, M. R., 61, 63
Lingoes, J., 375, 398
Little, R. J. A., 220, 241
Livesley, W. J., 41, 63, 86, 111, 164, 173, 342–343, 345, 347, 359
Loehlin, J. C., 238, 241, 271–272
Loevinger, J., 85, 210–211, 214, 403, 419
Loranger, A. W., 161, 163, 173, 271, 284
Lorenz, K., 323, 339
Lorr, M., 123, 132, 134, 188, 190–191, 193, 256, 263
Lubin, B., 378, 399
Lucke, J. F., 248, 261
Ludlow, L. H., 201, 214
Luiten, J. W., 75, 78
Lykken, D. T., 145, 156
Lyons, M., 42, 62
Lytton, H., 272, 284

MacAndrew, C., 387, 399
McCartney, K., 279, 285
McClearn, E. E., 271, 283
McClosky, H., 370–371, 387, 397
McClung, J. S., 189, 193
McCormick, C. C., 249, 262
McCrae, R. R., 40–41, 48, 62, 69, 71, 73–75, 77, 86, 111, 116, 129, 132, 135, 144, 155, 164–165, 170, 172–173, 191–192, 227, 231–233, 235, 240–241, 245, 254, 257, 262, 292–293, 305–306, 308–309, 311–313, 324, 340, 389, 399, 407, 418–419
McCully, E., 389, 396
McDonald, K., 201, 214
McDonald, R. P., 240–241
McEwen, J. L., 356, 358
McGlasan, T., 159, 174
McGue, M., 274, 285
McGuffin, P., 264, 285
McHugh, P. R., 162, 174
McKenna, T., 382, 388, 399–400
McKinley, J. C., 333, 339, 341, 358, 361, 363, 365–366, 370–371, 377, 379, 398–399
MacKinnon, D. W., 4, 25

Mackintosh, P., 273, 285
MacLean, C. J., 276, 278, 280, 285
MacLean, M., 344, 359
McLemore, C. W., 114, 116, 122–123, 126, 133–134, 253, 256, 258, 261–262
McNair, D. M., 123, 134
McNulty, J. L., 311, 313, 393, 398
McQuitty, L. L., 179, 184, 193
Magaro, P. A., 356, 359
Maier, W., 163, 173
Malloy, P. F., 388, 399
Mangan, G., 145, 156
Mardia, K. V., 248, 254, 262
Marini, S. L., 61, 63
Marks, P. A., 369, 399
Marks, P. D., 189, 190, 193
Markus, H., 317, 340
Martin, C. L., 247, 253, 263
Martin, N., 13, 20, 23, 264, 272, 284
Martin, N. G., 43, 62
Maslow, A., 93–94, 96, 99, 101
Matarazzo, J., 378, 394, 399
Maxwell, A. E., 9–10, 16, 25, 295, 313
Meagher, R. B., Jr., 102, 104–105, 111
Medin, D. L., 84, 87, 112
Mednick, S., 150–151, 157
Meehl, P. E., 148, 155–156, 191–193, 342–343, 358–359, 364–368, 370–373, 383, 387, 392, 394, 397–400
Megargee, E. I., 387, 399
Mellsop, G., 42, 63
Mendelsohn, F., 171–172
Mendelsohn, G. A., 387, 399
Merikangas, K. R., 162, 173, 264, 285
Merry, J., 253, 263, 357, 360
Mershon, B., 293, 313
Messick, S., 344, 359
Meulman, J., 197, 213
Mezzich, J., 161, 172, 254, 262
Mezzich, J. E., 184, 190, 194
Michener, C. D., 185, 194
Miele, G. M., 121, 133
Miller, E. N., 150, 155
Miller, T. R., 132, 135
Milligan, G. W., 184–186, 189, 190, 194
Millon, C., 102, 105–107, 112

Millon, T., 41, 63, 71, 78, 81, 85–86, 88,
    92–94, 102–108, 112, 132, 135,
    256, 258, 262, 342–343, 357,
    359–360
Mirmegawa, 382
Mischel, W., 164, 173
Mitchell, D. A., 150, 157
Mitchell, L. E., 270, 285
Mitchell, S. A., 307, 313
Mojena, R., 185, 190, 194
Moldin, S. O., 265, 268, 285–286
Montgomery, S. A., 139, 156
Morey, L. C., 123, 135, 161, 173, 191,
    194, 256, 263, 324, 333, 335, 340,
    343, 360, 377, 389, 400, 402,
    404–406, 411, 413–417, 419
Morey, S. A., 265, 285
Morris, C. A., 267, 285
Morton, N. E., 276, 285
Mount, M. K., 71, 76
Moyer, K. E., 306, 313
Mulaik, S. A., 217, 241
Mulder, R. T., 41, 62
Murray, H. A., 318, 352, 360
Murray, J. H., 336, 340

Naboisek, H., 116, 134, 251, 262
Nduaguba, M., 40, 63
Neale, M. C., 276, 285
Nediger, W., 205, 214
Neisser, U., 307, 313
Nelson, C., 201, 214
Nestadt, G., 162, 174
Neuman, R., 265, 286
Nichols, K. E., 68, 77
Nichols, R. C., 272, 284
Nielsen, A. T., 150, 156
Nikelly, A. G., 161, 164, 174
Norman, W. T., 292, 306, 313
Novy, D. M., 184
Nowicki, S., 328, 339
Nowicki, S., Jr., 203–204, 214, 246,
    263
Nunnally, J., 227, 241
Nunnally, J. C., 188, 194
Nurnberg, H. G., 265, 285
Nutt, D., 139, 156

Odbert, H. S., 66, 76
O'Dell, J. W., 69, 77–78
Oetting, E. R., 369, 397
Offer, D., 79, 112, 344, 360
Ohman, K., 333, 340
Oldham, J. M., 160, 163, 173–174, 265,
    271, 284–285
Oliveto, A. H., 166, 173
Olweus, D., 306, 314
Oreland, L., 276, 283
Orford, J., 121, 135, 249, 263
Ornduff, S. R., 406, 419
Osgood, C. E., 304, 314
Ossorio, A. G., 116, 133, 243, 262
Ostendorf, F., 292, 295, 313
Ott, J., 273, 278, 285
Overall, J. E., 184, 188–189, 194, 408
Overholser, J. C., 159, 174

Paddock, J. R., 203–204, 214, 246, 263
Pancoast, D., 379, 400
Pantony, K., 161, 164, 174
Paulhus, D. L., 247, 253, 263
Peabody, D., 231, 233, 241, 293, 314
Pearson, K., 217, 241
Pelphrey, A., 161, 172
Petersen, N. E., 150, 156
Peterson, C. D., 388, 400
Peterson, D. R., 123, 135
Pfohl, B., 41, 48, 63, 164, 175
Phillips, K., 161, 164, 174
Phillips, N., 123, 125, 136, 246, 263
Piaget, J., 307, 314
Pilkonis, P., 161, 172
Pincus, A. L., 41, 64, 115–116, 125, 128–
    129, 132, 135–136, 170, 175, 197,
    204, 212, 214, 227, 242–243, 250,
    253, 256–257, 261, 263, 306, 309,
    315, 317, 324, 334, 338, 340
Pinkston, K., 256, 261
Plomin, R., 145, 154, 156, 264, 279,
    285
Plutchik, R., 249, 261
Pope, K. S., 379, 387, 400
Popper, K. R., 265, 280, 285
Powell, S., 25
Prell, D. B., 13, 23

Prentice, R. L., 274, 287
Procidano, M. E., 410, 419
Przybeck, T., 41–43, 45, 62–63, 162, 174

Quay, H. C., 145, 156
Quiaoit, F., 274, 287
Quine, W. V. O., 87, 112

Rachman, S., 139, 156
Rahe, R. H., 410, 419
Raine, A., 150–151, 157
Raman, A. C., 151, 157
Ramsey, J. O., 197, 214
Rand, W. M., 189, 194
Rao, D. C., 270, 274, 279, 285
Raulin, M. L., 276, 283
Reddon, J. R., 342, 344–345, 358, 360
Reed, P. L., 344, 360
Reich, J., 40, 63
Reich, T., 267–268, 278, 285–286
Rende, R., 264, 285
Rescorla, R. A., 307, 314
Rest, J. R., 210–211, 214
Rice, J. P., 265, 267, 276, 278, 282, 285–286
Rinaldi, M., 168, 175
Risch, N., 270, 285–286
Robbins, S., 211, 213
Roberts, G. W., 139, 157
Robins, L. N., 162, 174
Rogers, C. R., 94, 101, 112
Rogers, R., 406, 419
Rohlf, F. J., 188, 194
Rojdev, R., 378, 400
Romanoski, A. J., 162, 174
Romesburg, H. C., 179, 194
Romney, D. M., 246, 256–257, 263, 293, 308, 314
Roper, B. L., 394, 400
Rosenberg, S. E., 123, 128, 133, 201, 204, 213–214, 253, 262
Rosnick, L., 160, 163, 173–174
Ross, B. E., 145, 155
Rounds, J., 246, 260, 263
Rounds, J. B., Jr., 206, 214
Royce, J. R., 11, 25
Rubin, D. B., 220, 241

Rubin, J., 186, 193
Rubinstein, P., 273, 282, 284
Rush, J. A., 48, 63
Russell, J. A., 260, 263
Russell, J. M., 274, 285
Rutter, M., 343, 360
Ryder, L. R., 273, 286

Sabshin, M., 79, 112, 158, 172, 344, 358, 360
Safran, J. D., 122, 135
Samuels, J. F., 162, 174
Sanderson, C., 160, 170–171, 175, 191, 195
Sass, L. A., 140, 157
Saucier, G., 233, 241, 248, 260, 263
Saunders, D. R., 228, 241
Schacht, T., 165, 174, 320, 322, 339
Schaefer, E. S., 318, 336, 340
Schalling, D., 146, 154
Schippers, G. M., 324, 339, 414, 419
Schlenger, W. E., 388, 400
Schmidt, H. O., 366, 400
Schmidt, J. A., 115, 135
Schneewind, K. A., 75, 77
Schonemann, P. H., 349, 360
Schroeder, M. L., 41, 63, 347, 359
Schulsinger, F., 151, 157
Schwartz, G. F., 370, 397
Schwartz, R. M., 170, 172
Scoltock, J., 179, 194
Seelen, J., 379, 387, 400
Seeman, W., 189, 190, 193, 369, 399
Seery, J. B., 205, 213
Selzer, M. L., 409, 419
Serlin, R. C., 238, 242
Sewell, K., 406, 419
She, 333
Sheard, M. H., 61, 63
Shepard, R. N., 187, 194
Sherman, J. L., 75, 78
Sherwood, N. E., 389, 396
Shoukri, M. M., 274, 286
Shrout, P., 171–172
Siever, L. J., 147, 151, 157, 271, 286, 308, 311, 314
Sigvardsson, S., 43, 63
Sikes-Nova, V. E., 129, 134

Silverman, J. M., 271, 286
Silverstein, A. B., 203, 205, 214
Six, B., 201, 214
Skay, C. L., 198, 203, 205, 208–210, 213
Skinner, H. A., 188–189, 191, 194, 344, 349–351, 359–360, 409, 419
Skodol, A. E., 42, 62, 159–161, 163, 171–174, 294, 314
Slater, E., 5, 25
Slater, P., 5, 25
Sletton, I. W., 370, 398
Slutske, W. S., 394, 396
Smith, A. F. M., 280, 284
Smith, D. T., 383, 401
Smith, E. E., 87, 112, 254, 261
Smith, L., 161, 164, 174
Smith M. L., 196, 214
Smith, P., 356, 359
Smith, R. L., 370, 397
Sneath, P. H. A., 184–185, 187, 189, 194
Snell, W. E., Jr., 201, 212, 214
Snyder, M., 191, 193, 343, 358
Sokal, R. R., 185–186, 189, 194
Soldz, S., 253, 256, 263, 357, 360
Sorbom, D., 276, 284
Spanier, G. B., 381, 400
Spearman, C., 217, 242
Spencer, H., 94, 112
Spielberger, C. D., 407, 410, 420
Spiro, A., 382, 396
Spitzer, R. L., 42, 62, 159, 161, 166–167, 173–175, 294, 314
Spoont, M. R., 308, 312, 314
Sprock, J., 85, 112, 256, 261
Sprouse, C. L., 201–202, 214
Srichantra, N. 204, 213
Stangl, D. , 41, 48, 63, 164, 175
Star, B., 75, 78
Steer, R. A., 408, 418
Steiger, J. H., 246, 263
Stephenson, W., 187, 194
Stern, G. G., 233, 242
Stock, W. A., 201, 214
Stone, M. H., 142, 157
Strack, S., 102, 106, 112, 191, 193, 204, 214, 256, 263
Strauss, J. C., 189, 192

Strelau, J., 143–144, 157
Stricker, L. J., 295, 314
Strupp, H. H., 123, 135, 320, 322, 339
Suarez, B. K., 278, 286
Suci, G., 304, 314
Suczek, R. F., 116, 125, 134
Sullivan, H. S., 115, 121–122, 135, 244, 263, 317–320, 336, 340
Sutker, P. B., 170, 174
Suziedelis, A., 190, 193
Svejgaard, A., 273, 286
Svrakic, D. M., 41–43, 45–46, 59, 61–63
Swanson, D., 211, 213
Szasz, T., 168, 174

Takemoto-Chock, N. K., 292, 306, 312
Talley, P. F., 123, 135
Tannenbaum, P. H., 304, 314
Tatsuoka, M. M., 67, 77
Taylor, K. L., 407, 419
Taylor, M. A., 142, 157, 369, 392, 396
Tellegen, A., 41, 63, 86, 111–112, 120, 125–126, 135, 145, 156, 212, 215, 292–293, 296, 300, 305–309, 311, 314–315, 361–362, 369, 380–381, 383, 385–387, 392, 395–397, 400
ten Berge, J. M. F., 221, 242
Teyber, E., 328, 340
Thapar, A., 264, 285
Tharp, R. G., 61, 63
Thomas, D. C., 280, 286
Thomas, J. A., 201, 214
Thompson, E. A., 280, 286
Thorne, A., 295, 312
Thurstone, L. L., 66, 78, 217, 242
Timbrook, R. E., 383, 386, 392, 397–398
Tipp, J., 162, 174
Tolman, E. C., 307, 314
Torgersen, S., 20
Torgerson, W. S., 203, 214
Tracey, T. J., 246, 260, 263
Trapnell, P. D., 68, 75, 78, 120, 122, 125, 129, 135–136, 246, 263, 292, 308, 314–315, 411, 420
Trives, R. L., 98, 113
Trouton, D. S., 9–10

Trull, T. J., 41–42, 56, 58, 63, 158, 160, 163, 168, 170, 174–175, 196, 215, 265, 286
Tryon, R. C., 179, 186, 195
Tucker, L. R., 208, 214
Tuite, D. R., 75, 78
Tulis, E. H., 271, 284
Tupes, E. C., 292, 314
Tversky, A., 84, 113
Tyrer, P., 41, 63

Ulrich, R., 161, 172
Ureno, G., 128, 133, 204, 213, 253, 262

Vaillant, G. E., 40, 62
Van den Brink, W., 324, 339, 414, 419
Vandenberg, S. G., 271, 283
Van Denburg, T. F., 115, 129, 134
Van Eerdewegh, P. A., 278, 286
Varghese, F., 42, 63
Velicer, W. F., 222, 224, 238, 240–242
Venables, P. H., 147, 150–151, 156–157
Verma, R. M., 18, 25
Vernon, P. E., 4, 25, 231, 242
Villasenor, V. S., 128, 133, 204, 213, 253, 262
Vitkus, J., 115, 123, 133
Vivekananthan, P. S., 201, 214
Vogler, G. P., 274, 285
von Knorring, L., 276, 283
Voonk, R., 201, 214

Waddington, J. L., 279, 286
Wadsworth, G. W., 363, 398
Wagner, E., 61, 63
Wahler, H. J., 407, 420
Wakefield, J. A., 9, 23
Wakefield, J. C., 158, 166
Walker, L. E. A., 169, 175
Waller, N. G., 41, 62, 296, 305–309, 311, 362, 389, 396, 400
Ward, J. H., 185, 195
Ward, R. H., 274, 286
Watson, D., 164, 175, 300, 308, 314–315
Watson, D. L., 61, 63
Watts, D., 383, 392, 398

Watzlawick, P., 328, 340
Waugh, M. H., 333, 340, 377, 400
Webb, J. T., 378, 400
Wechsler, D., 203, 215
Weed, N. C., 388, 392, 398, 400
Weiller, 392
Weiss, D. S., 295, 312
Weiss, L., 102, 106–107, 112
Weissman, M. M., 162, 173–175
Welsh, G., 366–367, 370–371, 375, 379, 387, 397, 400–401
West, J. A. 170, 174
Wette, R., 270, 279, 285
Wetter, M. W., 383, 401
White, P. O., 228, 241
White, R. W., 97, 113
Whitehead, C., 41–42, 45, 63
Wicklund, R. A., 116, 135
Widiger, J. S., 324, 340
Widiger, T. A., 56, 63, 121, 133, 158–161, 164, 168, 170–172, 175, 191, 196, 215, 258, 261, 265, 286, 293, 311, 315, 343–344, 358, 360
Wiener, D. N., 371, 374–376, 392, 401
Wigdor, A. K., 70, 77
Wiggins, J. S., 41, 64, 68, 75, 78, 115–117, 120, 122, 125, 128–129, 132, 134–136, 170, 175, 197, 204, 212, 214–215, 227, 231, 242–243, 246–247, 250–254, 256–259, 261, 263, 292, 306, 308–309, 311, 315, 317–318, 324, 334, 371, 377, 388, 401, 411, 414, 420
Wilber, K., 61
Wilkins, S., 150, 157
Willerman, L., 271, 284
Williams, C. L., 370, 388, 396–397
Williams, D. R., 349–350, 359
Williams, H. L., 388, 401
Williams, J. B. W., 42, 62, 159, 161, 166–167, 173–174, 294, 314
Williams, J. M. G., 153, 157
Williams, S. E., 147, 157
Williams, W. A., 184, 193
Willner, P., 139, 153, 157
Wilson, E. O., 88, 98–99, 110, 113

Wilson, J. R., 271, 283
Wish, M., 197, 213
Wishart, D., 186–187, 195
Wohlwill, J. F., 210, 215
Wolfe, J. H., 187, 195
Wolpe, J., 407, 420
Woodrow, J. C., 278, 284
Woods, A., 161, 172
Woodward, K. L., 60, 64
Wormworth, J. A., 41, 63
Wrobel, T. A., 376, 399

Yates, W., 40, 63
Yee, S., 276, 285

Yerevanian, B. I., 41, 61
Young, F. W., 201–202, 205, 213
Youniss, R. L., 191, 193

Zanarini, M. C., 160, 175
Zegers, F. E., 221, 242
Zevon, M. A., 212, 215
Zhao, L. P., 274, 287
Zimmerman, M., 41, 48, 63, 161,
     163–164, 172, 175, 265, 287
Zubin, J., 363, 399
Zuckerman, M., 143, 145, 148, 157, 293,
     315
Zwick, W. R., 224, 242

Subject Index

AB5C (Abridged Big Five-dimensional Circumplex) model, 233, 237
Abnormality, criteria for, 79
Abnormal personality
  manifestation of, 337
  paradox, 329, 331–336
  pathology of, 336
Abuse, effect of, 75, 191, 331
Activity Preference Questionnaire (APQ), 145
Adaptation
  modes of, 94–98
  significance of, 90
Adaptive strategies, 90
Adaptive styles, 90
Adaptivity, 170–171
ADCLUS, 187
ADMIX program, 276
Adoption studies, 272, 274
Adult personality, influences on, 333
Affective disorder, 16, 18
Aggressiveness, 306–307, 309
Alcohol abusers, cluster analysis study, 191
Amygdaloid flight/fight system, 146
Anhedonia, 150
Antisocial behavior, 145
Antisocial personalities, 93, 100
Antisocial Personality Disorder (APD), 21, 49, 162, 354, 356
Antithesis, 320
Anxiety
  low, 145–146

surplus, 146
theories of, 140
Aristotle, 83
Arousal, 144
Assessment, dimensional
  generally 343–345
  research in, 345–349
Association studies, 272–274, 281
Assortative mating, 278–279
Asymmetry, 139–141
Attachment, 323, 331, 336
Avoidant personality disorders, 21, 49, 93, 159, 257
Axis I disorders
  continuity and, 140
  Five-Factor Model, 29
  MCMI and, 103
  psychopathology, 29
Axis II personality disorders
  continuity and, 140
  defined, 125
  Five-Factor Model, 29–31
  interpersonal approach to, 324
  MCMI and, 103
  passivity and, 96
  psychopathology, 29–31
  psychosocial alternatives to, 258

Baseline, 325
Basic Personality Inventory (BPI), 26, 344–345
Behavioral intensity, 118
Behavioral rigidity, 124

Behavioral theories, 320
Behaviorism, extreme, 138
Benjamin, L., *see* Structural Analysis of
    Social Behaviors (SASB)
Bias, self-report, 390
Biosocial knowledge, 137
Bootstrapping, 368
Borderline Personality Disorder, 21, 49,
    147–148, 170
Brain function
    psychobiological models and, 144, 147
    in psychopaths, 147
Brain-stem activation, 144

Caffeine dependence, 167
Caffeine withdrawal, 166
California Psychological Inventory (CPI),
    9, 71
Cartet Count, 186–187
Cattell, Raymond, personality theory, *see*
    Cattellian personality
Cattellian personality
    implications of, 75
    normal vs. abnormal personality, 71–75
    research history, 66–67
    structure of, 67–71
Character dimensions, 43–44
Check List of Interpersonal (or
    Psychotherapy) Transactions
    (CLOIT-CLOPT), 123
Child development, temperament, 144–
    145
Circular profile, 250–251
Circumplex
    behaviors, 123–124
    computational example, 254–256
    defined, 243, 245
    evaluation of, 245–249
    interpersonal adjustments and, 249–254
    overview, 114, 116–120
    personality disorders and, 256–260
    profiles, 129
    research, 31
    structure of, 244
    vector length, 125
Clinical Analysis Questionnaire (CAQ),
    67, 72

CLUSTAN, 186–187
Cluster analysis
    coefficients of association, 182–183
    clustering process, 180
    cluster methods, 183
    defined, 179
    density search method, 186–187
    divisive method, 185–186
    empirical studies of, 189–190
    hierarchical clustering, 183–184, 190
    illustrative studies, 190–191
    iterative partitioning method, 186
    linkage clustering
        average linkage, 185
        complete, 184
    minimum-variance method, 185
    overlapping clusters, 187
    overview, 191–192
    Q-analysis, method, 187–189
    similarity, measures of, 180–182
    single-linkage analysis, 184
Cognitive distortions, 33
Cognitive therapy, 153
Commingling analysis, 276–277
Comorbidity, 159
Complementarity, 121, 125, 132
Compulsive personality disorder, 21, 159,
    162, 170, 258
Computer-based test interpretation
    (CBTI) programs, MMPI-2, 394–395
Constraint, 308
Continuity, 139–141
Continuum theory, 5, 9
Coping behavior, 80–81
Covert behavior, 122
Criminality, 20
Criterion analysis, 8
Cross-dressing, 165
Cycloid personality, 4
Cyclothymia, 4

Darwin, Charles, 90
Defining Issues Test (DIT), 211
Delusional-dominating Personality
    Disorder, 161
Dependent personality disorders, 21, 96,
    101

Depression, 153
Depressive Personality Disorder, 161
Depressive Symptomatology-Self Report (IDS-S), 48
Developmental theories, 320, 322–324
Deviance, 143
Deviant traits, 141
Diagnostic and Statistical Manual of Mental Disorders (DSM)
  categorical system, 169–170
  dimensional analysis and, 20–23
  disorders of, 104
  function of, 324–326
  maladaptivity
    clinically significant, 165–169
    normative, 162–165
  MCMI and, 103
  nomenclature, 161
  personality disorder diagnosis, 158–160
  taxonomy and, 83–84
Differential Personality Inventory (DPI), 344
Dimensional Assessment of Personality Pathology (DAPP), 345–349
Distress, subjective, 168
Dizygotic twins, *see* Twin studies
DNA, analysis of, 138
Dominance-submission, 117
Dysthymia, 5
Dystonia, 4

Effectance, 97
Eigenvalues, 224–226
Electrodermal (EDA) orienting, 151
Elevation, 181–182, 251, 253
Emotionality, *see* Negative emotionality; Positive emotionality
Emotional stability, 164
Extraversion-introversion, 4
Extraversion, 146, 170, 308–309
Eysenck, H., personality theory, *see* Three-factor model of personality
Eysenck Personality Inventory, 11
Eysenck Personality Questionnaire (EPQ), 11, 43, 203

Factor analysis
  component vs. factor analysis model, 221–223, 236
  data collection
    association index selection, 221
    cleansing the data, 220–221
    measurement format selection, 219–220
    subject selection, 218–219
    variables selection, 218
  dysthymia and, 5
  evolutionary model and, 85
  factor rotation, 227–229
  factor scores, calculation of, 229
  optimal number of factors, 223–227, 236
  overview, 216–218
  research, 66
  trait structures
    horizontal approaches, 231, 233–236
    vertical approaches, 231, 233–235
Familial correlations, 273–274
Family studies, 274
Family violence, 75
Fb scale, 383
Five Factor Model (FFM)
  Axis I psychopathology, 29
  Axis II psychopathology, 29–31
  configural analyses, 129, 132
  diagnosis and, 170
  generally, 10
  interpersonal circumplex and, 248
  as latent mathematical taxa, 86
  MMPI-2 and, 393
  normal, 292–293
  overview, 26–28
  personality structure, 67–68
  psychobiology and, 144
  psychopathology, 357
  trait analyses, 129, 132
Forme fruste, 148
F (p) scale, 384
F scale, 372–373, 383–384
Functional psychoses, 16, 18

GABA hypothesis, 140
Gating hypothesis, 146–147

Genetic analysis
  analytic approaches
    challenges to, 278–280
    commingling analysis, 276–277
    familial correlations, estimation of,
      273–274
    linkage analysis, 277–278
    path analysis, 274–276
    segregation analysis, 277
  assortative mating, 279
  developmental changes and, 279
  familial transmission models, 266
  gene-environment interactions, 279–
    280
  logistic models for, 278
  mathematical models, 281
  mixed model, 269
  multifactorial models, 267
  multigenic control of behavior, 280
  oligogenic model, 269–270
  overview, 264–265
  personality theory and, 280
  phenotypic measurement, latent
    measurement vs., 270
  phenotypic variation, 266
  research
    adoption studies, 272
    association studies, 272–273
    family studies, 271
    twin studies, 271-272
  single major locus model, 267–268

Headache patients, cluster analysis study,
  191
Hereditarianism, 138
Hierarchical personality models, 325
Hippocrates, 83, 316
Histrionic Personality Disorder, 21, 30,
  49, 97, 159, 170
Homostat clusters, 183
Hostility-affiliation, 117
Hyperthymic Personality Disorder, 161
Hysterical personality, 30

Identification, 329
Illness, 141–142
Immature Personality Disorder, 160

Immunological defenses, 81
Impact Message Inventory, 127
Impairment
  clinically significant, 169
  domain of, 171
  functional, 34, 158
  level of, 165
  threshold, 171
Impulsive Personality Disorder, 160
Individuation, 101, 138
Insomnia, 166
International classification of mental
    disorders (ICD-10), 142
Internalization, 322–323, 329
Interpersonal Adjective Scales (IAS), 125
Interpersonal Behavior Inventory (IBI),
  123
Interpersonal Check List (ICL), 125, 203
Interpersonal Circle, 123
Interpersonal Circle Acts Version (1982),
  123
Interpersonal circumplex, *see* Circumplex
Interpersonal relations, reciprocal, 121
Interpersonal theory
  abnormal personality, 324–326
  normal personality, 317–318
  support for, 334–335
  traits and, 125–127
Interpersonal trait, 119, 126
INTREX questionnaire, 319, 332, 334
Introjection, 320, 322, 329
Introversion, 144, 170
Inventories, *see also specific inventories*
  normal personality, applications with,
    352–355
  scoring system, 344–345
Inventory of Interpersonal Problems, 128
IPIR (important people or their
    internalized representations), 323

Jaccard coefficient, 183
Jackson Personality Inventory (JPI), 352,
  355
Jet lag syndrome, 166

Kaiser Foundation Health Plan, 116
Kappa coefficient, 183, 189

K-correction, 373, 392–393
Kraepelin, Emil, 26, 83
Kraepelinian nosology, 368
K scale, 374, 383
K-strategy, 98

Lateralization, 147
Laws of physics, 82
Life enhancement, 91–94
Life preservation, 91–93
Life Styles Inventory, 205
Linkage analysis, 277–278
LISREL, 276
Logistic regression, 278

Maladaptive personality
  defined, 115
  internalization and, 329, 331
  interpersonal assessment trends
    configural analyses, 129, 132
    interpersonal problems, 128–129
  traits and, 125–127
Maladaptive Transaction Cycle, 122
Manic-depressive illness, 4
MAPCLUS, 187
Mask of Sanity, The, 147
Mature personality, 99
Maudsley Medical Questionnaire, 11
Mendellian traits, 267–268
Mental disorders, *see specific types of
  disorders*
Millon Adolescent Clinical Inventory
  (MACI), 102, 105–106
Millon Adolescent Personality Inventory
  (MAPI), 102, 105–106
Millon Behavioral Health Inventory
  (MBHI), 102, 104–105
Millon Clinical Multiaxial Inventory
  (MCMI), 26, 102–104
Millon Index of Personality Styles
  (MIPS), 102, 107–110
Millon, T., personality theory
  aims of existence, 91–98
  clinical instruments, 102–106
  overview, 88–91
  personality instruments, 106–110
  replication strategies, 98–102

Minkowski metric, 181
Minnesota Multinhasic Personality
  Inventory (MMPI)
  construction of, 365–366
  content-based personality assessment,
    371–373
  empirical assessment, 370–371
  evolution of, 366–367, 377–378
  generally, 9, 333
  interpretation of, codebook approach,
    368–370
  item subtlety, 364
  normal/abnormal personality and, 71
  psychometric perspective, 361–362
  scales of
    content scales, 376–377
    critical items, 376
    generally, 374–375
    Harris-Lingoes subscales, 375–376,
      387
    validity, 364
    Welsch Factor scales 375
  significance of, 361
  social behavior and, 333
  theoretical underpinnings, 363–365,
    367–368
Minnesota Multiphasic Personality
  Inventory-2 (MMPI-2)
  computer technology and, 393–395
  empirical correlates, 390–391
  five factor models, 393
  goals of, 380–381
  interpretation of, configural vs. linear,
    391–392
  item subtlety, 392
  methods of, 381–382
  outcome of, 382
  problematic items, 380
  problematic norms, 379–380
  rationale for, 378
  scales
    clinical, 385–387
    content, 388–389
    supplementary, 387–388
    validity, 382–385
  status of, 389–390
  subject defensiveness, 392–393

Minnesota Normals, 365, 373
Mixed Personality Disorder, 160
MMPI Restandardization Committee,
    380, 385
MMPI-2, Personality Psychopathology
    Five (PSY-5) and, 311
MMPI-AX, 381
Monolithic clusters, 186
Monozygotic twins, see Twin studies
Multidimensional Personality
    Questionnaire, 362
Multidimensional scaling (MDS)
    basic concepts
        input data, 197–199
        models, 199–201
        sampling subjects/stimuli, 197
    overview, 196–197
    person perception, 201–202
    tests and test items
        component solutions, 204–207
        correlation matrices, components
            analysis of, 203–204
        factor model, 207–208
        unfolding model, 210–211
        vector model 208–210, 212
Multiple Affective Adjective Checklist-
    Revised (MAACL-R), 48
Multiple Personality Disorder, 160

Narcissistic Personality Disorder, 21, 49,
    97, 100, 170
National Institute of Mental Health
    (NIMH), Epidemiologic Catchment
    Area (ECA) study, 162
Needs, hierarchy of, 93, 99
Negative emotionality, 308–309
Negativistic Personality Disorder (NEG),
    interpersonal etiology of, 331
NEO Personality Inventory, 26, 32, 40
Neurosis, diathesis-stress theory of, 5
Neuroticism, 4, 8, 144, 164–165, 170,
    257, 308–309
Nonforgetannia Personality Disorder,
    161
Normality
    criteria for, 79
    models of, 342–343

Normal personality
    defined, 80
    dimensions of, 164
NORMAP, 187
NORMIX, 187
Nosological systems, 83
Nosology, 83–84

Obsessive-compulsive personality, 34–35,
    49, 96
Overt behavior, 122

Paranoid Personality Disorder, 21, 49,
    148
Parent–child relationship, 334
Partitioning, 186
Passive–active polarity, 95–96
Passive–aggressive Personality Disorder,
    21, 258, 331–332
Pathological personality
    dimensional assessment in, 345–349
    modal profile analysis of, 350–352
Pavlovian theory, 22, 138
Pedigree analysis, 266
Perceptual Aberration Scale, 276
Persona, 80
Personality
    conceptualizing
        generally, 82
        latent mathematical taxa, 84–86
        latent theoretical taxa, 86–88
        manifest and latent taxa, 83
    definition of, 80, 125, 127
    models of, 13
Personality Adjective Check List (PACL),
    102, 106
Personality Assessment Inventory (PAI)
    Five-Factor Model and, 26
    normal/abnormal personality,
        differentiation of
        feature distribution, 412–414
        personality traits, 417–418
        scoring patterns, 416
        social desirability, 415–416
    normative data, 404–405
    overview of, 402–404
    reliability of, 405

scales
  clinical, 406–409
  generally, 405–406
  interpersonal, 410–411
  treatment considerations, 409–410
  validity, 406
Personality disorder
  classification of, 142
  comorbidity, 159
  conceptualization of, 42, 59
  defined, 59
  diagnosis of, 5, 27, 51, 59–60
  diagnostic threshold, 165–167
  dimensional models, 61
  medical model, 5, 21, 80, 142
  obsessive-compulsive, 34–35
  prescientific, 80
  psychosis and, 147–152
  screening of, 59
  symptomatology, 162
  symptoms, number of, 52
  treatment of, 60–61
  types of, 22
Personality Disorder Questionnaire-
    Revised, 32
Personality disorder not otherwise
    specified (PDNOS), 160–161
Personality factors, 85
Personality models
  construction of, 4–9
  integration of, 61
  interpersonal circumplex, 114, 116–
    120
  interpersonal theory, 114, 120–123
  measurement
    heuristic model, 9–12
    hierarchical model, 13
  psychobiological, 42–46
Personality pathology, defined, 81
Personality Psychopathology Five
    (PSY 5)
  constructs, 306–309
  five factor model, comparison with,
    309–311
  study of, *see* Personality
    Psychopathology Five (PSY-5)
    study

Personality Psychopathology Five
    (PSY 5) study
  analyses, 297, 300
  materials, 296
  procedure, 296–297
  results/discussion, 300, 302, 304–306
  subjects, 296
Personality Research Form (PRF), 352,
    354
Personality traits
  continuity of, 27
  discrete, 266
  distribution of, 28
  inflexible, 158–159
  maladaptive, 158–159, 164
  organization of, 80, 124
  structure of, 230–231, 233–235
Personality-related disorders
  DSM and, 35–36
  models of, 31–34
Personology, 89
Phobias, 20
Pleasure-pain polarity, 91–94
Pleonexic Personality Disorder, 161
Polygenes, 267–269
Positive emotionality, 308–309
Probands, 271
Project for a Scientific Psychology
    (Freud), 88
Prototypes, 258–259
Prototypical Personality Disorder, 159
Psychasthenia, 5
Psychiatric Epidemiology Research
    Interview (PERI), 171
Psychic pathology, 81
Psychobiological models
  asymmetry, 139–141
  cognitive therapy and, 153
  continuity, 139, 141
  deviance, 143
  personality, 143
  reductionism, 139–141, 144
  temperament, 143–145
Psychological deviance, 138
Psychopathic Personality Disorder, 170
Psychopathology model, need for,
    293–295

Psychopathy Checklist, 151
Psychotherapy, group, 117
Psychoticism, 4, 13, 16, 18–20, 149–150, 307, 310
Psychotic states, as organic disease, 139

Q-analysis, 187–189

Racist Personality Disorder, 161
Rand coefficient, 183, 189
Recombinant personality, 98
Reductionism, 139–141, 144
Reproductive nurturance, 99–100
Reproductive propagation, 100–101
r-strategy, 98–99
R-technique factor analysis, 210, 212

Sadistic Personality Disorder, 49, 160–161
Scatter, 181–182
Schizo-affective disorders, 18
Schizoid Personality Disorder, 21, 49, 148, 257, 311
Schizophrenia, 148–149, 342–343
Schizothymia, 5
Schizotypal Personality Disorder, 33, 311
Schizotypy, 4, 21, 148, 150
Segregation analysis, 276–277, 281–282
Self-actualization, 96, 101
Self-defeating Personality Disorder, 49, 160–161, 170
Self-fulfilling prophecy, 126
Self-other polarity, 98–101
Sensation seeking scales (SSS), 145
Seven Factor Personality Model
    diagnostic assessment and, 54–58
    normal vs. deviant personality, 46–53
    overview, 40–42
    personality disorders and, 42–46
Sixteen Personality Factors
    Questionnaire, 16 PF, 16, 68–69, 227
Sociability, 145
Sociobiology (Wilson), 88
Spearman, Charles, 66
Squared Euclidean model (SEM), 198
Squared loading index (SQLI), 248
Stigmatization, 165

Structural Analysis of Social Behavior
    (SASB): Lorna Benjamin's
    personality model
    clinical example, 331–334
    normality/abnormality, defined, 326–328
    overview, 318–319
Structured Clinical Interview for DSM-
    III-R Personality Disorders (SCID), 163
Structured Interview for DSM-III
    Personality Disorders (SIDP), 48, 163
Substance abuse, 75
Subtle L scale, 373, 382–383
Syntonia, 4
Syntonic traits, continuous, 141

Taxonomy, 83–84
Temperament, 42–43, 143–145
Temperament and Character Inventory
    (TCI), 40
Thinking Disorder scale, 33
Three-factor model of personality, 3, 11, 13, 20–22
Trait interpersonal theory, 116–117
Trait ontology, 120
Transvestic fetishism, 165
Treatment, outcomes of, 41
Tridimensional Personality Questionnaire
    (TPQ), 43
True Response Inconsistency (TRIN)
    scale, 384, 394
T scores
    MMPI-2, 385–387
    Personality Assessment Inventory
        (PAI), 404–405
Twin studies, 271–272, 274, 280
Type A Personality Disorder, 170

Variable Response Inconsistency (VRIN)
    scale, 383–384, 394
Vocational Preference Inventory, 205, 209

Watson, J. B., 138
Wechsler Adult Intelligence Scale, 152
Wechsler Intelligence Tests, 205
Weighted Euclidean model (WEM), 200, 202